RESEARCH HANDBOOK ON THE ECONOMICS OF LABOR AND EMPLOYMENT LAW

RESEARCH HANDBOOKS IN LAW AND ECONOMICS

Series Editors: Richard A. Posner, *Judge, United States Court of Appeals for the Seventh Circuit and Senior Lecturer, University of Chicago Law School, USA* and Francesco Parisi, *Oppenheimer Wolff and Donnelly Professor of Law, University of Minnesota, USA and Professor of Economics, University of Bologna, Italy*

Edited by highly distinguished scholars, the landmark reference works in this series offer advanced treatments of specific topics that reflect the state-of-the-art of research in law and economics, while also expanding the law and economics debate. Each volume's accessible yet sophisticated contributions from top international researchers make it an indispensable resource for students and scholars alike.

Titles in this series include:

Research Handbook on Public Choice and Public Law
Edited by Daniel A. Farber and Anne Joseph O'Connell

Research Handbook on the Economics of Property Law
Edited by Kenneth Ayotte and Henry E. Smith

Research Handbook on the Economics of Family Law
Edited by Lloyd R. Cohen and Joshua D. Wright

Research Handbook on the Economics of Antitrust Law
Edited by Einer R. Elhauge

Research Handbook on the Economics of Corporate Law
Edited by Brett McDonnell and Claire A. Hill

Research Handbook on the Economics of European Union Law
Edited by Thomas Eger and Hans-Bernd Schäfer

Research Handbook on the Economics of Criminal Law
Edited by Alon Harel and Keith N. Hylton

Research Handbook on the Economics of Labor and Employment Law
Edited by Cynthia L. Estlund and Michael L. Wachter

Research Handbook on the Economics of Labor and Employment Law

Edited by

Cynthia L. Estlund

New York University School of Law, USA

Michael L. Wachter

University of Pennsylvania Law School, USA

RESEARCH HANDBOOKS IN LAW AND ECONOMICS

Edward Elgar
Cheltenham, UK • Northampton, MA, USA

Published by
Edward Elgar Publishing Limited
The Lypiatts
15 Lansdown Road
Cheltenham
Glos GL50 2JA
UK

Edward Elgar Publishing, Inc.
William Pratt House
9 Dewey Court
Northampton
Massachusetts 01060
USA

A catalogue record for this book
is available from the British Library

Library of Congress Control Number: 2012940992

MIX
Paper from
responsible sources
FSC
www.fsc.org   FSC® C018575

ISBN 978 1 84980 101 0 (cased)

Typeset by Servis Filmsetting Ltd, Stockport,Cheshire
Printed and bound by MPG Books Group, UK

Contents

Contributors

Rachel Arnow-Richman is Professor of Law at the University of Denver, Sturm College of Law, and Director of the Workplace Law Program.

Simon Deakin is Professor of Law at the University of Cambridge and Program Director in the Cambridge Centre for Business Research.

Zev J. Eigen is Assistant Professor of Law at Northwestern University School of Law.

Richard A. Epstein is the Laurence A. Tisch Professor of Law, New York University; the Peter and Kirsten Bedford Senior Fellow, The Hoover Institution; and the James Parker Hall Distinguished Service Professor of Law Emeritus and Senior Lecturer, The University of Chicago.

Cynthia L. Estlund is the Catherine A. Rein Professor of Law at New York University School of Law.

Samuel Estreicher is the Dwight D. Opperman Professor of Law and Director, Center for Labor and Employment Law, New York University School of Law.

Barry T. Hirsch is the W.J. Usery Chair of the American Workplace and Professor of Economics at Georgia State University.

Alan Hyde is Distinguished Professor and Sidney Reitman Scholar, Rutgers University School of Law, Newark, NJ.

Samuel Issacharoff is the Reiss Professor of Constitutional Law at the New York University School of Law.

Christine Jolls is the Gordon Bradford Tweedy Professor of Law and Organization at Yale Law School.

Bruce E. Kaufman is Professor of Economics, Andrew Young School of Policy Studies, Georgia State University; Senior Research Associate, Centre for Work, Organization and Wellbeing and Department of Human Resources and Employment Relations, Griffith University, Brisbane, Australia; and Research Associate, Work and Employment Research Unit, Business School, University of Hertfordshire, Hatfield, UK.

Morris M. Kleiner is the AFL-CIO Professor of Public Affairs, Humphrey School of Public Affairs at the University of Minnesota; Research Associate at the National Bureau of Economic Research; and Visiting Scholar at the Federal Reserve Bank of Minneapolis.

Benjamin I. Sachs is Professor of Law at Harvard Law School.

Erin Scharff is Acting Assistant Professor of Tax Law, New York University School of Law.

Stewart J. Schwab is the Allan R. Tessler Dean and Professor of Law at Cornell Law School.

Michael L. Wachter is the William B. Johnson Professor of Law and Economics and Co-Director, Institute for Law and Economics at the University of Pennsylvania.

David Weil is Professor of Markets, Public Policy, and Law and Everett W. Lord Distinguished Faculty Scholar, Boston University School of Management; and Co-Director and Senior Research Fellow Transparency Policy Project, Harvard Kennedy School of Government.

PART I

FOUNDATIONS

1. Introduction: the economics of labor and employment law

Cynthia L. Estlund and Michael L. Wachter

The law governing the employment relationship and labor relations is a natural field for the application of economic analysis. At bottom, labor and employment law governs voluntary contractual relations within labor markets and firms. That law is often bound to affect both the price and the cost of labor – whether or not it aims to do so – and thus to affect both the supply of and demand for labor. The price, cost, supply and demand for labor are all crucially important for firms, workers and the society at large. So it might seem inevitable and uncontroversial that economic analysis would make up a major part of legal scholarship in this area.

Although the integration of these two disciplines may have been inevitable, it was hardly uncontroversial. The entry and gradual integration of neoclassical economic analysis into the field of labor and employment law, beginning some 30 years ago, looked very different from the perspective of the two disciplines – law and economics. One reason for early controversy was that the two disciplines were far more distinct 30 years ago than in today's cross-disciplinary era. The first foray of modern economic analysis into labor law came from a particular wing of economics – one that was far more sanguine about the competitiveness of labor markets, and more critical of the body of labor and employment law that had evolved since the New Deal, than the median labor economist, not to mention the majority of labor law professors. The latter were especially disposed to stress the differences between labor markets and other markets.

Today, however, economic analysis in diverse forms has become widely accepted and integrated into labor and employment law scholarship. This volume reflects both the integration of economic analysis into the field of labor and employment law as well as the diverse forms of economic analysis that take place in the field. By way of introduction it is worth briefly recounting the recent history of economic analysis of labor and employment law, both as it played out in the law schools and as it appeared from the vantage point of modern labor economics. We say "recent history" because economic analysis of a different sort was crucial in shaping labor law in its formative period of the New Deal. We will return to this point below.

The initial foray of law-and-economics scholars of the modern era – what we may call the "Posnerian Era" – into the field of labor law in the early 1980s was fraught with acrimony, but also innovation.[1] For this University of Chicago-based wave of law-and-economics scholars, labor law was emblematic of the ill-conceived New Deal approach to economic activity: It rejected the elegant logic of property, contract, and the market in favor of government-sponsored cartelization of the labor supply (Epstein, 1983, 1984; Posner, 1984). For established scholars in the field of labor law, the intervention of law and economics appeared shockingly oblivious to the history, institutional realities, and values that animated labor law (Getman & Kohler, 1983; Verkuil, 1983). The quest for economic efficiency seemed to sweep away traditional labor law concerns like labor-management cooperation, industrial democracy, fairness and solidarity.

This acrimony, however, was partly a conflict over methodology. Posner's innovative project was to see how far economic analysis could go to shed light on legal issues. His approach was to take the competitive model, with few transaction costs, as his starting point for legal reasoning. As a benchmark, the predicated competitive outcomes were thus a gauge for evaluating other outcomes. In some areas of law such as contract and corporate law, the new cross-disciplinary approach caught on quickly and with few fireworks. In these fields, the relationship between the primary parties is entirely consensual, and the law provides a set of defaults that the parties can adopt as a low transaction form for contracting. In the economic paradigm, parties can then easily contract around the legal defaults to gain the private ordering that they seek. But the assumption of voluntary relationships within competitive markets is hardly a good starting point for analyzing labor law, where relationships need not be consensual and markets – especially, the internal labor markets where people are actually employed – are not competitive.

In the initial clash of values and disciplines in the early 1980s, labor law scholars and law-and-economics scholars found little common ground, and both retreated to their respective strongholds or moved on to other battlegrounds. But the disciplinary walls had been breached, and labor law scholarship would never be the same. The opening skirmish between labor law traditionalists and the law-and-economics scholars marked a watershed not only in labor law scholarship but in the policy environment for labor and employment issues in the early Reagan era, shortly after the pivotal PATCO showdown.[2] Economically inspired scholars, particularly those with limited institutional knowledge of the labor market, along with deregulatory policymakers, took the offensive and put the proponents of labor market regulation and of collective bargaining on the defensive. The former had defined a new battlefield with unfamiliar rules of engagement, and the latter had to decide whether to cede that ground or to join the fray – to become conversant with the assumptions and analytical tools of economic analysis.

The academic labor lawyers who decided to join the fray soon found that the Chicago School was far from the last word on the economics of labor markets. Richard Freeman and James Medoff, with their 1984 book *What Do Unions Do?*, introduced much of the labor law academy to more congenial strains of thinking and research within labor economics and industrial relations. Building on the pioneering work of Albert Hirschman, and especially his highly influential (1970) book, *Exit, Voice, and Loyalty: Responses to Decline in Firms, Organizations, and States*, Freeman and Medoff applied the insights to the labor union as an organization and gave a vocabulary to those who sought to defend unions and collective bargaining against the economic critique: Unions promoted worker *voice* in response to discontent, and those voice mechanisms offered a constructive alternative to *exit*, or quitting. Indeed, by rewarding experience, reducing turnover, and inducing workers to share their skills, collective voice (and the job security, seniority protections, and greater benefits that voice allowed workers to secure) could actually contribute to productivity. If unions could raise wages, could they also assist workers in raising productivity to offset the cost of the higher wages?

Freeman and Medoff surveyed the existing empirical research and found some support for a union productivity effect, though not enough to offset the union wage premium.[3] They also made the case for other positive societal contributions of unions such as representation of workers in the democratic political process.

The contributions of Freeman and Medoff on the economics of unions, although perhaps new to those in the field of labor law, were as well known in standard labor economics as were the works of Posner and the Chicago School. Whereas Posner stressed the forces of competitive markets in labor law, Freeman and Medoff helped in part to elaborate the idea that additional factors (both economic and non-economic) outside of the traditional competitive market analysis are important in considering the economic effects of unions. The standard economics model and the similarly standard notion of externalities were now joined. To the labor law scholars who favored collective bargaining as the best regime for governing employment relations (including those who criticized the labor laws from the left for its inadequate support for workers' collective activity), this body of research appeared for a time to offer a simple answer to the law-and-economics critics of unions and collective bargaining: If unions could boost output while increasing workers' share of that output, then society had good reason to promote unionization even though employers might have reason to oppose it.[4] Beginning in the mid-1980s, Freeman and Medoff quickly became a standard cite in the labor law literature for the virtues of collective voice over exit and the potential productivity benefits of unions, and a standard rejoinder to the law-and-economics critics.

Alas, the positive productivity story suggested by early studies proved to be "overly optimistic," as subsequent empirical research showed productivity gains in the union sector to be small or non-existent (Freeman, 2007; Hirsch, Chapter 4 in this volume). As a consequence any such gains were too small to offset the union wage premium, or the gap between the collectively bargained wage in the union sector and the prevailing market wage, consistent with Freeman and Medoff's conclusion about unions' negative effect on profits. Not coincidentally, the non-union sector of the economy continued to grow and prosper as the union sector declined.

The decline in union membership, well underway by the 1980s, was one of the most important institutional changes in the American economy over the past 60 years. As the slide continued, it became increasingly clear that, if labor unions did provide positive externalities to the American economy and polity, then their protection and promotion would require affirmative societal intervention – and intervention that was strong enough to counter powerful *and rational* employer resistance arising from higher labor costs.

The first comprehensive response to the law-and-economics critique in the legal academy was mounted by Paul Weiler (1990) in his important book *Governing the Workplace*. Weiler was not the first labor law scholar to take up the cudgels, but his extended critique of the Chicago School view of labor markets, and his vigorous defense of the proposition that human labor is different from other factors of production, marked an important point in the evolution of labor and employment law scholarship. Weiler took the economic critique of labor law seriously, and he responded seriously. In the process he helped to familiarize many labor law scholars with currents of labor economics and industrial relations scholarship that could be marshaled in support of laws protecting employees and fostering collective bargaining, and helped to promote engagement among labor and employment law scholars with economic analysis.

The prospects for such engagement were aided by the entry of a second wave of law-and-economics scholars into the field. Their deeper schooling in contemporary neoclassical labor economics led to more nuanced and less thoroughly critical economic analyses of labor law doctrines (Dau-Schmidt, 1992; Hylton & Hylton, 1989; Hylton, 1993; Wachter & Cohen, 1988; Schwab, 1987). In particular, this group of scholars was more attentive to the nature of internal labor markets, in which firm-specific investments, information asymmetries, and transaction costs were pervasive and labor market competition was muffled. Collective bargaining was recognized as a potential solution to some market failures (even if it had other costs). This second wave of law-and-economics scholarship also corresponded to the rise of "employment law" as a field, and quickly began to shape debates over employment-at-will and its exceptions (Freed & Polsby, 1989; Schwab, 1993, 1996; Verkerke, 1995). Since employers in internal labor markets are only constrained from opportunism by reputational sanctions, there is a greater potential field for welfare-improving intervention in non-union labor markets.

The civil rights laws soon came under economic scrutiny as well, initially in the influential work of Chicago School professor Gary Becker. Becker's core argument was that personal preferences could and indeed did include preferences for certain racial or ethnic groups over others in personal relationships, but that markets would punish employers that indulged such racialized preferences (Becker, 1957). His conjecture was that, without any legal intervention against discrimination, race-based differences in income would narrow over time as non-discriminating employers found that they could successfully compete by hiring workers scorned by others at lower wage rates. The great bulk of the cross-disciplinary work during this period, however, concluded otherwise. It appeared that history – specifically the history of slavery and Jim Crow – had left deep institutional marks and, in the economists' terminology, produced sticky Nash equilibria. As in other areas of law and economics, however, the competitive theorizing of the Chicago School garnered much of the attention among labor law scholars.

Richard Epstein's libertarian-style economic critique of antidiscrimination law (1992) provoked a wave of economically informed and empirically grounded defenses of the antidiscrimination mandate in the legal literature (Donohue, 1992; Issacharoff, 1992; Strauss, 1991; Verkerke, 1992). As new facets were added to the antidiscrimination mandate, they attracted further economic analysis, much of which raised questions about whether the laws were serving their intended beneficiaries or perhaps generating counterproductive labor market responses. Some scholars suggested, for example, that costly legal restraints on discharge or accommodation requirements for certain "protected" groups might induce employers to restrict their hiring of individuals from those groups (Donohue & Siegelman, 1991; Issacharoff & Rosenblum, 1993; Jolls, 2000).

The calculus of private market efficiency, however, was never the ultimate lodestar of economic analysis (although it sometimes seemed so to the legal scholars). Although economists prefer competitive outcomes and policy initiatives based on cost-benefit analysis, they understand that the best outcome is the one that leads to the highest position on society's social welfare ordering. The theory of the second-best, which was introduced early into the economics paradigm, showed that, in the face of impediments to "first-best" conditions of perfect competition, a move toward "freer" competition did not necessarily promote efficiency. Moreover, economists recognized that society might prefer noncompetitive outcomes on distributional grounds. To well-schooled economists, labor law reforms would still need to be defended on cost-benefit grounds as the best solution to a well-identified market problem, or forthrightly on distributional grounds; but the idea of reforming labor markets faced no special burden of justification.

By the mid-1990s, economic analysis had become almost impossible for labor and employment law scholars to ignore, and at the same time easier to reconcile with arguments for legal intervention on behalf of employees. It was particularly difficult to ignore the economists' predictions about the unintended labor market consequences of legal interventions for the workers they were designed to benefit. Mandatory benefits such as job security, for example, were predicted to decrease wage levels, employment levels or both. Some forms of antidiscrimination protections – particularly those that required "accommodation," but also those that significantly increased the expected costs of discharging individuals from protected groups – might effectively tax the hiring of those individuals. The economists succeeded in drawing the attention of legal scholars to the incentives that were likely to drive market actors' responses to regulations and that could defeat or confound well-intentioned reforms.

As more researchers entered the cross-disciplinary field, it was only natural that a broader view of the economic model would replace a strict adherence to the perfectly competitive version. The economic analysis of transaction costs, public goods and collective action problems, information deficits and asymmetries, and the like have all been standard fare within labor economics since the 1970s; but they did not filter into economic analysis within the legal academy, at least in labor and employment law, until after the first Posnerian foray. Armed with those concepts, it became easier to deploy economic analysis in the defense of some existing and proposed policy interventions. It became increasingly clear to legal scholars in the 1990s and thereafter that economic analysis was no longer a one-way ratchet against legal intervention in markets, nor did it necessarily entail swearing fealty to the goal of efficiency above all.

Economics has always been a mixture of theory and empirical work; and as labor law researchers adopted a broader range of economic models, they adopted econometric analysis as an important tool. Models, conjectures, and institutional details need to be tested to see if they are predictive of how labor markets function. This work has included methodologically sophisticated data-driven studies of litigation behavior, judicial decisions, and the economic correlates of legislation or other legal developments. These empirical studies have sometimes confirmed and sometimes confounded the predictions of theorists, and have sometimes contradicted each other, for example, with regard to the economic consequences of judicial erosion of the employment-at-will rule. Facts rarely speak for themselves, and theory does not readily surrender to empirically based challenges, which are often clouded by methodological disputes. But facts and data have always brought about significant changes in economic theory across the board, notably in labor economics.

Three major and interrelated scholarly currents have also compounded the heterodoxy of economic analysis of legal rules, doctrines and institutions, both in the field of labor and employment law and beyond. One major scholarly development that has complicated and fragmented the field of law and economics – the rise of behavioral analysis – may turn into a case study of the power of facts to alter theory (though the jury is still out). Based on a growing multitude of laboratory and field experiments, behavioral scholars have drawn attention to a collection of tendencies in actual human decision making that diverge in somewhat predictable ways from the "rational actor" model on which neoclassical economic theory is based (Jolls, 2007; Jolls, Sunstein & Thaler, 1998). Evidence of widespread patterns of "bounded rationality," "bounded will-power," and "bounded self-interest," for example, helped to enrich the law-and-economics field, questioning the realism of neoclassical economic theory and blunting or contradicting many of its policy prescriptions in the labor field as elsewhere (Sunstein, 2001; Williamson, Wachter & Harris, 1975). Some consumers of behavioral analysis seemed to take this new research as a grab bag of justifications for "paternalistic" forms of legal intervention; some of the behavioral scholars themselves were more cautious in their prescriptions (Camerer et al., 2003; Thaler & Sunstein, 2008).

Two other related scholarly currents that have enriched the field of law and economics are the rise of game theory and the role of "norms." Norms shape behavior in ways that seem both to defy the "rational actor" model and yet to facilitate private ordering. The power of norms of fairness and reciprocity in shaping human behavior was widely observed, both in laboratory experiments and in the world, including in the workplace; and those norms were seen to play an important role in sustaining the trust and cooperation on which many actual markets depended. These observations seemed to pose a serious challenge to the rational actor model at the heart of neoclassical economic theory. In one way, game theory came to the rescue, and allowed economic theorists to reclaim trust and cooperation as rational, at least among "repeat players." That had important implications for the workplace (Rock & Wachter, 1996). At the same time, game theory and the norms literature played a potentially subversive role, for they reintroduced squishy concepts of fairness, trust and reciprocity that had been virtually banished from economic discourse in the early years of the law-and-economics revolution.

The growing influence of these newer currents in economic research and thought has made law and economics a far richer and more diverse intellectual stream than it was in the 1970s and 1980s. That has been true across the board – in the law and economics of corporate governance, consumer law, contracts, torts, property, criminal law and civil procedure – indeed, everywhere that clever and ambitious young legal scholars ply their trade. But the heterodoxy of economic analysis in the field of labor and employment law has additional roots in the field of labor economics and its role in the history of labor and employment law.

Labor economics has always been open to the rich institutional realities of the labor market. The great labor economists of the 1950s and 1960s, including John Dunlop, Clark Kerr, H. Gregg Lewis, Mel Reder, and Albert Rees, were also institutionalists who borrowed from neoclassical theory to enrich their view of the functioning of labor market institutions. It was primarily these economists who were instrumental in shaping the origins of modern labor and employment law in the U.S. Indeed, from the foundational days of economics until the current period, the study of labor issues by the giants such as Adam Smith, Thomas Malthus, Karl Marx, and John Commons has always been rooted in institutionally grounded hypotheses. The ascendency of pure economic theory was a short-lived episode in labor economics.

In the decisive New Deal battles in which both modern labor law and the beginnings of modern employment law were forged, the then-ascendant institutionalist economic thinkers joined forces with legal realist scholars to contend for the legitimacy and wisdom of both legal support for collective bargaining and legislation of minimum labor standards (Kaufman, Chapter 3 in this volume; Hovenkamp, 2011). Although the modern neoclassical theory of labor markets and wages was percolating during the New Deal and was about to transform economic thinking about employment relations, the institutionalists' pivotal policy role and the durability of some of the reforms that they advocated during the New Deal probably helped sustain a greater diversity of views among labor economists, compared to the rest of the economics field. This integration of theory and institutions was repeated in the 1960s and 1970s when labor economists, using cost-benefit analysis, argued forcefully in favor of many programs such as employment training, antidiscrimination policy, and welfare reform, while arguing against some reforms of the New Deal, such as industry-specific labor rules, believed to have outlived their usefulness.

Still, there are divisions between economists and most labor law scholars. Consider for example, the proposition that individual employment relations are plagued by an "inequality of bargaining power" between workers and employers. The generalized "inequality of bargaining power" claim is a bête noire of most neoclassically trained economists (see, e.g., Schwab, 1997; Wachter & Wright, 1990). In neoclassical analysis, external labor markets are considered competitive or competitive enough so that a worker's "bargaining power" depends on cyclical labor market conditions and supply and demand for his particular skills. Some workers have significant bargaining power. Yet at least in the midst of the Great Depression, the proposition that employers generally had more bargaining power than employees seemed self-evident to many observers, and it was a founding premise of the New Deal labor legislation.

The idea of unequal bargaining power continues to appeal intuitively to many citizens, and it continues to animate much of labor and employment law policy and scholarship.[5] Indeed, it remains enshrined in the U.S. Code: The preamble to the National Labor Relations Act (NLRA) declares that there is an "inequality of bargaining power between employees who do not possess full freedom of association or actual liberty of contract, and employers who are organized in the corporate or other forms of ownership associations."[6] Of course, saying this does not necessarily make it so, even if Congress is the one saying it. Congress' particular conception of the inequality of bargaining power and how to redress it is in fact the subject of close and critical scrutiny in the present volume (Wachter, Chapter 2 in this volume).

The remarkable staying power (or "ossification") of the NLRA in particular – if not of its collective bargaining model of labor relations – is testimony to the fact that labor economists have always needed to study institutions in order to understand the workings of markets and to be able to propose reforms. Although the NLRA has many negative features in the eyes of economists, the number of economists who favor repeal of the Act is very small. It is the libertarians rather than the economists who want wholesale repeal of labor and employment law. Economists recognize that the difference between mostly competitive and perfectly competitive markets is vast in terms of its policy implications.

Neoclassical economic analysis has been enriched by its attention to transaction costs, the lessons of game theory, the importance and robustness of norms, and even the complications of behavioral economics. Some of the major innovations in neoclassical labor economics since the 1960s underscore the proposition that human labor is different from other factors of production. For example, the "efficiency wage hypothesis" posits that paying workers more than the "competitive" market wage can elicit greater work effort – out of both loyalty and reciprocity to the firm and a stronger incentive to keep the better paid job – which can potentially pay for itself in the form of higher productivity. The theory, and the underlying idea that trust, reciprocity and cooperation among workers and managers are major factors in labor productivity, is widely accepted by labor economists (at least in the non-union sector).[7] Moreover, the labor economist's elaboration of the market failures that are endemic within internal labor markets opens the theoretical door to legal interventions that could improve efficiency and fairness in employment relationships.

In assembling the present volume, we have taken a broad view of "economic analysis" of labor and employment law. We include producers of economic theory and of empirical research and neoclassical and institutional economists. We include scholars whose training and primary point of departure is in economics and positive economic analysis of legal rules, as well as scholars whose training and focus is more normative and attentive to the economic consequences, predicted in theory or demonstrated empirically, of policy interventions.

We begin, and complete Part I of this volume, with two accounts of the economics of labor markets and some of the policy implications of those accounts. The first is by Michael Wachter on the modern neoclassical economic theory of labor markets. The second, by Bruce Kaufman, offers a counterpoint in the form of a range of skeptical observations about the neoclassical account of labor markets, especially the "Chicago School" account, from the "institutional" or industrial relations perspective. Both accounts are attentive to the transaction costs and other frictions that may skew real labor markets from the competitive ideal, but they differ sharply on the extent to which these various "market failures" interfere with the competitiveness of external labor markets in the U.S. Wachter shares the consensus view within neoclassical economics, that external labor markets are basically competitive but that market imperfections are endemic to internal labor markets. Kaufman, on the other hand, sees market failure as pervasive in labor markets, both internal and external. Wachter shares the economists' "rebuttable presumption" in favor of labor market outcomes; thus, while he considers many legal mandates to be justified on efficiency grounds or otherwise, he resists legal enforcement of the terms of employment-at-will contracts and contends that non-legally enforceable norms can be effective in ensuring basic fairness within internal labor markets. Kaufman, by contrast, indulges no presumption in favor of market outcomes given the systematic advantages employers have over workers. From these two accounts and their engagement with each other, readers can discern the main lines of agreement and disagreement between the dominant and recessive wings of labor economics.

Parts II and III track the familiar division between "labor law," or the law of union organizing and collective bargaining, and "employment law." In Part II, we take up the field of "labor law." We begin with Barry Hirsch's comprehensive analysis of the economic literature – and particularly the empirical evidence – on the impact of unions on economic performance of firms. The picture is not encouraging for organized labor. Significant union wage premiums, and little or no offsetting productivity gains, reduce the profitability and competitiveness of union firms and facilities, and reduce investment in those facilities, with the inexorable result of declining union density. This economic story does not refute so much as it helps to explain intense management opposition to unionization, which in turn contributes to declining union density.

On Hirsch's account, the data do not support the more hopeful scenario of union productivity gains in a cooperative labor relations climate; but neither do they rule out that scenario. When non-union labor relations as well as management opposition to unions become the norm, cooperative collectivized labor-management relations become exceptional and precarious, especially in dynamic and growing sectors of the economy. Hirsch's chapter underscores the challenge that unions face in the U.S. labor law regime, which, unlike many European labor law systems, does not attempt to take wages and other labor costs out of competition, except at the very bottom of the market. The chapter also underscores the difficulty in such a labor law regime of realizing workers' right to form unions and engage in collective bargaining, to which U.S. public policy remains formally committed.

The next two chapters take up that issue from two radically different perspectives on the law of union organizing. Benjamin Sachs offers a novel analysis of what is wrong with both the current law of union organization under the NLRA *and* with the leading (and lately defeated) reform proposal, the Employee Free Choice Act (EFCA). Building on the recognition that union organization can be seen as an effort to alter the "default" status of no union representation, Sachs mines a rich literature on defaults and default-altering rules in statutory interpretation and in corporate governance to illuminate the problem of realizing employee preferences regarding union representation. The basic problem lies in the asymmetric stickiness of the non-union default, which stems from both strong employer opposition to unionization and the collective action problems that employees face in countering that opposition. Sachs argues that the law's neutrality regarding employees' free choice regarding unionization calls for the adoption of an "altering rule" – or a union organizing process – that corrects for the asymmetric stickiness of the non-union default by minimizing employer intervention in unionization campaigns. At the same time, and to the likely chagrin of EFCA supporters, Sachs questions the virtue of an open (versus secret) *decision making* process such as card check, which does not reduce the role of employer intervention but does potentially allow for interference with employee choice from the pro-union side. In closing, Sachs briefly previews the sorts of labor law reforms that would maximize employee free choice under his analysis.

Richard Epstein approaches much the same territory from quite another point on the political spectrum, reaching sharply different conclusions. His characteristic no-holds-barred blend of libertarianism and economic analysis leads him to a highly critical account of existing labor law, and an even more critical view of the major recent labor law reform proposals, including the recently deceased EFCA. He celebrates the failure of that proposal, which he contends would have made a bad law worse in terms of its interference with individual contractual liberties and its impact on the economy. Epstein would return, rather, to the pre-New Deal "common law for labor relations" (Epstein, 1983), including the "yellow-dog contract" and the right of employers not only to refuse to deal with unions but to refuse to employ union members. He would return, in short, to the liberty of individual contract within barely regulated labor markets.

The remaining two chapters in Part II begin to touch on issues of employment law as well as labor law. Morris Kleiner and David Weil compare remedies under the NLRA with remedies under other labor statutes, as well as with the demands of "deterrence theory," and find the remedies under the NLRA to be seriously deficient. In short, a rational employer who weighs the expected economic consequences of unionization

against the paltry remedies that may follow an illegal campaign to discourage unionization will not be much deterred from violating the law. The Kleiner and Weil chapter
explores one set of implications of the economics of unionization (which the Hirsch
chapter develops at greater length) for a public policy that purports to enable employees
to choose unionization in the face of employer opposition. The chapter also illustrates
one way in which the "rational actor" model, and simple assumptions about the economic incentives that drive private market actors, may support stronger public intervention in private behavior. If we take as given the law's definition of certain conduct as
wrongful, such as anti-union discrimination, the standard deterrence model may support
stronger remedies or enforcement policies.

Stewart Schwab's chapter explores a potential role for unions as "brokers" of their
members' employment law rights. By serving as gatekeeper to greater flexibility in the
terms and conditions of employment, and to a less costly and disruptive means of adjudicating employment law disputes, unions might be able to offer something of value to
both employers and workers. Schwab usefully reviews the economic and non-economic
rationales for existing employee rights and labor standards laws, explaining how the logic
of those rationales tends to dictate the non-waivability of the protections. For example,
if a workplace safety law aims to secure public goods for workers, it does not make sense
to allow individuals to waive those protections, for that would reintroduce the very collective action problems the law was designed to avoid. In some cases, however, unions
may be able to overcome those problems and to waive legal rights only when doing so
makes workers better off in the exchange. Schwab explores a range of cases in which
union waiver of employment rights is permitted under existing law, and contends for a
cautious expansion of this strategy for introducing flexibility and vitality into the law.

In Part III we turn directly to the field of employment law – once the arriviste and
now the dominant component of the labor and employment law field. Employment law
is obviously a diverse field, but much of it consists of mandates which can usefully be
sorted into two categories: minimum labor standards such as the Fair Labor Standards
Act (FLSA), the Occupational Safety and Health Act (OSHA), and the Family and
Medical Leave Act (FMLA); and individual employee rights such as those embodied
in Title VII of the Civil Rights Act and other antidiscrimination statutes, various anti-
retaliation statutes and doctrines, and a smattering of employee liberties and privacy
rights. The economics of employer mandates has long been grist for the law-and-
economics mill.

At the heart of employment law, however, is the employment contract; and at the heart
of the employment contract in the U.S. is the reigning presumption of terminability-at-
will. Employment-at-will, and the employer's power to condition continued employment
on acceptance of its chosen terms, makes the employment contract largely modifiable
at will and non-legally enforceable. Employment-at-will also sets the default position
against which all employer mandates, employee rights, and constraints on "wrongful
discharge" operate. Indeed, the distinctively American proliferation of antidiscrimination and anti-retaliation laws and doctrines, as well as wrongful discharge litigation,
are historical by-products of the employment-at-will default rule, which in its original
and absolute form tolerates the exercise of employer power that society has found to be
intolerable. Economic analysis has long been a major element of debates between the
defenders of employment-at-will, more or less absolute, and the proponents of some

version of "just cause" protection that prevails in nearly every other developed country in the world.

We begin the book's treatment of employment law from a methodological perspective. Christine Jolls' chapter, "Bias and the Law of the Workplace," looks at some major features of the employment law landscape through the lens of behavioral economics, and in light of well-documented deviations of actual human cognition from the "rational actor" construct at the heart of neoclassical economics. In particular, she shows how the law of the workplace sometimes works – and might work better – by reducing or counteracting widely shared cognitive biases. For example, the law of employee handbooks might respond to "optimism bias" in employees' apprehension of disclaimers, and better alert them to their lack of legally enforceable job security, by requiring employers to include actual examples of unjustified discharges that courts had found to be lawful. Turning to the stubborn problem of implicit racial biases, Jolls shows that the law of employment discrimination already does help to reduce such biases, most importantly by increasing workforce diversity. Exposing potentially biased individuals to African-American (or female) co-workers – or even to positive images of African-Americans or women – can reduce not only conscious biases, as the venerable "contact hypothesis" would have it, but implicit or unconscious biases as well. Through her exploration of a few bodies of behavioral research, and their implications for a few crucial areas of employment law, Jolls shows the broad potential value of behavioral economics in improving the law's capacity to achieve its goals.

Rachel Arnow-Richman's chapter, "From Just Cause to Just Notice in Reforming Employment Termination Law," focuses directly on the law of the employment contract and the debate over employment-at-will. Finding the debate to be at a bit of a stalemate, Arnow-Richman charts a new direction for reform. She observes that much of the critique of employment-at-will is based on the burden and dislocation that a summary discharge visits upon the employee, while much of the defense of employment-at-will revolves around the difficulty and cost of reviewing the employer's reasons for discharge – costs that would likely be passed on to employees. She argues that both concerns can be addressed by shifting the goal of reform from "just cause" to "just notice" – from allowing employees to contest the adequacy of the employer's reasons for discharge to guaranteeing employees a fair period of advance notice, or payment in lieu of notice, during which they can find their next jobs. Arnow-Richman argues that a "just notice" regime would entail much lower administrative costs than a "just cause" regime, and arguably lower than the existing "at-will plus exceptions" regime (although higher than a hypothetically pure at-will regime that almost no one currently defends). Moreover, a "just notice" regime would benefit not only the fraction of employees who are fired without adequate cause, but also the many more employees whose jobs are eliminated for economic reasons. Arnow-Richman brings a comparative dimension to the debate, not only to point out the familiar fact that U.S. law is a lonely outlier in its adherence to employment-at-will, but also to explore the Canadian experience with what amounts to a "just notice" regime.

Simon Deakin approaches the same set of issues from an empirical and comparative perspective in his chapter, "The Law and Economics of Employment Protection Legislation." Deakin traces the law-and-economics analysis of "employment protection laws" (EPL) – that is, unjust dismissal laws and laws relating to lay-off and redundancy

– through a series of stages. "First generation" analyses were highly critical of EPL as an inefficient and unjustified imposition on party autonomy. "Second generation" analyses reflected the teachings of modern neoclassical labor economics on transaction costs, asymmetric information and adverse selection, and produced a more mixed assessment of the economic impact of EPL. A "third generation" of "evolutionary models" builds on the "varieties of capitalism" literature, and views the varying approaches to EPL as "endogenously generated solutions to coordination problems arising in labour markets." That is, different nations' labor market institutions generate different solutions to the problem of dismissals and redundancies. Based on a review of recent empirical studies of EPL, which use new time-series datasets to supplement earlier cross-sectional studies, Deakin finds qualified support for an efficiency case for EPL-type interventions, at least in certain institutional contexts and under certain market conditions. For example, job security protections may contribute to productivity and innovation at the firm level by complementing and reinforcing a commitment (by trade unions, employer groups and government) to training and workforce development.

Alan Hyde focuses not on legal restrictions on employers' power to discharge employees but on contractual restrictions on employees' right to quit and compete with the employer. The latter are closely intertwined with the definition and allocation of property rights to the information that employees acquire and enhance through employment. Hyde's review of the extensive empirical literature on innovation, growth and employee mobility finds a striking consensus: "This literature finds *no* provable social advantages in intellectual property-based restrictions on employee mobility." Indeed, limiting employers' proprietary claims to workplace know-how and their power to restrict employee mobility – as California law does, for example – is associated with greater innovation and economic growth.

It is interesting to compare the Deakin and Hyde chapters. In some respects the two studies reinforce each other. Both review an extensive empirical literature and reach conclusions at odds with the predictions of first-generation law-and-economic analysis. The latter in both cases had come down firmly on the side of "freedom of contract," and for allowing employers both to freely fire their employees and to restrict their employees' mobility. Deakin and Hyde both find that restricting employer power – to fire employees or to restrict their mobility respectively – can promote economic growth and innovation (although Hyde is far more categorical in his conclusions than Deakin).

If we focus on the relative value of job stability and job mobility, however, the two studies seem to point in opposite directions, at least at first blush. Hyde's strong conclusions about the economic benefits of unrestricted employee mobility may seem to be at odds with Deakin's more qualified claim that job security and stability may promote productivity and innovation. Or perhaps there is an efficiency case to be made – at least in some industries and some institutional settings – both for ensuring employees' freedom to voluntarily move from one job to another and for legally restricting employers' power to discharge employees. There is no logical inconsistency – though there may be an irony in some eyes – in the notion that ensuring both employees' freedom to quit and their freedom from unjustified discharge, against employers' contractual claims to the contrary, might serve larger societal interests. At the very least these two chapters illustrate the vigor and heterodoxy of modern law-and-economic analysis.

Turning next to employment discrimination law, Samuel Issacharoff and Erin Scharff in their chapter, "Antidiscrimination in Employment: The Simple, the Complex, and the Paradoxical," argue that employment discrimination law encountered increasing strain as it progressed from Title VII's relatively straightforward attack on irrational discrimination to more redistributionist challenges to some forms of economically rational discrimination. Initially with the advent of disparate impact doctrine, then with the extension of the antidiscrimination mandate to older, pregnant, and disabled workers, and finally in the rise of explicit demands for accommodation, it became increasingly clear that employers were expected to bear significant costs in order to improve the employment prospects of some economically disadvantaged groups. But employers operating within markets cannot be expected simply to absorb those costs; they will try to avoid them or to pass them on, and in either case the losers may be the very groups the law sought to benefit. So, for example, if legal demands for accommodation of disabilities are made largely by incumbent employees, employers might rationally avoid hiring disabled workers. This result may be illegal but it is very hard to prove and rarely litigated.

Issacharoff and Scharff stress that, where society seeks to alter employment practices that are economically rational, it must consider how employers are likely to respond, and it may have to explicitly engineer the distribution of costs to avoid counterproductive responses. A forthright reckoning with the costs of promoting equal employment opportunity – and sometimes the use of vehicles other than antidiscrimination law, such as social insurance schemes – will allow society to better achieve its equal employment objectives.

The final chapter of Part III, Samuel Estreicher and Zev Eigen's "The Forum for Adjudication of Employment Disputes," elaborates another aspect of the costs associated with employment rights. Forum and process obviously affect the cost of adjudicating rights claims, and are obviously critical to the realization of whatever rights the law confers on parties to the employment relationship. The direct costs to employee-claimants affect employees' ability to vindicate their formal legal rights; that takes a toll especially on low- and middle-income workers. Some of those costs may be shifted to losing employer-defendants, but whatever adjudication costs are borne directly by employers may in turn be shifted back to employees in indirect forms, through lower wage packages or reduced employment. To be sure, the high cost of being sued – including the forum-related costs of litigation – can help to motivate employers to comply with the law. But employers' efforts to avoid costly litigation may take either productive or counterproductive forms.

Estreicher and Eigen are on balance critical of the heavy reliance on courts, juries and lawyers in U.S. employment law. In principle that reliance is counterposed by the traditional use of arbitration within the once-robust collective bargaining sphere, and the availability of administrative agencies for some rights enforcement. But in view of the ever-shrinking scope of collective bargaining and the chronic underfunding of administrative agencies, Estreicher and Eigen argue that the real alternative to the costly and slow judicial forum lies in employer-initiated arbitration and other dispute resolution systems. They review the main currents of controversy over mandatory arbitration, and come down in favor of preserving and improving these private dispute resolution systems. They close with suggestions for reform, including some that can be achieved through private ordering (such as improvements to the influential Due Process Protocol to which reputable employers and arbitrators largely adhere) and some that borrow from recent experience in the United Kingdom.

Part IV closes the volume with two economically inflected perspectives on the field, one from each of the editors, both of which straddle the divide between labor law and employment law. Michael Wachter's ironically titled chapter, "The Striking Success of the National Labor Relations Act," begins in the cauldron of widespread and often violent labor conflict in which the NLRA took shape, but concludes with the resurgence of a non-union sector that has met workers' needs, at least well enough, to virtually eliminate serious industrial unrest. On Wachter's account, the NLRA ultimately accomplished its most widely shared, abiding and coherent objective of "industrial peace." But it did so, not so much by supporting unionization and collective bargaining as the original Wagner Act set out to do, but by curbing union power and allowing the emergence of a robust non-union sector that was almost inevitably able to outcompete unionized firms in an increasingly competitive economy. As for the other major objectives of the Wagner Act, "industrial democracy" and increasing employees' bargaining power through union representation, they were plagued from the start, says Wachter, by a built-in contradiction: The more unions increase employees' bargaining power and deliver a wage premium, the more they raise the costs and hurt the competitiveness of unionized employers, thus depressing union density and the spread of "industrial democracy" through collective bargaining.

The contradiction that Wachter identifies between increased union bargaining power and wider union representation is not universal to all labor relations systems. Wachter's primary thesis is that the workings of today's labor markets are largely a product of political choices in favor of freer market competition. After a brief failed experiment with corporatist coordination of wages and prices under the National Industrial Recovery Act, the movement from "fair competition" to "free competition" progressed with the gradual dismantling of industry regulation in transportation, communication and utilities, and the increasing commitment to free trade and globalization of product markets. But among the crucial political choices was the choice in 1947 to curb organized labor's strongest economic weapons, and thus to curtail both its ability to disrupt commerce and its ability to extend its organizing gains across the primary sectors of the economy. Thereafter, neither corporatist coordination nor industry regulation nor private collective action was going to take wages out of competition. Thus the die was cast and the long slide in union density began.

Wachter's account is a depressing one from the perspective of organized labor in the United States. Whether it is depressing to most American workers turns on the soundness of his relatively sanguine portrayal of modern non-union workplace governance. More sophisticated and worker-friendly human resource (HR) policies, and self-enforcing informal norms of fairness, have managed to keep workers at least satisfied enough to keep them in the non-union fold – that was a major purpose of those policies, after all – and to keep them from taking to the streets in large numbers. Sure, many non-union workers say they would like to have a union or some other kind of collective representation; but most of them do not seem to feel strongly enough about it to trigger the NLRA's process for union recognition, which nowadays functions largely as a kind of pressure valve to keep workers' discontent from spilling into more disruptive forms. Labor peace thus prevails.

Estlund's chapter, "Why Workers Still Need a Collective Voice in the Era of Norms and Mandates," takes a less sanguine view of the non-union workplace, at least for workers who lack scarce and valued skills and in firms with relatively little reputational capital. For employees at and below the middling levels of the labor market, there is evidence of widespread noncompliance with basic labor standards, deteriorating real wages, benefits and job security, and workplace pressures that are unbuffered by the internal labor market norms that supposedly protect workers in the non-union workplace. Estlund is also doubtful that employees' option of unionization is robust enough to activate the "union threat effect" that, on Wachter's account, helps to back up norms of fair treatment. As per Sachs' chapter, employers' aggressive resistance to unionization – economically rational though it may be – makes it enormously difficult for employees to choose union representation and collective bargaining.

If we purport to ensure employees' free choice regarding unionization and collective bargaining, and particularly if we rely on that free choice – and the real threat of unionization – to induce non-union employers to behave decently, the law must do more to restrain employers' use of threats and coercion – sticks rather than carrots – to discourage unionization. Otherwise, "labor peace" may signify not employee contentment and basically fair and decent working conditions but rather resignation in the face of employer resistance and powerful market forces and pessimism about the utility of collective action and the reality of the rights the law purports to grant employees.

In the end, what unites the contributions to this volume, and all that unites the varieties of economic analysis in labor and employment law, is that market forces – in labor markets, product markets, and capital markets – are powerful and cannot be ignored. Those forces both drive and constrain employer behavior in workplace governance, even as employers make choices that govern workers' lives. Market forces shape employer responses to, and thus the consequences of, legal rules – though not invariably as the economics textbooks would predict. Whatever goals policymakers pursue – redistribution, fairness, equality, or even efficiency, economic growth or innovation – they will be well served by serious attention to the economic incentives that operate on market participants and the aggregate consequences for economic performance and growth.

NOTES

1. One of us later described that initial confrontation, somewhat tendentiously, thus: "With the temporary zeal of missionaries, and with as little respect for the local culture, several law-and-economics scholars brought the harsh logic of the neo-classical gospel to . . . labor law and found it hopelessly mired in rent-seeking" (Estlund, 2002).
2. After the Professional Air Traffic Controllers Organization (PATCO) launched an illegal strike in 1981, President Reagan fired over 11,000 striking air traffic controllers. The incident is often credited with emboldening U.S. employers to take a more aggressive anti-union stance, and particularly to resort to permanent replacement of lawful economic strikers (e.g., Wachter, 2007, pp. 617–18).
3. Most empirical research on this point has found little or no net impact of unions on productivity (Hirsch, Chapter 4 in this volume). An important mediating variable may be the quality of labor relations: In a cooperative labor-management relationship, the positive effects of unionization might outweigh the negative, while labor-management conflict takes a toll on productivity in a variety of ways. In either case, however, the lower profitability of unionized firms and facilities has been associated with lower investment of capital and lower growth in those firms and facilities, and with the relative shrinkage of the unionized sector. *Id.*

4. The claim met skepticism in the law-and-economics camp: If unions boosted productivity, then employer resistance to unions was irrational – and that could hardly be the case (Posner, 1984). The answer to that "puzzle" was simple enough; unions increased wages and benefits by more than they increased productivity, and thus reduced profits. That answer both explained employer resistance to unions and foretold a gloomy outlook for the success of unionized firms insofar as profits were needed to thrive or even survive in competitive product and capital markets.
5. For thoughtful defenses of the "unequal bargaining power" thesis, see Michael H. Gottesman (1991) and Kaufman (Chapter 3 in this volume).
6. National Labor Relations Act, 29 U.S.C. §151.
7. Freeman & Medoff's theory of how unions can promote greater productivity can be seen as a variation on the efficiency wage hypothesis for the union sector. In general, the idea of efficiency wages has been more salient in the non-union sector. Higher wages are said to generate employee loyalty to the non-union employer, and greater work effort in return. In the union sector, the union claims credit for higher wages, thereby weakening the workers' motivation to reward employers with greater effort.

REFERENCES

Becker, Gary S. 1957. *The Economics of Discrimination*. Chicago, IL: University of Chicago Press.
Camerer, Colin, Samuel Issacharoff, George Loewenstein, Ted O'Donoghue, and Matthew Rabin. 2003. "Regulation for Conservatives: Behavioral Economics and the Case for 'Asymmetric Paternalism,'" 151 *University of Pennsylvania Law Review* 1211–54.
Dau-Schmidt, Kenneth G. 1992. "A Bargaining Analysis of American Labor Law and the Search for Industrial Peace," 91 *Michigan Law Review* 419–514.
Donahue, John J. III. 1992. "Advocacy Versus Analysis in Assessing Employment Discrimination Law," 44 *Stanford Law Review* 1583-1614 (reviewing Richard Epstein, *Forbidden Grounds: The Case Against Employment Discrimination Laws* (1992)).
Donahue, John J. and Peter Siegelman. 1991. "The Changing Nature of Employment Discrimination Litigation," 43 *Stanford Law Review* 983–1033.
Epstein, Richard A. 1983. "A Common Law for Labor Relations: A Critique of the New Deal Labor Legislation," 92 *Yale Law Journal* 1357–408.
Epstein, Richard A. 1984. "In Defense of the Contract at Will," 51 *University of Chicago Law Review* 947–82.
Epstein, Richard A. 1992. *Forbidden Grounds: The Case Against Employment Discrimination Laws*. Cambridge, MA: Harvard University Press.
Estlund, Cynthia L. 2002. "Reflections on the Declining Prestige of American Labor Law Scholarship," 23 *Comparative Labor Law and Policy Journal* 789–800.
Freed, Mayer G. and Daniel D. Polsby. 1989. "Just Cause for Termination Rules and Economic Efficiency," 38 *Emory Law Journal* 1097–144.
Freeman, Richard B. 2007. "What Do Unions Do? The 2004 M-Brane Stringtwister Edition," in James T. Bennett and Bruce E. Kaufman. *What Do Unions Do? A Twenty-Year Perspective*. New Brunswick, NJ: Transaction Publishers.
Freeman, Richard B. and James L. Medoff. 1984. *What Do Unions Do?* New York: Basic Books.
Getman, Julius G. and Thomas C. Kohler. 1983. "The Common Law, Labor Law, and Reality: A Response to Professor Epstein," 92 *Yale Law Journal* 1415–34.
Gottesman, Michael H. 1991. "Wither Goest Labor Law: Law and Economics in the Workplace," 100 *Yale Law Journal* 2767–810 (reviewing Paul C. Weiler, *Governing the Workplace: The Future of Labor and Employment Law* (1990)).
Hirschman, Albert O. 1970. *Exit, Voice, and Loyalty: Responses to Decline in Firms, Organizations, and States*. Cambridge, MA: Harvard University Press.
Hovenkamp, Herbert J. 2011. "Coase, Institutionalism, and the Origins of Law and Economics," 86 *Indiana Law Journal* 499–542.
Hylton, Keith N. 1993. "Efficiency and Labor Law," 87 *Northwestern University Law Review* 471–522.
Hylton, Keith N. and Maria O'Brien Hylton. 1989. "Rational Decisions and Regulation of Union Entry," 34 *Villanova Law Review* 145–207.
Issacharoff, Samuel. 1992. "Contractual Liberties in Discriminatory Markets," 70 *Texas Law Review* 1219–59 (reviewing Richard Epstein, *Forbidden Grounds: The Case Against Employment Discrimination Laws* (1992)).
Issacharoff, Samuel and Elyse Rosenblum. 1993. "Women and the Workplace, Accommodating the Demands of Pregnancy," 94 *Columbia Law Review* 2154–221.
Jolls, Christine. 2000. "Accommodation Mandates," 53 *Stanford Law Review* 223–306.

Jolls, Christine. 2007. "Behavioral Economics Analysis of Employment Law," October 2007 Princeton University Behavioral Economics and Public Policy Conference. Available at: http://www.law.yale.edu/documents/pdf/Faculty/Jolls_BehavioralEconomicsAnalysisofEmploymentLaw1-18-10.pdf.

Jolls, Christine, Cass R. Sunstein, and Richard Thaler. 1998. "A Behavioral Approach to Law and Economics," 50 *Stanford Law Review* 1471–550.

Posner, Richard. 1984. "Some Economics of Labor Law," 51 *University of Chicago Law Review* 988–1011.

Rock, Edward B. and Michael L. Wachter. 1996. "The Enforceability of Norms and the Employment Relationship," 144 *University of Pennsylvania Law Review* 1913–52.

Schwab, Stewart J. 1987. "Collective Bargaining and the Coase Theorem," 72 *Cornell Law Review* 245–87.

Schwab, Stewart J. 1993. "Life-Cycle Justice: Accommodating Just Cause and Employment at Will," 92 *Michigan Law Review* 8–62.

Schwab, Stewart J. 1996. "Wrongful Discharge Law and the Search for Third-Party Effects," 74 *Texas Law Review* 1943–78.

Schwab, Stewart J. 1997. "The Law and Economics Approach to Workplace Regulation," in Bruce E. Kaufman, ed., *Government Regulation of the Employment Relationship*. Madison, WI: Industrial Relations Research Association.

Strauss, David A. 1991. "The Law and Economics of Racial Discrimination in Employment: The Case for Numerical Standards," 79 *Georgetown Law Journal* 1619–57.

Sunstein, Cass R. 2001. "Human Behavior and the Law of Work," 87 *Virginia Law Review* 205–73.

Thaler, Richard H. and Cass R. Sunstein. 2008. *Nudge: Improving Decisions about Health, Wealth, and Happiness.* New Haven, CT: Yale University Press.

Verkerke, J. Hoult. 1992. "Free to Search," 105 *Harvard Law Review* 2080–97 (reviewing Richard Epstein, *Forbidden Grounds: The Case Against Employment Discrimination Laws* (1992)).

Verkerke, J. Hoult. 1995. "An Empirical Perspective on Indefinite Term Employment Contracts: Resolving the Just Cause Debate," 1995 *Wisconsin Law Review* 837–917.

Verkuil, Paul. 1983. "Whose Common Law for Labor Relations?," 92 *Yale Law Journal* 1409–14.

Wachter, Michael L. 2007. "Labor Unions: A Corporatist Institution in a Competitive World," 155 *University of Pennsylvania Law Review* 581–634.

Wachter, Michael L. and George M. Cohen. 1988. "The Law and Economics of Collective Bargaining: An Introduction and Application to the Problem of Subcontracting, Partial Closure, and Relocation," 136 *University of Pennsylvania Law Review* 1349–417.

Wachter, Michael L. and Randall D. Wright. 1990. "The Economics of Internal Labor Markets," 29 *Industrial Relations* 240–62.

Weiler, Paul. 1990. *Governing the Workplace: The Future of Labor and Employment Law*. Cambridge, MA: Harvard University Press.

Williamson, Oliver E., Michael L. Wachter, and Jeffrey E. Harris. 1975. "Understanding the Employment Relation: The Analysis of Idiosyncratic Exchange," 6 *The Bell Journal of Economics* 250–78.

2. Neoclassical labor economics: its implications for labor and employment law

Michael L. Wachter[1]

The application of economics to labor and employment law trails its application in virtually all other areas of business and commercial law. Topics such as contracts, torts, corporations, commercial law, and tax have all readily integrated economic reasoning as an assist to legal reasoning. In almost all these cases, moreover, the economics concept of efficiency has been accepted as one of the goals of the law. This is decidedly not the case in labor law or, for the most part, in employment law.[2] Disagreement over fundamental principles serves as an important explanation for this relative lack of emphasis on economic reasoning.

Most labor law scholars believe deeply that collective bargaining is the preferred framework for the employment relationship.[3] They tend to share the original goal of the National Labor Relations Act (NLRA), which remains on the books today, of equalizing bargaining power by enabling workers to engage in collective bargaining with their employers. The NLRA's goal of equalizing bargaining power encompassed both procedural and substantive ends: it sought to promote the *mechanism* of collective bargaining and, in doing so, *to raise wages above the market wage* that would prevail absent unionization.

Achieving both procedural and substantive ends simultaneously turned out to be the challenge. As unions helped workers gain a wage premium, unionized firms became less competitive and nonunion firms fought harder to stay nonunion. Modern neoclassical economic theory offered a simple explanation based on the most basic principle of economics. The inverse relationship between quantity (i.e., employment) and price (i.e., wage), works in the labor market as in every other market. If unions succeed in raising wages above competitive levels by using the economic weapons available to them in collective bargaining, union employment is likely to suffer. The result is a tradeoff between the number of workers covered by collective bargaining agreements and the size of the union wage premium. As a consequence there is an inconsistency within this goal of the NLRA.

Several attempts have been made to formulate alternative theories that erase this dismal tradeoff between the size of the unionized workforce and the union wage premium in order to resuscitate the twin goals of high union employment and a higher union wage. Most variants are built around the efficiency model. Workers are not like other commodities or inputs in that they can respond to incentives. Perhaps higher wages could call forth greater cooperation and higher productivity. To date, however, this line of research has not been successful in resuscitating the normative appeal for the union sector because its assumptions only hold for the nonunion sector.

Research has moved beyond this threshold issue to other labor market issues, particularly those arising in the internal labor market, or, in other words, the employment relationship that exists inside the firm. Here workers are less mobile and the firm is less constrained by market forces. Consequently, there is at least potentially greater room for policy intervention that would improve the protection accorded to workers. Even here, however, economic theory which emphasizes the transaction costs of collective bargaining offers more caveats than encouragement. The lack of integration of economics into labor and employment law is thus not surprising at all. If one's agenda is to promote collective bargaining or provide more procedural rights to nonunion employees, neoclassical economics is not a promising starting point.

The task of this chapter is to analyze the tradeoff between wages and employment and to evaluate other policies and policy prescriptions in the context of a neoclassical model of the labor market. That model is different from the simplified textbook portrayal. Yet it is not new, as its basic building blocks have been available for several decades. For example, portions of this chapter are drawn from two articles that I co-authored (Wachter and Wright, 1990; Rock and Wachter, 1996), citing to the original articles that developed the concepts.

The chapter is organized in the following sections. Section I describes the foundations of the neoclassical model, starting with the textbook model of the union and nonunion labor markets. These are the external labor markets (ELM) where workers seek jobs and employers fill vacancies. This section presents the core issue; namely the tradeoff between union wages and union employment. It then explores the fundamental theorems of welfare economics that allow us to attach welfare implications to alternative market outcomes and investigates the various theoretical attempts to refute the existence of the tradeoff between union wages and employment. Section II develops the model of the internal labor markets (ILM), which represents the employment relationship inside the firm. It also presents the connections between the ILM and the ELM and presents the four central economic factors in the ILM; namely job-specific training, risk aversion, information asymmetries and transaction costs. Sections III and IV discuss how the parties deal with the four factors of the ILM either through union contracting (Section III) or nonunion contracting or norms (Section IV). The last section, Section V, concludes the chapter and discusses policy implications.

I.   FOUNDATIONS OF THE NEOCLASSICAL MODEL

A.   Textbook Model of a Competitive Labor Market

I start with the simple competitive equilibrium textbook model of the labor market (see Figure 2.1). Although simple, it is all that is needed to engage much of the debate. This is the external labor market (ELM), where firms hire workers into new jobs and unemployed workers search for jobs after an existing job turnover or an entry into the labor market. The key prediction is that wages are determined by market forces, labor supply (denoted by S), and labor demand (denoted by D). Market-equilibrating forces lead the labor market toward the equilibrium solution, where S and D intersect, with employment at E_C and the wage at W_C. At this point wages cannot be higher without employment being lower. The equilibrium point is thus efficient.[4]

Suppose, however, that the labor market were out of equilibrium, with a low wage of

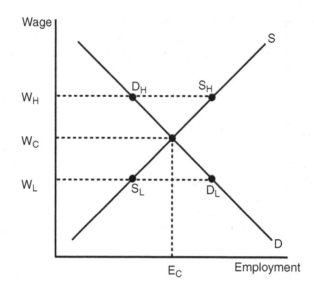

Figure 2.1   Competitive labor market

W_L (where the subscript L denotes the low wage). At this low wage level, demand for labor (D_L) would be far in excess of the supply of labor (S_L). Since labor markets are competitive, employers would offer higher wages to compete for workers in order to fill the high demand for labor. Wages would rise toward W_C, and the labor supply would increase as more individuals joined the labor force seeking jobs at the higher wage levels. At the same time, labor demand would begin to decline because the higher pay of the work force would mean that workers were less profitable. Thus the equilibrating process would continue until the wage had increased from W_L to W_C and demand had declined from D_L to the competitive equilibrium level of employment (denoted by E_C).

Alternatively, suppose the labor market were out of equilibrium with a high wage of W_H. At this point labor demand would be at D_H, which would be much lower than the supply S_H. Market-equilibrating forces would again come into operation. Now workers would compete for the jobs at the high wage rate. As a consequence of the labor competition, the wage rate would begin to decline. As the wage declined, employment would begin to pick up, reflecting the lower wage rate. The process would continue until the wage had declined to W_C and employment had increased to E_C.

The above discussion of labor supply and demand presents a partial equilibrium view. Labor supply and demand functions fit into a structural model of the overall economy. In the structural model, wage effects ripple through other markets and in turn feed back to influence the location of the labor supply and demand curve.

The labor demand curve discussed above is referred to as a derived demand because it is derived from the demand for the firm's products. The location of the demand curve depends on the productivity and skill of workers in producing the product or service that the employer is selling in the market. The greater the productivity of workers, the greater is the equilibrium wage. Demand curves slope downward because of substitution effects and diminishing returns as consumers switch away from expensive products and employers substitute inexpensive factors of production for expensive factors. At this level of abstraction the diagram refers to the overall labor market; however it can be generalized to any number of different skill levels and geographical regions. This discussion assumes the existence of competitive labor markets.

The supply curve's location depends on the work/leisure choice made by individuals. Supply curves are generally viewed as being upward sloping; that is, more individuals enter the labor market in search of jobs when the wage is high. However, whereas the demand curve is always downward sloping, the supply curve need not always be upward sloping. For the purposes of this chapter, I assume the labor supply is upward sloping, but nothing of importance in the chapter turns on this assumption.

It is the existence of an inverse relationship between wages and employment that is at the heart of the debate. There are some changes in the economy, such as an expansionary monetary and fiscal policy in the midst of a recession, that can allow employment to increase even as wages are increased. But changes of this type are not contested. The debatable issue is a very specific one, namely whether an exogenous increase in union wages above the market-clearing wage, as a result of collective bargaining, will have a negative effect on union employment. Deconstructing the wage/employment tradeoff thus becomes critical for traditional labor scholars who want to undo the claim that higher union wages are inversely related to union employment levels.[5]

In this chapter I assume, as do most other economists, that external labor markets in the nonunion sector are generally highly competitive. I do not assume that product markets are necessarily competitive nor do I assume that internal labor markets are perfectly competitive. Although the textbook model above assumes perfect competition, perfection is not needed for the efficiency and welfare conclusions to hold. Labor markets that are highly competitive, but not perfectly so, can have frictions and information gaps at any point in time, and can be in disequilibrium in the short run. None of the policy conclusions is changed by acknowledging these short-run market imperfections.

The model I use here, the neoclassical theory, is the standard model used in economic analysis. It can be criticized for ignoring many institutional features of the labor market, but its goal is testable predictions. And that it does with excellence. Wages do generally rise at a faster rate during expansions and decrease or rise at a slower rate during recessions. More skilled workers will generally have higher wages than less skilled workers. Growing regions will tend to have faster wage growth than declining regions. There are discrepancies, of course, because no theory is perfect, but the overall predictive picture is strong. Moreover – and this is key – there is no alternative theory which offers a similar range of predictions. Certainly there are many variants of the neoclassical model, but all share the assumption that prices and quantities are determined in markets by pressures of supply and demand. Moreover, whenever markets are out of equilibrium, there are equilibrating forces that push the market toward equilibrium. The equilibration is not instantaneous and it can even take years to recalibrate, as was the case in the early 20th century, where workers from the southern regions of the United States moved north in search of newly created manufacturing jobs.

Another key component of the neoclassical model consists of the fundamental general equilibrium theorems. The first fundamental theorem, stated in its most simple form, says that competitive markets are efficient because they maximize the total income that the economy can produce.[6] The second fundamental theorem, again in its simplest form, is that there are many different income-maximizing states, each corresponding to a different distribution of income across individuals.[7] The government, through tax and expenditure policies, is given the job of choosing among the alternative income-maximizing states to determine the welfare-maximizing income distribution. The policy implication drawn from these theorems is that policymakers should first attempt to make markets as competitive as possible, and then should seek to improve income distribution to reach the optimal distribution of income or welfare.

A number of interesting, albeit highly stylized, policy implications can be drawn from the above description of the labor market. First, there is no need for government policy (or for unions) to ensure that wages rise over time with worker productivity. Competitive markets will lead to that result. Instead, if unions raise wages above competitive levels, the economy will be less productive. Second, when changes in the income distribution are deemed desirable, they should generally be achieved through tax and government expenditure programs rather than by dictating noncompetitive outcomes in markets through government regulation. Industrial policy should be confined to making markets as competitive as possible.[8] Thus policies that improve the efficiency of particular labor markets are generally favored in neoclassical economics.

Although no one believes that markets are perfectly efficient, the neoclassical textbook model assumes that markets are perfectly competitive as a simplifying assumption (Ehrenberg and Smith, 2011) and as an ideal against which policy improvements can be judged. Notably, over the last several decades neoclassical models have incorporated job-search frictions, job-specific training, information asymmetries, and other market realities that might allow for policy improvements.

The neoclassical model has also been extended to account for monopsony, in which one firm can exercise labor market power.[9] Unlike in the competitive labor market, in which firms are "wage takers" when they hire workers, in the monopsony model the firm is a wage setter. It needs to raise its wage if it wants to increase hiring and can lower its wage when it is reducing employment. I will not illustrate this model or discuss it in any detail, however, because there is little evidence of material monopsony power in U.S. labor markets so that whatever monopsony power exists is unlikely to change any of the conclusions reached in this chapter. If monopsony were dominant in the labor market, higher union wages could lead to higher employment.

Labor markets tend to be more competitive than product markets. The reason is that employers, regardless of their product market, still hire workers from the same external labor market. Prospective workers have no firm-specific training and their skill level depends mainly on their level of education and general training, whether they are high school graduates, college graduates, or professional school graduates. If employers are hiring locally, then each would hire blue-collar workers from the same high schools and entry-level engineers or managers from the same colleges. In other words, even if labor markets were entirely local, they would be more competitive than the local product markets. However, labor markets are not local. While workers incur costs in moving from one locality to another in search of jobs, in today's society labor markets are more national than local.

B.   Textbook Model of a Union Labor Market

The primary goal of labor unions is to "take wages out of competition." Labor is not just another commodity and, in this line of reasoning, workers should not be treated as a commodity and have their pay determined by market forces. A key question for labor economics is what consequences will follow union efforts to raise wages above what the market would otherwise dictate.

The textbook union labor market uses a simple variant of the supply and demand model used in Figure 2.1. Figure 2.2 starts by duplicating the wage and employment levels that exist in a competitive market. As noted above, the equilibrating forces of competitive markets push the labor market toward the intersection of the S and D curves. The union market works very differently because the equilibrating market forces are replaced by the collective bargaining mechanism. The wage set through collective bargaining, denoted W_U, is higher than the market-clearing, or competitive, wage, W_C. With its legally protected strike weapon, the union can extract a wage premium from employers in return for not striking.

As a result of the higher union wage, firms set labor demand at D_U. The societal cost of the union wage being higher than the competitive wage is a lower level of employment (E_U rather than E_C). Furthermore, at the higher union wage, not only does the number of jobs decrease, but the number of workers seeking those jobs increases. The result is unemployment, measured by the horizontal distance at W_U between the supply of workers to the union sector, S_U, compared to labor demand, D_U. Without the equilibrating force of competitive markets the resulting social loss of reduced output and higher unemployment can persist in the union labor market.[10]

The union labor market is sometimes referred to as a cartelized market in that the union as the agent of the workers allows labor (workers or suppliers of labor) to act in

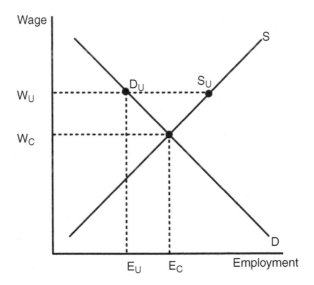

Figure 2.2   The union market

concert so that the wage is set above competitive levels (Posner, 1984; Wachter, Chapter 15 in this volume). From an economics vantage point, there is nothing controversial about calling the unionized labor market a cartelized market. The use of the term simply fits the economic definition of a cartel. Since cartels in product markets, however, are generally viewed negatively, the term cartel may have acquired negative connotations. Its use here, however, is entirely descriptive. Cartels seek to take prices, or in this case wages, out of competition, and that is perhaps the best single sentence stating unions' broad economic goal.[11]

The problem for the union sector is to maintain the cartel and prevent the equilibrating market forces from operating. This was a more likely event under the original Wagner Act, which favored unionization.[12] After the Taft-Hartley Act was passed it became easier for nonunion firms to form, remain nonunion, and thus compete, using their lower labor cost structure, with the unionized firms. The result was the growth of nonunion sectors in virtually all United States product markets. The emergence of international competition has only worsened an already bad situation for unions (Wachter, Chapter 15 in this volume).[13]

In terms of Figure 2.2, this shift of work from the union sector to the nonunion sector means that the labor demand curve shifts gradually to the left over time, resulting in steadily declining union employment. The union firm can either lower its product price to the nonunion price (to the detriment of profits) or try to maintain a price premium to cover the union wage. In either case, the union firm is likely to cut employment as it loses market share. Where the competition is greatest, the unionized firm is unlikely to earn a competitive return on its capital so that it is unlikely to continue to invest in updating its capital equipment in its high cost plants. As its capital becomes obsolete, the plants' production becomes uncompetitive so that output falls, causing a continuing erosion in union employment (Linneman, Wachter, and Carter, 1990; Hirsch, Chapter 4 in this volume).

Union wage setting in the labor market does not repeal product market pressures: wages are not actually taken out of competition in competitive product markets. The extent of the union wage premium, which is the percentage difference between W_U and W_C, will affect the fortunes of the firm, and if there are nonunion firms in the same product market, the union firm will be disadvantaged. That is invariably the case today: there are essentially no product markets that lack a nonunion sector.

One of the explicit goals of the Wagner Act was to equalize bargaining power. As Wachter (Chapter 15 in this volume) points out, the substantive element of that goal was to push the collectively bargained wage higher than the market wage. If the Wagner Act had also succeeded in the procedural element of that goal of spreading unionization throughout the economy, then the general equilibrium result of unionization would be not only to raise wages throughout the economy, but also to generate unemployment. The results would be akin to those shown in Figure 2.2.

The framers of the Wagner Act did not anticipate that the goal of raising wages above market levels and increasing union employment at the same time would prove to be inconsistent. The neoclassical economic model was not developed enough during the 1930s for it to be a useful policy tool. The three components of the theory not available to commentators in the 1930s were, first, a partial equilibrium theory of the labor market; second, a general equilibrium theory that pointed out the efficiency gains achieved by competitive outcomes; and third, a business cycle model.

The partial equilibrium theory of the labor market, which posits that labor demand moves inversely with the wage rate, was first sketched out by Marshall (1890)[14] at the turn of the last century, but its complete statement awaited the work of Sir John Hicks. Although Hicks' book was published in 1932,[15] Hicks was a 28 year old, hardly known budding star at the time. Consequently, the theory did not make its way out of university communities until the 1940s and it is not clear what Congress believed to be the appropriate microeconomic theory to use in evaluating the effect of an increase in wages resulting from collective bargaining.

Since the competitive wage was not a well-understood concept, it is fair to believe that the theory adopted by Congress may have been more one of Commons than of Hicks. Commons, one of the great labor economists of his time, thought that unemployment would be a constant problem and that, absent either government intervention or collective bargaining, the unemployed would bid down wages until they were at or immediately below a living wage (Commons and Andrews, 1927).

Until the advent of the modern neoclassical theory of labor markets, there was little support for the notion that society could be wealthy enough to generate a derived demand for labor that, in intersection with labor supply, would generate and maintain a socially acceptable wage. Yes, real wages had risen substantially over time in the 1800s, and took off with the industrial revolution. But a series of cyclical crises culminating in the Great Depression suggested an unpleasant dynamic story that capitalism was prone to excess competition which would inevitably generate depressions and "reserve armies" of unemployed workers. If the Great Depression had been the story of the future, then Commons rather than Hicks might still be taught in Econ 1.

The economic inefficiency of cartels was also largely unknown at the drafting of the NLRA. Showing that unions may cause unemployment in one market does not necessarily prove that the economy is worse off. Adam Smith (1776) conjectured that that was true in 1776, and Leon Walras (1874) developed the initial theory for it (if you could read French); but it was not until the 1950s that general equilibrium theory, and the proposition that competition produced efficient results, took hold through the works of Arrow and Debreu (1954), Debreu (1959), and McKenzie (1981), among others.

A piece of the puzzle was still missing, and that was the macroeconomic analysis of cyclical unemployment. This was provided by Keynes (1936) in the midst of the Great Depression. What Keynes showed and post-Keynesians have further developed is that a combination of monetary and fiscal policies could dampen the severity of business cycles. Although the Real Business Cycle model has raised questions about Keynesian theory and even the efficacy of monetary and fiscal policy, the state of the debate between New Keynesian versus Real Business Cycle theories leaves policymakers with far greater countercyclical tools than were available during the Great Depression (Mankiw, 1989; Abel, Bernanke, and Croushore, 2011).

The current macroeconomic debate has both the Keynesians and the Real Business Cycle theorists agreeing upon one critical feature of modern business cycles, namely, wage rigidity. That nominal wages are rigid in the union sector is not surprising. They are a key feature of the collective bargaining agreement. But wages also do not decline during recessions in the nonunion sector, at least since the Great Depression (Dobrescu, 2012).[16]

The finding of wage rigidity during recessions in the nonunion sector puts to rest concerns raised by the old economic greats like Malthus and Commons. Even during a recession and a period of high unemployment, market wage rates do not fall. One explanation for this wage rigidity is that firms are less risk averse than workers and are thus willing to offer insurance against income instability due to the business cycle. The other argument, and the one advanced in this chapter (see Section IV), stresses that wage cutting is not done even by nonunion firms because wage reductions in the face of declining demand is not a self-enforcing adjustment to declining product demand.

The upshot of this brief historical analysis is that, from the perspective of modern labor economics, the theory available to policymakers at the time of the passage of the Wagner Act in 1935 was flawed or not yet developed. It lacked the microeconomic foundations of labor markets being developed by Hicks and others; it lacked the fundamental welfare theorems of general equilibrium theory; and it lacked a modern business cycle theory. The Act's fear that absent unions there was nothing that could prevent recurring depressions was out of date by the late 1930s, and there is nothing in modern business cycle theory to suggest that unions help to prevent recurring business cycles.[17]

Indeed prevailing economic opinion had already moved away from this position by the late 1940s, when the Taft-Hartley Act was passed, moving labor policy from favoring unionization to neutrality.[18] Unions might sometimes be part of the problem rather than being part of the solution.

Still, many labor law scholars ignore the economic effects of unions even though the neoclassical model is so widely accepted in other areas of legal scholarship. What accounts for the widespread resistance to this conclusion in labor markets? One answer is the hope that a competing theory, the efficiency wage theory, might be used as an economic argument for favoring unions.

The heart of the efficiency wage model is the idea that if you pay workers a higher wage they will work harder and be more productive. It is, after all, a plausible outcome. Workers are not like any other commodity because they can adjust their behavior to incentives. As a consequence, instead of worker productivity explaining the wage, the wage determines worker productivity by providing incentives to work more productively.

C.   Efficiency Wage Model

The efficiency model can be viewed loosely as repealing the harsh predictions of the inverse relationship between the union wage and union employment. In the labor law literature, this has always been a favored line of thinking. The original example of the efficiency wage model was Henry Ford's decision to pay wages far above competitive levels in order to secure a more reliable and productive labor force.

The seminal efficiency wage model centers on the idea of a "gift-exchange" (Akerlof, 1984). The gift is a wage above the market-clearing wage. The basic theory is that the worker understands that she is receiving a gift in the form of a wage above the market-clearing wage. What is often neglected when scholars apply this model to the union sector is the importance of identifying the gift-giver. If the gift is coming from the firm, workers reciprocate by becoming more loyal to the firm, putting out more work effort and thus becoming more productive. Workers who are being treated well by their employer may, for example, respond to a busier than usual schedule by putting out more effort. The converse is also true: workers who think they are being badly treated may respond by putting forward less effort.

To see how the theory is likely to operate it is useful to describe the paradigmatic example of the efficiency wage; that is, Henry Ford's $5 a day wage. There are various stories of the famous episode.[19] If one is to take Henry Ford at his word, which was cited in the famous case of *Dodge v. Ford Motor Company*, he indicated: "'My ambition . . . is to employ still more men; to spread the benefits of this industrial system to the greatest possible number, to help them build up their lives and their homes. To do this, we are putting the greatest share of our profits back into the business.'"[20] In this story, Henry Ford is just a good, very rich capitalist who wants to share part of the good fortunes of the corporation with the workers rather than just with the shareholders.

The historically more grounded story is more complicated and less encouraging. Henry Ford was one of the first of the great entrepreneurs of the industrial age. He was rapidly expanding the business to meet a burgeoning demand for the low-cost cars he was producing. This required a concomitant rapid increase in employment. The problem was that, in 1920, he was primarily hiring workers off the farm who were unaccustomed to the discipline and on-time performance of manufacturing jobs. Workers were often not on time or strayed from the assembly line. Others just left to go back to the farm. The $5 a day wage, which was roughly double the competitive wage at that time, was an attempt to reduce turnover and make existing workers more productive.

The $5 a day wage required no elaborate monitoring, for if the boss did not think workers were meeting the standard, they could be freely fired under the then and now existing employment-at-will rule. In other words, the efficiency wage model requires that workers increase work effort as a response to the higher wage. The efficiency wage is thus an incentive story. Ford paid a higher wage, but the cost of that higher wage was offset by a more productive workforce. Besides requiring no monitoring, Ford could set the wage at whatever level he thought maximized profits. The goal of the $5 wage was not to lose money; it was to make greater profits.

How does this story play out in a unionized firm? First, to stay faithful to history, I note that Ford was vehemently antiunion. The violence that erupted when the United Auto Workers organized the Ford Motor Company is well known in labor history. Henry Ford hired a security force that engaged in battles with union organizers. Obviously, the creator in real life of the efficiency wage concept did not take kindly to having his facilities organized. And that fact is important.

The efficiency wage story simply does not fit in a unionized company. First, the idea that workers will work harder because the job pays better than their next best job prospect depends on low-cost monitoring. The efficiency wage is itself an implicit contract: higher wages for higher effort. For this deal to work, the company must be able to discharge a shirking worker quickly and at low cost. The efficiency wage pays for itself by encouraging workers, who find the above-market wage sufficiently compelling, to work hard to keep the job, whether this means on-time arrival, few absences, and no shirking on the job. That mechanism will be disrupted if the worker found to be shirking can mount and sustain a claim of unfair dismissal. From the worker's standpoint, the claim makes sense: for some workers caught shirking, it may have been a one-time lapse or the supervisor may have made a mistake in rendering the discharge. The presence of a union with a grievance-arbitration process in the collective bargaining agreement protects workers from these mistakes; but at the same time it forces the employer either to engage in costly monitoring or to tolerate a certain amount of "shirking," thus reducing the benefits to the employer that are promised by the efficiency wage theory.

Second, "who gets credit" for the gift? In collective bargaining, the gift-giver is the union. After all, it is the union that fought for the higher wage. The press rings with stories in which union leaders claim that their gains were "won" at the bargaining table and had to be wrung out of the boss. The stories are quite plausible. However, for the gift-exchange version of the efficiency wage theory to make economic sense, the gift has to be seen to come from the employer, for it is the employer's willingness to pay the above-market wage that encourages workers to be more loyal and grateful.

The efficiency story is alive and well, however, in many nonunion sectors of the economy. None of the economic models of the efficiency theory sees the efficiency wage as the product of collective bargaining where the parties can use their economic weapons to achieve the best contract for their side. To generate greater efficiency to cover the cost of the higher wage, the efficiency wage is calculated based on offsetting the higher cost with greater effort. It is entirely an incentive device. Nonunion firms may pay higher than market wages, both to reduce their turnover and monitoring costs but also to avoid unionization.

Elements of the efficiency wage model can be found in Freeman and Medoff in their book *What Do Unions Do?* (1984). They argued that higher union wages might encourage higher productivity among workers by providing workers with a voice that could affect the workplace environment. As a consequence of voice, workers might gain improvements in job seniority and security that would encourage workers to pass on skills to junior workers and to work more productively in general. Freeman and Medoff provided little evidence that unions could raise productivity high enough to offset the union wage premium. The only empirical support for the effect was provided by Brown and Medoff (1978). Indeed Freeman and Medoff acknowledged that any positive effects of unions on productivity would probably not be sufficient to undo the detrimental effect of the union pay premium. Consequently, they argued that the gains from the good face of unions could only be achieved by policy intervention such as amending labor law.

The vast literature on the subject of the efficiency effects of unions, much of it stimulated by the Freeman and Medoff book, showed a negative rather than a positive effect on productivity (although not statistically significant). This is summarized in Chapter 4 of this volume by Hirsch.

In sum, unions raise pay, and consequently union firms are at a cost disadvantage when competing with nonunion firms. There is no discernible offsetting increase in worker productivity. The great loss of union employment has been more than offset by the growth in domestic nonunion employment. This is not a story about low wages in emerging countries. Instead it is about the existence of a sizeable nonunion sector in every American industry that is able to compete successfully with its union competitors on the basis of lower labor costs. (See Hirsch, Chapter 4 in this volume.)

II.   UNDERSTANDING THE INTERNAL LABOR MARKET

Thus far, I have stressed that the external labor market is generally efficient. The external labor market is where individuals search for jobs when they either enter the labor force or leave their current employment, and where firms look for new employees. It is "external" in the sense that it is outside of the firm. What makes the external labor market competitive is that firms in numerous different industries are all looking for entry workers with generalized skill sets. A high school graduate could become a semi-skilled worker at Caterpillar, or at JP Morgan, or at a small firm. A college graduate could become a management trainee at General Electric or a web designer for a small firm. The workers' general skills may be more or less specialized and better suited for some industries than others; but they are not firm specific. Hence these workers can work in a range of industries or for any firm within the industry. The same story can be told of the MBA graduate who can be hired into management at Caterpillar or at JP Morgan, or at a small firm.

Once a worker is hired into a firm, she leaves the external labor market and enters the internal labor market (ILM). The internal labor market is the relationship between the firm and its employees. The ILM consists of a set of explicit or implicit rules governing wages, promotion opportunities, grievance procedures and other terms and conditions of employment. In large firms, the ILM can be highly formalized; in small firms, it may barely exist.

A.   Basic Principles of Internal Labor Markets

The ILM comes in two broad types: unionized and nonunionized. In the union ILM, the rules governing the workplace are largely a matter of express contract; they are written in the form of a collective bargaining agreement and are enforceable before an arbitrator, a court or the NLRB. In the nonunion ILM, the agreements are not contractual; that is, most of their terms cannot be enforced by a third-party arbitrator or judge. Rather, the nonunion ILM relationship is generally one of employment-at-will, and most of its terms are subject to modification at will.

Both types of ILMs are generally governed by similar broad principles, whether legally enforceable or not. Most hiring takes place at entry-level jobs which connect the ILM to the ELM. Based on performance or job tenure, workers can then be promoted into higher level jobs. Earnings typically rise with job tenure. In a product market decline, adjustments are typically made by reducing hours or laying off workers rather than by reducing wages; and resulting layoffs or discharges generally are inversely related to seniority. The difference between the union and nonunion ILMs is that these characteristics are contractually mandatory in the union ILM, whereas they are non-mandatory, frequently followed norms in the nonunion ILM.

What is described here is a somewhat idealized version of an ILM – or perhaps a historically contingent ILM, such as that which existed at "blue chip" companies like IBM and AT&T until the 1980s. Many observers have described changes in the nature of ILMs since the 1980s, characterizing them as an erosion or even an outright collapse of the long-term employment relationship and mutual expectations that are central to the idealized ILM (Stone, 2004). But none has convincingly shown that ILMs function anything like external "spot" markets for labor. So we will stick with the idealized ILM for analytic purposes, while recognizing that this overstates the difference on the ground between ILMs and ELMs.

From a policy perspective there is a huge difference between external and internal labor markets. Whereas ELMs are generally efficient because market forces discipline the parties ex ante, there is no reason to assume that internal labor markets are efficient. Most importantly, whereas workers are mobile in the ELMs, they are less mobile in the ILMs, in part because of the firm-specific training they undertake. Consequently, market discipline is muted in ILMs.

The analysis of ILMs began during the 1950s when Kerr (1954) and Dunlop (1958) described the institutional realities of internal markets. This pioneering work did not attempt to integrate the ILM as an institution into the neoclassical theory of labor markets. But that integration has come about since 1970 as the efficiency aspects of the ILM were developed by Doeringer and Piore (1971); Williamson, Wachter and Harris (1975); Okun (1981); and Freeman and Medoff (1984). The ILM is thus no newcomer to neoclassical labor economics. It has been an integral part of labor economics for over 30 years.

B.   Relationship between Internal and External Labor Markets

An important feature for both the union and the nonunion ILM is the manner in which they connect with the ELM. As noted, the ELM is differentiated in worker skills largely by the amount of education workers have received, and workers are hired into the ILM at entry-level jobs. This is true for all levels of education, though the ports of entry differ. Upon hiring, workers receive job-specific or firm-specific training, which enables them to move up the promotion ladder. Employees tend to receive higher wages based on seniority and the amount of specific training they have undertaken. Hourly pay tends to fluctuate little over the business cycle. Instead, the stage of the business cycle is manifested in hours worked.

Whereas the market discipline of the ELM controls entry wages for entry-level jobs, it has only indirect control over the great variety of jobs filled by internal promotions in the ILMs. Over the innumerable job titles that exist in the United States economy, very few are determined solely by the ELM. Yet the ELM does discipline all the ILM jobs because employees always have the right to quit and are likely to do so if job opportunities are more favorable at other firms. As expected, job turnover is higher for workers with little job tenure since starting over with a new employer typically means starting at that firm's entry-level position and entry pay; that usually represents a significant loss for more senior workers. Since young entry-level workers are mobile, they are likely to earn a market-based wage, while the older, less mobile workers are vulnerable because market discipline imposes little direct constraint on the employer.

Nevertheless, the external markets matter a great deal in controlling the pay and working conditions in internal labor markets. Few workers need to be mobile. As is true in economics generally, it is the worker on the margin of stay versus quit who wields influence. The worker on the margin will have the best information on alternative job opportunities and is likely to share it with other workers. The employer whose ILM is inconsistent with the relevant ELMs, in terms of wages, benefits and other terms and conditions of employment, will not be able to hire and retain a qualified workforce.

With the exception of wages, benefits, and other terms of conditions of employment, employers retain discretion over other matters whether the firm is unionized or not. Employers retain broad discretion, for example, to choose the firm's technology and to construct job descriptions in accordance with that technology. Virtually all product market decisions are decided unilaterally by the employer. Relations with the firm's other stakeholders are also typically determined by the employer without any input from employees.

C.   Four Central Economic Factors that Affect the ILM

The ILM has four foundational factors that distinguish it from ELMs and that create potential inefficiencies: firm-specific training, risk aversion, asymmetric information and transaction costs.[21]

1.   Firm-specific training

Firm-specific training is the core rationale for long-term attachments and thus for the ILMs (Wachter and Wright, 1990). Without firm-specific training, there would be no advantage to the firm in retaining a current employee as compared to hiring a new employee each day. Firm-specific training makes workers more valuable to their current employer than to other employers. The result is a wedge or surplus between their value to their current employer versus their value in the ELM. When this surplus is shared between the firm and the employee, the firm has an incentive to retain workers with job-specific training and workers have a similar incentive to stay with the employer. The surplus from firm-specific training is also perhaps the most important single factor enabling firms to pay efficiency wages or wages above competitive levels.

The problem is that, while the employer and employee are disciplined initially by the usual ELM forces, firm-specific investments in training create a lock-in because the investments are sunk and have no value outside of the match. This creates a bilateral monopoly bargaining situation and the prospect of inefficient rent-seeking as each party attempts to take more of the surplus than might have been agreed to. This lock-in is a clear break with competitive markets that require that workers be mobile. The ILM can thus be efficient, where the surplus is made as large as possible by cooperative behavior, or it can be reduced or eliminated by adversarial behavior. Although the parties have an incentive to maximize the size of the surplus, there is no market mechanism that guarantees this behavior. Consequently, the ILM is vulnerable to market failures.

Ironically, for those who identify the Chicago School with the assumption of perfectly competitive markets, the lock-in problem created by ILMs was originally identified by some of the greats of the Chicago School; namely, Becker (1964), Mincer (1962) and Oi (1962), among others.

The nature of the market failure is easily described. If the parties could trust each other and prevent rent-seeking, each would have an incentive to make the optimal level of investment in the relationship. However, each party has an incentive to act opportunistically once the training is completed. The incentive to act opportunistically is great if the costs of the investment are not shared. Suppose, for example, that the employer could get the employees to bear all the training costs. Once trained, the employees would be in a vulnerable position. The employer could attempt to divert almost the entire surplus to itself by threatening to fire the workers unless they accepted a minimal return. Pushed against the wall, the employees would have little choice but to remain with the employer and take any wage above the market wage paid in the ELM. Hence, the employer has a potential gain from acting opportunistically. Similarly, if the employer paid the entire training costs with the expectation of getting all of the resulting surplus, the employees, once trained, could threaten to quit unless the employer agreed to give up its return on the joint investment. Pushed against the same wall, the employer would be willing to take a very low return on its investment if the workers agreed to stay, because it could not secure equally productive employees on the external market.

In the face of the risk that opportunistic behavior might undo the mutual gains from investment in firm-specific training, the parties can develop self-enforcing norms that prevent opportunistic rent-seeking.[22] The key characteristic of the self-enforcing norm or contract was described by Becker (1964). Becker's solution was for the employer and the employee to share in the costs of the investment. In a simple model with one employer and one employee, the cost sharing would create an incentive-compatible contract where the incentive for opportunistic behavior might be eliminated. Cost-sharing takes the form of a "training wage" that is lower than what the employee could earn in an ELM without job-specific training, but higher than the employee's current productivity which is very low as he first acquires specific training. With the current costs shared, the payoff for both parties would come after the training is complete. In this case, the employer would have no incentive to fire the worker and the worker would have no incentive to quit because each would only receive a return on their investment if the relationship were maintained.

Unfortunately, a threat of employer opportunism remains even if the job investment costs are shared. Assume there are a number of employees. If the workers are not organized and cannot act in concert, the employer could pick off one vulnerable employee at a time, and threaten to fire the employee absent a wage reduction. For each individual worker, the threat to fire that worker is real because the employer might secure its expected return on the joint investment from the continued employment of the other workers. Each worker could be put individually in that position, and would both stay on the job and accept a lower wage, as long as the employer allows the worker to receive some benefit from the investment. That is, workers are better off by not quitting as long as they are paid any premium, however small, over the wage available in the ELM. Since each worker believes that the others will be offered the same bargain, each worker knows that quitting is suboptimal. Hence, the employer can successfully act opportunistically by getting the employees to accept a lower, though still positive, return on their investment.

This inequality in bargaining power is reduced if the workers can act in concert by becoming unionized. Forced to deal with the workers as a single unit, the employer's threat to fire the workers does not ring true because the threat would also cause the employer to lose whatever it invested in the relationship. One of the important rationales for labor unions is that they can protect workers from opportunistic behavior by employers who might otherwise seek to divert the portion of the surplus that belongs to workers.

Can the same results be achieved without a union? Arguably they can. Where the employment relationship is ongoing or where the employer must regularly hire workers in the ELM, the sharing of costs can be a self-enforcing norm. If the employer and its employees need to make ongoing investments in their relationship, employer opportunism in the initial period will discourage the employees from agreeing to the second set of investments. Hence, repeat play reduces the potential for opportunism. Similarly, if the employer must return to the ELM to hire additional workers, the employer's concern for its reputation will deter it from behaving opportunistically; otherwise it will be difficult to hire new employees or to get these employees to invest in their relationship. Consequently, the importance to the employer of retaining a reputation for fair play, both externally and within an ongoing relationship, can make the arrangement self-enforcing. The self-enforcing feature of the arrangement will be greatest, obviously, where both are present – the employer needs to return regularly to the ELM and the relationship with each employee is ongoing (or repeat-play).

The option to unionize provides additional protection against opportunism by a nonunion employer. As noted above, the evidence is overwhelming that controlling for skill, job tenure, education, demographics, and location, unionized workers are paid more than comparable nonunion workers. This suggests that, in the unionized workplace, a large share of the investment in firm-specific training is paid for by the employer in the form of above-market wages. Given the higher labor costs associated with a unionized labor force, it may not be necessary for the nonunion workers to actually form a union, for the ever-present threat of unionization can be particularly effective in discouraging employer opportunism.

Ironically, although the union sector is struggling due to nonunion competition, the nonunion sector has benefitted from the existence of the union sector because of a deterrent effect on nonunion employers who might otherwise act opportunistically if not for the fear of being unionized.

2.   Risk aversion

If the parties to the employment relationship were risk neutral, the great bulk of pay as well as promotions would be strictly performance based. That is because pay-for-performance creates the greatest incentives for employees to work at their highest level of performance, and is therefore wealth maximizing. The evidence, however, is that workers are more risk averse than are employers. That is, employees prefer to receive a stable income, rather than an amount that varies with the fortunes of the firm, even if the variable pay has a higher expected value than the steady stream. This risk aversion may be a function of employers' better access to financial markets to smooth out the consequence of revenue fluctuations; but it simply may be due to the fact that workers don't like fluctuations in their income. Stable does not mean constant; in fact, workers tend to prefer a steadily rising wage profile. That is, workers make more investments in the form of reduced income when they are younger, and receive the returns on those investments when they are older. The value of firm-specific investments thus only partly explains the widely observed fact that workers' income tends to be higher as they get older.

If employees were not risk averse, the great bulk of pay would be performance based. Wage increases, bonuses, etc. would all be based on performance. Promotions too would be based on performance. The preference for pay-for-performance is that it is wealth maximizing. It creates the greatest incentives for employees to work at their highest sustainable level of performance.

Almost all businesses work to find the best tradeoff in their compensation arrangements between stable wages and the high-powered incentives provided by pay-for-performance. This is the same problem that the firm solves to determine the best efficiency wage level. Pay-for-performance may take the form of stock options or bonuses, or it may take the form of annual salary increases or promotions based on performance. In this regard, unionized firms tend to have the least amount of pay-for-performance. This might be due to a greater distrust of employers, higher-than-normal risk aversion, or a preference for minimizing pay disparities across workers.

3.   Asymmetric information

Another important feature of ILMs is the presence of information asymmetries. Asymmetric information exists in the ILM when it is relatively more costly for one of the parties to observe or monitor the quantity and quality of worker inputs. Although the employee is involved in an ongoing relationship with the employer, the firm has information advantages over employees. In particular, the employer has superior information about the productivity of its workers. Remember that the labor demand curve depends on the marginal productivity of the worker. Except in the unusual case where the worker produces a good or service from scratch and sells it herself to the customer, the worker's marginal productivity will be unobservable to the worker. The worker, however, has an information advantage over another key item; namely, the worker's effort. Because monitoring is costly, employers can only estimate their employees' work effort.

One answer to the problem of asymmetry of information has been provided by government regulation of the ILM in cases where employers have a significant information advantage and the stakes for employees are large. That is the case for both workplace safety and deferred compensation in the form of retirement pay. Moreover, employer reputation may not be a sensitive control in such cases because of the difficulty and complexity in observing existing safety conditions and deferred compensation, and in separating out the role of employer opportunism from changes in technology or the product market. The problem of asymmetric information is resolved here by government regulation in the form of the Employee Retirement Income Security Act (ERISA) and the Occupational Safety and Health Act (OSHA).[23]

Outside of these areas where government information fills an existing gap, what explains the lack of complex contracting to control other information asymmetries more generally? The same question can be asked about job-specific training, which might also benefit from contracts that protect each party's vulnerable investments. The union contract, although lengthy, hardly covers all possible contingencies. In the nonunion sector, there is no contracting at all. The answer to the existence of limited contracting rather than complex contingent claims contracts to deal with every contingency has to be the transaction costs inherent in contracting in the ILM.

4.   Transaction costs

Transaction costs involve the costs associated with writing and enforcing agreements that govern the relationship between employers and employees. As noted in the section above, the presence of asymmetric information leads one to expect complex contingent-state contracts. As described by Wachter and Wright (1990),

[s]uch contracts would specify what happens in the face of potential exogenous changes in technology or in the demand for the firm's output, and hence inputs. Combined with risk aversion and match-specific investments, such contracts would also describe the parties' agreed-upon tradeoffs between income smoothing and the provision of appropriate incentives for correct reporting of asymmetric information.

This is no simple task; it would challenge even the best drafter of contracts. The term "bounded rationality" can be used to describe the inability of contract drafters to anticipate all the potential states of the world that might emerge, and how the parties should respond to each particular state of the world.

Several factors make contracting in the ILM particularly costly. First, many jobs are idiosyncratic to the ILM. Besides the large number of different jobs, workers within the same job will differ in their amount of firm-specific training. Second, the number of interactions is large. ILM contracts are not for a single delivery of a product on a date and time to be contracted for. The employee's performance is continuous over the work time and over the days of employment. There is not one deliverable; there are many. Third, jobs are also interconnected. One worker's performance affects the potential performance of workers who are in the same team, the same office, the same assembly line, etc. Finally, jobs evolve over time, fundamentally with changes in technology, or in more minor but continuous ways with changes in product demand.[24]

The importance of transaction costs makes labor and employment law central to the modern theory of the firm, which begins with Coase (1937) and is elaborated by Williamson (1985), Hart (1989), and other scholars. In the theory of the firm, simply stated, the firm faces "make or buy" decisions at every turn. Take the firm that makes computers. It must decide as to each part, for example, the microprocessor, the operating system, and the keyboard, whether to make it internally or purchase it through suppliers. Much of that make-or-buy decision is based on technology, patents, and similar factors. For example, the firm will normally produce for itself computer parts over which the firm has patent protection and has developed the technology.

In this decision-making process, a single question reappears: how easy is it to contract for any individual part or input? The prevailing view is that holding other factors constant, a firm is likely to buy in the market when the input being purchased is standard rather than idiosyncratic. It is likely to make rather than to buy when the input is more specialized or idiosyncratic. Also, the firm is more likely to make rather than buy when information asymmetries are important. Information asymmetries make third-party enforcement of a contract difficult and error-prone because key facts are not observable or verifiable by an arbitrator or judge. Finally, the higher the cost of specifying terms in advance – as in the case of repeated interactions, interconnected tasks, and evolving tasks and technology – the more likely the firm is to make rather than to buy.

All of these make/buy decisions turn on the amount of transaction costs, which is why transaction costs are central to the boundaries of the firm. What results is the following conclusion: buy when the transaction costs of contracting are low. When transaction costs are low, the parties can write a contract that is likely to be largely complete. Holes in the contract will still occur when an unexpected event happens over which the parties have not contracted. But, given sufficient existing contractual completeness, the court can usually fill the hole by inferring a contract term based on what the parties themselves would have done if they had anticipated the event. On the other hand, if an event occurs for which there are no relevant contract terms, the court will assume that the event is outside of the four corners of the contract and is therefore not covered by the contract.

Hence, the theory of the firm resolves a paradox that is created by the four factors discussed above. Specifically, the economic theory suggests that, with idiosyncratic products (or, in labor market terms, workers with different amounts of job-specific training on tasks that may be unique to the firm) and high information asymmetries, the parties have an incentive to write complex state-contingent contracts. Yet these very same factors that contribute to high transaction costs make the contract more costly to write, more incomplete than complete, and hence more likely to be subject to judicial error. Consequently, the theory of the firm provides a different answer: instead of using complex state-contingent contracts, use no contract at all. Instead, "make" rather than "buy" by bringing that activity inside the firm and use the firm's hierarchy to control that input (Coase, 1937; Williamson, Wachter, and Harris, 1975).

A transaction cost theory of the firm and the make/buy distinction is generally successful. One almost never observes complex contracting inside the firm, whether in the ILM or elsewhere. The firm might write simple employment contracts for some executive officers or specialized employees; but these contracts are usually short and straightforward, and mostly deal with the possibility of termination.

The collective bargaining contract is the one great exception to the non-contractual nature of the firm. It is the only detailed enforceable contract that the firm writes to deal with activities and with actors that are wholly inside the firm. Its policy implications, discussed in the next section, are extremely important.

III.   CONTRACTING IN THE UNION ILM

As noted above, one way to deal with the complexity of the ILM and the potential for opportunism is to meet it head on; that is, to write or at least attempt to write the complex state-contingent contract that describes each potential state of the world that might occur and, for each possible state of the world, what the parties wish to happen. Bounded rationality and the many contingencies that the parties to an employment relationship face make that task impossible. But that is what union contracts attempt to do. And that is why those contracts often run to hundreds of pages. Even so, they are notoriously incomplete. The proof of the degree of contractual incompleteness in union contracts is the number of grievances that often occur and the costs of resolving them. These costs can include the fees of outside arbitrators, the time of lawyers (or managers and stewards) representing the parties, the work-time loss, and the ill-will that often continues beyond the conflict's resolution.

Beyond dispute resolution costs, however, a frequently cited cost of union contracting is the rigidity imposed by the collective bargaining agreement. All of the factors cited above make rigid contract terms expensive, especially in a world where there are constant changes in technology, competitive pressures on the firm, and the state of the economy. Fixed contract terms cannot be the low-cost answer to these conditions.

Take the seemingly most easily resolved type of dispute: was the employee's performance or behavior acceptable or sufficiently below contract levels as to merit the employee's dismissal? Each of the elements that make contract writing difficult comes into play.

First, what level of performance is to be expected? Jobs are idiosyncratic as is the amount of specific training undertaken by the employee. In the extreme, standards may have to be set on an employee-to-employee basis. Second, the employee's performance may be acceptable, even consummate some of the time, while other times performance is below that contemplated by the contract. It is no easy task to write a contract that defines what percentage of below-par performances merits discharge. The third factor, job interconnectedness, makes the task that much more difficult. Was unsatisfactory performance truly the fault of the employee or did another employee's behavior, or even the supervisor's behavior, lead to the unsatisfactory performance? Finally, how is the question of discharge to be resolved if the technology has changed to make the job more difficult, or if the product market has declined to make the employee's performance less productive even for the same level of work effort?

All of these factors contribute to making dispute resolution difficult even for the core question of worker performance. The employee may claim that her work effort was high. The employer may complain that the employee's productivity was low. Both may be true in the complex ILM, where work effort and productivity are not one and the same. Even apart from the difficulty of specifying the weight that each should have in judging performance, a problem is that the employer cannot easily determine the worker's effort and the worker cannot easily determine her productivity.

If this were not complex enough, add yet another factor. Since effort and productivity are not easily observable and verifiable, they are subject to the parties' manipulation. At the moment of dispute resolution, the neutral arbitrator or judge must rely on the parties' representations about the facts. Even if the parties were acting in good faith, the dispute would be difficult to judge reliably. If the parties can manipulate the data to their own advantage with little risk of detection, the task of reaching the correct judgment is very difficult indeed.

Another interesting feature of the union ILM, to which I have already alluded, is that it handles the tradeoff between incentives and risk aversion with a near polar solution. Maximizing the value of the corporation and making workers as productive as possible is best accomplished by making pay dependent on performance. But in union ILMs, pay for performance is almost entirely absent. Pay increases are based almost entirely on job tenure and not on performance; even promotions may be based largely on seniority. In addition, the union "just cause" provision and grievance procedures make it very costly for the employer to penalize workers who are underperforming. These two factors alone – no extra pay for good performance and little penalty for poor performance – suggest a very negative effect of unions on firm productivity.

Union preference against pay-for-performance is partly ideological and partly based on distrust fed by asymmetric information. Unions typically favor narrow wage differentials on ideological grounds. Indeed a general finding in the union premium literature is that the most skilled workers get the smallest union wage premium, while the least skilled receive the highest premium. Distrust also plays a key role. Data on productivity are available to the company, but not the union. Even if the company makes information available to the union, it cannot be verified. If the parties are not in a relationship of trust and confidence, it is unlikely that they will agree to base pay on information that cannot be verified by both parties.

Another factor making the union ILM atypical in the contract world is that the relationship is not a voluntary one as far as the employer is concerned. Generally, contracts are entered into voluntarily by the parties. Contract law serves as "the handmaiden of the parties" and supplies a set of default terms, most of which the parties can change voluntarily. Parties can restrict or expand the scope of the contract to fit their needs. There are few mandatory terms, with the exception of an implied obligation of "good faith and fair dealing." Commercial contracts typically run for a limited term so that, if the parties do have a falling out, the contract can be terminated.

The collective bargaining contract is also unlike any other commercial contract. First of all, once a union is selected by a majority of bargaining unit members, the company is required by law to bargain with the union even if it prefers to bargain with another union or with no union at all. The employer must bargain in good faith over a set of mandatory topics, including wages, hours, and other terms and conditions of employment. The parties can also deploy "economic weapons" – the union can strike or the employer can lock out the workers – to pressure the other party should they reach an impasse in their bargaining. Although the law's goal may be peaceful labor relations, that peace is achieved and punctuated by the use of these "weapons."

None of this is meant as criticism of the NLRA in terms of its overall effect on the economy. In another chapter in this volume I argue that the NLRA was justified, and has in fact been extraordinarily successful. The argument brings in issues of political economy that are beyond the scope of this chapter, but its main point is worth noting here. Before the passage of the NLRA, labor history in the United States, as elsewhere, was filled with stories of violent strikes. At times revolution was in the air. Only the NLRA, and its nationwide legitimization of unions, collective bargaining, and peaceful strikes, was able to bring a close to that violent chapter of history.

Putting aside the social value of labor law, however, the union ILM has elements that are clearly costly to employers. Apart from raising wages and benefits above competitive levels, unions also bring about a degree of formalization in contract writing and enforcement that is inherently costly.

IV. ILM CONTRACTING IN THE NONUNION FIRM

Whereas the union sector takes on the complexities of the ILM by writing explicit contracts, the nonunion sector does not. This lack of contracting raises two questions. First, why does the nonunion ILM do virtually no contracting at all, versus, for example, some contracting but less than the union sector? Second, how can the nonunion ILM be successful in mitigating or eliminating the potential for employer opportunism?

Before answering these questions it is important to explain how I am using the word "contract." Economists use the term contract to mean an agreement by the parties, which can be implicit or explicit and is not necessarily enforceable. Indeed the question of enforceability is not raised, nor is it of particular interest to economists, particularly since the contracts are often constructed to be self-enforcing. In this chapter, the difference between judicial enforceability and unenforceability is an important distinction. I will use the term "contract," whether explicit or implicit, to mean a judicially enforceable agreement, and I will use the term "norm" to mean a mutual expectation that is not intended to be judicially enforceable.[25]

What then explains the difference between the use of enforceable contracts in the union ILM and the almost exclusive use of non-enforceable norms in the nonunion ILM? At a theoretical level, the answer is given by the theory of the firm discussed above. Recall that the boundaries of the firm are drawn specifically so that the activities brought inside the firm are those where formal contracting is too difficult or costly, and where decision making can more efficiently be done unilaterally through the firm's hierarchical structure. The union ILM is the great exception, in that the activity is carried out inside the firm and the employees bargain collectively with the employer and reach an enforceable agreement governing the employment relationship (Dau-Schmidt, 1992).

The implication of this divide is enormously important. If the transaction cost-based theory of the firm is correct, the unionized firm has a large competitive disadvantage. But there is a big "if" attached to that proposition. In the late 1800s, employees who were dissatisfied with their terms and conditions of employment would, from time to time, attempt to organize a union and engage in concerted activities. Some of those activities were illegal under state law, and the police or National Guard, or even the regular army, was brought in to subdue or crush them (Wachter, Chapter 15 in this volume). Indeed, the most compelling rationale for the passage of the NLRA was to end this industrial strife, which was harmful to the nation's economy.

The point that can be drawn from the history is that, prior to the NLRA, the nonunion sector was a frequently dysfunctional organizational type. For the affected employer, the costs of strikes were just the tip of the iceberg. Disgruntled employees had many ways to penalize a firm if they chose to do so. Since monitoring is not and cannot be continuous, employees in manufacturing or construction, for example, could harm the firm by sabotaging equipment or simply ignoring the need for repairs. Although documenting such activity is impossible, it is likely that, even prior to an outbreak of overt concerted activity, disgruntled employees had many ways to hit back at an employer who was acting unfairly or opportunistically. This point was emphasized by institutionalists such as Dunlop (1958) and Kerr (1954) and theorists like Becker (1964).

The militancy of workers in the early organizing drives of the 1930s and before appears to reflect intense worker unhappiness with the existing nonunion ILMs of the time. It is no surprise that worker unrest escalated in the Depression, given that employers have greater potential to act opportunistically during economic depressions, thus provoking increased industrial strife.

Conditions seem to be very different today. At least the extremely low levels of strike activity would seem to suggest that the nonunion ILM operates with less opportunism than in the past.[26] How does the nonunion ILM now operate so as to defuse industrial unrest? At this point, we return to the theory of the firm and the core concept that activities brought inside the firm are both susceptible to norm-based governance and involve activities too costly for effective contract enforcement.

The norm-based governance of the nonunion ILM is integrally tied to the judicial doctrine of employment-at-will (Rock and Wachter, 1996). According to the employment-at-will doctrine, "an employer can fire an employee for good reason, bad reason, or no reason at all." This doctrine can be criticized for appearing to condone employer opportunism; but this criticism entirely misses the point. The point of the phraseology is to signal a jurisdictional boundary rather than a legal rule that is applied in its literal meaning (Rock and Wachter, 1996). By stating the employer's prerogatives as broadly as possible, the employee who believes herself to be wrongfully discharged cannot sustain a claim. The only exception is a worker who falls into a policy exception such as race or gender discrimination, or illegal retaliation.

How can a legal regime that allows workers to be discharged for "no reason at all" be either fair or efficient? The answer lies in the reason behind the stark and unforgiving language.

To understand that reason, compare this actual standard with a counterfactual one where the firm states that "it can lower wages for a good reason, a bad reason, or no reason at all." The wage reduction rule is not self-enforcing, and any firm adopting it would soon find it impossible to hire workers and difficult to retain them. This rule would be entirely self-serving and not joint profit maximizing. The reason is that a firm can quickly raise its profits by reducing wages; but the increase in profits comes entirely from the lower wages. Workers would obviously respond negatively to such clearly opportunistic behavior. Indeed, much of the industrial strife in nonunion firms of the 1930s arose when companies adopted just this kind of policy. Even though such policies were primarily adopted during severe downturns in the economy, firms could not convince workers of the need to accept the reductions.

The underlying reason for the workers' distrust of a norm that allows firms to lower wages, even during a recession, goes back to information asymmetries: the firm's economic condition is known to the firm, but not to the workforce. Even if the workers know that there is a recession and that production has fallen, they do not know how much of a wage reduction is merited. If the firm says that a 10 percent reduction is needed, the workers have every reason to distrust that assertion; maybe a 5 percent reduction would be sufficient to save the plant and the jobs at the plant. The firm has every incentive to overstate its problem to improve profits, while the workers have every reason to distrust the firm. This is precisely why a norm of "reducing wages to deal with a recession" is not an efficient, joint profit-maximizing norm. And, indeed, such a policy is rarely used.[27] Instead, the almost universal response to a reduction in product demand is to reduce hours of work. This is an efficient and self-policing norm because the firm does not have a reason to overstate its case or overshoot the mark. If the firm reduces hours more than is merited by the reduction in demand, output will fall and profits will suffer more than they would with a smaller reduction.

Employment-at-will is more like the self-policing norm of "reducing hours in response to a recession" than it is like the inefficient norm of "reducing wages." Discharging a productive worker for no reason is counterproductive for the firm. It may lower the wage bill, but the firm will lose the efforts of the worker (who is presumably more productive than the next new hire). The rational firm will not discharge a worker for no reason at all because it will suffer in the product market. Hence, a norm of employment-at-will is altogether different from a norm of lowering wages in response to a recession.

To many readers, the idea that product market pressures ensure that the rational firm would not discharge a worker for no reason might not be reassuring enough. However, there are other dynamics endemic to the nature of the ILM itself that tend to ensure that norms work well. There is now an established literature describing the conditions in which non-legally enforceable norms are a better choice for the parties than legally enforceable contracts (Ellickson, 1991). Those conditions, as discussed below, are those of the ILM.

A puzzle remains: if no rational firm would actually fire a worker "for a bad reason or no reason," what is the purpose of the language stating that they can do so? The answer is that the language is intended to be a signal to the courts; namely, it is intended to draw a jurisdictional boundary that leaves a firm's internal business judgments beyond the scope of judicial review (Rock and Wachter, 1996). From a firm's vantage point such a jurisdictional boundary promotes efficiency by leaving internal employment decisions to the discretion of the firm. From a social welfare perspective the jurisdictional boundary is also efficient (putting aside the regulatory protections offered to certain groups and activities) because of the high costs and risk of error associated with adjudicating discharge decisions.

Suppose that the employer needed to prove "just cause." Monitoring is costly, but it would be necessary if the decision were subject to judicial review. As noted above, it is always more difficult to prove a point to a court than to learn the facts. Even flagrant bad play such as theft may be hard to prove, but what about the more prevalent cases where the employee does not perform well enough? How many examples of poor performance would be sufficient? How harmful does each incident have to be to be worthy of discharge for cause? The correct decision would require the judge to learn the norms of the workplace and to sort through facts that are proffered by the firm, and that are often not verifiable by the court. Job specificity makes these decisions even more difficult. In contract disputes, the value of the actual performance is measured against the value paid. Idiosyncratic valuations make this task difficult, but this is exactly the same problem raised in the ILM where workers have firm-specific training. Market values of the appropriate wage rate and productivity are not available.

If judicial review is contemplated, the parties in the ILM would have to write contingent claims contracts to cover the many different states of the world that could result. The contract, no matter how complete, would necessarily be highly incomplete, particularly as more time elapsed. Courts deal with incomplete contracts in two different ways. When the contract is largely complete, the court may plug the gap with a term that the court believes the parties would have adopted had they known of this exact contingency. The more complete the contract, the better the court knows how a gap would be filled. However, if the contract is highly incomplete, the court takes a passive stance, and will typically rule that there is no contract for that event (Schwartz, 1992).

The labor contract involving the ILM, no matter how great the ambitions of the parties, is likely to be highly incomplete. A court faced with this type of incompleteness is thus likely to say that there is no contract for that event. And that would be the right response. By stating the employment-at-will doctrine in a form that amounts to saying that the employer can do whatever it wants, the firm is simply seeking a judicial finding that there is no contract. This jurisdictional boundary ensures that the courts will stay out of disputes in internal labor markets and leave the resolution to the norms of the workplace.

Clearly there is still potential for opportunism in an employment-at-will world where judicial enforcement is not available to employees. Recall that job-specific training leaves both parties potentially exposed because of their investments in the match. I have already discussed the potential solution to this problem above, but it is worth addressing in somewhat greater detail. The key is that safeguards against opportunism have to be self-enforcing since legal enforcement is ruled out.

The traditional solution emphasized in the neoclassical literature is reputational effects. Most employers have to make frequent trips to the external market. Reputational effects are the first constraint on employer opportunism. Employers with reputations for treating their workers unfairly will find it difficult to recruit and maintain a qualified work force. Even if employees do not learn about an employer's reputation before hire, they will quickly learn it after being hired. Quit rates are very high in the first year of employment. Newly hired workers have made few investments in the job and lose relatively little by quitting and searching for another job. Even firms with declining employment are subject to this check if they must replace some of their departing workers.

The second check on employer opportunism is that dissatisfied employees can trigger their rights to organize and bargain collectively, thus replacing norms that are intended to be self-enforcing with legally enforceable contracts. This is a very powerful threat given that the newly unionized firm may find its labor costs increasing sharply (assuming a standard union wage premium). In a competitive, largely nonunionized industry, unionization may be fatal to the firm. It can be argued, given low rates of unionization in the private sector, that the threat to unionize is not much of a deterrent to employer opportunism. Perhaps that is true, but an employer would have to be highly risk tolerant to take that bet.

The final deterrent against opportunism is the self-enforcing norms themselves. The literature on norms has identified the characteristics that are most likely to lead to successful norm-based governance (Ellickson, 1991). Workable norms are joint profit maximizing. Since they are voluntary, they have to satisfy both parties. If norms with this characteristic can be developed, they are superior to contracts given the cost of contract writing and enforcement. This is particularly true in contracting over labor relations within a firm, where the frequency of interactions, the connectedness of events, and the evolutionary nature of the relationship make it impossible to write even a moderately complete contract. Fortunately, features that make contracting expensive in the ILM context are very similar to the factors identified by Ellickson as likely to give force to successful norms-based enforcement, such as being part of a closely knit group. Therefore, in the ILM, norms governance has the potential to be very successful, while contract writing and enforcement will be very costly.

In addition, Ellickson notes that the ability to apply sanctions is an important feature of norm governance. In the ILM, employees are empowered to apply sanctions by exercising their ability to quit, as noted in the groundbreaking article by Gary Becker (1964), as well as by participating in negative gossip, which has become increasingly damaging in today's Internet world. The employee's ability to apply sanctions in the ILM to deal with employer opportunism highlights the idea that ILMs are likely to generate self-enforcing employment norms that can ultimately trump contracting as a method of workplace governance.

The primary point of the theory of the firm is that contract writing in the ILM is inefficient. If it were efficient to contract over the terms of a particular activity, then it could be left to contracting in the external market, which benefits from the discipline and high-powered incentives of market forces. The ILM is internal to the firm precisely because it is too costly to do otherwise.

The point is underscored by the rising use of "outsourcing" today, which amounts to using the market to purchase labor services. Indeed, outsourcing of the labor function, as an alternative to a union ILM, has become a major cost-cutting strategy, and thus a major profit producer for many firms. Anything that significantly increases the cost of employing union labor internally (such as judicial imposition of high contract enforcement costs) increases the attractiveness of outsourcing. The nonunion firm rarely finds outsourcing attractive because its norm-based enforcement system is less expensive than writing a contract with a firm that provides outsourcing labor. The "make or buy" choice is a very active area for decision making today regarding labor usage inside the firm.

Hence, norms start with a huge advantage over contract writing inside the firm. Because contract writing and enforcement are so costly and difficult, neither norms nor their enforcement have to be perfect; they just have to get over that low bar to succeed.

V. CONCLUSION AND POLICY IMPLICATIONS

Labor law and law and economics have not been close bedfellows. From one perspective, this is surprising. Labor law is primarily about negotiating and writing collective bargaining contracts, and contract law quickly embraced law and economics when Richard Posner showed that important contract questions could be answered by applying economic contract theory (Posner, 1973).[28] Similarly, labor law is about one of the firm's key inputs, labor, much as corporate law deals with another of its key inputs, capital. Corporate law found law and economics to be useful for thinking about relations between the firm and its sources of capital, yet labor law remains resistant to law and economics.

The explanation for the hostility of labor law to law and economics is apparent. First, labor law, unlike many areas of law, is inherently normative. The Wagner Act was itself pro-union and many of its supporters believed that unions would become the dominant industrial relations system. The law arguably became neutral between union and nonunion industrial relations systems after the adoption of the Taft-Hartley Amendments, but labor law scholarship retained its strong normative edge in favor of unions. Most labor law scholars believe that collective bargaining is the appropriate mechanism for governing the employment relationship for working men and women.

The clash with law and economics was bound to be fierce, or at least spirited. The basic finding of labor economics – uncontroversial in every other area of law and economics – is that the quantity purchased of a good (e.g., labor) varies inversely with its price (e.g., wage). In labor law, such an assertion is a cause for battle, for it puts the central aims of the NLRA at odds with each other. The NLRA's goal of equalizing bargaining power was to be realized by workers joining unions, and by unions raising wages. However, modern labor economics teaches that if union wages are increased above market levels, union employment falls. The goal is thus internally inconsistent.

The union movement's hope was that wages were to be taken out of competition, so that the collective wage could be higher than the market wage. But this is unachievable in a competitive economy with a significant nonunion sector. Labor cost differentials between union and nonunion firms matter a great deal.

Over the past several decades, several attempts have been made to controvert the conclusion that if unions, through collective bargaining, force employers to pay more than the market wage, union employment will decline. The efficiency wage theory suggested that if an employer paid workers an above market wage it could build a more loyal, experienced, and productive workforce. But if the high wage is to be a gift that calls forth greater productivity, it has to be given freely by the firm. In the context of collective bargaining, the union is seen as securing the gains for the workers from recalcitrant management; so in unionized firms, the workers' primary loyalty is likely to go to the union and not the firm. The efficiency wage story makes much better sense in the nonunion labor market, where the gift of the high wage can be claimed by management. After all, the efficiency wage is simply another form of incentive payment which needs to be set by the employer at the level where the cost of the higher wage is equal to the productivity benefit that results from the higher wage.

The empirical test of the efficiency wage claim for the union labor market has produced negative results. A plethora of academic research found no positive relationship between unions and productivity (Hirsch, Chapter 4 in this volume). While unions raise wages above competitive levels, there is no offsetting productivity effect.

Traditional labor law scholars have tended to view the neoclassical model to be opposed to almost all policy improvements, even in the nonunion sector. There is much to this position, but the neoclassical model itself does allow for a number of policy interventions. To begin with, measures that improve the functioning of markets (i.e., that improve information flows and aid mobility) are supported by neoclassical economics. Moreover, given the problem of asymmetric information, modern neoclassical economic theory can support policy measures to improve occupational health (e.g., OSHA) and the security of deferred compensation arrangements (e.g., ERISA). Policy economists might disagree with each other as to whether specific regulations pass muster under benefit-cost analysis or whether the procedural elements are unnecessarily costly, but, as a theoretical matter, the existence of information asymmetries can justify regulatory oversight.

Regulations such as OSHA and ERISA, as well as the Fair Labor Standards Act, have another feature that makes them acceptable to policy-oriented neoclassical economists: because they apply throughout the economy, they do not cause cost discrepancies among union and nonunion firms.

The anti-intervention tilt of economic analysis comes back into force when policies attempt to improve the lot of workers by providing more procedural rights, such as restrictions on employment-at-will. Here, transaction cost theory is central. In particular, third-party enforcement of procedural rights inside the ILM is very costly as described in this chapter. Process is expensive, especially if it involves third-party review. Talk is not cheap, thus mandating more process is likely to lead to more outsourcing of the labor function.

A broader question is whether traditional neoclassical arguments miss the positive redistributional or welfare-enhancing effects of unions. This raises several complex claims. One is that, when labor unions raise wages, the effect is redistributional toward the bottom end of the income distribution. Putting aside the empirical question as to the position of union workers in the income distribution, neoclassical theory has a potent response. It tells us that using unions to redistribute income is a bad idea. The fundamental theorems of welfare economics tell policymakers to adopt policies that improve efficiency and then redistribute income through taxes and government expenditures.

Hence, even if unions have a positive effect on income distribution, those goals are better and more efficiently handled by other policy mechanisms.

There remain, however, several critical areas for policy reform and welfare improvements. The first concerns laws to combat discrimination or to give special protection to certain vulnerable groups. Whether or not there is a strong efficiency case for such laws – there may be for some and not for others (Issacharoff and Scharff, Chapter 13 in this volume) – they may have strong welfare justifications beyond the scope of economic analysis. The second opening for reform is at the bottom of the labor market. In the nonunion sector, employers are encouraged to play by the rules because of reputational effects and the threat of unionization. But some employers are not deterred by these forces. Small employers and those who are on a path to go out of business are not as likely to be deterred, nor are employers who hire undocumented workers. For these workers, there is no back-stop even to prevent such core breakdowns as the nonpayment of wages for work performed.

A more fundamental point involves the distinction between normative and positive analysis noted above. Much of traditional labor reform is normative and articulates societal values or what commentators believe the values ought to be. Normative analysis is not antithetical to law and economics, nor does normative analysis provide a critique of the positive theory of the neoclassical model. The fundamental theorems of neoclassical economics, as discussed in the first section, recognize the existence of a social welfare function, which incorporates societal values. Economists, as economists, have little to say directly about the contours of the social welfare function. For example, many labor law scholars favor collective bargaining as a goal in itself. Expressed as a societal value, that is, as an input into the social welfare function, these positions are not open to the positive critique of the neoclassical model.

At issue, however, is whether pro-union normative preferences are captured by the political economy that society has chosen. As stressed in Wachter (Chapter 15 in this volume), society's choice of a political economy is more a political choice than an economic one. The neoclassical model takes the political economy or the social welfare function as a given. Its analysis of the positive or negative effects of union pay premiums or other outcomes takes place in the context of the accepted political economy. Today, the political economy of the United States is highly competitive. Hence, it is at this level that the normative argument in support of unions' traditional goals loses support. That unions cannot take wages out of competition is a consequence of society's choice of a political economy that stresses free competition.

NOTES

1. The author gratefully acknowledges the contribution of the criticisms and suggestions made by Cynthia Estlund, Barry Hirsch, Bruce Kaufman, and Howard Lesnick. The author also thanks Natalie Ditomasso, Sarah Edelson and Marisa Kirio for research assistance.
2. The initial text that started the debate in labor law was the first edition of Posner's book, *The Economic Analysis of Law* (1973).
3. See for example Estlund (2003), Gould (1993), Stone (2004) and Weiler (1984). For a traditionalist critique of the neoclassical model's application to labor law, see Getman and Kohler (1983) and Verkuil (1983).

4. This follows the introductory treatment of labor markets. See, for example, Parkin (2012). For an intermediate-level treatment, see Varian (2010).
5. The neoclassical model was developed from earlier classical models that came to similar conclusions, but in less complete or rigorous ways. Adam Smith's (1776) was the most well known. Thomas Malthus (1803) had a theory of the labor market which predicted that wages would always be pushed to the subsistence level because of the inability of individuals to control their fertility. More central to this chapter, Karl Marx (1867) had a theory that all value was created by labor and thus could be returned to workers, presumably in the form of higher wages. His theory was contested by Böhm-Bawerk (1889), who believed, correctly as it turned out, that savings was a form of postponed consumption and required a return (interest) in order to occur. If there were no return for savings, there would be little savings and little capital. The value of capital was thus not embedded labor as Marx had theorized.
6. See Katz and Rosen (1994), stating the first fundamental theorem: "As long as producers and consumers act as price takers and there is a market for every commodity, the equilibrium allocation of resources is Pareto efficient. That is, the economy operates at some point on the utility possibilities frontier."
7. See Katz and Rosen (1994), stating the second fundamental theorem: "[P]rovided that all indifference curves and isoquants are convex at the origin, for each Pareto efficient allocation of resources there is a set of prices that can attain that allocation as a general competitive equilibrium."
8. Labor economists are sometimes labeled as conservative because they disfavor direct government intervention in specific markets. This is a misguided labeling from my perspective. Such individuals may well be very liberal overall but prefer that redistribution be achieved through tax and expenditure policy.
9. In a recent study Ashenfelter, Farber, and Ransom (2010) conclude that firms have some wage-setting or monopsony power due to imperfect information and job differentiation. Although this line of research is just beginning, the prevailing assumption remains that, except in the very short run, the amount of monopsony power available to firms is small and therefore unlikely to affect the conclusions reached in this chapter.
10. For a standard microeconomic treatment of the union sector see Parkin (2012) for introductory treatment. See Varian (2010) for an intermediate-level treatment of fixing wages or prices above competitive levels. Union pay or total compensation consists of both the wage and nonwage benefits. For ease of exposition I use the term wage in place of total compensation.
11. Cartelization, although descriptive in economics, can be interpreted as pejorative in law. Cartelization is unlawful as a violation of the antitrust laws. However, the Clayton Act specifically provides a safe harbor for union activity. Consequently, as a semantic matter, if cartelization indicates unlawful antitrust behavior, then unions do not cartelize the labor market. To use cartelization pejoratively in the labor context thus requires a separate justification for why cartelization is harmful.
12. The National Labor Relations Act of 1935, sponsored by Senator Robert F. Wagner, is also known widely as the Wagner Act. When I use the term Wagner Act, I am referring to the Act as originally passed. When I refer to the NLRA, I am referring to the Act as amended, most importantly by the Labor Management Relations Act of 1947, popularly known as the Taft-Hartley Act.
13. The decline in union employment was, of course, due to a number of factors. For an accounting, see Farber and Western (2002).
14. The version of *Principles of Economics* used here was published in 1920; however the original version of the book was first published in 1890.
15. The version of *The Theory of Wages* used here was published in 1963; however it contains an original reprint of the first edition of the book published in 1932.
16. Indeed, although the economy has still not fully recovered from the financial crisis of 2008 and the resulting steep recession, arguably the worst since the Great Depression, the evidence to date is that wages have not only not declined, rather they have also continued to grow (Daly, Hobijn and Lucking, 2012).
17. This is from the preamble to the Wagner Act: "The inequality of bargaining power between employees who do not possess full freedom of association or actual liberty of contract, and employers who are organized in the corporate or other forms of ownership association substantially burdens and affects the flow of commerce, and tends to aggravate recurrent business depressions, by depressing wage rates and the purchasing power of wage earners in industry and by preventing the stabilization of competitive wage rates and working conditions within and between industries."
18. Moreover, between the passage of the Wagner Act and the Taft-Hartley Act, influential commentators such as Simons (1944) and Hayek (1944) had begun to question whether concentrated economic power, even in the hands of labor unions, was socially beneficial.
19. See Henderson (2009) for a detailed description of the facts and story behind the *Dodge v. Ford Motor Company* case.
20. *Dodge v. Ford Motor Co.*, 170 N.W. at 671.
21. This section draws heavily from Wachter and Wright (1990).

22. The economics literature on self-enforcing labor market contracts is extensive. See for example Carmichael (1989), Lazear (2000), and Gibbons (1998).
23. See for example Ehrenberg (1989) for a discussion of these issues.
24. See Williamson, Wachter, and Harris (1975) for a broader discussion of transaction costs in the ILM and the use of the term bounded rationality to describe the difficulty of writing detailed contingent-state contracts.
25. *Black's Law Dictionary* (8th ed., 2004, p. 341) defines a contract as "an agreement between two or more parties creating obligations that are enforceable or otherwise recognizable at law."
26. Stone (2004) disagrees, claiming that, in the digital age, workers are exposed to a host of new challenges and insecurities, and thus unionism is more important now than it has ever been. However, the problem is that unionism itself has yet to adapt to this new era.
27. Wage rigidity refers specifically to wage rates. Workers who also receive bonuses or any other form of pay for performance will find their income varying with the size of the bonus or other pay for performance. As expected from the theory, for bonuses to work well they have to be based on information observable by the workers. A common technique is to base bonuses on firm-level income or other measures that are required as part of the firm's federal filing requirements under the Securities Exchange Act of 1934 as amended.
28. The first edition of Posner's *Economic Analysis of Law* was published in 1973. The latest edition is the eighth, which was published in 2011.

REFERENCES

Abel, Andrew B., Ben S. Bernanke, and Dean Croushore. 2011. *Macroeconomics* (7th ed.). Boston, MA: Addison-Wesley.

Akerlof, George A. 1984. "Gift Exchange and Efficiency Wage Theory: Four Views," 74 *American Economic Review* 79–83.

Arrow, Kenneth J. and Gerard Debreu. 1954. "Existence of an Equilibrium for a Competitive Economy," 22 *Econometrica* 265.

Ashenfelter, Orley C., Henry Farber, and Michael R. Ransom. 2010. "Modern Models of Monopsony in Labor Markets: Tests and Estimates," 28 *Journal of Labor Economics* 203.

Becker, Gary S. 1964. *Human Capital*. Chicago, IL: University of Chicago Press.

Böhm-Bawerk, Eugen von. 1889 (1891). *Positive Theory of Capital*. London: Macmillan and Co.

Brown, Charles and James Medoff. 1978. "Trade Unions in the Production Process," 86 *Journal of Political Economy* 355.

Carmichael, H. Lorne. 1989. "Self-Enforcing Contracts, Shirking and Life Cycle Incentives," 3 *Journal of Economic Perspectives* 65.

Coase, Ronald. 1937. "The Nature of the Firm," 4 *Economica* 386.

Commons, Sir John R. 1913. *Labor and Administration*. New York: Macmillan.

Commons, Sir John R. and John B. Andrews. 1927. *Principles of Labor Legislation* (rev. ed.). New York: Harper & Bros.

Daly, Mary, Bart Hobijn, and Brian Lucking. 2012. "Why Has Wage Growth Stayed Strong?," Federal Reserve Bank of San Francisco Economic Letter. Available at: http://www.frbsf.org/publications/economics/letter/2012/el2012-10.html (accessed July 17, 2012).

Dau-Schmidt, Kenneth. 1992. "A Bargaining Analysis of American Labor Law," 91 *Michigan Law Review* 419.

Debreu, Gerard. 1959. *Theory of Value: An Axiomatic Analysis of Economic Equilibrium*. New Haven, CT: Yale University Press.

Dobrescu, Monica. 2012. "The New Keynesian Approach to Business Cycle Theory: Nominal and Real Rigidities," 2 *International Journal of Economic Practices and Theories* 13.

Doeringer, Peter B. and Michael J. Piore. 1971. *Internal Labor Markets and Manpower Analysis*. Lexington, MA: Heath.

Dunlop, John. 1958. *Industrial Relations Systems*. Carbondale, IL: Southern Illinois University Press.

Ehrenberg, Ronald G. 1989. "Workers' Rights: Rethinking Protective Labor Legislation," in D. Lee Bawden and Felicity Skidmore, eds., *Rethinking Employment Policy*. Washington, DC: Urban Institute Press.

Ehrenberg, Ronald G. and Robert S. Smith. 2011. *Modern Labor Economics: Theory and Policy* (11th ed.). Upper Saddle River, NJ: Prentice Hall.

Ellickson, Robert C. 1991. *Order Without Law: How Neighbors Settle Disputes*. Cambridge, MA: Harvard University Press.

Estlund, Cynthia. 2003. *Working Together: How Workplace Bonds Strengthen a Diverse Democracy*. New York: Oxford University Press.
Farber, Henry S. and Bruce Western. 2002. "Accounting for the Decline of Unions in the Private Sector, 1973–1998," in James T. Bennett and Bruce E. Kaufman (eds.), *The Future of Private Sector Unionism in the United States*. Armonk, NY: M.E. Sharpe.
Freeman, Richard and James Medoff. 1984. *What Do Unions Do?* New York: Basic Books.
Getman, Julius G. and Thomas C. Kohler. 1983. "The Common Law, Labor Law, and Reality: A Response to Professor Epstein," 92 *Yale Law Journal* 1415.
Gibbons, Robert. 1998. "Incentives in Organization," 12 *Journal of Economic Perspectives* 115.
Gould, William B. 1993. *Agenda for Reform: The Future of Employment Relationships and the Law*. Cambridge, MA: MIT Press.
Hart, Oliver. 1989. "An Economist's Perspective on the Theory of the Firm," 89 *Columbia Law Review* 1757.
Hayek, Friedrich A. 1944 (2007). *The Road to Serfdom*. Chicago, IL: University of Chicago Press.
Henderson, M. Todd. 2009. "The Story of *Dodge v. Ford Motor Company*: Everything Old is New Again," in J. Mark Ramseyer (ed.), *Corporate Law Stories*. New York: Foundation Press.
Hicks, John R. 1932 (1963). *The Theory of Wages* (2nd ed.). New York: St. Martin's Press.
Kahn, Lawrence M. 1980. "Union Spillover Effects on Organized Labor Markets," 15 *The Journal of Human Resources* 87.
Katz, Michael L. and Harvey S. Rosen. 1994. *Microeconomics* (2nd ed.). Burr Ridge, IL: Irwin Professional Publishing.
Kerr, Clark. 1954. "The Balkanization of Labor Markets," *Labor Mobility and Economic Opportunity* 92.
Keynes, John Maynard. 1936 (2009). *The General Theory of Employment, Interest, and Money*. New York: Classic Books America.
Lazear, Edward P. 2000. "Performance Pay and Productivity," 90 *American Economic Review* 1346.
Linneman, Peter D., Michael L. Wachter, and William H. Carter. 1990. "Evaluating the Evidence on Union Employment and Wages," 44 *Industrial and Labor Relations Review* 34.
Malthus, Thomas R. 1803 (1958). *An Essay on the Principle of Population; or, a View of its Past and Present Effects on Human Happiness; with an Enquiry into our Prospects respecting the Future Removal or Mitigation of the Evils which it occasions*. London: J.M. Dent & Sons Ltd.
Mankiw, N. Gregory. 1989. "Real Business Cycles: A New Keynesian Perspective," 3 *Journal of Economic Perspectives* 79.
Marshall, Alfred. 1890 (1920). *Principles of Economics* (8th ed.). London: Macmillan and Co.
Marx, Karl. 1867 (1990). *Capital, Volume I*. Trans. Ben Fowkes. London: Penguin Books.
McKenzie, Lionel W. 1981. "The Classical Theorem on Existence of Competitive Equilibrium," 49 *Econometrica* 819.
Mincer, Jacob. 1962. "On-the Job Training: Costs, Returns, and Implications," 70 *Journal of Political Economy* 50.
Oi, Walter. 1962. "Labor as a Quasi-Fixed Factor," 70 *Journal of Political Economy* 538.
Okun, Arthur M. 1981. *Prices & Quantities: A Macroeconomic Analysis*. Washington, DC: The Brookings Institution.
Parkin, Michael. 2012. *Microeconomics* (10th ed.). Boston, MA: Addison-Wesley.
Posner, Richard A. 1973. *Economic Analysis of Law* (1st ed.). Boston, MA: Little, Brown.
Posner, Richard A. 1984. "Some Economics of Labor Law," 51 *University of Chicago Law Review* 988.
Posner, Richard A. 2011. *Economic Analysis of Law* (8th ed.). New York: Aspen Publishers.
Rock, Edward B. and Michael L. Wachter. 1996. "The Enforceability of Norms in the Employment Relationship," 144 *University of Pennsylvania Law Review* 1913.
Schwartz, Alan. 1992. "Relational Contracts in the Courts: An Analysis of Incomplete Agreements and Judicial Strategies," 21 *Journal of Legal Studies* 271.
Simons, Henry C. 1944. "Some Reflections of Syndicalism." 52 *Journal of Political Economy* 1.
Smith, Adam. 1776 (1991). *An Inquiry into the Nature and Causes of the Wealth of Nations*. New York: Prometheus Books.
Stone, Katherine V.W. 2004. *From Widgets to Digits: Employment Regulation for the Changing Workplace*. New York: Cambridge University Press.
Varian, Hal R. 2010. *Intermediate Microeconomics: A Modern Approach* (8th ed.). New York: W.W. Norton & Co.
Verkuil, Paul R. 1983. "Whose Common Law for Labor Relations?," 92 *Yale Law Journal* 1409.
Wachter, Michael and Randall D. Wright. 1990. "The Economics of Internal Labor Markets," 29 *Industrial Relations* 240.
Walras, Leon. 1874. "Eléments d'économie politique pure, ou théorie de la richesse sociale," first installment. Paris: Guillaumin.

Weiler, Paul. 1984. "Striking a New Balance: Freedom of Contract and the Prospects for Union Representation," 98 *Harvard Law Review* 351.

Williamson, Oliver E. 1985. *The Economic Institutions of Capitalism: Firms, Markets, and Relational Contracting*. New York: The Free Press.

Williamson, Oliver E., Michael L. Wachter, and Jeffrey E. Harris. 1975. "Understanding the Employment Relation: The Analysis of Idiosyncratic Exchange," 6 *The Bell Journal of Economics* 250.

Cases and statutes cited

Clayton Act, 15 U.S.C. §§ 12–27, 29 U.S.C. §§ 52–3 (2006).

Dodge v. Ford Motor Co., 170 N.W. 668 (Mich. 1919).

Labor Management Relations (Taft-Hartley) Act, Pub. L. No. 80-101, 61 Stat. 136 (1947) (codified as amended at 29 U.S.C. §§ 141–87, (2006)).

National Labor Relations (Wagner) Act, Pub. L. No. 74-198, 49 Stat. 449 (1935) (codified as amended at 29 U.S.C. §§ 151–69 (2006)).

Securities Exchange Act of 1934, 15 U.S.C. §§ 78a –78pp (2006 & Supp. IV 2011).

3. Economic analysis of labor markets and labor law: an institutional/industrial relations perspective
Bruce E. Kaufman

I. INTRODUCTION

In the 20th century two intellectual traditions were the most influential in the American field of labor economics. The first was the tradition of institutional economics (IE) and its close offshoot industrial relations (IR), the second was the tradition of neoclassical economics (NE). This cleavage is refracted into the modern field of labor law where on one side is an IE/IR-oriented traditional approach to labor law (e.g., Deakin and Wilkinson 2005; Estlund 2006; Arthurs 2007) and, on the other, a largely NE-inspired law and economics (L&E) approach (Schwab 1997; Posner 2007; Medema 2010).

The institutional economics/industrial relations (IE/IR) approach had its original home base at the University of Wisconsin and was led by John Commons; after the 1930s it evolved and expanded to include a neo-institutional branch centered in industrial relations and headed by non-Wisconsin labor economists such as John Dunlop, Clark Kerr, Richard Lester, and Lloyd Reynolds (McNulty 1980; Segal 1986; Kaufman 1988, 2006). Johnson (1975) refers to this tradition as the "old labor economics" and notes that it was partially separated from the main body of economics by its cross-disciplinary approach to theory-building, critical stance toward the competitive core of neoclassical theory, and neutral-to-sympathetic attitude toward trade unions and labor law. Other intellectual traditions, such as socio-economics, economic sociology, and comparative institutional analysis from political science, also feed into modern-day IE/IR.

The cross-disciplinary dimension of original IE/IR included considerable attention to the role of law as a determinant of an economy's institutional infrastructure and economic performance, making it a central player in what Hovenkamp (1990; also Pearson 1997) identifies as the 20th century's *first law and economics movement* (FL&EM). The FL&EM was closely linked to the legal realist tradition in law (Mercuro and Medema 1997; Fried 1998); within the FL&EM the subfield of labor law occupied a central place, illustrated by Commons and Andrews' pioneering text *Principles of Labor Legislation* (1916). After World War II many writers in traditional labor law field, as well as some of the nation's best-known labor mediators, arbitrators and policy officials, came from the IE/IR camp. Examples are Henry Aaron, Archibald Cox, John Dunlop, and Arthur Goldberg; outside the USA are people such as Otto Kahn-Freund, Roger Blanpain, and Manfred Weiss.

The neoclassical economics tradition in American labor economics goes back to the early 20th century with principal roots in the work of English neoclassical economists, such as Alfred Marshall, John Hicks, and Joan Robinson; after World War II, however, NE research in labor economics shifted to America and soon acquired a well-recognized home base at another Midwestern university – the University of Chicago (McNulty 1980; Boyer and Smith 2001; Kaufman 2010a). Illustratively, Chicago professor H. Gregg Lewis is widely considered the "father" of modern labor economics and one reviewer (Biddle 1996) labels his style of economics "uncompromising neoclassicism" (p. 184). The neoclassical approach to the study of labor economics was until the 1970s largely an application of Marshallian partial equilibrium price theory to labor markets and wage determination; since then, however, contributions by Gary Becker and several other Nobel prize-winning economists at Chicago (and elsewhere) have greatly broadened its domain and explanatory power by applying the tools of rational choice and equilibrium to an ever-widening range of non-market and imperfect market topics (Becker 1976, 1993; Lazear 2000). The neoclassical approach in American labor economics was overshadowed by the IE/IR paradigm through the 1950s, and the events of the Great Depression and New Deal in the eyes of many economists appeared to considerably discredit and marginalize NE's competitive "demand/supply" theoretical core. In hindsight, however, this was only a temporary setback. From the 1970s onward the "new" labor economics (aka, modern labor economics) of the NE school grew in strength and influence until by century's end it had become so dominant across American universities that younger researchers could be forgiven for thinking no earlier IE/IR approach had ever been mainstream (Pearson 1997; Boyer and Smith 2001; Cahuc and Zylberberg 2004).

The University of Chicago was also home to what Hovenkamp (1990) refers to as the *second law and economics movement* (SL&EM). It was fathered by Chicagoans Ronald Coase and Richard Posner, is anchored (particularly the Posnerian version) in neoclassical price theory, and seeks at a positive level to analyze how law influences economic activity and at a normative level how law should be constructed in order to promote economic efficiency. For reasons explained shortly, Chicago L&E is wary-to-skeptical of government interference with private contracting and market outcomes (Schwab 1997; Medema 2010). The exemplar work is Posner's *The Economic Analysis of Law* (2007). In the labor law field Posner's article "Some Economic Aspects of Labor Law" (1984) was an early contribution, complemented by influential articles on subjects such as critique of the New Deal labor legislation and defense of employment-at-will by fellow Chicagoan Richard Epstein (e.g., Epstein 1983, 1984). In the last 20–30 years the Chicago-based law and economics (L&E) movement has grown rapidly and now has a presence in many economics departments and law schools; naturally, in this process it has evolved beyond its Chicago and NE price theory roots but with many continuing linkages thereto in terms of theoretical and policy orientation (Mercuro and Medema 1997).

This chapter compares and contrasts the theoretical foundations of the first and second L&E movements, the former located in IE/IR and the second in NE, and the respective implications these theories have for analysis and evaluation of labor law. The chapter then demonstrates why, from an IE/IR perceptive, the NE model used in SL&EM has serious logical flaws and leads to unduly negative conclusions about the potential of labor law to enhance social welfare.

Before proceeding, several points of context are usefully established. First, IE/IR and NE are not monolithic constructs. As indicated above, NE now covers a very heterogeneous territory and, indeed, has expanded via a Coasean-inspired new institutional economics (NIE) to include a comparative study of institutions (Williamson 1985; Furubotn and Richter 2005). Hence, I define and use the two terms in the following delimited sense: IE/IR typifies the people and ideas associated in the USA with the FL&EM and NE similarly typifies people and ideas associated with the SL&EM. Also, IE/IR and NE are not the endpoints in the spectrum of labor market theory, for other intellectual traditions occupy these positions, such as Marxist/radical and post-Keynesian labor economics to the left of IE/IR and Austrian (libertarian) economics to the right of NE.

Similarly, the terms "Wisconsin" and "Chicago" are best regarded in this chapter as metaphors or allegorical symbols for two broader constructs, IE/IR and FL&EM on one hand and NE and SL&EM on the other, that now extend far beyond their original home bases. The qualifier "in the USA" is also important since the IE/IR and NE traditions discussed here, along with their parallel labor law traditions, are in a number of respects distinctively American products (Jacoby 2005). Finally, the term "labor law" is used in the expansive sense of covering collective and individual dimensions, the latter sometimes separately distinguished as employment law.

The reader may wish to consult an earlier review by this author of the first and second L&E movements (Kaufman 2009), as this chapter builds and expands on it. Also, to avoid unnecessary duplication with other articles by this author on the IE/IR analysis of unions (e.g., Kaufman 2007b, 2012a), the analysis in this chapter is oriented to labor and employment law broadly considered.

II.   THE FUNDAMENTAL DIVIDING LINE: "ASSUME A COMPETITIVE LABOR MARKET"

Modern economics, as indicated above, theorizes an immense range of institutions and behaviors, many of which do not even involve a market per se. When it comes to evaluation of labor law, however, people in NE and SL&EM typically start the analysis from the same foundational concept, a concept I paraphrase as "assume a competitive labor market." This often takes the pure form of a perfectly competitive labor market, with attendant demand/supply diagram; other times frictions and imperfections are introduced, such as in the NIE, but with the common assumption that competitive selection pressures remain strong enough that employers and employees are led to adopt (mostly) efficient contract terms. In the words of Nobel laureate Robert Solow (1990: xvi), "in today's preferred style the labor market is usually modeled as just clearing or, more subtly, producing efficient contracts." Thus, economists use the terms "competitive market" and "competitive theory" in both a narrow (zero friction) and broad (positive friction) sense. By conventional agreement, however, the core property that any such model must preserve in order to remain "competitive" is that prices (including wage rates) are parametric (a "given") and therefore individual firms and workers are price-takers and have no ability to set an alternative price and still find willing buyers and sellers (Varian 2010: 603).

Figure 3.1 illustrates the competitive demand/supply labor market model; it is an application to the labor market of the generic competitive market model that is a ubiquitous feature of scholarly expositions of modern L&E (e.g., Mercuro and Medema 1997; Posner 2007; Cooter and Ulen 2010). The labor demand curve D and supply curve S determine an equilibrium wage W and employment level L. This conclusion by itself is

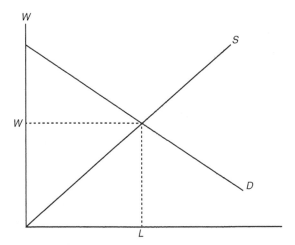

Figure 3.1   Competitive labor market

not of great significance for analysis of labor law; what matters are the implications for
social welfare.

One desirable social welfare property, mentioned in the Solow quote, is that competitive markets yield market-clearing prices and quantities. This means that competition
causes wage rates to rise or fall until equilibrium is established where demand and supply
are evenly balanced and neither a shortage nor excess of labor prevails. The beneficial
aspect of market clearing is most apparent at the aggregate level; that is, the implication
is that a competitive market economy automatically and without government guidance
("as if by an invisible hand") tends to correct demand/supply imbalances and yield an
equilibrium where the number of jobs available matches the number of people wanting
to work (a definition of full employment).

A second desirable property, also alluded to in the Solow quotation, is that a competitive market economy leads to an efficient use of resources. Full employment of labor
is clearly one dimension of efficiency (unemployment is a waste of labor resources).
Another dimension is that competition and competitive wage rates sort and assign the
nation's heterogeneous labor resources to their most productive use (e.g., the people
with a comparative advantage at plumbing end up being plumbers). Yet a third dimension is that competition prevents employers from exploiting (underpaying) workers and
provides employers with strong incentives to treat workers fairly (e.g., ill-treatment leads
to a high turnover rate, a reputation as a bad employer, and less loyal and committed
employees). A final dimension of efficiency, known as Pareto optimality, is that the
nation's resources are allocated and utilized with no slack or waste; that is, the production of goods and services (or "wealth") is at the economy's maximum limit and one
person therefore can get more goods and services only if another gets less.

The demand/supply model and the conditions and implications that come from it are,
of course, highly idealized; further, as described in more detail below, economists in the
NE/NIE tradition have persuasively argued that many seeming labor market problems
(e.g., unemployment, gender wage differentials) are actually efficient or competitive-like

responses to underlying productivity, cost, and taste differentials. Not all economists, however, accept either the standard competitive model or the extended NE/NIE efficient contract version as useful interpretations of labor markets; others use them only as rough-and-ready benchmarks to get the analysis started. Hence a wide spectrum of opinion exists among economists regarding two related questions. The first is how well the competitive model and its various extensions and generalizations serve as a useful device for understanding and explaining labor markets and employment relationships; the second is to what degree the outcomes of a competitive labor market, even if attained, are beneficial for human welfare and therefore a desired object of public policy.

Here is located, I believe, a central dividing line between FL&EM and SL&EM. As a general statement (documented in what follows), the position of people affiliated with the First L&E movement mostly answer "no" to both of these questions while those with the Second mostly answer "yes". For this reason Rodrik (2007; also McCloskey 1997), calls those in the neoclassical-affiliated group "first-best" economists (market-generated outcomes are typically the best that are realistically attainable) and those in groups such as the institutional "second-best" economists (market-generated outcomes can be improved upon through government regulation/coordination). Given this position, economists of the Second L&EM believe it is appropriate to start off analysis of labor law with the proposition "assume a competitive labor market;" second-best economists, however, believe that the "assume a competitive labor market" proposition is by itself likely to lead to significant error in evaluating the pros and cons of labor law and must, therefore, either be used with significant qualifications or replaced with a different model.

III.   THE COMPETITIVE LABOR MARKET MODEL IN THE SECOND L&E MOVEMENT

In this section I take a deeper look at the role and significance of the "assume a competitive labor market" theme in the Second L&E movement – where "competitive" is defined broadly to include efficient contract generalizations.

The effective birth date of both IE/IR and NE is the 1880s (Blaug 1985; Hovenkamp 1990; Jacoby 2005). The marginal revolution had begun in the 1870s in the work of Jevons, Menger and Walras, and by the 1880s had mostly displaced the classical approach of Malthus, Ricardo and Marx. Not unrelatedly, this decade also saw the emergence of the *Methodenstreit* (i.e., "battle over method") – a fierce debate over the pros and cons of two rival approaches to the science of economics. On one side were the proponents of classical/neoclassical economics, principally located in Britain, Austria and to some degree France; on the other were proponents of historical/social economics, located principally in Germany but with a strong presence in heterodox circles in Britain and other countries (Koot 1987; Pearson 1997). The historical/social economics proponents were the insurgents and they sought to substantially modify the orthodox economics developed by Ricardo, Mill and Walras; considerably to their left were various Marxists and radicals, who sought to completely replace orthodoxy and thus fall outside our purview.

The battle was ostensibly over the merits of a deductive versus inductive approach to theory-building in economics; under the surface, however, were also political consider-ations about individualism vs. collectivism and the extent of government regulation and redistribution (Ekelund and Hebert 2007, Chs. 9, 10). The main body of English deduc-tive economists, for example, placed tight limits on government regulation of labor (some opposed maximum hour limits for women and children), while most historical/social economists supported Germany's pioneering program of workmen's compen-sation, unemployment insurance and old-age pensions. The deductive approach was favored by the classical/neoclassical side, exemplified in the abstract and mathematical theories of Ricardo and Walras, respectively. This approach to theorizing relied on a few general propositions about human nature and markets – typically portrayed as self-evident and akin to laws of nature (e.g., the "economic man" model of rational and self-interested behavior; the law of supply and demand) – and proceeded to derive a corpus of cause-effect propositions. The spirit is well captured by Walras (1900/1954) who declares,

> In fact, the whole world may be looked upon as a vast general market made up of diverse special markets. Our task then is to discover the laws to which these purchases and sales tend to conform automatically. To this end, we shall suppose that the market is perfectly competi-tive, just as in pure mechanics we suppose, to start with, that machines are perfectly frictionless. (p. 84)

This quote highlights several features of the early neoclassical approach that have remained prominent over the decades and still inform the core of neoclassical micro-economics as taught to today's students and used in neoclassical-oriented treatises on law and economics (Rizvi 2007); indeed, it is from these historical roots that the "assume a competitive labor market" proposition originates. These features include a conceptual model of the economy derived from physics and classical mechanics where economic relations are closely akin to natural laws (e.g., the "law of demand"); a core model of human beings based on rationality and self-interest; a core model of markets based on demand and supply and competitive equilibrium; a core set of tools including constrained maximization, equilibrium and efficiency; and adherence to the ideas of Adam Smith and Jean Baptiste Say – enshrined in the invisible hand idea and Say's Law – that self-interest and competition cause a market economy to automatically gravitate through flexible price adjustments toward a full-employment equilibrium (Kates 1998). These ideas are then rounded out with the Pareto welfare principle, described earlier.

These insights were formalized in the 1950s by Arrow and Debreu into the *first welfare theorem* of neoclassical economics (Blaug 2007). The first welfare theorem (FWT) is also often called the "invisible hand" theorem. It states that a perfectly competitive economy is able to generate a Pareto-optimal (aka, efficient) allocation of resources, meaning that the flexible price system puts the economy on its production possibility frontier (full utilization of resources, including labor) such that all gains from trade are exhausted and no readjustment of production/distribution can make one person better off without harming the welfare of another. Another characterization of Pareto optimality is "best feasible outcome," given the initial distribution of wealth and existing set of rules, laws and other constraints. The first welfare theorem is often regarded as the most important result of economic science, per this statement by Just, Hueth and Schmitz (2004):

> This conclusion [the first welfare theorem] is probably the single most powerful result in the theory of market economies and is widely used by economists who believe that markets are competitive and that governments should not intervene in economic activity. Milton Friedman and the "Chicago School" are the best known defenders of this position. In addition, because of its efficiency properties, competitive equilibrium offers a useful standard for policy analysis. (pp. 27–8)

Not surprisingly, the first welfare theorem leads to distinctly conservative-to-libertarian conclusions regarding policy and institutional interventions in labor markets. Illustratively, Mas-Colell, Whinston and Green (1995) state, "Under perfectly competitive conditions . . . the only possible welfare justification for intervention in the economy is the fulfillment of distributional objectives" (p. 524). The last part of this statement introduces the *second welfare theorem* (SWT). It states that attainment of efficiency in a competitive market system is independent of the distribution of income and other endowments, the upshot of which is that any desired redistribution for equity and fairness reasons should be done "before the market" in the form of ex ante lump-sum taxes and payments rather than through use of methods that in some way interfere with demand/supply (e.g., a minimum wage law, collective bargaining) or endeavor to alter market outcomes ex post. Thus, the FWT and SWT effectively establish the prima facie case that in a competitive market economy the appropriate role of government is limited to certain basic functions such as maintenance of law and order, enforcement of contracts, provision of public goods, and lump-sum income transfers; otherwise, markets and employers and employees are best left to operate on their own with laissez-faire the general but not necessarily universal rule. As the quote above indicates, this position is particularly associated with the Chicago School of economics and many of the Chicagoans who founded and participated in the development of modern law and economics (Overtfeldt 2007; Freedman 2008; Medema 2010).

One rarely sees the first and second welfare theorems mentioned in the labor economics literature or even in most NE discussions of labor law and policy. A reason is that NE-style labor economics is essentially applied microeconomics and the FWT and SWT are therefore typically presumed or implicit. Illustrative is the recent book *The Economics of Imperfect Labor Markets* (Boeri and van Ours 2008). In Chapter 1 they follow the standard theoretical line of argument in NE and SL&EM: they state that the theoretical model economists use as the benchmark for evaluating labor market institutions and laws is the competitive demand/supply model. They then lay out this model and demonstrate (1) why competition maximizes allocative efficiency and (2) how laws and institutions (e.g., unions) interfere with demand/supply and create welfare losses. Without invoking the FWT and SWT in name, they nonetheless reach a minimalist verdict on the appropriate role of labor law and institutions. In their words,

> Because all labor market institutions introduce a wedge between labor demand and supply, they reduce the size of labor markets [and gains from trade]. If the labor market is competitive, the total surplus to be shared between firms and workers will be reduced after the introduction of any labor market institution . . . it should be possible to make everybody happier (or at least as happy) without them. (p. 18)

These pro-market conclusions rest, of course, on the supposition that real world labor markets are indeed approximately competitive or, more generally, that the outcomes are efficient *as if* the market were competitive. Reder (1982) claims the early Chicago economists who founded the SL&EM took precisely this view. He states that their position was, ". . . in the absence of sufficient evidence to the contrary, one may treat observed prices and quantities as good approximations to their long-run competitive equilibrium values" (p. 12). The implication is that labor markets, while having a variety of short-run frictions and imperfections, nonetheless yield outcomes that in the longer run are approximately competitive. An implication is that most alleged employment problems, such as discrimination, exploitation and bad treatment, are of a surface or transitory nature that will get ironed out by competition without government intervention (Friedman and Friedman 1990).

In the last two-to-three decades many economists with the SL&EM have moved to a more generalized version of this proposition, particularly due to the influence of Coase and the NIE. Coase (1937) and later writers such as Williamson (1985) point out that a significant share of economic exchange takes place inside firms, where there is no competitive market and where management (in the absence of a union) decides employment matters by fiat. What, then, is to prevent managers from taking advantage of workers?

NE/NIE admits that sometimes workers are taken advantage of, but denies that in most cases this is a widespread problem (Dow 1997). The line of argument proceeds along two levels. The first invokes the *Coase theorem*, an idea inspired by Coase (1960), but named and formally articulated by Stigler (1966). The theorem asserts that, in a situation of zero transaction cost (frictionless/zero-cost trading), individual economic agents have an incentive to exchange property rights to scarce resources until they are fully allocated to the people who value them most. The key insights SL&EM proponents take from the Coase theorem are (1) with low transaction costs individuals can bargain and trade their way to a competitive-like and surplus-maximizing outcome even in the absence of markets, and (2) where employment problems occur, government regulation or labor unions are not the only or necessarily best option; rather, an alternative is to make existing markets more competitive by reducing transaction costs and creating new or better-protected property rights (Cooter and Ulen 2010).

The second line of thought also comes from Coase (1937) and the NIE. The argument is that firms, employment relationships and internal labor markets (ILMs) come into existence in order to economize on the costs of allocating and coordinating resources through direct exchange in labor markets. That is, using managers to coordinate and allocate labor (employees) inside firms can be the more efficient solution when transaction costs of market exchange are relatively high. Since internal labor markets are coordinated by management and not demand/supply, one might think that considerable room therefore opens up for discrimination, exploitation and other maladies. However, these economists argue that competition in external labor and product markets in most cases effectively regulates and polices the practices and conditions of labor inside firms. They cite three reasons. The first is that workers can quit if they do not get market-going pay and conditions; a second is that firms lose profit if they do not adopt efficient employment structures and practices; and, third, even though explicit market prices do not exist in internal labor markets, the managers and workers have substitute "shadow prices" (opportunity costs) to guide them toward outcomes that are surplus maximizing. Illustratively, Wachter and Wright (1990) argue that "economic pressures [from external markets] on the ILM are not repealed; they are simply rechanneled . . ." (p. 244) and, hence, employers and employees are led to adopt efficient and self-enforcing contract practices and understandings that "serve the optimizing goals of the firm and the workers" (p. 242) and "promot[e] the joint surplus through savings on contract costs" (p. 256).

The point to be stressed is that the NE paradigm, either in terms of standard competitive price theory or a transaction cost efficient contract theory, does *not* rule out use of labor law per se; rather, it creates a general presumption against interference. This position rests on other propositions that are implicit in the first welfare theorem and a mainstay of Second L&EM analysis – the benefits of *free trade* and legal corollary of *freedom of contract* in competitive markets. The virtues of free trade and freedom of contract are that *all sides gain from trade* and *resources flow to the contracting party who values them most* (the core idea of the Coase theorem). Based on this reasoning, Frank Knight of the Chicago School comments, "All good economists since Smith have favored free trade, that is, laissez-faire against protectionism" (Emmett 1999: 439). From this perspective, the danger with labor law – and certainly with unions – is that despite their well-intentioned goals they often create undesirable protectionism and monopoly in labor markets. The free trade sentiment among NE economists is also captured in these comments by Charles Plott (2010). He states (p. 14), "[A] consensus [exists] within the scientific community that is spreading to the general public that free markets . . . are in everyone's best interest." He immediately cautions that "The principle [of free markets] does not say that government should do nothing" (p. 14), but also concludes in the next sentence that in free markets "there are natural tendencies and that the most productive policies are those that will harmonize with them." These "harmonizing policies" are not zero regulation but regulation only when clearly needed, per his observation that "Our economy is built on the idea that competition can protect the consuming public" (p. 8). Members of SL&EM would amend this statement only by expanding it to include *the working public*.

Hence, mainstream economists start off analysis of labor law from the presumption that free trade in labor is desired; therefore, to make the case for an abridgement of free trade, one must demonstrate clear evidence that markets for some reason are malfunctioning. That is, one must demonstrate *market failure* (Addison and Hirsch 1997; Boeri and van Ours 2008).

A market failure, traditionally defined, arises when some feature of labor markets diverges in a substantively important way from the ideal of perfect competition. Oft-cited examples are monopsony, imperfect/asymmetric information, externalities, public goods, principal–agent problems, match-specific investments, and barriers to mobility. However, the extended efficient contract form of NE, as described above, has been able to demonstrate that many of these (alleged) departures from competition are not likely to pose significant social concern. One reason is that they often reflect an efficient adaptation to underlying technological and cost constraints (Dow 1997). For example, low turnover may not mean a firm has monopsony power but rather that workers choose to stay with the employer to reap the benefits of specific on-the-job training. Likewise, if women are mostly employed in a group of low-paying occupations while men are mostly employed in different group of high-paying occupations, this is not necessarily a sign of discrimination but instead efficient sorting by comparative advantage (due to different biological endowments and gender-related tastes) and differences in human capital investment (due to different occupational choices and family roles).

A second reason not to worry about alleged departures from the competitive ideal is that employers and employees are often able to create self-enforcing contract provisions and safeguards that protect against potential opportunism and exploitation on account of these non-competitive elements. For example, match-specific investments (e.g., firm-specific job skills and training) create sunk costs for both the firm and worker and the two sides are therefore restrained from opportunistically taking advantage of each other by the prospect of losing these costs if the relationship ends. Wachter (2004) points out these contract safeguards are not always fully effective and are necessarily a second-best solution relative to a world of perfect competition, yet broadly viewed they are often first-best solutions in light of prevailing costs and constraints. He states:

> However, second-best solutions are not necessarily market failures that give rise to policy improvements. Information asymmetries, potential opportunism, and moral hazard are real economic costs just like any other economic cost, such as workers' insistence on being paid to work. Consequently, the self-enforcing arrangements worked out by the parties are arguably first-best, given the restricted set of solutions available to them. (pp. 169–70)

It is a fair generalization to say that economists associated with the SL&EM are for these reasons predisposed to regard labor markets – absent compelling evidence to the contrary – as approximately competitive and employment contracts as generally efficient (Mercuro and Medema 1997; Schwab 1997; Huang 2009). This leads them, in turn, to favor maximum scope for free markets, competition and private ordering in firms and, conversely, to take a skeptical "first show me the market failure" argument toward proposed extensions of labor law, government regulation, or trade unions and collective bargaining. Their minimalist view on labor law is reinforced by practical considerations. That is, in an ideal world government regulation could potentially pinpoint instances of workplace exploitation or discrimination and fashion cost-effective remedies; in the real world, however, government regulation is slow, cumbersome and politically driven, and therefore can entail very large costs for fixing a social problem. Society, therefore, may find that the costs from intervening in markets far outweigh the benefits.

IV.   A CASE STUDY: POSNER'S ECONOMIC ANALYSIS OF LAW

Exhibit A of the general approach I am describing is Richard Posner's *Economic Analysis of Law* (2007); the approach there is, in turn, mirrored in practically every other book and journal article with "law and economics" in the title. My purpose is to illustrate in a concrete way (1) reliance of the Second L&E movement on the competitive model and (2) the marked tendency of the model to yield "guilty until proven innocent" conclusions about labor law. The remainder of the chapter then demonstrates why this approach is theoretically flawed and normatively unbalanced (also Kaufman 2012b).

The title of Chapter 1 is "The Nature of Economic Reasoning." The first sentence reads, "This book is written in the conviction that economics is a powerful tool for analyzing a vast range of legal questions . . ." (p. 3). I highlight this sentence because it suggests that economics is a singular entity, mirroring the mainstream presumption à la Becker that there is only one corpus of economic theory (Becker is cited in Posner 2007, p. 1, footnote 1.1). The next sentence reads, "A student takes a course in price theory . . ."

Price theory is another term for standard NE microeconomic theory, suggesting that, while mainstream economics may indeed encompass a huge domain of non-standard topics, the core remains the same price theory that earlier Chicagoans, such as Friedman and Stigler, popularized a half-century ago. The innovation of the SL&EM, however, is to treat legal rules as establishing another vector of prices facing economic agents.

At the end of the first paragraph there follows a new heading, labeled "Fundamental Concepts." The first fundamental concept is "man is a rational utility maximizer" (p. 4). From this flows what Posner (p. 4) calls the "three fundamental principles of economics." The first is the law of demand (price and quantity are inversely related); the second is the economic meaning of cost (often measured by a market price but more generally by the economic value of resources devoted to an alternative use, called opportunity cost or shadow price); the third is that resources tend to gravitate toward their most valuable uses if voluntary exchange and market trading are allowed (markets tend to promote efficient outcomes).

These concepts are supplemented with three fundamental NE tools: the law of demand, illustrated by a downward-sloping demand curve (Figure 1, p. 4); a competitive demand/supply model of markets (Figure 2, p. 8); and the welfare criteria of Pareto superiority and the Kaldor-Hicks compensation principle. The next-to-ending section of Chapter 1 is devoted to "The Realism of Assumptions in Economics." Posner here follows Friedman (1953) and argues that the neoclassical theories and tools he uses are not to be judged by whether they are realistic (characterized as a demand on the part of critics for "descriptiveness completeness" (p. 16)) but by their predictive power. People have cognitive limitations (bounded rationality) and cannot as a factual matter make all the calculations competitive theory presumes; nonetheless, observed market outcomes typically approximate competitive predictions and therefore analysts may use the model "as if" it is a description of reality.

Posner only briefly examines the effect of government regulation on markets in Chapter 1. The specific example chosen – rent control in a competitive housing market – illustrates the general points that regulation is frequently demanded by special interest groups as a form of rent-seeking behavior, often has undesirable market consequences (shortages, higher prices, etc.), and entails an overall reduction in social welfare through resource misallocation and deadweight loss.

Chapter 11 is devoted entirely to regulation of the employment relationship. Posner considers a number of staple topics in labor law: unions, employment-at-will, minimum wages, occupational safety and health, mandated benefits, discrimination, and pensions. Space precludes a detailed review of this chapter; I thus summarize below salient points, roughly following the order in the book.

- Labor markets are broadly competitive in nature since "labor monopsony . . . is not a serious problem in this country" (p. 342) and "monopolies and cartels carry within them the seeds of their own destruction" (p. 343). Even where competition is not fully effective due to imperfect information or other frictions, one can nonetheless presume that labor outcomes are (mostly) efficient because otherwise unexploited gains from trade "would be negotiated voluntarily" (p. 349). The baseline for analysis, therefore, is "an efficient common law of labor relations" (p. 341).
- Unions act as a labor cartel and win higher wages for their members but at the

cost of economic inefficiency and "reduction in the demand for labor caused by union wage scales" (p. 343). The National Labor Relations Act (NLRA) "is a kind of reverse Sherman Act, designed to encourage cartelization of labor markets" (p. 344).

- Workers were not victimized by early 20th century "yellow-dog contracts" (a provision by which a worker agrees as a condition of employment to refrain from joining a labor union) because in a competitive labor market "the worker presumably would demand compensation for giving up his right to join a union" (p. 341).

- "Further evidence that job security is inefficient is that . . . employment-at-will is the normal form of work contract in the United States. The worker can quit when he wants . . . An employer who gets a reputation for arbitrarily discharging employees will have to pay new employees a premium . . ." (p. 348).

- A legal minimum wage "reinforces the effect of unionization on wage rates" (p. 352), and thus represents another form of monopoly influence in labor markets; it also is ineffective in poverty reduction and most harms the job prospects of the workers who are most disadvantaged (e.g., black teenagers).

- "The Occupational Safety and Health Act . . . is arguably superfluous. The employer has a selfish interest in providing the optimal . . . level of worker health and safety" (p. 354).

- Women's lower wages relative to men are mostly due to their different human capital and occupational choice decisions, made in light of different family roles and preferences. These differences "would have narrowed even without government intervention." Moreover, "not all employment discrimination on grounds of sex is inefficient" (p. 357).

- Pension protection may well not be necessary because (in part) "[t]he employer's incentive to abuse the power that incomplete vesting conferred on him by reneging on his unwritten contract to deal fairly with his employees would be held in check by his concern for preserving a reputation for fair dealing" (pp. 363–4).

I cite these examples from Posner's book to illustrate what I am here calling the NE paradigm in the analysis of labor law and to its various properties and characteristics. One may also consult labor economists such as Boeri and van Ours (2008) and legal scholars such as Jolls (2006) to see the same model and mode of reasoning in action. I believe it is clear that *"assume a competitive labor market"* is the starting point for this type of economic analysis of law, and that the structure and operationalization of this theory – either in perfectly competitive or extended "demand/supply with frictions" form – by its very nature leads to a *guilty until proven innocent* verdict on labor law. The entire point of this chapter, in turn, is to question whether this *a priori* negative-leaning verdict on labor law rests on solid and evenly balanced theoretical ground.

V.   THE COMPETITIVE MODEL IN THE FIRST L&E MOVEMENT

IE/IR economists do not deny supply and demand; further, they recognize that competition is often a beneficial force that protects and advances the conditions of labor and leads firms to efficiently produce goods and services for consumers. These are part of the success story of capitalism. However, institutional economists also claim that there is a darker side to labor markets in capitalism that the neoclassical side neglects, assumes away, or fatalistically attributes to inexorable economic law. Craypo (1997) captures the IE/IR viewpoint and critique, for example, when he states,

> Institutional labor economics in America appeared before the turn of the century in response to neoclassical failure to study labor markets rather than labor theories and therefore to address chronic unemployment and low wages among hourly workers . . . At the heart of the institutional perception . . . is the conviction that society gets the labor market outcomes it wants, not those determined by some economic law, and that society therefore must assume a responsibly interventionist position. (p. 231)

The term the early institutional economists gave to the darker side of the world of work is "labor problems" (also called "evils") and many of the labor textbooks written by these economists through the 1960s had the term "labor problems" somewhere in the title (e.g., Watkins 1922; Shultz and Coleman 1961). Commonly cited labor problems were poverty-level wages, long work hours, industrial accidents, child labor, and unemployment; the package of "visible hand" measures to solve these problems included labor law, collective bargaining, social safety net insurance programs, and counter-cyclical fiscal and monetary policies (Kaufman 1997, 2003a). As the old-style institutional labor economics was replaced by new-style neoclassical labor economics, the term "labor problems" faded from sight and is today never encountered. One may fairly speculate that part of the explanation is that the concept of labor problems carries a connotation of sub-optimality which goes against the maximization hypothesis central to neoclassical economics; arguably another explanation is that the concept of labor problems provided institutional economists with a rationale for government intervention in labor markets which neoclassical-trained writers typically regard as unpersuasive and counter-productive.

The position of institutional economics is that a laissez-faire or "state of nature" capitalist economy, such as in the early 20th century United States, is certain to be unbalanced, unstable and inhumane, and therefore conducive to considerable inefficiency, injustice and social conflict (Commons and Andrews 1916; Budd 2004; Isaac 2007; Kaufman 2010b; Rutherford 2011). The purpose of FL&EM, accordingly, is to discover and implement labor law and the other policy measures in a manner that promotes greater balance, stability and social harmony. This does not mean IE/IR economists have in mind a one-way street of ever-greater regulation of labor markets; it does mean, however, that they think much of the labor legislation and regulation enacted over the 20th century was on balance a good idea and has well-served the nation and, correlatively, that it would be a mistake to dismantle large parts of it as counseled by the neoliberal and "first-best" part of NE and SL&EM (Osterman, Kochan, Locke and Piore 2001; Kochan 2005; Befort and Budd 2009).

The difference of opinion between the First and Second law and economics movements revolves around different assessments of the benefits and costs of labor law, unions, and other such measures (compare Freeman and Medoff 1984 vs. Epstein, 1983; Craypo 1997 vs. Dow 1997; Kaufman 2010c vs. Neumark and Wascher 2008). The latter see few if any benefits because they look at labor markets as highly competitive, put considerable faith in the invisible hand, and judge performance mostly (or solely) by the criterion of economic efficiency (Lazear 2000); on the other hand, they see large costs in the form of fewer jobs, less competitive industry, higher consumer prices, a larger government bureaucracy, and a less efficient allocation of resources.

IE/IR, on the other hand, looks at labor law and associated employment programs and sees greater benefits and lower costs (e.g., Belman and Belzer 1997; Block, Roberts, and Clark 2003; Arthurs 2006; Dau-Schmidt and Traynor 2009; Estlund 2010). On the benefit side are six factors unduly discounted or neglected in NE:

- Frictions, impediments and market failures are inherent to and widespread in labor markets and, therefore, invisible hand forces are present but attenuated and unable to fully protect and advance the interests of labor.
- Labor markets and employment relationships are (in general) a tipped playing field favoring employers' (and consumers') interests over workers' because of built-in social, legal and economic inequalities; hence, employment outcomes may be "competitive" but also considerably unequal, inefficient, and socially undesirable.
- Competition in labor markets, more so than in product markets, can become excessive and actually retard rather than promote efficiency and industrial performance.
- Firms often have market power to set wages and this opens up space for non-competitive outcomes in employment relationships that may contain a significant element of discrimination, exploitation, or unfairness.
- Institutions in labor markets are not well-viewed as primarily inefficient wedges and distortions; rather, they are also essential to a high-performing employment relationship because they promote higher static and dynamic efficiency through encouragement of cooperation and trust, organizational citizenship and loyalty, security of investment in training and hard work, and voice and involvement in problem-solving.
- Efficiency is important in evaluating employment outcomes but so are human rights for workers, democracy in the workplace, respect and fair treatment by employers, and jobs that are safe, satisfying and meaningful.

IE/IR economists also believe the costs of labor law are not as large or serious as NE portrays. For example,

- Job losses are smaller (or not at all) for a moderate increase in labor costs from new or expanded employment law and regulation, in part because labor demand curves are more inelastic and "looser" due to non-NE features such as production indivisibilities and interdependencies (e.g., team forms of production; positive wage/effort effects).
- Labor law and regulation are often "distortion-correcting" rather than "distortion-creating" so at least over a range the efficiency costs of labor law emphasized in NE are minimal or non-existent.
- Labor markets and firms frequently have resource slack and organizational buffers that can help absorb the cost effect of labor law.
- Unfairness, exclusion, and ill-treatment in employment procedures and outcomes generate many economic and social costs that NE omits or under-emphasizes (e.g.,

greater absenteeism, less work effort, more strikes, waste of human resources) and which labor law can help reduce.
- Government law and regulation can be administered more efficiently than NE portrays and, similarly, government leaders/workers are not just self-interested rent-seekers.

As discussed above, the FL&EM has its roots in the 1880s and was much inspired by the historical/social type of economics done in late 19th century Germany (Hovenkamp 1990; Pearson 1997; Jacoby 2005; Rutherford 2011); in the labor area it was also closely linked with the creation of the International Labor Organization (ILO) at the end of World War I (Kaufman 2004). The beginnings of industrialization brought with it numerous employment problems, mounting strikes and capital-labor conflict, and the rise of radical trade unions and socialist political parties. These individual problems became known collectively as "The Labor Problem." The economists and fellow social reformers who started the FL&EM believed that the Labor Problem, if allowed to fester and intensify, threatened the survival of American capitalism and democratic form of government (Fried 1998). They sought to defuse it by a middle-way program of reform that steered a course between laissez-faire on one side and socialism on the other.

Two fathers of FL&EM, Richard Ely and Henry Carter Adams, both did graduate work in Germany in the 1880s and wrote on the intersection of law and economics, particularly with regard to contracts and property rights (Rader 1966; Dorfman 1969). Just as Walras (1900/1954) enunciated certain themes that capture the essence of NE, Adams and Ely do the same for IE/IR. I start with Adams.

Adams' presidential address to the American Economic Association is titled "Economics and Jurisprudence" (1897). Adams states that law is "the background of all associated activity; it provides the framework that limits and controls the exercise of liberty . . . [and is] the expression of the ethical sense of a community crystallized about the problem of common living" (p. 138). The fundamental objective of law is to "understand justice, . . . explain the evolution of justice, . . . and formulate those rules of conduct essential to the realization of justice." (ibid.). Adams emphasizes justice as the chief goal of law because justice is a prerequisite for a stable and harmonious social order and such an order is, in turn, a prerequisite for a prosperous economy.

The major domestic problem Adams addresses in his paper is the Labor Problem. He says, "the workings of self-interest in the industrial field do not in all respects appear to be in harmony with the ideals of justice, and . . . it places in jeopardy material progress itself" (pp. 142–3). His diagnosis for the growing disharmony in society is that the structure of relations between employers and employees shifted in ways that strongly favor employers (e.g., the growth of large corporations, a wage labor force dependent on employers for jobs and the means of production; substantial unemployment in labor markets); this growing inequality – and the insecure and frequently oppressive employment experiences that accompanied it – created a growing sense of individual and class injustice; and the solution, therefore, was to realign the legal order and set of property rights to achieve a better bargaining balance, such as through new protective labor laws and collective bargaining. Adams (1887: 90) referred to this process as "raising the plane of competitive action," with the idea that this does not replace competition but raises the floor on competition so it yields more just outcomes and therefore more cooperation and harmony in industry and higher economic performance.

Ely's book *The Labor Movement in America* (1886) stands as the first work in what later became the American field of industrial relations. He argues that trade unions and labor law are required to "remove disadvantages under which the great mass of workingmen suffer, and must continue to suffer unless they get relief either by voluntary combination or by combined political action" (p. 96). He notes in the same paragraph that orthodox economists maintain that promoting free competition in labor markets protects and advances workers' interests; but, he claims, this is a false view.

Ely cites two fallacies in the orthodox view. The first is the NE view that competition creates an open playing field where the ordinary worker can get ahead through individual action. In reality, legal, social and economic inequalities tip the contest in favor of employers and make it difficult for the mass of workers to escape from dangerous, low-paid, and onerous jobs. The result, therefore, is "absence of actual equality between the two parties to the labor-contract, and the one-sided determination of the price and other conditions of labor" (p. 100). The second NE fallacy is that labor is essentially similar to other commodities, and that free competition, therefore, leads to beneficial outcomes. Ely argues that because labor is embodied in human beings, competition in labor markets does not work as demand/supply theory predicts. Fluctuation in wages and jobs makes workers feel insecure, demoralized, and antagonistic toward employers, all of which undercuts efficiency and harmony in the workplace. Similarly, competition in labor markets can be destabilizing – "If the demand falls, labor cannot be withdrawn from the market like other wares. On the contrary, . . . the supply must increase by reason of competition of a greater number of laborers . . . [as] children and women seek labor to eke out the father's income" (p. 101). And, finally, workers are forced by mobility costs and lack of alternative jobs to "risk health in ill-ventilated rooms . . . and [their] lives . . . by [employers'] failure to fence in dangerous equipment" (p. 106).

In 1905 Ely took the lead in founding the American Association for Labor Legislation (AALL). The AALL soon became the most important research and lobbying group in the country for expanded labor law and social insurance programs (Moss 1996). The group actively promoted workmen's compensation, unemployment insurance, old-age pensions, minimum wages, maximum hour limits, a ban on child labor, workplace safety legislation, universal health insurance, and counter-cyclical public works spending. A variety of economic and social arguments were advanced in favor of these measures. To illustrate I take two examples (Commons and Andrews 1916; Moss 1996; Kaufman 1997).

The first is workmen's compensation; that is, employer-financed payments out of a general fund to employees who have suffered loss of work due to a workplace accident. From an IE/IR perspective, unregulated competition in labor markets leads to excessive injuries because workers possess poor information about safety risks and are often constrained from leaving unsafe jobs by mobility costs. On the employer side, firms often have small incentives to invest in safety because of a public goods problem (workers do not speak up about unsafe conditions out of fear of employer retaliation and therefore act as free riders in the hope someone else will do so) and the availability in most years of an ample supply of unemployed workers eager to replace the injured. Making employers pay an injury tax, therefore, gives them an incentive to improve safety; it forces employers to bear the cost of accidents as part of their total cost of production (rather than shift the cost to workers, families, or the community). And, finally, accident compensation is a humane and just payment to help unfortunate workers who because of a workplace accident can no longer work to put food on the table. Thus, labor law serves to increase both efficiency and fairness.

A second case is a legal minimum wage. It has a number of virtues that conventional economics mostly ignores. For example, a minimum wage puts a floor under labor markets and prevents sweatshop wages; stops a destabilizing fall in wages during recessions and depressions; provides an incentive to employers to improve operational efficiency, helps reduce income inequality; increases household income and aggregate demand in the economy; improves wages for the groups most exploited and discriminated against; draws people into the labor market and legitimate employment, and helps ensure that workers get at least a social minimum of income.

IE/IR and the FL&EM dominated intellectual thought and policy making on labor law into the 1960s and 1970s. High-water marks were the Progressive era (1900–14), the New Deal (1933–45), and the New Frontier/Great Society period (1961–8). Ely passed on the IE/IR baton to his student and colleague at Wisconsin, John Commons. Commons, like Ely before him, was elected by his peers to be president of the American Economic Association (1917) and was widely recognized as the nation's foremost labor economist. Commons was a tireless advocate for the AALL program of expanded labor law, social insurance, collective bargaining, and government counter-cyclical fiscal and monetary policy. Economist Kenneth Boulding (1957) declared Commons was, "the intellectual father of the New Deal, of labor legislation, of social security, of the whole movement in the country toward a welfare state" (p. 7).

A puzzling question from today's neoliberal/SL&EM perspective is this: how could Commons, presumptively considered by his peers to be a good economist, champion these interferences with the free market? The answer is that he considered but rejected the "assume a competitive labor market" proposition as a sound place (by itself) for theorizing and evaluating labor law. Illustratively, he stated, "The commodity theory of labor . . . is not false, it is incomplete" (Commons 1919: 17). Later he explained (1950),

> Interference with the law of supply and demand has always been the main objection raised against all collective action, whether against protective tariffs, against immigration restriction, against labor unions, or against corporations; but these interferences have nonetheless been repeated and cumulated for a hundred years, *because the alternatives of noninterference under the circumstances were deemed worse than the interferences.* Public programs and policies cannot be evaluated in terms of logical consequences of isolated assumptions or similarities. They must be judged by the practical consequences of their operations. This requires a subtle *balancing of many parts – some of which are necessarily contradictory.* (p. 137; emphasis added)

Note in the first italicized part of the quote the IE/IR proposition that the costs associated with labor law intervention in markets are positive but less than the costs incurred from continued laissez-faire. In the second italicized part is another IE/IR theme: Labor law cannot be considered in isolation from historical and social context, but, rather, must be evaluated in terms of the conditions of the time, as part of a system of industrial relations institutions and practices, with the goal of achieving economic and social balance, and recognition that not all parts of an industrial relations system can always work together smoothly.

Later generations of IE/IR economists have staked out the same position. I provide three examples. All three concern the case for unions and collective bargaining, but the implications are identical for labor law. The first is Harry Millis, professor of economics at Chicago, president of the American Economic Association (1934), and a pre-World War II institutional-oriented economist. In testimony to Congress on the proposed NLRA, he states (National Labor Relations Board 1985: 1553–4):

> Of course, if there were perfect mobility of labor, keen competition for labor, and no concerted control of wages and hours by employers, the situation would be substantially different from what it has been and the case for collective bargaining would be less conclusive in modern industry. I am aware that many of my academic brethren assume that these conditions just mentioned are generally true, and reason that in the absence of such friction in the market, wages, hours, and all the rest of it rather steadily adjust themselves to what industry, and consumers, should and can bear.

But he then goes on to explain (pp. 1553–4),

> The truth, as I see it, is . . . that the competitive demand for labor, while important, does not go far in protecting the workers against long hours, excessive overtime, fines, discharge, without sufficient cause, and objectionable working conditions . . . One is thus driven to the conclusion that . . . hours of work and conditions of work – things which intimately concern workmen, are best decided collectively – through legislation or through collective bargaining, and some of them are not easily subject to legislative control. This is particularly true of a reasonable degree of security of tenure. The case for collective bargaining is only less strong with respect to wages.

A second example is economist Lloyd Reynolds, a president of the Industrial Relations Research Association (1955). He states as a general principle, "[I]t is apparent that local labor markets in this country . . . are not highly competitive" (Reynolds 1954: 543). He goes on to amplify on this observation (p. 549):

> Only in theory, then, does the "competitive labor market" provide an alternative to wage determination through collective bargaining. The practical alternative is collective bargaining *versus* wage-setting by employers with rather weak competitive checks. Under non-union conditions, the immobility of the majority of workers plus the unsystematic selection of jobs by those in search of work gives employers wide latitude in determining wage rates and other conditions of employment. An employer can offer terms considerably below those generally prevailing in the area and still secure an adequate labor force. He is subject to serious competitive pressure mainly at the peak of business cycles, when job opportunities in other plants are relatively plentiful. Even after years of high unemployment, one still finds large differences in the wages offered by different employers for the same jobs.

A third example of the IE/IR perspective comes from John Dunlop. In an interview published in 2002 (Kaufman 2002: 338) he states,

> I would surely agree that in some cases unions and collective bargaining have made wage rates uneconomic. This is undesirable. But I have several problems with the view you have just stated [the neoclassical critique of unions]. I reject out of hand any argument that the economy would be better off without unions. Unions do not come into the picture and distort some "perfect" wage structure, because there is no such thing. In the real world there are all kinds of distortions and inequities built into the wage structure, as any person who has set wages knows. To assume in a model that wages are "competitive" is to assume away a large part of the reality.

In an earlier essay, Dunlop explicitly takes the same position that Commons enunciated more than six decades earlier regarding the "assume a competitive labor market" proposition. That is, the model by itself is too narrow and simplistic to serve as an adequate tool for understanding labor markets and labor law. Thus, Dunlop declares, "the competitive model, or economic considerations alone, are not an adequate tool unassisted by ... industrial relations tools and concepts" (Dunlop 1984: 23). Several years later "second-best" macroeconomist Robert Solow repeats the same theme: "It does not follow from any of this that the ordinary forces of supply and demand are irrelevant to the labor market, or that we can do without the textbook apparatus altogether. It only follows that they are incomplete and need completing" (Solow 1990: 22).

As reviewed earlier in this chapter, mainstream economists have in the last two-to-three decades substantially generalized and extended the competitive model and incorporated many frictions and imperfections, including the existence of hierarchical firms and structured internal labor markets. From an IE/IR perspective, this is all to the good and helps bring NE and IE/IR together toward a middle ground.

There remains, however, a divide along several dimensions. One is methodologically based. The way that many NE/NIE economists have incorporated labor market frictions and internal firm structures into standard demand/supply theory is to add them as additional constraints in an optimization model (Becker 1976; Lazear 2000). By the nature of optimization, however, the resulting outcomes (e.g., unemployment because of job search costs; discrimination because of imperfect information) are efficient in the sense they cannot be improved upon (anything less, by definition, is not optimization). If, in turn, they cannot be improved upon, then evidently no opportunity exists in labor markets for labor law or unions to improve the situation. Hence, NE/NIE incorporates frictions and imperfections, but in a way that still leads to (mostly) non-interventionist conclusions. Gregory Dow, in a review article of NIE, well articulates this situation. He explains (Dow 1997: 60),

> A great deal of intellectual effort has gone into the construction of economic rationales for existing organizational practices ... This reflects a tendency among most NIE writers to assume, at least prima facie, that actual employment practices represent efficient solutions to complex contracting problems. This efficiency assumption is useful in generating explanatory hypotheses of a functionalist kind (employment practice X exists because it satisfies efficiency criterion Y under environment conditions Z). However, it also places a heavy burden of proof on advocates of labor market regulation by obliging them to identify specific market failures that warrant government intervention. One must often read between the lines (and squint hard) in order to discover a rationale for regulatory policy in the NIE.

IE/IR scholars recognize we do not live in a perfect, frictionless world and therefore some employment problems are bound to arise as the nature of things. They also worry, however, that this type of optimization modeling can end up being an *ex post* rationalization; that is, if we observe it, then it must be efficient (since people have an incentive to maximize joint surplus and exhaust gains from trade). They also believe it is impossible to explain many features of employment relationships as an efficient contract outcome of economizing behavior. Thus, Dunlop (1994) concludes that, "the new institutional economics has little to contribute ... to an understanding of internal labor markets" (p. 395); he finds it "unacceptable...to define an internal labor market simply as a 'set of explicit or implicit, more or less long-term agreements between a firm and its workers'."

The second divide concerns the role of inequality. SL&EM scholars typically give little research attention or weight in policy evaluation to inequality of outcomes, partly based on the SWT (efficiency is independent of distribution) and partly on the ground that distributional fairness is an ethical and subjective matter and therefore not one amenable to economic analysis. Posner (2007: 14–15), for example, argues that economists cannot resolve normative debates over fairness, but can generally agree on the more delimited normative goal of maximizing the value of output (i.e., attaining efficient outcomes).

Work in the FL&EM and institutional economics tradition, however, insists that a separation between distribution and efficiency is untenable on theory grounds because fairness is a fundamental determinant of workplace relations and, therefore, productivity and firm performance (e.g., Commons 1934; Akerlof 1990; Bewley 1999; Befort and Budd 2009). Further, distribution determines the location of supply and demand curves in the labor market diagram (e.g., high or low) and, thus, the level of wages and conditions of employment. This is particularly important for evaluating labor law since the position of supply and demand determines the size of compensating wage differentials that are relied on in FL&EM to provide correct incentives to firms in matters such as workplace safety and fair treatment. Likewise, IE/IR notes that efficiency also has an ethical and subjective dimension – because it rests on opportunity costs that are a function of individual preferences and valuation – and is in this respect on no firmer theoretical ground than fairness (Samuels and Schmid 1981). Finally, to put aside distributional fairness is to privilege the status quo of income and wealth inequality in society.

A third divide concerns the relevant variables to be included in the social welfare function for evaluating public policy in general and labor law in particular (Budd and Scoville 2005; Gross and Compa 2009). Maximizing the value of output privileges consumers' interests in abundant low-priced goods but slights workers' interests since labor is considered in the NE framework as simply another factor input whose pay, conditions, and treatment should be the minimum the market allows. IE/IR insists, by contrast, that because labor is embodied in human beings, workers' interests in good pay, reasonable hours and conditions, and a satisfying work life must be weighed in the social welfare function; otherwise the material objects made in the economy are given higher priority than the human beings who make them (Kaufman 2005). Giving attention to workers' interests, in turn, means that efficiency in production has to be balanced with other workplace considerations that SL&EM slights, such as human rights at work, democratic firm governance (e.g., due process, voice), and jobs that build up the capabilities and character of the nation's people.

VI.   IE/IR PRINCIPLES AND CONCEPTS

Given this introduction, I want to move toward greater development and analytical representation of the theoretical framework used by IE/IR to examine and evaluate labor law and labor institutions. This builds on earlier work by this author (e.g., Kaufman 1997, 2003a, 2007a, 2007b) and other relevant studies. A general overview of the institutional approach to L&E is provided by Samuels and Schmid (1981) and Mercuro and Medema (1997). I proceed in a two-step process: first, delineation of key concepts and principles in this section and, second, in the next section a diagrammatic exposition.

Certain points described above are reiterated for purposes of emphasis and inclusiveness. Also, certain complementary concepts and ideas of Coase and the NIE are brought over to IE/IR. The list of IE/IR principles given below starts with philosophical/normative underpinnings and then transitions to theoretical concepts and ideas important at the individual, firm and economy level.

Purpose of an economy.   The purpose of an economy is to serve human ends. One way it does this is to operate efficiently so people have the maximum of goods and services. But the grand objective of human existence is not efficiency or the largest GDP (gross domestic product) but the "good life" (Slichter 1931). What exactly constitutes the good life is subject to debate, but it certainly includes greater economic security, procedural and distributive justice, and opportunities for self-development and self-actualization than are provided by the efficiency criterion alone (Lutz 1999; Budd 2004; Sunstein 2004). IE/IR proponents agree that economic policy should seek to get society on the production possibility frontier, but only if the "goods" (or "social wealth") included in calculating the frontier include economic security, social justice, fulfilling jobs, and healthful working conditions. Without this broader perspective, the interests of people (including workers) get subordinated by a narrow efficiency/materialist welfare objective to doing what is best for the economy, rather than structuring and operating the economy to benefit people.

Liberty.   The NE version of liberty is *negative liberty* – i.e., absence of restraint – which leads these economists to advocate minimal government market regulation. From an IE/IR perspective, however, "liberty to starve" or "liberty to work a 14 hour day" is not an attractive conception of liberty; likewise, to say that both a poor person and rich person have an equal freedom to quit a dangerous or dirty job empties the concept of freedom of meaningful significance (Adams 1897; Samuels, Medema and Schmid 1997; Fried 1998). Seen in this light, freedom of contract may hide the whip of economic coercion wielded by one person over another; an example is an employer with scarce job opportunities facing individual workers who either trade their labor or go hungry. Proponents of IE/IR, therefore, base their theory and policy program on a concept of *positive liberty*. Each person has positive liberty when they have the resources needed to command the essentials of life, thus giving them not only the legal space to construct their life but also the economic space (Sen 1999).

Labor is human.   In NE labor is modeled as not substantively different from other factor inputs or goods and services; hence, labor markets are modeled like other kinds of markets (Addison and Hirsch 1997). In IE/IR the fact that labor services are embodied in human beings fundamentally changes theorizing about labor (Commons and Andrews 1916; Budd 2004; Kaufman 2010b). Unlike inanimate inputs such as steel or wheat, the amount of productive services rendered by labor is volitional and thus subject to many more motivational influences than price. Likewise, labor is inseparable from the person selling it, unlike the supply of other factor inputs, and hence the conditions and treatment at the work site are certain to significantly affect employees' work choices. The human dimension of labor also endows the operation of the labor market and employment relationship with greater moral significance than other buy-sell transactions.

Behavioral/social model of the human agent.   People are modeled as largely purposeful and self-interested, but their behavior is subject to "bounded rationality" and is influenced by emotions, social interdependencies, and ethical precepts (Jolls, Sunstein, and Thaler 1998; Kaufman 1999; Schmid 2004). A key part of bounded rationality is that many future events are subject to fundamental uncertainty – that is, cannot be represented by even a probability distribution; in such cases, human beings cannot even hypothetically solve a maximization model since the choice set is not well-defined. Even when rational calculation is possible, it may be partly or wholly displaced by emotions such as anger, hate, love and pride.

Transactions and transaction cost.   A transaction is a legal transfer of ownership; transaction cost is the real resources used to effectuate and enforce this transfer (Commons 1934; Coase 1937).

Ownership and property rights.   Institutional economics is built on the concept of ownership and correlative concept of property rights, per the statement of Commons (1934: 5) that "ownership becomes the foundation of institutional economics." Property rights also figure prominently in the NIE (Coase 1992; Furubotn and Richter 2005). Without prior specification of property rights and ownership, fundamental economic constructs such as commodities, production functions, and demand and supply curves have no basis. These property rights also include not only ownership of economic goods but fundamental human and social rights.

Institutions.   Institutions are bodies of rules, both formal and informal and explicit and tacit, that are built out of property rights (broadly defined) and define the rules of the economic game and the constraints, opportunity sets, incentives, and strategic interdependencies faced by economic agents (Commons 1934; Coase 1992; Groenewegen, Spithoven, and Van Den Berg 2010). All economic activity is "institutional" since it takes place within and is structured and guided by human-made institutions, such as markets, firms and families. These institutions through laws, rules, norms and customs apportion not only economic goods but also justice, power and social standing.

The employment relationship.   Workers most often provide labor services in an institution called the employment relationship (ER). Because slavery is illegal and labor services cannot be separated from the person providing them, firms are able to own physical capital but they must rent human labor from employees. This difference in property rights means that firms typically have a greater incentive to conserve and care for their physical capital (e.g., a truck they own) than their human capital (the truck driver they rent). Unlike in competitive ("spot") product markets, the buyer and seller of labor are also embedded in a personal, long-term and socially interdependent relationship where many things besides price mediate and coordinate the exchange (Dunlop 1994; Befort and Budd 2009).

Incomplete employment contracts.   Because of bounded rationality, imperfect and asymmetric information, fundamental uncertainty, and the interdependent and complex nature of production tasks, transaction costs are both positive and large in most ERs. As a result, employment contracts are necessarily incomplete, contingent and open-ended and subject to numerous forms of externality, public good, moral hazard, opportunism, principal–agent problem, and tacit bargaining (Simon 1951; Marsden 1999).

Labor time vs. labor power.   Due to the incomplete nature of employment contracts it is necessary to distinguish between labor time and labor power (Thompson and Newsome 2004; Kaufman 2010b). Labor time is the 60 minutes that workers are required to be on the employers' premises in return for the hourly wage; labor power is the amount of work (physical, mental and emotional effort) the employees do during the 60 minutes to produce goods and services. The goal of firms is to extract the maximum labor power for the minimum of cost and push-back; the goal of workers is to get the highest return for their labor power with a reasonable limit on the maximum amount of labor power to be delivered. In some branches of IE/IR the extraction of labor power is called the labor process; in others it is called the wage/effort bargain (Baldamus 1961). The labor process and wage/effort bargain create an inherent, if partial, conflict of interest in the employment relationship. They also set up a Prisoner's Dilemma-type bargaining game (Miller 1991) with the possibility of a win-win outcome (e.g., employees provide high labor power and employers provide good paying secure jobs) but also a strong built-in tendency for the two sides to gravitate to a less productive and rewarding win-lose outcome (e.g., employees provide high labor power, firms lay off surplus workers; firms provide workers with job security, employees get lackadaisical). Employers create a human resource management system for the purpose of maximizing extracted labor power through a variety of control, supervisory and disciplinary devices (Edwards 1979; Edwards 2009).

Cooperation, trust, fairness and job security.   Production is in most cases an interdependent process that requires active cooperation among workers and managers. The degree of cooperation (including work effort) is a choice variable for workers; low cooperation typically means low productivity and profits and high cooperation means the reverse. Many factors influence workers' willingness to cooperate but among the most important are trust, fairness and job security (Akerlof 1990; Budd 2004; Schmid 2004) – all likely to be missing in a competitive-style labor market.

Modes of coordination.   Economies have alternative institutional modes for coordinating transactions; the two most important for theory are (1) markets and price, and (2) organizations and command (Williamson 1985; Coase 1992; Kaufman 2003b; Groenewegen, Spithoven and Van Den Berg 2010).

Power.   Power is the ability to satisfy one's desires and obtain a greater share of an institution's scarce goods (material and non-material). Power is influenced by how greatly an economic agent needs/wants an outcome and how long the agent can hold out in the bargaining vis-à-vis the other side (Samuels, Medema and Schmid 1997).

Imperfect competition.   Labor markets are by their nature not only imperfect (in the economist's sense) but among the most imperfect in the economy (Lester 1941; Thurow 1983). Competitive forces are present, and the demand/supply model has some degree of explanatory power; nonetheless, in the short to medium run most labor markets exhibit substantial wage rigidity, constraints on labor mobility, and in most years excess labor supply (involuntary unemployment). These conditions mean labor markets are not self-regulating via flexible wages and are therefore partially coordinated by other means (e.g., labor quantity and quality adjustments); likewise, market outcomes may depart widely from competitive or efficient contract predictions such that conditions of discrimination, exploitation, and unfair treatment have significant space to emerge and persist in employment relationships.

Segmented labor markets.   Labor markets are divided into segments more complex and variegated than the standard competitive versus monopsony categories (Kerr 1977; Dunlop 1994). Segmentation arises from factors that impede competitive forces and the flow of labor across firms and markets, including institutional rules (e.g., seniority systems, occupational licensing), different educational requirements, firm-specific skills, discrimination and social norms, and job search costs, and the human desire for security. Segmentation impedes and replaces competitive demand/supply forces; hence, wage rates and other terms and conditions of employment exhibit considerable diversity across firms and market segments. Some elements of this dispersion are equalizing (or "compensating" in the competitive sense), but many others are non-equalizing.

Internal labor markets.   A major form of segmentation is the internal labor market (Doeringer and Piore 1971; Osterman 1987; Dunlop 1994). Firms create ILMs because they contribute to greater productivity and profit (e.g., by coordinating and controlling labor power and upgrading skills) and positive employee relations; they therefore have a strong efficiency rationale. They are also a major instrument for controlling/coordinating labor power. ILMs, however, also partially supplant and replace coordination via competition and market forces with a hierarchical system of management command and administration. Within ILMs, the quit option affords workers with only partial protection, particularly with regard to items not easily divisible and fungible into money (e.g., collective aspects of working conditions and treatment).

Inequality of bargaining power.   Employers in laissez-faire labor markets both individually and as a group typically have a power advantage over individual workers in both external wage bargaining and internal firm governance due to their legal authority over work (the "master-servant relationship"), control of the supply of jobs, the perishability of labor services (inability to inventory), workers' limited hold-out ability (from limited financial reserves, significant fixed costs of family subsistence), costly job search and restricted job opportunities, and tilted legal rules and resource endowments (Commons and Andrews 1916; Kaufman 2010c). These conditions create a "tipped playing field" both "within the market" and "before the market" that favors firms' interests in exchange and governance relationships, and allows employers to capture a disproportionate and possibly unjust/unreasonable share of economic surplus, workplace control, and life satisfaction. As noted later, the breadth and depth of these problems diminish as the economy gets closer to full employment.

Sovereignty.   Economics is always "political economy" because the institutions and their derivative rules which guide and structure economic activity are in part determined through a political process in which people individually and collectively seek to capture and use the power of sovereignty to shape the institutions and rules to promote their interests (Commons 1950).

Reasonable value.   Economic agents individually and collectively have a notion of what is fair and reasonable; whenever an outcome/process falls outside the bound of reasonableness they undertake action to alter the institutional matrix of rules and rights (Adams, 1897; Commons, 1934; Mercuro and Medema, 1997; McIntyre and Ramstad, 2002).

Labor demand curves and employment effects.   Labor demand curves are relatively inelastic and, indeed, in the short run and for a modest increase in the cost of labor the employment effect may be zero or even slightly positive (Card and Krueger 1995; Kaufman 2010c). IE/IR does not deny the law of demand and has always recognized that price and quantity demanded are – at a broad level – inversely related (see Webb 1912). Rather, IE/IR qualifies the law of demand along four dimensions. First, since labor is embodied in human beings, a rise in the wage may lead to increased employee work effort and cooperative behavior, thus mitigating the cost increase. Second, because labor markets are non-competitive, microeconomic theory demonstrates that firms do not have a well-defined labor demand curve (just as in a monopoly product market a firm does not have a well-defined supply curve), thus introducing some indeterminacy into the law of demand. Third, even if a higher wage *ceteris paribus* leads to a reduction in jobs, this negative effect is often offset by other adjustments in the firm, such as improved management, more attention to product quality, and skills upgrading. Fourth, a decrease in jobs, say due to a higher union wage, may actually promote efficiency in the economy to the extent employers' private labor costs are below social labor costs due to imperfections such as externalities and public goods (Kaufman 2010c). Over the longer run, however, and particularly for a relatively large labor cost increase, capital-labor substitution and other adjustments will lead to an eventual decrease in employment – a negative outcome that then has to be weighed against other potentially positive outcomes before a normative welfare judgment is rendered.

Say's Law and under-consumption.   For all the reasons cited, flexible wages cannot and do not act as an effective equilibrating mechanism except perhaps in the very long run. Contrary to the macroeconomic principle known as Say's Law, labor markets often remain out of equilibrium (in the sense of a demand/supply imbalance) for months and years, and restoration of equilibrium comes about as much from labor quantity and quality adjustment (e.g., demand/supply curve shifts) as from wage adjustment. Wage adjustments are slow, not because of unions or minimum wage laws – the usual parties blamed in NE – but because firms know that cutting wages depresses worker morale and productivity (Bewley 1999; Fehr and Falk 1999). At a macro level, even with completely flexible wages the aggregate labor market is not self-correcting, since wage cuts reduce household income and aggregate demand and, hence, cause production and employment to depart even further from full-employment equilibrium (Keynes 1936; Levendis 2007). Likewise, a free market economy is prone to under-consumption in the medium-to-long run because the bulk of the fruits of productivity growth are distributed to a relatively small group in the top part of the income distribution who have more inelastic labor supply curves (due to scarcity of unique talents, skills, positions) and thus reap a proportionately large part of real wage gains from economic growth (e.g., CEOs).

VII. ANALYTICAL FRAMEWORK: AN IE/IR MODEL OF LABOR MARKETS

This section puts these general principles into an analytical framework, shown in Figure 3.2. This model of labor markets has five parts. I describe them in order here, in the next section set them in motion to explain labor/employment outcomes, and then in the final section consider the model's implications for labor law both past and present.

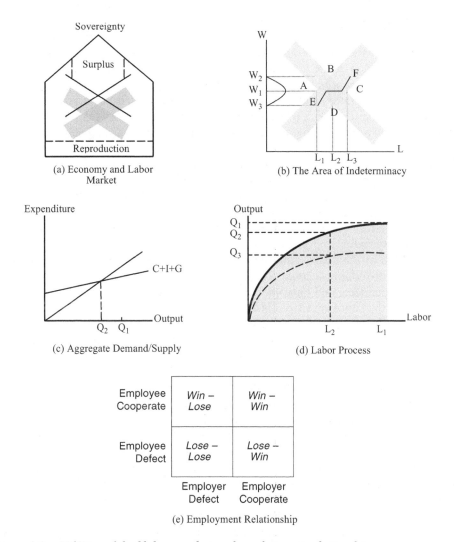

Figure 3.2   IE/IR model of labor market and employment relationship

The baseline economy represented by this model is free market capitalism without labor law, trade unions, social safety net programs, or macroeconomic guidance – in other words, something close to the American labor market in the early 1900s when FL&EM took shape (Fishback 1998; Kaufman 2008). Applications to today's economy are then sketched.

First panel (a). It has numerous distinguishing features. The area of the pentagon shape represents the size of GDP, usually represented in NE by a pie diagram. Part of the annual GDP has to go toward reproduction of the system – that is, a minimum necessary amount to replenish capital, maintain the fertility of the land, and feed and clothe the workforce. Sometimes the reproduction level for labor is called the "social minimum" or "social wage." The remainder of the GDP is available as a surplus or "discretionary income" that can be distributed to alternative uses and people; for example, it may be distributed as wages or profit or used for consumption, capital accumulation, or defense. The area under the horizontal dashed line represents the reproduction part of GDP, the part above it is the economic surplus (Davis 1992). The process of economic growth expands the pentagon shape and the size of the surplus; it contracts during recessions and depressions. The reproduction amount of GDP also grows over time, partly to cover greater capital depreciation and also because labor's social minimum is in part culturally and historically conditioned. For example, the social minimum in real terms is greater in 2000 than 1900 because of higher needs and expectations regarding education, health care, and housing.

The pentagon shape also represents the institutional infrastructure that coordinates and regulates the economy; it is the human-created command and control function. Institutional economists call it the *governance system* (Commons 1950; Williamson 1985). The pentagon shape captures five important IE/IR ideas.

The first is that all economic activity is embedded in an institutional infrastructure of laws, property rights, and social relations that collectively set the rules of the game, the endowments of the actors, and the objectives they pursue (Mercuro and Medema 1997; Deakin and Wilkinson 2005). These factors determine whether markets exist, their structure and operation, and outcomes of demand and supply. This idea is illustrated in panel (a) where the pentagon represents the "institutional space" (or "regulatory space") that surrounds and embeds the labor market and demand/supply within a "web of rules" (Kerr and Siegel 1955; Dunlop 1958). The institutional infrastructure and web of rules are taken as a "given" in NE microeconomics and, for most purposes, omitted from consideration (e.g., it is an invisible, passive, and status quo condition in Figure 3.1).

The second idea is that the institutional order is politically determined through some social choice process (e.g., dictatorship, monarchy, democracy) and contending factions and classes endeavor to use the political power of sovereignty to shape the rules of the game to promote their interests (Samuels and Schmid 1981). Here is the political economy dimension of IE/IR, illustrated in two ways in panel (a). The first is denoted by the word Sovereignty at the apex of the governance structure, indicating that the web of rules inside the pentagon is politically determined by a social group in control of the sovereign power of the nation state. In addition, two dashed lines are drawn in panel (a) extending from the governance structure (the "roof" over the labor market) to the top set of demand/supply curves, indicating the control that the visible hand of government exercises over the location and movement of both curves.

A frequent argument in SL&EM is that the common law evolves to promote efficiency and groups wanting to displace the common law with legislated labor law are often engaged in non-productive rent-seeking. This is a common charge leveled against the political activity of labor unions, for example (Epstein 1983). IE/IR, however, argues that the common law refracts the constellation of political power in society and evolves through political contestation between insiders and outsiders (Mercuro and Medema 1997). It is important to ask, therefore: whose interests are being served by wealth maximization and is society satisfied with the resulting distribution of income and wealth? These questions are not answered by neutral economic law but by the governance structure that determines endowments, the web of rules, and thus whether demand and supply curves are located high or low in the pentagon structure (a high- or low-wage outcome). The nature and reasonableness of economic outcomes, therefore, hinges critically on the distribution of power in society and whether its political and social institutions are open and egalitarian or segmented and oligarchic. If the latter, then what may look to NE as rent-seeking looks to IE/IR as a social reform movement led by progressive groups such as trade unions on behalf of disadvantaged outsiders demanding equal rights – be they workers' rights for protection from unfair dismissal, women's rights for equal pay, African-Americans' rights for a discrimination-free workplace, or gay-lesbian rights for employment regardless of sexual preference.

The third idea is that, as a command and control system, the institutional infrastructure inherently creates asymmetric power and authority relations: a relatively small group at the top of the pentagon are power-holders and order-givers and a much larger group toward the bottom have little power and follow orders. Since competition in labor markets is attenuated, they cannot provide a complete check and balance to the exercise of power and authority and, accordingly, society must ensure that the governance structure meets reasonable standards for due process, voice and representation. In IE/IR this was historically expressed as a demand for *industrial democracy* (Webb and Webb 1897; Derber 1970).

The fourth idea is that the economy is not a natural law-like mechanism where some unseen gravity-like invisible hand automatically and without friction coordinates economic activity to an a-historical equilibrium; rather, it is an organic human-made structure that evolves over time along with the institutional infrastructure, and that depends on not only impersonal market forces for coordination but also the visible hand of administration, governance, management and planning (Commons 1934; Galbraith 1967; Chandler 1977; Rutherford 2011).

The fifth is that the pentagon-shaped governance system applies not only at the macro level of the economy but also at the micro level of the firm. That is, the NE firm exists as a technological production function run by an invisible entrepreneur who changes the mix of factor inputs in response to shifting market prices. In some branches of the NIE, firms are a locus of efficient contracts that get adjusted in a similar manner to changing market and shadow prices (Furubotn and Richter 2005). In IE/IR and other branches of NIE, on the other hand, the firm is a politically constructed entity with a property rights regime that is coordinated through a hierarchical "visible hand" process of administration, management, planning and strategic choice by a chief executive officer, descending order of vice-presidents and directors, and various line and staff managers (e.g., human resource managers). The pentagon, invisible in the NE theory of the firm, creates an internal labor market (ILM), where human resources management (HRM) acts as a "ministry of labor" and through central planning sets pay rates and assigns jobs (Doeringer and Piore 1971; Rubery and Grimshaw 1998). This process is broadly constrained by competitive forces in the ELM, but not deterministically so.

Panel (a) shows two sets of demand-supply curves, a set of pencil-thin lines and a set of broad bands. The former represent demand/supply in the competitive model (as earlier depicted in Figure 3.1) and the latter represent demand/supply in the IE/IR model. A detailed explanation is provided shortly. Panel (b) takes the demand/supply bands from panel (a) and adds two further features. The first is that the band-like nature of the demand and supply functions creates an area of indeterminacy in wages and other terms and conditions of employment, illustrated in the figure by the bell-shaped curve. The idea is that organizational and institutional frictions partially obstruct competitive forces and give individual firms some discretion regarding the wages and conditions they provide (Lester 1952; Dunlop 1957). The average wage in the market is W_1; it is bounded, however, by a dispersion ranging from W_2 at the highest-wage firm to W_3 at the lowest-wage firm. The size of the area of indeterminacy may narrow somewhat in the long run but it is quite persistent.

Panel (b) also depicts the labor supply curve facing the typical individual firm in this market. In the competitive model the firm has a perfectly elastic (horizontal) labor supply curve (not illustrated in Figures 3.1 or 3.2); the firm pays whatever is the market wage. IE/IR argues, however, that the firm's labor supply curve typically resembles the kinked line EF. Assume this firm is paying the average market wage W_1 and has hired L_2 workers. The kinked supply function indicates three things: first, the firm can pay inframarginal workers a wage lower than W_1 (the downward-sloping portion) without losing many of these employees. Hence, the firm has some monopsony power (Manning 2003; Erickson and Mitchell 2008). Second, the firm can modestly expand its workforce with new hires of roughly the same effective labor at the prevailing rate of average hourly earnings. This is depicted by the horizontal segment of the supply line, the length of which is partly determined by the amount of involuntary unemployment in the local labor market. Past a certain point, however, additional workforce expansion necessitates either paying a higher money wage or hiring new workers with a lower level of effective labor (e.g., fewer skills or less desirable work habits), either of which is equivalent in production cost terms. In this range the firm's labor supply function is upward sloping, as in monopsony.

Panel (c) of Figure 3.2 introduces the macroeconomic dimension of the employment relationship. NE has no need to feature such a model in Figure 3.1 because it assumes that flexible prices and the invisible hand automatically steer labor markets and the aggregate economy to an equilibrium position of full employment via Say's Law. IE/IR, however, claims that an economy has no such automatic tendency toward full employment and, indeed, the baseline condition is persistent excess supply of labor (Atkinson and Oleson 1998). A convenient representation of the IE/IR position is the "Keynesian cross" model. Aggregate demand determines the level of output and employment, given by the intersection of the C+I+G schedule (consumption + investment + government spending) and the aggregate supply line (45 degree line). The full-employment level of GDP is Q_1 but in most years the economy suffers from insufficient aggregate demand and hence an actual output of only Q_2 with consequent overhang of unemployment in the labor market. Market forces do not eliminate the excess labor supply, partly because wages have a large degree of rigidity and partly because a fall in wages reduces purchasing power and therefore further reduces aggregate demand and employment (the C+I+G line shifts downward).

Panel (d) captures the IE/IR distinction between labor time and labor power. Pictured there are two short-run production functions; they show how output increases with additional labor input (holding capital constant). In NE the economy has one unique output curve, such as the dashed line. The reason is that NE treats labor as a homogeneous commodity that generates a well-defined marginal product in a technologically determined production process. Thus, for a given labor input level L_2 output is a single-valued number, such as Q_3. At full employment the maximum labor input is L_1 and the NE production function predicts a single-valued output of Q_1 (Q_1 corresponding, in turn, to Q_1 in panel (c)).

In IE/IR, on the other hand, what the employer buys is L_2 amount of labor time, but the amount of output produced is a function of the amount of labor power obtained. The result is that, in panel (d), a purchased amount of labor time L_2 can yield a wide range of different labor powers, depending on the outcome of the wage/effort bargain and the extraction effectiveness of the employer's HRM program. The solid line production function shows that the maximum attainable labor power is Q_2; the shaded area under this line shows all the other feasible levels of labor power. The employer who buys L_2 units of labor time may get zero labor power (a point on the horizontal axis) if, for example, the workers stage a spontaneous walkout or are all asleep in their trucks; alternatively, if workers are induced to go "all out" then output is Q_2.

Panel (e) illustrates a pay-off matrix of employment relations outcomes. It represents the Prisoner's Dilemma nature of the ER. Employers and employees, respectively, can either choose to cooperate with each other or defect from the relationship and pursue narrow self-interest. This choice set creates the pay-off matrix shown in the figure where the employment relationship can take one of four possible outcomes for the employer and employees: lose/lose, win/lose, lose/win, and win/win.

VIII.   IE/IR MODEL IN ACTION: HOW LABOR MARKETS *REALLY* WORK

The next step is to put Figure 3.2 into action to analyze how labor markets and employment relationships work and the nature of the outcomes they generate. The end product is a portrait of the employment world considerably different than one gets from "assume a competitive labor market," with correspondingly different implications for labor law.

An employment relationship presumes as a matter of definition that firms have at least two people, a boss and a worker. Coase (1937) and the NIE have explained that this agglomeration into a firm arises only if transaction costs are positive; the implication, therefore, is that in a situation of zero transaction costs all the firms disagglomerate to single-person proprietorships and independent contractors. They have not, however, carried this insight to its logical conclusion (Kaufman 2010b).

With zero transaction costs the entire GDP in panel (a) is produced by single-person firms. In this case, however, the economy has no need for a labor market or employment relationship since firms get labor services from other single-person firms in product markets. That is, rather than go to a labor market and hire Joe Smith to be an employee truck driver, the firm hires Joe Smith Trucking, Inc. to provide the service. (Joe can get the funds to buy the truck since capital markets are also perfectly competitive.) An implication of Coasean logic, therefore, is that the demand/supply diagram in panel (a) actually represents buying and selling of labor services in product markets, not labor markets. In other words, to say "assume a competitive labor market" – which is the foundational premise of NE and SL&EM that drives their analysis of labor law – is theoretically incoherent. For if the presumed conditions of zero transaction costs, frictionless trade, and complete contracts were to exist, all performance requirements could be written into a complete sales contract and enforced at zero cost, and there would be no economic rationale for hiring employees (Dow 1997).

Taking the logic in reverse, multi-person firms, labor markets, and an employment relationship only exist with positive transaction costs and market frictions (e.g., bounded rationality, uncertainty, imperfect information). The implication is that labor markets are *always and everywhere imperfectly competitive*. If labor markets are imperfectly competitive, however, the first welfare theorem is no longer applicable and one cannot presume that market outcomes are efficient. Further, by the theory of the second best (Lipsey and Lancaster 1956), one cannot presume that selective re-engineering of labor markets to make them more competitive will actually improve efficiency; it may worsen it. The production of the nation's GDP in panel (a), therefore, takes place in a mixed economy with a combination of markets and firms and price and planning coordination. Competitive forces are present but necessarily attenuated and therefore offer only partial protection to employees.

Critics of the IE/IR position may object at this point that, when more deeply examined, this alleged "labor problem" (e.g., an area of indeterminacy in wages with attenuated competition) is not a problem in any substantive sense and that employees have no need of labor law protection. They are likely to invoke one or a combination of two arguments (Mercuro and Medema 1997; Dow 1997). The first is that alleged anomalies in labor markets, such as dispersed wage rates and costs of job mobility, are themselves rational economizing outcomes in the face of various costs and constraints not included in the simple competitive model (e.g., imperfect information); the second is that these observed labor market outcomes can be assumed on prima facie grounds to approximate efficient outcomes since, if they are not, economic agents have incentives to modify arrangements in order to capture additional gains from trade. As indicated earlier, IE/IR does not completely discount these arguments, but suggests that they carry the danger of turning into a tautology and an apologia for the status quo. That is, if nearly any significant labor market anomaly can be explained as an economizing outcome (and it is worth noting that Becker (1976) claims the extended NE model can explain *all* human behavior in market and non-market contexts), then NE/NIE theory may become a vehicle for rationalizing whatever is observed. Opinions differ on this matter; the position of IE/IR, however, is that labor markets and employment relationships are imperfect in a substantively important sense, and that these imperfections open up space in economic relations for labor law and labor institutions to do good as well as harm.

The merits of the IE/IR case for labor law are strengthened by giving further consideration to the ramifications of positive transaction cost in labor markets. As explained above, the pencil-thin demand and supply lines in panel (a) have no logical existence; hence, the labor market cannot determine an equilibrium wage and set of terms and conditions. Instead, the lines are replaced in panels (a) and (b) by demand and supply *bands*. On the demand side, this change is a logical outcome of the indeterminate nature of the wage/effort bargain in the labor process in panel (d). That is, the amount of labor time purchased is determinate, but the amount of labor power and the size of the marginal product is uncertain and takes a range of possible values (Kaufman 2010a). Imperfect information and job search costs make the labor supply curve a band.

The indeterminate nature of the labor demand curve means that the law of demand does not locally hold; for example, a modest rise in the minimum wage may not cause a decline in employment (Doucouliagos and Stanley 2009). Likewise, employers have some discretion regarding the wage and conditions they provide, and the threat of exit by workers is only partially effective in determining employers' HRM and employee relations practices. These implications are reinforced when panel (b) is considered.

The rising portion of firms' labor supply curve gives them some degree of monopsony power over inframarginal employees (because of mobility costs for workers if they quit). Monopsony power, in turn, means that firms gain the upper hand in wage bargaining and can practice some degree of labor exploitation (underpayment of workers). In the IE/IR theory of labor markets, nearly all firms have some degree of potential monopsony power. Although writers such as Posner (2009) in the First L&EM routinely dismiss the practical importance of monopsony, organizers of a recent symposium on the subject conclude, "the remarkable feature of all the studies here is the high 'monopsony power' implied by the firm-level estimates of labor supply . . . The articles provide remarkable evidence that labor markets are *far* from competitive (Ashenfelter, Farber, and Ransom 2010: 208–9, emphasis added). Some firms, however, do not exercise this power because they know it will harm employee morale and result in lower productivity (in panel (d)), and because it will undermine a win-win employment relationship (in panel (e)) (Bronfenbrenner 1956); others selectively exercise it through, for example, salary compression for long-service but immobile employees. Other employers, including those following a low-road HRM strategy or for which production is not much affected by positive employee feelings – use their monopsony power to practice labor exploitation in a number of ways ranging from low wages to work intensification to abuse of civil liberties and human rights (Shulman 2003).

The ubiquity of monopsony, and the fact that labor markets are always and everywhere imperfect, also calls into doubt the logical coherence of the neoclassical labor demand curve. As earlier noted, standard price theory shows that a firm in an imperfectly competitive labor market does not have a well-defined labor demand curve (Fleischer and Kniesner 1980). Thus, the demand/supply diagram *and* the standard labor demand curve diagram (e.g., Posner 2007, Figure 1.1) – the two most important theoretical constructs in the Second L&EM's analysis of labor law – are *both* logically defective and need to be replaced by an alternative model. The IE/IR solution is depicted in panels (a) and (b); that is, to replace the labor demand curve *line* with a labor demand curve *band*. The band idea illustrates the absence of a one-to-one correspondence between the wage rate and quantity demanded of labor (as with a conventional NE labor demand line), yet allows for an inverse relation for relatively large wage changes. Thus, a modest and phased-in increase in the minimum wage or union wage premium may have no negative employment effect – it may even be positive (Card and Krueger 1995) – while a large one-time increase is more likely to have a negative effect.

Not only do the demand and supply curves change from lines to bands, their location also changes. This is represented in panel (a) where both bands are shifted down relative to the NE lines. The labor demand curve is shifted down (to the left) because in the macroeconomy pictured in panel (c) the economy typically suffers from insufficient aggregate demand; less demand for economy's products means a smaller derived demand for its labor. Likewise, the labor supply curve is shifted down (to the right) because the employer class (and associated property/power elites) use their dominant political influence to create an institutional infrastructure that weakens workers' bargaining position, forcing them to offer their labor time at a lower wage. For example, in a laissez-faire labor market dominated by employer interests (perhaps facilitated by a limited franchise and corruption in the legislative process), the state provides no unemployment insurance. This reduces workers' hold-out ability and forces them to lower their reservation wage to quickly get work, thus shifting the labor supply curve rightward (Fehr and Falk 2006). Similarly, employers use their power to secure employment law that creates an unequal relationship of "master and servant" and gives them authority to terminate workers at-will (Deakin and Wilkinson 2005). The macroeconomic overhang of unemployed workers also forces down workers' reservations wages and induces them to provide more effort (Bowles and Boyer 1988).

Yet another change in the demand/supply model regards the shape of the labor supply curve near the reproduction level of wages. NE theory draws the labor supply curve as forward-sloped throughout, implying that, as wages fall, workers substitute from market work to other now-cheaper activities, such as leisure, attending school, and raising children. The theory does not explain, however, where workers get the income for food, shelter and family care if they do not have a paycheck. This consideration becomes paramount as wages approach the reproduction (social minimum) level; at that point, and without a modern welfare state and social safety net programs, the average worker is in a "work or starve" situation and has no choice but to get work at any price. Hence, the labor supply curve at low wages is kinked and develops a negative-sloped (forward-falling) segment with considerable elasticity (not depicted in Figure 3.2 to avoid cluttering the diagrams): as the wage goes below the subsistence level (the dashed line in panel (a)), workers and family members increase labor supply in order to collectively bring home a survival income level (Sharif 2000; Dessing 2002). It is probable that in this region the labor supply curve becomes more elastic than the labor demand curve (target income behavior leads to a unit elastic labor supply curve); therefore, as wages are bid down by cut-throat competition among desperate workers, the demand and supply imbalance only worsens and the market becomes dynamically unstable – as in a depression situation. At the same time, the nation's human resources start to deteriorate as labor income no longer fully covers minimum social cost (Prasch 2005).

NE and the Second L&EM portray the labor market and employment relationship as a level playing field where demand and supply set efficient and fair wages and workers cannot be exploited because they can quit one job for another. IE/IR claims, however, that they get to this conclusion only by unduly ignoring the very frictions and governance structures that lead to the existence of labor markets. The reality, according to IE/IR, is that the governance structure – absent countervailing social reengineering – is tilted in favor of employers since workers do not enter the market with the same rights and endowments. Employers are frequently corporations, or aggregations of capital, with ownership of large, valuable and long-lived assets and a workforce of perhaps hundreds or thousands. Workers, on the other hand, bargain as individuals; they cannot diversify their risks and dependency beyond one job (or, perhaps, two), typically have few fall-back assets, and have only one commodity to sell. Hence, workers are under considerable pressure to find a buyer because each day's labor has zero value if not sold and, in addition, they face a minimum daily income requirement for family survival. In most years workers' bargaining power is further undercut because the labor market has an excess of unemployed jobseekers (Webb and Webb 1897; Craypo 1997; Kaufman 2003a, 2007a).

The result in an early capitalist laissez-faire labor market, as pictured in panel (a) of Figure 3.2, is that workers as a class – particularly the less skilled/educated and labor force minorities – are put in a disadvantaged and dependent position in wage determination. Not surprisingly, the entire structure of wages, work conditions, and treatment of workers is lower e.g. given by the demand/supply bands than the NE theory is wont to portray. This situation also leaves little room for the compensating wage differentials that are supposed to penalize employers for – and protect employees from – unsafe conditions, work intensification, and unfair treatment. Further aggravating things is that, as earlier noted, firms own capital, but rent labor and accordingly give more attention to reducing capital waste than labor waste (Kaufman 2010b). The choice for many workers, given mobility constraints, boils down to "work at a low wage dissatisfying job at Company A or quit and get the same kind of job at Company B" (Appelbaum, Bernhardt, and Murnane 2003).

Indeed, the imbalance between wages and profit, and lifestyles of employers and workers, may be so starkly different that one cannot help but conclude the latter are *exploited*. In the NE "level playing field" world, the economic surplus is typically portrayed as relatively evenly divided between profit income and wage income, making market outcomes look fair and square (i.e., the demand and supply lines are drawn so they intersect somewhere in the middle of the diagram, such as Figure 3.1). In the IE/IR world of structural inequality, however, a disproportionate share of the economy's surplus – absent redistributive taxes and transfers – goes to a relatively small group of people in the upper strata of the income and wealth distribution (in 2010 the top 1 percent of households owned 42 percent of financial wealth and received 21 percent of national income (Domhoff 2012)).

Definitions of what constitutes exploitation differ (see Taylor 1977; Roemer 1982; Hahnel 2006). At a general level, IE/IR contends, and most people would agree, that some degree of income inequality between capital and labor is acceptable and legitimate (reflecting a differential reward to entrepreneurship, risk-taking, saving, etc.); as inequality increases, however, at some point the distribution of income crosses over into "unfair," or even exploitative. Suppose, for example, that the demand and supply curves intersect in panel (a) on the dashed line so that labor gets only a reproduction level of income and capital gets the entire surplus. Since this is a "competitive outcome," NE declares it free of exploitation. IE/IR, however, considers this a case of exploitation since the bulk of workers get only enough of their product to survive and return each day to the nation's factories, mills and stores to create and pass on to the upper class of property owners, employers and affluent consumers the remainder of the GDP.

A central purpose of FL&EM is to change endowments and rules of the game so that the governance structure is more egalitarian, accessible, and democratic, and yields more balanced and reasonable terms and conditions of employment in the labor market and distribution of income in society. In terms of panel (a), the object is to re-engineer and rebalance the governance structure so the demand and supply bands shift upward to the position of the pencil-thin lines and yield a wage and conditions of employment that would have existed if the original playing field had not been so tipped. This illustrates Adams' (1887) idea of "raising the plane of competitive action" and the institutional contention, illustrated in the earlier quote by Craypo (1997), that society and not economic law decides the labor outcomes yielded in labor markets.

Raising the plane of competition can be achieved through a variety of means, many of which also correct market failures. Minimum wages and collective bargaining, for example, set a wage floor in the labor market closer to the pencil-thin DS lines (and offset monopsony power); unemployment insurance and old-age pensions allow workers to have a higher reservation wage (and help cover labor's social overhead costs), and government training and manpower development programs give workers more valuable skills and greater bargaining power (and correct for the free market's undersupply of training due to companies' free-riding behavior). Since all such labor programs redistribute power and income from employers and the affluent (who as consumers with the largest per capita expenditures benefit proportionately most from low-priced goods), they inevitably arouse considerable political opposition from these groups.

Part of the IE/IR program for balanced capitalism and employment relationships, therefore, is to ensure that the parties with the most money (e.g., corporations, the affluent) are not allowed to buy the governance system (including labor laws) that promotes their private interests. Tellingly, this form of upper class rent-seeking gets little attention in the SL&EM while rent-seeking by unions (agents of the working class) gets much. Likewise, it is important that suffrage rights in the polity are widespread and equally protected for all groups. The presumption is that elected officials are more likely to create a balanced governance system, including employment laws and regulations and protection of collective bargaining rights, when they face a broader, more representative, and equally financed constituent base. Labor law and a just society, therefore, are undermined by court decisions, such as *Citizens United v. Federal Election Commission* (2010), that give corporations and the wealthy far more ability to influence government (to "buy votes") than workers.

This political economy aspect of labor law, particularly the insight regarding how rules influence the position of the labor demand/supply curves, is mostly neglected and discounted in the Second L&EM. Instead, this group emphasizes that labor laws and social welfare programs are a form of collectivist wealth redistribution, confiscation of private property, and unwise interference with *given* demand/supply curves in competitive markets. Similarly, SL&EM regards labor law as (mostly) an anti-competitive form of protectionism. FL&EM sees the same "protectionism" as a social virtue that guards workers against substandard and unfair terms and conditions of employment made possible by externalities, monopsony, and other market imperfections, a tipped institutional playing field, and an excess supply of jobseekers. The idea, therefore, that labor unions exercise monopoly power and cartelize labor markets is not in dispute; what *is* in dispute is the one-sided negative account given by SL&EM proponents which mostly omits these contingencies. The First L&EM also regards a certain degree of wealth equalization as a useful way to avoid a Latin American type of society with political rule by a rich oligarchy, great extremes in social outcomes, and a class-conscious and politically radicalized segment of the labor force.

Now transition attention to panel (e). Pictured are four alternative employment relation outcomes: win-win; win-lose; lose-win; and lose-lose. NE and SL&EM assume the invisible hand guides employers and employees to adopt (approximately) efficient contracts where the joint surplus is maximized. Further, in a competitive market economy factor inputs receive a return proportional to their marginal value contribution to production; in the case of labor this means the wage rate paid workers is equal to the part of the output they help produce (the marginal product). Definitions of fairness differ and economists are reluctant to make judgments on this matter; nonetheless, many believe competitive outcomes pass the ethical test because labor receives its share of the fruits of production (called by Budd (2004) "marginal productivity justice") and suffers no exploitation at the hands of employers. Since the size of the economic pie is as large as possible and distributed in what seems like an ethically satisfactory manner, one may judge that employers and employees are in the cell of panel (e) marked win-win. Here is another virtue of a competitive private-ordered economy and, presumably, another reason why trade unions and protective labor law are not needed in most situations.

From an IE/IR perspective these conclusions are very inaccurate because they neglect the fundamentally human nature of labor. If labor was an inanimate commodity, it would have no consciousness of fairness and justice and, hence, no objection to alternative and perhaps quite unequal allocations. Labor is a unique factor input, however, because it is embodied in human beings (Edwards 2003; Kaufman 2010a). Accordingly, the structural inequality built into capitalism, and the resulting asymmetric outcomes, inevitably lead workers to regard the state-of-nature situation as unfair and unjust. This structural inequality is manifest at the market level in terms of the distributive process just reviewed. It is also manifest inside the workplace where employers and their hired managers (the "suits") have high salaries, secure jobs, interesting work, social status, and power to issue and enforce orders, while the rank and file of employees (with blue and pink collars) experience the opposite on all these dimensions.

A common finding in laboratory experiments is that, in an "ultimatum game," the party who is put into a highly unequal take-it-or-leave-it position often refuses to accept the minimalist pay-off because it violates the standard of fairness (Miller 1991; Falk, Fehr and Fischbacher 2003). IE/IR predicts the same for the employment relationship. That is, because of the large asymmetry in both market-level and workplace outcomes workers come to view the deeper reality of the employment relationship not as win-win but as win-lose. So viewed, workers naturally pull back on cooperation, commitment, and hard work; in panel (c), therefore, the same labor input of L_1 yields less labor power. Employers, in turn, experience lower productivity and profit as labor power falls and come to see workers as uncooperative and lazy; they react, therefore, with a harsher attitude, tighter regime of workplace controls, and more punitive sanctions. This process creates a polarized dynamic in which the two sides regard each other as adversaries embedded in a zero-sum game (Edwards 2003).

From an IE/IR perspective, the nature of the capitalist employment relationship makes the baseline outcome in panel (e) the win-lose or even lose-lose option. In all companies the employment relationship (ER) features elements of both cooperation and conflict, and to various degrees this translates into a win-lose (or lose-win) pay-off; some companies, however, are able through forward-looking management, progressive HRM, and an accommodative economic environment to restructure the ER into a win-win. The modern-day exemplar is variously known as the mutual gains enterprise, high involvement workplace, and high performance work system (HPWS) (Kochan and Osterman 1994; Appelbaum, Berg, Kalleberg, and Bailey 2000). Empirical research finds that these transformed work systems have distinctly higher productivity and financial performance (Combs, Liu, Hall and Ketchen 2006), suggesting they outperform the win-lose or zero-sum type of ER. Yet research also finds that they represent a distinct minority of all workplaces (Blasi and Kruse 2006). This seems to suggest that, for some reason in the labor markets of real life, competition is not moving employers to capture available gains from trade by creating HPWS systems.

The IE/IR model points to a particular reason (among others) why HPWS firms are relatively rare. That is, their performance edge hinges on achieving a win-win ER, but this outcome is unstable and difficult to maintain. The explanation goes back to panel (c), where shifts in the aggregate demand curve create boom and bust cycles. A mutual gain outcome requires that both capital and labor reap the benefits of cooperation, workers have secure jobs in return for loyalty and hard work, and employers live up to their promises – particularly when the going gets tough (Thompson 2003). However, employers are often forced (or say they are forced) by pressures of cost-cutting and short-term survival to renege on their commitments and institute actions, such as large lay-offs, wage and benefit cuts, and harsher discipline. If these actions appear to workers to one-sidedly advance the interests of profit-making and shareholders over the interests of employees, the "we are partners" psychological contract quickly deteriorates (Edwards 2009). Workers may respond with grudging performance or even strikes, sabotage, union organizing, and street protests.

IE/IR depicts involuntary unemployment as a crucial feature and weakness of capitalism. It is a crucial feature because it gives employers a cheap but effective device to motivate and discipline labor (Edwards 1979; Bowles and Boyer 1988). A logically contradictory part of the NE model is the firm's perfectly elastic labor supply curve (not shown). The curve indicates that workers can at no cost quit one employer and immediately find another job at the same wage with a different company; the contradiction is that the workers have no incentive to provide more than a minimum of labor power and, hence, competitive equilibrium is not efficient. The problem is that this part of the NE model ignores the wage-effort bargain in panel (d). One device to extract labor power is for the firm as part of its HRM strategy to pay a higher than market wage, as theorized in mainstream efficiency wage models (Shapiro and Stiglitz 1984; Akerlof 1990). Doing so increases labor power; but if numerous firms do this it also raises the wage above the market-clearing level and creates a permanent reserve army of the unemployed. One may follow NE, cast this model in an optimization framework, and conclude that this kind of unemployment is not a "labor problem" because it creates the largest joint surplus (Boyer and Smith 2001); from an IE/IR perspective, however, it *is* a labor problem if the structure of capitalism requires perhaps several million people to go without jobs in order to motivate those who do have jobs to work hard and obey the rules.

A principle of IE/IR, as pointed out earlier, is that labor markets are divided into segments with partially attenuated mobility across them (Kerr 1977). A major purpose of anti-discrimination legislation has been to reduce these barriers and the structural inequality they give rise to. The most popular NE theory of discrimination claims, for example, that free market forces will automatically erode discriminatory employment practices arising from employers' bigotry or prejudice (Becker 1957). This theory has difficulty, however, explaining why, in the free market and mostly non-union era before the New Deal, stark and pervasive discrimination existed in wages, occupations, promotion and training (Leonard 2003). To explain (or rationalize) this anomaly, the Second L&EM is prone to point the finger of blame at government (e.g., segregation laws) for interfering with competitive forces (Epstein 1992). Certainly government was partially responsible but, from an IE/IR perspective, the blame more appropriately rests with the interest groups in the polity who pressured legislators to enact the discriminatory laws. Also, historical evidence indicates that if government had not instituted "legalized" discrimination then the likely outcome would be not fair play for jobs in a now-free labor market but overt enforcement of discrimination at the workplace and community level through violence, intimidation, racist/sexist social norms, and institutional stratification in schools, neighborhoods, and companies (Brown and Philips 1986).

Equally difficult to explain purely on efficiency grounds is why professional schools in law, medicine and business into the 1970s so clearly discriminated in their admission policies on the basis of race, gender and religion (Epstein 1981). A popular NE theory attributes the small number of female doctors and lawyers in this era to the fact that they voluntarily decided to not go to professional schools so they could better accommodate work and family (Polachek 1981). As in all matters discussed in this chapter, this NE theory has insight and explanatory power; the problem, however, is that it also neglects that part of the "voluntary choice" made by these women is based on opportunity costs, relative market prices, and preferences that are distorted by the tipped, discriminatory, and patriarchal nature of the governance structure within which demand/supply are embedded (Albelda 1997; Gottfried 2009).

The labor market segmentation arising from discrimination is amplified by other forms of segmentation in the economy's institutional infrastructure. The efficiency wage idea discussed above, for example, explains the existence of a dual labor market economy with high-wage firms and well-developed ILMs in a primary labor market and low-wage firms with highly externalized and insecure jobs in a secondary labor market (Bulow and Summers 1986). The factor that differentiates the two is the technology of production and the structure of the labor process. That is, if the technology entails jobs with considerable firm-specific skill, autonomy and effort discretion, then firms create ILMs and use high wages to elicit effort; if the jobs are unskilled, easily learned and can be tightly controlled, then the firms pay low wages and extract labor power through tight supervision, fast-paced assembly lines, and so on (Edwards 1979). Discrimination, therefore, leads to differential access to the good jobs in the labor market. Over time this gap further widens; that is, favored workers accumulate higher-level skills and move up job/career ladders in ILMs and primary firms, while disfavored workers stall out in dead-end occupations or jobs with limited advancement opportunities in secondary firms.

From an IE/IR perspective, the most serious market defect and cause of labor problems in capitalist economies is widespread unemployment (Commons 1934; Kaufman

1997, 2003a). NE typically omits this consideration since it starts evaluation of labor law with the assumption that labor markets are in equilibrium (where the DS curves cross) and the only unemployment, therefore, is frictional and short term in nature, related to job search and geographic mobility (both good for the economy). In the half-century before World War II, however, labor markets in all but a few years had millions of excess jobseekers (Lescohier 1919; Long 1958). The excess labor supply was not remedied by flexible wages nor was it caused by impediments such as minimum wage laws or unions (widespread only after the mid-1930s); rather, the economy suffered from a general situation of demand-deficient unemployment. In tandem with structural sources of inequality, pervasive excess supply of labor considerably worsened many of the labor problems of that era by undercutting workers' power to bargain for reasonable wages and conditions, short-circuiting the protective force of competition, and enabling employers to manage employees in an autocratic and oppressive manner.

IX.   LABOR LAW TODAY: THE IMPORTANCE OF HISTORICAL CONTEXT

Neoclassical economic principles are considered independent of time and place; that is, principles such as the law of demand and competitive determination of price by demand/supply are "universals" that predict economic behavior across centuries, countries and peoples. The implications for labor law, in turn, are also universalistic. For example, one can equally well predict that a government-induced higher price for labor reduces employment in 16th century France (via the restrictions of the guild system) and early 21st century America (via a rise in the legal minimum wage); similarly, opening up labor markets to more competition predictably increases wealth regardless of country because of the (alleged) truism that "all sides gain from trade."

IE/IR argues, on the other hand, that the strength, direction and applicability of (so-called) economic "laws" are inherently contingent and contextual. For example, in some situations (e.g., unskilled workers in competitive markets) a higher price of labor often lowers employment, but in others (e.g., knowledge workers in imperfect markets) it leads to higher (or no less) employment; likewise, in some situations more competition improves efficiency, but in others it harms efficiency. In this final section, the IE/IR analysis of labor law is extended to consider this type of contingency, albeit limited to the case of the United States and historical change in its economic institutions since the 1930s.

I start with the 1930s because this is the pivotal decade that opened the policy doors to the IE/IR-promoted expansion of labor and employment law; it is likewise the pivotal decade that economic/social conservatives are seeking to fundamentally reinterpret in order to justify rolling back the New Deal labor regulation program (e.g., privatizing social security, abolishing the National Labor Relations Act). Consideration of the pros and cons of labor and employment law today, therefore, cannot be understood by drawing a demand/supply curve diagram for the present year and considering these laws in isolation from the events and ideas that preceded them. In particular, consideration of the depression decade of the 1930s is crucial to balanced thinking about modern-day labor law because it brings into the picture the link between the macroeconomy and conditions in labor markets that the SL&EM omits with its "assume a competitive labor market" type of analysis.

Today's system of labor and employment in America was in many respects institutionally born in the depression decade of the 1930s during the New Deal recovery and reform program of the Roosevelt administration. A growing number of conservative and neoliberal scholars argue the government's expanded labor regulatory role initiated by the New Deal was a huge mistake at the time and has since compounded the damage to the economy by opening the door in later decades to an ever-expanding octopus of new labor laws and social welfare programs (Epstein 1983; Ohanian 2009). Since more competitive (free) labor markets are a universal good from an NE perspective, the prescription of scholars in the Second L&EM is, not unexpectedly, to rejuvenate the American economy by greatly paring back the present-day regime of labor regulation in favor of free markets and private ordering of employment outcomes (Galloway 2010).

Since the neoliberal critique has enjoyed considerable visibility and success, it is important in this kind of exposition of IE/IR principles to examine and appropriately rebut it (Kaufman 2012c). As indicated earlier, IE/IR scholars consider unemployment the most serious defect of capitalism and greatest cause of labor problems. From this perspective, the economist who probably made the greatest contribution in the 20th century to improved employment relations was Englishman J.M. Keynes. Like IE/IR economists, Keynes believed the "assume a competitive labor market" theory does not work in real life and, therefore, the invisible hand of competition needs to be stabilized, regulated and balanced by the visible hand of government. Not coincidentally, Keynes advanced these then-heretical ideas in the middle point of the Great Depression, most notably in his famous book *The General Theory of Employment, Interest and Money* (1936).

IE/IR and Keynesian macroeconomics have close intellectual ties, in part because Keynes wrote the *General Theory* with ideas from earlier works by Commons and other American institutional economists in mind (Whalen 2008; Kates 2010; Rutherford 2011). In other writings, Keynes also endorsed the New Deal labor program of the Roosevelt administration, including minimum wages, expanded collective bargaining and social insurance programs such as unemployment insurance and social security (Moggridge 1982, Vol. 21: 438). The central message of both IE/IR and Keynesian macroeconomics is that a laissez-faire economy is prone to serious boom and bust cycles, and that government needs to offset this instability by using both fiscal and monetary policies to keep aggregate demand at a steady full-employment level, and stabilizing and redistributive programs in the labor market (e.g., unemployment insurance, progressive income taxes) to maintain steady wage growth among working class and middle class households. According to Keynes (1936), these views were so outside the orthodox mainstream in economics that it put him amongst the "brave army of heretics" (p. 371).

Although Keynesian economics enjoyed considerable professional and popular acceptance through the 1960s, in the last three-to-four decades Keynesianism – along with intellectual fellow travelers IE/IR and traditional labor law – have come under sustained criticism, lost much support, and again have an aura of "bad economics" (Estlund 2006; Ohanian 2009). The attack on Keynsianism, institutionalism, and traditional labor law has roots at Chicago and, in particular, the highly revisionist reinterpretation of the Great Depression by Friedman, Stigler, and Lucas.

The standard post-World War II view of the Great Depression was the IE/Keynesian "unstable, unbalanced, and imperfect capitalism" thesis; the corollary policy conclusion is that unregulated product and (particularly) labor markets can be dysfunctional and need regulation, social welfare programs, and countervailing power for workers. The first influential attack on this thesis was by Friedman and Schwartz (1963); over the years a number of other economists have advanced this argument, including people such as Nobel laureate Edward Prescott (1999). They have collectively done what an earlier generation of economists would have thought impossible; that is, they have reversed the (apparent) lesson of the Great Depression with the claim that the length and severity of the debacle was *not* the fault of free market capitalism but was instead caused by labor law, unions, unwise government macroeconomic intervention, and government-supported market rigidities. Thus, from their point of view it is highly ironic for the IE/Keynesian side to use the Great Depression as justification for "more government" when it was precisely government and allies (unions, etc.) that started the downturn and then transformed it into a decade-long depression.

Regarding labor markets and labor law, for example, Chari, Kehoe and McGrattan (2003) claim, "These poor [labor] policies turn what otherwise would be modest downturns into prolonged depressions" (p. 3); in a similar vein Ohanian (2009) concludes "the key to understanding the Depression is understanding and quantifying this labor market distortion" (p. 2314). These economists arrive at these conclusions using "assume a competitive labor market" reasoning. That is, involuntary unemployment means the price of labor is too high and therefore the demand for workers is less than the supply; the evident solution to unemployment is to reduce wage rates (and other employment costs) until labor is cheap enough that employers are willing to hire all who want to work. The New Deal labor program, however, (allegedly) thwarted the labor market's self-correcting process by preventing wages from falling; in fact, it made the depression worse because minimum wages, social security, expanded collective bargaining and the other parts raised the price of labor and thus further reduced employment.

This argument has increasingly gained traction; IE/IR, however, claims it is quite inaccurate and misleading because these principles are in important ways contradicted or invalidated by the historical circumstances of that period. In evaluating the free market argument one has to appreciate that in the first half of the Great Depression both unions and labor law were a very small presence. The nation did not even have a federal child labor law when the depression started in 1929 (it came in 1938, along with a minimum wage); likewise, union density was about 10 percent and nearly all of the mass production part of the economy was essentially union-free. It is true that Franklin Roosevelt's 1933 National Industrial Recovery Act encouraged an expansion of unions and minimum wages; but this can have had nothing to do with the initial collapse of the economy into depression or the next four years of stagnancy. Indeed, money wage rates were relatively flexible and declined by over one-quarter between 1929 and 1933. Moreover, Roosevelt strongly resisted greater government deficit spending in his first term in office (until 1936).

So, given this context, how were free labor markets operating in the early 1930s? Were they promoting efficiency and fairness and helping the economy get back to full employment? It helps to start the IE/IR rebuttal with these two quotations from case studies of employment conditions during the 1930s. This type of case study evidence is an important way institutionalists try to confront theory with historical facts. The first comes from a study of auto workers (Peterson 1987: 133):

> Foremen met workers' complaints about worsening working conditions with the perennial request to look out the window at the line of job seekers and the standard refrain of, "if you cannot do the job, there is somebody in that line who can." Many plants combined speed-up with a shift from piecework to day rates, keeping wages low as production increased at a rate that one study estimated from two to three times its predepression rate. Some workers were even forced to work overtime for no pay in order to keep their jobs.

The second quotation comes from a study of San Francisco dockworkers (Nelson 1988: 106–07):

> In San Francisco, the Embarcadero was known as the "slave market," but to many who witnessed it the shape-up bespoke of an even lower form of existence . . . One longshoreman recalled that "for thirty-five days, rain or shine, I was out there, on the waterfront from five in the morning till all the crews were filled, but I never got a job." Of course, the shape-up system invited abuse, ranging from petty corruption to systematic extortion . . . where the men regularly kicked back 10 percent of their wages to the gang boss.

Here from an IE/IR perspective is the dark side of a free labor market system that the Second L&EM proponents tend to ignore or rationalize away. The IE/IR perspective is quite different because such employment outcomes are not treated as anomalies or the fault of government and unions, but, rather, as a predictable outcome of laissez-faire capitalism.

In IE/IR and Keynsian theory, the one-quarter drop in money wages and one-third drop in prices from 1929 to 1933 unleashed a deflationary process of "destructive competition" or "race to the bottom" that is potentially quite destabilizing (Kaufman 1997, 2012c). The idea that competition can turn destructive is antithetical to NE theory; a fall in wages and prices is seen as a normal and desirable way to bring the economy back to full-employment equilibrium.

In IE/IR theory, however, competition can turn destructive in a recession or depression for several reasons. Strong competition, for example, brings on wage cuts; but wage cuts reduce aggregate demand (in panel (c) of Figure 3.2) and drive the economy deeper into recession and unemployment. Also, as earlier described, wage cuts can become destabilizing because, as they reduce family income toward the survival level, labor supply expands, thus further driving down wages (the kinked labor supply curve idea). Moreover, as wage rates and family income fall below the social minimum (in panel (a)), workers' physical and human capital begins to deteriorate. A situation of falling wages and prices also increases the real debt burden of firms, which react by cutting costs wherever possible. Since labor is typically the largest part of variable cost in the short run, the brunt of cost reduction falls on workers in the form of lay-offs, speed-ups, deteriorating working conditions and harsher treatment. The labor market provides them little protection in this scenario, however, because compensating wage differentials are compressed or eliminated and many hungry jobseekers are available to employers. A final negative effect of strong competition in this situation is that the ratcheting down of wages and conditions of employment leads to feelings of unfairness, insecurity and bitterness among the employees, all of which aggravate conflict and undermine cooperative and high-productivity win-win employment relationships (in panel (e)).

Frances Perkins, Labor Secretary in the Roosevelt administration, summed up the IE/IR perspective when she said (quoted in Craypo 1997: 226):

> As a nation, we are recognizing that programs long thought of as merely labor welfare, such as shorter hours, higher wages, and a voice in terms and conditions of work, are really essential economic factors for recovery and for the technique of industrial management in a mass production age.

Consonant with the theme of this chapter, once again the "assume a competitive labor market" proposition is seen to be a substantially defective tool for understanding the behavior of labor markets and social welfare effect of labor laws; likewise, again illustrated is the superior explanatory power and insight of the alternative IE/IR theory. A second virtue of the IE/IR approach is that it does not repeat another mistake of NE and SL&EM; that is, the assumption that its model of labor markets has universal applicability to all historical epochs ("one size fits all"). Instead, IE/IR takes an evolutionary point of view and works into its theory changes in the institutional structure of the economy (e.g., via the "roof" and government-legislated changes in endowments and rules of the game in panel (a)); doing so, in turn, means its evaluation of labor law and social welfare programs is also historically contingent.

FL&EM and IE/IR look at the seven decades since the Great Depression and see great progress along three major fronts of attack on labor problems: ameliorating labor market failures, balancing the institutional governance structure and reducing unemployment. President Reagan famously asserted that the nine most dangerous words in the English language are "I'm from the government and I'm here to help." IE/IR asks, however, that we look below the surface of appealing free market rhetoric and consider the record of what has been accomplished by government in labor markets. Consider, for example, the major labor and employment laws enacted since World War II, including the Equal Pay Act, Civil Rights Act, Age Discrimination in Employment Act, Employee Retirement and Income Security Act, Occupational Safety and Health Act, Worker Adjustment and Retraining Act, Family Medical Leave Act, Americans with Disabilities Act, and the Patient Protection and Affordable Care Act.

The opinion on these laws of, respectively, the American public and neoclassical/SL&EM scholars is noticeably discordant. Hamermesh (2009) reports that the most researched labor policy issue in labor economics is the minimum wage. According to a 2006 national poll (reported at http://pewresearch.org/pubs/18/maximum-support-for-raising-the-minimum), 83 percent of Americans said they favored a $2.00 increase in the minimum wage. Economists Neumark and Washer, however, reflect a large body of economic opinion when they conclude in their new book *Minimum Wages* (2008), "we find it very difficult to see a good economic rationale for continuing to seek a higher minimum wage." The belief of most IE/IR economists is that the public has the correct position not only on the minimum wage but on all of the other labor laws cited above. They do not claim that these laws are perfect or cannot be improved, nor do they deny that regulation could go too far or minimum wages too high. But IE/IR believes the public accurately perceives that these laws have helped solve significant labor problems. Evidence in support of this belief is taken from the fact that efforts to repeal old labor laws (e.g., the move to privatize Social Security in the Bush administration) and block several new laws (e.g., President Obama's health care law) have thus far failed.

Nonetheless, clearly the political tide in the last three decades has on balance favored giving a greater role to markets and paring back government regulation and collective bargaining. In this respect SL&EM has clearly dominated FL&EM. The decision of the state of Wisconsin in early 2011 to rescind collective bargaining rights for public sector employees is emblematic, as is (at this time of writing) the near-death experience of Obama's health care legislation. An IE/IR interpretation is the following, with emphasis on two themes articulated by Commons: the inevitability of contradictions in labor policy and the need to look at labor law as one part of a larger industrial relations system.

Here Keynes re-enters our historically contingent story. After World War II the American government gradually started to practice Keynesian-inspired full-employment fiscal and monetary policies. The effect was dramatic – recessions were shallower and further apart, economic growth was fast-paced into the early 1970s, and the labor market stayed closer to full employment. If the economy is at or near full employment, then the NE "assume a competitive labor market" theory comes a step closer to reality and its implications for labor law and unions have more relevance. In particular, in a full-employment economy workers do not need as much labor law protection, unions gradually transition from a protector of the underdog to a source of monopoly wages, and both protective laws and unions begin to appear unnecessarily restrictive and cost-increasing. The apparent success of Keynesian full-employment macroeconomic practices, therefore, undercut some of the need for the wage-raising and protective parts of the New Deal labor program. This was most true concerning protection and support of trade unions, since new labor laws are mostly a one-time structural change in labor markets, but the collective bargaining system they promote has a built-in dynamic push for "more" that in a full-employment economy creates a growing problem of monopoly wages and benefits and cost-push inflation pressures (Mitchell 1980; Kaufman 2007c, 2012a).

Union density in the private sector gradually declined over the years until in 2010 it was less than 8 percent (Hirsch and Macpherson 2011). This decline was partly an automatic economic response as higher-cost unionized firms gradually lost market and employment share to non-union competitors and foreign firms; partly it was also a product of an effort by the Reagan and Bush administrations to weaken unions through a variety of regulatory rulings, shifts in labor law enforcement, and budget reallocations (actions also applied to other areas of labor law, such as occupational safety and health). Here emerge contradictory forces, however.

On one hand, the decline of private sector unions, selective weakening of existing labor laws, growth of flexible work arrangements (e.g., contract and temporary employment), and process of globalization succeeded in creating a more competitive labor market since the early 1980s, exactly as NE and SL&EM have advocated. The accompanying outcomes, however, were exactly what IE/IR theory would predict – re-emergence of an inequality of bargaining power for the middle-to-lower part of the workforce and growing structural inequality in the nation's governance structure and institutional rules governing the labor market. Inequality of bargaining power re-emerged because workers lacked a viable union threat effect, and American workers were now competing with low-wage workers in China, India and other countries; the lack of good jobs in America put workers into more of a "take it or leave it" situation. The governance structure also gradually tipped in favor of the interests of employers and the affluent due to growing political and financial clout by conservative and pro-business groups, declining clout by unions and other groups on the progressive/left side of the political spectrum, and a growing flood of mostly "right-learning" money into political lobbying and elections (Phillips 2008).

These two structural shifts created a more competitive labor market, but "competitive" in this case is manifest not by removal of government restraints and movement to the equilibrium of supply and demand (Figure 3.1) but a shifting down of both curves (Figure 3.2 panel (a) from the pencil-thin lines to the bands), and indeed the entire plane of competition in the American labor market. Two important examples are decisions of the American government since 2000 (explicit or tacit) to live with large-scale illegal immigration and an undervalued Chinese currency, both of which in effect expand the supply of labor competing against American workers and increase profits relative to wages (if labor demand curves are inelastic, which evidence (Hamermesh 1993) suggests they are). Accordingly, real wages and family incomes stagnated for the middle and working classes, most of the productivity gains generated by the economy went to corporate profits and top-tier earners, and the income distribution gradually moved to greater inequality in favor of the rich (Stiglitz 2010; Economic Policy Institute 2011).

The rising income share for employers, property owners, and the affluent creates buoyant financial markets, construction spending, and capital goods spending, all of which expand the supply side of the economy. The downside, however, is that a stagnant-to-modestly rising real wage and a falling income share for labor leads to anemic growth in household income, consumer spending, and aggregate demand – propped up for a time, perhaps, by a run-up in household debt. Eventually a structural shortfall of demand develops that price adjustments cannot solve, precipitating a sustained bout of overproduction (output Q_1 in Figure 3.2 panel (c), but demand of Q_2), a large rise in unemployment, popping of real estate and financial market bubbles, and, in a worst-case scenario, descent into economic crisis.

These events, from an IE/IR perspective, describe the economic crisis of 2007–10. They are also eerily reminiscent of the economic crisis of the 1930s. As in the 1930s, more unions and redistributive labor laws are blunt and often costly measures to solve the problem of structural imbalance and economic inequality that afflicts the American labor market of the early 2010s. If these tools are not used, however, then society needs to come up with some other mechanism that preserves a reasonable balance in bargaining power and income distribution. What IE/IR and FL&EM are absolutely certain of is that a strategy of deregulation, deunionization and wage-cutting will not solve American competitive problems but will only worsen matters.

Free market theories of the "assume a competitive labor market" type are intellectual works of beauty and have insights not to be ignored; nonetheless, they are also a recipe for labor problems and economic mal-performance because they envision labor markets as operating no differently than commodity and financial markets. If the field of industrial relations has a central theme, it is that this doctrine is dangerously inaccurate in theory and harmful in practice.

X.   CONCLUSION

From one point of view labor markets are highly competitive, employment practices are (mostly) efficient adaptations to underlying costs and constraints, and government solutions are typically inefficient and coercive. This point of view, most closely identified in the post-World War II period with the neoclassical economics and Second L&E tradition at the University of Chicago, leads to the conclusion that in most cases labor law and employment regulation should be kept to a minimum and used only when evidence of market failure is clear and compelling and other pro-market solutions are infeasible.

From another point of view – most closely identified with the institutional economics/industrial relations and First L&E tradition born in the early part of the 20th century at the University of Wisconsin – laissez-faire external and internal labor markets are considerably imperfect and structurally unbalanced and, hence, wages, conditions and managerial employment practices tend to have significant elements of inefficiency, injustice and inhumanity, absent purposeful corrective action. Further, from this point of view, even if labor markets could be made highly competitive it is undesirable to do so since they are harmful to cooperative high-productivity employment relations and the life interest of workers in jobs with reasonable security, stability and advancement opportunities. So viewed, capitalism and the work world can be materially improved by a complementary program of labor law, social insurance, availability of collective bargaining, and macroeconomic guidance that together deploy the visible hand of government to supplement, strengthen and in some cases restrain the invisible hand of self-interest and competition.

It is generally the case in employment disputes, as arbitrators, mediators and judges come to learn full-well, that neither side to an argument has a monopoly on facts and truth. Hence, the verdict has to be established by a careful and objective weighing of the evidence. In this chapter I have endeavored to present to the jury both the positive case for the IE/IR and FL&EM side of the labor law debate and a critical account (albeit hopefully fair and balanced) of the gaps and shortcomings in the NE and SL&EM argument. Without question labor law, labor unions, and social safety net programs entail costs and sometimes cause economic inefficiency; the IE/IR position, however, is that the "assume a competitive labor market" proposition that grounds the NE and SL&EM evaluation of these institutions is logically flawed, because its principle theoretical tools (labor demand curve, demand/ supply model) lack a solid micro foundation, and is empirically biased because it accentuates their costs and minimizes their benefits. In effect, the "anti" side of the labor law debate asks the jury to evaluate labor law with a theoretical framework that inevitably leads to a baseline verdict of "guilty until proven innocent." It does this by committing what Demsetz (1969) calls the "nirvana fallacy;" that is, evaluating imperfect human-made institutions against the outcomes of a (mostly) first-best set of markets and contracts. The essence of IE/IR is to model labor markets and employment relationships in a more realistic and hence imperfect manner, with the effect of opening intellectual space for labor law and labor institutions to do good as well as harm. IE/IR proponents have considerable faith, in turn, that if American social policy were to actually follow the deregulation regime explicit or implicit in SL&EM – for example, the list of recommendations/conclusions cited earlier from Posner's *Law and Economics* – the nation would soon see a return of all the labor problems that FL&EM worked so hard over the 20th century to solve.

REFERENCES

Adams, Henry. 1887. "The Relation of the State to Industrial Action," 1 *Publications of the American Economic Association* 7–85. Reprinted in Joseph Dorfman, ed., 1969, *Two Essays: The Relation of the State to Industrial Action and Economics & Jurisprudence*. Boston: Kelley.

Adams, Henry. 1897. *Economics and Jurisprudence*. New York: Macmillan.

Addison, John, and Barry Hirsch. 1997. "The Economic Effects of Employment Regulation: What Are the Limits?" in Bruce Kaufman, ed., *Government Regulation of the Employment Relationship*. Ithaca, NY: Cornell University Press, pp. 125–78.

Akerlof, George. 1990. "The Fair Wage-Effort Hypothesis and Unemployment," 105 *Quarterly Journal of Economics* 255–84.

Albelda, Randy. 1997. *Economics and Feminism: Disturbances in the Field*. New York: Twayne.

Amsden, Alice, and Ajit Singh. 1994. "The Optimal Degree of Competition and Dynamic Efficiency in Japan and Korea," 38 *European Economic Review* 941–51.

Appelbaum, Eileen, Peter Berg, Arnie Kalleberg, and Thomas Bailey. 2000. *Manufacturing Advantage: Why High-Performance Systems Pay Off*. Ithaca, NY: Cornell University Press.

Appelbaum, Eileen, Annette Bernhardt, and Richard Murnane. 2003. *Low Wage America: How Employers are Reshaping Opportunity in the Workplace*. New York: Russell Sage.

Arthurs, Harry. 2006. *Fairness at Work: Federal Labor Standards for the 21st Century*. Ottawa: HRSDC.

Arthurs, Harry. 2007. "Compared to What? Reflections on the Future of Comparative Labor Law," 28 *Comparative Labor Law & Policy Journal* 591–612.

Ashenfelter, Orley, Henry Farber, and Michael Ransom. 2010. "Labor Market Monopsony," 28 *Journal of Labor Economics* 203–10.

Atkinson, Glen, and Theodore Oleson. 1998. "Commons and Keynes: Their Assault on Laissez-Faire," 32 *Journal of Economic Issues* 1019–30.

Baldamus, Wilhelm. 1961. *Efficiency and Effort*. London: Tavistock.

Becker, Gary. 1957. *The Economics of Discrimination*. Chicago, IL: University of Chicago Press.

Becker, Gary. 1976. *The Economic Approach to Human Behavior*. Chicago, IL: University of Chicago Press.

Becker, Gary. 1993. "Nobel Lecture: The Economic Way of Looking at Behavior," 101 *Journal of Political Economy* 385–409.

Befort, Stephen, and John Budd. 2009. *Invisible Hands, Invisible Objects: Bringing Workplace Law and Public Policy into Focus*, Stanford, CA: Stanford Economics and Finance.

Belman, Dale, and Michael Belzer. 1997. "Regulation of Labor Markets: Balancing the Benefits and Costs of Competition," in Bruce Kaufman, ed., *Government Regulation of the Employment Relationship*. Ithaca, NY: Cornell University Press, pp. 179–220.

Bewley, Truman. 1999. *Why Wages Don't Fall in a Recession*. Cambridge, MA: Harvard University Press.

Biddle, Jeff. 1996. "H. Gregg Lewis," in Warren Samuels, ed., *American Economists of the Late 20th Century*. Cheltenham, UK and Brookfield, VT, USA: Edward Elgar, pp. 174–93.

Blasi, Joe, and Douglas Kruse. 2006. "U.S. High Performance Work Practices at Century's End," 45 *Industrial Relations* 457–78.

Blaug, Mark. 1985. *Economic Theory in Retrospect*, 4th ed. New York: Cambridge University Press.

Blaug, Mark. 2007. "The Fundamental Welfare Theorems of Modern Welfare Economics, Historically Contemplated," 39 *History of Political Economy* 185–207.

Block, Richard, Karen Roberts, and R. Oliver Clark. 2003. *Labor Standards in the United States and Canada*. Kalamazoo: Upjohn.

Boeri, Tito, and Jan van Ours. 2008. *The Economics of Imperfect Labor Markets*. Princeton, NJ: Princeton University Press.

Boulding, Kenneth. 1957. "A New Look at Institutionalism," 47 *American Economic Review* 1–12.

Bowles, Samuel, and Robert Boyer. 1988. "Labor Discipline and Aggregate Demand: A Macroeconomic Model," 78 *American Economic Review* 395–400.

Boyer, G., and R. Smith. 2001. "The Neoclassical Tradition in Labor Economics," 54 *Industrial and Labor Relations Review* 199–223.

Bronfenbrenner, Martin. 1956. "Potential Monopsony in Labor Markets," 9 *Industrial and Labor Relations Review* 577–88.

Brown, Martin, and Peter Philips. 1986. "Competition, Racism, and Hiring Practices among California Manufacturers, 1860–1882," 40 *Industrial and Labor Relations Review* 61–74.

Budd, John. 2004. *Employment with a Human Face: Balancing Efficiency, Equity, and Voice*. Ithaca, NY: Cornell University Press.

Budd, John, and James Scoville. 2005. *The Ethics of Industrial Relations and Human Resources*. Champaign, IL: Labor and Employment Relations Association.

Bulow, Jeremy, and Lawrence Summers. 1986. "A Theory of Dual Labor Markets with Application to Industrial Policy, Discrimination, and Keynesian Unemployment," 4 *Journal of Labor Economics* 376–414.

Cahuc, Pierre, and André Zylberberg. 2004. *Labor Economics*, Cambridge, MA: MIT Press.

Card, David, and Alan Krueger. 1995. *Myth and Measurement: The New Economics of the Minimum Wage.* Princeton, NJ: Princeton University Press.

Chandler, Alfred Jr. 1977. *The Visible Hand: The Managerial Revolution in American Business.* Cambridge, MA: Harvard University Press.

Chari, V., Patrick Kehoe, and Ellen McGrattan. 2003. "Accounting for the Great Depression," 27 *Federal Reserve Bank of Minneapolis Quarterly Review* 2–8.

Coase, Ronald. 1937. "The Nature of the Firm," 4 *Economica* 386–405.

Coase, Ronald. 1992. "The Institutional Structure of Production," 82 *American Economic Review* 713–19.

Combs, J., Y. Liu, A. Hall, and D. Ketchen. 2006. "How Much Do High-Performance Work Practices Matter? A Meta-Analysis of their Effects on Organizational Performance," 59 *Personnel Psychology* 501–28.

Commons, John. 1919. *Industrial Goodwill.* New York: McGraw-Hill.

Commons, John. 1934. *Institutional Economics: Its Place in Political Economy.* New York: Macmillan.

Commons, John. 1950. *The Economics of Collective Action,* Madison, WI: University of Wisconsin Press.

Commons, John, and John Andrews. 1916. *Principles of Labor Legislation,* New York: Harper.

Cooter, Robert, and Thomas Ulen. 2010. *Law & Economics,* 6th ed. New York: Pearson.

Craypo, Charles. 1997. "Alternative Perspectives on the Purpose and Effects of Labor Standards Legislation," in Bruce Kaufman, ed., *Government Regulation of the Employment Relationship.* Madison, WI: Industrial Relations Research Association (IRRA), pp. 221–52.

Dau-Schmidt, Kenneth, and Arthur Traynor. 2009. "Regulating Unions and Collective Bargaining," in Kenneth Dau-Schmidt, Seth Harris, and Orly Lobel, eds., *Labor and Employment Law and Economics.* Cheltenham, UK and Northampton, MA, USA: Edward Elgar, pp. 96–128.

Davis, John. 1992. *The Economic Surplus in Advanced Economies.* Aldershot, UK and Brookfield, VT, USA: Edward Elgar.

Deakin, Simon, and Frank Wilkinson. 2005. *Law of the Labor Market: Industrialization, Employment, and Legal Evolution.* New York: Oxford University Press.

Demsetz, Harold. 1969. "Information and Efficiency: Another Viewpoint," 12 *Journal of Law and Economics* 1–22.

Derber, Milton. 1970. *The American Idea of Industrial Democracy.* Champaign-Urbana, IL: University of Illinois Press.

Dessing, Markye. 2002. "Labor Supply, the Family and Poverty: The S-Shaped Labor Supply Curve," 49 *Journal of Economic Behavior and Organization* 433–58.

Doeringer, Peter, and Michael Piore. 1971. *Internal Labor Markets and Manpower Analysis.* Lexington, MA: Lexington Books.

Dorfman, Joseph. 1969. "Henry Carter Adams: Harmonizer of Liberty and Reform," in Joseph Dorfman, ed., *Two Essays by Henry Carter Adams.* New York: Kelly, pp. 3–55.

Dornhoff, William. 2012. *Who Rules America?* www.usc.edu/whorulesamerica/power/.

Doucouliagos, Hristos, and Thomas Stanley. 2009. "Publication Selection Bias in Minimum Wage Research? A Meta-regression Analysis," 47 *British Journal of Industrial Relations* 406–28.

Dow, Gregory. 1997. "The New Institutional Economics and Employment Regulation," in Bruce Kaufman, ed., *Government Regulation of the Employment Relationship.* Madison, WI: IRRA, pp. 57–90.

Dunlop, John. 1957. "The Task of Contemporary Wage Theory," in George Taylor and Frank Pierson, eds., *New Concepts in Wage Determination.* New York: McGraw-Hill, pp. 117–39.

Dunlop, John. 1958. *Industrial Relations Systems.* New York: Holt.

Dunlop, John. 1984. "Industrial Relations and Economics: The Common Frontier of Wage Determination," in *Proceedings of the Thirty-Seventh Annual Meeting,* Madison, WI: IRRA, pp. 9–23.

Dunlop, John. 1994. "Organizations and Human Resources: Internal and External Markets," in Clark Kerr and Paul Staudohar, eds., *Labor Economics and Industrial Relations: Markets and Institutions.* Cambridge, MA: Harvard University Press, pp. 375–400.

Economic Policy Institute. 2011. *The State of Working America.* Washington, DC: Economic Policy Institute.

Edwards, Paul. 2003. "The Employment Relationship and the Field of Industrial Relations," in Paul Edwards, ed., *Industrial Relations: Theory and Practice,* 2nd ed. Oxford: Blackwell, pp. 1–36.

Edwards, Paul. 2009. "The Employment Perspective in Strategic HRM," in John Storey, Patrick Wright, and David Ulrich, eds., *The Routledge Companion to Strategic Human Resource Management.* London: Routledge, pp. 40–51.

Edwards, R. (1979). *Contested Terrain: The Transformation of Work in Twentieth Century America.* New York: Basic Books.

Ekelund, Robert, and Robert Hebert. 2007. *A History of Economic Thought and Method*, 5th ed. Long Grove, IL: Waveland.

Ely, Richard. 1884. *The Past and Present of Political Economy*. Baltimore, MD: Johns Hopkins University Press.

Ely, Richard. 1886. *The Labor Movement in America*. New York: Crowell.

Emmett, Ross. 1999. *Selected Essays by Frank H. Knight*, Vol. 2. Chicago, IL: University of Chicago Press.

Epstein, Cynthia. 1981. *Women in Law*. New York: Basic Books.

Epstein, Richard. 1983. "A Common Law for Labor Relations: A Critique of the New Deal Labor Legislation," 92 *Yale Law Journal* 1357–408.

Epstein, Richard. 1984. "In Defense of the Contract at Will," 51 *University of Chicago Law Review* 947–87.

Epstein, Richard. 1992. *Forbidden Grounds: The Case against Employment Discrimination Laws*. Cambridge, MA: Harvard University Press.

Erickson, Christopher, and Daniel Mitchell. 2008. "Monopsony as a Metaphor for the Emerging Post-Union Labor Market," 146 *International Labor Review* 163–87.

Estlund, Cynthia. 2006. "The Death of Labor Law?" 2 *Annual Review of Law and Social Science* 105–23.

Estlund, Cynthia. 2010. *Regoverning the Workplace: From Self-regulation to Co-regulation*. New Haven, CT: Yale University Press.

Falk, Armin, Ernst Fehr, and Urs Fischbacher. 2003. "On the Nature of Fair Behavior," 41 *Economic Inquiry* 20–26.

Fehr, E., and A. Falk. 1999. "Wage Rigidity in a Competitive Incomplete Contract Market," 107 *Journal of Political Economy* 106–34.

Fehr, E., and A. Falk. 2006. "Fairness Perceptions and Reservations Wages – The Behavioral Effects of Minimum Wage Laws," 121 *Quarterly Journal of Economics* 1347–81.

Fishback, Price. 1998. "Operations of 'Unfettered' Labor Markets: Exit and Voice in American Labor Markets at the Turn of the Century," 36 *Journal of Economic Literature* 722–65.

Fleischer, Belton, and Thomas Kniesner. 1980. *Labor Economics: Theory, Evidence and Policy*, 2nd ed. Englewood Cliffs, NJ: Prentice Hall.

Freedman, Craig. 2008. *Chicago Fundamentalism: Ideology and Methodology in Economics*. Hackensack, NJ: World Scientific.

Freeman, Richard, and James Medoff. 1984. *What Do Unions Do?* New York: Basic Books.

Fried, Barbara. 1998. *The Progressive Assault on Laissez-Faire: Robert Hale and the First Law and Economics Movement*. Cambridge, MA: Harvard University Press.

Friedman, Milton. 1953. "The Methodology of Positive Economics," in Milton Friedman, ed., *Essays in Positive Economics*. Chicago, IL: University of Chicago Press, pp. 3–43.

Friedman, Milton, and Rose Friedman. 1990. *Free to Choose*. New York: Harcourt Brace.

Friedman, Milton, and Anna Schwartz. 1963. *A Monetary History of the United States, 1867-1960*. Princeton, NJ: Princeton University Press.

Furubotn, Erik, and Rudolf Richter. 2005. *Institutions & Economic Theory*, 2nd ed. Ann Arbor, MI: University of Michigan Press.

Galbraith, John. 1967. *The New Industrial State*. Boston, MA: Houghton-Mifflin.

Galloway, Lowell. 2010. "Unions, the High-Wage Doctrine, and Employment," 30 *Cato Journal* 197–213.

Gottfried, Heidi. 2009. "Gender and Employment: A Global Lens on Analyzing and Theorizing of Labor Markets," 3 *Sociological Compass* 1–16.

Groenewegen, John, Antoon Spithoven, and Annette Van Den Berg. 2010. *Institutional Economics: An Introduction*. New York: Palgrave Macmillan.

Gross, James, and Lance Compa. 2009. *Human Rights in Labor and Employment Relations*, Champaign-Urbana, IL: Labor and Employment Relations Association.

Hahnel, Robin. 2006. "Exploitation: A Modern Approach," 38 *Review of Radical Political Economics* 175–92.

Hamermesh, Daniel. 1993. *Labor Demand*. Princeton, NJ: Princeton University Press.

Hamermesh, Daniel. 2009. "Comment," in John Siegfried, ed., *Better Living through Economics*. Cambridge, MA: Harvard University Press, pp. 36–9.

Hirsch, Barry, and David Macpherson. 2011. *Union Coverage and Data Book*. Washington, DC: BNA.

Hovenkamp, Herbert. 1990. "The First Great Law and Economics Movement," 42 *Stanford Law Review* 993–1058.

Huang, Peter. 2009. "Emotional Reactions to Law and Economics: Market Metaphors, and Rationality Rhetoric," in Mark White, ed., *Theoretical Foundations of Law and Economics*. New York: Cambridge University Press, pp. 163–83.

Isaac, Joe. 2007. "Reforming Australian Industrial Relations," 49 *Journal of Industrial Relations* 411–35.

Jacoby, Sanford. 2005. "Economic Ideas and the Labor Market: Origins of the Anglo-American Model and Prospects for Global Diffusion," 26 *Comparative Labor Law & Policy Journal* 43–78.

Johnson, George. 1975. "Economic Analysis of Trade Unionism," 65 *American Economic Review* 23–38.

Jolls, Christine. 2006. "Law and the Labor Market," 2 *Annual Review of Law and Social Science* 359–85.

Jolls, Christine, Cass Sunstein, and Richard Thaler. 1998. "A Behavioral Approach to Law and Economics," 50 *Stanford University Law Review* 1471–550.

Just, Richard, Darrell Hueth, and Andrew Schmitz. 2004. *The Welfare Economics of Public Policy*. Cheltenham, UK and Northampton, MA, USA: Edward Elgar.

Kates, Steven. 1998. *Say's Law and the Keynesian Revolution*. Cheltenham, UK and Lyme, NH, USA: Edward Elgar.

Kates, Steven. 2010. "Influencing Keynes: The Intellectual Origins of the General Theory," 18 *History of Economic Ideas* 33–64.

Kaufman, Bruce. 1988. *How Labor Markets Work: Reflections on Theory and Practice by John Dunlop, Clark Kerr, Richard Lester and Lloyd Reynolds*. Lexington, MA: Lexington Books.

Kaufman, Bruce. 1997. "Labor Markets and Employment Regulation: The View of the 'Old' Institutionalists," in Bruce Kaufman, ed., *Government Regulation of the Employment Relationship*. Madison, WI: IRRA, pp. 11–56.

Kaufman, Bruce. 1999. "Expanding the Behavioral Foundations of Labor Economics," 52 *Industrial and Labor Relations Review* 361–91.

Kaufman, Bruce. 2002. "Reflections on Six Decades in Industrial Relations: An Interview with John Dunlop," 55 *Industrial and Labor Relations Review* 324–48.

Kaufman, Bruce. 2003a. "John R. Commons and the Wisconsin School on Industrial Relations Strategy and Policy," 56 *Industrial and Labor Relations Review* 3–30.

Kaufman, Bruce. 2003b. "The Organization of Economic Activity: Insights from the Institutional Theory of John R. Commons," 52 *Journal of Economic Behavior and Organization* 71–96.

Kaufman, Bruce. 2004. *The Global Evolution of Industrial Relations: Events, Ideas, and the IIRA*. Geneva: International Labor Organization.

Kaufman, Bruce. 2005. "The Social Welfare Objectives and Ethical Principles of Industrial Relations," in John Budd and James Scoville, eds., *The Ethics of Human Resources and Industrial Relations*. Champaign-Urbana, IL: Labor and Employment Relations Association, pp. 23–59.

Kaufman, Bruce. 2006. "Labor Institutionalism and Industrial Relations: A Century of Boom and Bust," 47 *Labor History* 295–318.

Kaufman, Bruce. 2007a. "The Institutional Economics of John R. Commons: Complement and Substitute for Neoclassical Economic Theory," 5 *Socio-Economic Review* 3–46.

Kaufman, Bruce. 2007b. "Historical Insights: The Early Institutionalists on Trade Unionism and Labor Policy," in James Bennett and Bruce Kaufman, eds., *What Do Unions Do: A Twenty-Year Perspective*, New Brunswick, NJ: Transaction Press, pp. 46–78.

Kaufman, Bruce. 2007c. "What Do Unions Do? Evaluation and Commentary," in J. Bennett and B. Kaufman, eds., *What Do Unions Do: A Twenty-Year Perspective*. New Brunswick, NJ: Transaction Press, pp. 520–62.

Kaufman, Bruce. 2008. *Managing the Human Factor: The Early Years of Human Resource Management in American Industry*. Ithaca, NY: Cornell University Press.

Kaufman, Bruce. 2009. "Labor Law and Employment Regulation: Neoclassical and Institutional Perspectives," in K. Dau-Schmidt, S. Harris, and O. Lobel, eds., *Labor and Employment Law and Economics*. Cheltenham, UK and Northampton, MA: Edward Elgar, pp. 3–58.

Kaufman, Bruce. 2010a. "Chicago and the Development of Twentieth Century Labor Economics," in Ross Emmett, ed., *The Elgar Companion to the Chicago School of Economics*. Cheltenham, UK and Northampton, MA, UK: Edward Elgar, pp. 128–51.

Kaufman, Bruce. 2010b. "The Theoretical Foundation of Industrial Relations and Implications for Labor Economics and Human Resource Management," 64 *Industrial and Labor Relations Review* 74–108.

Kaufman, Bruce. 2010c. "Institutional Economics and the Minimum Wage: Broadening the Theoretical and Policy Debate," 63 *Industrial and Labor Relations Review* 427–53.

Kaufman, Bruce. 2012a. "An Institutional Economic Analysis of Labor Unions," 51 *Industrial Relations* 338–71.

Kaufman, Bruce. 2012b. "Some Coasian Problems with Posnerian Law & Economics," 46 *Journal of Economic Issues* 745–64.

Kaufman, Bruce. 2012c. "Wage Policy, the Great Depression, and New Deal Labor Policy: Were Government and Unions to Blame?" 66 *Industrial & Labor Relations Review*.

Kerr, Clark. 1977. *Labor Markets and Wage Determination*. Berkeley, CA: University of California Press.

Kerr, Clark, and Abraham Siegel. 1955. "The Structuring of the Labor Force in Industrial Society: New Dimensions and New Questions," 8 *Industrial and Labor Relations Review* 151–68.

Keynes, John. 1936. *The General Theory of Employment, Interest, and Money*. London: Macmillan.

Kochan, Thomas. 2005. *Restoring the American Dream: A Working Families' Agenda*. Cambridge, MA: MIT Press.

Kochan, Thomas, and Paul Osterman. 1994. *The Mutual Gains Enterprise*. Cambridge, MA: Harvard Business School Press.

Koot, Gerald. 1987. *English Historical Economics, 1870–1926*. Cambridge: Cambridge University Press.

Lazear, Edward. 2000. "Economic Imperialism," 115 *Quarterly Journal of Economics* 99–145.

Leonard, Jonathon. 2003. "Advancing Equal Employment Opportunity, Diversity, and Employee Rights: Good Will, Good Management, and Legal Compulsion," in Bruce Kaufman, Richard Beaumont, and Roy Helfgott, eds., *Industrial Relations to Human Resources and Beyond: The Evolving Process of Employee Relations Management*, Armonk, NY: M.E. Sharpe, pp. 258–92.

Lescohier, Don. 1919. *The Labor Market*. New York: Macmillan.

Lester, Richard. 1941. *The Economics of Labor*. New York: Macmillan.

Lester, Richard. 1952. "A Range Theory of Wage Differentials," 5 *Industrial and Labor Relations Review* 433–50.

Levendis, John. 2007. "The Fallacy of Wage Cuts and Keynes' Involuntary Unemployment," 29 *Journal of the History of Economic Thought* 309–29.

Lipsey, Richard, and Kevin Lancaster. 1956. "The General Theory of the Second Best," 24 *The Review of Economic Studies* 11–32.

Long, Clarence. 1958. *The Labor Force under Changing Income and Employment*. Princeton, NJ: Princeton University Press.

Lutz, Mark. 1999. *Economics for the Common Good: Two Centuries of Social Economic Thought in the Humanistic Tradition*. New York: Routledge.

Manning, Alan. 2003. *Monopsony in Motion*. Princeton, NJ: Princeton University Press.

Marsden, David. 1999. *A Theory of Employment Systems*. Oxford: Oxford University Press.

Mas-Colell, Andreu, Michael Whinston, and Jerry Green. 1995. *Microeconomic Theory*. New York: Oxford University Press.

McCloskey, Deirdre. 1997. "The Good Old Coase Theorem and the Good Old Chicago School: A Comment on Zerbe and Medema," in Steven Medema, ed., *Coasean Economics: Law and Economics and the New Institutional Economics*. Boston, MA: Kluwer, pp. 239–48.

McIntyre, Richard, and Yngve Ramstad. 2002. "John R. Commons and the Problem of International Labor Rights," 36 *Journal of Economic Issues* 293–302.

McNulty, Paul. 1980. *The Origins and Development of Labor Economics*. Cambridge, MA: MIT Press.

Medema, Steven. 2010. "Chicago Law and Economics," in Ross Emmett, ed., *The Elgar Companion to the Chicago School of Economics*. Cheltenham, UK and Northampton, MA: Edward Elgar, pp. 160–74.

Mercuro, Nicholas, and Steven Medema. 1997. *Economics and the Law: From Posner to Post-Modernism*, Princeton, NJ: Princeton University Press.

Miller, Gary. 1991. *Managerial Dilemmas*. Cambridge: Cambridge University Press.

Mitchell, Daniel. 1980. *Unions, Wages, and Inflation*. Washington, DC: Brookings.

Moggridge, Donald. 1982. *The Collected Writings of John Maynard Keynes*, Vol. 21. London: Macmillan.

Moss, David. 1996. *Socializing Security: Progressive-Era Economists and the Origins of American Social Policy*, Cambridge, MA: Harvard University Press.

National Labor Relations Board. 1985. *Legislative Hearings on the National Labor Relations Act*, Vols. 1 and 2. Washington, DC: Government Printing Office.

Nelson, Bruce. 1988. *Workers on the Waterfront: Seamen, Longshoremen, and Unionism in the 1930s*. Champaign-Urbana, IL: University of Illinois Press.

Neumark, David, and W. Wascher. 2008. *Minimum Wages*. Cambridge, MA: MIT Press.

Ohanian, Lee. 2009. "What – or Who – Started the Great Depression?" 144 *Journal of Economic Theory* 2310–35.

Osterman, Paul. 1987. "Choice of Employment Systems in Internal Labor Markets," 26 *Industrial Relations* 46–67.

Osterman, Paul, Thomas Kochan, Richard Locke, and Michael Piore. 2001. *Working in America: A Blueprint for a New Labor Market*. Cambridge, MA: MIT Press.

Overtfeldt, Johan van. 2007. *The Chicago School: How the University of Chicago Assembled the Thinkers that Revolutionized Economics and Business*. Chicago, IL: Agate.

Parker, Randall. 2007. *The Economics of the Great Depression*. Cheltenham, UK and Northampton, MA: Edward Elgar.

Pearson, Heath. 1997. *Origins and Law and Economics: The Economists' New Science of Law 1830-1930*. Cambridge: Cambridge University Press.

Peterson, Joyce. 1987. *American Automobile Workers, 1900-1933*. Albany, NY: State University of New York Press.

Phillips, Kevin. 2008. *Bad Money: Reckless Finance, Failed Politics, and the Global Crisis of American Capitalism*. New York: Viking.

Plott, Charles. 2010. "Overview: Highlights of the Benefits of Basic Science in Economics," in John Siegfried, ed., *Better Living through Economics*. Cambridge, MA: Harvard University Press, pp. 6–35.

Polachek, Solomon. 1981. "Occupational Self-Selection: A Human Capital Approach to Sex Differences in Occupational Structure," 63 *Review of Economics and Statistics* 60–69.

Posner, Richard. 1984. "Some Economics of Labor Law," 51 *University of Chicago Law Review* 988–1011.

Posner, Richard. 2007. *Economic Analysis of Law*, 7th ed. Austin, TX: Wolters-Kluwer.

Prasch, Robert. 2005. "The Social Cost of Labor," 39 *Journal of Economic Issues* 1–7.

Prescott, Edward. 1999. "Some Observations on the Great Depression," 23 *Federal Reserve Bank of Minneapolis Quarterly Review* 25–9.

Rader, B. 1966. *The Academic Mind and Reform: The Influence of Richard T. Ely in American Life*, Lexington, KY: University of Kentucky Press.

Reder, M. 1982. "Chicago Economics: Permanence and Change," 20 *Journal of Economic Literature* 1–38.

Reynolds, Lloyd. 1954. *Labor Economics and Labor Relations*, 2nd ed. Englewood Cliffs, NJ: Prentice Hall.

Rizvi, S. Abu Turab. 2007. "Postwar Neoclassical Microeconomics," in W. Samuels, J. Biddle, and J. Davis, eds., *A Companion to the History of Economic Thought*. Oxford: Blackwell, pp. 377–94.

Rodrik, Dani. 2007. "Why Economists Disagree," web blog at http://rodrik.typepad.com/dani_rodriks_web log/economists_blindspots/.

Roemer, John. 1982. *A General Theory of Exploitation and Class*. Cambridge, MA: Harvard University Press.

Rubery, Jill, and Damian Grimshaw 1998. "Integrating the Internal and External Labor Markets," 22 *Cambridge Journal of Economics* 199–220.

Rutherford, Malcolm. 2011. *The Institutionalist Movement in American Economics, 1918–1947*. New York: Cambridge University Press.

Samuels, Warren, and A. Allan Schmid. 1981. *Law and Economics: An Institutional Perspective*. Boston, MA: Kluwer-Nijhoff.

Samuels, Warren, Steven Medema, and A. Allan Schmid. 1997. *The Economy as a Process of Valuation*. Cheltenham, UK and Lyme, NH, USA: Edward Elgar.

Schmid, A. Allan. 2004. *Conflict and Cooperation: Behavioral and Institutional Economics*, Malden, MA: Blackwell.

Schwab, Stewart. 1997. "The Law and Economics Approach to Workplace Regulation," in Bruce Kaufman, ed., *Government Regulation of the Employment Relationship*. Madison, WI: IRRA, pp. 91–124.

Segal, Martin. 1986. "Post-Institutionalism in Labor Economics: The Forties and Fifties Revisited," 39 *Industrial and Labor Relations Review* 388–403.

Sen, Amartya. 1999. *Commodities and Capabilities*. New York: Oxford University Press.

Shapiro, Carl, and Joseph Stiglitz. 1984. "Equilibrium Unemployment as a Worker Discipline Device," 74 *American Economic Review* 433–44.

Sharif, Mohammed. 2000. "Inverted 'S' – The Complete Neoclassical Labor Supply Function," 139 *International Labor Review* 379–408.

Shulman, Beth. 2003. *The Betrayal of Work: How Low-Wage Jobs Fail Thirty Million Americans and their Families*. New York: New Press.

Shultz, George, and John Coleman. 1961. *Labor Problems: Cases and Readings*, 2nd ed. New York: McGraw-Hill.

Simon, Herbert. 1951. "A Formal Theory of the Employment Relationship," 19 *Econometrica* 293–305.

Slichter, Sumner. 1931. *Modern Economic Society*, 2nd ed. New York: Holt.

Solow, Robert. 1990. *The Labor Market as a Social Institution*. New York: Blackwell.

Stigler, George. 1966. *The Theory of Price*, 3rd ed. New York: Macmillan.

Stigler, George. 1982. *The Economist as Preacher and Other Essays*. Chicago, IL: University of Chicago Press.

Stiglitz, Joseph. 2010. *Freefall: America, Free Markets and the Sinking of the World Economy*. New York: Norton.

Sunstein, Cass. 2004. *The Second Bill of Rights*. New York: Basic Books.

Taylor, James. 1977. "Exploitation through Contrived Dependence," 11 *Journal of Economic Issues* 51–9.

Thompson, Paul. 2003. "Disconnected Capitalism: Or Why Employers Can't Keep their Side of the Bargain," 17 *Work, Employment and Society* 359–78.

Thompson, Paul, and Christy Newsome. 2004. "Labor Process Theory, Work, and the Employment Relationship," in Bruce Kaufman, ed., *Theoretical Perspectives on Work and the Employment Relationship*. Champaign-Urbana, IL: Labor and Employment Relations Association, pp. 133–62.

Thurow, Lester. 1983. *Dangerous Currents: The State of Economics*. New York: Random House.

Varian, Hal. 2010. *Intermediate Microeconomics: A Modern Approach*, 8th ed. New York: Norton.

Wachter, Michael. 2004. "Theories of the Employment Relationship: Choosing between Norms and Contracts," in Bruce Kaufman, ed., *Theoretical Perspectives on Work and the Employment Relationship*. Champaign-Urbana, IL: Labor and Employment Relations Association, pp. 163–94.

Wachter, Michael, and Randall Wright. 1990. "The Economics of Internal Labor Markets," 29 *Industrial Relations* 240–62.

Walras, Leon. 1900/1954. *Elements of Pure Economics*. Translated by William Jaffé. Homewood, IL: Irwin.

Watkins, Gordon. 1922. *An Introduction to the Study of Labor Problems*. New York: Thomas Crowell.

Webb, Sidney. 1912. "The Economic Theory of a Legal Minimum Wage," 20 *Journal of Political Economy* 973–98.

Webb, Sidney, and Beatrice Webb. 1897. *Industrial Democracy*. London: Longmans, Green.

Whalen, Charles. 2008. "John R, Commons and John Maynard Keynes on Economic History and Policy: The 1920s and Today," 42 *Journal of Economic Issues* 225–42.

Williamson, Oliver. 1985. *The Economic Institutions of Capitalism*. New York: Free Press.

PART II

UNIONS AND COLLECTIVE BARGAINING

4.   Unions, dynamism, and economic performance
Barry T. Hirsch

I.   INTRODUCTION

The relationship between unions and economic performance is necessarily central to understanding changes in union membership, the role of unions in the workplace, and public policy. It is central first because union impacts on performance enter into the policy calculus of costs and benefits associated with policies that enhance or constrain union organizing and collective bargaining coverage. Second, whatever the publicly desired level and role for unions in the workplace, the realized level of coverage is heavily influenced by how unionized businesses perform in an increasingly competitive and dynamic global economy.

Maintaining a large union workforce in the US requires financially healthy unionized employers. Competitive pressures limit the size of the union sector if higher union compensation is not fully offset by higher productivity. Compared to nonunion workplace governance, where there is substantial managerial discretion constrained by market forces and law, union governance is more formal, deliberate, and often sluggish. Union companies, therefore, often fare poorly in highly dynamic and competitive economic settings. Union density, defined as the percentage of employees who are union members, has declined sharply in the US private sector, from just over a third in the mid-1950s to only 6.9 percent in 2010. Among a host of reasons for declining private sector union density, the most fundamental explanation appears to be an increasingly dynamic US economy coupled with the relatively poorer economic performance among union than nonunion establishments and firms.

Collective bargaining in the public sector operates under different labor laws and in different economic and political settings than does private sector collective bargaining. The proportion of public sector workers who are union members in 2010 is 36.2 percent as compared to the 6.9 percent seen among private sector workers. Union density for public workers has remained steady for some 30-plus years as private sector density has declined. Just over half of all US union members are now government employees. The success of public relative to private sector unionism lends support to the thesis that dynamism and competitive pressures serve as the principal limiting force on collective bargaining. Although the public sector is not immune to financial pressures, as the last several years have shown, competition and dynamism play far larger roles in the private sector, while long-term employment and constituent ("customer") relationships are more prevalent in the public sector.

This chapter explores the relationship between economic performance and unionism in the US, focusing first on what we do and do not know based on empirical research. Evidence on the relationship of unions with wages and benefits, productivity, profitability, investment, debt, employment growth, and business failures are all relevant in assessing the future of unions and public policy with respect to unions. A coherent story

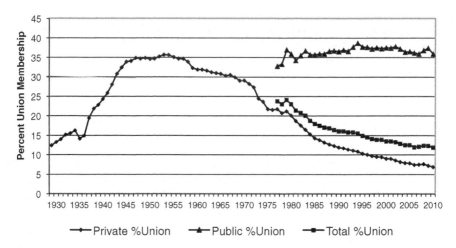

Figure 4.1   *US private sector union density, 1929–2010: total and public sector union density, 1977–2010*

emerges from the empirical literature, albeit one that relies heavily on data that are neither as current nor as comprehensive as one would like. The chapter's principal thesis is that union decline has been tied to competitive forces and economic dynamism. The implications of these findings are discussed briefly in a final section.

II.   US UNION MEMBERSHIP AND DENSITY: A TALE OF TWO SECTORS[1]

Without too much overstatement, the 20th century can be characterized as having experienced the rise and fall of private sector unionization. The rise was sudden, the result of major economic, social, and political upheaval followed by public policy support for union organizing. The 1935 passage and subsequent Court approval and federal implementation of the National Labor Relations Act (NLRA) provided the legal and administrative framework that facilitated a rapid transition to an industrial US economy in which union governance became the norm. Major industries – coal, steel, automotive – became unionized over a brief period, a transition encouraged by New Deal corporatist policies during the 1930s and reinforced by the industrial buildup for World War II in the 1940s.[2] Following World War II, inflation and widespread strikes shifted majority opinion toward support for greater limits on union power. The Taft–Hartley Act in 1947 outlawed union practices like closed shops and secondary boycotts, allowed states to pass "right-to-work" laws, and gave the federal government the power to block or end strikes that might have national safety or health implications.

Figure 4.1 shows US private sector union density from 1929 through 2010. The proportion of private sector workers who were union members rose from about 12 percent in 1929 to 24 percent by 1940 and to 35 percent by 1947. Union density was largely flat through the mid-1950s, with a peak at 36 percent in 1953 and 1954. Private sector union

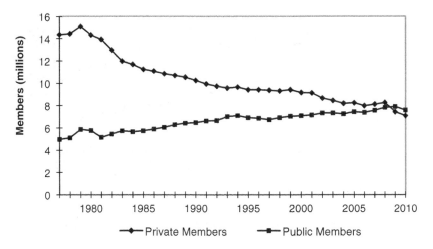

Figure 4.2   Private and public union membership, 1977–2010

density edged slightly downward during the late 1950s and 1960s, and then began its long-term decline in the 1970s. The decline has been gradual, but unrelenting. Private sector union density was 24.5 percent in 1973, 16.5 percent in 1983, 11.1 percent by 1993, and stood at 6.9 percent in 2010. The number of private sector union members was 15 million in 1973, roughly maintained through the end of that decade, but subsequently fell to just over 7 million in 2010. As private union membership fell by nearly half, nonunion wage and salary employment in the private sector more than doubled from 47 million in 1973 to 103 million in 2010 (down from 108 million in 2008).

At the same time that private sector unionism was in decline, public sector unionism increased rapidly in the 1960s and 1970s following enactment of enabling public sector labor laws within (most) states and for federal employees. Figure 4.1 shows public sector union density beginning in 1977 (the first year that permits a time-consistent definition of membership). Although the size of the public sector has grown considerably since the 1970s, density has remained relatively constant, rising from 32.8 percent in 1977 to 36.7 percent in 1983 to a current level of 36.2 percent in 2010. Union density for all wage and salary workers (the weighted average of the private and public figures), also shown in Figure 4.1 for years since 1977, has declined from 23.8 percent in 1977 to 11.9 percent in 2010.

The growth of membership in the public sector combined with decline in the private sector has resulted in a union movement increasingly populated by public sector workers. Private and public membership since 1977 is shown in Figure 4.2. Whereas in 1977 only a quarter (25.8 percent) of US union members were public employees, public member-ship overtook private membership during 2009. Data for 2010 show that 52 percent of members are government employees, with 7.6 million public sector versus 7.1 million private sector union members.

As shown in Hirsch (2008), *all* the private sector decline in private sector union mem-bership since the 1970s can be accounted for by three large sectors of the economy – manufacturing, construction, and transportation, communications and utilities. (Union

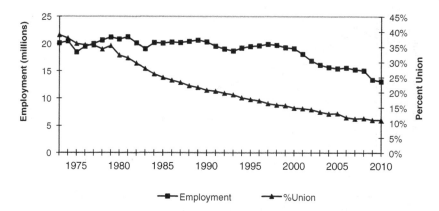

Figure 4.3a   Employment and union density in private manufacturing, 1973–2010

membership in the very large remainder of the private sector economy remained flat at roughly 3.5 million as employment grew enormously.) Figures 4.3a–4.3c show total private sector employment and union density in these three traditionally unionized sectors. In manufacturing (Figure 4.3a), total employment was relatively constant at about 20 million from 1973 through the late 1990s, but since then has fallen sharply to about 13 million in 2010. Much of the decline has been in union employment, from 7.8 million in 1973 to 1.4 million members in 2010. Union density in manufacturing fell from 38.9 percent in 1973 to 10.7 percent in 2010 as the dominant norm in the industrial sector shifted from union to nonunion governance.

Among the sectors that have historically been highly unionized, only manufacturing shows a long-run decline in employment. In the other heavily unionized industries, there was rapid growth in total employment, as seen in Figures 4.3b and 4.3c for the private transportation, communications, and utility (TCU) sectors and construction. In con-struction (Figure 4.3b) , wage and salary employment rose from 4.1 million to a high of 8.6 million in 2007 before falling sharply to 6.1 million in 2010. As union density declined in construction, membership stayed roughly flat at between 1.0–1.2 million from 1983 through 2008, falling to 0.8 million in 2010. Union density fell from 39.5 to 13.1 percent between 1973 and 2010. TCU total employment (Figure 4.3c) also rose sharply, from 4.4 to 7.9 million between 1973 and 2010 (following an 8.7 million 2007 peak). Union density declined from 51.4 to 17.6 percent, with membership falling from 2.3 to 1.4 million.

Despite the sharp decline in private sector density, the union wage advantage relative to similar nonunion workers has remained fairly stable over time, with a modest decline in recent years (shown in Figure 4.4). Union pay is determined by a collective bargaining process shaped by the preferences of union members and the bargaining power of the parties, the latter influenced by product and labor market conditions. Union leaders are elected and union contracts must be approved by a majority of rank-and-file members. Basic models of union behavior treat the decisions of union leaders as responsive to the preferences of the median voter or member (see Farber (1986) for a comprehensive discussion). Members face a tradeoff between wages and employment (although settle-ments need not strictly lie on the labor demand curve), with the tradeoff influenced by

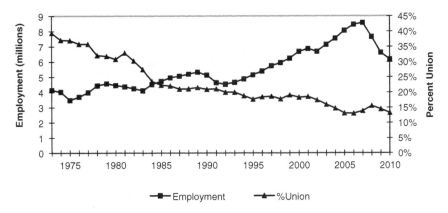

Figure 4.3b   Employment and union density in private construction, 1973–2010

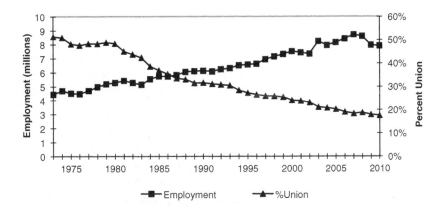

Figure 4.3c   Employment and union density in private transportation, communications, and utilities, 1973–2010

the ability of firms and customers to substitute between union and nonunion workers, establishments, and goods. Incumbent workers may place low weight on the greater employment opportunities that could exist at a lower wage, while median (often older) members may feel insulated from layoffs based on seniority, except when establishment closings or bankruptcies are a threat.

In contrast to the highly limited information available on company unionization and economic performance, worker data on union and nonunion wages (but not benefits) are readily available. These data permit estimation of union wage premiums – the percentage difference in the wages of similarly skilled union and nonunion workers in similar jobs. Changes in union wage gaps (premiums) over time provide a rough but useful measure of changes in relative labor costs of union firms. Although the focus here is wages, it is total compensation (wages plus benefits) that is the more relevant measure.

Hirsch and Macpherson (2011, table 2) provide regression estimates of union–nonunion wage premiums (gaps) for the years 1973–2010 from the Current Population

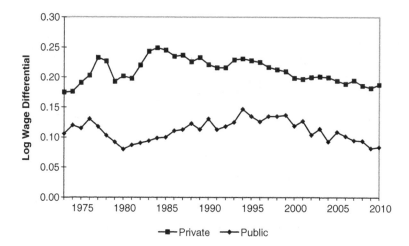

Figure 4.4   Private and public sector union wage premiums, 1973–2010

Survey (CPS) using a time-consistent specification. Estimates of the union gaps are obtained from annual wage equations, where the natural log of the wage is the dependent variable, while union status and controls for worker/job/location characteristics are included as independent variables.[3] The regression coefficient on union status provides a measure of the union wage premium, as shown in Figure 4.4 for both private and public sector workers. Because wages are measured in natural logs, the coefficient on union status can be interpreted as a proportional or percentage difference.[4]

Have private sector union wage premiums declined over time as density, union organizing strength, and bargaining power have diminished?[5] Yes – but by surprisingly little and only following the run-up in the union wage premium and sharp drop in union employment during the early 1980s (Linneman et al., 1990). Since the estimated peak premium of 0.249 (about 25 percent) in 1984, there has been a modest downward trend to an estimated 2010 union wage gap of 0.188. Although it is generally argued that union wage premiums are countercyclical due to the use of multiyear contracts (Blanchflower and Bryson, 2003), there is only weak evidence of this in these estimates. The most important point to bring away from Figure 4.4 is that union wage premiums in the private sector remain high, on the order of 20 percent, well above the level found in most developed economies (Blanchflower and Bryson (2003) and included references).[6] As discussed below, the typical union workplace does not generate sufficiently higher productivity to offset the costs of higher compensation; as such, union premiums reinforce the array of forces leading to private sector unionism's long-run decline.

Evidence on union–nonunion differences in benefits is limited, but that available points clearly to a union benefits premium larger than the wage premium (Freeman and Medoff, 1984; Budd, 2007). In *What Do Unions Do?* Freeman and Medoff provide estimates for 1974–7 indicating a 20 percent union wage premium, a larger benefits premium (68 percent absent control for wages and 30 percent controlling for wages), yielding a 25 percent union compensation premium (Freeman and Medoff, 1984, p. 64). Looking at 2010 data from the Employer Costs for Employee Compensation (ECEC) program, benefits as a percentage of total compensation among private sector workers in goods-producing industries is 41.4 percent for union and 30.7 percent for nonunion workers. Equivalent figures in service-providing industries are 37.4 and 27.2 percent for union and nonunion workers, respectively (US Department of Labor, 2011, table 13, p. 22).[7]

The private sector is our principal interest, but estimates of union–nonunion wage gaps among public sector workers (conditioned on controls) warrant brief mention. Consistent with prior studies, Hirsch and Macpherson (2011) find that union wage effects in the public sector are considerably smaller than in the private sector – more of the order of 10 than 20 percent. As seen in Figure 4.4, their estimates rise to about 13–14 percent in the mid-to-late 1990s, but subsequently drop to under 10 percent. These aggregate estimates represent some sort of weighted average across local, state, and federal employees, as well as across a diverse set of occupations (teachers, police, firefighters, administrators, etc.). Freeman (1986) suggests that public sector unions, while having more limited wage effects than their private counterparts, may be effective in increasing employment for their members via the political process.

This chapter argues that a mismatch between a relatively rigid and costly system of union governance and a highly competitive and dynamic economy has been a fundamental reason for the long-term decline of private sector unionism.[8] Compensation premiums not fully offset by productivity increases are a key element of this process. Increasing economic dynamism, say from rapid technological change or shifting trade patterns, reinforces cost disadvantages for union companies that respond slowly to changes in the economic environment. Of course, there are other important reasons for private sector union decline. Complementary to the competitive thesis are structural and legal explanations. I define "structural" as the change in aggregate union density resulting from shifts over time in the types of jobs (industry and occupation) and their geographic location. The legal explanation emphasizes the role of labor (and employment) law, its interpretation and enforcement, and the conduct of union elections. The legal explanation can be broadened to include the role of union "sentiment" among workers, management, and the public. Worker sentiment toward unions is influenced by past and present unionization in one's community and by workplace protections offered workers absent unionization (e.g., antidiscrimination law). The competitive, structural, and legal explanations are not independent. For example, neither worker nor management sentiment regarding unions is unrelated to the economic performance of union and nonunion companies. I return briefly to these issues in the final section of the chapter.

III.   UNIONS AND ECONOMIC PERFORMANCE: THEORY

Two theoretical frameworks, a standard microeconomic approach and Freeman and Medoff's (1984) collective voice/institutional response (CV/IR) approach, have been widely used to organize discussion of union effects on wages, employment, and economic performance. Brief discussion is provided below, first of the economic approach and then of CV/IR.

The standard microeconomic approach treats the labor demand curve as the "labor constraint" or "tradeoff curve" between wages and employment facing labor unions within firms. A firm labor demand curve shows the profit-maximizing employment level at each wage rate. All else the same, unions and their members fare better the higher rather than the lower the level of demand for union labor (i.e., outward rather than inward shifts of the demand curve) and the less elastic (i.e., less wage sensitive) is demand for union labor.[9]

Although the standard model and its underlying assumptions are simplistic and often violated, the "labor constraint" framework is helpful in understanding union behavior and outcomes. For example, policies that shift labor demand outward through an increase in industry-wide product demand are beneficial to both firms and their unions, increasing firms' output and price and at the same time permitting both wage and employment increases for workers. Stated alternatively, there is a commonality of interest by shareholders and labor in the financial health of the firm and in those policies perceived as helping the firm or industry. Such examples might include mutual industry and union support for an industry-specific policy, be it trade protection, government subsidy or favorable tax treatment (e.g., rebates for new car purchases were supported by the UAW and their employers).

The more elastic the demand for union labor, the larger the employment (membership) loss resulting from a wage increase. Marshall's laws of derived demand show that long-run labor demand is more elastic (more wage sensitive) (a) the more elastic or price sensitive is product demand, implying difficulty in passing wage increases through to consumers in the form of higher prices; and (b) the easier is substitution of capital for labor or nonunion for union labor. The first "law" helps explain union support for or opposition to trade liberalization (union policies vary depending on whether union members are employed in predominantly export or import industries), and vehement opposition in the 1970s among affected unions to removing airline and trucking regulations restricting entry and price competition. The second "law" helps explain union resistance to labor-saving technologies and unions' strong interest in implicit or explicit limits to on-site use of nonunion workers or outsourcing (i.e., shifting production to nonunion suppliers in the US or abroad).[10]

The standard framework offers a normative basis to evaluate the effects of unionism, using economic efficiency as the outcome criterion. By this criterion, unions create a distortion (i.e., a welfare loss) from the efficient competitive outcome, causing the price of labor to rise above opportunity costs and leading to too little employment and output in the union sector, and thus too much elsewhere. The ability of unions to raise wages above opportunity cost is made possible by the representation and bargaining rights granted to unions in US labor law. The standard micro theory approach to unions also addresses the possibility of monopsony or oligopsony (i.e., a single or few employers, with minimal worker mobility across markets). In the monopsony model, a union wage increase over a particular range can increase efficiency by raising both wages and employment toward competitive levels.[11] The micro distortion approach to evaluating unions and collective bargaining is far too narrow, however, basically making unionism equivalent to an exogenous wage increase. Taken alone, such an approach fails to account for the many other ways in which unions and collective bargaining affect economic performance, positively and negatively, which is the subject of this chapter. The standard framework also ignores the difficulty in measuring the value to workers and society resulting from the option for workers to choose workplace democracy and formalized governance.

Since the 1984 publication of Freeman and Medoff's *What Do Unions Do?*, their 'two faces of unions' framework has been used to evaluate unions. The approach provides a broad umbrella under which scholars can describe union effects on the workplace, cataloguing the effects as either monopoly effects based on standard micro theory summarized above or (often positive) collective voice/institutional response (CV/IR) effects. The monopoly face emphasizes the role of bargaining power, recognizing that the ability of unions to extract monopoly gains for its members is determined by the degree of competition and constraints on substitution facing both the employer and union. This face includes not only the distortionary effects on relative factor prices and factor usage resulting from union wage premiums. Unions may cause losses in output through strikes and decrease productivity in some workplaces through contractual work rules, reduced worker incentives, and limited managerial discretion. The monopoly face of unionism has expanded to include other union effects that reduce efficiency or total value (the "size of the pie") for firm stakeholders (workers and owners) and consumers. Theoretical and empirical literature, discussed subsequently, has emphasized unions' role in taxing returns on tangible and intangible capital and the resulting effects on profitability, investment, and growth (Hirsch 2007b).

The "collective voice/institutional response" (CV/IR) face of unions described by Freeman and Medoff focuses on value-enhancing aspects of unions, emphasizing the potential role unions can play in the operation of internal labor markets. Legally protected unions may make it possible for workers to express their preferences and exercise workplace collective voice. Collective bargaining can be more effective than individual bargaining or regulation in overcoming free-rider problems and underproduction of public goods in the workplace. As the workers' agent, unions may facilitate the exercise of the workers' rights to free speech, acquire information, monitor employer behavior, and formalize the workplace governance structure (Weil, 2005). Unions are more likely to represent average or inframarginal workers, whereas nonunion employers are most responsive to their more mobile employees and potential hires. The exercise of effective voice potentially can increase workplace productivity, an outcome depending not only on voice but also on a constructive "institutional response" and a cooperative labor relations environment. Freeman and Medoff emphasize that a supportive management response to union voice is a necessary condition for positive union outcomes. Where management is inherently hostile to union governance, regardless of union behavior, one cannot expect unions and CV/IR to produce positive performance outcomes.

Freeman and Medoff broadened not only the theoretical lens through which economists viewed unions, but also the scope of empirical evidence. Rather than focus primarily on union wage effects and strike behavior, the staples of older literature, empirical labor economists (and others) extended the literature to include union effects on wage inequality, benefits, productivity and productivity growth, profitability, investment, and turnover, among other things (for a comprehensive retrospective of the CV/IR framework, see the papers in Bennett and Kaufman (2007)). Most of the empirical evidence summarized in Freeman and Medoff has held up rather well, with two important exceptions (see Freeman, 2007; Hirsch, 2007b). Freeman and Medoff were overly optimistic regarding the rather mixed evidence on unions and productivity, relying heavily on a study by Brown and Medoff (1978) that suggested large positive effects across US manufacturing. As discussed below, subsequent evidence indicates that union-productivity effects in the US are not only variable, but on average close to zero.[12] The second exception regards unions and investment, an important measure of performance about which Freeman and Medoff had little evidence. They did not anticipate subsequent literature finding unions associated with significantly lower investment in long-lived physical and innovative (R&D) capital.

In what follows, I borrow from both the monopoly and CV/IR approaches, emphasizing the importance of union governance and how it operates in a competitive and dynamic economic environment. The role of competition in sustainability is well understood. For union companies operating in competitive, largely nonunion, industries, cost increases cannot be passed forward to consumers through higher prices. Substantial union wage premiums in such settings, absent productivity improvements that largely offset labor cost increases, should lead establishments to contract over time.[13] Unions have greater ability to acquire and maintain wage gains in less competitive economic settings, but there are fewer and fewer such settings in an increasingly competitive global economy. Also emphasized is a point not widely expressed in the union performance literature: highly formalized, deliberate union governance and reduced managerial discretion can prove particularly disadvantageous the more dynamic the economic environment.[14]

IV.   UNIONS AND PERFORMANCE: MEASUREMENT AND INTERPRETATION

Because theory provides reasons why unionization can improve and harm economic performance, both the qualitative and quantitative effects of unions are largely an empirical question. Before turning to issues of measurement and evidence in this section, it is worth emphasizing three related points. First, union effects on performance are typically measured by union–nonunion differences in outcomes across firms or sectors within an economy. Such differentials, however, do not measure union effects on aggregate or economy-wide performance because resources move across sectors. For example, evidence summarized below establishes that unionized companies have had lower profits and growth than similar nonunion companies. The relatively poorer performance of union businesses leads to a shift of production and employment out of union and into nonunion sectors. Overall union effects on economy-wide performance are likely to be modest.

A second point is that what are referred to as "union effects" on performance are the results of the interactions between management and unions (i.e., executives, managers, union leaders, rank and file) within the collective bargaining process as compared to some nonunion counterfactual. Measured union–nonunion differences in performance reflect these joint actions and not just the actions or behavior by unions. Were management (union) attitudes and actions with respect to unions (management) different, "union effects" on performance would no doubt differ. Value-added unionism and a stronger CV/IR face would be more likely if the collective bargaining process were less adversarial, were management less ideologically hostile to unions, and were unions (and rank and file workers) more far sighted and less focused on capturing rents. The third point follows naturally. The effects of unions on productivity and other aspects of performance will vary substantially across companies, industries, time, and countries given that both the collective voice and monopoly activities of unions depend crucially on the labor relations and economic environments.

As in other areas of study, the empirical literature on union performance effects in the US is imperfect. The most serious impediment to progress in this field is the almost total absence of current, publicly available data on collective bargaining coverage at the establishment and firm level. Data are more readily available for other developed countries, but results from other countries cannot be readily generalized given the considerable variability in labor institutions across countries. The US has publicly available data on individual worker union membership and coverage from CPS household surveys that can provide union density estimates for industries, occupations, and localities (Hirsch and Macpherson, 2003; the www.unionstats.com database), but not measures of establishment or firm-level union coverage. Labor unions provide reports of their membership and finances to the Department of Labor, but membership cannot fully be allocated across specific establishments and companies based on these reports.[15] The National Labor Relations Board (NLRB) reports on union elections and outcomes, but these data have several limitations.[16] The empirical literature on unions and performance has therefore relied on unique data sets containing measures of unionism; for example, coverage among establishments in a single industry or coverage among a nationwide sample of companies responding to a researcher's survey questionnaire. And much of the evidence for the US, including that in recently published studies, is based on older data on unions and performance, most often from the 1970s and 1980s. Absent readily available data on past and current union coverage among US establishments and firms, it has been difficult to provide broad-based descriptive evidence on union–nonunion differences in performance, let alone reliably estimate causal effects.

Although never fully achievable, the goal of empirical studies (and theory) is to make possible reliable inferences about the causal effects of unionization on economic performance throughout the economy. In principle, we would like to observe something equivalent to a laboratory experiment in which some establishments or firms were randomly "treated" or assigned collective bargaining coverage while others were not. We could then compare subsequent performance outcomes of the "treated" union businesses with the non-treated "control" group of nonunion businesses. Of course, unionization is not randomly determined. Today's union coverage is the result of past and present preferences, decisions, and interactions among workers, unions, and management, all occurring within environments heavily influenced by economic, legal, political, and cultural forces.[17] Empirical studies attempt to condition on measurable differences across businesses when comparing union and nonunion outcomes. But even when one can control for a large number of covariates, estimation issues remain.

A large number of existing studies utilize cross-sectional data at a single or multiple points in time, where differences in outcomes (productivity, profits, etc.) across establishments, firms or industries are associated with different levels of union coverage. Regression analysis is then used to provide estimates of union relative to nonunion differences in performance, conditioned on other measurable covariates. Such results are highly informative, but caution must be used before inferring that estimated differentials provide good measures of causal union effects. Among the key issues here are whether there is omitted variable bias, union endogeneity, measurement error, and external validity.

As applied to unions and performance, omitted variable bias results when one is unable to control for an important performance determinant correlated with union density. For example, if older plants have lower productivity and union density is higher in older plants, inability to control for plant age (or its correlates) in a production function would bias downward estimates of the union impact on productivity. A second concern is that union status may be determined endogenously rather than independently of the outcome measure. For example, unions are most likely to organize, obtain contracts, and sustain employment in firms (or industries) with higher potential profitability. Standard estimates of union effects on profitability would thus be biased upward, understating the negative impact of unions on profits. It has proven difficult to account for union endogeneity in the union literature. It is less clear whether or not this produces any substantial bias in estimates of union effects.

A third concern is external validity. Even when a study is internally valid, it need not follow that its results are externally valid; that is, that its results can be generalized beyond the particular setting from which the data are drawn. Some of the more reliable estimates of union effects on productivity are based on specific industries (e.g., cement, sawmills) where output is homogeneous and measured in physical units rather than by value added. Yet it is not clear whether results for, say, the western sawmill industry (Mitchell and Stone, 1992) can be generalized to the economy as a whole, particularly given that we expect union effects to differ across time, establishment, and industry.

In short, the unions and performance literature is limited by the paucity of US data sets containing data on establishment and firm-level union coverage and performance outcomes. Among the studies that do exist, most cannot be strictly interpreted as measuring the causal effects of union coverage. But it does not follow that the empirical literature is uninformative. Depending on the question and data analysis at hand, it is sometimes possible to make reasoned inferences about the direction and size of bias in the estimates. Moreover, the studies can be interpreted as measuring partial correlations; that is, the correlation between union coverage and performance outcomes holding constant other measured covariates. Such "descriptive" evidence is informative and relevant. For example, evidence that unionized companies have, on average, substantively higher wages, at most modestly higher productivity, and lower profitability, can help explain why private sector unionism has declined in an increasingly competitive economy, even if these partial correlations are biased measures of causal union effects. Biased estimates may be less helpful for policy evaluation. If we are considering labor law policies that either enhance or restrict union organizing, it would be preferable to know the causal effects of unions on economic performance.

V.   UNIONS AND PERFORMANCE: EVIDENCE

Rather than provide an encyclopedic survey of the empirical literature, this section will interpret what I believe are some of the more important or representative studies and assess what we can and cannot say about unions and performance. Readers can refer to existing surveys for a comprehensive set of references.[18] The focus is on US studies, with some attention given to studies from Canada where evidence on unions and performance aligns well with that from the US. Union data at the enterprise level are less readily available in the US than in several other countries, but it is difficult to generalize results across countries given that union effects can vary with the economic and institutional environments.

A.   Productivity and Productivity Growth

The unions and performance literature has rightly emphasized the importance of how unionism affects productivity. If collective bargaining in the workplace were to systematically increase productivity along with worker compensation, but not retard investment and growth, a much stronger argument could be made for policies that encourage union organizing.

Most studies have estimated some variant of a modified Cobb-Douglas production function developed by Brown and Medoff (1978),

$$Q=AK^{\alpha} (Ln+cLu)^{1-\alpha} \tag{1}$$

where Q is output; K is capital, Lu and Ln are union and nonunion labor; A is a constant of proportionality; and α and $(1-\alpha)$ are the output elasticities with respect to capital and labor. The parameter c reflects productivity differences between union and nonunion labor. If $c > 1$, union labor is more productive, in line with the collective-voice model; if $c < 1$, union labor is less productive, in line with conventional arguments concerning the deleterious impact of such things as union work rules and constraints on merit-based wage dispersion. Manipulation of equation (1) yields the estimating equation

$$\ln(Q/L) \approx \ln A + \alpha \ln(K/L) + (1-\alpha)(c-1)P, \tag{2}$$

where P represents proportion unionized (Lu/L) in a firm or industry or (in some studies) the presence or absence of a union at the plant or firm level. Equation (2) assumes constant returns to scale, an assumption relaxed by adding $\ln L$ as a control variable. The coefficient on P measures the logarithmic productivity differential of unionized establishments. If it were assumed that the union effect on productivity solely reflects the differential efficiency of labor inputs, the effect of union labor on productivity would be calculated by dividing the coefficient on P by $(1-\alpha)$.

The conclusion that unions substantially raise productivity rests primarily on Brown and Medoff's results using aggregate two-digit manufacturing industry data cross-classified by state groups for 1972. Brown and Medoff's preferred coefficient estimates on union density are from 0.22 to 0.24 (approximately 22–24 percent), implying values (obtained by dividing the union coefficient by $1-\alpha$) for $c-1$ of from 0.30 to 0.31. Such large union-productivity effects, if correct, would more than offset union wage effects. Using alternative assumptions about relative union to nonunion capital usage (i.e., allowing for higher rather than equivalent capital/labor ratios within industry-by-state groups), Brown and Medoff obtain sharply lower estimates of union-productivity effects.

The production function approach has limitations, many of which are identified by Brown and Medoff. In particular, the use of value added as an output measure confounds price and quantity effects, since part of the measured union-productivity differential may result from higher prices in the unionized sector, particularly in those markets sheltered from nonunion and foreign competition. Estimated effects of unions on productivity tend to be lower following price adjustments, possible in industry-specific studies such as construction (Allen, 1986) and western sawmills (Mitchell and Stone, 1992). Use of value added is less a concern in firm- or business-level analyses that measure firms' union status plus industry union density or other industry controls (Clark, 1984; Hirsch, 1991a). The Brown-Medoff results are also inconsistent with other pieces of evidence. As argued by Addison and Hirsch (1989), parameter estimates from Brown and Medoff would imply an increase in profits resulting from unionism, contrary to widespread evidence of lower firm and industry profitability, on average, associated with union coverage.

Subsequent studies using the Brown-Medoff approach have been as likely to find negative as positive union effects on productivity. Two studies with manufacturing-wide data and firm- or business-level measures of union coverage are Clark (1984) and Hirsch (1991a). Clark uses data for 902 manufacturing lines of business from 1970 to 1980 to estimate value-added production functions, among other things. He obtains marginally significant coefficients on the union variable between -0.02 and -0.03. The Clark study has the advantage of a large sample size over multiple years, business-specific information on union coverage, and a detailed set of control variables. A similar study by Hirsch (1991a), examines over 600 publicly-traded manufacturing firms during 1968–80, with 1977 (retrospective) firm-level union coverage data collected by the author. A strong negative relationship between union coverage and productivity is found when including only firm-level controls, but the union effect drops sharply with the inclusion of detailed industry controls, a result highly comparable to that in Clark. Hirsch interprets his results as providing no evidence for a positive economy-wide productivity effect and weak evidence for a negative effect. Regrettably, recent US firm- or business-level data with measures of union coverage similar to those used by Clark and Hirsch have not been readily available.

Both Clark (1984) and Hirsch (1991a) find considerable variability in union-productivity effects across manufacturing industries.[19] These results support the expectation that union effects on productivity vary with the labor relations environment. Several studies provide evidence showing that productivity or quality suffers as a result of strikes and labor unrest. Kleiner et al. (2002) conclude that negative productivity effects from strikes and slowdowns at a commercial airline manufacturer are temporary. Krueger and Mas (2004) find that tire defect rates were particularly high at a Bridgestone/Firestone plant during periods of labor unrest. Using auction data, Mas (2008) finds that construction equipment produced by Caterpillar at its US plants during periods of labor unrest was more likely to be subsequently resold and sold at a deeper discount.

A largely distinct literature examines how productivity is related to human resource management (HRM) practices (e.g., incentive pay, intensive screening of hires, team-work, flexible job assignments, skills training, etc.) and workplace culture within establishments. This literature offers some insight into the relationship between union governance and productivity. Ichniowski et al. (1997) examine how productivity differs with respect to individual HRM practices and bundles of practices across steel-finishing line plants. Although union effects on productivity were not their principal interest, they did have a measure of union coverage. They found that union plants or lines of production were somewhat less productive overall than were nonunion lines, but that this result was due to the HRM practices (largely not) adopted in union plants. Among those steel-finishing lines that adopted the most productive bundles of HRM practices, union lines were more productive than were nonunion lines. These most productive bundles of workplace practices, however, were least likely to be adopted in union plants.

Black and Lynch (2001) provide a similar finding. They estimate production functions for a sample of US manufacturing plants over the period 1987–93, focusing not on union effects but on the effects of workplace practices, information technology, and management procedures. Absent interaction terms, Black and Lynch find slightly lower productivity in unionized plants following inclusion of detailed controls, a result equivalent to that found throughout manufacturing by Clark and Hirsch, and by Ichniowski et al. for steel production lines. Black and Lynch conclude that the negative union result is driven by low productivity among unionized plants using traditional management systems. Union plants that adopted human resource practices involving joint decision-making (i.e., total quality management or TQM) and incentive-based compensation (i.e., profit sharing for nonmanagerial employees) were found to be more productive than their nonunion counterparts, which in turn had higher productivity than union plants using traditional labor-management relations. But the Black-Lynch sample contains few union plants adopting the most productive HRM systems.

Economy-wide, union plants are among those least likely to adopt modern human resource practices and incentive-based compensation (Verma, 2007). This stylized fact is consistent with the strong rise in such HRM practices during a period of declining unionism and by relatively compressed pay in union as compared to nonunion companies.[20]

In summary, the conclusion of this section is that average union-productivity effects are close to zero. This conclusion is reinforced in other surveys. The authors of a meta-analysis of the unions-productivity literature conclude that the average effect in the US is very small but positive, while negative in the UK (Doucouliagos and Laroche, 2003). Interestingly, a survey of labor economists at leading universities asking for an assessment of the union effect on productivity produced a median response of zero and mean of 3.1 percent (Fuchs et al., 1998).[21]

No less important than the effect of unions on productivity levels is the dynamic effect of unions on productivity growth. Productivity growth is typically measured as a residual; that is, by the growth in output that cannot be accounted for by changes in factor inputs (e.g., labor and stocks of tangible and intangible capital). Some studies (Hirsch, 1991a) measure not only the "direct" effect of unions on growth, but also indirect effects that work through union effects on profits and investment (discussed in a subsequent section). Union effects on productivity growth need not match the evidence on productivity levels. For example, unionization might initially be associated with higher levels of productivity owing to "shock" or voice effects, but at the same time retard rates of growth. Of course, over time low (high) rates of productivity growth will produce low (high) productivity levels.

Analysis in Freeman and Medoff (1984) suggested lower but not statistically significant union-productivity growth effects using alternative industry-level data sets, evidence they regarded as inconclusive. A more comprehensive analysis using firm-level data (with control for industry effects) was provided by Hirsch (1991a) based on a sample of 531 firms and covering the period 1968 to 1980. Following control for company size and firm-level changes in labor, physical capital, and research and development (R&D), union firms have substantially lower productivity growth than nonunion firms. Accounting for *industry* sales growth, energy usage, and trade, however, cuts the estimate of the union effect by more than half. Addition of industry dummies cuts the estimates further, while remaining effects are fragile when subjected to econometric probes regarding the error structure. Hirsch concludes that unionized companies during these years displayed substantially lower productivity growth than nonunion firms. But most of the difference was an indirect effect resulting from lower profits and investment among union firms or from operating in industries with slower growth.

Despite the contentiousness surrounding the effects of unions on productivity levels and growth, the most comprehensive studies find little evidence that unions substantially increase or decrease productivity once one accounts for non-labor factors of production, among other determinants. The conclusion that unions have a minimal average effect on productivity runs counter to the belief that unions decrease productivity, the conventional wisdom among economists prior to Freeman and Medoff. And it runs counter to a conventional wisdom arising in some circles following Freeman and Medoff's (1984) overly rosy assessment of the productivity evidence in *What Do Unions Do?*[22]

Assuming that one accepts (as I do) the conclusion that average union-productivity effects are small, several caveats attach to interpretation of this result. First, the finding that union firms have lower productivity and productivity growth absent detailed industry controls is important in its own right, even if it tells us little about unions' causal effects. Second, the critical finding is that unionization fails to produce a positive effect on productivity sufficiently large to offset union compensation gains. This implies lower profitability and, indirectly, lower investment among union businesses. Third, a small or zero union-productivity effect is difficult to interpret. This could mean that all or most channels through which union coverage might affect productivity are unimportant, or that both positive and negative channels matter but cancel out. Fourth, studies reporting average effects of unions almost certainly mask considerable diversity in outcomes across firms and industries. Fifth, studies of productivity and productivity growth control for differences in levels or changes in factor-input usage. But unionization is associated with lower rates of investment and accumulation of physical and innovative capital. These indirect effects of unionization appear to be an important route through which union companies and sectors in the US have realized slower growth.

B.   Profitability

Evidence on unions and profits is reasonably clear-cut, indicating lower profitability in union than in nonunion companies. This is not surprising as long as union-productivity (output) effects do not fully offset union increases in compensation. Absent such an offset, the only way profits would not decline is if union companies could shift higher costs to consumers through higher prices. In some US industries, this once may have been possible.[23] In today's competitive markets where union companies compete with nonunion domestic companies and traded goods, there is limited ability to pass forward higher costs to consumers. Nor can it be argued that unions are simply capturing monopoly or super-normal profits and thus have limited effects on resource allocation.

Such an argument had some plausibility 30 years ago, but a careful evaluation of the evidence failed to support this thesis (see Hirsch and Connolly, 1987). The argument is implausible in today's competitive economic environment.

Differences in profitability should lead to a movement of resources out of union into nonunion sectors over the long run, thus mitigating differences in returns. Specifically, investment in and by union operations should decline until these firms' rates of return (after a union "tax" on profits) are equivalent to nonunion returns. Remaining union coverage (companies) should be restricted to economic sectors realizing above-normal, pre-union rates of returns and those where unionization provide some special advantage and/or where competitive entry is difficult. Such an adjustment process may be rather drawn out, particularly in less competitive environments where quasi-rents accruing to long-lived capital have provided a principal source for union gains. Resource movements should be accelerated the more dynamic and competitive the economic environment.

The process described above appears to approximate the long-run de-unionization process seen in the US private sector. The gradual nature of this transition coupled with data limitations (i.e., the absence of publicly available data on firm unionization) make it difficult to empirically establish, isolate, and quantify the specifics of such a process. The paucity of such evidence, however, does not rule out such a characterization of the US experience.

Lower profits among union companies should be evident in current earnings, measured by rates of return on capital or sales, and in lower stock market valuation of firms' assets. Ex ante returns on equity (risk-adjusted) should not differ between union and nonunion companies, since stock prices adjust downward to reflect lower expected earnings (for evidence, see Hirsch and Morgan, 1994). Lower profits are found using alternative measures of profitability. Studies have used industry price-cost margin, accounting profit measures of rates of return on capital and sales, and market-value measures such as Tobin's q (market value divided by the replacement cost of assets). "Event studies" have examined changes in stock market returns associated with union election wins (and losses) relative to predicted market returns based on estimated parameters from capital asset pricing models (CAPM). The body of existing evidence points unambiguously to lower profitability among union companies.[24]

Estimates from a prototypical study suggest that unionized firms had profits 10 to 20 percent lower than in nonunion firms during the late 1960s through early 1980s (e.g., Hirsch, 1991b). Economists are understandably skeptical that large profit differentials could survive in a competitive economy. Because rates of profit are not typically large, small absolute differences can produce large percentage differences. Whether one believes 10–20 percent differences in profitability can be sustained for "long" periods of time may hinge on one's beliefs regarding how closely the US economy is approximated by the competitive model. One interpretation of the evidence is that union–nonunion differences in profitability did survive for a long period, but that the very long run has now arrived with the competitive process having largely played itself out.[25] Absent the ability to fund union compensation premiums from super-normal profits, the alternative is for labor to capture a share of firms' quasi-rents; i.e., the normal returns to prior investments in long-lived physical and intangible capital. If this is how union premiums are funded, it has serious implications for investment and long-term growth, a topic addressed in the next section.

C.   Investment

Union effects on investment were not a focus of work by Freeman and Medoff (1984) or others summarized in *What Do Unions Do?* This is not surprising given the absence of empirical work on unions and investment at that time. Subsequent research has concluded that investment is an important route through which unions affect economic performance. The earliest empirical paper appears to be Connolly et al. (1986), who proffered a rent-seeking framework in which unions appropriate (i.e., tax) the returns from investments in tangible and intangible capital. Their framework relied on theoretical papers by Baldwin (1983) and Grout (1984). Connolly et al. found unionization, measured at the industry level, associated with lower firm-level investments in R&D.

As developed further in Hirsch (1991a, 1992), it is argued that average and more senior union members may be "rationally myopic" in that their time horizons are shorter than those of owners. This leads unions to "tax" or "capture" a share of the returns on past investments in long-lived, nontransferable capital (e.g., a large plant). Union wage premiums are thus funded in part by appropriation of a share of the quasi-rents that make up the normal return to past investment in long-lived physical capital and R&D.[26] Knowing this, firms reduce their investment in vulnerable capital until marginal returns on investment are equalized across the union and nonunion (i.e., taxed and non-taxed) sectors.[27] Contraction of the union sector, it is argued, results from the long-run response by firms to such union rent seeking.[28]

The union tax or rent-seeking framework has rather different implications than does the standard economic model of unions. In the standard model, a union wage increase causes a firm to move up and along its labor demand schedule by decreasing employment, hiring higher quality workers, and increasing the ratio of capital to labor. Capital investment can increase or decrease owing to substitution and output effects working in opposing directions. In the rent-seeking framework, a high union wage need not decrease the relative cost of capital if the union wage is funded in part by taxing capital (Hirsch and Prasad, 1995). Thus, there should be no presumption that higher union wages increase capital intensity (the ratio of capital to labor, K/L). The little empirical evidence that we have finds no significant effect of union coverage on the capital-labor ratio (Clark, 1984; Hirsch, 1991a).

Empirical analysis of union effects on investment in tangible and intangible capital by Hirsch (1991a) distinguishes between the "direct" and "indirect" investment effects of unions. The direct effect stems from the union tax that leads firms to decrease investment until the marginal post-tax rate of return is equated with the marginal financing cost. The indirect union effect on investment arises from the higher financing costs owing to reduced profits (and, thus, reduces internal funding of investment). Using data for 1968–80 for approximately 500 publicly traded manufacturing firms and a model with detailed firm and industry controls, including profitability, Hirsch estimates the effect on investment for a typical unionized company compared to a nonunion company. Other things equal, the typical unionized company has 6 percent lower capital investment than its equivalent nonunion counterpart. Adding in the indirect effect of lower profits on investment increases the estimated union effect to about 13 percent. For annual investments in R&D, Hirsch finds that the average unionized company has 15 percent lower

R&D, holding constant profitability and the other determinants. Allowing for indirect effects induced by lower profitability raises the estimated effect only modestly.

Subsequent empirical studies for the US provide strong support for the conclusion that unions are associated with lower physical and intangible capital investments (for references, see Hirsch, 2007b; and Doucouliagos and Laroche, 2011).[29] More broadly, evidence consistent with the rent-seeking model should be evident from wage studies as well as investment studies. The labor economics literature suggests that rent sharing (i.e., higher wages associated with higher profits) exists in nonunion as well as union establishments, but collective bargaining provides a formal mechanism to identify and capture above-normal returns.[30] A recent paper by Felix and Hines (2009) uncovers the interesting empirical finding that, in states with lower corporate income taxes, union wage premiums are higher. They interpret this outcome as evidence of rent sharing. A more nuanced explanation might be that low corporate income tax leads to higher capital intensity and creates a pool of quasi-rents susceptible to union bargaining power and wage demands.

A related literature has arisen on debt financing, arguing that unionized companies will maintain higher debt-to-equity ratios to hold down union bargaining power.[31] Support for this was found in an early paper by Bronars and Deere (1991). Recent studies include Matsa (2010) and Klasa et al. (2009).

D.   Employment Growth and Survival

The effects of unions on employment growth and survival are not independent of their effects on productivity, profits, and investment. It would be surprising were lower profits and investment not accompanied by slower growth, and this is what the evidence shows. Leonard (1992) found that unionized California companies grew at significantly slower rates than did nonunion companies. In a study using longitudinal plant-level data, LaLonde et al. (1996) show that employment (and output) decrease following a vote in favor of union certification.[32] More broadly, Linneman et al. (1990) showed that much of what had been represented as a "de-industrialization" of America was largely "de-unionization" – within most narrowly defined manufacturing industries during the 1980s nonunion employment grew while at the same time there were substantial decreases in union employment (for an update and extension, see Bratsberg and Ragan, 2002). Not explored in the literature owing to data limitations is the extent to which companies with both union and nonunion plants tend to shift production toward their nonunion operations over time. Although it seems likely that the expectation of lower financial returns is the chief explanation for slower growth in union than in nonunion employment and output, one cannot rule out that noneconomic factors (say, union animus among corporate decision makers) play a role in investment decisions.

There exists a small but related literature focusing on unions and business closings. Given that we observe slower growth among union than nonunion businesses, we would expect to observe higher business failure rates as well. Such a pattern is not readily evident in the few, albeit dated, studies available. Dunne and Macpherson (1994) utilize longitudinal plant-level data (grouped by industry by size) to show that there are more employment contractions, fewer expansions, and fewer plant "births" in more highly unionized industries. Yet they find that unions have no effect upon plant "deaths," even after controlling for plant size. Freeman and Kleiner (1999) analyze two sets of data, one including insolvent and solvent firms, each with information on union status, and a second on individuals surveyed in the CPS Displaced Worker Surveys. Using the first data set, Freeman and Kleiner conclude that failed firms or lines of business (most lines of business remain in operation following bankruptcy) have similar union density as do solvent firms and lines of business. Using individual data, they find that being a union worker does not lead to a higher probability of permanent job loss from plant closure or business failure. DiNardo and Lee (2004) examine survival rates for establishments following union certification elections. Using a regression discontinuity design, they compare survival rates for establishments that have just under and just over a 50 percent vote in union elections. Combining NLRB election data for 1983–99 with a matched listing of whether establishments named in the NLRB file continue to exist at that address in May 2001, they conclude that the effects of a successful union-organizing drive on survival are negligible. For that matter, they find few differences in any economic outcomes, including wages, between businesses with close union wins and those with close losses.[33]

In short, the rather limited empirical literature that exists finds that US unions are associated with slower employment growth, but the data appear to exhibit little difference in rates of business failure or survival. At first blush, these results appear inconsistent and require some explanation. One possibility is that survival rates are affected by union status but that we have not had sufficiently rich and reliable data to establish this. For example, not all studies have been able to control for firm age and size. Older and larger firms are both more likely to survive and to be unionized. None of the studies cited above examines recent years in which bankruptcies and plant closings among large union companies have been quite visible (see discussion below on the airline and automotive industries).

An alternative explanation (Freeman and Kleiner, 1999; Kuhn, 1998) is that rent-seeking unions will drive enterprises toward the cliff but rarely over it.[34] In an uncertain world, however, it would be surprising if unions and management did not sometimes miscalculate location of "the cliff" and thus have "accidental" business failures. This appears to be exactly what has happened in the airline and automotive industries, as discussed below. But even in these industries, most businesses have survived following their restructuring through bankruptcy. Hirsch (2008) has argued that union governance has often proven sluggish or insufficiently flexible (i.e., too little, too late) in the face of dynamic competitive changes. The next section addresses this broader question regarding union versus nonunion governance, an area in which we have little systematic evidence.

VI.   UNION GOVERNANCE, DYNAMISM, AND COMPETITION

This section first discusses differences in union and nonunion governance and how each operates in dynamic and competitive economic environments. The airline and automotive industries are then examined as case studies of how union governance has operated in the face of rapid change and increased competition. A brief final section addresses differences between the public and private sectors.

A.   Union Workplaces and the Economic Environment

Collective bargaining once provided the dominant workplace governance structure in the private industrial sectors of the US economy. This is no longer so. Although there are many reasons why private sector unions have been in decline, the discussion below emphasizes the relative disadvantage faced by union governance in highly competitive and dynamic economic environments.

In the nonunion private sector, the dominant governance structure is employer-fiat personnel systems wherein outcomes are determined by some combination of employer norms, government regulations and mandates, and the incentives and constraints produced by market forces, in particular, financial viability coupled with the need to attract and retain qualified employees. Subject to economic constraints, plus governmental constraints with respect to discrimination, minimum pay, hours of work, safety, and the like, nonunion employers are free to dictate pay and governance methods.

Unionized companies face largely the same external legal and economic constraints as do nonunion businesses. Union workplaces, however, are characterized by relatively formalized governance structures that rely on collective bargaining, explicit contracts, and structured channels for worker voice. As envisioned in the NLRA, industrial workplaces are typified by top-down control moving from managers to workers, the latter having minimal need for discretion or decision-making. Such a characterization may have been defensible during the NLRA's formative years, but not today. In contemporary workplaces, job hierarchies are not so clear-cut and worker decision-making, often done in teams, is essential at most levels of production. HRM practices intended to encourage smart decisions by workers and teams, such as incentive pay, flexible job assignments, and the like, are widespread within nonunion companies, but far less likely in union establishments (Verma, 2007; Ichniowski et al., 1997; Bloom and Van Reenen, 2011). Although collective bargaining contracts permit considerable employer authority in the daily operation of a workplace and certainly could permit management to bargain for modern HRM practices that diffuse some of that authority, managerial discretion and flexibility are constrained, with substantive changes in wages and methods of pay, benefits, job assignments, and working conditions requiring negotiation with the union.

Union governance by its very design is deliberative and often slow – what is here called "sluggish" – in responding to changes in the economic environment. This stems in part from the adversarial nature of traditional unionism and the limited opportunity for worker voice outside of formal union channels. Sluggish governance and high "transaction costs" are also the inevitable result of unions' democratic structure. Contracts have to be negotiated and usually approved by the rank-and-file. In order to gain and maintain their positions, union leaders cannot steer far away from the preferences of their members. When product and labor market conditions change, contractual revisions in the workplace relationship must await sufficient acceptance by workers of the need for or inevitability of such changes. Contracts are typically negotiated every three years or so when an expiring contract is to be replaced or when there are substantial unanticipated shocks requiring concessions by workers or changes by management. Formal contracts have advantages, among them increasing certainty about the future and limiting opportunistic behavior by employers. But they come with a cost, reducing the ability of employers to make needed adjustments in the face of unanticipated shocks.[35]

More generally, all workplaces confront a set of contractual issues that must be addressed through its governance structure, be it union or nonunion. Neither a union nor nonunion governance structure is uniformly superior to the other, a priori. As discussed by Wachter and Wright (1984), Wachter (2004), and Williamson et al. (1975), critical factors in any labor-contracting relationship include the ability to effectively deal with match-specific investments, asymmetric information, and risk (each being discussed below), and to do so in a relatively low cost manner (i.e., with low transaction costs). Wachter (2004) argues that the predominance of nonunion enterprises is primarily the result of low transaction costs. In a related vein, I have emphasized that formalized and deliberate union governance may not be particularly disadvantageous in a static, non-competitive economic environment, but that it becomes increasingly costly the more competitive and dynamic the environment (for earlier presentation of this view, see Hirsch and Hirsch, 2007; and Hirsch, 2008). As the economic environment has become more dynamic (i.e., rapidly changing) and competitive, traditional union governance has become more disadvantageous. Note a subtle but important point. What is being emphasized here is that slow-moving union governance and the exercise of voice may limit firms' ability to adjust in highly dynamic and competitive economic environments. This argument neither contradicts nor negates points made earlier that competitive market pressures serve to limit union rent-seeking and may spur productivity enhancements.

One contractual issue concerns match-specific investments in human and physical capital not valued by or transferable to other firms. As workers acquire firm-specific skills, they become more valuable to their current employer than to alternative employers. As firms acquire long-lived capital, some of it will be specific to the firm and not readily transferable to other companies. A problem associated with match-specific investments is the possibility of hold-up; once a party makes such investments, the other party can behave opportunistically and capture ex post "quasi-rents." One solution for firm-specific human capital is for workers and firms to jointly invest in these skills, with wages greater than those same workers can earn elsewhere but below the marginal revenue product of the workers to the firm. This arrangement creates a self-enforcing implicit agreement that gives both parties an interest in continuing the employment relationship so as not to lose returns on their investments. Opportunistic behavior by employers may be constrained by concern for their reputation among current and potential workers. As discussed previously, not so easily solved is the hold-up problem faced by union firms with respect to long-lived firm-specific investments.

Asymmetric information between workers and management creates a risk that the advantaged party will behave opportunistically. For example, firms possess information on product demand superior to that of workers, providing firms with the opportunity to misstate market conditions and gain an advantage in workplace negotiations. A result of the product-demand asymmetry has been the widespread norm under which firms are relatively free to adjust employment levels, but rarely adjust wages downward (Bewley 1999).[36] This self-enforcing mechanism reduces opportunistic use of the information asymmetry by generally taking off the table the option of understating the level of demand to achieve wage cuts. With wages fixed, employers lack incentive to misstate demand because they do not want to cut employment if demand is strong. In union workplaces, this process is somewhat more formal. Most collective-bargaining agreements allow employment-level changes, but not wage adjustments, absent negotiation.

Unions may grant employer requests for wage concessions, but generally only if financial records are disclosed to union representatives. Unions serve the useful purpose of verifying employer claims.

Risk bearing is a third contractual issue addressed in the employment relationship. Because workers have much of their income tied to their jobs with little ability to diversify, they are in a poor position to bear company-specific earnings risk through variable hours (including job loss) and compensation. Moreover, variability in company earnings is largely beyond the control of its workforce. Investors, in contrast, can readily diversify investments and bear such risk. Efficient risk bearing would largely insulate the compensation of (nonmanagerial) workers from variability in firm revenue and profit. Consequently, both union and nonunion workplaces have relatively fixed wage rates, in the union case through collective bargaining agreements and in nonunion companies through largely self-enforcing implicit contracts or norms.

Any advantage of nonunion over union pay and governance determination is not likely to arise from the above factors – match-specific investments, asymmetric information or risk bearing – but, rather, from lower transaction costs in adjusting to contractual changes associated with these and other issues. Were changes in the economic environment very gradual and competitive pressures weak, a formal and highly deliberate union governance structure might pose few problems.[37] The costs of deliberate or sluggish union governance, however, increase with the speed of change and the degree of competition. New information is constantly coming to a firm and its workers and it is prohibitively costly to have explicit contract terms for every possible contingency. Revising formal contractual terms is costly. Although many collective bargaining agreements have broad management rights clauses, formalized contractual governance limits flexibility and managerial discretion in union companies.

It is widely believed that the US industrial sector operates in a highly competitive and dynamic environment. Arguably, the US economy has become more competitive and dynamic over time, increasing the cost of union relative to nonunion governance. There is no single definition or measurement for the competitiveness and dynamism of an economy.[38] In the discussion below, I briefly look at measures of concentration, trade, productivity growth, and job creation and destruction.

A common, albeit imperfect, measure of product market competition is a concentration ratio, which measures the share of value added, sales, employment, etc. by the largest companies (often the share of the largest four companies).[39] Concentration ratios for value added, employment, and payroll, both economy-wide and in manufacturing, have remained steady or decreased over the last 50 years, suggesting steady or increasing competitiveness in the US (White, 2002). Moreover, most measures of concentration do not account (or fully account) for international trade, thus understating the level and increases over time in competiveness. Competitive pressures from international trade are strong and have grown over time. The value of imports as a percentage of GDP increased from 5.4 percent in 1970 to 17.8 percent in 2008, falling sharply to 13.9 percent in 2009 due to the worldwide recession, and rebounding to 16.0 percent in 2010 (the latter figure a preliminary estimate) (US Council of Economic Advisers, 2011, table B-1).

An economy's dynamism can be evidenced by high rates of productivity growth (due to technological change and a host of other factors) and high levels of job creation and destruction (Schumpeter's "creative destruction" or what labor economists refer to as "job churn"). Output per work hour in the nonfarm business sector of the economy has more than doubled since 1970, from an index (with 2005=100) of 50.2 in 1970 to 111.0 in the third quarter of 2010 (US Council of Economic Advisers, 2011, table B-49). Productivity growth in manufacturing exceeds that economy-wide. As further evidence on productivity, one could point to relatively high growth rates in research and development expenditures and patents granted.

The US labor market is characterized by high rates of job churn. Between 1990 and 2005, the private sector (manufacturing sector) had a job destruction rate of 7.6 (4.9) percent per quarter and job creation rate of 7.9 (5.3) percent, implying a net employment growth rate per quarter of 0.3 (–0.4) percent (Davis, Faberman, and Haltiwanger, 2006, table 2A). High rates of employment growth and job churn make it difficult for unions to maintain their share of covered workers. To maintain density at, say, 7 percent as total employment is increasing, unions must organize enough existing and newly created jobs to offset union members lost plus 7 percent of the net employment growth. Maintaining union density is particularly difficult because most new jobs and all new businesses are "born" nonunion, and because declining union membership decreases the financial base from which organizing is funded. And of course organizing workplaces is difficult in the US given widespread management opposition and mixed support among workers.

Evidence directly linking union decline to competition or dynamism is limited. Magnani and Prentice (2010) use a data set on US manufacturing industries from 1973–96 and simulate the effects of unions on flexibility and average costs. They conclude that more highly unionized industries have lower flexibility and higher average costs, the latter due mainly to higher fixed costs (e.g., worker benefits), than do less unionized industries. Slaughter (2007) shows that union density is lower in manufacturing industries with a high degree of global engagement, in particular those with inward foreign direct investment. His interpretation is that increased capital mobility has raised labor demand elasticities and weakened union bargaining power. An implication of the competitive thesis is that a highly competitive economy not only constrains union density, but also limits the economy-wide costs of unionism since resources are more readily reallocated to sectors with the highest expected returns.

Recent research by Bloom and Van Reenen (2007, 2010) on differences in management practices across firms and countries has found that productivity and financial performance are associated with differences in management practices. Moreover, more favorable management practices (i.e., those with better outcomes) are associated with competitive market environments and a relatively "light touch" in labor market regulations. Although Bloom and Van Reenen's work provides little direct evidence on union effects on performance, it is suggestive given that changes in management practices, the expansion in use of incentive pay schemes, and increasing market competition have coincided with declines in unionization in the US and elsewhere.

B.   Case Studies: A Sluggish Response to Shocks in the Automotive and Airline Industries

Although it is difficult to link in a systematic way deliberative union governance and union decline in the face of increasing competition and dynamism, case studies can illustrate such a possibility. Examples include Hirsch's discussion of collective bargaining in the automotive and airline industries (Hirsch, 2007a, 2008). The US automotive industry is emblematic of the narrative provided in this chapter. The industry was almost completely unionized and faced little international competition in the decades following World War II. There was then increasing penetration of imported vehicles (in particular from Japan) and, subsequently, the establishment of numerous assembly plants by foreign-owned producers in the US. The latter were often located in southern states; all of them started out, and nearly all remained, nonunion establishments. At the same time, more and more production moved out of assembly plants and into a growing and increasingly nonunion auto parts supply chain, with plants clustered within a one-day drive of assembly plants.

Prior to the Great Recession and the concomitant restructuring of the US auto industry, total US employment in motor vehicle and equipment manufacturing had remained relatively constant over a nearly 35-year period, a period over which there was a considerable increase in productivity and production. Calculations from Current Population Survey (CPS) data for 1973–2006 by Hirsch (2008) show employment in the automotive industry moving from 1.2 million in 1973 to 1.0 million in 1983, 1.1 million in 1990, 1.3 million in 2000, and 1.4 million in 2006. At the same time, union membership (and density) dropped sharply from 830 000 (71.0 percent) in 1973, to 590 000 (58.8 percent) in 1983, 540 000 (48.4 percent) in 1990, 470 000 (35.9 percent) in 2000, and just 360 000 (26.0 percent) in 2006. By 2010, employment in the automotive industry stood at 945 000, of whom only 192 000 (20 percent) were union members (Hirsch and Macpherson, 2011; also shown at www.unionstats.com). In short, the US maintained a large automotive industry, but one with a much smaller union presence. Michigan, Ohio, and a few other states had sharply reduced shares of automotive industry employment over this period, with states such as Tennessee, South Carolina, Alabama, and Kentucky gaining employment shares of 2–3 percentage points each.

Technological change in the automotive industry over this period was rapid, with substantial increases in productivity and decreases in quality-adjusted prices. After falling well behind their Japanese and European competitors in productivity and quality, US companies made considerable progress in narrowing these gaps. But change was not nearly fast enough. Competitive prices are set at the margin – and in the automotive industry it was increasingly the "Toyotas" and "Hondas" rather than "Detroit" that determined market prices (US branded vehicles in fact sold at a discount based on perceived quality differences). In order for the Big Three to have prospered, they would have needed to maintain their market shares and avoid substantial price discounting. Had they been able to do so, they could have spread their legacy retiree pension and health commitments over a larger number of automobiles and employees. This scenario did not play out. Instead, the Big Three US companies (in particular, General Motors) lost market share, while at the same time paying higher wages and benefits than their competitors and retaining the commitment to pay retiree health and pension costs. Their ability to cut labor costs was further limited because workers displaced due to technology or restructuring were paid while in a "jobs bank" (now eliminated). Vehicle manufacturers trimmed costs of inputs by putting pressure on their auto parts suppliers to lower prices, at the same time demanding improved product quality and just-in-time delivery.

Something had to give. During the mid-2000s auto parts suppliers Delphi (a corporate spin-off of GM), Dana, Collins & Aikman, and others filed for bankruptcy and worker wages and benefits were lowered substantially. GM and Ford structured various lump-sum buyouts of workers in order to reduce employment. UAW contracts, which had maintained generous health plan coverage with no employee or retiree cost sharing, introduced cost sharing. The UAW subsequently assumed the administering of health benefits through a voluntary employees' beneficiary association (VEBA) fund financed by promised lump-sum payments from the companies. When the Great Recession hit in 2008, neither GM nor Chrysler could maintain solvency. GM went into a federal structured bankruptcy that broke out its "dead" assets (abandoned plants, etc.) into a separate company (Motors Liquidation or "Old GM") supported by federal loans, while shaping what is hoped to be a viable entity with the federal government as principal (non-active) shareholder. In order to help make the "New GM" viable, not only were equity owners wiped out, but bondholders took large losses, a two-tier wage structure was adopted for use once GM hires new employees, brands were eliminated, dealers thinned out, and numerous plants were closed. Chrysler was reorganized with ownership from Fiat, a UAW VEBA, and minority ownership shares from the US and Canadian governments. Ford was able to avoid bankruptcy because it had taken on a very large amount of debt (i.e., had a large infusion of cash) just prior to the collapse of sales.

While the Great Recession's severity could not have been anticipated, the underlying structural problems facing the Big Three were widely acknowledged for years, if not decades. Had the Big Three not been unionized or had the UAW been more flexible far earlier, what might have happened? Of course we cannot observe such a counterfactual. It is at least possible that rather than "hitting the (bankruptcy) wall" and thus producing substantial employment and compensation decreases, an earlier and more gradual adjustment process might have occurred. Over time, plants and dealerships might have been closed, staffing levels decreased, and compensation growth slowed. As seen elsewhere in the private sector, employee health plans would have included considerable cost sharing, and promises for retiree pension and health benefits would have been more constrained. Of course, there is no assurance that management at the Big Three, absent the constraints of the union governance process, would have steered their companies toward healthy financial outcomes. What is clear is that the collective bargaining process could not shield employees from long-run market forces or company-specific strategic failures.

The automotive industry, it should be noted, is typified by large and medium-sized companies and plants. Whether union or nonunion, US or foreign-owned, employee governance will be relatively formalized in all but the smallest organizations. But a formalized governance structure need not produce rigidity. What I am suggesting is that adversarial union governance has proven a disadvantage relative to nonunion human resource management and greater managerial flexibility, in particular when facing technological advances, domestic and international competition, market demand shocks, and the like. The tendency of union governance to be sluggish is not an economic law. Some union workplaces have well-functioning employee governance, good labor relations, and respond well to economic change. No doubt more workplaces would fit this characterization were not antipathy toward unions so widespread among US managers. But adversarial union governance, both economy-wide and in an automotive industry characterized by a generally stable labor relations system, too often fails the market test. This conclusion is not intended as a critique (or endorsement) of behavior by union leaders, rank-and-file or management, but as criticism of the current US labor relations system.

In contrast to most US industries, unions in the airline industry have largely maintained coverage and retained substantial bargaining power, subject to economic conditions in the industry. Roughly half of all workers in air transportation were unionized before deregulation in the mid-1970s and about half remained unionized through 2006 (Hirsch, 2007a), although density has since fallen to 39 percent in 2010 (www.unionstats.com). All major carriers, including Southwest, are unionized (Delta pilots but not other workers are unionized), while mid-size national and regional carriers include a mix of union and nonunion companies. The high union density is in part a carryover from the pre-1978 regulatory period. More fundamentally, density was maintained because strong bargaining power makes representation attractive to workers; a profitable nonunion carrier paying well below other carriers would quickly be organized. Bargaining power is substantial because of the strike threat. A strike by a carrier's pilots, flight attendants or mechanics (and possibly other workers) can shut down all flight operations. A shutdown in a service industry like this can be particularly costly. Unlike consumer durables, transport services cannot be stored or shifted in time. Many customers can switch to non-struck carriers. Because shutdowns are so costly, strikes are rare, but unions are able to capture rents for their members.

What has emerged in the airline industry is compensation that reflects a "union tax" cycle. Union airline workers, particularly pilots among the larger carriers, realize substantial wage premiums (Hirsch and Macpherson, 2000; Hirsch, 2007a). Following periods in which airlines have been relatively profitable, such as the late 1990s, union contracts "tax" those profits and premiums rise. Following substantial losses, unions provide contract concessions. But union response to changing economic conditions takes time. In the perfect storm that hit the airline industry in the early 2000s, the response was too slow. Adverse conditions faced by airlines included a recession hitting in 2001 as high contract wages were taking force; the 9/11 attacks and a 20 percent reduction in flights; a stock market downturn destroying pension wealth; Internet pricing that lowered carrier margins; increasing market shares of "low-cost carriers"; and later, increasing fuel prices. US Airways and United entered bankruptcy protection in 2002 (and US Airways again in 2004), while Delta and Northwest entered bankruptcy on the same day in 2005.[40] American Airlines, the only legacy carrier that had not disappeared, been acquired or entered bankruptcy since deregulation in 1978, faced a bankruptcy filing in 2003 until it received concessions from its unions. America entered bankruptcy in November 2011.

In most industries, companies that have high costs and respond slowly to economic shocks are likely to wither as customers switch to goods produced by domestic or foreign competitors. Emerging successfully from bankruptcy may not be a viable option for such companies. In the airline industry, however, carriers continued operations and retained much of their customer base, emerging from bankruptcy with a lower cost structure that in turn set the pattern for much of the industry. There has been industry consolidation, with recent mergers by US Airways/America West, Delta/Northwest, United/Continental, and Southwest/AirTran, coupled with removal of capacity from the system.

Despite a long-run relationship between the major carriers and their unions, labor relations throughout much of the industry have remained contentious, with the notable exception of Southwest. As this narrative is written, airlines are beginning to show profitability following a period of unusually high oil prices followed by the Great Recession. Because airlines operate under the Railway Labor Act (RLA), union contracts remain active at existing terms absent a new contract or either the union or firm asking for release from the existing agreement following a mediation process. That made the process of adjustment slow but its effects more durable. Absent agreement on new contracts or desire among workers to call a strike, much of the industry has maintained its low-cost structure (by historic standards) and allowed the airlines to earn modest profits despite relatively low prices and traffic. Airline unions and their members, however, are now determined to recover wages and benefits lost through bankruptcy and poor market conditions. A key factor determining future labor compensation will be product market competition and prices. The recession and increased penetration and competition from domestic low-cost carriers (some union and some nonunion) have constrained prices and labor compensation. Recent mergers among major carriers, however, may increase their pricing power if air travel demand is robust.

It remains to be seen whether there can emerge a reasonably cooperative labor relations environment in the airline industry, with agreements on new contracts providing sustainable labor costs. One scenario would have the parties learning a common set of lessons from their decade-long roller-coaster ride and then finding their way toward sustainability. A more likely scenario may be a return to the past – a strained labor relations environment, resumption of lagged wage-profit cycles, and eventually an upending of the status quo following the failure to respond quickly to future market shocks.

The examples of the automotive and airline industries are based on very different types of industries operating in different economic environments. Yet each of their histories provides examples where lack of flexibility by management and sluggishness in union governance failed to respond in a timely fashion to large economic shocks. It might be argued that the shocks faced in these two industries were unusual and extreme, although this does not strike me as a good argument. Shocks occur throughout the economy. The point is that economic shocks are generally dealt with continually through resource movements (including business failures) in response to price signals, where "price" includes product prices, wages, interest rates, profits/losses, etc. The thesis here is that governance within unionized companies has often been sluggish in responding to such shocks and this has proven disadvantageous in an increasingly dynamic and competitive economy.

C.   A Note on the Public Sector

A brief look at the public sector provides support for the thesis that a competitive and dynamic economic environment has been a fundamental constraint on unionization in the private sector. Since federal and state labor laws cleared the way for collective bargaining for government employees, public sector union density has greatly exceeded private density and has been maintained over time as private density has fallen. In 1977, the first year in which current union variable definitions were adopted in the CPS, union membership density in the public sector was 32.8 percent, versus 21.7 percent in the private sector. By 2010, private sector density had fallen sharply to only 6.9 percent, whereas public sector density remained largely unchanged at 36.2 percent.[41] As noted above, the number of public sector union members overtook private sector membership during 2009. In 2010, government workers accounted for 52.0 percent of all union members (www.unionstats.com).

The public sector is not immune to economic forces and pressure from voters to hold down taxes, as has been readily evident in recent years. But competitive forces and change (dynamism) are far less important in the public than in the private sector. In much of the public sector, be it unionized or not, there exists a highly formalized workplace structure with civil service or other codified personnel systems. Governance is deliberate and often sluggish in the face of economic (and political) shocks. Because of this, governance differences between union and nonunion government entities are typically smaller than are the private sector union–nonunion differences that have been a major focus of this chapter.

In the private sector, large employers with well-defined internal labor markets and low turnover are often those most likely to have unionized employees or well-developed HRM systems. It is therefore not surprising that the public sector has highly formalized workplace governance and that collective bargaining is widespread where permitted or facilitated by law. Most public employees display relatively low turnover (strong attachment) and lengthy tenure. Part of the explanation for this is the widespread use of defined benefit pension plans in the public sector. More fundamentally, for many public workers (in education, law enforcement, social assistance, etc.), there are few private employers and limited ability to move across government jurisdictions, an immobility often reinforced by seniority-based pay.

The presence of gradual rather than rapid change in the public sector also emanates from the "product market." In comparison to private employers, local, state, and federal jurisdictions see far more limited movement of "consumers" (constituents) to competitive jurisdictions, face little risk of competitive "entry," and face a lower threat of bankruptcy (or going out of business if bankrupt). Whereas the goals of for-profit firms in the private sector are reasonably clear, the goals of public agencies are diverse and inherently political. As emphasized long ago by Freeman (1986), union power and outcomes in the public sector occur in no small part via the political process and they may influence expenditures and employment as much or more than they do wages.

VII.   CONCLUDING REMARKS

This chapter argues that traditional union governance in the US private sector has proven poorly suited to flourishing in an increasingly competitive and dynamic world. Evidence on unions and economic performance – wages and benefits, productivity, profitability, investment, employment growth, and business failure – are relevant in assessing public policy and the future of unions.

Unions increase wages and benefits for their members, substantially so in many sectors of the economy. These union premiums are not offset (or not offset fully) by higher productivity. Rather, average union-productivity effects within establishments and firms are close to zero, although likely positive. These average effects mask what is a high variance across economic environments, with outcomes sensitive to the state of labor relations. Because union wage premiums are not offset by productivity enhancements, profitability is lower in union companies, whether measured by accounting profits or market valuation measures. Investors' risk-adjusted expected returns must equalize, which occurs through a lower market valuation of equity in union than in nonunion companies.

Union premiums cannot be funded (or fully funded) from sustained super-normal profits because such profits are rare in a highly competitive economy. A principal way that wage premiums are funded is through appropriation of a share of the normal returns from prior investment in long-lived physical and innovative capital (so-called quasi-rents). In response to the tax on the returns to long-lived capital, union companies invest less in physical capital and R&D. Investment is reduced further due to lower profits among union firms, which limits the ability to finance investment internally. Lower investment in physical and innovative capital by union companies has led to slower growth in productivity, sales, and employment (i.e., union membership). A simple way to think about the long-run decline in US private sector union density is that it is part of a broader shift in resources (capital and land as well as labor) away from union and toward nonunion companies and establishments both within and across economic sectors, inside and outside the US. More competitive and dynamic economic environments accentuate this process, while at the same time limiting the potential costs of unionism economy-wide by speeding the movement of resources to their most valued uses. In the US economy of today, the macroeconomic (i.e., aggregate) effects of private sector unionism are likely to be minimal.

There is little basis for expecting private sector unionism in its current form to increase substantially over time, absent a strong shift in worker and voter attitudes and adoption of policies that would greatly ease union organizing and obtaining first contracts. Indeed, it will be difficult for unions to maintain density at its current 7 percent level. This conclusion follows naturally if one accepts this chapter's thesis that the fundamental constraint on the size of the union sector is the growing competitiveness and dynamism of the US economy, epitomized by globalization (i.e., international flows of goods, capital, and people) and technological change. Advances in information technology, among other technologies, have led to shifts in the occupations, industries, and locations of jobs. These "structural" shifts in jobs account for perhaps a quarter of the long-run union decline. Most of the union density decline, however, has not been due to employment shifts but to union density decline within narrowly-defined industries and occupations (Hirsch, 2008, pp. 159–61). In a highly competitive world, neither traditional unions nor any other worker voice institution can flourish unless it has high value added and limited rent seeking.

Of course there are other explanations for declining private sector unionization – strong management opposition, unfair labor practices, a less favorable labor law environment during recent Republican administrations, and weaker sentiment among nonunion workers to join unions as they recognize the prospects of strong management opposition, are exposed to fewer union community members, and receive protections offered by federal and state employment laws (antidiscrimination laws, pension insurance, etc.).[42] But these explanations appear to be less fundamental and of second-order importance compared to the role played by a competitive, dynamic economic environment. Opposition to union organizing by management, lack of enthusiasm for unions among many workers, and limited political support among the public for union-supported policies that would enhance organizing are not unrelated to beliefs (some correct) as to how unions affect economic performance.

Although this chapter has focused on the economic links between changes in union density and economic performance, it is informative to think about union density in an accounting sense. Changes in density are arithmetically determined by the magnitude of union and nonunion "flows" into and out of employment relative to the existing "stocks" of union and nonunion employment. To maintain a given level of union density, more organizing of new workplaces is needed the higher is the existing level of density and the higher the rate of job churn (i.e., job creation and destruction). For example, beginning around the early 1980s, organizing rates fell substantially below the level needed to maintain density. Private sector union density declined sharply and over a sustained period, as seen in Figure 4.1. But far less organizing is necessary to maintain union density at, say, 5 percent than at 15 percent. Depending on assumptions about union and nonunion job destruction, coupled with overall employment growth, rates of organizing achieved prior to the Great Recession can probably support a steady-state private sector density close to 5 percent, not too far below current rates (Farber and Western, 2002).

While maintaining density close to current levels might be possible with organizing rates seen prior to the recession, it will not be easy to achieve these rates. Low current unionization begets low organizing of new members. First, organizing is costly and declining membership decreases the financial base that funds it. Second, union services are an "experience good" – those exposed to unions in their community, among family members or friends, or in early jobs are more likely to be union members. Lower density today therefore implies less union experience and less positive union sentiment among potential future members (Holmes, 2006; Budd, 2010).

Under any likely scenario, union governance in the private sector will remain a minority model largely restricted to a few sectors of the economy. This is not necessarily a terrible outcome, at least not if the alternative were to have a large, uncompetitive union sector in a highly competitive world. But it is far from a first-best outcome. The current system provides too little worker voice, participation, and worker–management cooperation in both union and nonunion workplaces. The adversarial relationship envisioned and reinforced by the NLRA holds little appeal for workers (Freeman and Rogers, 1999).[43] While desirable levels of voice and cooperation have evolved in some, perhaps many, US companies, enhanced worker voice and participation on a larger scale is likely to require (politically difficult) labor and employment law initiatives. For any initiative to be successful, it would need to produce new forms of voice and workplace governance within the large nonunion sector, creating new options short of full collective bargaining rights. Rather than being a substitute for traditional unionism, movement in this direction might reinvigorate the union movement and help create a larger set of participatory workplace institutions, traditional unions being one of several available options.

The discussion of possible reforms of this sort is well beyond the scope of this chapter. In previous work (Hirsch and Hirsch, 2007), possible expansion of nonunion voice via reforms in the NLRA has been proposed (building on Estreicher, 1994), along with a speculative proposal to move the labor law default from nonunion status to a worker option for a governance structure akin to German works councils. Traditional NLRA collective bargaining or the absence of any formal voice mechanism – "all" or "nothing" – would remain options that workers could adopt. Sachs (2010) examines the issue of labor law defaults more broadly, his principal focus being changes in the NLRB election process that would facilitate workers' ability to express their preferences for a union under strict confidentiality and free of management influence.[44] More in line with the emphasis in this chapter, Estlund (2010) recognizes that, with the decline in collective bargaining, workers have many legal rights, but little representation at work, depending instead on self-regulation within firms. Estlund accepts that self-regulation, in more or less regulated forms, is here to stay, and discusses ways in which effective worker voice and participation can be secured within a nonunion or self-regulatory process.

Specific workplace institutions, human resource management practices, and vehicles for voice and participation that may emerge in the coming decades cannot be reliably identified. What can be said with some confidence is that, whatever the forms of workplace governance, they will have to provide value added in the workplace in order to flourish in what will likely remain a highly competitive and dynamic economic environment.

NOTES

1. Unless stated otherwise, all figures on union membership and density beginning in 1973 are from calculations by the author from the Current Population Survey (CPS) monthly files. Data are provided at the Union Membership and Coverage Database from the CPS (www.unionstats.com) and described in Hirsch and Macpherson (2003). Pre-1973 union figures shown in Figure 4.1 are derived from Troy and Sheflin (1985), as explained in Hirsch (2008).
2. Wachter (2007) argues that the NLRA, while setting up the administrative machinery that facilitated union organizing and governance, at the same time planted the seed for union decline. The NLRA constituted a break from the cooperative corporatist framework envisioned by the New Deal and instead recognized collective bargaining as an adversarial system that would operate within a market economy. In doing so, the NLRA allowed union power to be constrained and eventually marginalized by competitive pressures.
3. Control variables include years of schooling, potential years of experience and its square (interacted with gender), and variables for marital status, race and ethnicity, gender, part-time work, large metropolitan area, public sector, region, broad occupation, and broad industry.
4. The log differential is an approximate proportional difference, the union minus nonunion wage ($Wu - Wn$) divided by some "average" wage between Wu and Wn. The percentage differential $[(Wu - Wn)/Wn]100$ is typically approximated by $[\exp(d) - 1]100$, where d is the log differential. Estimation issues regarding union endogeneity, two-sided (employer and employee) selection on unmeasured skill, and earnings imputation, inter alia, are discussed in the literature (Hirsch, 2004).
5. There is no standard measure of union bargaining power. Union density and wage premiums are the most readily available measures. Firm-level (inverse) labor demand elasticities would be a reasonable proxy, but are not generally available. Cramton and Tracy (1998) construct a model in which weak bargaining power leads to less use of strikes and greater use of holdouts (working with an expired contract). As measured by the ratio of strikes to holdouts, bargaining power fell sharply during the 1980s. They conclude that much of the decline was due to employers' increased willingness to use replacement workers. Bargaining power should be correlated with union success. Pencavel (2009) provides a weighted average of union density and the wage premium to measure union "utility" over time. Union well-being rises and then falls over 1922–2005, peaking in the early 1950s but with little change through the late 1960s, and then declining continuously thereafter to values slightly below those in the 1920s.
6. Estimates of the union wage premium for 2011 show a substantive decline, possibly indicating a new lower level for union wages. In countries with broad sector-wide bargaining and where union gains are viewed as a right for all workers, union–nonunion differences are expected to be smaller than in the US.
7. The ECEC includes paid leave and supplemental pay as benefits rather than part of wage and salary earnings.
8. For a related argument, see Wachter (2007), described in note 2.
9. Changes in employment due to wage changes represent movement along the labor demand curve, all else the same, while shifts of the curve (i.e., greater or less employment at each given wage) depend on the level of output and the price of substitute factors – capital and nonunion labor. Of course, unions may move the employer up the demand curve to a wage (employment) level higher (lower) than the competitive outcome, or may move the firm off of its labor demand curve (for a discussion of "efficient contract" models, see Farber, 1986).
10. If union wage gains derive in part from a "tax" on the returns to long-lived capital, as discussed

subsequently, it need not follow that union companies increase capital intensity (i.e., the ratio of capital to labor).

11. There exist few examples of "classic" monopsony in today's economy, but a "new" monopsony literature has arisen that emphasizes labor supply frictions that tie workers to firms (Manning, 2003). Unlike the classic monopsony model, the welfare and policy implications of new monopsony models are rather opaque.

12. Freeman and Medoff argue that a competitive environment may be a necessary condition for positive productivity effects. "Higher productivity appears to run hand in hand with good industrial relations and to be spurred by competition in the product market, while lower productivity under unionism appears to exist under the opposite circumstances." (Freeman and Medoff, 1984, p. 180).

13. By the same reasoning, union companies that prosper in a competitive environment are not a random draw from among all possible (and largely unobserved) union–company experiences.

14. The clearest precursors are Wachter and Wright (1984) and Wachter (2004, 2007), the first two papers comparing internal versus external labor markets and union versus nonunion governance, and the third the fundamental role competition plays in limiting union strength. Dynamism and the sluggishness of union governance is emphasized in Hirsch (2008) and Hirsch and Hirsch (2007). For a related discussion on contracts and workplace governance, including an application to unions, see MacLeod (2011).

15. Holmes and Walrath (2007) provide a careful and enlightening longitudinal analysis of such data. Among the issues that arise are that figures provided by union locals sometimes include members for a single establishment, sometimes for a single firm across establishments, and sometimes for members across multiple employers.

16. NLRB reports do not include small election units, union election wins need not translate into collective bargaining coverage (i.e., a contract), aggregating from elections up to the firm level is difficult, flows into union membership via elections for a given year (or set of years) are a small proportion of the total stock of members and there is no obvious way to account for flows out of union employment.

17. It can be argued that unionism is an "experience good" for workers, organizers, and management (Gomez and Gunderson, 2004). Holmes (2006) provides evidence on the geographic link between past and current unionization, consistent with the experience good framework.

18. Early surveys and interpretations of the US literature include Addison and Hirsch (1989), Booth (1995), and Kuhn (1998), while recent surveys include Hirsch (2007b) and MacLeod (2011). Greater emphasis on non-US studies is provided in Aidt and Tzannatos (2002) and Metcalf (2003). Doucouliagos and Laroche (2003, 2009, 2011) provide meta-analyses of the literatures on unions and productivity, profits, and innovative activity, respectively.

19. A recent survey article by Syverson (2011) examines productivity differences across firms. He emphasizes that there exist large differences in productivity at any point in time, even among firms producing homogeneous products in the same product markets (e.g., cement). Much of the variance in productivity cannot be accounted for by measurable factors; union status is one of many unmeasured factors. Over the long run, firms with the lowest productivity tend to be weeded out of the market.

20. For comprehensive US and international evidence on HRM practices, see Bloom and Van Reenen (2011).

21. The specific question asked was: "What is your best estimate of the percentage impact of unions on the productivity of unionized companies?" (Fuchs et al., 1998, pp. 1392, 1418). The larger purpose of the study was to compare how economists differ in their views on public policies versus their assessment of market relationships or parameters.

22. Controversy did not surprise Freeman and Medoff. They end their productivity chapter stating: "This 'answer' to the debate over what unions do to productivity is probably the most controversial and least widely accepted result in this book…While the new work deals with these [listed reasons for] problems, at least in part, the controversy is unlikely to disappear. Age-old debates do not often end with a bang, even with computerized evidence." (Freeman and Medoff, 1984, p. 80).

23. The most obvious examples were regulated industries with restricted entry (e.g., airlines, trucking, and utilities) where prices were administratively determined to approximate average costs. Substantial pass-through of costs to consumers also may have occurred in oligopolistic industries facing little foreign or domestic nonunion competition (e.g., the 1950–70s automotive industry).

24. See Hirsch (2007b) and Doucouliagos and Laroche (2009) for references. A notable exception to the negative profit result is DiNardo and Lee's (2004) regression discontinuity analysis, which finds virtually no significant outcome effects (including wages) associated with close union wins versus close union losses. Their methodology is designed to estimate the causal effects of collective bargaining, holding constant union sentiment among workers (i.e., roughly 50/50 support). It is not clear that the effects of union wins with "marginal" support can be generalized to union effects more generally. A substantial extension of their analysis by Lee and Mas (2009) shows that the equity value of companies is substantially reduced following average and large-margin union wins.

25. The title of Addison and Hirsch's (1989) paper on union effects on performance asks: "Has the long run arrived?"

26. Using firm-level union data from Hirsch (1991a) matched to Compustat financial data, Cavanaugh (1998) shows that deleterious union effects on market value and investment are directly related to the ease with which quasi-rents can be appropriated.

27. Chen et al. (2011) provide rather direct evidence on this point. They find that firms with "reduced operating flexibility" (measured by whether a firm is unionized) face a higher cost of capital.

28. The "hold-up" models of unions and investment proffered by Baldwin (1983) and Grout (1984) involve inefficient contracts. In principle, worker wages could be reduced during the investment period in order to "pre-finance" the subsequent rent sharing (i.e., tax on investment returns). Card et al. (2010) carefully test such a rent-sharing model using matched employer-employee data from the Veneto region of Italy (the data contain no information on union status). The authors conclude that there is evidence for efficient dynamic bargaining, with workers paying upfront for the returns to sunk capital that they will capture in later periods. The evidence on unions and investment summarized in this section suggests that one should be cautious in generalizing the Card et al. results to union contracts in the US.

29. Consistent with US evidence, Odgers and Betts (1997) conclude that in Canada unions significantly reduce investment in physical capital, while Betts et al. (2001) conclude likewise for R&D. In a comparative study of the US and Britain, Menezes-Filho et al. (1998) conclude that the US evidence for a deleterious union effect on R&D investment is robust, but that unions have little effect in the UK following detailed industry controls. They speculate that British unions have fewer deleterious effects than do American unions owing to more explicit bargaining over employment levels and a preference for longer contracts than in the US. The R&D evidence is also consistent with the evidence finding far smaller union wage effects in Britain than in the US (Blanchflower and Bryson, 2003).

30. Guertzgen (2009) uses linked employer-employee data from Sweden and shows that wage contracts are related to firm quasi-rents, but that industry-wide agreements (common in Sweden but not the US) have much lower responsiveness to firm-level profitability than do local agreements.

31. Similar reasoning is used to argue that union companies have an incentive to underfund pensions (Ippolito, 1985).

32. Studies of Canada (Long, 1993; Walsworth, 2010) and Britain (Addison et al., 2003) likewise find unionization associated with slower employment growth.

33. As mentioned previously, Lee and Mas (2009) provide data refinements and extend the DiNardo and Lee analysis to examine how the effect of union wins on equity value varies with the strength of union support. They conclude that union wins with average and large margins are associated with large declines in market value. They do not examine how survival rates are affected by the strength of union support.

34. "Unions reduce profits but they do not 'destroy the goose that lays the golden egg'" (Freeman and Kleiner, 1999, p. 526). "Like successful viruses, unions are smart enough not to kill their hosts" (Kuhn, 1998, p. 1039). More formally, Kremer and Olken (2009) provide an evolutionary biology model of unions, noting that parasites that kill their hosts do not spread, whereas those that do little harm spread and may evolve to become essential to their hosts. They conclude that unions maximizing the present value of members' wages are likely to be displaced by more moderate unions. In their model, exogenous firm turnover lowers equilibrium union density since unions must work harder (organize more) to stay in place.

35. Sluggish union governance is a strong tendency and not an iron law. As noted subsequently, some companies have productive and responsive labor relations environments.

36. Sharp, widespread downturns such as the Great Recession beginning in December 2007 provide the exception to the general rule of no unilateral pay cuts. Such downturns in business are readily evident to workers, in which case employers' stated need to impose pay cuts, reduced benefits, furloughs, etc. are credible and more readily accepted by workers.

37. Our attention here is focused on differences in governance structure in union and nonunion workplaces. We ignore here any costs (or benefits) associated with union monopoly or employer monopsony power.

38. The term "dynamism" has become increasingly associated with 2006 Nobel laureate Edmund Phelps, whose use of the word has a broader emphasis than in this chapter (Phelps, 2007). Phelps' discussion of dynamism emphasizes, among other things, innovation (which changes jobs), entrepreneurship, openness, and inclusion and self-realization through one's work. Phelps argues that dynamism can serve to increase self-realization among the disadvantaged and that economies without dynamism cannot be just.

39. A concentration ratio need not be a good measure of monopoly power, which we expect to be associated with restricted output and high prices, since some firms grow very large relative to their competitors because of low prices and/or high quality. But concentration ratios are informative.

40. Delta's experience is instructive. Prior to 2001, Delta had a strong balance sheet with low indebtedness and, with the exception of its pilots, a nonunion workforce, although pay for nonunion workers had to be similar to that for union workers to deter union organizing. By 2003, Delta faced deteriorating product

market conditions coupled with industry-leading pay for its pilots and other workers. Financial viability required that Delta sharply reduce labor and other costs, but this could not be done without substantial concessions from pilots. Despite its initial advantages, the company was unable to steer a path to financial viability, instead accumulating massive debt and finally resorting to use of the costly bankruptcy process to achieve lower costs. For an analysis of the use of corporate debt by airlines to limit union bargaining power, see Benmelech et al. (2011).

41. The numbers for union *coverage* were as follows: In 1977, 32.8 percent in the public sector versus 23.3 percent in the private sector; and, in 2010, 40 percent in the public sector versus 7.7 percent in the private sector.

42. As emphasized in work by Weil (2005), unions facilitate the enforcement of workplace regulations and use of employment-based social insurance programs.

43. Freeman and Rogers (1999) administered worker surveys in the US in the early 1990s, along with subsequent surveys in other countries. My reading of their results is as follows. First, many workers want greater voice and participation in workplace decision-making, but the voice they desire is as much an individual voice as the collective voice associated with traditional unions. Second, workers want a more cooperative and less adversarial worker–management relationship, coupled with management support for worker participatory organizations. Third, workers who desire voice do not only want to express themselves but want their views to affect workplace outcomes. And fourth, workers see management resistance as the primary obstacle to worker participation and cooperation. Despite some differences, workers' expressed wants and concerns are surprisingly similar in union and nonunion workplaces.

44. I find appealing Sachs' proposals to utilize electronic voting, protect worker confidentiality, and adopt procedures used by the National Mediation Board (NMB) in the airline and railroad industries. While Sachs emphasizes steps that would fully insulate workers from management influence, my preference would be for procedures that would enhance the quality of information that workers receive during campaigns from both unions and management. Claims by both parties might be moderated if subjected to rebuttal and discussion. Although not currently feasible, I would like to see NLRB-sponsored forums, perhaps akin to a political debate, with representatives from the union and management, an NLRB moderator, and worker Q&A. Eligible workers could attend such forums or view them later on-line. Bodie (2008) likewise emphasizes the need for improved information to workers. He argues that required disclosure by unions and management would be feasible and provide at least some useful information to workers. More promising may be Internet-based channels of information that evolve over time, a process that could be enhanced by the NLRB (Hirsch, 2011).

REFERENCES

Addison, John T. and Barry T. Hirsch (1989), "Union Effects on Productivity, Profits, and Growth: Has the Long Run Arrived?" 7 *Journal of Labor Economics* 72–105.

Addison, John T., John S. Heywood, and Xiangdong Wei (2003), "New Evidence on Unions and Plant Closings: Britain in the 1990s," 69 *Southern Economic Journal* 822–41.

Aidt, Toke and Zafiris Tzannatos (2002), *Unions and Collective Bargaining: Economic Effects in a Global Environment*, Washington, DC: World Bank.

Allen, Steven G. (1986), "Unionization and Productivity in Office Building and School Construction," 39 *Industrial and Labor Relations Review* 187–201.

Baldwin, Carliss Y. (1983), "Productivity and Labor Unions: An Application of the Theory of Self-Enforcing Contracts," 56 *Journal of Business* 155–85.

Benmelech, Efraim, Nittai K. Bergman, and Ricardo Enriquez (2011), "Negotiating with Labor under Financial Distress," NBER Working Paper No. 17192 (July).

Bennett, James T. and Bruce E. Kaufman (eds) (2007), *What Do Unions Do? A Twenty-Year Perspective*, Piscataway, NJ: Transaction Publishers.

Betts, Julian R., Cameron W. Odgers, and Michael K. Wilson (2001), "The Effects of Unions on Research and Development: An Empirical Analysis Using Multi-Year Data," 34 *Canadian Journal of Economics* 785–806.

Bewley, Truman (1999), *Why Wages Don't Fall During a Recession*, Cambridge, MA: Harvard University Press.

Black, Sandra E. and Lisa M. Lynch (2001), "How to Compete: The Impact of Workplace Practices and Information Technology on Productivity," 83 *Review of Economics and Statistics* 434–45.

Blanchflower, David G. and Alex Bryson (2003), "Changes Over Time in Union Relative Wage Effects in the UK and the US Revisited," in John T. Addison and Claus Schnabel (eds), *International Handbook of Trade Unions*, Cheltenham, UK and Northampton, MA: Edward Elgar, pp. 197–245.

Bloom, Nicholas and John Van Reenen (2007), "Measuring and Explaining Management Practices across Firms and Countries," 122 *Quarterly Journal of Economics* 1351–408.

Bloom, Nicholas and John Van Reenen (2010), "Why Do Management Practices Differ across Firms and Countries?" 24 *Journal of Economic Perspectives* 203–24.

Bloom, Nicholas and John Van Reenen (2011), "Human Resource Management and Productivity," in Orley C. Ashenfelter and David Card (eds), *Handbook of Labor Economics, Vol. 4B*, Amsterdam: Elsevier, pp. 1697–767.

Bodie, Matthew T. (2008), "Information and the Market for Union Representation," 94 *Virginia Law Review* 1–78.

Booth, Alison L. (1995), *The Economics of the Trade Union*, Cambridge, UK: Cambridge University Press.

Bratsberg, Bernt and James F. Ragan, Jr. (2002), "Changes in the Union Wage Premium by Industry," 56 *Industrial and Labor Relations Review* 65–83.

Bronars, Stephen G. and Donald R. Deere (1991), "The Threat of Unionization, the Use of Debt, and the Preservation of Shareholder Wealth," 106 *Quarterly Journal of Economics* 231–54.

Brown, Charles and James Medoff (1978), "Trade Unions in the Production Process," 86 *Journal of Political Economy* 355–78.

Budd, John W. (2007), "The Effect of Unions on Employee Benefits and Non-Wage Compensation: Monopoly Power, Collective Voice, and Facilitation," in James T. Bennett and Bruce E. Kaufman (eds), *What Do Unions Do? A Twenty-Year Perspective*, Piscataway, NJ: Transaction Publishers, pp. 160–92.

Budd, John W. (2010), "When Do U.S. Workers First Experience Unionization? Implications for Revitalizing the Labor Movement," 49 *Industrial Relations* 209–25.

Card, David, Francesco Devicienti, and Agata Maida (2010), "Rent-sharing, Holdup, and Wages: Evidence from Matched Panel Data," NBER Working Paper No. 16192 (July).

Cavanaugh, Joseph K. (1998), "Asset Specific Investment and Unionized Labor," 37 *Industrial Relations* 35–50.

Chen, Huafeng (Jason), Marcin Kacperczyk, and Hernán Ortiz-Molina (2011), "Labor Unions, Operating Flexibility, and the Cost of Equity," 46 *Journal of Financial and Quantitative Analysis* 25–58.

Clark, Kim B. (1984), "Unionization and Firm Performance: The Impact on Profits, Growth, and Productivity," 74 *American Economic Review* 893–919.

Connolly, Robert A., Barry T. Hirsch, and Mark Hirschey (1986), "Union Rent Seeking, Intangible Capital, and Market Value of the Firm," 68 *Review of Economics and Statistics* 567–77.

Cramton, Peter and Joseph Tracy (1998), "The Use of Replacement Workers in Union Contract Negotiations: The US Experience, 1980–1989," 16 *Journal of Labor Economics* 667–701.

Davis, Steven J., R. Jason Faberman, and John Haltiwanger (2006), "The Flow Approach to Labor Markets: New Data Sources and Micro-Macro Links," 20 *Journal of Economic Perspectives* 3–26.

DiNardo, John and David S. Lee (2004), "Economic Impacts of New Unionization on Private Sector Employers: 1984–2001," 119 *Quarterly Journal of Economics* 1382–441.

Doucouliagos, Christos and Patrice Laroche (2003), "What Do Unions Do to Productivity? A Meta-Analysis," 42 *Industrial Relations* 650–91.

Doucouliagos, Christos and Patrice Laroche (2009), "Unions and Profits: A Meta-Regression Analysis," 48 *Industrial Relations* 146–83.

Doucouliagos, Christos and Patrice Laroche (2011), "Unions, Innovation, and Technology Adoption: New Insights from the Cross-Country Evidence," working paper.

Dunne, Timothy and David A. Macpherson (1994), "Unionism and Gross Employment Flows," 60 *Southern Economic Journal* 727–38.

Estlund, Cynthia (2010), *Regoverning the Workplace: From Self-Regulation to Co-Regulation*, New Haven, CT: Yale University Press.

Estreicher, Samuel (1994), "Employee Involvement and the 'Company Union' Prohibition: The Case for Partial Repeal of Section 8(a)(2) of the NLRA," 69 *New York University Law Review* 125–61.

Farber, Henry S. (1986), "The Analysis of Union Behavior," in Orley C. Ashenfelter and Richard Layard (eds), *Handbook of Labor Economics, Vol. II*, Amsterdam: Elsevier, pp. 1039–89.

Farber, Henry S. and Bruce Western (2002), "Accounting for the Decline of Unions in the Private Sector, 1973–1988," in James Bennett and Bruce Kaufman (eds), *The Future of Private Sector Unionism in the United States*, Armonk, NY: M.E. Sharpe, pp. 28–58.

Felix, R. Alison and James R. Hines, Jr. (2009), "Corporate Taxes and Union Wages in the United States," NBER Working Paper No. 15263 (August).

Freeman, Richard B. (1986), "Unionism Comes to the Public Sector," 24 *Journal of Economic Literature* 41–86.

Freeman, Richard B. (2007), "What Do Unions Do? The 2004 M-Brane Stringtwister Edition," in James T. Bennett and Bruce E. Kaufman (eds), *What Do Unions Do? A Twenty-Year Perspective*, Piscataway, NJ: Transaction Publishers, pp. 607–36.

Freeman, Richard B. and Morris M. Kleiner (1999), "Do Unions Make Enterprises Insolvent?" 52 *Industrial and Labor Relations Review* 510–27.

Freeman, Richard B. and James L. Medoff (1984), *What Do Unions Do?* New York: Basic Books.

Freeman, Richard B. and Joel Rogers (1999), *What Workers Want*, Ithaca, NY: Cornell University Press.

Fuchs, Victor R., Alan B. Krueger, and James M. Poterba (1998), "Economists' Views about Parameters, Values, and Policies: Survey Results in Labor and Public Economics," 36 *Journal of Economic Literature* 1387–425.

Gomez, Rafael and Morley Gunderson (2004), "The Experience Good Model of Trade Union Membership," in Phanindra V. Wunnava (ed.), *The Changing Role of Unions: New Forms of Representation*, Armonk, NY: M.E. Sharpe, pp. 92–112.

Grout, Paul A. (1984), "Investment and Wages in the Absence of Binding Contracts: A Nash Bargaining Approach," 52 *Econometrica* 449–60.

Guertzgen, Nicole (2009), "Rent-Sharing and Collective Bargaining Coverage: Evidence from Linked Employer-Employee Data," 111 *Scandinavian Journal of Economics* 323–49.

Hirsch, Barry T. (1991a), *Labor Unions and the Economic Performance of US Firms*, Kalamazoo, MI: Upjohn Institute for Employment Research.

Hirsch, Barry T. (1991b), "Union Coverage and Profitability Among US Firms," 73 *Review of Economics and Statistics* 69–77.

Hirsch, Barry T. (1992), "Firm Investment Behavior and Collective Bargaining Strategy," 31 *Industrial Relations* 95–121.

Hirsch, Barry T. (2004), "Reconsidering Union Wage Effects: Surveying New Evidence on an Old Topic," 25 *Journal of Labor Research* 233–66.

Hirsch, Barry T. (2007a), "Wage Determination in the US Airline Industry: Union Power under Product Market Constraints," in Darin Lee (ed.), *Advances in Airline Economics, Volume 2: The Economics of Airline Institutions, Operations and Marketing*, Amsterdam: Elsevier, pp. 27–59.

Hirsch, Barry T. (2007b), "What Do Unions Do for Economic Performance?" in James T. Bennett and Bruce E. Kaufman (eds), *What Do Unions Do? A Twenty-Year Perspective*, Piscataway, NJ: Transaction Publishers, pp. 193–237.

Hirsch, Barry T. (2008), "Sluggish Institutions in a Dynamic World: Can Unions and Industrial Competition Coexist?" 22 *Journal of Economic Perspectives* 153–76.

Hirsch, Barry T. and Robert A. Connolly (1987), "Do Unions Capture Monopoly Profits?" 41 *Industrial and Labor Relations Review* 118–36.

Hirsch, Barry T. and David A. Macpherson (2000), "Earnings, Rents, and Competition in the Airline Labor Market," 18 *Journal of Labor Economics* 125–55.

Hirsch, Barry T. and David A. Macpherson (2003), "Union Membership and Coverage Database from the Current Population Survey: Note," 56 *Industrial and Labor Relations Review* 349–54, and accompanying data site http://www.unionstats.com/.

Hirsch, Barry T. and David A. Macpherson (2011), *Union Membership and Earnings Data Book: Compilations from the Current Population Survey*, Washington, DC: Bureau of National Affairs.

Hirsch, Barry T. and Barbara A. Morgan (1994), "Shareholder Risk and Returns in Union and Nonunion Firms," 47 *Industrial and Labor Relations Review* 302–18.

Hirsch, Barry T. and Kislaya Prasad (1995), "Wage-Employment Determination and a Union Tax on Capital: Can Theory and Evidence be Reconciled?" 48 *Economics Letters* 61–71.

Hirsch, Jeffrey M. (2011), "Communication Breakdown: Reviving the Role of Discourse in the Regulation of Employee Collective Action," 44 *UC Davis Law Review* 1091–152.

Hirsch, Jeffrey M. and Barry T. Hirsch (2007), "The Rise and Fall of Private Sector Unionism: What Next for the NLRA?" 34 *Florida State University Law Review* 1133–80.

Holmes, Thomas J. (2006), "Geographic Spillover of Unionism," NBER Working Paper No. 12025.

Holmes, Thomas J. and Michael Walrath (2007), "Dynamics of Union Organizations: A Look at Gross Flows in the LORS Files," NBER Working Paper No. 13212 (July).

Ichniowski, Casey, Kathryn Shaw, and Giovanna Prennushi (1997), "The Effects of Human Resource Management Practices on Productivity: A Study of Steel Finishing Lines," 87 *American Economic Review* 291–313.

Ippolito, Richard A. (1985), "The Economic Function of Underfunded Pension Plans," 28 *Journal of Law and Economics* 611–51.

Klasa, Sandy, William F. Maxwell, and Hernán Ortiz-Molina (2009), "The Strategic Use of Corporate Cash Holdings in Collective Bargaining with Labor Unions," 92 *Journal of Financial Economics* 421–42.

Kleiner, Morris M., Jonathan S. Leonard, and Adam M. Pilarksi (2002), "How Industrial Relations Affects Plant Performance: The Case of Commercial Aircraft Manufacturing," 55 *Industrial and Labor Relations Review* 195–218.

Kremer, Michael and Benjamin A. Olken (2009), "A Biological Model of Unions," 1 *American Economic Journal: Applied Economics* 150–75.

Krueger, Alan B. and Alexandre Mas (2004), "Strikes, Scabs, and Tread Separations: Labor Strife and the Production of Defective Bridgestone/Firestone Tires," 112 *Journal of Political Economy* 253–89.

Kuhn, Peter (1998), "Unions and the Economy: What We Know; What We Should Know," 31 *Canadian Journal of Economics* 1033–56.

LaLonde, Robert J., Gérard Marschke, and Kenneth Troske (1996), "Using Longitudinal Data on Establishments to Analyze the Effects of Union Organizing Campaigns in the United States," 41/42 *Annales d'Économie et de Statistique* 155–85.

Lee, David and Alexandre Mas (2009), "Long-Run Impacts of Unions on Firms: New Evidence from Financial Markets, 1961–1999," NBER Working Paper No. 14709 (February).

Leonard, Jonathan S. (1992), "Unions and Employment Growth," in Mario F. Bognanno and Morris M. Kleiner (eds), *Labor Market Institutions and the Future Role of Unions*, Cambridge, MA: Blackwell Publishers, pp. 80–94.

Linneman, Peter D., Michael L. Wachter, and William H. Carter (1990), "Evaluating the Evidence on Union Employment and Wages," 44 *Industrial and Labor Relations Review* 34–53.

Long, Richard J. (1993), "The Effect of Unionization on Employment Growth of Canadian Companies," 46 *Industrial and Labor Relations Review* 691–703.

MacLeod, W. Bentley (2011), "Great Expectations: Law, Employment Contracts, and Labor Market Performance," in Orley C. Ashenfelter and David Card (eds), *Handbook of Labor Economics, Vol.4B*, Amsterdam: Elsevier, pp. 1591–696.

Magnani, Elisabetta and David Prentice (2010), "Did Reducing Unionization Create More Flexible American Industries?" 63 *Industrial and Labor Relations Review* 662–80.

Manning, Alan (2003), *Monopsony in Motion: Imperfect Competition in Labor Markets*, Princeton, NJ: Princeton University Press.

Mas, Alexandre (2008), "Labor Unrest and the Quality of Production: Evidence from the Construction Equipment Resale Market," 75 *Review of Economic Studies* 229–58.

Matsa, David A. (2010), "Capital Structure as a Strategic Variable: Evidence from Collective Bargaining," 65 *Journal of Finance* 1197–232.

Menezes-Filho, Naercio, David Ulph, and John Van Reenen (1998), "R&D and Unionism: Comparative Evidence from British Companies and Establishments," 52 *Industrial and Labor Relations Review* 45–63.

Metcalf, David (2003), "Unions and Productivity, Financial Performance and Investment: International Evidence," in John Addison and Claus Schnabel (eds), *International Handbook of Trade Unions*, Cheltenham, UK and Northampton, MA: Edward Elgar, pp. 118–71.

Mitchell, Merwin W. and Joe A. Stone (1992), "Union Effects on Productivity: Evidence from Western Sawmills," 46 *Industrial and Labor Relations Review* 135–45.

Odgers, Cameron W. and Julian R. Betts (1997), "Do Unions Reduce Investment? Evidence from Canada," 51 *Industrial and Labor Relations Review* 18–36.

Pencavel, John (2009), "How Successful Have Trade Unions Been? A Utility-Based Indicator of Union Well-Being," 62 *Industrial and Labor Relations Review* 147–56.

Phelps, Edmund S. (2007), "Macroeconomics for a Modern Economy (Nobel Address)," 97 *American Economic Review* 543–61.

Sachs, Benjamin I. (2010), "Enabling Employee Choice: A Structural Approach to the Rules of Union Organizing," 123 *Harvard Law Review* 655–728.

Slaughter, Matthew J. (2007), "Globalization and Declining Unionization in the United States," 46 *Industrial Relations* 329–46.

Syverson, Chad (2011), "What Determines Productivity?" 49 *Journal of Economic Literature* 326–65.

Troy, Leo, and Neil Sheflin (1985), *U.S. Union Sourcebook: Membership, Structure, Finance, Directory*, West Orange, NJ: Industrial Relations Data and Information Services.

US Council of Economic Advisors (2011), *Economic Report of the President*, Washington, DC: US Government Printing Office (February).

US Department of Labor (2011), "Employer Costs for Employee Compensation, December 2010," News Release, USDL-11-0304, Bureau of Labor Statistics, March 9.

Verma, Anil (2007), "What Do Unions Do to the Workplace? Union Effects on Management and HRM Policies," in James T. Bennett and Bruce E. Kaufman (eds), *What Do Unions Do? A Twenty-Year Perspective*, Piscataway, NJ: Transaction Publishers, pp. 275–312.

Wachter, Michael L. (2004), "Theories of the Employment Relationship: Choosing between Norms and Contracts," in Bruce E. Kaufman (ed.), *Theoretical Perspectives on Work and the Employment Relationship*, Champaign, IL: Industrial Relations Research Association, pp. 163–93.

Wachter, Michael L. (2007), "Labor Unions: A Corporatist Institution in a Competitive World," 155 *University of Pennsylvania Law Review* 581–634.

Wachter, Michael L. and Randall D. Wright (1984), "The Economics of Internal Labor Markets," 29 *Industrial Relations* 240–62.

Walsworth, Scott (2010), "Unions and Employment Growth: The Canadian Experience," 49 *Industrial Relations* 142–56.

Weil, David (2005), "Individual Rights and Collective Agents: The Role of Old and New Workplace Institutions in the Regulation of Labor Markets," in Richard Freeman, Larry Mishel, and Joni Hersch (eds), *Emerging Labor Market Institutions for the Twenty-First Century*, Chicago, IL: University of Chicago Press, pp. 13–44.

White, Lawrence J. (2002), "Trends in Aggregate Concentration in the United States," 16 *Journal of Economic Perspectives* 137–60.

Williamson, Oliver E., Michael L. Wachter, and Jeffrey E. Harris (1975), "Understanding the Employment Relation: The Analysis of Idiosyncratic Exchange," 6 *Bell Journal of Economics* 250–78.

5. Union organizing and the architecture of employee choice

*Benjamin I. Sachs**

I. INTRODUCTION

It is a central aim of our federal labor law to offer employees a choice on the question of unionization. But designing a legal regime that, in fact, protects employees' ability to choose whether they wish to bargain individually or collectively with their employers has long proven an elusive goal.[1]

The question of how to enable employee choice gained renewed attention in the opening months of the Obama Administration. The interest centered around the Employee Free Choice Act (EFCA), a bill that would have changed the process through which workers organize unions and enable employees to form unions through a procedure known as "card check." Under card check, if a majority of workers in a relevant unit sign authorization cards, the employer would be legally obligated to recognize the union as the employees' collective representative.[2] Senate negotiators also entertained possible alternatives to card check, including a "rapid elections" regime which would mandate that union elections take place almost immediately after the completion of a union organizing drive (Greenhouse, 2009a).

Irrespective of EFCA's fate, the debate over the legislation allows for reexamination of a set of questions at the conceptual core of labor law. As I will explain in this chapter, card check and rapid elections both aim to advance employee choice by minimizing or eliminating managerial intervention in union organizing efforts. Accordingly, the central substantive question raised by the EFCA debate is whether it is appropriate for federal law to enable employees and unions to minimize, or avoid entirely, managerial intervention in organizing efforts. This issue is foundational for labor law.[3]

We could answer the question in a relatively easy and straightforward way if labor law had a normative preference for unionization. But because labor law neither favors nor disfavors unionization, instead allowing employees to decide which form of bargaining they prefer, the appropriateness of curtailing managerial intervention in union organizing efforts must be investigated as part of an overall analysis of employee choice. To this end, I will address this question by drawing on two contemporary theories of legal default rules: the preference-eliciting default theory of statutory interpretation and the reversible default theory from corporate law (Bebchuk, 1989; Bebchuk and Hamdani, 2002; Elhauge, 2008).

In brief, both of these theories shed light on how legislatures (or courts) should choose default rules for a legal regime designed to maximize the satisfaction of some relevant preference set. Both theories, moreover, share a key insight: because of asymmetric impediments of one kind or another, it is often more difficult for parties to "depart" from one default rule than it would be for them to depart from another. Both theories then suggest the same answer: when the legislature (or court) does not know with certainty which default rule will maximize satisfaction of the relevant preference set, and when it is more difficult to depart from one default than it would be from the other, the legislature (or court) should choose the default from which it is easier to depart (Bebchuk and Hamdani, 2002; Elhauge, 2008). That way, if the initial placement of the rule turns out to be wrong, the parties will be best positioned to exercise their preferences and correct the misplacement.

But changing the default rule is not the only means to maximize satisfaction of preferences. In certain contexts, the same preference-maximizing goals that can be achieved by adopting a reversible or preference-eliciting default can also be secured by changing the *process* through which parties depart from the default. More specifically, by changing the process through which parties depart from a default in a manner that mitigates the asymmetry that called for the reversible default in the first place, legislatures (or courts) can maximize the preferences that are the aim of the legal regime. Ayres (2006) has named the processes through which parties depart from defaults "altering rules."[4] I will name a rule that corrects an asymmetric ability to depart from the default an "asymmetry-correcting altering rule."

Card check and rapid elections are best understood as asymmetry-correcting altering rules. The good to be maximized by the rules governing employee decisionmaking on the union question is employee choice.[5] As in the corporate law and statutory interpretation contexts, moreover, labor law must choose a default rule: workplaces must either be union or nonunion by default (Sunstein, 2001; Weiler, 1990; Barenberg, 1994). Preference-eliciting and reversible default theory suggest a way to approach this decision. First, when it comes to maximizing employee preferences on the union question, we must be – by definition – entirely uncertain whether employees prefer the union or nonunion option.[6] Second, because of collective action problems and managerial opposition to unionization, which I describe below, employees have an asymmetric ability to depart depending on where the default is set. It is at least somewhat more difficult for employees to depart from the nonunion default and choose unionization than it would be for employees to depart from a union default and choose nonunion bargaining.

In this setting, then, we have two options to maximize employee choice. First, labor law could impose a new default rule of union bargaining. While this approach may be conceptually justified, it is unlikely to be viable for a host of political and pragmatic reasons discussed below. Second, we could change the altering rule – the process through which employees depart from the nonunion default – in a way that mitigates the asymmetric ease of departure. Because the relevant asymmetry here flows from management's opposition to unionization and its ability to intervene in the employee organizing process, an altering rule – like card check or rapid elections – that minimizes management's ability to intervene can correct the relevant asymmetry and maximize employee choice.

Of course, an approach to maximizing employee choice that depends on minimizing managerial participation in union organizing campaigns raises two related questions. The first is whether labor law ought to provide employers with an affirmative right to intervene in the employee organizing process. As I will show, however, the argument in favor of an affirmative right for employer intervention depends on a flawed conception of what unionization entails. Unionization, for better or worse, does not effect a shift in sovereignty over the firm. It is a far more limited process, one in which employees decide to bargain collectively, rather than individually, with their employers and to name their agent for these purposes.[7] And while the outcome of the employees' decisionmaking process will impact employers, this fact does not entitle employers to an affirmative right to intervene in that process.

The second question returns us to the focus on employee choice and concerns the loss of information available to employees in an organizing effort conducted with a minimum of managerial involvement. A decrease in the quantity of information available to employees – information concerning the demerits of unionization – is a cost of adopting an asymmetry-correcting altering rule that minimizes employer intervention. But, as I will show, the cost to employee choice is likely to be marginal and will not outweigh the benefits to choice that flow from the new altering rule. This is so for several reasons, including the fact that neither card check nor rapid elections would deprive management of its ability to mount an argument against unionization, but would change only the time frame in which it is likely to do so.

Because minimizing managerial intervention in union campaigns is a legitimate means of advancing employee choice, labor law must resolve the question of how to design an altering rule that achieves this goal. In particular, the debate over EFCA presents the question of whether an *open* decisionmaking process – like card check – is an appropriate mechanism for minimizing managerial intervention. This chapter argues that openness in decisionmaking is unrelated to any legitimate asymmetry-correcting goal and, moreover, that an open decisionmaking process can expose employees to forms of union and coworker interference at the moment of decision. Because, for reasons described below, rapid elections are not the optimal approach, the chapter briefly sketches two new designs – alternatives to both card check and rapid elections – that would accomplish the legitimate function of minimizing managerial intervention while at the same time preserving secrecy in decisionmaking.

This chapter proceeds as follows. Section II provides, by way of background, a stylized description of the union organizing process under traditional National Labor Relations Act (NLRA) rules, under a rapid elections regime, and under card check. Section III explains the preference-eliciting and reversible default theories and applies these theories to the union organizing context. It then suggests card check and rapid elections as asymmetry-correcting altering rules. Section IV addresses the questions of management's affirmative right to intervene in the employee organizing process and employees' interest in receiving information from employers about unionization. Section V discusses the merits of an open voting system and proposes alternatives to card check that preserve secret voting while minimizing managerial intervention in union campaigns. Section VI concludes.

II.   THREE REGIMES FOR UNION ORGANIZING

In this section, I offer a highly stylized model of union organizing under current NLRA rules and then provide a model of organizing under two alternative regimes: rapid elections and card check.

A.   The NLRA

Under federal labor and employment law, individual employment contracting is the default rule in U.S. workplaces – bargaining over terms and conditions of work in the default position takes place between individual employees and their employers (see, e.g., Weiler, 1990). The NLRA gives employees the right to depart from this default by forming labor unions and bargaining collectively with their employers over terms and conditions of employment.[8] Under traditional NLRA procedures, the process of departing from the default rule involves two discrete phases: the organizing phase and the decisional phase.

During the organizing phase, union organizers along with sympathetic employees attempt to build support for the union among the workforce. Although some discussions between employees take place at work, the effort consists primarily of visits with employees when they are not at work through so-called "house calls."[9] Through these discussions, organizers and pro-union employees field questions from employees about the process of forming a union and about the likely results if unionization should succeed, and they relate the merits of unionization. Ultimately, organizers urge employees to commit to voting in favor of unionization and to signing authorization cards, which are later used to request that the NLRB conduct a union representation election.[10]

Because of the intensity of employer opposition to unionization, a subject I take up below, unions try to complete as much of the organizing phase as possible before the employer becomes aware of the effort. Thus, union organizing guides instruct organizers on maintaining as low a profile as possible for as long as possible (see, e.g., American Federation of State, County, and Municipal Employees, 1999).

Under current NLRA rules, although a union can avoid managerial intervention for a time, the union is required to give management notice of the organizing campaign well before the vote on unionization takes place. An employer is only obligated to recognize a union as its employees' collective representative if and when a majority of employees vote for union representation in a secret ballot election conducted by the NLRB.[11] In order to secure such an election, employees must "petition" the Board by submitting authorization cards signed by at least 30 percent of the employees in the relevant bargaining unit,[12] and once this petition is filed, the Board notifies the employer of the organizing effort. On average, an NLRB election is scheduled forty-one days after the employees' petition is filed, meaning that the campaign is public for approximately six weeks prior to the time employees vote (see Ferguson, 2008).

Once the organizing campaign becomes public, employers – in nearly all cases – mount a campaign of their own designed to discourage employees from choosing unionization.[13] As has been documented both in the scholarly literature (Bronfenbrenner, 2000; Estlund, 2002; Weiler, 1983) and in congressional hearings on the matter (House Report No. 110-23, 2007), employers have at their disposal a variety of mechanisms, both legal and illegal, for discouraging unionization, and they use these tools with some frequency. For example, firms often schedule one-on-one meetings between employees and their supervisors along with mandatory meetings of the entire workforce, during work time, to convey their view that unionization is not in the interests of the employees or the firm (see, e.g., Lafer, 2007). Employees can legally be subject to discipline or discharge if they refuse to attend these meetings.[14] Quite often, though prohibited by federal law, employers threaten that unionization will result in job loss and in the closing of the firm.[15] Finally, in many organizing campaigns, employers discharge union supporters as a means of nipping an organizing campaign "in the bud."[16]

Under current rules, when the organizing phase is complete, employees are called on to make their choice about unionization through a secret ballot election. On a day designated by the Board, employees are directed to a location on the employer's property where they cast their ballots. If more than 50 percent of voting employees vote in favor of unionization, the employer is required by law to recognize the union as the employees' bargaining agent. If fewer than 50 percent vote in favor of unionization, the firm continues with the default arrangement of individual employment contracting.[17]

B.   Rapid Elections

A second, longstanding proposal for reform would require the NLRB to conduct union elections almost immediately after a union has filed its election petition. A so-called rapid elections regime would leave nearly all of the current rules for union organizing and recognition in place, and thus union campaigns under such a regime would proceed largely in the manner described immediately above. Unions, as they do now, would attempt to keep their organizational activity underground for as long as possible. As under current law, in order to unionize under a rapid elections regime, employees would be required to petition the Board for an election once they had gathered cards signed by 30 percent of the relevant bargaining unit.[18] When employees have filed the petition, the Board would notify the employer of the campaign. Employees would vote, as they do now, in a secret ballot election conducted on the employer's property.

Unlike the current regime, however, a rapid elections regime would call on the NLRB to hold representation elections within a strictly limited period of time following the filing of the petition. Proposals range from five days to two weeks (see, e.g., Greenhouse, 2009a). As such, rapid elections aim to reduce dramatically the period of time during which a union campaign must be public and thus to minimize the amount of time that employers have to intervene in organizing efforts. As Weiler (1990) describes it, in a rapid elections regime:

> The Board would . . . conduct an immediate election in five days or so [following the petition] . . . . [B]ecause the vote would be conducted so close to the time the union surfaced from its organizational drive, the die would largely be cast as far as the employer was concerned. There would be no extended campaign during which management could try either to persuade or to pressure its employees to change their minds.

Two points bear mention. First, although rapid elections aim to limit the window of opportunity for managerial intervention in union campaigns, the proposal would still statutorily guarantee employers some minimum window of time – again, five days to two weeks – during which they could oppose unionization. Second, rapid elections would restrict managerial intervention to this statutory minimum only if employees succeed in keeping their campaigns "private" until the moment the petition is filed. Should management learn of union organizational activity prior to the filing of a petition, its interventions could begin at that point.

C.   Card Check

Card check would offer employees a substantially different process for organizing unions. Under a card check regime, employees would register their choice on the question of unionization by signing a card indicating that they want a union to serve as their agent for purposes of collective bargaining with the employer. Unlike an NLRB election, in a card check regime there is emphatically no requirement of secrecy. To the contrary, cards may be solicited by a union supporter and signed in the presence of the union supporter who solicited the card. Moreover, although the validity of a card can be challenged ex post on the ground that it was obtained through coercion or fraud, there is no contemporaneous oversight of the card solicitation process. Under a card check regime, if a majority of employees in the relevant bargaining unit sign authorization cards, the employer is then required to recognize the union as the employees' agent and to bargain collectively with the union. If fewer than 50 percent of employees in the unit sign cards, the firm remains in the default position of individual employment contracting.[19]

For our purposes, the most salient difference between these two decisional mechanisms – between card check and an NLRB election – is secrecy.[20] The openness of card check as a decisional mechanism has generated enormous criticism. Critics assert that card check impedes autonomous employee choice because an open decisional mechanism exposes employees to coercive pressure from the coworkers and union organizers who solicit cards (see, e.g., Yager et al., 1998). Craver (1995), for example, writes that a card check process opens "the possibility that employees may have signed authorization cards due to social pressure, misunderstanding, or outright coercion."[21]

Proponents of the legislation argue that card check advances autonomous employee choice; they do not, however, trumpet card check's attributes as a decisional mechanism. Few defend openness in decisionmaking,[22] or critique the secret ballot as an unfair means for employee voting. Rather, supporters argue that card check enhances employee choice because it corrects what they see as flaws in the union organizing process that precedes the casting of ballots.[23] Namely, in their support of card check, proponents point to management's ability to intervene in the employee organizing process and through various means to interfere coercively with employee decisionmaking on the question of unionization.

The framing of the card check debate, though, raises a puzzle. If card check is a different way for employees to register their choice on the question of unionization – if it is simply a different *decisional mechanism* – how can it affect the ways in which management does or does not intervene in the union organizing process? The answer to this puzzle lies in the observation that card check is more than a decisional mechanism. In fact, and more importantly, card check is what I will call an organizing technology: it is a device that enables employees to conduct union organizing campaigns without giving notice to management that a campaign is underway and thus to limit, or avoid entirely, managerial intervention.

Card check functions in this way because, under a card check regime, unions have no affirmative obligation to disclose the existence of the organizing drive to the employer until the union has successfully gathered cards from a majority of employees. Once a majority of employees have signed union authorization cards, however, the organizing drive is complete and the employer is obligated to recognize and bargain with the union.[24] The window for employer intervention has, accordingly, closed. To be sure, card check's organizing technology cannot always accomplish this objective perfectly. Even under card check, no union can ensure that in every campaign management will not learn of its organizing efforts: most obviously, an employee opposed to unionization can inform management of the organizing drive as soon as she is visited by a union organizer. But these imperfections do not alter the underlying logic and purpose of the technology.

Although many proponents of card check legislation do not make the point explicitly, the fact that card check functions as an organizing technology of this sort is made clear by academic observers. Barenberg (1994), for example, describes card check as a "samizdat" approach to labor law reform. According to Barenberg (1994):

> [Card check is designed] to preempt the employer's use of its machinery of communication and incentives by allowing workers to organize unions secretly through whatever underground or external communication network they currently can muster. . . . The employer would therefore have no opportunity to interfere with the workers' collective organizing – unless it got wind of the underground card solicitations.

Epstein (2008) characterizes the organizing phase under card check as "clandestine," while Weiler (1983) (see also Estlund, Senate Committee Testimony, 2007) describes the Canadian card check regime by explaining that "[t]he employer is afforded no opportunity to campaign against the union," because "when the union surfaces with a majority of the bargaining unit signed up, the statutory condition for certification is satisfied."

In sum, both rapid elections and card check aim to restructure the union organizing process in order to minimize or eliminate employer intervention in that process. The question posed by these regimes, therefore, is whether this goal is an *appropriate* one for federal law. It is to this question, one of the central issues for labor law, that I turn now.

III.   A NEW ALTERING RULE FOR LABOR LAW

Federal labor law neither mandates nor prohibits unionization. Rather, it establishes the default position of individual, nonunion employment contracting, a nondefault alternative of collective bargaining through unions, and an "altering rule."[25] An altering rule, as Ayres (2006) defines it, specifies the "means of opting" for a nondefault alternative; it "tell[s] private parties the necessary and sufficient conditions" for moving from the default position to the nondefault alternative. Labor law's current altering rule – the *means* through which workers opt out of nonunion bargaining and opt into unionized collective bargaining – is the NLRB secret ballot election process.

Neither card check nor a rapid elections regime would change labor law's default rule; the default position would still be individual, nonunion employment contracting. Nor would card check or rapid elections change the statutory alternative to the default rule; collective bargaining through unions over terms and conditions of employment would remain the nondefault alternative. Both alternatives would, however, change labor law's altering rule in order to minimize management's ability to intervene in the unionization process. Under rapid elections, employees would vote on the union question almost immediately following the completion of their organizing efforts. Card check would effect a more pronounced change: under card check, employees could move from the nonunion default to the union alternative by signing authorization cards.

Card check and rapid elections, moreover and more to the point, are not simply modified altering rules; they are *easier* altering rules than those provided by current law. By allowing employees to complete organizing campaigns with a minimum of managerial intervention and opposition, card check and rapid elections make it significantly easier than it is under current law for employees to opt out of the nonunion default and choose unionization.

A.   Preference-Eliciting and Reversible Default Theory

In his recent work on statutory interpretation, Elhauge (2008) argues that, under conditions of uncertainty and asymmetric power, courts should interpret unclear legislation by using "preference-eliciting default rules." These default rules are most likely to maximize "political satisfaction" because they are most likely to result – at the end of the day – in statutory language that most fully captures the "enactable preferences" of the polity.[26] Although preference-eliciting defaults are designed to maximize enactable preferences, these default rules do *not* call on courts to choose the statutory interpretation they believe is most likely to capture those preferences. Rather, a preference-eliciting default requires courts to choose the interpretation "more likely to be corrected by the legislature because it burdens some politically powerful group with ready access to the legislative agenda" (Elhauge, 2008). That is, a preference-eliciting default requires courts to choose the interpretation that would be disfavored by the party to the interpretive debate with the greatest capacity to force the legislature to correct an erroneous interpretation.

Elhauge provides the following illustration. Suppose that a court can interpret a statute in two different but plausible ways: interpretation *A* or interpretation *B*. There is a 60 percent chance that interpretation *A* captures enactable preferences, and there is a 40 percent chance that interpretation *B* gets it right. Now suppose, Elhauge continues, that if interpretation *A* does *not* capture enactable preferences, there is a 0 percent chance that the legislature will correct the court's interpretation. Conversely, if interpretation *B* is incorrect, there is a 100 percent chance that the legislature will react by correcting the court's interpretation.

In this example, should the court choose interpretation *A*, it can expect that overall "expected political satisfaction" will be 60 percent. However, should the court go with interpretation *B*, expected political satisfaction will be 100 percent: the court will choose the right interpretation 40 percent of the time, and in the 60 percent of the cases in which the court chooses the wrong interpretation, the legislature will correct the court. As such, "[c]hoosing preference-eliciting option *B* will . . . ultimately increase the expected satisfaction of enactable preferences, even though option *B* itself is less likely to reflect enactable preferences than *A*" (Elhauge, 2008).

Elhauge shows that preference-eliciting default rules are appropriate when certain conditions are met: first, there must be uncertainty regarding enactable preferences; and second, there must be an asymmetry in the likelihood that the legislature will correct the judicial interpretation depending on which interpretation the court chooses.[27] In fact, the appropriateness of employing a preference-eliciting default depends primarily on an interaction between these conditions. Where there is complete certainty about the legislature's preferences, there is no justification for a preference-eliciting default. In these cases, a court knows what the legislature prefers, and it should interpret the statute accordingly. Where there is uncertainty about legislative preference, however, a preference-eliciting default rule is appropriate if there is sufficient asymmetry between the likelihood that the legislature will correct one option or another. Most useful for our purposes, Elhauge shows that when a court is completely uncertain about what interpretation the legislature would prefer – if, following the illustration above, the court believes there is a 50 percent chance that the legislature would choose interpretation *A* and a 50 percent chance that the legislature would choose *B* – then a preference-eliciting rule is appropriate if there is any asymmetry in the likelihood of correction.

In the context of statutory interpretation, asymmetry in the likelihood of legislative correction flows from differentials in the political power of groups on either side of the interpretive dispute (Elhauge, 2008). These power differentials might be explained, as Elhauge shows, because one side has a better ability to shape the legislative agenda, to intervene in drafting, to raise issues with the legislature, or to block legislative change. But "[w]hatever the cause, preference-eliciting analysis provides a reason for favoring" the party with less political power in the interpretive dispute. This conclusion is, in some respects, deeply counterintuitive. After all, if courts were to choose a default rule geared toward most accurately estimating enactable preferences, they would do far better by choosing the interpretation favored by the most politically *powerful* side of the debate. But again, Elhauge shows that by choosing the interpretation favored by the politically *weaker* side of the interpretive debate, the court can invite legislative correction in the event that it chooses wrongly, and thereby maximize political satisfaction.

Finally, Elhauge (2008) stresses that the reason it is appropriate for courts to choose a default rule that favors the politically weaker party in an interpretive debate is definitively not because those with less political power are more likely to support benevolent policies, nor because politically weak groups deserve any kind of special solicitude, nor because the politically weak are likely to reflect enactable preferences of the polity as a whole. It is not because the politically weak are likely to be "right" in any sense. To the contrary, the point of favoring the politically weak is that doing so "will produce a precise legislative appraisal of the weight the political process wishes to give those interests." That is, the point of favoring the politically weak is that doing so will more likely result in an outcome that maximizes enactable preferences, even though enactable preferences may well ultimately prove to be contrary to the policies the politically weak would have chosen.

For Elhauge and statutory interpretation, the question is how to design a default rule that maximizes enactable preferences when there is uncertainty regarding those preferences and the distribution of political power between the parties to the interpretive dispute produces an asymmetric ability to depart from the default. Bebchuk and Hamdani (2002) (see also Bebchuk, 1989) take up a similar question in the context of corporate law and come to a similar conclusion.

As Bebchuk and Hamdani (2002) explain, the challenge for corporate law is to select default rules that are most likely to maximize shareholder value or shareholder preferences.[28] The traditional approach to default rules in corporate law is the "hypothetical bargains" approach (Bebchuk and Hamdani, 2002). Here, where there is uncertainty regarding which of two rules would maximize value, the court or the legislature is to choose the rule that it believes "fully informed and rational shareholders would have most likely chosen had they considered this question." Bebchuk and Hamdani (2002), however, reject the hypothetical bargains approach to corporate defaults because, as they explain, this approach "overlooks a fundamental asymmetry in the process of opting-out of default rules." The asymmetry of concern to Bebchuk and Hamdani flows from management's control over the process by which corporate charter amendments are initiated. Although a corporate charter can be amended by a vote of the corporation's shareholders, such a vote "take[s] place only on amendments initiated by management." Thus, this managerial "veto power over charter amendments" creates an asymmetry between those arrangements that management favors and those it disfavors.

In particular, should a legislature or court choose a default rule that turns out to decrease shareholder value, and management disfavors the rule, shareholders will be able to depart from the default rule because management will likely initiate a charter amendment. In contrast, should the legislature or court choose a value-decreasing default rule that management favors, it is less likely that shareholders will be able to depart from the default because it is less likely that management will initiate the amendment process. According to Bebchuk and Hamdani (2002), this asymmetry between the reversibility of defaults favored and disfavored by management suggests that the hypothetical bargains approach will often fail to maximize shareholder value. To correct this failing, the authors suggest the "reversible defaults" approach. Under the reversible defaults rule:

> [W]henever there is uncertainty over the identity of the value-maximizing arrangement, a preference should generally be given to the alternative that is more restrictive of managers. This restrictive alternative would be reversed if it turns out to be value decreasing [and left in place if not], whereas the alternative favored by managers would remain in place if chosen as default even if it turned out to be value decreasing.

So far, the theory of reversible defaults points to the same conclusion as the theory of preference-eliciting defaults. According to both approaches, the combination of uncertainty regarding the relevant preference set and an asymmetric ability to depart from the default calls for choosing the default from which it is easiest to depart. But Bebchuk and Hamdani (2002) provide an additional insight that is important here. Namely, the authors explain that although a charter amendment is required to opt out of *most* corporate default arrangements, in some instances the default can be reversed by amending the corporate bylaws. And unlike a charter amendment, bylaws can be amended by shareholders without board approval – that is to say, without a need for management to initiate the amendment process. Accordingly, in instances where default reversal can be accomplished through bylaw amendment, management no longer enjoys an asymmetric ability to block a departure from the default rule. As Bebchuk and Hamdani (2002) put it, "[w]ith respect to such issues [governed by bylaw amendment], . . . the asymmetry between arrangements favored and disfavored by managers in terms of ease of reversibility would largely disappear." And so they conclude that "[b]y allowing opting out via a bylaw amendment, public officials would ensure that, if the chosen default turned out to be value decreasing, shareholders would be able to reverse it easily and not be stuck with a value-decreasing arrangement."

Although Bebchuk and Hamdani do not use the following language, what they identify here are two different altering rules for corporate law defaults – two different "means of opting" for a nondefault alternative (Ayres, 2006). What their theory reveals, moreover, is that when a court or legislature is faced with uncertainty regarding which rule shareholders would prefer, and there is an asymmetric ability to depart depending on which rule is chosen as the default, the court or legislature can maximize value in one of *two* ways. First, the court or legislature can choose the reversible default, the one from which it is easiest to depart. Or second, the default can be set according to the traditional hypothetical bargains approach, and the altering rule can be changed in a manner that mitigates the asymmetric ability or power to depart from the default. The key insight here is that value – or shareholder preference – can be maximized *either* by choosing the default rule from which it is easiest to depart *or* by adopting an asymmetry-correcting altering rule.[29]

B.   Choosing Default and Altering Rules to Maximize Employee Choice

For preference-eliciting default theory, the question is how to design default rules to maximize the enactable preferences of the legislature. For reversible default theory, the question is how to design a default regime to maximize shareholder value or preference. In our context, the question is how to structure the rules governing organizing campaigns in a manner that maximizes the satisfaction of employee preferences on the union question. What might preference-eliciting and reversible default theory tell us about the appropriate choice of default and altering rules in this context? Again, a preference-eliciting or reversible default approach is appropriate when there is uncertainty regarding how to maximize the good sought by the regime and there is an asymmetric ability to depart from the default depending on where the default is set. In our context there is uncertainty – indeed definitional uncertainty – regarding actual employee preferences. Further, as I discuss in this section, there is an asymmetric ability to depart depending on where the default is set. Because of a series of collective action problems and market failures that disproportionately affect employees who wish to move from nonunion to union governance, and because of managerial opposition to unionization, it is more difficult for employees to depart from a nonunion default (to choose unionization) than it would be for employees to depart from a union default (to choose nonunion, individual employment contracting).

1.   Asymmetric impediments to unionization

Management generally opposes unionization. This fact is essentially undisputed and is evident from a host of empirical studies (see, e.g., Bronfenbrenner, 2009). The fact of employer opposition creates a series of asymmetric impediments to unionization and thereby makes it more difficult for employees to choose to unionize than to remain nonunion. The first set of impediments flows from traditional collective action problems. Employers have the discretion to ban much speech about unionization on company property (since rules prohibiting employees from discussing unionization during working time are presumptively valid)[30] and can bar nonemployee union organizers from company property entirely.[31] As such, employees who wish to communicate information in support of unionization bear the substantial transaction costs of identifying and then contacting all other prospective supporters during nonwork time (Barenberg, 1994). Management, on the other hand, is immune from such collective action problems. For example, managers have access to complete information about bargaining unit members and have the ability (and the legal right) to conduct one-on-one and company-wide captive audience meetings during working time to discourage unionization.[32] Management, moreover, has a "centralized capacity to overcome free-rider problems among individual workers" (Barenberg, 1994). Although much of this conduct would constitute an unfair labor practice,[33] management can provide resources – including communicational, logistical, and financial resources – to workers who oppose unionization, while withholding similar resources from pro-union employees. For example, management often provides support to "vote no" committees during organizing drives.[34] Finally, management can help employees opposed to unionization overcome "second-order" collective action problems by imposing punishment on pro-union employees – a coordination cost that the anti-union employees would otherwise have to bear (Barenberg, 1994).

In addition to these traditional collective action problems, an "intrapersonal collective action problem" (Sunstein, 1991) also makes it more difficult for employees to depart from the nonunion default. Here, the problem arises because "the costs and benefits, for a particular person, of engaging in an activity change dramatically over time" (Sunstein, 1991; Frederick et al., 2002). Because "[m]any workers greatly discount the future, sometimes treating it as irrelevant," they may be prone to one particular form of intrapersonal collective action problem: "[A] refusal, because the short-term costs exceed the short-term benefits, to engage in activity having long-term benefits that dwarf long-term costs" (Sunstein, 1991).[35] In our context, for the individual employee considering whether to support a union organizing effort, the short-term costs of supporting unionization almost always exceed the short-term benefits. As we have seen (and as I will discuss in more detail below), workers bear a substantial risk of losing their jobs should they support a unionization effort (see, e.g., Schmitt and Zipperer, 2007), and among those union supporters who are not discharged or formally disciplined for their activity, many face softer forms of retaliation that are nonetheless quite significant and can diminish career prospects (see, e.g., Barenberg, 1994). In the short term, moreover, there are often no benefits from unionization; even when a campaign is successful, it takes many months to bargain a first contract and usually much longer to realize the full gains of that contract.[36] And although the long-term benefits may well be substantial (in the form of wage and benefit gains, for example) (see generally Budd, 2007; Card et al., 2007), these benefits are likely to be substantially discounted (Sunstein, 2001).

Accordingly, intrapersonal collective action problems can impede the move from a nonunion default to the union alternative. But the same problems would not hinder the move in the opposite direction – from a union default to nonunion, individual employment contracting. Here, the short-term costs to employees are likely to be *de minimis* and to be outweighed by short-term benefits. Employers likely would not punish employees who supported this departure from the default, and might indeed reward such workers either through explicit benefits or through softer forms of promotion.

The intrapersonal collective action problem is similar to, and exacerbated by, a dynamic that Barenberg (1994) terms an "intertemporal market failure." Here, the problem is not that workers highly discount the future benefits of unionization, but rather that the workers who bear the upfront costs of unionization are not able *in fact* to recapture those costs through downstream rewards. So, "[e]mployees who, as union pioneers and activists, risk their careers and bear other material and psychic costs cannot generally capture the stream of benefits flowing to workers who subsequently enter the already unionized workplace" (Barenberg, 1994). Again, this market failure will reduce the likelihood that workers will depart from the nonunion default, but its logic does not apply to the union default. In that context, again, upfront costs are unlikely: employees who support the departure from the union default will not bear risks to their careers or other "material and psychic costs" but can expect, if anything, enhanced career prospects along with other material and psychic benefits that come from an approving management.

As such, these sets of collective action problems make it more difficult for employees to depart from a nonunion default than it would be for them to depart from a union default. But beyond these impediments, management can, and does, intervene directly in the employee decisional process in order to deter unionization.[37] I will briefly discuss two particular forms of intervention: first, managerial threats or predictions that a successful unionization campaign will result in closure of the enterprise; and second, the discharge of employees in retaliation for support of unionization. Both forms of intervention are prevalent and both have the intended effect of deterring unionization.[38]

With respect to threats of closure, the Bronfenbrenner (2009) study finds that 57 percent of the 1004 employers in the sample made threats to close all or part of the firm if the employees decided to unionize.[39] With respect to discharge of workers for union activity, estimates of the frequency of discharge rates vary. Bronfenbrenner (2009) finds that employers discharged union activists in 34 percent of campaigns, whereas Schmitt and Zipperer (2007) estimate that nearly one in five workers who takes an active role in union organizing is discharged for doing so. Morris (1998) estimates that between 1992 and 1997, one in eighteen workers involved in organizing activity faced illegal retaliation. The lowest end of the estimate range comes from a study prepared by the Center for Union Facts, a "union watchdog" dedicated to educating the public about "union officials' abuse of power."[40] This study reports that in 2.7 percent of campaigns where the union filed an election petition, an employee was illegally fired for union activity (Wilson, 2008).[41]

Wherever the actual discharge rate falls in this spectrum of estimates, and however frequent threats and predictions of closing are, several pieces of evidence suggest that these forms of management opposition to unionization are "extremely effective in reducing union election win rates" (Bronfenbrenner, 2000). Making modest assumptions about the rationality of employer spending, these findings should not be surprising. Employers expend a great deal of resources combating union organizing drives, and it would be puzzling if they did so without in fact deterring unionization. Most specifically, employers frequently subject themselves to legal liability (in the form of back wage payments and reinstatement orders) in order to discourage unionization. Although monetary damages under the NLRA are limited to compensatory relief (Sachs, 2008), backpay orders are certainly not free.[42]

Empirical studies on the impact of employer interventions into the employee organizing process support the conclusion that these interventions have their intended effect. In her 2009 study, Bronfenbrenner (2009) found that employer anti-union activity was associated with declining union win rates. Thus, when employers used no anti-union tactics, the success rate of worker organizing efforts was 72 percent. When employers deployed one to four of the anti-union tactics identified by Bronfenbrenner – some of which are legal, but many of which are illegal under the NLRA – the union win rate was 65 percent. And when an employer used ten or more anti-union tactics, the win rate was just 45 percent. Of particular relevance here, Bronfenbrenner (2009) finds that threats of plant closings and discharges of union activists (when the worker is not reinstated before the election) are associated with union win rates lower than in campaigns where these tactics are not deployed.[43]

2.　Employee free choice and managerial intervention

I have argued that two sets of factors make it at least somewhat more difficult for employees to depart from the nonunion default than it would be for them to depart from a union default. The stickiness of the nonunion default is due, first, to collective action problems (and intertemporal market failures) that hinder employee efforts at unionization but would not hinder efforts to deunionize. Second, I have argued that a nonunion default is stickier than a union default because employer intervention in the organizing process moves employee preferences in the nonunion direction. Yet, with respect to this second set of factors, if employees are more likely to choose nonunion bargaining following employer intervention because they have legitimately formed a preference for nonunion bargaining, then the increased stickiness of the nonunion default attributable to direct managerial intervention (as opposed to that caused by asymmetric collective action problems) would simply be a legitimate product of altered employee preferences. If, however, this shift in employee preferences reflects an illegitimate influence on preferences, then the stickiness here would not reflect employee free choice and would call for correction.

In what sense might employer intervention in the union organizing process be inconsistent with employee free choice? A straightforward way to conceive of this dynamic begins with the observation that the commitment to employee "free" choice reflects the idea that employees' choices on the question of unionization should be autonomous. As is conventionally understood, force and fraud impede the autonomy of choices (cf. Sunstein, 1986; see generally Farnsworth, 2004).[44] Thus, where managerial intervention involves either force or fraud – coercion or misinformation – the influence of such intervention on employee preference expression should not be understood as contributing to free employee choice.[45]

Not all managerial interventions in union campaigns amount to force or fraud, and certain forms of employer communication – regarding, for example, the bargaining positions management is likely to take should unionization occur – can legitimately contribute to the formation of employee preferences. Nonetheless, several types of employer interventions are properly understood as constituting force or fraud and thus as illegitimately inhibiting departures from the nonunion default. The discharge of union activists is a particularly stark example of managerial intervention that takes this form. Here, employees who are openly supportive of union organizing efforts face "the [employment] equivalent of capital punishment."[46] The effect on the employees actually discharged is literally to deprive them of the option of unionization: no longer employed by the employer, the discharged worker has lost her chance to support and ultimately join the union. But the signaling effect of such discharges extends beyond those workers actually removed from the workforce. The message sent by such discharges to the workforce as a whole is that support for unionization carries with it the very real risk that one's employment at the firm will end.

Of course, discharging an employee for supporting unionization is an unfair labor practice, and reinstatement is available as a remedy.[47] The weakness of the NLRB's remedial arsenal, however, has rendered this unfair labor practice charge nearly meaningless (Sachs, 2008). Even in cases where the Board pursues and successfully prosecutes a discharge case, it takes the Board approximately two years to issue a reinstatement order (Sachs, 2008). Thus, in almost every instance, a union supporter discharged for organizing activity will remain out of the workforce for the entire life of the unionization effort.[48] To the extent that other employees involved in an organizing effort understand discharge as the potential price for supporting unionization, their choice on the question should not be understood as autonomous or free.

While the discharge of union activists is a form of coercive intervention, employer threats that they will close all or part of the firm if the employees choose to unionize – which occurred more than half the time in Bronfenbrenner's (2009) sample – can be a form of misinformation that interferes with autonomous employee choice. Here, the message is that unionization will lead not just to the discharge of certain union supporters, but also to the loss of all employees' jobs. Although predictions based on economic facts that unionization will lead to firm closure do not constitute misinformation, several pieces of evidence suggest that employer statements regarding firm closure made during organizing drives are more likely to be threats, lacking a grounding in economic fact, than they are to be genuine predictions. To start, what employees will demand through collective bargaining and what an actual contract will require can only be known at the conclusion of bargaining and is indeterminate during the course of an organizing effort. As such, it is rarely the case that employers can predict that unionization *simpliciter* will lead to any specific outcome.[49] Second, there is ample theoretical and empirical support for the view that unions will not – and most often do not – make wage demands that threaten the continued viability of the firm, at least in the short to medium term. Unions generally do not push for contractual gains that "destroy the goose that lays the golden egg" (Freeman and Kleiner, 1999; see also Freeman and Medoff, 1984). Third, Bronfenbrenner (2000) finds that actual threats of plant closure are unlikely to be related to the financial condition of the firm. In her recent study, Bronfenbrenner (2009) reports that although 57 percent of employers in the sample threatened full or partial closure in the event of unionization, only 15 percent of firms actually closed any part of their businesses following the union drive.

Finally, research regarding the general effects of unionization on firm survival and employment levels lends support to these conclusions. Thus, as reflected in a recent survey of the contemporary literature, studies report that while unionization may lead to slower growth, fewer expansions, and fewer firm "births," unionization has no effect on firm "deaths" or on employment levels (Hirsch, 2007). In a 2004 study, for example, DiNardo and Lee (2004) examined firms where the NLRB ran a union election between 1984 and 1999, a data set that allowed the authors to examine business survival and employment effects over periods ranging from two to seventeen years. The authors report that unionization had no significant impact on business survival. Similarly, the authors found that the effect of unionization on employment was also statistically insignificant – ranging from slightly positive to slightly negative. Dunne and Macpherson (1994) and Freeman and Kleiner (1999) also conclude that unionization does not increase the likelihood of firm death.[50] Accordingly, Hirsch (2007) concludes his review of the contemporary literature by writing that "the empirical literature finds that U.S. unions are associated with slower employment growth but exhibit little or no difference in rates of business failure or survival."[51]

Like discharges of union supporters, employer statements connecting unionization to plant closure may violate the Act.[52] Three factors, however, suggest that the potential for unfair labor practice liability is insufficient to alleviate concerns with threats of this kind. First, remedial weakness again renders deterrence from the unfair labor practice insufficient. Second, in *NLRB v. Gissel Packing Co.*, the Supreme Court held that while "threats" of closure violate the Act, there is no unfair labor practice liability if an employer predicts "on the basis of objective fact" that the "demonstrably probable consequence[]" of unionization is closure.[53] But the doctrine has not remained faithful to this distinction, and the Board on numerous occasions has permitted employers to imply a causal connection between unionization and plant closure without the kind of support that *Gissel* seems to require.[54]

Third, neither the employees nor the union involved in an organizing drive has a right to information about the actual financial condition of the firm.[55] Regardless of what claims an employer makes concerning the likely effects of unionization, it is under no obligation to provide employees with information to verify these claims. As such, if management raises the prospect that unionization will lead to closure or loss of jobs, employees have no way of knowing whether the suggestion is likely to be accurate – that is, whether it is a "prediction" or a "threat."[56]

Although coercive, discharges and threats of closure may contain some information relevant to employees who are forming their preferences on unionization. In particular, employer actions of these kinds may signal to employees that the employer will take an adversarial position vis-à-vis the union should the union be certified – suggesting, for example, that the employer will "bargain hard" and refuse to reach agreement with the union unless compelled to do so by employee economic action. Having gained an indication of what the employer's conduct is likely to be post-unionization, employees could "adapt" their preferences and decide that remaining nonunion is the better course.

The point, however, should not be overstated. First, an employer's campaign conduct is an imperfect signal of what its post-unionization approach will be. Namely, employers who fight unionization vigorously may relent if the union wins, and employers who are less aggressive during the campaign might nonetheless take tough bargaining positions. More important, though, is the relative magnitude of the legitimate and illegitimate effects of coercive employer actions on employee preference formation. Although impossible to quantify with precision, it seems likely, for example, that the coercive effect of employee discharges on employee preference formation will be more pronounced than the effect of the information about post-unionization conduct that such discharges convey.

In sum, when management intervention in the employee organizing process takes the form of discharge of union activists or the threat that unionization will result in closure of the firm, the intervention can be expected to influence employee choice on the union question. But these interventions influence employee preferences in ways that are inconsistent with autonomous choice and, thus, employer interventions in the organizing process that take this form make departing from the nonunion default more difficult in a manner that we should not attribute to free employee choice.

3.   The stickiness of the nonunion default

Because we must assume complete uncertainty regarding actual employee preferences on the union question, as long as the factors discussed above make it any more difficult for employees to choose union rather than nonunion bargaining (if these factors make a nonunion default even 1 percent more "sticky" than a union default), a preference-eliciting or reversible default approach is appropriate (see Elhauge, 2008). And, indeed, given the evidence we have on the effectiveness of employer interventions and given the asymmetric nature of the collective action problems discussed above, a 1 percent differential seems a conservative estimate.

Of course, in the context of a union default rule, we should expect unions to discourage employees from choosing nonunion bargaining just as – under the nonunion default – employers intervene to discourage unionization. In a unionized firm, for example, the union could deploy social sanctions against anti-union employees and might also decline to provide vigorous representation in grievance proceedings to employees who favor decertifying the union.[57] These dynamics could mitigate some of the asymmetric stickiness of the two default rules, but several factors suggest that they would not eliminate the asymmetry. First, whatever force these forms of union authority have, they are not as powerful as those possessed by the employer in the nonunion workplace – exemplified by the ability to control wages and working conditions, discharge employees, and credibly threaten to terminate operations.[58] Second, in considering the *comparative* stickiness of the different default rules, it is relevant that the employer's authority in a unionized workplace – and thus its ability to encourage decertification – is far greater than the union's authority in a nonunion workplace. Finally, irrespective of the results of a campaign to certify or decertify a union, the employer will remain the employees' employer. In contrast, the union's existence at the firm is contingent on the outcome of the campaign, another asymmetric dynamic that increases the salience of threats made by an employer relative to those a union might deliver. As noted above, a preference-eliciting or reversible default approach is appropriate so long as there is a *slight* differential in the ease of departure between the two default rules. Accordingly, so long as the employer's ability to deter unionization is slightly greater than the union's ability to deter decertification, the approach advanced here is appropriate.[59]

4.   A new altering rule

As I have shown, the preference-maximizing aims of a preference-eliciting or reversible default regime can be accomplished in two ways. First, labor law could impose a default rule of union bargaining. Second, Congress could change labor law's altering rule in a way that minimizes the asymmetric stickiness of the nonunion default. In our context, because the relevant asymmetry flows from management's opposition to unionization and its ability to intervene in the employee organizing process, an altering rule that eliminates or minimizes management's ability to intervene in the unionization effort can correct the relevant asymmetry.

Although the argument here provides conceptual justification for either a new default of unionized collective bargaining or a new altering rule, several considerations point in the direction of adopting a new altering rule and not a new default. The first of these considerations flows from the dynamic nature of workforces. That is, even if a firm begins its life with a union default, each time a workforce decides to depart and choose nonunion bargaining, the "default" position for all future workforces at that firm becomes nonunion bargaining (see, e.g., Barenberg, 1994). Without an asymmetry-correcting altering rule, this nonunion position will exhibit precisely the same problems vis-à-vis future workforces – precisely the same stickiness – as a nonunion default set by law. As such, even were we to adopt a union default rule, we would *also* need an asymmetry-correcting altering rule.

Given dynamic workforces, therefore, the choice is not between adopting a union default or an asymmetry-correcting altering rule. Rather, to maximize employee choice we must choose between adopting either a union default *and* an asymmetry-correcting altering rule or adopting just the new altering rule.[60] Although there is no conceptual reason to favor a nonunion over a union default – so long as either is paired with an appropriate altering rule – there are clear pragmatic reasons to favor the nonunion default coupled with an asymmetry-correcting altering rule. To state the obvious, under current conditions, a union default would encounter practical and political obstacles of such scale as to render the prospects for such a proposal exceedingly improbable.

Beyond the lack of political potential, moreover, a union default would encounter practical problems that stem from current levels of union density. More than 92 percent of private sector workers in the United States are now nonunion (Bureau of Labor Statistics, 2009), and thus a union default would require nearly all of the private employers in the country to reorganize their labor-management relations systems in relatively short order. Of equal concern, the imposition of default unionism would cause deep practical problems for workers and unions. Unlike a change to a default rule of statutory interpretation or corporate governance, a new default rule for labor law would depend upon a massive increase in the organizational and representational capacity of worker organizations, an increase that would not be achievable in the foreseeable future.

An asymmetry-correcting altering rule that minimizes employer intervention in union organizing avoids these problems while accomplishing the same preference-maximizing aims. First, under card check or rapid elections, employers would only be required to recognize a union when the union demonstrates that it has the support of a majority of the relevant workforce; change would be incremental, and there would be no requirement that 92 percent of the nation's private businesses do anything all at once. Similarly, union growth would be far more organic under a new altering rule than under a union default. This result is significant because, as is the case today, union growth would be constrained by unions' capacity to organize new workers. This constraint implies that as new workers are added to union membership, unions concomitantly will develop the organizational capacity to represent them effectively. And politically, of course, changing labor law's altering rule is far more viable than imposing a union default.

Because we can maximize employee preferences with an asymmetry-correcting altering rule, and because a union default would not be sufficient, maximizing employee choice with a new altering rule makes pragmatic sense.

IV.   MINIMIZING MANAGERIAL INTERVENTION

I have argued that an asymmetry-correcting altering rule that minimizes employer intervention can maximize employee choice. But enabling employees to conduct and conclude organizing campaigns with a minimum of managerial intervention raises a discrete set of questions. The first is whether Congress should provide employers an affirmative right to intervene in the employee organizing process. This question is implicated most starkly by card check which, again, aims to enable employees to complete organizational efforts before the employer is aware that a campaign is underway. But the question is also relevant for a rapid elections proposal. As noted above, a rapid elections regime would provide employers with some minimum window of time during which they could intervene in unionization campaigns. Nonetheless, if management ought to enjoy an affirmative right to intervene in employees' organizing efforts, restricting the scope of that participation to a period as short as five days would require justification. Because, as I argue below, labor law need not provide employers with an affirmative right to intervene, a decisional mechanism – like rapid elections – that limits the scope of such intervention does not deprive management of a right that it ought otherwise to possess. The second question, implicated by both card check and rapid elections, concerns the loss of information available to employees in an organizing effort conducted with less managerial involvement. In this section, I address these two questions in turn.

A.   Should Management Have an Affirmative Right To Intervene?

With respect to the first question, the claim that employers should enjoy an affirmative right to participate in the employee organizing process is grounded in the view that a union representation election, like a political election, is a contest between management and the union over firm governance.[61] As Weiler (1983) puts it, under this view, "the employer is legitimately entitled to play the same role in a representation campaign against the union that the Republican Party plays in a political campaign against the Democrats."

And indeed, if a union election actually resolved which party governed the firm, or if unionization amounted to a shift in firm governance from sole to joint sovereignty, the argument in favor of employer participation would be strong. But for better or worse, sovereignty in the workplace is not at stake in a union election (see, e.g., Stone, 1981).[62] To the contrary, employees decide through the union representation process only whether they wish to bargain individually or collectively with their employer. If employees choose to unionize, the law then imposes on the employer a duty to bargain "in good faith" with the union on behalf of the employees in the bargaining unit over "wages, hours, and other terms and conditions of employment."[63] But that is all the law requires: good faith collective bargaining, instead of individual bargaining, over terms and conditions of employment. As many scholars already have observed, and as the scope and content of this duty make clear, employees' decision to bargain collectively will undoubtedly have an impact on management, but collective bargaining amounts to neither sovereignty nor control (see, e.g., Weiler, 1990; Becker, 1993; Bodie, 2008; Stone, 1981; Weiler, 1983).

To start, the duty to bargain in good faith extends only to "mandatory subject[s] of bargaining."[64] With respect to any topic that is not a mandatory subject – so-called permissive subjects – the employer is under no obligation to engage with the union in any way.[65] The Supreme Court, moreover, has interpreted this statutory list of mandatory subjects narrowly. Most importantly for our purposes, the Court has excluded from the duty to bargain precisely those decisions that most directly implicate control of the firm. Under this rule, the Board and the courts have held that an employer has no duty to bargain over investment decisions, financing decisions, advertising decisions, or product design decisions.[66] Perhaps most profoundly, the employer has no obligation to bargain over a decision to cease operating entirely.[67]

Next, even regarding those subjects that fall within the scope of the bargaining obligation – for example, wages or work schedules – the rules concerning "management rights clauses" further clarify the nature of unionization's impact on firm sovereignty. In short, although an employer is obligated to bargain in good faith over these mandatory subjects, the Supreme Court has held that an employer's bargaining position may be to maintain unilateral control over the subject.[68]

Given the limited impact of unionization on firm governance, labor scholars have proposed a slew of metaphors to describe what they view as the anomalous nature of the proposition that Congress should afford management an affirmative right to intervene in union organizing efforts. Bodie (2008) puts it most simply: "Whether I hire Joy to represent me in my negotiations with Earl is really no business of Earl's." Whatever analogy one favors, however, the relevant observation is that unionization is a process through which employees choose to bargain collectively, rather than individually, with their employers and through which employees designate an agent for these purposes. The law entitles unions to bargain (though not over many of the most important decisions a firm will make), but unionization is not a process through which employees decide whether to assume joint sovereignty in the firm. Although employers will be impacted by the choice employees make on the unionization question, that fact does not provide the basis for an affirmative right to intervene in the employees' decisionmaking process.

B. Information Loss

The second question raised by an altering rule that minimizes employer intervention concerns the loss of information available to employees. The argument here is that full employer participation is required in order to ensure that employee choice on the union question is fully informed. For example, Epstein (2009) argues that:

> Employer speech provides valuable information to workers. Workers need to be able to form an educated view on the long-term implications of union representation, which includes some estimate as to how well employees think the union and employer will work together on points of common concern. Employees can form that judgment only by collecting information from all sides.

Outside the legal academy, former NLRB member Charles Cohen (House Committee Testimony, 2002) contends that only the NLRB election process, with employer participation, can ensure a "fully informed electorate."

Provision of information is generally good (see Estlund, Senate Committee Testimony, 2007) and, in an employee organizing campaign conducted with less employer intervention, employees may receive less information from their employer regarding management's views on unionization. Indeed, in forming their own views about unionization, employees might legitimately wish to know management's position on the question. For example, the knowledge that management was strongly opposed to unionization – or that management intended to engage in "hard bargaining" should a union campaign succeed – might alter some employees' preferences on the union question. Accordingly, loss of information of this sort would constitute a cost of an asymmetry-correcting altering rule that minimizes employer intervention. But, for several reasons, the cost to employee choice from this information loss is not likely to be high and is unlikely to outweigh the choice-maximizing advantages that flow from an asymmetry-correcting altering rule.[69]

First, even under a card check regime, in which management would have no statutorily guaranteed window to intervene prior to a demand for recognition, management would remain free to, and indeed would have a new incentive to, present its views on unionization on a more continuous basis. In this sense, card check and similar altering rules would require that management change the timing of its messages about unionization, but would not affect management's ability to communicate. Mark Barenberg accordingly writes that, even under card check, management could weave its views on unionization "into the organizational warp and woof of the enterprise" (Barenberg, 1994), informing employees when they are hired, as well as during regular intervals, why it believes that unionization is not in the interests of the firm and the position it would take should unionization occur. In a rapid elections regime, management not only could conduct such ongoing communicational efforts, but also would be entitled to campaign against unionization between the filing of the petition and election day. This last window of time would be short – again, somewhere between five days and two weeks – but it would nonetheless provide management with an opportunity to express its views.

Second, employers are not the only source of information for the "nonunion" side of the argument. To the contrary, there is a set of third-party organizations whose raison d'être is providing employees with information about and arguments against unionization. The Center for Union Facts, for example, has compiled a database that "contains more than 12.5 million facts about the American labor movement[,] [f]rom the smallest local to the largest international union."[70] And organizations including the National Right to Work Committee (and its affiliated Legal Defense Foundation) and the Center for Union Facts offer comprehensive data about every major union in the United States along with reports that highlight the deleterious effects of unionization. These latter organizations also engage in affirmative outreach to employees when they learn that an organizing campaign is underway.[71] Such third-party organizations usually cannot provide information about an individual firm, or the particular impact that unionization will likely have on that firm, but the type of general information that third parties provide is the type that employers most often communicate during organizing campaigns.[72] This phenomenon is due largely to the fact that it is never possible to predict during an organizing campaign the specific impact that unionization will have on a firm: what a union will demand in bargaining cannot be known prior to the commencement of bargaining, particularly because union bargaining demands are shaped by the financial information management is obligated to disclose only after bargaining begins. Thus, during the organizing phase, employers must rely primarily on general arguments about the effects of unionization, evidence gathered from past campaigns involving the same union, or more general information about the particular union involved in the campaign. Particularly when employers rely on consultants to direct their interventions, the information provided to employees follows something approaching a predesigned script focusing on these general themes.[73]

To be sure, third-party organizations are not a perfect substitute for employer intervention. As noted, these organizations lack firm-specific information and, except in instances in which the organizations are successful in their outreach efforts, the information provided by third parties can be accessed only if an employee takes the initiative to access it. But for employees who seek out the information – and for those contacted through third-party organizational outreach – these nonprofit organizations can provide a substantial part of the information that otherwise flows from employer interventions.

Third, as demonstrated most recently by Bodie (2008), employers are not ideally suited to present to employees the "nonunion" side of the unionization argument. Bodie (2008) shows that employers have different incentives to convey information about the drawbacks of unionization depending upon the employer's view of the union's potential strength. When the employer believes that the union is likely to be particularly strong – that it will bargain effectively on behalf of employees – the employer will have the "strongest incentive to defeat the union" and will "therefore put on the fiercest campaign." In contrast, when the employer estimates that the union is likely to be weakest – in Bodie's (2008) terms, when "the union will not be all that effective in improving terms and conditions" – the employer's incentives to provide information change in an important way. Most important, when faced with an organizing campaign by a "sweetheart union" – one that has no intention of attempting to secure gains for employees but will merely collect dues – the employer may have an incentive to provide information to employees that encourages them to *support* the union drive (Bodie, 2008). This is so because when employees join a "sweetheart union" they may be foreclosed from electing a legitimate union for a significant period of time.[74] Bodie (2008) accordingly characterizes employers' incentives to provide information to employees about unionization as "inverse" to employees' interests.

Two final points bear mention. First, although a decline in employer interventions will limit the amount of information about unions and unionization that would otherwise come from management, employees will still have a great deal of information about the nonunion default, by virtue of living and working in a regime of nonunion bargaining prior to the organizing effort. Thus, "the employer that hired and has managed all its employees for a considerable time before the union even appeared on the scene has had ample opportunity to demonstrate the advantages of the individual employment relationship" (Weiler, 1990).[75] Second, the type of information that employers and third parties provide during organizing campaigns is not likely to be new information for employees deciding whether to support unionization. Far from being novel, the arguments that unions are corrupt, that they charge high member dues and then waste them, that they are prone to violence, that they strike irresponsibly, and that they threaten the viability of the firm and cause job losses are part of our common cultural and political discourse. They are reflected in news media reporting on unions and unionization (see, e.g., Greenhouse, 2009b; and Puette, 1992) and popular film and television accounts of unions.[76]

With less managerial intervention in the union organizing process, employees may receive less negative information about unions. But given the factors outlined here, the decline in the quantity of information is not likely to be great and the cost of limiting this information will not outweigh the choice-maximizing benefits that an asymmetry-correcting altering rule can offer.

V.   A NEW ALTERING RULE FOR LABOR LAW'S ASYMMETRIC DEFAULT

If minimizing managerial intervention through an asymmetry-correcting altering rule is a legitimate goal for labor law, the question of how best to design such an altering rule remains. The debate over card check also poses the particular question of whether an open decisional mechanism is necessary to the purpose of minimizing managerial intervention and, more broadly, whether an open decisional mechanism is an appropriate means to achieve that goal.

Although a full discussion of these issues is beyond the scope of this chapter, it is apparent that openness in decisionmaking is unrelated to the substantive goal of minimizing employer intervention in union campaigns. To the contrary, what is required for the asymmetry-correcting function of minimizing managerial intervention is a decisional mechanism that enables employees to register their choice on the union question without providing notice to management that the campaign is underway. Although such a mechanism must enable employees to vote at home or in some other nonworkplace location, openness in decisionmaking is unrelated to this requirement.

Openness, however, can expose employees to certain forms of union and coworker interference at the moment of decision. While claims of physical intimidation by union organizers do not find support in the evidence (Sachs, 2010), the potential for interference inherent in an open voting procedure – and, perhaps more importantly, the significant public concern over this potential – raises legitimacy issues for unions organized through such processes. Moreover, if voting is open, organizers and coworkers will often enjoy other, nonphysical but effective forms of influence, including the kind of "epistemological authority" that Professor Lynn Sanders (1997) describes.

The appropriate institutional design question for labor law, therefore, is how to construct a decisional mechanism that minimizes managerial intervention in employee organizing efforts while at the same time preserving secrecy in decisionmaking. Rapid elections offer a potential step in this direction. Such a regime would provide employees with a confidential decisional mechanism, and, by reducing the window for managerial involvement in the employee organizing effort, would constitute an improvement over the status quo. Despite their merits, however, rapid elections are not the best approach for a set of reasons. First, a rapid elections regime depends upon the NLRB to ensure that elections are carried out within the statutorily prescribed time frame. And while legislation could mandate that the NLRB conduct elections within five or ten days, for example, it is far from certain that the agency would be able to run elections that rapidly. Indeed, the last fifty years of experience suggest strongly that there is nothing "rapid" about the NLRB, and despite repeated attempts to speed up various Board proceedings, the agency remains plagued by delay (Sachs, 2008). Second, the extent to which rapid elections can minimize managerial intervention in employee organizing efforts is inherently limited. In a rapid elections regime, as under current law, once employees file a petition for an election, the employer is given notice of the organizing campaign and thus has a statutorily guaranteed window of time to campaign against unionization. Should the employer become aware of organizing efforts before the petition is filed, of course, managerial intervention could begin at that point.

As such, neither rapid elections nor card check is the optimal approach to enabling employee choice. But there are other possibilities. One potential approach would borrow technologies used in union elections in airline and railroad industries, and permit employees to cast secret ballots in their homes over the phone, via the internet, or through the mail. A second approach would draw on the model of early voting now used in U.S. political elections and allow employees to cast ballots – at a polling place established by the Board – throughout the course of the organizing campaign. In neither case would the NLRB inform the employer of the existence of the campaign while organizing was underway. But, in both proposals, union organizers would be barred from interfering with employee voting, and the employer would be entitled to the information it needs to challenge the outcome (Sachs, 2010). Accordingly, both of these designs preserve the secret ballot while also accomplishing the asymmetry-correcting function of minimizing employer intervention in union organizing drives. Both approaches therefore offer a way to redesign the rules of union organizing and employee decisionmaking consistent with contemporary legal theory on maximizing choice.

VI.   CONCLUSION

How to enable employee choice on the question of unionization, and the appropriateness of managerial intervention in the union organizing process, are issues that have long been central to federal labor law. This chapter has offered a new way to approach these questions. By building on contemporary theories of default rules, and developing the concept of the "asymmetry-correcting altering rule," the chapter has shown how a decisional mechanism like card check, or an alternative like rapid elections, can advance employee choice. Managerial opposition to unionization, along with the collective action problems involved in employee efforts to unionize, make it more difficult for workers to unionize than it would be for employees to depart from a union default and choose individual employment contracting. The legal regime can address these asymmetries by adopting an altering rule that minimizes employer intervention in the employee organizing process. By designing an altering rule that minimizes such intervention while also preserving secrecy in decisionmaking, labor law can maximize employee choice.

NOTES

*   This chapter is derived in large part from Sachs (2010).
1.   This chapter takes as given federal labor law's project of attempting to ensure employee choice on the union question. The chapter does not address whether unionization itself is in the economic interests of employees, employers, or the economy as a whole. For a recent treatment of those questions, see Bennett and Kaufman (2008).
2.   See Employee Free Choice Act of 2009, H.R. 1409, 111th Cong. (2009). EFCA was passed by the House of Representatives in 2007 but died in the Senate after a closure vote failed 51–48 (Source: Govtrack.us, accessed Nov. 22, 2009 at http://www.govtrack.us/congress/bill.xpd?bill=h110-800).

3. A seminal treatment is found in Weiler (1983). For additional discussion, see Barenberg (1994), Becker (1993), and Weiler (1990).
4. Ayres (2006) has identified the role played by altering rules – and has named them – but has not yet provided a comprehensive treatment of the subject.
5. This statement is not a claim that the only good sought by the entire regime of labor law is free employee choice, but only a claim that choice is the good sought by those labor law rules that govern employee decisionmaking on the union question. See, for example, *NLRB v. A.J. Tower Co.* 329 U.S. 324 (1946).
6. 29 U.S.C. § 157 sets out employees' right to form and join labor unions and an equal "right to refrain from any or all of such activities."
7. The move from individual to collective bargaining describes the change in the relationship between employees and employers effected by unionization. Unionization can also create new possibilities for community among workers, modify employees' perceptions of themselves in important ways, and – particularly in immigrant communities – alleviate conditions of intense social isolation (see, e.g., Delgado, 1993; Fantasia, 1988; Flores, 1997). But the ways in which unions can reconstitute employee-to-employee relationships and alter workers' self-perceptions cannot provide a justification for employer intervention in the union organizing process, so I do not consider those dynamics here.
8. See 29 U.S.C. §§ 157, 158(a)(5), 159(a).
9. The prevalence of and need for off-site contacts is largely a product of NLRA rules. Under current law, employers are entitled to prohibit discussions of unionization during work time and in working areas. See, for example, *Peyton Packing Co.* 49 N.L.R.B. 828 (1943), cited in *Republic Aviation Corp. v. NLRB*, 324 U.S. 793 (1945). Moreover, union organizers have no right to access employees on company property. See *Lechmere Inc. v. NLRB* 502 U.S. 527 (1992).
10. See 29 U.S.C. § 159.
11. See, for example, *Linden Lumber Div., Summer & Co. v. NLRB* 419 U.S. 301 (1974).
12. See 29 U.S.C. § 159(c)(1)(A); 29 C.F.R. § 101.18.
13. In her study of 1004 NLRB certification elections, Bronfenbrenner (2009) found that employers mounted some form of anti-union effort in 96 percent of the campaigns.
14. See, for example, *Litton Sys., Inc.* 173 N.L.R.B. 1024 (1968); *Babcock & Wilcox Co.* 77 N.L.R.B. 577 (1948).
15. See, for example, *Shearer's Foods, Inc.* 340 N.L.R.B. 1093, 1094 (2003). See also Bronfenbrenner (2000; 2009).
16. See, for example, *Lloyd's Ornamental & Steel Fabricators, Inc.* 197 N.L.R.B. 367 (1972). As I note below, the data on the specific level and rate of discharges are contested. For example, Schmitt and Zipperer (2007) report that one in five union activists is discharged, Morris (1998) puts the number at approximately one in eighteen, and a report by Wilson (2008) arrives at one in thirty-seven. For reasons explained in Section II.B.1, our concern will be less with the precise frequency of discharge and more with the general phenomenon.
17. See 29 U.S.C. §§ 158(a)(5), 159(a).
18. In some proposals, the move to rapid elections entails a concomitant increase in the percentage of employee support necessary for a petition. Weiler (1990), for example, suggests requiring 55 or 60 percent employee support for a rapid-election petition.
19. See Employee Free Choice Act of 2009, H.R. 1409, 111th Cong. (2009).
20. Separate objections are discussed later in this chapter.
21. EFCA proponents, on the other hand, point to the rarity of reported incidents of union coercion during card gathering conducted under voluntary card check agreements. See, for example, Estlund, Senate Committee Testimony (2007), Brudney (2005), Eaton and Kriesky (2003), and Lafer (2008).
22. Lafer (2008) is one exception.
23. For example, the AFL-CIO tells readers of its webpage that card check responds to the fact that "employers routinely harass, intimidate, coerce and even fire workers struggling to gain a union." (AFL-CIO, n.d).
24. See Employee Free Choice Act of 2009, H.R. 1409, 111th Cong. (2009).
25. As several authors have noted, there is nothing inevitable or natural about the choice of a nonunion default rule. Weiler (1990), for example, explains that the rule has "its roots in the common law background of the NLRA: the tacit legal assumption that the 'natural' status for a workplace is nonunion." See also Barenberg (1994) and Sunstein (2001).
26. Elhauge's argument for preference-eliciting defaults depends on a conclusion that enactable preferences are the "good" that statutory interpretation should maximize. It is unnecessary to take a position on this debate here. What Elhauge's theory of preference-eliciting defaults shows us is how to design a default rule (in conditions of uncertainty and asymmetric power) in order to maximize a good once we have determined what that good is. The *how* question can be pursued independently of the *what* question, and that is what I intend to do here.

27.　Elhauge (2008) adds a third condition: the interim costs of choosing the wrong rule must be tolerable.
28.　In developing a theory of default rules for this context, Bebchuk and Hamdani make two normative assumptions, both of which are worth noting here, but neither of which is important for our purposes. First, the authors assume that the good to be maximized by the law of corporate governance is shareholder value (Bebchuk and Hamdani, 2002). This is a contestable – though fairly widely held – view. But again, our concern here is not *what* good corporate law seeks to maximize, but rather *how* a default regime can maximize that good. Second, the authors assume that "market players and investors in any given company are more likely than public officials to identify the superior [that is, value-maximizing] arrangement for their company" (id.). This assumption is necessary to justify the choice of some default rule rather than a mandatory one; where the public officials "know better" than market actors what the right outcome is, mandatory rules are appropriate (id.). Again, this assumption – though widely held – is also contestable, but we need not engage with this debate either. Our question is not *whether* a default arrangement is appropriate in the labor law context, but *which* default arrangement best maximizes employee choice. We can therefore accept both assumptions for the purposes of this discussion.
29.　The two approaches may not be perfect substitutes. For example, collective action problems can impede shareholders from pursuing bylaw amendments, even in the absence of managerial interference (see Bebchuk and Hamdani, 2002). For Bebchuk and Hamdani (2002), the implication of these coordination problems is that – even when opting out of the default is possible through bylaw amendment – there should still be a presumption, though not as strong, in favor of setting the default rule against management.
30.　See, for example, *Peyton Packing Co.* 49 N.L.R.B. 828 (1943), cited in *Republic Aviation Corp. v. NLRB* 324 U.S. 793 (1945).
31.　See, for example, *Lechmere, Inc. v. NLRB* 502 U.S. 527 (1992). See generally Estlund (1994).
32.　See, for example, *Peerless Plywood Co.* 107 N.L.R.B. 427 (1953).
33.　See 29 U.S.C. § 158(a)(2).
34.　In one study, Bronfenbrenner (2000) found that such support was provided in 31 percent of the campaigns.
35.　Sunstein calls this "myopic behavior" (1991).
36.　On average, it takes ten months for the parties to bargain a first contract (Ferguson, 2008). More importantly, many contracts delay or stagger the implementation of, for example, wage gains over the life of the contract, increasing the distance between the costs of union organizing and the benefits of a union contract (see, e.g., Bureau of National Affairs, 2009).
37.　If all employer anti-union conduct designed to influence employee decisionmaking is taken to be a legitimate part of how employees form their preferences, then the "stickiness" of the nonunion default caused by direct managerial opposition is attributable to legitimately altered employee preferences. I address this question in the next section, arguing that some employer interventions cannot be understood as contributing to autonomous employee choice.
38.　The data available on the specific prevalence of these interventions are contested (see, e.g., Epstein, 2009). As noted above, however, we are concerned here not with the magnitude of the asymmetry created by employer opposition, but more simply with the existence of the asymmetry.
39.　In her 2000 study, Bronfenbrenner (2000) found that in mobile industries (including manufacturing and communication), employers threatened closure in 68 percent of the organizing campaigns.
40.　Source: Center for Union Facts, "About Us," http://www.unionfacts.com/aboutUs.cfm (accessed Nov. 22, 2009).
41.　The substantially lower rate reported in this last study might be explained by the fact that by looking only at cases where an election petition was filed, the study excludes all instances in which union activists were discharged and the union was never able to gather sufficient support to file a petition. Nor does this study attempt to capture those illegal discharges of union supporters – after the filing of a petition – for which an unfair labor practice charge was not filed.
42.　"In fiscal year 2009, for example, the Board awarded $76,337,306 in backpay for 'lost wages caused by unlawful discharge and other discriminatory action.'" And while some fraction of this figure may reflect discriminatory actions taken outside the context of organizing campaigns, the point remains the same (National Labor Relations Board, 2009). Available at: http://www.nlrb.gov/annual-reports.
43.　These data do not capture instances in which a union organizing drive fails before an election petition is filed. Nor do they, of course, account for organizing drives that never begin. As such, the "win rates" reported here may overstate the actual degree of union success. In an earlier study, Professor William Dickens found that the typical employer anti-union campaign, involving both legal and illegal tactics, reduced by 5–10 percent the probability that the average employee would vote "yes" on the question of unionization (Weiler, 1983). Comstock and Fox (1994), summarizing the results of more than 150,000 interviews with workers in nonunion firms, report that 22 percent of white workers and 48 percent of African American workers cited "management pressure" as the primary impediment to union support.

44. The relevant point here is only that force and fraud impede autonomy, not that force or fraud (as conventionally defined) are the only sources of such interference.
45. A different way to conceive of the inconsistency between certain forms of employer influence and employee choice is through the lens of "adaptive" preferences. According to Sunstein (1991), *autonomous* choices are those made with "a full and vivid awareness of available opportunities, with reference to all relevant information, and without illegitimate or excessive constraints on the process of preference formation." Following this line of argument, then, preferences are not autonomously formed if individuals believe that some part of the universe of options, which is in fact open to them or in some normatively compelling sense should be open to them, is unavailable (see, e.g., Barenberg, 1994). Preferences formed under these conditions can be described as "adaptive" rather than autonomous (Elster, 1983). Sunstein (1986) provides several examples of adaptive preference formation, one of which relates specifically to unionization. He writes that:

    > Workers seem not to be willing to trade much in the way of money for self-government. But that preference may be a product of a belief that self-government in the workplace is unavailable. Were the option to be one that workers conventionally thought available, the option might be highly valued.

    Indeed, much employer intervention in the union organizing process has the intent and the effect of signaling to workers that unionization, although available as a formal legal matter, is unavailable as a practical matter.
46. *Complete Auto Transit, Inc. v. Reis* 451 U.S. 401 (1981) .
47. 29 U.S.C. §§ 158(a)(1), 158(a)(3) (2006); id. § 160(c).
48. In Bronfenbrenner's 2000 study, employees discharged for union activity were reinstated before the election was held in only 3 percent of the cases where unfair labor practice charges were filed (Bronfenbrenner, 2000, p. 74, table 9).
49. There are, however, reported cases where a firm's customers have a policy of not dealing with unionized employers, in which case unionization itself might lead to a loss in the firm's income and thus job loss. See, for example, *DTR Indus., Inc*, 311 N.L.R.B. 833 (1993).
50. See also Hirsch (2007), reviewing this literature. But see LaLonde et al. (1996), reporting negative employment effects.
51. Of course, it is something of a puzzle how or why unions could cause slower employment growth but not affect survival rates. Freeman and Kleiner (1999) propose one explanation: unions will push for contract gains but will not kill the "goose that lays the golden egg." Or, in Hirsch's (2007) characterization, unions are "willing to drive enterprises toward the cliff but not over it." Another possibility is that the wage premiums that unions bargain allow firms to respond to economic downturns by cutting wages (through concessionary bargaining) rather than by contracting (Hirsch, 2007).
52. See *NLRB v. Gissel Packing Co*. 395 U.S. 575 (1969). See also, for example, *Guardian Indus. Corp. v. NLRB* 49 F.3d 317 (7th Cir. 1995), *Shearer's Foods, Inc*. 340 N.L.R.B. 1093 (2003), and *Be-Lo Stores* 318 N.L.R.B. 1 (1995).
53. *NLRB v. Gissel Packing Co*. 395 U.S. 575 (1969).
54. For several particularly stark examples, see *Smithfield Foods, Inc*. 349 N.L.R.B. 1225 (2006), *Stanadyne Auto. Corp*. 345 N.L.R.B. 85 (2005), and *Mt. Ida Footwear Co*. 217 N.L.R.B. 1011 (1975).
55. Employers have a duty to furnish information to the union during collective bargaining, but this obligation arises only when there is a duty to bargain – that is to say, *after* the union has been recognized as the exclusive representative of employees in the bargaining unit. See, for example, *NLRB v. Truitt Mfg. Co.* 351 U.S. 149 (1956).
56. See *NLRB v. Gissel Packing Co*. 395 U.S. 575 (1969).
57. Such conduct would likely constitute a breach of the union's duty of fair representation. See, for example, *Vaca v. Sipes* 386 U.S. 171 (1967).
58. In the contemporary setting, the social sanctions available to unions are often notoriously weak. For a theoretical account, see generally Bacharach et al. (2001).
59. In the context of a union default, an altering rule like card check would enable employees to minimize *union* intervention in their decertification efforts.
60. Bebchuk and Hamdani (2002) point out that in certain contexts an asymmetry-correcting altering rule may not be a perfect substitute for the reversible default. This is true where the coordination costs involved in departing from one default are greater than those involved in departing from the other default, even when an appropriate altering rule is in place. In our context, the introduction of the asymmetry-correcting altering rule should minimize the asymmetry in these costs.
61. For a thorough treatment of the political election analogy in labor law, see Becker (1993).
62. Stone's (1981) piece marked a departure from earlier scholarship that advanced a theory of industrial pluralism, which she discussed in her article. See, for example, Leiserson (1959) and Cox (1947).
63. 29 U.S.C. § 158(d). See also 29 U.S.C. § 158(a)(5), and 29 U.S.C. § 159(a), which makes it an unfair labor

practice to refuse to bargain in good faith. The law concurrently prohibits the employer from bargaining directly with individual employees. See, for example, *J.I. Case Co. v. NLRB* 321 U.S. 332 (1944).

64. *NLRB v. Wooster Div. of Borg-Warner Corp.* 356 U.S. 342 (1958). For a more recent discussion, see *Pall Corp. v. NLRB* 275 F.3d 116 (D.C. Cir. 2002).
65. See *NLRB v. Wooster Div. of Borg-Warner Corp.* 356 U.S. 342 (1958).
66. See *First Nat'l Maint. Corp. v. NLRB* 452 U.S. 666 (1981), listing subjects that are clearly beyond the scope of the bargaining obligation because they "have only an indirect and attenuated impact on the employment relationship."
67. See *Textile Workers Union v. Darlington Mfg. Co.* 380 U.S. 263 (1965).
68. See, for example, *NLRB v. American National Insurance Co.* 343 U.S. 395 (1952).
69. Weiler (1990) reaches the same conclusion: "My reading of the evidence about how the current lengthy representation campaign has actually operated in practice leaves me quite unpersuaded of [the] net social value [of employer intervention]."
70. Source: Center for Union Facts, "Find Your Union: Union Profiles," http://www.unionfacts.com/unions/ (accessed Nov. 22, 2009).
71. In some cases, the Foundation mails literature directly to employees of the firm where the unionization effort is taking place (National Right to Work Foundation, n.d.). In other instances, the Committee has garnered press attention for its efforts. See, for example, National Right to Work Legal Defense Foundation (2003) and *Cincinnati Enquirer* (2003).
72. See, for example, Bodie (2008), DeMaria (2001). For some illustrative accounts of third parties providing information during organizing campaigns, see Lafer (2007, pp. 13–28).
73. For example, the Labor Relations Institute offers a set of thirteen preprinted posters that address "[t]he questions most commonly asked during a union organizing campaign," campaign flyers designed to "help you to further focus on issues common to most organizing campaigns," and union-specific publications that "highlight[] the many restrictive rules and regulations contained in the international unions [sic] constitution" (Source: Labor Relations Institute, accessed Nov. 22, 2209 at http://www.lrionline.com/union_avoidance/campaign_literature.htm).
74. The recognition of a union bars a decertification vote – and hence the possibility for another organizing effort – for a period of one year. See 29 U.S.C. § 159(e)(2).
75. Given that the unionization rate among private sector workers is now below 8 percent, the vast majority of employees in the United States will have spent their entire careers in the nonunion setting (see Bureau of Labor Statistics, 2009).
76. For contemporary television examples, see *The Sopranos: No Show* (Sept. 22, 2002) and *The Wire* (2003). For an example from cinema, see *On the Waterfront* (1954). Not all film depictions are negative, perhaps most notably *Norma Rae* (1979).

REFERENCES

AFL-CIO. n.d. "Employee Free Choice Act: The System for Forming Unions is Broken." Available at: http://pennfedbmwe.org/docs/legislative/efca/employee_free_choice_act.html.
American Federation of State, County and Municipal Employees. 1999. "Organizing Model & Manual."
Ayres, Ian. 2006. "Menus Matter," 73 *University of Chicago Law Review* 3–15.
Bacharach, Samuel B., Peter A. Bamberger, and William J. Sonnenstuhl. 2001. *Mutual Aid and Union Renewal: Cycles of Logic of Action*. Ithaca, NY: ILR Press.
Barenberg, Mark. 1994. "Democracy and Domination in the Law of Workplace Cooperation: From Bureaucratic to Flexible Production," 94 *Columbia Law Review* 753–983.
Bebchuk, Lucian Arye. 1989. "Foreword: The Debate on Contractual Freedom in Corporate Law," 89 *Columbia Law Review* 1395–415.
Bebchuk, Lucian A. and Assaf Hamdani. 2002. "Optimal Defaults for Corporate Law Evolution," 96 *Northwestern University Law Review* 489–519.
Becker, Craig. 1993. "Democracy in the Workplace: Union Representation Elections and Federal Labor Law," 77 *Minnesota Law Review* 495–603.
Bennett, James T. and Bruce E. Kaufman, eds. 2008. *What Do Unions Do? A Twenty-Year Perspective*. New Brunswick, NJ: Transaction Publishers.
Blakey, G. Robert and Ronald Goldstock. 1980. "'On the Waterfront': RICO and Labor Racketeering,"17 *American Criminal Law Review* 341–65.
Bodie, Matthew T. 2008. "Information and the Market for Union Representation," 94 *Virginia Law Review* 1–78.

Bronfenbrenner, Kate. 2000. "Uneasy Terrain: The Impact of Capital Mobility on Workers, Wages, and Union Organizing," ILR Collection: Research Studies and Reports. Available at: http://digitalcommons.ilr. cornell.edu/cgi/viewcontent.cgi?article=1002&context=reports.

Bronfenbrenner, Kate. 2009. "No Holds Barred: The Intensification of Employer Opposition to Organizing," Economic Policy Institute (EPI) Briefing Paper No. 235. Available at: http://epi.3cdn.net/ edc3b3dc172dd1094f_0ym6ii96d.pdf.

Bronfenbrenner, Kate and Tom Juravich. 1998. "It Takes More than House Calls: Organizing to Win with a Comprehensive Union-Building Strategy," in Kate Bronfenbrenner, Sheldon Friedman, Richard W. Hurd, and Rudolph A. Oswald, eds., *Organizing to Win: New Research on Union Strategies.* Ithaca, NY: ILR Press.

Brudney, James J. 2005. "Neutrality Agreements and Card Check Recognition: Prospects for Changing Paradigms," 90 *Iowa Law Review* 819–86.

Budd, John W. 2007. "The Effect of Unions on Employee Benefits and Non-Wage Compensation: Monopoly Power, Collective Voice, and Facilitation," in James T. Bennett and Bruce E. Kaufman, eds., *What Do Unions Do?* New Brunswick, NJ: Transaction Publishers.

Bureau of Labor Statistics. 2008. "Current Population Survey," United States Department of Labor. Available at: http://www.bls.gov/cps/cpsaat42.pdf.

Bureau of Labor Statistics. 2009. "Economic News Release: Union Members Summary," United States Department of Labor, Jan. 29. Available at: http://www.bls.gov/news.release/union2.nr0.htm.

Bureau of National Affairs. 2009. "CNA Members Ratify Four-Year Contract with Two Hospitals Covering 1,450 Nurses," 23 *Labor Relations Week*, Aug. 13, 1290.

Card, David, Thomas Lemieux, and W. Craig Riddell. 2007. "Unions and Wage Inequality," in James T. Bennett and Bruce E. Kaufman, eds., *What Do Unions Do?* New Brunswick, NJ: Transaction Publishers.

Cincinnati Enquirer, 2003. "Group Says Unions Pressure Workers," Sept. 18, 1D.

Comstock, Phil and Maier B. Fox. 1994. "Employer Tactics and Labor Law Reform," in Sheldon Friedman, Richard W. Hurd, Rudolph A. Oswald, and Ronald L. Seeber, eds., *Restoring the Promise of American Labor Law.* Ithaca, NY: Cornell University Press.

Cox, Archibald. 1947. "Some Aspects of the Labor Management Relations Act, 1947," 61 *Harvard Law Review* 1–49.

Craver, Charles B. 1995. "Rearranging Deck Chairs on the Titanic: The Inadequacy of Modest Proposals To Reform Labor Law," 93 *Michigan Law Review* 1616–44.

Delgado, Héctor L. 1993. *New Immigrants, Old Unions: Organizing Undocumented Workers in Los Angeles.* Philadelphia, PA: Temple University Press.

DeMaria, Alfred T. 2001. "Learning Lessons (Good and Bad) from a Real-Life Campaign," *Management Report*, Apr., 3.

DiNardo, John and David S. Lee. 2004. "Economic Impacts of New Unionization on Private Sector Employers: 1984–2001," 119 *Quarterly Journal of Economics* 1383–441.

Dunne, Timothy and David A. Macpherson. 1994. "Unionism and Gross Employment Flows," 60 *Southern Economic Journal* 727–38.

Eaton, Adrienne E. and Jill Kriesky. 2003. "No More Stacked Deck: Evaluating the Case against Card-Check Union Recognition," *Perspectives on Work* 19–21.

Eaton, Adrienne E. and Jill Kriesky. 2009. "NLRB Elections versus Card Check Campaigns: Results of a Worker Survey," 62 *Industrial and Labor Relations Review* 157–72.

Elhauge, Einer. 2008. *Statutory Default Rules: How to Interpret Unclear Legislation.* Cambridge, MA: Harvard University Press.

Elster, Jon. 1983. *Sour Grapes: Studies in the Subversion of Rationality.* Cambridge, UK: Cambridge University Press.

Elster, Jon. 1986. "Comments on Krouse and McPherson," 97 *Ethics* 146–53.

Epstein, Richard A. 2008. "The Employee Free Choice Act is Unconstitutional," *Wall Street Journal*, Dec. 19, A15.

Epstein, Richard A. 2009. "The Case Against the Employee Free Choice Act," University of Chicago Law & Economics, Olin Working Paper No. 452. Available at: SSRN http://papers.ssrn.com/sol3/papers. cfm?abstract_id=1337185.

Wilson (2008), Cynthia L. 1994. "Labor, Property, and Sovereignty after *Lechmere*," 46 *Stanford Law Review* 305–59.

Estlund, Cynthia L. 2002. "The Ossification of American Labor Law," 102 *Columbia Law Review* 1527–612.

Estlund, Cynthia L. 2005. "Rebuilding the Law of the Workplace in an Era of Self-Regulation," 105 *Columbia Law Review* 319–404.

Fantasia, Rick. 1988. *Cultures of Solidarity: Consciousness, Action, and Contemporary American Workers.* Berkeley, CA: University of California Press.

Farnsworth, E. Allan. 2004. *Contracts*, 4th edition. New York, NY: Aspen Publishers.

Ferguson, John-Paul. 2008. "The Eyes of the Needles: A Sequential Model of Union Organizing Drives, 1999–2004," 62 *Industrial and Labor Relations Review* 3–21.

Flores, William V. 1997. "Mujeres en Huelga: Cultural Citizenship and Gender Empowerment in a Cannery Strike," in William V. Flores and Rina Benmayor, eds., *Latino Cultural Citizenship*. Boston, MA: Beacon Press.

Frederick, Shane, George Loewenstein, and Ted O'Donoghue. 2002. "Time Discounting and Time Preference: A Critical Review," 40 *Journal of Economic Literature* 351–401.

Freeman, Richard B. and Morris M. Kleiner. 1999. "Do Unions Make Enterprises Insolvent?" 52 *Industrial and Labor Relations Review* 510–27.

Freeman, Richard B. and James L. Medoff. 1984. *What Do Unions Do?* New York, NY: Basic Books.

Gould, William B. IV. 1993. *Agenda for Reform: The Future of Employment Relationships and the Law*. Cambridge, MA: MIT Press.

Greenhouse, Steven. 2009a. "Democrats Drop Key Part of Bill to Assist Unions," *New York Times*, July 16, A1.

Greenhouse, Steven. 2009b. "At Labor Gathering, Luxury, Jockeying and Applause for Secretary," *New York Times*, Mar. 8, A22.

Hirsch, Barry T. 2007. "What Do Unions Do for Economic Performance?" in James T. Bennett and Bruce E. Kaufman, eds., *What Do Unions Do?* New Brunswick, NJ: Transaction Publishers.

House Committee on Education and the Workforce, Subcommittee on Employer-Employee Relations. 2002. "Emerging Trends in Employment and Labor Law: Labor-Management Relations in a Global Economy," 107th Congress, Second Session, Oct. 8, 29–30.

Lafer, Gordon. 2007. "Neither Free nor Fair: The Subversion of Democracy under National Labor Relations Board Elections," American Rights at Work Report. Available at: http://www.americanrightsatwork.org/publications/general/neither-free-nor-fair.html.

Lafer, Gordon. 2008. "What's More Democratic than a Secret Ballot, *WorkingUSA: The Journal of Labor and Society* 71–98.

LaLonde, Robert J., Gérard Marschke, and Kenneth Troske. 1996. "Using Longitudinal Data on Establishments to Analyze the Effects of Union Organizing Campaigns in the United States," 41–2 *Annales d'Économie et de Statistique* 155–85.

Leiserson, William M. 1959. *American Trade Union Democracy*. New York, NY: Columbia University Press.

Lopez, Steven Henry. 2006. *Reorganizing the Rust Belt: An Inside Study of the American Labor Movement*. Berkeley, CA: University of California Press.

Milkman, Ruth. 2006. *L.A. Story: Immigrant Workers and the Future of the U.S. Labor Movement*. New York, NY: Russell Sage Foundation.

Morris, Charles J. 1998. "A Tale of Two Statutes: Discrimination for Union Activity under the NLRA and RLA," 2 *Employee Rights and Employment Policy Journal* 317–60.

National Labor Relations Board. 2009. *Seventy-Fourth Annual Report of the National Labor Relations Board for the Fiscal Year Ended September 30, 2009*. Available at: http://www.nlrb.gov/annual-reports

National Right to Work Foundation. n.d. "Why Is Johnson Controls Giving Your Home Address and Telephone Number to Union Organizers?" Available at: http://www.nrtw.org/neutrality/na_ad3.pdf (accessed Nov. 22, 2009).

National Right to Work Legal Defense Foundation. 2003. "Legal Foundation To Assist Cintas Employees Harassed by UNITE Union Organizers," Sept. 17. Available at: http://www.nrtw.org/press/2003/09/legal-foundation-assist-cintas-employees-harassed-unite-union-organizers.

Puette, William J. 1992. *Through Jaundiced Eyes: How the Media View Organized Labor*. Ithaca, NY: ILR Press.

Sachs, Benjamin I. 2008. "Employment Law as Labor Law," 29 *Cardozo Law Review* 2685–748.

Sachs, Benjamin I. 2010. "Enabling Employee Choice: A Structural Approach to the Rules of Union Organizing," 123 *Harvard Law Review* 655–728.

Sanders, Lynn M. 1997. "Against Deliberation," 25 *Political Theory* 347–76.

Schmitt, John and Ben Zipperer. 2007. "Dropping the Ax: Illegal Firings during Union Election Campaigns," Center for Economic and Policy Research (CEPR). Available at: http://www.cepr.net/documents/publications/unions_2007_01.pdf.

Senate Committee on Health, Education, Labor, and Pensions to consider H.R. 800, the Employee Free Choice Act. 110th Congress, First Session, Mar. 27, 2007, pp. 12–17.

Specter, Arlen and Eric S. Nguyen. 2008. "Policy Essay: Representation without Intimidation: Securing Workers' Right to Choose under the National Labor Relations Act," 45 *Harvard Journal on Legislation* 311–34.

Stone, Katherine Van Wezel. 1981. "The Post-War Paradigm in American Labor Law," 90 *Yale Law Journal* 1509–80.

Sunstein, Cass R. 1986. "Legal Interference with Private Preferences," 53 *University of Chicago Law Review* 1129–74.

Sunstein, Cass R. 1991. "Preferences and Politics," 20 *Philosophy and Public Affairs* 3–34.

Sunstein, Cass R. 2001. "Human Behavior and the Law of Work," 87 *Virginia Law Review* 205–76.

Weiler, Paul. 1983. "Promises to Keep: Securing Workers' Rights to Self-Organization under the NLRA," 96 *Harvard Law Review* 1769–827.

Weiler, Paul. 1990. *Governing the Workplace: The Future of Labor and Employment Law*. Cambridge, MA: Harvard University Press.

Wilson, Justin J. 2008. "Union Math, Union Myths: An Analysis of Government Data on Employees Fired during Union Organizing Campaigns," Center for Union Facts. Available at: http://www.unionfacts.com/downloads/union_math_union_myths.pdf.

Yager, Daniel V., Timothy J. Bartl, and Joseph J. LoBue. 1998. *Employee Free Choice: It's Not in the Cards*. Washington, DC: LPA.

6. The deserved demise of EFCA (and why the NLRA should share its fate)

*Richard A. Epstein**

INTRODUCTION

For the past several years, Democratic majorities in both houses of Congress have championed the passage of the Employee Free Choice Act (EFCA). Some defenders of the proposed legislation did not see it as a sea change. But that position was belied by the vast amounts of energy and money that the dominant players on both sides invested in the battle. Those expenditures are more consistent with the view that passage of the bill would have revolutionized management and labor relations over at least some substantial portion of the labor force, most likely in low-paying jobs in the service industries.

When Barack Obama was elected President in November 2008, the odds were good that EFCA would be enacted quickly into law. Obama was elected with strong majorities in both houses of Congress, and the public had soured on American business and had accepted much of the populist critique that attributed the great financial crisis in the fall of 2008 to corporate greed and the nonstop financial machinations on Wall Street. Relationships between the administration and organized labor were close, and the two groups showed every sign of working effectively together on a powerful Congressional campaign to turn the bill into law. Unlike the then pending health care legislation that introduced extensive changes throughout the health care system,[1] EFCA is a short bill whose implementation does not require levying any new taxes or creating any major new administrative agency. Intellectually and emotionally, EFCA fed off the widespread and determined perception within pro-labor circles, both those in practice and those in the academy, that the feeble union remedies available under the National Labor Relations Act (NLRA) – usually holding new elections or issuing bargaining orders – leave employers who consciously breach the statute better off than they would have been if they had complied with the law. Time after time, pro-union scholars have identified the NLRA's weak remedial side as the major explanation for the rapid decline of labor union membership in the private sector. Those numbers had leveled off in 2006 and 2007, only to plummet again in the post-2008 meltdown to a new low of 6.9 percent of the private workforce today (BLS, 2010). That figure is down from a high of about 35 percent in 1954. Indeed, so great is the transformation in union membership that today there are more members of public sector unions than private sector unions, by a respectable margin of 7.9 million to 7.4 million workers (*id.*).[2]

There are, of course, other ways to explain the decline in union representation. One point worth noting is that the basic legal framework has changed only in modest ways since 1954. If the system could support high levels of unionization then, it is fair to ask, why not now? Other explanations point to the increase in labor market fluidity, deregulation, and the rise in foreign competition. These other explanations are consistent with the observation that the decline in union density is not unique to the United States but is paralleled in other advanced industrialized countries (Estreicher, 2008).

However, one point seems clear. As of the end of 2012, EFCA seems dead in the water, and given the Republican control in the House and a filibuster position in the Senate, there is no likely prospect of its revival. The change in sentiment is apparent. In the first two years of the Obama presidency, the enthusiasm of labor for the bill was matched every step of the way by the undying hostility of employer groups toward the legislation. With few exceptions,[3] these groups acted with a unity of purpose that is not normally found in the fractious ranks of American industry, where businesses are often at logger-heads with each other. One sign of that unity is that these organizations funded my own book, *The Case Against the Employee Free Choice Act* (Epstein, 2009a).[4] To be sure, not all firms were equally opposed to EFCA. Those businesses that were already unionized could obtain, at least in the short run, some compensatory advantage if their rivals were subject to similar (or even more burdensome) union contracts. But that small advantage was not enough to swing many employers into the pro-EFCA camp, for EFCA also held out the distinct possibility of further unionization of firms in which unions had already acquired a foothold. It is no deep secret that, within their gates, employers do not welcome unions with open arms. Whether these employers could have succeeded against a full-court press from the Obama administration remains unclear. But employers were surely aided by its decision to subordinate labor law reform to health care legislation,[5] financial legislation[6] and climate control legislation, the first two of which have passed, and the third of which is not going anywhere soon.

However, the full explanation for the stalemate over EFCA does not rest solely in the relative strength of management over labor in this struggle. All partisan disputes take place in arenas where neutral third parties can choose sides. On this particular occasion, the unions faced intense public antipathy to the most conspicuous portion of EFCA, which allowed unions to gain representation by a card-check, without going through secret-ballot elections. The obvious risks of fraud and coercion in such a pro-cedure brought out such individuals as George McGovern, the Democratic presidential nominee in 1972, against the bill (McGovern, 2008). I regard these developments as both welcome and long overdue. EFCA represented a potentially catastrophic federal inter-vention in already fragile labor markets, perhaps on par with the 1935 NLRA. Rather than compound that New Deal mistake, I would urge a position that goes against the dominant political ethos both in the United States and overseas: the NLRA should be repealed in favor of a return to the common law system of labor relations that prevailed prior to the New Deal (see Epstein, 1983; Getman and Kohler, 1983).[7]

Needless to say, this normative outlook is not shared widely by the academics who specialize in labor relations, most of whom are highly supportive of the basic NLRA model and of some if not all of EFCA's major innovations, especially the effort to boost the remedies against employers during organization drives. The purpose of this chapter is to critique the recent arguments that pro-labor scholars have advanced for labor law reforms that would strengthen the NLRA and make up for its remedial shortfalls. Make no mistake about it: the adoption of EFCA would have been a more dramatic develop-ment than a return to the 1935 Wagner Act[8] by the repeal of the Taft-Hartley Act of 1947. In particular, EFCA's first-contract arbitration provision would eliminate the employer's ability to stand firm against union demands during the collective bargaining process, which even the original Wagner Act allowed employers to do.[9] Front and center for proponents are the questions of how to increase the odds of union success in organizing drives, as well as their ability to gain, as of right, first contracts thereafter. These measures are the only way to stem the rapid decline in unionization that takes place through the unrelenting attrition of large unions in old-line industries. It is no surprise, therefore, that EFCA has nothing to say regarding other key issues associated with labor relations, such as the operation of the grievance process or the use of the strike and lockout as economic weapons in labor disputes. The abortive strike by the Communications Workers of America against Verizon offers strong evidence that under current conditions, employers are better able to withstand strikes than they were in earlier times.

Notwithstanding unions' current vulnerability, their effort to transform established law has proven a bridge too far to cross. The Democratic and union-backed effort to transform American labor law by strenuous political efforts failed in the face of unanimous business opposition and widespread public uneasiness with the bill. That demise is to be welcomed, and the same is true for the present dysfunctional structure of the NLRA. The deserved repeal of that law is not on the cards. Indeed, the pressure is on to expand the reach of the NLRA. To be sure, labor forces have, for the moment, given up the effort to introduce either the card-check or compulsory first-contract arbitration. But they have not given up on the effort to shorten the time allowable for union elections. Indeed, however dormant EFCA is politically, it continues to garner major support inside labor unions and among its many academic backers. It is important, therefore, to give close attention to the arguments for unionization in general and for this bill in particular, given that EFCA could be reintroduced at any time, be it as freestanding legislation or as a rider to some other bill. The purpose of this chapter is to examine and refute the case that has been made for the legislation. On this issue, I see no virtue in taking the middle ground: none of the provisions in EFCA should be enacted into law, ever.

EFCA itself consists of three separate provisions. The first two, which are best considered together, have as their objective the exclusion or reduction of employer influence in the union organization process. The first departure from current law, benignly described as "Strengthening Enforcement," modifies the rules governing employer unfair labor practices (ULPs) during organization campaigns.[10] This section increases the penalties for ULPs committed by employers during an organization drive without touching the penalties for unfair labor practices by labor unions. The second provision, which under the EFCA goes by the soothing name of "Streamlining Union Certification," allows, at the option of "either the union or any group of employees,"[11] the routine substitution of the card-check for the NLRB-supervised secret election that now represents the preferred approach under the Act. That card-check procedure effectively allows unions to undertake organization campaigns in relative secrecy, thus neutralizing, without prohibiting, much of the employer's influence in an organization campaign. These first two elements are considered together because each is meant to reinforce the other.

The third major reform, described as "Facilitating Initial Collective Bargaining Agreements," calls for the use of a two-year mandatory "contract" that is determined by an arbitral board selected by the Federal Mediation and Conciliation Service (FMCS), if the parties fail to come to an agreement after a negotiation process lasting as little as 130 days, all stages included.[12] This mandatory arrangement is imposed even when both the union and management have, in good faith, bargained to impasse under the present NLRA. The cumulative effect of these three provisions would lead to a massive shift in the balance of power between labor and management and, I fear, to new levels of mutual animosity in an area where political relations between the two sides are, to put it mildly, already frayed.

My analysis proceeds in four steps. In Section I, I look at two sets of arguments that have been made to strengthen the union position in organizing drives. The first of these was written in 1993 by Craig Becker, who came to prominence thanks to determined Republican opposition to his presidential recess appointment to the board, much of it stemming from his article "Democracy in the Workplace: Union Representation Elections and Federal Labor Law." A more recent effort that builds on the Becker work is a recent article of Professor Benjamin Sachs (2010), who explicitly addresses EFCA in his analysis of the organizational process. In Section II, I turn to a recent defense of the system of mandatory arbitration offered by Professors Catherine Fisk and Adam Pulver (2009). Section III offers an overall examination of EFCA. Section IV examines some estimates of the probable negative effects of EFCA on job formation and retention. A brief conclusion follows.

I.   EMPLOYEE ORGANIZATIONAL DRIVES

A.   Becker and Employee Autonomy

Becker's critique of modern labor law makes no bones about where he stands in his suspension of the operation of market forces in labor markets. In his conclusion, he quotes from the famous article of Roscoe Pound (1909), which deplored the Supreme Court for its ostrich-like behavior in cases like *Lochner v. New York*.[13] To Becker, as to Pound, the thought that individual employees could bargain effectively with employers sacrificed all practical wisdom for some misguided fascination with an outdated notion of formal equality. "Actual industrial conditions" just did not square with the naïve view of the world held by the defenders of laissez-faire (pp. 454, 487). Becker's leitmotif was that Pound's basic orientation should carry through to understanding and interpreting American labor law.

In Becker's view, the NLRB's halcyon period was the heady time between 1935 and 1939 when there was much judicial support for the view that, under the NLRA, employers did not have any right to be involved in any way during the representation proceedings prior to the employees' selection of the union either by election or otherwise (Becker, 1993). Becker goes on to argue that this policy established the right set of legal relationships on the ground that the employer played no proper role in trying to influence the creation, internal affairs and operation of the union. And he further notes that in the early years after the passage of the NLRA, the Board was sympathetic to union efforts to exclude the employer from worker deliberations over selecting union representatives. A union did not have to be chosen solely through a secret-ballot election, but could be chosen via a card-check, which had the advantage that "[m]embership cards could be solicited without employers knowing that their employees were organizing" (p. 535). His bottom line, therefore, was that employers should be relegated to the role of observers in union elections, without any participation in the basic process, and without any rights of speech associated with the campaign process. To implement that position, said Becker, the NLRB "should exercise [its] discretion by specifying that the only parties to both pre- and post-election hearings are employees and the unions seeking to represent them" (p. 586). He concludes: "One thing therefore is certain. So long as the law construes employers and unions as equals in union elections, industrial democracy will remain as much a legal fiction as liberty of contract" (p. 603).

I believe that Becker is correct in his claim that, as a matter of first principle, any selection of a union should be a matter for potential workers to decide for themselves. After all, no other business organization has to gain the consent of its negotiating adversary in order to decide how to form its ranks. Becker notes that appeals to this notion of internal autonomy were commonly made by supporters of the Wagner Act, who wanted to insulate union deliberations from any management influence: "suppose the United States and Mexico were seeking to adjust a boundary matter by negotiation through commissioners. How would it be regarded if the United States sought to influence the selection of certain commissioners to represent Mexico?" (Becker, 1993, p. 531).[14] This meddling would be totally improper. But, then again, under the strong conceptions of state sovereignty that dominate international law, the United States did not have the power to force the Mexican government to negotiate with it in good faith. Note, therefore, Becker's astute rhetorical ploy: he uses the strong theory of individual autonomy for internal workers affairs, but rejects that same theory for employers by accepting the NLRA's mandatory duty to bargain with the recognized union and its representatives. His goal therefore is *not* to apply an even-handed theory of individual choice to all participants in labor market. It is to celebrate some conception of collective autonomy for workers that necessarily limits the autonomy interests of employers. The paramount difficulty with using this approach to employee activities is that it does not take into account the other profound adjustments that the NLRA imposes on the institutional arrangements between an employer and employee.

It would be perfectly acceptable to follow Becker's striking position in a world in which freedom of association and economic liberty governed every aspect of management/labor relationships. In that world, it is clear by parity of reasoning that labor groups could exert no influence in the way in which employers choose to govern their businesses or in the policies that they choose to pursue in relation to their employees and to the labor unions that wish to represent them (except of course to the extent that the employer voluntarily agreed to such restrictions). In particular, those principles would allow the employer not to deal with any union representatives at all, and to insist that any worker agree not to join any union or promise to join any union so long as they continue to work for the employer. These "yellow dog" contracts, in effect, would force a firm's workers to be loyal to one side or the other. But no worker could, in a regime that honors strong autonomy, have his cake and eat it too, by forcing the employer to hire him when he is a union member or has committed to joining the union on its request (Epstein, 1983).

A second precondition for the Becker approach that denies an employer a special voice in worker affairs is that the union could not bind those workers who decided to resist union membership. Any accurate rendition of the principle of freedom of association does not allow for majorities in some state-determined bargaining unit to bind other individuals by a combination of administrative fiats and majority votes, including one that abrogates their prior individual contracts.[15]

In order to avoid these conclusions, the NLRA, in line with the view of Pound and others, adopts the dubious rhetorical ploy that workers do not have "full" or "actual" freedom of contract so long as they are opposed by firms that consist of an aggregation of shareholders.[16] As Becker himself notes, Senator Robert Wagner constantly appeals to the notions of individual freedom to defend the statute: "It is the next step in the logical unfolding of man's eternal quest for freedom. . . . Only 150 years ago did this country cast off the shackles of political despotism. And today, with economic problems occupying the center of the stage, we strive to liberate the common man . . . ." (Becker, 1993, p. 496).[17] And so the Constitution of limited government becomes a justification for massive interference into the economy. Wagner's argument that the NLRA somehow advances the principle of freedom of association has become a staple of the academic literature (see, e.g., Cox, 1956).[18] Nor is its appeal local, for that same ad hoc version of "freedom of association" has been endorsed by the International Labor Organization and its 183 member nations (see ILO, 2011).

Notwithstanding the overwhelming political consensus on this issue, as a matter of first principle, the argument does not play out as Wagner suggests. The modern rhetoric makes repeated reference to the ideal of "employee choice." Yet the repeated use of that idea in this context[19] is the homage that vice pays to virtue. Quite simply, the traditional principle of freedom of association, both actual and full, bears no relationship to that which is invoked under the Labor Act. Justice Brennan, in *Roberts v. United States Jaycees*, wrote, "Freedom of association . . . plainly presupposes a freedom not to associate,"[20] only to restrict the application of that principle to a narrow set of intimate associations.[21] That right not to associate is not honored today in the antidiscrimination laws, for example, in many economic settings. Yet there is no principled reason why the gains from free association should be available to some types of transactions but not to others. Properly understood, that principle in its generalized form also negates government efforts to impose any duty to bargain on an employer in a competitive market. Any agreement between workers can bind only those agreeing; it cannot increase their rights against third persons, employers included. If an employer can refuse to bargain with individual workers, in principle it should certainly be able to refuse to bargain with a collectivity of workers, whose monopoly power has long been criticized by economists and other observers for its tendency to lower output, raise wages and reduce overall social welfare.

Thus, it is misguided for defenders of the NLRA to appeal to the expanded notion of employee choice under the guise of the principle of freedom of association. The NLRA violates that neutral principle of freedom of association in both cases, by stripping from employers rights that principle should grant them, and conferring unwarranted advantages on unions that do not deserve them. Removing this linguistic veil makes clear that, far from advancing "actual" freedom of contract, the Wagner Act carried out its main purpose – the creation of union monopoly power – without ever using the term. Indeed, given their monopoly position, unions should be prohibited from discriminating against some workers in favor of others. In my view, the antidiscrimination norm has no place in competitive labor markets (see Epstein, 1992);[22] but that norm should apply against monopolist unions. The most obvious axis of discrimination is of course race, which is why the Supreme Court grafted onto the basic statute a duty of fair representation to protect minority workers from majority exploitation in *Steele v. Louisville & Nashville R.R. Co.*,[23] only to have to grapple with the implications of that duty in race cases for over a decade afterwards.[24]

The principle of freedom of association for workers cannot be invoked to defend the NLRA when that statute has irrevocably altered all the background conditions under which a claim of freedom of association becomes defensible. Thus in ordinary cases, any group of market actors that decides to organize is subject to the constraints of antitrust law to the extent that it seeks to dominate one side of the market and constrain competition. The collective refusal to deal counts today as a per se violation of the antitrust laws,[25] just as it did in the case of unions before the passage of the Clayton Act. Indeed, on this point there has been an instructive set of historical reversals. In the so-called Danbury Hatters' Case, *Loewe v. Lawlor*, a union was held liable in a unanimous decision under the Sherman Act for organizing a nationwide secondary boycott against dealers who traded in hats made by the Danbury Hat Co.[26] Chief Justice Melville Fuller held that the same principles that governed boycotts in ordinary commerce applied to labor unions.[27] His concern was not based on formal principles in blithe disregard to facts on the ground. In fact, that secondary boycott had real teeth and led seventy of eighty-two hatters in the United States to capitulate to the union demands.[28] As a matter of straight antitrust law, there is no serious argument that the decision was incorrect. Progressive forces, however, quickly overturned *Loewe v. Lawlor* in 1914 by passing Section 6 of the Clayton Act,[29] which largely immunized the efforts of unions to organize workers,[30] at least insofar as they did not collaborate with unionized firms to drive non-unionized firms out of business.[31] That exemption from the general antitrust law is both a major and ad hoc boon to labor unions, which fundamentally alters the background conditions under which the claim for strong union autonomy should be examined. Yet even that strong pro-union position did not last, because one of the major reforms of the Taft-Hartley Act was to reinstate the prohibition against secondary boycotts.[32]

But Taft-Hartley left intact the right of a union to bargain collectively on behalf of non-member workers, such that non-consenting members of a "bargaining unit" are subjected to the unions' exclusive representation. Indeed, if the logic of freedom of association had prevailed under the NLRA, there would be no need for a union to show that the workers who do choose to join its ranks are members of some bargaining unit determined by occult statutory rules such as those found in Section 9 of the NLRA.

In the name of employee choice, the NLRA also confers upon unions a second privilege that flies in the face of the orthodox principle of freedom of association. No agreement between A and B, however voluntary, can give them additional rights against C. I cannot agree with my best friend that a third person will sell his house to us for $10. That contract may, after a fashion, be binding on the two of us, but it in no way alters the right of C to refuse to deal with either of us on the terms stated. The same would be true of an agreement between my friend and me to force C to negotiate with us "in good faith" in order to reach the terms and conditions on which the house could be sold. The labor statutes flatly reject this necessary and standard side-constraint to the robust account of freedom of association, by explicitly authorizing a majority of employees, by forming a union, to force the employer to negotiate with it against its will.[33]

Union defenders like to describe these extraordinary statutory privileges as a commendable form of realism in the face of the employer's overwhelming market power. Indeed, Becker treats these built-in union advantages as given by some state of nature, but cannot, in an article of 49,296 words, once utter the phrases "statutory monopolist" or "worker cartel" to describe the union's position vis-à-vis the employer. To be sure, the level of monopoly power that any union holds today has been eroded, in part, by the more open market in trade on both the domestic and international fronts. But site-specific gains remain possible (and if they did not, unions would not bother to seek passage of EFCA because strong competitive forces would hold wages at or close to their pre-unionization levels). Unions could make real inroads in domestic markets for restaurants and hotels, for instance, shifting the wage curves upward without worrying, at least in the short run, about direct forms of foreign competition. It is, therefore, proper to think of EFCA as a way to obtain those economic advantages.

In entering those markets, there remains the question of whether the union, with its current panoply of statutory rights, works under some systematic disadvantage in seeking to organize workers. That proposition is commonly advanced, as it is by Becker (and Pound before him). But the facts fall short. That is not to say that unions do not face steep odds. Of course, it is easy to collect, as Professor Sachs does, evidence of strong employer resistance to unionization.[34] Indeed, to no one's surprise, over 96 percent of employers oppose union organization drives (Bronfenbrenner, 2009, p. 10, table 3), and they spend, in the aggregate, close to $1 billion annually in defensive efforts to ward off these union drives, including about $200 million in external payments to third parties and the rest in the company time of managers and supervisors (Logan, 2006).[35]

Who would expect otherwise? Such behavior is only rational in light of the complex bargaining arrangements to which unionization commits employers under the current law. But that does not amount to a showing that unions labor under a systematic disadvantage. Unions themselves can bring formidable resources to organizing campaigns, and are able to win a substantial fraction of contested elections. To be sure, this figure does not reflect the organizing efforts that unions do not mount because they expect to lose. But by the same token, they may expect to lose many campaigns in which there are no unfair labor practices. And employers may well throw in the towel with respect to those campaigns that they expect to lose as well. There is nothing therefore in these numbers that points to serious irregularities in the practice. Nor is there any independent evidence that points to such irregularities. What is most notable is that unions that are thwarted in election drives often resort to other tactics, including publicity drives, to discredit firms outside the collective bargaining field. They can also find political allies who will help pass zoning laws to keep non-union firms out of local markets. These tactics cannot be ignored in evaluating the relative bargaining strength of the parties. Faced with these and other tactics, stout resistance to union initiative is always rational and often effective. Does *anyone* think that unionization makes the unionized firm better off?[36]

It is possible to go still further. Given the size of the stakes, the conventional estimates of the costs that businesses expend to resist unionization are in all likelihood far too *low*. First, these estimates do not include the costs that the United States incurs in overseeing these complex processes. Second, even with respect to private expenditures, both direct and indirect, the full total should include not only those that kick in once a union drive is in the offing, but those that occur in anticipation of possible union activity. An astute employer and its internal legal team will never wait until union activity is underway to make their influence felt on company decisions. In a world that allows yellow dog contracts, employers have little need to take these costly defensive actions. But once those sensible, pro-competitive contracts are made illegal, the employer, fearing the loss of both management prerogatives and overall productivity, is well-advised to choose plant locations, to design its plants and other facilities, to structure assembly lines and to contract out in ways that minimize vulnerability to union initiatives. These expenditures are not easily quantifiable because they all involve decisions that mix union-related with non-union motivations. Furthermore, no prudent employer would ever broadcast these elements, lest it bring the wrath of reformers, unions and the NLRB down on its shoulders. But employers take these union avoidance measures because they are conscious of the seriousness of the threat that unionization poses to the efficiency of the firm, which is some measure of the *social* losses of unionization. If matters were otherwise, and unions helped firms, the opposition would instantly melt away. But so long as unionization relies on coercive mechanisms, that opposition will persist because forced associations can never generate the same levels of trust as are found in voluntary associations.

At this juncture, the purpose is not (only) to put in a plea for a repeal of established labor law. It is also to point out that there has to be some limit to the legal advantages that unions should receive. Indeed, the better reading of the history shows that many of the major adjustments in the law, both by the Taft-Hartley amendments and by judicial interpretation, were perceived as countervailing responses to the advantages the unions received under the original Wagner Act.[37] I will discuss three examples below. The message here is clear. The adoption of a collective bargaining system requires multiple adjustments elsewhere to make sure that neither side receives too great an advantage. That form of calibration is hard to achieve, and one reason to repeal this statute is to allow the government to get out of the business of generating new countervailing benefits.

1. Secondary boycotts

Consider the position of the secondary boycott, open to challenge in federal court under the Supreme Court's construction of the Clayton Act but then insulated by the Norris-LaGuardia and Wagner Acts. The power of these boycotts is only increased if the boycotts can be combined with the direct pressure that unions can place on employers through the collective bargaining process. In the end, the one-two combination proved to be too powerful for Congress to accept. Once unions had gained the statutory right to compel employers to bargain collectively, the added pressure of secondary boycotts proved too great. The Taft-Hartley law thus included an elaborate statutory provision in Section 8(b)(4), which sought to limit such boycotts' scope and control their influence. The boycotts that might have been tenable when unions had little power against their primary employer had proven much more ominous when those powers were in place (see Meltzer and Henderson, 1985; Fisk and Pulver, 2009).

2. Labor injunctions

To progressives, the labor injunction against organizing activities was one of the great abuses of the pre-1932 period. This alleged abuse was rectified by the Norris-La Guardia Act,[38] which greatly narrowed the federal courts' power to issue injunctions in all labor disputes by abolishing their use, for example, to enforce yellow dog contracts. But the question arises as to whether that hostile attitude toward injunctions makes sense when the union has agreed to a "no-strike clause" – that is, a collective bargaining provision that prohibits any "cessation or stoppage of work, lock-out, picketing or boycotts."[39] In *Boys Markets, Inc. v. Retail Clerks Union, Local 770*,[40] Justice William Brennan held that the injunction should issue in these circumstances. He knew full well that many state courts could issue injunctions in labor disputes because they were not covered by Norris-La Guardia or by any parallel state statute.[41] He was, therefore, most uneasy about any law that encouraged unions to remove state court suits for injunctive relief to federal court, where Norris-La Guardia would apply.[42] Yet his larger reason for allowing the injunction paralleled all the arguments that courts had adopted prior to Norris-La Guardia:

> Any incentive for employers to enter into such an arrangement is necessarily dissipated if the principal and most expeditious method by which the no-strike obligation can be enforced is eliminated. While it is of course true, as respondent contends, that other avenues of redress, such as an action for damages, would remain open to an aggrieved employer, an award of damages after a dispute has been settled is no substitute for an immediate halt to an illegal strike. Furthermore, an action for damages prosecuted during or after a labor dispute would only tend to aggravate industrial strife and delay an early resolution of the difficulties between employer and union.[43]

His argument offers a textbook account of why injunctions should issue when damages are inadequate. Once again, the advent of collective bargaining requires a fundamental realignment of other portions of the law. The labor injunction (which was the object of such wrath in 1932) rightly became the preferred legal remedy in 1970, at least when the labor contract had been formed. The hostility to labor injunctions in other cases still remains, in ways that were consistent with the statutory scheme.

3.   Employer speech

Closer to the Becker thesis is the evolution of law governing employer speech during organization campaigns. Today, the basic statutory compromise, which is said to reflect the requirements of the First Amendment,[44] reads as follows:

> (c) *Expression of views without threat of reprisal or force or promise of benefit.* The expressing of any views, argument, or opinion, or the dissemination thereof, whether in written, printed, graphic, or visual form, shall not constitute or be evidence of an unfair labor practice under any of the provisions of this Act [subchapter], if such expression contains no threat of reprisal or force or promise of benefit.[45]

Becker disapproves of this section because he thinks that it resurrects the false equivalence between employer and employee speech that the original Wagner Act had rejected (Becker, 1993).[46] But look at the question from the other side. How, one might ask, does Section 8(c) meet the normal constitutional standard of robust and uninhibited debate, generally characteristic of democratic institutions? "Democracy" is the first word in the title of Becker's article. So where is the disconnect between Section 8(c) and "democracy"? Not in its use of the term "force," at least if that is confined to physical force or the threat thereof. The term "reprisal," however, is filled with studied ambiguity because it covers simultaneously managerial resistance and bodily harm, which give rise to widely divergent responses at common law. So why can't an employer take reprisals by firing workers who don't want to work on the (non-union) terms that the employer finds acceptable? It is only because it would undermine the collective bargaining structure envisioned under the Act.

The same is true for the benefit side of this statutory equation. Outside the area of labor law, offering benefits is the antithesis of coercion, and the proper way to elicit the support of others. But in the context of collective bargaining agreements, offering benefits to workers cannot be allowed if the statutory scheme is to function well. Suppose, for example, that at the outset of a union organization drive, the employer vows to match, term-for-term, the best union offer, so long as workers do not join the union. Within the framework of the act, that strategy is rightly deemed too potent because few unions will initiate an organization drive if they know that employers can take advantage of this powerful counterstrategy. So the survival of the collective bargaining process depends on backing off from the extensive traditional protections offered to free speech outside the labor context. (It would be odd to defend that move by calling disputes that arise in the context of industrial democracy mere commercial disputes similar to those in which a merchant offers goods for sale.)

The key question is how far to back off standard First Amendment conceptions of freedom of speech. The gist of the Becker proposal is to take 8(c) one step further: just keep the employers from speaking at all about the internal affairs of unions, or the employees' decision whether to choose union representation, as part of the grand statutory recalibration of labor law. Against the backdrop of pre-New Deal common law rules, the position is tenable so long as the employer can refuse outright to deal with organized workers. But now that option is gone, as the duty to bargain gives the workers a real club against the employer. Faced with that reality, why should the employer be powerless to speak on its own behalf about an institution with which it will be obliged to bargain if the outcome of the election goes against its interest? Silencing employers who are obligated to bargain shifts the advantage too far to one side and allows unions to make claims that undecided workers could have little chance to critically examine. Right now, employers get their opposing message through by describing firms that failed after unionization, only to predict that the same thing will happen here. The message is effective and tends to change minds and votes, which is why it should remain legal, at least so long as it is not tainted by an implicit threat to close the business if the union should win the recognition election.

To be sure, this system is not perfect. But unions also have countermeasures. If the information in question is thought to be incorrect, the union can seek to counteract it, often outside the purview of the workplace, unfettered by the restrictions parallel to those contained in Section 8(c). To be sure, unions cannot get all the information that they desire about the employer's financial status. Yet note that this information would, in general, be irrelevant in a competitive market, where the only question that matters is whether the employer can match the bid of rival firms. The need to force information transfer is thus another unhappy consequence of the collective bargaining regime. Given the changes in the background rules of negotiation wrought by the labor statute, the speech rules should stay exactly where they are. In its own way, the current law makes the appropriate adjustments in light of the initial statutory commitment to collective bargaining.

B.   Sachs and Default Rules

Writing seventeen years after Becker, Professor Sachs' article mounts a defense for EFCA on unfair labor practices during organizational campaigns coupled with a flirtation, but not an outright endorsement, of the card-check. In writing about this subject, he deals only obliquely with EFCA, about which he expresses certain reservations. But on the basic question of empowering unions, he is determined to ride the flawed notion of "employee choice" as hard as he can in order to persuade his readers to adopt that set of labor rules that will reduce management interference with employee choices, and thus increase the odds of union success in organizational activities.

Of course, two issues that matter on this topic are the relatively rapid and "under the radar" organizational campaigns, which Sachs strongly endorses, and card-check, on which, to his credit, he expresses more ambivalence. On the latter issue, Sachs expresses concern with what he calls the "open" nature of the card-check decisionmaking process, which he thinks renders workers vulnerable to union pressure. Sachs does not address the compulsory arbitration piece of the labor relations puzzle, and he does not think that EFCA offers the solution to the current defects in the NLRA.

Where Sachs comes closest to Becker is in his endorsement of efforts to minimize the employer's role in representation campaigns, by allowing organizing to proceed in secret without an open, formal campaign. In support of that position, he seeks to identify certain key "asymmetries" in the representation process that give an unfair advantage to employers. As with Becker before him, he accepts as given the soundness of the original commitments of the Wagner Act, insofar as it allows a single union to be the exclusive bargaining representative of workers within a given unit. And, as with Becker again, the words "statutory monopoly" never appear in Sachs' 37,915-word article. Rather, Sachs denies this market reality by claiming what no one would care to dispute: "Unionization, for better or worse, does not effect a shift in sovereignty over the firm. It is a far more limited process, one in which employees decide to bargain collectively, rather than individually, with their employers and to name their agent for these purposes" (p. 661). This statement is only half right. The evocative word "sovereignty" would apply only if the union took over the firm lock, stock, and barrel. But it is false if it is meant to say that the employer should be indifferent to the arrival of a union to whom it must necessarily yield some of its prerogatives. The law does not merely allow employees to "decide to bargain collectively," but to force the employer to the bargaining table, which amounts to a partial takeover of its operations and a potential lien on its assets. Once the union is established, it has a stake that is tantamount to part ownership in the business. Given that level of power, it is hard to conclude (as Sachs does) that this "impact" on employers does "not entitle employers to an affirmative right to intervene in that [unionization] process" (p. 662). The impact in this case is not just that of a competitor, for the union has a positive claim against firm assets, which only increases in value as its bargaining rights become more powerful.

At its core, the Sachs plea for revised unionization procedures repeats the Becker error. The union can have explicit claims against employers but should also be immune from any employer counterclaims on workers. As before, the case against the employer's additional speech rights under the NLRA disappears in the face of its duty to bargain with the union. At that point, its legal interest in the union election, and thus its right to speak about union elections, is not zero. The right is at least as great as any random outsider who wishes to comment on the union position. Indeed, given that unions and management are joined at the hip, its stake is surely larger. None of this matters to Sachs' enterprise, which is premised on the unquestioned soundness of some collective bargaining regime, with this caveat: it must lead to an increase of unionized workers over the current level, by limiting the employer's role during union organization drives. Yet those drives often fail not because sanctions are weak but because whatever the union offers by way of gains is offset by the risky nature of collective bargaining negotiations and the precariousness of the unionized firm. Consistent with the objective to expand the unionized workforce, Sachs' political objective is to minimize or eliminate the influence that employers can exert over the question of whether workers will be represented by unions. In his view, the card-check organizing process serves that goal admirably because it is designed "to allow workers to complete a unionization effort before management is aware that such an effort is underway" (Sachs, 2010, p. 657).[47] Note that the choice of the word "workers" is somewhat disingenuous, for Sachs is well aware that, under EFCA, any union is allowed to initiate the card-check process without any showing of union support among the rank of employees. He also quotes at length from the organizing manuals of the American Federation of State, County and Municipal Employees (AFSCME) and the Teamsters to the effect that secrecy is a premium virtue (Sachs, 2010).

The ostensible targets of that secrecy are, moreover, not just the employer, but also those members of the employer's workforce who would likely be opposed to unionization. The system that allows a majority – or even a supermajority – of cards to settle the question of union organization could freeze out these workers from the deliberative process, which still has some faint aspiration of full participation by all persons within the unit. But all that is only a fig leaf. The processes chosen have no neutral valence to them.

Consistent with his basic orientation, Sachs discusses two separate strategies for reformulating the structure of American law. They deal, respectively, with what he calls the initial *default* position, and the *alteration* rules that might be adopted to flip the default to the opposite position. Under the current law, the non-union position is regarded as the default, and a successful organization drive by the union is needed to flip the presumption to a unionized state. Sachs has serious reservations on both counts. He thinks that the law has settled on an uncomfortable (if unavoidable) default provision, and that the current secret-ballot position makes it far too difficult to flip over to the opposite position. Let us look at these two points in order.

1. The default position

Sachs' basic position is to support "employee choice" (Sachs, 2010, p. 656), which he thinks "provides conceptual support for either a new default rule of unionized collective bargaining or a new altering rule that minimizes managerial intervention in organizing" (p. 660). Ultimately, he understands that it is not possible to ask workers to opt for a unionized workforce without having any idea of who that union might be. He therefore goes through this conceptual analysis to explain why, in the real world, the protection of that employee choice requires that the law minimize employer participation in the unionization process. To soften up the defense of the current non-unionized baseline, Sachs relies heavily on "Human Behavior and the Law of Work," the well-known article by

Cass Sunstein (2001). Sunstein argues that the common law baseline rules should be critically reexamined in light of the new learning from behavioral economics, which in his view should render us much more sympathetic to for-cause labor contracts at common law and to unionization under the NLRA.[48]

Sunstein's work builds on the assertion of Paul Weiler (1990) that there is no reason for modern legislatures to accept what Weiler calls "the tacit legal assumption that the 'natural' status for a workplace is non-union." That point is developed in more systematic fashion in a slightly different context by Sunstein's well-known, but misguided, critique of the contract at will: "In the workplace, as elsewhere, the law cannot 'do nothing.' . . . [I]t is necessary to start somewhere – not with nature or voluntary arrangements but with an initial allocation of legal rights" (Sunstein, 2001, p. 208). To Sunstein, the place to start is with the recognition that the common law reflects a number of what he terms "waivable employers' rights." These are rights that the common law confers on the employer, which the employee could then decide to purchase if they were of greater value to him. Yet Sunstein contends that the endowment effect, whereby people value what they own more than what they do not, could easily interfere with the transaction by creating sticky default rules (Sunstein, 2001). He takes issue with my views in favor of the common law's baseline rules of individual autonomy, by insisting that "[w]hat Epstein does not sufficiently acknowledge is the extent to which a number of rights are conferred on the employer by the common law; any suggestion that the common law reflects 'laissez-faire,' or promotes 'voluntary interactions,' should be prefaced with this point" (p. 209 note 10). The stark model of individuals as rational economic calculators, he suggests, should give way to a more complex behavioral model that recognizes the imperfections in workers' evaluation of their own interests on all matters, from their asymmetrical attitude towards gains and losses, to their ignorance of legal rules, to a tendency toward "excessive optimism," to an improper lack of attentiveness to the future, among other issues (p. 206).

In dealing with this issue, I start with the conventional account of default rules, which indicate that either side to some future agreement can insist that they be switched for the transaction to go forward. On that assumption, the more salient the issue, the less likely it is that any default rule will hold. In employment contracts, no background contract term is more important than the choice between at-will and for-cause contracts, so the confident conclusion is that setting the default against the employer will not matter, given its intense preference to undo any for-cause requirement. Employers will make it clear to employees in a thousand ways that this is the rule of engagement, so much so that switching a default rule has no consequence at all – unless it is only the employee who has the right to switch out of the for-cause default position.

Today's labor law takes the at-will option off the table. It is not possible, under the law, for any employer to tell his workers, "I will only hire you if you agree to sign away all rights to join a union under procedures set out by the NLRA." The issue here has nothing to do with default provisions and everything to do with the invalidity of contract provisions that are against public policy. At this point, it is also illegal, once the employment relationship is formed, to attempt to interfere with the statutory machinery by offering each worker $10,000 to avoid the union drive. We can be relatively agnostic about the setting of contract default provisions that are easily reversible. But we cannot be indifferent to the choice of default arrangements like those contained in the NLRA, which reshape an industry.

In dealing with these statutory requirements, it is a huge mistake to claim that the defenders of common law rules think that "the common law system of property rights has some natural, preconventional status" (Sunstein, 2001, p. 209). No one thinks that. The common law of property establishes a set of individual baselines that will reduce the costs of voluntary transactions, and the common law of contract seeks to facilitate and enforce those transactions. Together, they form the foundations of a competitive market economy, which is needed in order to reach the system that has, on average, the highest output. As noted, this drives the antitrust law as well as the common law.

Once we recognize that nature is not the source of the common law baseline, what's next? That piercing insight does not exonerate the attackers of the common law rules from the duty to explain why their normative baseline, from which the pro-union position can work, is superior to the baseline that they dislike. That is a task that they have *never* attempted to undertake, in part because of the practical difficulties of knowing which union would represent which workers when. Instead, they push their case for the reform of labor law under the guise of employee choice, which is somehow thought to lead to a higher likelihood of union activity, if only those pesky employer influences could be put to one side. Yet even at that conceptual level, the difficulties of these supposedly neutral positions are fatal to the proposed reform efforts. Start with the cognitive difficulties: once we know that people are subject to biases and have limited ability to assimilate information, the last thing that we need is a unique and convoluted labor law whose many features people cannot understand. Does anyone think that impaired workers are better off deciding on the benefits of having a union that could negotiate a contract that may or may not pay off, rather than just having an offer of a job at a stated salary? The simpler the legal system (and the fewer the relevant players), the better the information. The so-called "employee choice" baseline that leads to a strengthening of the union position only makes things worse for imperfect minds. Do they really have information as to how their union agent will behave over long periods of time? And should they pre-commit to that representation without knowing how union policies and leaders will shift?

But, just for the sake of argument, assume that the common law baseline is wrong, and that some thought experiment urges that a strengthened collective bargaining regime be put in its place. Again, the question is: what's next? At a minimum, that baseline must have the same degree of universality found under the common law rules so that it explains how parties should proceed in each and every employment relationship subsumed under the new rule. The common law rule specifies that the owner has his capital and the worker has his labor. They can exchange these on whatever terms and conditions they see fit. They are not obligated to fit themselves into some predetermined category of employee and employer, but could easily choose to work as partners or as independent contractors. Their joint intention, as expressed in public language, controls all matters of contractual interpretation. The rule works to cover everything from small two-person businesses to large and complicated corporations. Each set of contracts builds on those that went before it. The secret of the system is to have clarity in terms (for which intelligent default provisions help) and consistency in enforcement. The hope in all cases rests on two fundamental propositions. The first is that voluntary trade between the parties produces mutual gain. The second is that greater levels of wealth for both parties increase opportunities for third persons. The antitrust laws remain a limitation that sometimes bites against contracts in restraint of trade, which should properly, as in *Loewe v. Lawlor*,[49] be a nontrivial binding constraint against unions.

So just what baseline might be proposed in the common law baseline's place? I cannot conceive of any pro-union default rule that could be made operational, for example, in the context of a new firm that has hired two or a dozen workers. By no stretch of the imagination could anyone insist that it is impermissible for a prospective employer to hire a worker unless he first receives the permission of some union. To which one should he turn, and why? In the event of some jurisdictional dispute, should one union be able to insist that it has the right to represent workers to this nascent firm even before it is formed? Do the workers, or prospective workers, have to be polled in advance to see whether they would like to join that union? And must that poll be taken multiple times, as new workers are added and current ones leave? It is not necessary to insist that the ordinary contractual regime is natural, God-given, or, in some mysterious sense, pre-political. It is enough to show that it is blessed with a versatility and simplicity that no ad hoc pro-union baseline could hope to achieve.

Ultimately, Sachs does well not to pin down any new default position. You can't beat one well-established baseline with a philosophical objection to its intrinsic desirability without offering the prospect of setting some better one. The critique of the status quo has to articulate an alternative baseline that is able to withstand the functional criticism of its common law opponents. Sachs' hypothetical ruminations for a union default serves mainly as an effort to soften up the opposition to his actual proposal, which is to make it easier to overturn the non-union default by minimizing employer involvement in the representation campaign. But that version of employee choice also fails, for he does not explain why a rule that gives the union essentially exclusive control over the bully pulpit is the correct way to reform labor relationships. True choice for all parties, employers included, can only occur by jettisoning the basic structure of collective bargaining.

Much of this troubled discussion on the proper baseline reflects the vast gulf that separates questions of contract interpretation from those of institutional design. The default position at stake in the representation context is very different from the proper default norm for contract interpretation. The former requires creating a set of institutions that can be put in place on the ground, which is a far more ambitious matter. There is little question that Senator Wagner sought to ease the path to unionization. Wagner did not envision a world in which a union could be regarded as the default position for all firms. Rather, like Sachs, he saw sufficient defects in the regime of individual bargaining under the common law rule that allows an employer to hire (and fire) workers on an at-will basis – a position that I have long defended (see Epstein, 1984). At this point, the NLRA's mission is not to find default rules intended to realize the intention of the parties. Rather, the NLRA supports institutional arrangements that are intended to drive outcomes to a preferred position that one party desires and the other opposes, namely the increase of union penetration in the workforce. Setting that alternative baseline by statute is a dead loser. Its downfall lies not just in the theoretical attacks on its inefficiency or even in the practical impossibility of that alternative baseline. It lies in the utter inability of its supporters to offer principled reasons of social welfare in support of their complex regime of protected labor monopolies. The invocation of "employee free choice" is not a principled reason, for one group of employees' choice to form a union necessarily deprives other employers of their free choice not to negotiate with a union. So the defenders of EFCA and labor law reform move on to the second point. If the statutory rules are where they are, what alteration in their content improves the employees' chances of success from its current low level?

2. Alteration

Sachs' second line of defense of EFCA and similar reforms thus focuses on the less ambitious – but still vital – task of easing the costs of transition from a non-unionized to a unionized firm. His endeavor assumes that, if the baseline must necessarily be set against the union, the law should make it easier to get to the right position by adopting one of two mechanisms: rapid elections or a card-check. To Sachs, the former is more obtainable. The latter is one on which he is ambivalent, but which has raised enormous controversy elsewhere. The impetus for adopting either is that they function as "asymmetry-correcting altering rules" – that is, as ways of "mitigating the impediments now available to employers, that block departure from the non-union default" (Sachs, 2010, p. 656). But this presupposes that we know who has the advantage in dealing with these elections – the calculus for which is tricky (Epstein, 2009b). It is quite clear that the analysis here is more complicated than in a political election where both parties compete, more or less, on a position of parity, subject to the imbalances that incumbency introduces. In this asymmetrical conflict, the union has advantages that management does not. It can usually formulate the bargaining unit of its choice. It can time the onset of the campaign to take advantage of short-term employer weaknesses or worker unrest. It is not bound by speech rules. It can sow discord with customers long before the election takes place. The employer, of course, can respond with speech on company time and a strong show of hostility. But who knows which set of advantages matters most? A look at actual elections shows that each side has its fair measure of success, with the unions winning somewhat fewer elections in somewhat larger units (*id.*).

Now that there are no huge 1930s-style assembly lines left to organize, how much any change in campaign rules can alter the labor landscape is an open question. But it is still worthwhile to analyze two proposed alternative schemes. The first common device is an expedited election that gives an employer less than two weeks after the campaign announcement to make its case, instead of the nearly six weeks typically allowed for an election campaign today. The major union reason for speeding up the election is to prevent the influence of employer speech from negating the union's initial advantage of surprise in timing the call for an election.

This proposal is one that shows life independent of EFCA. Along strictly partisan lines, the NLRB has proposed to shorten the period between the onset of a union organization campaign and the secret-ballot election.[50] The median election campaign now runs about 39 days, and the average around 57 days.[51] The new periods would, if implemented, be far shorter. AFL-CIO President Rich Trumka praised the move "as a modest step to remove roadblocks and reduce necessary and costly litigation – and that's good news for employers as well as employees."[52] The United States Chamber of Commerce denounced the administrative move as yet "another, not-so-cleverly-disguised effort to restrict the ability of employers to express their views during an election campaign, to inform employees of the pros and cons of unionization."[53] The National Retail Federation drew the explicit connection between the NLRB proposed rules and EFCA: "Unions weren't able to get the Employee Free Choice Act through Congress, so they're using administrative procedures at the NLRB to turn as much of the bill into law as possible."[54]

The union insistence on shorter organizational campaigns does *not* stem from a concern that the employer will say things that violate Section 8(c), but that the employer will be able to point out examples and make arguments that turn out to be persuasive to workers. In effect, the argument in favor of the expedited election is that incomplete information that favors unions is better than full information that does not, which is hard to square with any effort to ensure informed worker choice. The argument quickly blends into the view that *all* persuasive speech should be regarded as an improper threat rather than as sound argument (Epstein, 2009b). That claim is inconsistent with the revisions found in Taft-Hartley that give equal weight to the right to remain free of union influence. The card-check option is even worse than rapid elections because it allows the union campaign to proceed by stealth, and to produce a decision before the employer has any chance at all to have its say. Once again, the point here is to force the issue before full information is acquired by workers who might turn against the union, which is again inconsistent with any version of a full participation model.

The supposed reason for adopting either or both of these strategies is to overcome the coordination problem that workers have in getting a union in place against the implacable opposition of the employer (Sachs, 2010).[55] But the actual reasons are more complex than that (see Epstein, 2009b). The first point is that the union that runs the organizational campaign has no problems with its internal organization. It can promise the moon with little fear of legal pushback. And just as employers can resort to tactics that might involve unfair labor practices, so too can unions resort to all sorts of rough stuff on their side in order to make the position of the employer as painful as possible. They can hire picketers (who are not workers at the plant) to protest working conditions in efforts to drive away customers. They can file complaints, often anonymously, with regulators that bring snap inspections against employers. They can make direct political appeals to zoning boards to keep out firms that do not agree to accept union demands. They can isolate individual workers through intimidation via house calls. In these cases, a longer campaign period may increase the employer's chances in large measure because they can put out the opposite message and neutralize the advantage of union surprise. A union always wants the *option* for the early election, which it can waive if it chooses. Its reason is clear. They fear not only illegitimate coercion but also truthful information, which is exactly what election campaigns should encourage.

Most ironically, disorganized workers opposed to a union do badly under a card-check. Thus a worker whose first preference is to keep out of the union may well sign a card if he or she fears that the union will be selected over his or her opposition. The point is not fanciful, because right now workers often sign cards to support elections, only to vote against them on a secret ballot, which offers protection against reprisal of both sides. At this point, enough swing votes could put matters back the opposite way. One could quarrel about the relative strengths of these difficulties, given the current structure. But the overarching point is that eliminating the entire union election apparatus gets rid of this whole dilemma of deciding which side wields untoward influence and why. Right now most workers in the private sector function quite well. In sum, both parts of the reform campaign under EFCA are wrong. There is no case for altering the rules on union organization or adopting any form of card-check authorization.

II.   FISK AND PULVER AND THE ALLURE OF FIRST-CONTRACT ARBITRATION

The task of Fisk and Pulver is to defend the back end of the union agenda – namely, the push to mandatory arbitration. As with the organization phase of the campaign, the key objection to the current status quo is that determined employers just hold out too long against union demands (Fisk and Pulver, 2009). It is rarely stated that the unions, too, may be reluctant to moderate their demands, lest they lose the support of rank and file – even though it always takes two to make an impasse. The source of these drawn-out negotiations, moreover, lies in the NLRA's basic commitment to a collective bargaining regime that leaves both employer and union with no one to negotiate with but each other with respect to employees.

While these negotiations are supposed to be carried out in mutual good faith, this bilateral monopoly structure invites holdout and bluffing on both sides. The pattern of this bargaining game depends critically on the perceived size of the bargaining range. The union hopes to move the agreement toward a monopoly wage. The employer knows that it cannot go below the competitive wage. In the immediate New Deal period, the want of foreign competition (coupled with various domestic barriers to entry in such key industries as communications) created a large bargaining range (see Ohanian, 2010). The willingness of unions to go on strike and of employers to lock out made sense when there was a good deal to be gained or lost. But the corporatist model that relied on big government to regulate the relationships between big labor and big business led to a form of economic stagnation that, in the end, spelled that model's undoing (Wachter, 2007).[56] As the removal of entry barriers, both domestic and foreign, made labor markets more competitive, there was less to gain through either strikes or lockouts, so a greater measure of calm returned to labor markets. Prolonged negotiations no longer meant a disruption in production, so employers had much to gain from preserving the status quo ante. Unions, for their part, could not succeed with their members if they could not bring wage and benefit packages that mattered, which is a tall order in competitive product markets.

That pattern of decline has not held true for public unions. Their public employers face few or no competitive pressures, and they are often under explicit state law commands to bargain under the shadow of compulsory arbitration. As noted earlier, the union ranks of public employees have swelled to the point that they now exceed – in absolute terms – the number of union members in the private sector. These compulsory arbitration regimes usually offer a laundry list of relevant factors for arbitrators to consider, including comparable wages and benefits, conditions data in comparable markets, and often, ominõusly, "the financial ability of the unit of government to meet these costs" (Fisk and Pulver, 2009, p. 66). That is, the richer you are, the more we can demand – a form of wage discrimination that is consistent with the exploitation of monopoly power. Not surprisingly, the resort to these factors has led to constant wage and benefits increases to keep up with other places of employment, to the point where now the salary premiums and pension packages have ruined public finances, as unionized workers in the public sector comprise over 40 percent of the workforce.

For union supporters, unfortunately, the debate takes place on myopic terms. From their point of view, a forced first-contract regime is superior to the holdout game that the NLRA invites. In effect, Fisk, Pulver and others argue that there is little risk that savvy and conservative arbitrators will make a mess of first contract arbitration by imposing onerous terms on employers. From the union perspective, arbitration is preferable to the current bargaining system. Management, of course, regards the loss of control over vital labor functions as a risk that it cannot run no matter how soothing the assurance of arbitral neutrality and professional competence. But unions do not care whether compulsory arbitration is a positive sum game. The exit rights under the current system are just too valuable to a firm that could otherwise be forced to make adjustments in its labor practices whose consequences could easily outlast any two-year first contract. Nor in assessing the relative risks of holdout problems versus forced contracts do union supporters ever acknowledge that the best way to avoid *both* the holdout and the expropriation game simultaneously is to repeal the NLRA in its entirety, thereby removing both risks by creating a competitive market.

That possibility does not enter into Fisk and Pulver's discussion. Rather, the argument that they construct for compulsory arbitration is in the negative: don't worry about a wholly untested system that is loathed by one side of the transaction. There is no reason, they argue, to think that the arbitrators that will be appointed will be biased toward one side or another. Arbitration, after all, has been used in a number of contexts, including, most notably, with public employees, as under the Taylor Act in New York[57] and fifteen other states (Fisk and Pulver, 2009). It has also been used to deal with disputes over screen credits in Hollywood, and in interpreting and applying the grievance provisions of collective bargaining agreements under the current law. And final offer arbitration (FOA) has long been a staple for resolving salary disputes in professional sports. The clear implication is that the importation of this practice by statute into labor relations is no major departure. The gains from stopping holdouts are large. The dislocations from improvident bargains are small. Why then worry?

For many good reasons, it turns out. In critiquing their case, we can quickly dismiss any reliance on schemes of arbitration put into place by contract. In the case of arbitration under a contract, the terms of the contract will explicitly limit the arbitrator's discretion and provide safeguards against runaway arbitrators (who will not be hired a second time if they do badly the first). The best way to understand these arbitral agreements is as a voluntary substitution for litigation in order to reduce transaction costs and unpredictability in dispute resolution. The arbitration system is not a substitute for negotiation, because the function of the arbitrator is to enforce an agreement that the parties have already made, not to fashion an agreement out of whole cloth to a set of terms that neither side has accepted.

The real question is how compulsory arbitration works, as we leave the voluntary market behind. For this, the closest reference point is the disastrous experience with compulsory arbitration in the public sector, where industrial peace was purchased at the price of fiscal implosion. That expansive history shows that no list of relevant factors can control the upward pressure of individual agreements. Fisk and Pulver write as if the social objectives of any arbitration system are achieved by reaching final agreements that avoid holdouts without bankrupting private firms. Those goals certainly matter, but they are at best stepping-stones to a larger question of whether this system of arbitration will improve the overall operation of labor markets. It won't. The price for industrial peace in the public sector has been runaway increases in salaries and public pension programs that today are the major threat to the solvency of states like New

York, precisely because the Taylor Act is in place. The same story can be told about California (Malanga, 2010).

The clear pressure in the public arena is for arbitrators to impose unsustainable burdens on public bodies that cannot resist. It is quite likely that private employers – at least those large enough to put up a struggle – will put up stouter resistance than public employers, given that they face the short-term risk of bankruptcy. Some evidence suggests that the advent of unionization, on average, leads to a reduction in the value of the firm under the current regime by $60,000 per worker, a figure worth fighting over (Lee and Mas, 2009). That number may overstate the consequences, but whatever the right figure is, it will not get smaller with a compulsory arbitration program, in which it would be foolhardy to assume that adroit firms can prevent these losses from occurring. Even if these firms *are* more adroit, their margin of error is far smaller because they operate in an intensely competitive environment. Firms cannot thrive if for months they are uncertain as to how to assign and organize their workforce. Arbitrators, for all their supposed expertise, do not have a stake in the business. They could too easily hand out generous awards for other people to pay.

The unions may well be willing to take these risks because they will suffer only a small fraction of the losses if the firm goes insolvent, but will keep all the gains from a lucrative first contract. They will have, moreover, strong incentives to enter into cushy deals for the benefit of current employees, promising fiscal relief to the firm in concessions from *future* union members. That is the pattern of negotiation that took place in the recent face-off between then-Governor David Paterson and the public unions in New York, (see, e.g., Confessore, 2010), and the conflict has only intensified under current Governor Andrew Cuomo, who has initiated layoffs after his inability to get union acceptance for his compromise position.[58] All the pension reductions come from workers not yet hired. Fisk and Pulver think that FOA could salvage compulsory bargaining by allowing each side to submit a wage bid to an arbitral panel that is told to take one or the other, but not split the difference. The most obvious objection to this point is that, in professional sports, FOA is used only for single-year contract extensions under standardized terms. FOA is never used to arbitrate long-term contracts. Nor is it used to deal with contracts with many simultaneously moving parts. Fisk and Pulver (2009) think that this is possible with labor contracts, as it is possible to take, for example, the workers' wage demands and the employer's pension benefit system. The theoretical objection is that if the terms are considered separately, the interactions between them are necessarily ignored. That point is probably true even with two related terms, but it is surely true with the thousands of different issues that have to be resolved in negotiating a collective bargaining agreement, which has to cover hot button issues such as contracting out work, health care benefits, discipline and seniority, among others. Ultimately, even under FOA, arbitrators will end up splitting the difference, and that won't work when arbitrators lack detailed knowledge of firm-specific practices.

Public arbitrators do not have to deal with issues such as mergers and takeovers, because these activities are not features of the static public setting. Contracting out is an issue with respect to some peripheral services, but is not on the table with respect to the core functions of teachers, prison guards, and transportation workers. And public arbitrators do not have to consider how the pressures of innovation could require radical changes in workplace deployment to keep competitive. Renegotiation with the usual collateral concessions for waiving contract rights is either too little or too late. Fisk and Pulver (2009) note, with apparent approval, that arbitrators (in a field that arbitrators have practiced) tend to show a bias toward the status quo; but that is the kiss of death for innovative firms in competitive industries which regularly shake up job classifications. Fisk and Pulver thus underrate the need for rapid adaptive responses once competition appears. Unfortunately, the costs of renegotiation make it likely that the union responses will be sticky, even though unions in principle have some incentive to moderate their wage demands in the face of competition, which poses the risk of bankruptcy. But the internal conflicts of interest within unions matter, for senior workers are better able to withstand the downturn than recent members, and both are likely to do better than individuals who have yet to join unions. It is for that reason that two-tier pricing in many industries always works to the benefit of incumbent workers against outsiders (Epstein, 2009b). These devices, however, do not work so well from the management side. In the end, therefore, all union agreements suffer from want of flexibility. Those that are imposed from outside are likely to be further from the ideal than those that are negotiated. That, in turn, increases the need for adaptive responses both during the life of the contract and after it. Unilateral decisions are needed in these areas, for workers as well as employers. The hope to protect some workers from dismissal creates the far greater risk that the entire edifice will come tumbling down on employer and employees alike. That problem does not disappear when one looks more closely at the operational features of EFCA.

III.   THE INTERNAL OPERATIONS OF EFCA

Thus far I have examined in general form the arguments against making changes in the rules governing organizational drives, card-checks and compulsory bargaining. That critique took place on the assumption that it was possible to design each of these elements in some coherent fashion so that the means chosen would be calibrated to achieve their ends. Real statutory design always adds a second level of implementation problems, which can be quite daunting. Let me add a closer look at the operational particulars of EFCA in all three areas. What the statute sets out is a broad framework. What it lacks is a sense of how to fill in all the critical pieces.

A.   Unfair Labor Practices during Organizing Campaigns

This portion of EFCA is the least radical because it accepts the traditional framework in which union organizational campaigns precede union elections. But it adds three distinct turns of the screw. First, this provision grants a priority of enforcement resources to this class of violations over all other claims of misconduct, including any and all forms of union statutory violations. Second, the provision also trebles the back pay awards that are made to workers in the event of a finding of an employer unfair labor practice. Third, the statute, for the first time, authorizes fines up to $20,000 per "violation" – a term that receives no statutory definition – of either the overlapping provisions of Section 8(a)(1) or 8(a)(3) of the Act, dealing with employer coercion against employees or employer discrimination against pro-union workers. That per-violation fine is only triggered against employers who "willfully or repeatedly" commit these unfair labor practices.

In administering this section, EFCA only instructs the Board to "consider the gravity of the unfair labor practice and the impact of the unfair labor practice on the charging party, on other persons seeking to exercise rights guaranteed by this Act, or on the public interest."[59] That general language has a notable defect in that it gives no method for counting the number of violations, while the use of the word "repeatedly" opens up a legion of unexplored possibilities of how to count the number of violations in any particular dispute. Yet in the face of this massive uncertainty, the EFCA does not contain any provision which ensures any form of judicial review, or, if that review is somehow required, whether it should be de novo or only for an abuse of discretion.

B.   Card-check

The card-check provisions are every bit as one-sided as the organizational provisions. As noted earlier, there is no precondition for any type of deliberation by all union members before the union is authorized. EFCA allows "an employee or group of employees or any individual or labor organization acting in their behalf" to file the petition at any time, and to obtain success even if 49 percent of the workers had no idea of the pending union campaign.[60] In addition, there is nothing in the statute that indicates the time period in which the cards for any individual application may be signed, or whether a worker who has signed an authorization card is entitled to insist on its return if it is handed over to the union for safekeeping. EFCA contains no provision to deal with the treatment of cards that have been obtained by misrepresentation, trickery or coercion. There is no obvious answer to the question of what should happen if the union represents that the card is being signed in support of an election and then uses it to obtain recognition. Nor is there any statement of the burden of proof that would apply to these disputes. But I am aware of few, if any, successful challenges on these grounds under the card-check systems that are now in place. The gaps in the statute could, in principle, be filled by regulation, although there is no indication of any duty to do so. The only specific topics for discussion are the creation of an authorization form that serves as a safe harbor for a union, and the determination of criteria by which the validity of disputed cards would be determined. Whether those rules could go beyond the invalidation of forged cards is not clear. Nor is there any sense of what the appropriate burdens of proof are with respect to these cards. The huge level of administrative discretion thus adds to the basic uncertainty of the law.

C.   Compulsory Arbitration

The procedures of compulsory arbitration also raise serious questions. The initial provision requires the employer to commence collective bargaining within ten days of receiving notification of the card-check selection.[61] This short fuse applies even for an employer who had no knowledge of the card-check campaign before its success. Within that time (which includes at least one weekend), it becomes necessary to hire representation and organize all the document disclosure that is required for bargaining under EFCA. A large union has the huge advantage of having permanent teams that can be assembled in advance for individual cases. It seems clear, meanwhile, that many employers will not be able to meet the tight deadline, at which point EFCA gives no indication of what sanctions are available or what procedures should be used to enforce them.

The parties then have ninety days to seek out a collective bargaining agreement, regardless of the size of the unit or the complexity of the transaction.[62] Once again, it is not clear whether the usual rules for unfair labor practices apply or whether the ability of the aggrieved party to go to arbitration renders those determinations irrelevant. The statute then provides that the Federal Mediation & Conciliation Service (FMCS), a political branch of the Department of Labor, may "promptly" get involved in the case.[63] But once again it gives no indication of what happens to the statutory timetable if the FMCS is unable to supply that assistance. Is the statute tolled, or does the time continue to run toward compulsory arbitration? Nor does the statute specify what is to be done if the FMCS is alleged to favor one side or another in the mediation. Can its conduct be put under the microscope, and if so, what kind of showing has to be made to sustain the outcome?

The most controversial provision is the last, which requires that the case be referred to an "arbitration board established in accordance with such regulations as may be prescribed by the Service."[64] The difficulties here are legion. There are no time triggers that indicate when the Service must act, and no sense of what should be done in the event of any delay. Nor is there any limitation on the composition of the Board, which need not take the form of one arbitrator chosen by each side, with a third chosen by the other two. EFCA does not specify any of the arbitral procedures, nor does it require a final arbitral determination by a date certain; it does not even specify whether the two-year period runs from union recognition, the onset of arbitration, or the final resolution. Fisk and Pulver seek to sidestep this difficulty by insisting, correctly, that employers always have some incentive to settle in order to avoid the greater expense and risk of compulsory arbitration. The possibility of settlement can never justify the choice of any legal regime over another. Gains from settlement are available, no matter what the legal regime, from the combined effect of reducing the costs of both uncertainty and litigation. One settles disputes in market economies as well. But the key question is whether compulsory arbitration creates a sound framework so that the right settlements are reached – which is unlikely. In sum, the rigidities and uncertainties of compulsory arbitration are unacceptable in any legislation that introduces such fundamental changes.

IV.   AN ECONOMIC OVERVIEW OF EFCA

This effort to intensify the regulation of labor markets is peculiarly unfortunate in a time of economic distress. Compulsory arbitration on the heels of a card-check is likely to produce very pronounced declines in employment levels, which is the last thing needed today, when unemployment rates are wholly resistant to the stimulus programs that seek to create jobs in the public sector by priming the financial pump. It is all too easy to trace much of the decline in employment to short-run union victories that led to long-run labor dislocations. As Barry T. Hirsch has written, any effort to unionization suffers from systematic disadvantages that no intensification of regulation can cure.

Compared to nonunion workplace governance, where there is substantial managerial discretion constrained by market forces and law, union governance is more formal, deliberate, and often sluggish. Union companies, therefore, often fare poorly in highly dynamic and competitive economic settings. Union density, defined as the percentage of employees who are union members, has declined sharply in the US private sector, from just over a third in the mid-1950s to only 6.9 percent in 2010. Among a host of reasons for declining private sector union density, the most fundamental explanation appears to be an increasingly dynamic US economy coupled with the relatively poorer economic performance among union than nonunion establishments and firms.[65]

One clear implication of this position is that the change in industry structure has removed the large pockets of monopoly profits that were available to unions in such regulated industries as telecommunications and airlines during the height of the New Deal. In those cases, lower profits for firms did not necessarily signal lower levels of efficiency. But even in that environment, it is hard to think of any way in which the presence of unions could have improved substantially the productivity of union labor. Even if union workers are more productive than non-union labor, the wage differential is greater than the productivity differential, so that unions are bad deals for employers, which is why they are strenuously resisted. And in the modern setting, strong unions are far more likely to obtain their profits from firm-specific capital that arises from innovation which normally receives protection from the law of patents, copyrights and trade secrets. The clear implication here is that, in the absence of barriers to entry, unionization will reduce returns to investments in ways that pose serious risks to the profitability of union firms. In this environment, there is no case for strengthening the balky union governance system. A far better way to attack the problem is to relax the direct regulation of labor markets.

All these elements were at play in the automobile industry, which has bled workers in recent years. The colossal miscalculations of the United Auto Workers (UAW) in getting (and GM in accepting) a hugely favorable 1979 collective bargaining agreement presaged its implosion over a generation later. These are numbers worthy of note. The UAW had 1,500,000 members in 1979, a number which had dropped to 431,000 by the end of 2008, before the final crack-up of GM, and 355,000 members by the end of 2009, according to no less a source than the World Socialist Web Site (White, 2010).[66] The modest turnaround in the recent post-reorganization period, which led to an increase in UAW membership to 376,000 in 2010,[67] only took place with the aid of massive infusions of government capital, which have yet to be repaid (Davies, 2010).[68] Prior to that time, over 1,000,000 jobs disappeared without the commission of a single unfair labor practice. It is not possible to expect anything else, for when the price of labor goes up, product prices go up or profits go down; either way the quantity of labor eventually goes down. And in the case of the U.S. auto industry, the quantity of labor goes down by a whole lot. The natural restraint of arbitrators, real or imagined, will prove no check against major dislocations. The risks that occur with bargaining will surely occur with mandatory arbitration. There are no dots to connect in the relevant graph.

Yet another way to make the same point is to look at the job growth in non-unionized firms against the job growth of unionized firms. Here is one example. The unionized firm Safeway had 106,000 jobs in 1993 and 201,000 jobs in 2007, the last year before the 2008 market meltdown. By 2009 that number declined to 186,000.[69] For the non-union

Target, the numbers were 174,000 in 1993, 352,000 in 2007, which remained steady at 351,000 in 2009. Two points are worth noting here. The first is that, after the year 2007, the unionized firm lost about 8 percent of its workforce while the non-union firm held its ground. The second point involves the increase in the size of the workforce that ended in 2007. The Safeway increase is about 90 percent, that of Target around 110 percent. Not such a big difference, at first look. But of the 95,000 new Safeway employees, 75,000 were acquired by merger. The revised growth increase shrinks to about 11 percent. Not so good. It is tempting, of course, to chalk up these differences to some unknown confounding factor, such as unobserved differences in management style. But even these perceived differences in the behavior of both senior executives and boards of directors should not be treated as independent variables. A firm that faces unionization, collective bargaining negotiations and work rules needs a more stubborn and inflexible management than one that can concentrate on product development and customer relations. The fierce opposition of non-union firms to unionization stems, I believe, in large measure from the realization of the negative consequences of unionization on many other aspects of unionized firms.

Compulsory arbitration will only make unions more potent. As such, it will only aggravate, not ameliorate, the concerns of the current system. Consider the dynamic consequences. Facing the prospect of instant and costly unionization will dampen the rate of formation of new firms that fear a serious financial hit early on in their life cycles. It will also retard the expansion of existing firms that fear that a tide of new workers could bring in a unionized regime. Overall, the most adverse consequences are likely to fall on low-income, low-skill jobs; the price increases will prove most devastating to the total number of employees (Ohanian, 2010). The only question is the size of these effects, and the evidence suggests that it will be large. Here is some simple data evidence that should not be ignored. Ohanian presents evidence that for each 1 percent expansion in the level of the unionized workforce, overall employment rates will drop substantially, depending on the fraction of workers unionized and the market premiums that they can obtain.

The high estimate of four and one half million jobs does not seem credible, not because the premium is off, but because the share of union workers seems too high. Indeed, the general consensus is that in those cases where unions take hold, they can exert an increase of 15 to 20 percent in real wages over competitive numbers (Card, 1996). Those figures, however, are tricky to interpret, because they only address those firms that were able to survive with union representation, not those that fell by the wayside because they could not meet those premiums, or that never formed given the fear of an expensive labor market. But the 1.5 million jobs lost, or an increase of 1 percent overall in a workforce of 150 million workers, does have some plausibility.

Nor does Ohanian's work stand alone. Anne Layne-Farrar attacked the same question from a different point of view by asking the extent to which card-checks and first-contract arbitration (both of which have been deployed in Canada in times past) influenced levels of unemployment. Her analysis of the Canadian data led to a prediction that passing EFCA "would lead to a 1 percentage point increase in the unemployment rate for every 3 percentage points gained in union membership brought about by a system of card-checks and mandatory arbitration" (Layne-Farrar, 2009, p. 4). That conclusion can be, and has been, criticized for being too extreme, notably by Canadian labor law scholars who published a number of technical articles attacking her work (see, e.g., Johnson, 2009; Fortin, 2009; Saran and Stanford, 2009). But there is no conceivable way the data could be interpreted to suggest that somehow EFCA will *improve* the employment figures. Adding costs and reducing employer options is not a pro-growth signal to new businesses, where most job creation takes place. With unemployment levels stuck at close to 8 percent, and job creation in the private sector at low levels, this is hardly the time to move aggressively with new labor reforms. In general, the view that labor statutes create labor monopolies as their usual effect survives both theoretical and empirical attack (see, e.g., Kaufman, 2004).[70]

So why not reconsider the repeal of the NLRA? After all, unions represent only 7.2 percent of the private workforce (BLS, 2010). Ordinary competitive forces seem to work well for the other 92.8 percent – or would, if there were not so many other regulatory obstacles that stand in the way of the operation of free labor markets. Why not try competition across the board – which would lead to the repeal of virtually every labor law that regulates wages and terms of employment, except perhaps with respect to health and safety? A modest topic for another day.

CONCLUSION: AN ECONOMIC MENACE

EFCA represented a concerted effort by organized labor to regain much of the power that it had lost over the last fifty years. In some real sense, this concerted political campaign was quixotic because the liberalization of product markets, both at home and abroad, reduces the possibility that any union could extract huge settlements from any employer. But that does not mean that EFCA could not cause a great deal of harm along the way. All of its provisions together create a seamless structure in which unions can lodge powerful sanctions against employers that oppose their organization drives, which end in recognition through card-check, without the full participation of all workers in the discussion, let alone a secret-ballot election. Once a union is chosen, it can force a contract through arbitration, again (potentially) without consulting the rank and file. Taken as a whole, the workers lose the two major checks that the current law and practice gives them against their union representatives: the secret-ballot election (which is protected by law) and contract ratification (which is a common, but not required practice). The huge shift in power allows the union to impose on firms terms that, in the best of circumstances, impede their operation and may well reduce their ability to expand or, at worst, drive them from the marketplace altogether.

Labor supporters ask for us to trust them with this power, promising not to abuse it. But the institutional constraints built into EFCA are so weak that the doomsday scenario is all too likely to occur. Higher rates of unionization mean fewer jobs and lower levels of production. EFCA tightens that screw several notches. None of its overall consequences will work for the benefit of employers or union members, no matter how much power the statute confers on the union hierarchy. Defenders of labor unions spin out all sorts of clever theories to explain why the world would be a better place with more extensive union representation. But the grim truth is that no one profits from legal complexity, higher costs and transactional confusion, all of which attend the current labor law system, and which EFCA would exacerbate.

NOTES

*   I should like to thank Brett Davenport, Maxine Sharavsky, and Christopher Tan, of the NYU Law School Class of 2012, and Isaac Gruber, University of Chicago Law School, Class of 2012, for their valuable research assistance, and to Cynthia Estlund for her detailed editorial comments on earlier drafts of this chapter.

1.   Patient Protection and Affordable Care Act, Pub. L. No. 111-148, 124 Stat. 119 (2010) (to be codified as amended in scattered sections of 42 U.S.C.).

2.   More public than private sector employees are unionized, "despite there being 5 times more wage and salary workers in the private sector" (BLS, 2010).

3.   *See* Business Leaders for a Fair Economy (2009), which included SEIU as its Featured Employer. For the dominant sentiment, *see* U.S. Chamber of Commerce (2011).

4.   By way of full disclosure, these organizations have nothing to do with the writing of this chapter. I also wrote several independent pieces toward the same end. *See, e.g.*, Epstein (2008, 2009b, 2009c).

5.   Patient Protection and Affordable Care Act, Pub. L. No. 111-148, 124 Stat. 119 (2010) (to be codified as amended in scattered sections of 42 U.S.C.).

6.   Dodd-Frank Wall Street Reform and Consumer Protection Act, Pub. L. No. 111-203, 124 Stat. 1376 (2010).

7.   My abiding antipathy to the NLRA dates back to my student days. *See* Epstein (1968).

8.   National Labor Relations (Wagner) Act, 29 U.S.C. §§ 151–69 (2006).

9.   Labor Management Relations (Taft-Hartley) Act, 29 U.S.C. §§ 141–97 (2006).

10.   Employee Free Choice Act of 2009, H.R. 1409, 111th Cong. § 4 (2009).

11.   *Id.* § 2.

12.   *Id.* § 3.

13.   198 U.S. 45 (1905).

14.   Quoting *Nat'l Labor Relations Board of 1935: Hearing on S. 1958 Before the S. Comm. on Educ. and Labor*, 74th Cong. 150 (1935) (statement of Charlton Ogburn, Counsel, AFL) (internal quotation marks omitted).

15.   *See* J.I. Case Co. v. NLRB, 321 U.S. 332 (1944).

16.   29 U.S.C. § 15 ("The inequality of bargaining power between employees who do not possess full freedom of association or actual liberty of contract and employers who are organized in the corporate or other forms of ownership association substantially burdens and affects the flow of commerce, and tends to aggravate recurrent business depressions, by depressing wage rates and the purchasing power of wage earners in industry and by preventing the stabilization of competitive wage rates and working conditions within and between industries.").

17.   Quoting 79 Cong. Rec. 7565 (1935), *reprinted in* 2 NLRB, Legislative History of the National Labor Relations Act, 1935, at 2321 (1949)).

18.   Cox argues that labor law instantiated the sound view of freedom of contract. His views were adopted in large measure in Vaca v. Sipes, 386 U.S. 171 (1967), per Justice White, who was strongly pro-labor during his entire tenure of service. *Vaca* denied any individual worker the right to press his own grievance under a collective bargaining agreement if the union in good faith did not go along. For my student response, *see* Epstein (1968, pp. 563–4, 577–8) (attacking both Cox's account of freedom of association and White's rule in *Vaca*). I stand by that student note today.

19.   *See* discussion of Sachs, *infra* at Section I.B.

20.   468 U.S. 609, 623 (1984) (noting tension between the principle of freedom of association with a general antidiscrimination law).

21.   For my critique of this subject matter specific view of freedom of association, *see* Epstein (2010).

22.   In *Forbidden Grounds: The Case against Employment Discrimination*, I argue against antidiscrimination laws in the private sector, and in favor of the per se legalization of all affirmative action programs.

23.   323 U.S. 192 (1944).

24.   *See, e.g.*, Conley v. Gibson, 355 U.S. 41 (1957), which had to clean up fair representation cases under *Steele*.

25.   Fashion Originators' Guild of Am. v. FTC, 312 U.S. 668 (1941) (applying per se rule notwithstanding the Guild's purpose to stop production of knock-off garments).

26.   Loewe v. Lawlor, 208 U.S. 274 (1908).

27.   *Id.* at 294–6.

28.   *Id.* at 305.

29.   Clayton Antitrust Act of 1914, 15 U.S.C. § 17 (2006). By its terms, Section 20 of the Clayton Act limited the ability of courts to issue injunctions against unions or their members in various labor disputes "unless necessary to prevent irreparable injury to property, or to a property right." In *United States v. Hutcheson*,

312 U.S. 219 (1941), the Supreme Court held that Section 20 also barred criminal prosecutions in light of the Norris-La Guardia Act's intention to boost union organizing efforts. Justice Frankfurter never stopped to ask whether the attack on the labor injunction rested on the institutional risk of allowing a private party to use the labor injunction, which is removed when the action is taken by the government. Frankfurter had insisted on that distinction in his own book, *The Labor Injunction*, written just before the passage of the Norris-La Guardia Act (Frankfurter and Greene, 1930, p. 220).

30. *See* Clayton Antitrust Act §§ 6, 20.
31. *See, e.g.*, Duplex Printing Press Co. v. Deering, 254 U.S. 443 (1921). For discussion, *see* Epstein (2006, pp. 87–8).
32. Labor Management Relations (Taft-Hartley) Act, 29 U.S.C. §§ 141–97 (2006).
33. The National Labor Relations Act § 157 reads: "Employees shall have the right to self-organization, to form, join, or assist labor organizations, to bargain collectively through representatives of their own choosing, and to engage in other concerted activities for the purpose of collective bargaining or other mutual aid or protection, and shall also have the right to refrain from any or all of such activities [subject to a closed shop exceptions]…"
34. Sachs (2010) collects recent references including Logan (2002, 2006) and Lawler (1990).
35. *See* Logan (2002, p. 198).
36. The point is pushed by Freeman and Medoff (1984), which posits that unions help mediate disputes between workers and employers and supply needed public goods to the firm. For my criticism of these arguments, *see* Epstein (2009a, pp. 125–32).
37. For example, consider the addition of new unfair labor practices against unions, including the restrictions on secondary boycotts, the insistence that substantial evidence support board decisions, and the broader definition of independent contractors.
38. 29 U.S.C. §§ 101–15 (2006).
39. *See, e.g.*, Boys Mkts., Inc. v. Retail Clerks Union, Local 770, 398 U.S. 235, 239 (1970), *overruling* Sinclair Ref. Co. v. Atkinson, 370 U.S. 195 (1962).
40. *Id.*
41. *See, e.g.*, McCarroll v. Los Angeles Dist. Council of Carpenters, 315 P.2d 322 (Cal. 1957), *cert. denied*, 355 U.S. 932 (1958).
42. *Boys Markets*, 398 U.S. at 245–46.
43. *Id.* at 248.
44. *See* NLRB v. Gissel Packing Co., 395 U.S. 575, 617 (1969).
45. 29 U.S.C. § 158(c) (emphasis added). For the constitutional acceptance of the statutory provision, *see* Chamber of Commerce v. Brown, 554 U.S. 60, 67 (2008).
46. Becker explicitly attacks the dicta in Justice Jackson's concurring opinion in Thomas v. Collins, 323 U.S. 516, 545–8 (1945)).
47. In this passage, Sachs appears to approve of the secret drive, which he later criticizes (see Sachs, 2010, p. 718).
48. Sachs also appeals to more general critiques of statutory construction that seek to use a public choice perspective to figure out the proper meanings of different languages such as Einer Elhauge's (2008) argument in favor of "preference-eliciting default rules," and Lucian A. Bebchuk and Assaf Hamdani's (2002) effort to construct optimal default rules for corporations. Ultimately, these intriguing positions take Sachs too far afield to be of much relevance to the issues at stake here.
49. 208 U.S. 274 (1908).
50. For the details, see NLRB, Proposed amendments to NLRB election rules and regulations fact sheet, http://www.nlrb.gov/news/board-proposes-rules-reform-pre-and-post-election-representation-case-procedures (June 21, 2011) Representation-Case Procedures, 76 Fed. Reg. 36812 (proposed June 22, 2011) (to be codified at 29 C.F.R. pt. 101 et seq.).
51. Steven Greenhouse, N.L.R.B. Rules Would Streamline Unionizing, N.Y. Times, June 21, 2011, available online at http://www.nytimes.com/2011/06/22/business/22labor.html?_r=1 (visited Oct. 27, 2011), Note that the Greenhouse term consciously echoes the term "streamline" as it appears in EFCA. http://www.nytimes.com/2011/06/22/business/22labor.html?_r=1.
52. *Id.*
53. *Id.*
54. Nat'l Retail Fed'n, 2011.
55. "Employees who wish to unionize therefore bear the coordination costs of identifying and contacting other employees during nonwork time and at nonwork locations" (Sachs, 2010, p. 697). So do anti-union workers, whom management helps at its peril.
56. Michael L. Wachter (2007) notes how the corporatist model fed union growth. For comment, see Cynthia L. Estlund (2007) (suggesting that unions could make new gains today in localized low-end labor markets).

57. Public Employees Fair Employment (Taylor) Act, New York Civil Service Law § 209 (McKinney 2000).
58. Associated Press, "Union's Board gives Early OK to NY Contract," *Wall Street Journal*, October 17, 2011, *available at* http://online.wsj.com/article/AP6ca3d8a488d6433082b46cb58957b74a.html.
59. Employee Free Choice Act of 2009, H.R. 1409, 111th Cong. § 4(b) (2009).
60. Employee Free Choice Act § 2(a).
61. *Id.* at § 3.
62. *Id.*
63. Employee Free Choice Act § 3.
64. *Id.*
65. Barry T. Hirsch, "Unions, Dynamism, and Economic Performance," Chapter 4 in this volume.
66. For further confirmation of the 2009 numbers, see Brent Snavely, "UAW seeks Technical, Professional Workers," *Detroit Free Press* (June 16, 2010), *available at* http://www.freep.com/article/20100616/BUSINESS01/6160380/UAW-seeks-technical-professional-workers. For additional membership numbers, see "UAW Membership Drops below 500,000," MSNBC (March 30, 2008), *available at* http://www.msnbc.msn.com/id/23869586/ns/business-autos/t/uaw-membership-drops-below/#.TqtMPFYu7Zk.
67. United Auto Workers, "UAW Membership Increases," March 31, 2011, *available at* http://www.uaw.org/articles/uaw-membership-increases.
68. The percentage increases were large, but the total units sold were small, at 12,181 units in April, 2010 (Rall, 2010). Chevrolet sold 135,369 units in the same period (*id.*).
69. My thanks to William Schwesig of the University of Chicago's D'Angelo Law Library for gathering much of the information about these two firms from 10-K forms filed with the Securities and Exchange Commission.
70. Kaufman outlines the familiar risks of rent seeking, monopoly wages, feather bedding, reduced investment and the like. See also the response of Richard B. Freeman (2004) claiming that worker savings under union pension plans offset the reduced levels of union firms. Note that all of the many fine essays in this volume were written before the recent labor market implosion.

REFERENCES

Bebchuk, Lucian A. and Assaf Hamdani. 2002. "Optimal Defaults for Corporate Law Evolution," 96 *Northwestern University Law Review* 489–519.
Becker, Craig. 1993. "Democracy in the Workplace: Union Representation Elections and Federal Labor Law," 77 *Minnesota Law Review* 495–603.
Bronfenbrenner, Kate. 2009. "No Holds Barred: The Intensification of Employer Opposition to Organizing," Briefing Paper No. 235, Economic Policy Institute.
Bureau of Labor Statistics (BLS). 2010. "Union Members – 2009." BLS News Release (Jan. 20). Available at: http://www.bls.gov/news.release/pdf/union2.pdf.
Business Leaders for a Fair Economy. 2009. "More than 225 Colorado Businesses Support the Employee Free Choice Act." News Release (Jun. 12). Available at: http://www.faireconomynow.org/more-than-225-colorado-businesses-support-the-employee-free-choice-act/.
Card, David. 1996. "The Effect of Unions on the Structure of Wages: A Longitudinal Analysis," 64 *Econometrica* 957–79.
Confessore, Nicholas. 2010. "Paterson Offers Choice: Furloughs or a Shutdown," *N.Y. Times* (May 4). Available at: http://cityroom.blogs.nytimes.com/2010/05/04/paterson-offers-choice-furloughs-or-shutdown/.
Cox, Archibald. 1956. "Rights under a Labor Agreement," 69 *Harvard Law Review* 601–57.
Davies, Richard. 2010. "Buick Makes a Big U-Turn, Leads U-Turn at GM," *ABC News* (Apr. 18). Available at: http://abcnews.go.com/Business/buick-leads-gm-turnaround/story?id=11428049.
Elhauge, Einer. 2008. *Statutory Default Rules: How to Interpret Unclear Legislation*. Cambridge, MA: Harvard University Press.
Epstein, Richard A. 1968. "Note: Individual Control over Personal Grievances under *Vaca v. Sipes*," 77 *Yale Law Journal* 559–77.
Epstein, Richard A. 1983. "A Common Law for Labor Relations: A Critique of the New Deal Labor Legislation," 92 *Yale Law Journal* 1357–408.
Epstein, Richard A. 1983. "Common Law, Labor Law, and Reality: A Rejoinder to Professors Getman and Kohler," 92 *Yale Law Journal* 1435–41.
Epstein, Richard A. 1984. "In Defense of the Contract at Will," 51 *University of Chicago Law Review* 947–82.

Epstein, Richard A. 1992. *Forbidden Grounds: The Case against Employment Discrimination*. Cambridge, MA: Harvard University Press.

Epstein, Richard A. 2006. *How Progressives Rewrote the Constitution*. Washington, DC: Cato Institute.

Epstein, Richard A. 2008. "The Employee No Choice Act," *Chief Executive Magazine* (Dec. 12). Available at: http://www.chiefexecutive.net.

Epstein, Richard A. 2009a. *The Case Against the Employee Free Choice Act*. Stanford, CA: Hoover Institution Press.

Epstein, Richard A. 2009b. "The Employee Free Choice Act: Free Choice or No Choice for Workers," Civil Justice Forum No. 45, The Manhattan Institute. Available at: http://www.manhattan-institute.org/pdf/cjf_45.pdf.

Epstein, Richard A. 2009c. "The Ominous Employee Free Choice Act," 32 *Regulation* 48–54.

Epstein, Richard A. 2010. "Church and State at the Crossroads: *Christian Legal Society v. Martinez*," in Ilya Shapiro, ed., *Cato Supreme Court Review 2009–2010*. Washington, DC: The Cato Institute.

Estlund, Cynthia L. 2007. "Are Unions Doomed to Being a 'Niche Movement' in a Competitive Economy?" 155 *University of Pennsylvania Law Review PENNumbra* 165-172. Available at: http://www.pennumbra.com/responses/02-2007/Estlund.pdf.

Estreicher, Samuel. 2008. "'Think Global, Act Local' Workplace Representation in a World of Global Labour and Product Market Competition," Paper No. 90, New York University Public Law and Legal Theory Working Papers. Available at: http://lsr.nellco.org/nyu_plltwp/90/.

Fisk, Catherine L. and Adam R. Pulver. 2009. "First Contract Arbitration and the Employee Free Choice Act," 70 *Louisiana Law Review* 47–95.

Fortin, Pierre. 2009. "Faulty Methodology Generates Faulty Results: Comments on the Paper Entitled 'An Empirical Assessment of the Employee Free Choice Act: The Economic Implications,'" 15 *Just Labour: A Canadian Journal of Work and Society* 26–8.

Frankfurter, Felix and Nathan Greene. 1930. *The Labor Injunction*. New York: The Macmillan Company.

Freeman, Richard B. 2004. "What Do Unions Do? The 2004 M-Brine String Twister Edition," in James T. Bennett and Bruce E. Kaufman, eds., *What Do Unions Do?: A Twenty-Year Perspective*. New Brunswick, NJ: Transaction Publishers.

Freeman, Richard B and James L. Medoff. 1984. *What Do Unions Do?* New York: Basic Books.

Getman, Julius G. and Thomas C. Kohler. 1983. "The Common Law, Labor Law, and Reality: A Response to Professor Epstein," 92 *Yale Law Journal* 1415–34.

International Labour Organization (ILO). 2011. "About the ILO." Available at: http://www.ilo.org/global/About_the_ILO/lang--en/index.htm.

Johnson, Susan. 2009. "Comments on 'An Empirical Assessment of the Employee Free Choice Act: The Economic Implications' by Anne Layne-Farrar," 15 *Just Labour: A Canadian Journal of Work and Society* 14–25.

Kaufman, Bruce E. 2004. "What Unions Do: Insights from Economic Theory," in James T. Bennett and Bruce E. Kaufman, eds., *What Do Unions Do?: A Twenty-Year Perspective*. New Brunswick, NJ: Transaction Publishers.

Lawler, John J. 1990. *Unionization and Deunionization: Strategy, Tactics, and Outcomes (Studies in Industrial Relations)*. Columbia, SC: University of South Carolina Press.

Layne-Farrar, Anne. 2009. "An Empirical Assessment of the Employee Free Choice Act: The Economic Implications," Working Paper. Available at: http://papers.ssrn.com/sol3/papers.cfm?abstract_id=1353305.

Lee, David and Alexandre Mas. 2009. "Long-Run Impacts of Unions on Firms: New Evidence from Financial Markets," NBER Working Paper No. 14709. Available at: http://www.nber.org/papers/w14709.pdf.

Logan, John. 2002. "Consultants, Lawyers, and the 'Union Free' Movement in the USA since the 1970s," 33 *Industrial Relations Journal* 197–214.

Logan, John. 2006. "The Union Avoidance Industry in the United States," 44 *British Journal of Industrial Relations* 651–75.

Malanga, Steven. 2010. "The Beholden State: How Public-Sector Unions Broke California," 20 *City Journal* No. 2.

McGovern, George. 2008. "My Party Should Respect Union Ballots," *Wall Street Journal* (Aug. 8).

Meltzer, Bernard and Stanley Henderson. 1985. *Labor Law: Cases, Materials, and Problems*. 3d ed. Boston: Little, Brown & Company.

National Conference of Commissioners on Uniform State Laws. 2010. "Model Employment Termination Act Summary." Available at: http://uniformlaws.org/ActSummary.aspx?title=Model%20Employment%20Termination%20Act.

National Retail Federation. 2011. "NRF Calls NLRB Proposal on Union Elections 'Backdoor Card Check,'" July 18, 2011, online at http://www.nrf.com/modules.php?name=News&op=viewlive&sp_id=1156 (statement of NRF CEO, Matthew Shay) (visited Oct. 27, 2011).

Ohanian, Lee E. 2010. "The Impact of Employee Free Choice Act on the U.S. Economy," American

Enterprise Institute for Public Policy Research. Available at: http://www.aei.org/docLib/OhanianEmployee FreeChoiceAct.pdf.

Pound, Roscoe. 1909. "Liberty of Contract," 18 *Yale Law Journal* 454–87.

Rall, Patrick. 2010. "April Sales Numbers: General Motors." *Examiner.com* (May 5). Available at: http://www.examiner.com/autos-in-detroit/april-sales-numbers-general-motors.

Rizzo, Mario and Douglas Glen Whitman. 2009. "Little Brother is Watching You: New Paternalism on Paternalist Slopes," 51 *Arizona Law Review* 685–739.

Sachs, Benjamin I. 2010. "Enabling Employee Choice: A Structural Approach to the Rules of Union Organizing," 123 *Harvard Law Review* 655–728.

Saran, Gary and Jim Stanford. 2009. "Further Tests of the Link between Unionization, Unemployment and Employment: Findings from Canadian National and Provincial Data," 15 *Just Labour: A Canadian Journal of Work and Society* 29–77.

Sunstein, Cass R. 2001. "Human Behavior and the Law of Work," 87 *Virginia Law Review* 205–73.

Sunstein, Cass R. and Richard H. Thaler. 2003. "Libertarian Paternalism is not an Oxymoron," 70 *University of Chicago Law Review* 1159–202.

U.S. Chamber of Commerce. 2011. "The Employee Free Choice Act – the 'Card Check' Bill." Available at: http://www.uschamber.com/issues/labor/employee-free-choice-act-card-check-bill.

Wachter, Michael L. 2007. "Labor Unions: A Corporatist Institution in a Competitive World," 155 *University of Pennsylvania Law Review* 581–634.

Weiler, Paul C. 1990. *Governing the Workplace: The Future of Labor and Employment Law.* Cambridge, MA: Harvard University Press.

White, Jerry. 2010. "UAW Membership Continues to Plummet," World Socialist Web Site (Apr. 1). Available at: http://www.wsws.org/articles/2010/apr2010/uawm-a01.shtml.

7. Evaluating the effectiveness of National Labor Relations Act remedies: analysis and comparison with other workplace penalty policies
Morris M. Kleiner and David Weil

I. INTRODUCTION

The National Labor Relations Act (NLRA) has been one of the most controversial pieces of labor legislation passed during the New Deal era. From management's perspective, the original form of this law, the Wagner Act of 1935, gave labor unions an easy method of organizing the firm's workforce using the government's enforcement mechanism and the legitimacy of a federal statute to promote union organizing. During the years following the passage of the Act, unionization grew markedly in the United States. In contrast, the 1947 Taft-Hartley Amendment to the Act was viewed by labor union leaders as a "slave labor act," because it stated that unions could also be found guilty of unfair labor practices that were similar to those that management might commit, and it included substantial monetary fines for potential restraint of business activity (Wagner 2002). These provisions were deemed so abhorrent from labor's perspective that former AFL-CIO president Lane Kirkland called for the repeal of the whole Act as amended, saying labor could do better without provisions of the NLRA (Apgar 1984).[1]

Workplace regulations – whether the NLRA, the Occupational Safety and Health Act, or any of the other major federal statutes – attempt to change private behavior so that it conforms with public policy objectives. Regulations provide for a means of monitoring behavior and providing incentives or penalties to move the regulated party in the desired direction. One way of evaluating the adequacy of any regulatory system is assessing how significant those incentives are in light of the benefits of maintaining status quo behaviors.

The goal of this chapter is to examine the remedial policies underlying the NLRA, and specifically their impact on the employer and union behaviors the Act addresses. We do so by providing a context and theoretical background for comparing the remedies arising from violations of the Act with the penalties arising from violations of other major federal workplace policies. We present a general framework for evaluating the manner in which workplace penalty policies affect employer behavior, particularly through deterrence effects. With this framework as a backdrop, we evaluate the level and the changes in extent of the remedies for violations of the Act against individuals by firms and unions and then estimate the impact of these remedies as a means of "making whole" workers affected by violations.

Using data from National Labor Relations Board (NLRB) back pay findings from 2000–09, we examine whether remedies provide sufficient incentives to companies and unions to comply with the law – that is, whether prospective remedies arising from unfair labor practices have potential deterrence impacts.[2] We find that the Act's focus on remedies provides insufficient incentives to deter unfair labor practices by employers, particularly given the considerable benefits arising from union avoidance. Given this finding, we examine other potential remedies to better attain the objectives of the Act, in particular, methods to address the impact of delays in enforcement (the length of time from the filing of the charge or the issuance of the charge to the time of its adjudication before an administrative law judge at the NLRB or through the federal courts) on the ability of workers to choose representation.

The chapter describes the economic costs of both labor and management violating the NLRA and suggests a method of determining appropriate remedies. In the first few sections, we describe the existing rationales for workplace penalties and develop a theory of optimal penalties from the perspective of both the firm and society. In the following sections, we apply the theory to the NLRA, provide new descriptive data on the adequacy of back pay awards to affected workers and the costs to firms and unions of violating the Act against individuals, and discuss its implications for union organizing. We also discuss the implications of providing industrial democracy in the workplace through unionization in the face of the relatively low costs to both labor and management of violating the Act. In the concluding sections, we examine the impact of delays on achieving the basic goals of the NLRA and explore remedies outside of potential penalties to improve performance of the Act. The final section summarizes our conclusions.

II.   CONCEPTUAL AIMS OF WORKPLACE PENALTY POLICIES

To evaluate the adequacy of remedies under the NLRA, it is useful to first examine the different justifications for workplace penalties generally.[3] Penalty policies (in particular those embodied in legislation) arise from the same political processes that drive legislation. Weil (2008) argues that passage of federal workplace legislation has been driven by distinctive dynamics, where successful efforts to pass workplace policies in the past 50 years have required two conditions: significant differences within the business community in opposition to legislation and particularly strong ties between the labor movement and other communities in support of legislation. One consequence of those dynamics is that penalty policies (as well as the recourse to criminal versus civil fines) reflect the particular political coalitions needed to pass specific legislation and their relative strengths.[4] This has led, for example, to exemption of small workplaces under many statutes as well as diminished enforcement authority or less draconian penalty policies (see Weil 2008, pp. 299–308; Fishback and Kantor 2000).

But even given the political context underlying penalty policies, there are other factors that may lead to inconsistent fines for seemingly comparable infractions of the law. Sunstein et al. (2002) argue that the administrative penalties across a variety of federal legislation exhibit substantial "incoherence," in that the penalties in one domain (for example, violation of the Wild Bird Conservation Act carrying a maximum penalty of $25,000) may appear far more draconian than those in another (serious violation of health and safety standards under the Occupational Safety and Health Act carrying a maximum penalty of $7,000).

The seeming incoherence of wider policies arises from the fact that administrative penalty policies are set within the context of specific *categories* (for example, the relevant category being penalties under a single act such as the Wild Bird Conservation Act) rather than on a larger, cross-category basis. Within a given category (for example, workplace safety), policymakers may anchor penalties based on "the intensity of emotions they evoke" (Sunstein et al. 2002, p. 1187). Incoherence between penalty policies therefore reflects the fact that when legislators draft, judges review, or regulators implement penalty policies, they are typically not required to look beyond the particular policy domain in which they operate.[5] The basis of a penalty system may therefore be anchored to different reference points that are inconsistent because those decisions were made in relative isolation.

Once a penalty policy has been anchored within a given category, policymakers structure gradations of violations based on factors like the severity of the violation or the past record of the regulated party. This aspect of penalty-setting, within a given policy context, may reflect more coherent ranking schemes: less serious violations typically have lower penalties than do serious ones; violations arising for the first time or which do not seem to reflect a clear intent to circumvent the law are dealt with less harshly than repeat violations or those which involve a party acting willfully to violate the law. Seen in this light, intra-category penalty policy appears more rational. However, since each category of policies constructs gradations of penalties around an anchor independent of other contexts, penalties in the aggregate diverge further; "moral intuitions [driving gradations] do not specify a scaling factor for the task of translating punitive intent into dollars" (Sunstein et al. 2002, p. 1187).

These forces may operate even within a single policy domain. Federal workplace policies are set by a variety of agencies under several different statutes. Most agencies that enforce workplace polices are part of the U.S. Department of Labor – for example, the Wage and Hour Division (WHD) for labor standards; the Occupational Safety and Health Administration (OSHA) for most private sector and some public health and safety issues, except, notably, the Mine Safety and Health Administration (MSHA), which oversees health and safety in underground and surface mining; and the Employee Benefits Standards Administration (EBSA) etc. Despite their common home department and the responsibility of the U.S. Secretary of Labor to ultimately set policy for them, penalty and other enforcement policies across those agencies vary widely because they were established by different pieces of legislation, in different eras, and operate fairly autonomously. Some of these agencies, like the Wage and Hour Division (WHD) and the Employee Benefits Standards Administration (EBSA), administer multiple pieces of major legislation, leading to varied policies even in the context of a single agency.

The forces leading to incoherence are even stronger for those agencies dealing with workplace policy but operating outside of the Department of Labor – notably the National Labor Relations Board (NLRB). The views of the top policymakers of such agencies may differ from those of the Secretary of Labor. As a result, there is remarkable variation in the penalties set even within the area of workplace policy.[6] It is therefore undeniable that the type of penalty policies will differ significantly as a consequence of the politics of enactment and institutional factors leading to incoherence.

III.   REMEDIES AS PENALTIES UNDER THE NLRA

A comparison of the NLRA with other workplace policies begins by recognizing that the U.S. Supreme Court has repeatedly held that the Act "is designed to perform a remedial function and that punitive sanctions may not be imposed for violations" (Gould 1994, p. 120).[7] In this sense, remedies are not intended to serve as penalties – at least in a strictly legal sense. However, since NLRA remedies represent real costs to employers or unions arising from violations of the Act, they operate as *de facto* penalties and can be evaluated as such.

In reviewing the rationale for penalty policies, how might one try to rationally judge what a coherent and consistent policy might look like? Although acknowledging that current policies reflect the political and institutional factors discussed above, we begin by thinking about the aims of an optimal policy. Given this, we look at other workplace regulations in light of what an optimal policy might require. Finally, we use insights from this wider analysis to evaluate current and prospective NLRA policies.[8]

Workplace policies, like most regulatory policies, attempt to change the behavior of individuals, organizations and markets. The underlying assumption of these policies is that regulated parties, left on their own, will make choices that are counter to the public interest. The instruments of regulation – whether penalties, incentives, disclosure, or market-related devices like carbon trading – attempt to change the benefits and costs of targets of public policy in order to change their choices and behaviors.

Analytically, the purpose of penalty policies is to increase the regulated party's costs of noncompliance in one of two ways. First, penalties have a direct effect when connected to the finding of a violation during an inspection. The penalty imposes a cost for past violations and often also imposes an ongoing cost for continuing noncompliance. (For example, the Mine Safety and Health Act imposes additional fines of up to $7,500 for each day the violation is not abated after the prescribed date for compliance.) Assessed penalties are also thought to change the subsequent behavior of the inspected firm, leading it to remain in compliance in the future. Affecting behavior of the parties being directly inspected is sometimes termed "specific deterrence."[9]

Second, penalties may change the behavior of regulated parties prospectively: the prospect of receiving a penalty creates potential costs that regulated parties seek to avoid through voluntary compliance. These *general deterrence* effects of penalties are particularly important when the government is unable to inspect all firms (or individuals) covered by the policy and must instead depend on deterrence to change behavior. The amount of penalties in this case could reflect the benefits of noncompliance or the harm imposed. But it should also reflect the probability of inspection and detection.

At the outset, we argue that *de facto* specific and general deterrence effects of penalty policies transcend their *de jure* basis. That is, legislation underlying regulations often has an explicit reasoning behind the system of penalties or remedies it establishes. The legislation might cite deterrence (or its equivalent) as the system's rationale. But the explicit intent of the legislation does not insure that the penalties will have such effects, for example, if those penalties are small in relation to the economic benefits arising from noncompliance. The reverse is also true, as argued above in the case of the NLRA: The fact that the Act explicitly authorizes only remedies rather than penalties does not itself diminish the potential deterrent impact of those remedies in practice. Depending on their size or cost, "remedies" may in fact deter misconduct.

A. A Simple Model of Enforcement

If the aim of penalty policy is to change behavior, what should be the basis by which penalties are set? Deterrence theory states that penalties should reflect the potential gains from failing to comply and the probability that noncompliance will be detected. A simple model of enforcement provides a useful basis to understand the components of setting an optimal penalty policy.[10]

Imagine that an agency in the Department of Labor is attempting to set a penalty level to induce compliance with a new law. Assume that the typical employer being regulated is risk neutral and that the costs of complying with the new law are known by the agency. If the government is seeking to bring the typical firm into compliance, it has two tools: inspections (occurring with a probability of p) and fines (F).[11] The government agency will need to set policy by seeking to change employer behavior, given that compliance with the new law is costly and employers are choosing not to comply prior to its passage.

The employer decides whether or not to comply with the new law, which will cost W. It makes this decision by minimizing the expected total costs of compliance $E(C)$, which are based on the costs of complying W and the expected fine for not complying ($p(F)$). Since our focus is on the optimal penalty level, assume that the probability of inspection p is set by the level of resources available to the agency.[12]

The firm's options are to comply and face the costs of compliance with a probability of γ or to not comply and face the expected penalty $p(F)$:

$$E(C)=\gamma(W)+(1-\gamma)p(F). \tag{1}$$

It can be shown that the optimal policy of the firm to minimize its expected costs given the cost of compliance and the expected penalties it faces is given by:

$$W=p(F) \tag{2}$$

that is, where the cost of compliance is equal to the expected cost of noncompliance.[13]

This analysis implies that the rational, wealth-maximizing, risk-neutral employer will choose not to comply when the expected penalty is less than the cost of complying with the law ($W>p(F)$), will choose to comply when the costs of compliance are less than the expected penalty ($W<p(F)$), and will be indifferent between complying and not complying when the costs of compliance are just equal to the expected penalty ($W=p(F)$). From the government's perspective, if it seeks to set the optimal penalty level F given a current level of enforcement (and, therefore, probability of inspection p), it should set the penalty where[14]

$$F\geq W/p. \tag{3}$$

That is, the penalty should increase linearly with the costs of complying but exponentially with the probability of detection. Specifically, equation (3) means that if it cost the employer $1,000 to comply with the new rule, then the expected penalty for violation

Table 7.1   Percentage of complaints that resulted in citations by the Regional Offices of the NLRB, 2000–2009

NLRA Section	% complaints yielding citations by Regional NLRB Offices
8(a)(2)	26.3%
8(a)(3)	25.7%
8(a)(4)	24.5%
8(a)(5)	24.9%
All Management	25.3%
8(b)(2)	32.2%
8(b)(3)	18.1%
All Labor	29.8%

Source: National Labor Relations Board data, analyzed by the authors.

should equal $2,000 if there is a 50 percent probability of investigation ($1,000/0.5); $4,000 if there is a 25 percent probability; and $10,000 if there is a 10 percent probability. For an agency like the MSHA, which undertakes a minimum of four inspections per mine per year, the optimal penalty should be close to that dictated by compliance costs. However, the annual probability of an investigation in most industries covered by the Occupational Safety and Health Act is far below 10 percent, meaning that optimal penalties should exceed the cost of compliance (e.g., the cost of adopting required machine guards) by a factor of more than 10 in light of deterrence theory.

Violations under the NLRA are identified and reported by workers, unions and employers.[15] Unfair labor practices arising from employer misconduct, such as dismissal due to involvement in organizing, will likely be identified by individual workers or by labor unions involved in organizing efforts and taken to the NLRB. Unfair labor practices by unions, such as intimidation of workers, will likely be identified by employers or employees and similarly taken to the Board. In both instances, the complaint will instigate some sort of response by the Board (akin to an enforcement action under other statutes). This agency role played by either unions or employers substantially raises the probability that an unfair practice will be identified.[16] This means that the probability of enforcement under the NLRA can be reasonably considered to be high for cases where a union is present, such as during an organizing drive or contract negotiations.[17]

Table 7.1 presents the percentage of complaints that were filed in regional offices in 2000–09 that were found to have merit by the director and the staff of those offices for each major section of the NLRA that involves individuals. The NLRB concluded that in about 25–30 percent of all these cases there was sufficient cause to take the claim forward to the next step of adjudication.[18] The fact that unions, companies and individuals filed so many claims that are not taken to the next step demonstrates that there is a significant inflow of potential cases to the Board.[19] If the agency role of unions in the case of employer violations or of firms in the case of union violations is sufficient, then this may imply a probability of detection close to 1.0; that implies in turn, as per equation (3), that the effectiveness of deterrence largely turns on the adequacy of remedies as a form of *de facto* penalties.

B. Rationales for Penalty Policies

In general, if the aim is to tip the balance of costs and benefits to the regulated party toward compliance, it does not strictly matter whether one changes the expected costs of noncompliance by increasing the probability of detection or the expected penalties, once a violation is detected. Given that enforcement is costly, optimal deterrence theory suggests that it makes more sense from the regulator's perspective to increase penalties as much as possible in order to maximize the impact of a constrained regulatory budget (Polinsky and Shavell 1998, 2000). However, this view suggests that there need not be a rationale for the size of the penalty beyond affecting expected costs of noncompliance.

An alternative basis for setting optimal penalty policies is to have the expected penalty for a given violation reflect something real about the basis of that penalty. Once such a rationale is chosen, the penalty can be further adjusted to reflect the underlying probability of inspection, or *enforcement.* This approach comports with the way that legislators write penalties (to solve problems clearly defined by the legislation), that judges tend to review penalties (in terms of whether they are reasonable, given the violation), and that investigators behave (often driven by notions – explicit or implicit – of what is fair).[20]

The above model of optimal policy reflects the case in which the government is seeking to induce the level of compliance implied by the employer's internal cost of compliance. This is not necessarily equivalent to the optimal level from society's point of view, since it does not tell us anything about the social costs associated with noncompliance. From this perspective, there are several bases for setting the optimal level of compliance.

In the simple model discussed above, the government is seeking to obtain compliance with the law given internal costs of the employer. Here, the government needs to assess the penalty in terms of the *benefits received* by the employer from noncompliance (which is equivalent to W). For example, by paying below the minimum wage under the Fair Labor Standards Act, an employer is able to achieve lower unit labor costs than if it complied with the law. As a result, a basic feature of a finding of violation under that Act is payment of back wages, equal to the amount of money owed to the workers during the time they were underpaid. Another optional feature of the finding of a Fair Labor Standards Act violation provides workers with liquidated damages equal to the amount of back wages owed. Liquidated damages can be thought of as additional compensation for the potential benefits received by the employer during the period of underpayment (for example, reflecting the return arising from the underpayment). Moreover, the ability in some states to bring class action lawsuits and to recover punitive damages can also serve as major deterrents.[21]

However, assume that the costs to society from noncompliance are greater than the costs to the employer of complying. This is plausible in cases in which there is a significant externality, that is, when the social costs of complying go significantly beyond those faced by the employer. In a case with significant externalities associated with noncompliance that go beyond the costs of complying, a penalty set on the basis of the costs of compliance will be too low. For example, imagine that the cost of installing a machine guard is $1,000 per worker affected, but the expected benefit to society is $2,000 when accounting for the prevention of productivity loss, and pain and suffering associated with an injury.

In such a case, the appropriate penalty level for consideration is not the benefits received from noncompliance W, but an amount reflecting the *harms inflicted* on society from noncompliance (H). In such a case, the optimal penalty should be

$$F=H/p, \tag{4}$$

with $H \neq W$.

It is also possible that H may be below W when the regulatory standard is too stringent – that is, the costs of compliance exceed the harms inflicted on society.[22] Many workplace policies attempt to remediate an externality. The Occupational Safety and Health Act, for example, is premised on the need to reduce workplace risks because employers' incentives to reduce injuries and illnesses fall below those desirable from a social perspective. Penalties in this sense should reflect the costs imposed on workers – for example, increases in morbidity and mortality arising from exposures.[23]

Penalties based on these two rationales – benefits received and harms inflicted – can in some cases be quite similar and in other cases diverge markedly. One can imagine cases (like minimum wage violations) in which the benefits received are close to the harms inflicted: back wages – the difference between what an individual was paid and what the Fair Labor Standards Act requires in terms of minimum wages or overtime – are a measure of both the direct benefits received from an employer failing to pay statutory wages and the harms inflicted on the worker not receiving them.[24] Similarly, one component of the penalties assessed for violations of the discrimination regulations administered by the Office of Federal Contract Compliance Programs is make-whole relief, which requires that a victim of discrimination be restored to the economic and status positions that the victim would have occupied had the discrimination never taken place. By requiring payment of this amount, the employer is essentially required to pay the equivalent of the direct amount of compensation and other benefits arising from the discriminatory practice (the benefits received from discrimination).[25]

Still, the benefits-received and harms-inflicted measures might differ significantly: failure to provide workers with information under OSHA's hazardous communication standard might provide only nominal direct benefits to an employer (and, therefore, call for only a small penalty under the benefits-received model), but impose large costs from additional risks borne by workers unaware of their exposures as a result of noncompliance. In general, any regulation that involves amelioration of an externality may imply penalties far larger from a harms-inflicted perspective than from a benefits-received perspective.

How well can the NLRA deter misconduct by employers or unions, given that penalties *per se* are eschewed and remedies under the Act are grounded in making the affected workers whole? Section 10(c) of the Act states this as the principal authority of the Board in the face of unfair labor practices:

> If upon the preponderance of the testimony taken the Board shall be of the opinion that any person named in the complaint has engaged in or is engaging in any such unfair labor practice, then the Board shall state its findings of fact and shall issue and cause to be served on such person an order requiring such person to cease and desist from such unfair labor practice, and to take such affirmative action including reinstatement of employees with or without backpay, as will effectuate the policies of this Act.[26]

If one thinks of remedies as *de facto* penalties, then those described in section 10(c) imply a penalty policy rooted in a benefits-received model – that is, that the benefits for noncompliance (committing an unfair labor practice (ULP)) can be seen as roughly equivalent to the losses imposed on those parties directly affected by the unfair labor practice (for example, the workers who are dismissed because of involvement in an organizing campaign or who quit because of intimidation by a union). As we discuss below, rooting remedies in a benefits-received model results in *de facto* penalties that are far below those required to "effectuate the policies of this Act" in the sense that they anchor them to the impacts of unfair labor practices on only those directly affected (e.g., a person fired for participation in an organizing drive) but do not capture the significant spillovers on other employees thereby denied an opportunity to elect union representation. A harms-based approach, on the other hand, requires considering the broader impacts of ULPs on the workforce as a whole, which is at odds with the remediation focus of the Act.

C.   Addressing Clear and Present Risks

The above discussion does not account for another dimension of penalty (or remediation) policy which may be important in cases involving clear and present risks or dangers or in which the persistence of violations could undermine public policy objectives. In this subset of cases, optimal policy has an important time dimension, in that it needs not only to change behavior, but also to distinguish between minor and major violations. This aspect of penalty policy is most explicitly recognized under MSHA: violations with a higher gravity – in terms of the severity of violations (defined by the number of lost work days associated with them), persons potentially affected, and likelihood of occurrence – have higher penalty levels associated with them. For example, for a large, underground coal operator, a violation involving no lost work days, fewer than 10 workers exposed, and an unlikely occurrence of the event at which the standard is directed would be between $100 and $125. If the same standard violation involved potentially disabling injuries, more than 10 workers, and a high likelihood of occurrence, then the penalty would be closer to $20,000.[27]

Both safety and health acts and a variety of workplace regulations overseen by the Employee Benefits Standards Administration also provide for a penalty per day that violations remain present, after the time set by the agency for abatement or compliance has been past: $7,500 per day for the Mine Safety and Health Act; $7,000 for the Occupational Safety and Health Act; and $1,100 for the Employee Benefits Standards Administration. The concepts underlying these daily penalties relate to the dangers or harms potentially faced by workers for each day that a cited violation persists.

If the problems arising from the violation are consequential enough that a failure to redress them promptly thwarts the public interest, then recourse beyond penalties under some statutes is also set out. MSHA is a prime example, not surprisingly, given the tremendous risks prevailing in underground mining. Its section 104(b) states that, in a follow-up inspection, if its official finds that a violation has not been abated within the time required (and that there is no basis for further extension), then the official can order that the operator "immediately cause all persons . . . to be withdrawn from, and to be prohibited from entering, such area until an authorized representative of the Secretary [of Labor] determines that such violation has been abated."[28] The Act also provides the MSHA with the authority to determine whether an imminent danger requiring immediate redress exists.[29] In general, violations that threaten health and safety or inflict significant damage on policy aims have this characteristic, and an optimal penalty policy may require a separate authority to invoke.

Other workplace laws provide means to address the persistent and time-sensitive violations that undermine their basic aims. The Fair Labor Standards Act allows the Wage and Hour Division to embargo goods produced when the employer has significantly violated minimum wage or overtime requirements or has used child labor. The provision has been commonly employed in the garment industry, where a manufacturer can have its goods embargoed (held from being sent, for example, to a retail customer) because a contractor to that manufacturer has violated one of the standards. (See Weil 2005 for a discussion of this provision.) The embargo authority has also been applied to other industry segments, most commonly to agriculture (Leonard 2000).

Another powerful tool to address significant breaches of workplace statutes, perhaps without the element of speed, lies in the use of the federal government's role as a major customer for services. Under several statutes with specific provisions governing federal contractors, like the discrimination laws administered by the Office of Federal Contractor Compliance Programs or the Davis-Bacon Act's prevailing wage laws for federally funded construction, administered by the Wage and Hour Division of the Labor Department, the federal government can threaten to debar the company – that is, deprive it of the right to do work for the government in the future. Given the size of contracts involved, this authority is significant and is wielded, appropriately, under exacting sets of conditions.

The ability to immediately shut down mining operations, embargo the flow of goods in commerce, or debar companies from doing business with the federal government involves the imposition of implicit penalties that far outweigh the explicit penalty policies discussed above. Studies show, not surprisingly, that these implicit penalties have substantial impacts on behavior when invoked. For example, Weil (2005) shows that the behavior of garment manufacturers in response to actual or threatened embargoes suggests an implicit penalty of over $100,000.[30]

The NLRB contains none of these powerful remedies. On the other hand, the requirement that the NLRB provide reinstatement for those affected by unfair labor practices in the NLRA's section 10(c), if it happens quickly, might function as a significant non-monetary deterrent to misconduct. The explicit prescription of reinstatement suggests that the Act recognizes the importance of time in redressing problems. In evaluating the adequacy of remediation policies under the Act, it is thus important to consider the Board's ability to provide for reinstatement in a timely manner, as we discuss below.

IV.   EVALUATING THE ADEQUACY OF REMEDIES UNDER THE NLRA

Virtually all federal workplace policies have a system of enforcement underlying them. These include a mechanism to surface problems (through complaints, audits, investigations, or combinations of these activities). They have some kind of adjudication process.

Statute	Underlying basis of penalty	Maximum penalties and basis for assessment[a]	Penalty based on benefits received or harms inflicted?	Probability of investigation?	Additional remedies for clear and present problems?
National Labor Relations Act (NLRA)[a]	Reinstatement and back pay for violations of rights	Reinstatement of all workers adversely affected by violation and full back pay compensation.	Unclear	High – Presence of collective agents to identify violations	Yes – Temporary injunctive relief requires expeditious relief
Fair Labor Standards Act (FLSA)[b]	Back wages for violations; civil monetary penalties for repeat violators	• $10,000 and/or 6 months for criminal violations of minimum wage, overtime, child labor, and record keeping laws. • Full back pay and an equal amount in liquidated damages for violations of minimum wage or overtime laws. • $11,000 per violation, or $50,000 per violation if it causes serious injury, for having child labor which violates the FLSA.	Benefits received	Low	Yes – Embargo authority for goods paid in violation of Act under some circumstances
Occupational Safety and Health Act (OSHA)[c]	Penalties related to number of workers affected, severity, past behavior of employer	• $5,000 minimum and $70,000 maximum per violation for willful or repeated violations. • Requires a penalty ("shall be assessed") up to $7,000 per citation for a serious violation. • $7,000 per day for a citation that has been issued within the period permitted for its correction (and as modified by appeals of the violation to the OSHA Review Commission), where there has been a failure to abate or the violation continues. • Maximum of $10,000 and/or 6 months in prison for willful violation where that violation caused death to any employee, given conviction. • Maximum of $20,000 and/or 1 year in prison for willful violation that caused death to any employee, given conviction and where the conviction is for a second conviction.	Harms inflicted	Low	No ability comparable to that of MSHA to close dangerous areas or workplaces

Figure 7.1   Comparative penalty policies for U.S. federal workplace statutes

Statute	Underlying basis of penalty	Maximum penalties and basis for assessment[a]	Penalty based on benefits received or harms inflicted?	Probability of investigation?	Additional remedies for clear and present problems?
		• Maximum of $10,000 and/or 6 months in prison for knowingly making false statements, representation, or certification in any application, record, report, plan, or other document filed or required to be maintained.			
Mine Safety & Health Act (MSHA)[d]	Penalties related to number of workers affected, severity, past behavior of mine operator	• $70,000 per violation of MSHA standards or other provisions. Each occurrence of a violation of a mandatory safety or health standard may constitute a separate offense. • $7,500 per day for failure to abate a cited violation by the time required by MSHA. • Minimum $5,000 and not more than $60,000 per violation for failure to provide timely notification to the Secretary for the following accidents: (1) The death of an individual at the mine, or (2) An injury or entrapment of an individual at the mine, which has a reasonable potential to cause death. • $220,000 per violation for flagrant failure to make reasonable efforts to eliminate a known violation of a mandatory health or safety standard that substantially and proximately caused, or reasonably could cause, death or serious bodily injury.	Harms inflicted	High – Minimum number of annual inspections required (2 for above ground, 4 for underground)	Yes – Ability to close sections, mines to restrict access to dangerous areas and conditions
Employee Polygraph Protection Act (EPPA)[e]	Penalties related to employer abuse of polygraph	• $10,000 per violation for employer who improperly forces employee to take a lie detector test. • Civil suit by employee for lost wages for employer forcing improper taking of lie detector test.	Harms inflicted	Low	No
Contract Work Hours and Safety Standards Act (CWHSSA)[f]	Loss of contracting ability with federal government	• Loss of contracting ability with government for contractors that have employees work in dangerous or unsanitary conditions.	Benefits received	Medium – Audits of federal contractors	Yes – Debarment from federal contracting

Family Medical Leave Act (FMLA)[g]	Back pay and liquidated damages	• Full back pay and an equal amount in liquidated damages for not allowing an employee leave or somehow injuring an employee who takes leave.	**Benefits received**	**Low**	No
Office of Federal Contract Compliance Policy (OFCCP)[h]	Back pay and reinstatement of workers; debarment	Full front pay, back pay for two years before filing, and possible reinstatement by federal contractor; mirrors Title VII of the Civil Rights Act.	**Benefits received**	**Medium – Audits of federal contractors**	**Yes – Debarment from federal contracting**
Employee Benefits Standards Act (EBSA)[i]	Penalties related to severity of violation	$1,100 per day for failure or refusal to provide a document. $150 per day, $50,000 maximum, for missing or deficient IQPA report. $100 per day, $36,500 maximum, for significant reporting errors. $300 per day, $30,000 per year maximum, cumulative $180,000 maximum, for failing to file an annual plan report.	**Harms inflicted**	Low	No

Notes: a   Citations for maximum penalties: NLRA: 29 U.S.C. § 160(c); FLSA 29 U.S.C. 216(a), (b), (e) / OSHA 29 U.S.C. 666(a), (b), (c), (d), (e), (f), (g) / MSHA 30 U.S.C. 820(a); 30 CFR 100.5(c); 30 CFR 100.4(c); 30 CFR 100.5(d) 30 U.S.C. 820(b) / EPPA 29 U.S.C. 2005(a)(1); (c)(1) / CWHSSA 40 U.S.C. 3704(b)(2) / FMLA 29 U.S.C. 2617(a)(1) / OFCCP Executive Order 11246 / EBSA 29 U.S.C. 1132(c)(8); 29 U.S.C. 1132(g)(2)(C)(ii); 29 U.S.C. 1132(c).

Figure 7.1   (continued)

And they have some combination of penalties and remedies that follow the adjudication of misconduct by the regulated entity.

Figure 7.1 provides an overview of the NLRA and other major workplace laws discussed above with respect to key dimensions of their penalty policies. In order to evaluate the adequacy of remedies under the NLRA relative to other workplace policies, we compare major workplace policies regarding the elements of optimal policy described above.[31] In this section, we also evaluate the adequacy of remedies under the NLRA to affect the behavior of management and unions in relation to the Act's objectives. We undertake this evaluation using both data on NLRB adjudication over the past decade and comparative analysis of the law in relation to other workplace statutes.

A.   Underlying Basis of NLRA Penalties

Unlike other workplace statutes administered by the U.S. Department of Labor, the NLRA does not empower its agency to initiate investigations to assess compliance. Instead, the NLRB merely responds to charges of unfair labor practices arising principally under the sections described above. This means that the probability of enforcement is largely contingent on the willingness of employees, firms, and unions to step forward if their rights under the NLRA are violated.

Since the NLRA itself is rooted in the notion of collective action, many of the problems arising from the use of employees to trigger enforcement under other statutes do not arise here (Weil 1991, 1999, 2005; Budd and McCall 1997; Fine and Gordon 2010). Again, unions play the critical agency role if employers commit unfair labor practices, and employers play that role in regard to allegations of union violations. That means that employer ULPs against employees who are not represented by or seeking to organize a union tend to go unaddressed. But with regard to the great majority of ULPs that directly affect unions, union organizing activities, or employers, violations are very likely to be investigated. In this sense, the NLRA is similar to the Mine Safety and Health Act, albeit for very different reasons; in the latter case, the law requires a minimum of four inspections per year for all underground mining operations. In contrast, only a small fraction of workplaces will receive an investigation under the FLSA, OSHA and other workplace laws listed in Figure 7.1.

The high probability of response to an alleged violation means that the incentives for specific or general deterrence are rooted in the magnitude of the penalty itself. As noted above, in the case of the NLRA, penalties consist of the remedies for violations of the Act. These remedies have two components. First, the remedies for unfair labor practices committed by employers (sections 8(a)(3), 8(a)(4)) are reinstatement and provision of lost back pay for the appropriate period. That is, if the NLRB (or an administrative law judge) finds that workers were dismissed because of their union activity (or because of complaining to or testifying for the NLRB), then the remedy is the amount of back pay owed the workers from the time they were dismissed until they were reinstated minus any earnings received from employment in the interim (not including unemployment compensation). Similarly, if a union causes the discharge of an employee (for example, a union dissident), then the penalty facing the union is to make whole the losses incurred by those workers. The NLRA only provides for explicit penalties in the case of contempt or defiance of a judicially enforced Board order. The magnitude of *de facto* penalties is, therefore, largely determined by the number of workers affected by the unfair labor practice and the amount of time that the action led to a loss of compensation. The Act affords no meaningful remedy (or penalty) on behalf of individuals who may have been threatened or intimidated by employer actions but who lost no wages.

This focus on the harms of only those workers directly affected by the ULP stems directly from the exclusive focus of the Act on remediation and not deterrence. From the standpoint of the deterrence model embodied in the remedy, one may assume that, when a company weighs its decision to comply or not, it considers largely the cost of compensating workers who were dismissed for the organizing activities – that is, the amount of their lost wages (but not benefiting from their services over that time period). If the harms inflicted on society by the unfair labor practice are greater than the lost compensation (that is, as in equation (4), $H > W$), then the penalty policy underlying the NLRA will be insufficient to deter unfair labor practices to the extent that is socially desirable.

This rationale for NLRA remedies contrasts with that for safety and health acts and other statutes listed in Figure 7.1, in which penalties represent a charge related to committing the violation of the law or standard itself. The criteria for successively higher safety and health penalties primarily center on the assessed gravity, or severity, of the violation. Judging the severity of the violation requires the inspector to assess the probability that the violation could lead to an injury or illness, the severity of that potential injury or illness (for example, a lost work day or death), and the number of workers potentially affected by it. In addition, the penalty reflects the underlying behavior of the employer: did the violation arise from an error or poor information, or was it done "knowingly and willingly"?

These criteria primarily regard the potential harm to workers arising from the employers' failure to follow safety and health standards. This harm-based rationale is important and consistent with the notion that those statutes address workplace externalities. The implied size of externalities differs dramatically in the sense of the degree to which they rise with violations. Even more, the variety of industries and workplace risks covered by the Occupational Safety and Health Act would suggest that a far more nuanced set of guidelines that reflect the very different size of externalities in industries like construction and financial services should guide penalty-setting using a harm-based approach.[32]

B. Magnitude of Remedies for NLRA Violations

Given that remedies are rooted in reinstating and making whole workers whose rights have been violated under the NLRA, the magnitude of remedies is important for analyzing their potential impact on employer behavior. For some perspective, Figure 7.1 lists the maximum penalties under other federal statutes as well as those under the NLRA. One striking contrast to note is that other workplace statutes – even those like the Fair Labor Standards Act which, like the NLRA, is primarily based on recovery of back pay – provide for explicit, maximum penalties for certain types of violations, separate from remediation of lost compensation. The NLRA has no such provision.

Academic studies and government reports have attempted to estimate the size of the penalties imposed for violating the NLRA. The implied penalties for violating the Act in these studies range from about \$3,000 to between \$10,000 and \$15,000 (Kleiner, McLean, and Dreher 1988 and Commission on the Future of Labor Management

Table 7.2   Values (in dollars) of back pay per individual and per citation, all years from 2000–2009*

	Back pay ($)[a]							
	Per individual				Per citation			
	No.	Mean	Median	Standard Deviation	No.	Mean	Median	Standard Deviation
8(a)(2)	8,034	4,192	5,557	38,998	69	488,053	32,946	2,618,416
8(a)(3)	29,128	10,956	12,437	44,164	1,355	235,519	46,986	1,389,840
8(a)(4)	3,370	15,904	16,295	55,252	171	313,423	55,523	1,259,712
8(a)(5)	43,685	8,452	5,436	74,895	768	480,783	71,191	2,078,826
8(b)(2)[b]	1,404	4,032	9,433	42,227	58	97,601	28,917	208,412
8(b)(3)[b]	135	1,450	2,461	17,934	6	32,628	22,897	39,722

Notes:
*   Values are adjusted by the consumer price index by year, with 2009 as the base. See Tables 7.3 and 7.4 for additional notes on these estimates.
a   Since 8(a)(1) violations are added to all other charges by the NLRB automatically because any such violations are considered to have necessarily "restrained or coerced" employees' Section 7 rights under the Act, we do not explicitly examine them. However, back pay for violations where this provision was included for the time period of our analysis for individuals was $9,136 (mean) and $8,716 (median) and for citations the mean was $245,923 and a median of $173,334. There were only 74 § 8(a)(1) only cases where remedies were awarded over the 10-year period. The awards for individuals were $26,381 (mean) and $19,339 (median) and for citations the mean was $135,460 (mean), with a median of $92,020. The average duration from the time of filing to adjudication was 2,048 days.
b   For these two sections, the means, medians, and standard deviations are based on only the years which had recorded cases.

Source: National Labor Relations Board data, analyzed by the authors.

Relations 1994). Unlike previous reviews of the remedies under the Act, we disaggregate the various substantive sections of the Act by the major violations and show how they have varied over time. Our approach provides a much more detailed and comprehensive analysis of the remedies than do previous examinations.

The four substantive sections of the NLRA that are most likely to be violated by management are sections 8(a)(2), which charges that a union is dominated by the employer; 8(a)(3), which focuses on violations of discrimination for union activity by employers; 8(a)(4), which includes violations for discrimination by an employer for providing testimony to the NLRB; and 8(a)(5), which involves violations by management for failing to bargain in good faith with representatives of labor organizations.[33]

Table 7.2 shows the number of individuals and citations for violations of each section of the NLRA for the 10-year period from 2000 through 2009. The largest number of violations occurred for section 8(a)(3), with 1,355 citations (about 56 percent of all violation types presented in the table) and more than 29,000 employees involved. Section 8(a)(5) had the largest number of individuals involved during the period of our data, with more than 43,600 workers receiving back pay from NLRB judgments.

Table 7.2, also provides the average – mean and median – costs of violating the NLRA over the 10-year period from 2000 through 2009 for both management and labor union violations, measured in terms of back pay per individual and per citation (with the latter being almost always a violation by a firm or a union).[34] The largest penalties per individual are for cases in which individuals were discharged for testifying or providing information to the NLRB (section 8(a)(4)), with a median penalty of over $16,000. The highest mean dollar violation per citation, however, was for violations arising from company-dominated unions or bargaining over wages, hours, and terms and conditions of employment outside the prescribed guidelines of collective bargaining (section 8(a)(2) and 8(a)(5)). Violations of the Act by unions (sections 8(b)(2) and 8(b)(3)) resulted in much smaller fines per individual and per citation.

There was considerable variation in the amount awarded to individual workers by NLRB administrative law judges, by both year adjudicated and section of the Act. Table 7.3 shows the values for each year and section of the Act as well as the mean and median amount of back pay per worker during 2000–09, adjusted by the consumer price index over that 10-year period. The data do not include settlements between the parties that may have occurred in anticipation of an award (those settlements remain private). Nevertheless, the data do provide a guide for what both labor and management may perceive as an upper bound for an award that goes to an administrative law judge.[35]

Over the entire 10 years, for section 8(a)(3), the most frequently violated section of the law against individuals; the median back pay per worker was almost $12,500, ranging from a low of $8,700 in 2008 to a high of almost $21,000 in 2007. The next column of Table 7.3 provides similar estimates for section 8(a)(4), which protects workers from discrimination because they provided testimony to the NLRB. The median awards for individuals of about $16,000 (ranging from about $6,900 in 2003 to more than $34,000 in 2005). The other sections of the Act had much lower settlements. The median levels of back pay for sections 8(a)(2) and 8(a)(5) (both involving violations by management) are both around $5,500. Most 8(a)(5) violations involve management making unilateral decisions during the course of negotiations or taking unilateral actions during a period covered by a collective bargaining agreement that may also involve individual workers.

Consistent with the move to level the labor–management relations playing field following a spike in strikes and labor disputes after World War II, the Taft-Hartley provisions of the NLRA also provide for penalties against unions that violate individual workers' rights under the Act. Under section 8(b)(2), unions are barred from attempting to cause an employer to discriminate against employees for their lack of union membership or participation. Section 8(b)(3) is violated by a union refusing to bargain collectively with an employer. (The Act also prohibits other actions by unions against businesses – such as secondary boycotts, picketing, or refusing to handle any product of any other employer – that may involve many workers and large awards. But because those awards are based on lost earnings of the firm due to the job action, they were not included in our data, which focus on an analysis of violations against individual employees.)

For section 8(b)(2), where the NLRB or courts found the unions guilty of violating the Act, the median back pay per individual during 2000–09 was slightly more than $9,400 (ranging over the years from a few thousand dollars to almost $74,000 in 2008 in Table 7.3). Given the relatively few violations of these provisions, it is not surprising that the spread is so large. Similarly, the final columns of Table 7.3 show violations by unions for failing to bargain in good faith, and reveal even larger variations across the years.

How far do these calculated remedies in Tables 7.2 and 7.3 go in regard to making

Table 7.3   *Back pay per individual, by year and by NLRA section involved, 2000–2009*
            (in dollars)*

Year Case Closed	Measure	8(a)(2)	8(a)(3)[a]	8(a)(4)	8(a)(5)[b]	8(b)(2)[c]	8(b)(3)[c]
2000	No. of Individuals	118	2,338	145	3,669	27	***
	Mean	$3,147	$11,246	$13,923	$8,584	$2,704	***
	Median	$1,406	$10,322	$13,485	$4,328	$1,259	***
	Std. Dev.	$6,555	$50,068	$61,465	$18,364	$14,526	***
2001	No. of Individuals	71	1,891	232	3,970	16	6
	Mean	$12,978	$13,465	$19,846	$5,700	$17,957	$6,951
	Median	$18,563	$13,013	$17,696	$5,115	$2,657	$6,951
	Std. Dev.	$79,193	$38,733	$46,575	$195,178	$15,236	—
2002	No. of Individuals	880	5,461	1,444	6,638	24	3
	Mean	$6,069	$8,036	$7,256	$5,845	$26,845	$596
	Median	$15,190	$10,714	$11,533	$4,477	$41,979	$596
	Std. Dev.	$39,661	$42,827	$95,806	$25,143	$102,643	—
2003	No. of Individuals	205	2,630	93	3,329	13	2
	Mean	$2,005	$11,384	$9,331	$8,236	$32,321	$25,028
	Median	$1,008	$11,746	$6,876	$5,061	$10,821	$25,028
	Std. Dev.	$9,242	$33,295	$32,727	$26,075	$53,636	$29,617
2004	No. of Individuals	42	1,823	601	4,463	4	***
	Mean	$16,563	$15,744	$16,142	$14,055	$55,199	***
	Median	$7,833	$14,237	$22,983	$9,188	$56,710	***
	Std. Dev.	$26,619	$32,861	$31,883	$29,393	$16,184	***
2005	No. of Individuals	96	2,692	273	4,155	106	***
	Mean	$3,024	$26,717	$57,738	$12,680	$8,075	***
	Median	$603	$15,317	$34,368	$5,146	$9,612	***
	Std. Dev.	$3,003	$46,454	$78,999	$21,132	$16,965	***
2006	No. of Individuals	115	2,578	102	3,331	1,105	***
	Mean	$8,584	$9,920	$36,381	$6,807	$2,280	***
	Median	$14,077	$13,762	$30,130	$6,497	$2,175	***
	Std. Dev.	$16,884	$45,680	$21,093	$26,707	$28,299	***
2007	No. of Individuals	6,307	7,557	111	8,867	30	2
	Mean	$3,480	$5,941	$33,000	$4,701	$11,801	$108
	Median	$2,873	$20,984	$29,087	$4,703	$2,794	$108
	Std. Dev.	$18,752	$66,913	$41,344	$47,756	$23,677	—
2008	No. of Individuals	78	915	154	3,128	79	***
	Mean	$21,952	$10,041	$13,155	$13,257	$3,621	***
	Median	$10,609	$8,747	$15,640	$5,706	$73,797	***
	Std. Dev.	$28,275	$30,780	$35,624	$33,126	$54,418	***
2009	No. of Individuals	122	1,243	215	2,135	***	122
	Mean	$8,161	$10,671	$3,547	$12,956	***	$836
	Median	$12,835	$14,653	$9,209	$5,692	***	$836
	Std. Dev.	$6,720	$40,922	$15,760	$24,280	***	—

Table 7.3   (continued)

Notes:

*   Values are adjusted by the consumer price index by year, with 2009 as the base.

a.   Reported mean and median reflect cases where just 8(a)(3) violations were cited and where both 8(a)(3) and 8(a)(5) citations were cited. Since the NLRB provides an overall remedy and does not separate out back pay for each citation, in those cases where both are cited, the back pay award is included in the tabulation for both sections. Excluding all cases where the employer was cited for both types of violations, the estimated average back pay per individual for 8(a)(3) for the time period is $19,343 (mean) and $16,303 (median). Similarly, where there were only citations for other 8(a) violations, the results were as follows for 8(a)(2): $2,842 (mean) and $3,180 median; for 8(a)(4): $8,725 (mean) and $2,008 (median).

b.   Reported mean and median reflect cases where just 8(a)(5) violations were cited and where both 8(a)(3) and 8(a)(5) citations were cited. In those cases where both are cited, the back pay award is included in the tabulation for both sections. Excluding all cases where the employer was cited for both types of violations, the estimated average back pay per individual for 8(a)(5) for the time period is $7,437 (mean) and $5,620 (median), Similarly, where there were only citations for other 8(b) violations, the results were as follows: for 8(b)(2) $17,931(mean) and $13,038 (median) and for 8(b)(3) $8,352 (mean) and $3,894 (median).

c.   For these sections, the means, medians, and standard deviations are based on only the years which have recorded cases.

Source: National Labor Relations Board data, analyzed by the authors.

affected workers whole? (That is, how large are median penalties with respect to the lost earnings experienced by workers?) For workers, the loss of a job is large in comparison to the back pay awarded by an NLRB administrative law judge long after the violation occurred. We do not have direct evidence of the replacement rate of these awards (that is, the amount of back pay settlements relative to the lost earnings of affected workers). However, Brudney (2010) provides estimates which suggest that a significant percentage of workers who ultimately received back pay remedies were not fully compensated for lost earnings, less the amount earned through interim employment. He estimates that 43 percent of all employees receiving back pay through formal Board orders received an amount less than what those workers' case files would indicate would fully compensate them for the earnings loss they experienced.[36] Older studies also indicate that a significant percentage of employees who were found to have been unlawfully discharged and won the right to be reinstated did not ultimately return to their employers or returned only briefly. This implies longer-term disruptions to earnings profiles arising from the discharge that would also not be recovered via the back pay award method used by the Board (U.S. General Accounting Office 1982; Kleiner 1984).[37]

C.   Evaluating Remedies as Deterrence to Employer Violations

What is the impact of remedies under the NLRA as a spur to changing employer behavior (that is, as a means of specific or general deterrence)? Answering this question requires consideration of the magnitude of costs that those remedies represent relative to the benefits of noncompliance, as depicted in the model earlier in the chapter. As we discuss below, the back pay remedies tend to be small in comparison to the perceived and actual gains by management of reducing the influence of a union or stopping an organizing drive (Freeman and Kleiner 1999).

To more fully understand the influence of the law on firm behavior, we present an analysis of the costs to firms of violations of the NLRA by citation (which represents firm-level penalties). Tables 7.2 and 7.4 also present the results by the major sections of the law by citation rather than the amount an individual worker would receive. These dollar values may reflect the costs to the firm of a strategy of trying to stop an organizing drive (8(a)(3) or 8(a)(4)) or weakening the union during the collective bargaining process (8(a)(5)) or the costs to the unions of disciplining their members or weakening an employer's bargaining position (8(b)(2) and 8(b)(3)). They do not include the costs of attorney fees or indirect costs such as the potential lost output due to a drop in productivity within a firm.

Table 7.2 shows that the median citation to firms for violations of section 8(a)(2) was about $33,000 over the 10-year period. Table 7.4 provides annual breakdowns for back pay per firm: median monetary awards ranged widely during that period, from about $9,300 in 2005 to nearly $500,000 in 2009. The second column shows similar data for the most widely used part of the NLRA, section 8(a)(3). There the median citation over the study period was about $47,000, ranging from nearly $28,000 in 2000 to about $63,000 in 2007.

In contrast to other violations against individuals, section 8(a)(4) focuses on violations against individuals for their participation in NLRB procedures. Median citations for these violations were slightly higher than for section 8(a)(3), but with a wider range, from almost $17,500 in 2003 to almost $242,000 in 2002. The composition of the payouts is largely determined by the number of individuals involved in the case and their previous earnings.

Finally, citations for section 8(a)(5), the provision that focuses on good faith collective bargaining. This section of the NLRA is the most widely used and has coverage for the largest number of individuals. During the 10-year period for which we were able to get data from the Board on decisions, the highest median value for this section was more than $140,000 in 2006. In contrast, the lowest value was just under $48,000 in 2005. This reflects in large part the larger coverage of workers per case in this section of the Act.

Do the remedies presented in Table 7.4 translate into an incentive to change behavior – that is, do they reduce the likelihood of worker rights under the Act being violated? Unlike safety and health act penalties, which consider the spillover elements of a violation (by accounting for the number of workers potentially affected by the violation), remedies under the NLRA do not account for losses incurred by workers who were impacted by a thwarted election procedure or collective bargaining attempt. Unlike the Fair Labor Standards Act, which provides for civil monetary penalties for repeat offenders, or the safety and health acts, which allow a direct modification of penalties due to patterns of noncompliance, the NLRA penalty policy does not explicitly escalate penalties due to past violations of the Act (although there might be related remedies, such as fines for repeat violations of the Board's ruling that translate into contempt and injunctive relief under circumstances we discuss below).

However, even if back pay fully compensated workers who were unjustly dismissed for exercising rights under the NLRA,[38] the logic underlying remedies is at odds with what is

Table 7.4 Back pay per citation, by year and by NLRA section involved, 2000–2009 (in dollars)*

Year Case Closed	Measure	8(a)(2)	8(a)(3)[a]	8(a)(4)	8(a)(5)[b]	8(b)(2)[c]	8(b)(3)[c]
2000	No. of Citations	7	134	9	80	6	—
	Mean	$53,049	$196,225	$699,101	$393,674	$12,166	—
	Median	$21,700	$28,350	$75,219	$65,980	$2,200	—
	Std. Dev.	$93,093	$545,467	$489,485	$807,636	$16,594	—
2001	No. of Citations	9	174	22	99	7	1
	Mean	$102,383	$146,338	$209,288	$228,573	$41,044	$41,708
	Median	$76,695	$39,791	$48,456	$48,456	$2,657	$41,708
	Std. Dev.	$91,339	$389,357	$679,720	$462,588	$79,771	
2002	No. of Citations	14	177	20	99	4	1
	Mean	$381,481	$247,932	$523,892	$391,932	$161,072	$1,789
	Median	$60,990	$56,645	$241,861	$76,521	$85,007	$1,789
	Std. Dev.	$700,027	$1,120,316	$767,879	$19,445,656	$200,001	
2003	No. of Citations	5	147	17	92	8	2
	Mean	$82,191	$203,673	$51,047	$298,020	$52,521	$25,028
	Median	$83,698	$46,986	$17,489	$77,175	$14,939	$25,028
	Std. Dev.	$94,712	$814,830	$63,774	$1,018,644	$109,032	$29,617
2004	No. of Citations	5	137	14	80	4	—
	Mean	$139,132	$209,499	$692,973	$784,071	$55,199	—
	Median	$30,590	$45,750	$85,529	$87,042	$56,710	—
	Std. Dev.	$172,215	$745,626	$2,082,966	$2,620,980	$16,184	—
2005	No. of Citations	6	143	21	78	9	—
	Mean	$48,376	$502,945	$750,596	$675,439	$95,103	—
	Median	$9,325	$48,234	$38,447	$47,760	$28,975	—
	Std. Dev.	$99,196	$3,372,335	$2,968,958	$4,304,585	$123,953	—
2006	No. of Citations	7	113	16	64	7	—
	Mean	$141,024	$226,309	$231,927	$354,285	$359,899	—
	Median	$32,297	$47,897	$42,006	$140,786	$68,662	—
	Std. Dev.	$155,043	$603,639	$387,014	$825,713	$489,939	—
2007	No. of Citations	5	133	19	62	9	1
	Mean	$4,390,041	$337,590	$192,792	$672,363	$39,336	$216
	Median	$43,653	$62,985	$99,083	$67,247	$5,387	$216
	Std. Dev.	$9,683,658	$1,895,009	$250,685	$2,958,019	$72,957	
2008	No. of Citations	9	111	19	64	4	—
	Mean	$190,246	$82,774	$106,623	$647,944	$71,515	—
	Median	$40,854	$40,854	$62,559	$66,705	$73,797	—
	Std. Dev.	$282,876	$125,119	$106,852	$1,810,452	$44,144	—
2009	No. Of Citations	2	86	14	50	—	1
	Mean	$497,821	$154,238	$54,477	$553,205	—	$102,000
	Median	$497,821	$52,719	$22,769	$77,576	—	$102,000
	Std. Dev.	$679,153	$308,842	$72,911	$1,782,295	—	

Table 7.4   (continued)

Notes:
*   Values are adjusted by the consumer price index by year, with 2009 as the base.
a.   Reported mean and median reflect cases where just 8(a)(3) violations were cited and where both 8(a)(3) and 8(a)(5) citations were cited. Since the NLRB provides an overall remedy and does not separate out back pay for each citation, in those cases where both are cited, the back pay award is included in the tabulation for both sections. Excluding all cases where the employer was cited for both types of violations, the estimated average back pay per individual for 8(a)(3) for the time period is $91,356 (mean) and $98,946 (median). Similarly, where there were only citations for other 8(a) violations, the results were as follows for 8(a)(2): $9,024 (mean) and $9,024 median; for 8(a)(4): $22,800 (mean) and $22,518 (median).
b.   Reported mean and median reflect cases where just 8(a)(5) violations were cited and where both 8(a)(3) and 8(a)(5) citations were cited. In those cases where both are cited, the back pay award is included in the tabulation for both sections. Excluding all cases where the employer was cited for both types of violations, the estimated average back pay per individual for 8(a)(5) for the time period is $710,546 (mean) and $319,430 (median). Similarly, where there were only citations for other 8(b) violations, the results were as follows: for 8(b)(2) $96,917 (mean) and $55,199 (median) and for 8(b)(3) $42,631 (mean) and $33,368 (median).
c.   For these sections, the means, medians, and standard deviations are based on only the years which have recorded cases.

Source: National Labor Relations Board data, analyzed by the authors.

required if the intention is deterrence. Using back pay as the primary basis for penalties makes sense under a statute like the Fair Labor Standards Act, since the benefits received by an employer from noncompliance arise from the savings from paying below-statutory minimum wage or overtime requirements. Penalties based on back wages (adjusted to reflect the probability of detection and the prior compliance history of the employer) make sense given the nature of the employer's compliance decision.

The results in the tables suggest that the expected costs to an employer over the past decade of attempting to thwart a unionization drive (thereby violating 8(a)(3)) are greater than $200,000 using the mean value from Table 7.2. In contrast, the benefits of *thwarting* unionization – that is, the cost savings arising from continued operation as a nonunion enterprise – are potentially much larger, since they include the present value of future increases in wages and benefits arising from unionization as well as other resulting transfers of surplus from shareholders and owners of the firm to the workforce. We can examine this in two ways.

As a first approximation of the limited deterrence impact of remedies, imagine a 200-person company in which current employees each receive total compensation of $30,000 each year. And imagine that the employer anticipates that, with a union in place, prospective annual compensation would grow annually by 5 percent rather than 2 percent without a union. By thwarting a union drive, the company would save about $6.8 million over the course of 10 years.[39] This also roughly represents the economic harm to the employees from employer ULPs that succeed in defeating a union drive but does not include whatever savings the employer may anticipate from avoiding the constraints that collective bargaining tends to place on managerial discretion and flexibility. The voluminous literature on union effects on wages and benefits provides more systematic evidence that the potential benefits of union avoidance to the employer (and costs to the employees) are very large relative to the small remedial costs portrayed in Table 7.4.[40]

This point is further borne out by a more plausible model of the employer calculus for assessing the benefits and costs of violating the Act. The estimates above make the strong assumption that using unfair labor practices results in the failure of an organizing drive. Using a less restrictive and probabilistic structural approach, we examine the impact of committing unfair labor practices if it has a lower probability of thwarting the union campaign. Using our results from the NLRB data and estimates by other researchers regarding the success of union organizing drives and the influence of unionization on profitability in recent years, we model employer incentives to comply with the Act in an appendix.[41] We show that the expected benefits of committing ULPs during unionization drive are substantial: For a typical organizing drive, a conservative estimate of the net value to an employer of committing ULPs is well over $300,000. It is therefore fully rational for firms to resist unionization in the face of the current public and private benefits and costs of doing so.

Since the benefits of union avoidance dwarf the costs of paying back wages to those workers directly caught in the cross hairs of union avoidance through unfair labor practices, the incentives for noncompliance are overwhelming. Many researchers, such as Weiler (1983), Freeman and Medoff (1984), and Gould (1993), have made similar arguments.[42] However, we emphasize that the incentives to commit unfair labor practices to thwart the NLRA arise from the basic structure of its *de facto* penalty policy, rooted in the notion of making whole only those workers directly affected by unfair labor practices rather than reflecting the wider harms inflicted through those actions.

Given the relatively low costs of violating the NLRA by firms and the potential benefits of stopping a union during an organizing drive (that include a lower wage bill and fewer constraints on management in the allocation of labor resources), it might not be surprising to find that violations of the Act are high or increasing. Recent studies document the increase in violations and their consequences on election win rates and the completion of first-time collective bargaining agreements (for example, Flanagan 2005; Freeman 1985, 2005; Ferguson 2008).

As a final illustration of the incentives for noncompliance under existing penalty policies, we examine data on the relative growth of two groups of workers from the early 1950s to the period 2006–09: workers who were fired and then offered reinstatement to their prior jobs as a result of NLRB actions, and all workers who voted in favor of unions in NLRB elections. Figure 7.2 presents the ratio of these two groups of workers. This gives a broad view of terminations relative to workers who supported unions in these elections over a long time period.

The ratio has increased strikingly over five decades: only about one worker was fired (and reinstated) for every 200 workers who voted in favor of a union in the 1950s. In contrast, during the last 10 years, the ratio has been close to 7 in 200, suggesting a sevenfold increase in management resistance to unionization since the 1950s using this broad metric. These results suggest that management may have been less deterred from using terminations to try to stop union organizing, a result that is also consistent with our structural approach to managerial incentives in the face of union organizing (Freeman 1985; Kleiner 2001). The simple correlation between the increase in terminations

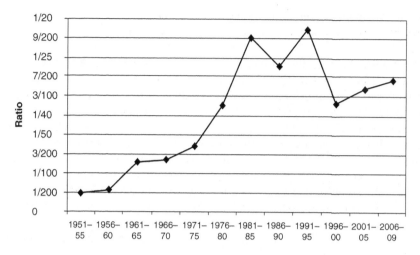

Source: NLRB Annual Reports, various years, analyzed by the authors.

Figure 7.2   Ratio of workers offered reinstatement to workers voting for unions, 1950–2009

by employers and the decline in unionization over the same period underscores the relationship between the two trends.

In essence, the penalties in Table 7.3 for employers represent relatively small costs that do not reduce their reluctance to use discriminatory activities to try to stop organizing drives. These results are also consistent with survey results by Freeman and Rogers (1999) indicating that while 32 percent of nonunion workers and 90 percent of current union workers would vote for a union in the private sector, only 6.9 percent of private sector workers belonged to a union in 2011 (Farber and Krueger 1993; Freeman and Rogers 1999; Bureau of Labor Statistics 2012).

D.   Evaluating Remedies as a Deterrent to Union Violations

Union violations of worker rights were less numerous than employer violations over the study period, and median citations on unions were much lower. The final two columns of Table 7.4 present similar data to that shown for management violations of the NLRA for violations of section 8(b)(2). This section of the Act focuses on union discrimination against individuals for their participation in union activities. Given that there were fewer cases, it is not surprising to learn that there were wider swings in the dollar payouts and in the duration of the awards from claims to settlement by the Board. The median citation over the period was about $29,000. The variation by year was large from $2,200 in 2000 to more than $85,000 in 2002. These payouts by unions were considerably smaller than those by firms.

The least used section of the NLRA was section 8(b)(3), which deals with union failure to bargain in good faith. The median back pay per citation equaled only about $23,000 for the five years with citations. There were no rulings by the NLRB on this provision for the years 2000, 2004–06, or 2008. Citation levels ranged from only about $200 in 2007 to $102,000 in 2009. These values should be read with much care because of the extremely small number of citations that were settled in each year and the small number of workers involved (135).

It is less clear how the penalties shown in Table 7.4 affect union behavior. The much lower back pay per citation for union unfair labor practice cases suggests that the prospective costs of violation are also lower for unions, which, in and of itself, would increase the incentives for noncompliance. However, recall also the very low incidence of citations brought against unions for unfair labor practices during the period 2000–09 (Table 7.2): only 58 citations for 8(b)(2) violations and a scant 6 for 8(b)(3) citations. The average number of workers receiving back pay per case was also much smaller for these unfair labor practices (ULP) relative to those committed by management.[43] This would suggest either lower recourse to the NLRB for such cases or a lower incidence of violations. The fact that the study period occurred largely during 2000–09, a period when the federal government placed great scrutiny on union activity in general, would suggest the latter explanation.[44]

V.   DEVELOPING AN ECONOMICALLY RATIONAL PENALTY APPROACH

The prior analysis suggests that the rationale for NLRA remedies provides insufficient incentives from a deterrence perspective to thwart employer violations of the Act. Because the harms inflicted by unfair labor practices go beyond the workers directly affected by discharge, the Act's remedies are ill-suited to a deterrence-based objective of curbing behaviors that thwart the ability of workers to make free choices regarding workplace representation.

Section 10(c) of the NLRA provides the NLRB with an ability to order parties to "cease and desist from such unfair labor practice, and to take such affirmative action including reinstatement of employees with or without back pay, *as will effectuate the policies of this Act*" (emphasis added).[45] An interpretation of the italicized phrase is that the Board has authority to pursue remedies that could be more compatible with a deterrence-oriented approach, while still operating under a remediation- rather than penalties-based model. Jumping off from this notion, Brudney (2010) argues for changes in the administration of remedies to push the Board to draw on its ability to set mandatory levels in response to violations of the Act, thereby raising the *de facto* expected penalties from a deterrence perspective. He argues that the U.S. Supreme Court in its *Phelps Dodge* decision of 1941 implies that the NLRB can pursue objectives beyond repairing injuries in setting back pay levels:

> The majority opinion in *Phelps Dodge* relies heavily on the Board's expansive powers to remedy unlawful employer discrimination – not only through the "limited function" of repairing private injuries but also by acting "in a public capacity to give effect to" the law's declared public policies, including "safeguarding . . . the right of self-organization."[46]

Brudney goes on to describe an approach to setting mandatory minimum back pay awards that would not require, in his view, changes to the statute since they draw on authority already granted to the NLRB. The mandatory minimums would provide that "employees discharged as a result of unlawful employer discrimination should receive at least one calendar quarter of back pay, to be awarded without regard to net loss or mitigation efforts."[47] In a related vein, the Board recently announced its decision to require that back pay awards should be adjusted to account for compounded (rather than simple) interest between the time the earnings losses occurred and the time the award was made to the worker.[48]

Brudney's (2010) mandatory minimum back pay approach and the proposed NLRB policies on interest could possibly redress the fact that individuals are not usually made whole under existing procedures. But it seems a stretch that these changes could sufficiently increase *de facto* penalties arising from remediation policies to the extent required from a deterrence perspective. In fact, given the calculations presented in the prior section, even the substantially increased remedies – including for the first time explicit penalties – that were incorporated into the recently proposed Employee Free Choice Act would reduce, but not close, the yawning gap between the benefits and the costs of noncompliance.[49]

It is also important to look at remedies linked to reducing the time between allegations of violations of the NLRA and rulings by various levels of the NLRB. As discussed earlier, many public policies have special procedures separate from (or in addition to) penalties to deal with imminent dangers posed by violations or in response to major or repeated violations of workplace laws (as displayed in the final column of Figure 7.1). Most strikingly, the Mine Safety and Health Act provide for mine closures in the event of failure to remediate dangerous conditions.

In the case of the NLRA, the objective of allowing employees to freely choose collective bargaining through a fair election requires that the election process move ahead in as unobstructed a manner as possible. As many have noted for several decades, the time required to process violation claims has a significant impact on election outcomes, with longer delays leading to diminished likelihood of election (and first contract) success.[50] Delays in processing unfair labor practices during 1960–80 are cited by Weiler (1983) and by Gould (1993). Our own evaluation of NLRB data also suggests significant delays between the filing of claims and their resolution by the Board. Table 7.5 presents the total time that elapsed between the filing of initial claims and final decisions by the Board (in those cases that are decided finally by the Board) under the six major sections of the NLRA between 2000 and 2009. The upper panel presents summary statistics for the overall 10-year period, while the lower panel provides them for each year. For violations by employers, the median ranged from 4.8 years for 8(a)(4) cases all the way up to 5.7 years for 8(a)(2) cases. The median delay for union violations cases was shorter for 8(b)(3) violations – 3.3 years – but about 4.7 years for 8(b)(2).[51]

To be sure, the large majority of NLRB cases are resolved prior to a decision by the Board. Still, delays are significant. Brudney (2010, p. 29, Table 1) provides estimates of time requirements for earlier steps of the process during the period 2004–08.[52] First, he shows that the average number of days from the time a worker is fired to the time the worker receives back pay ranges from 270 days for cases handled via a non-NLRB settlement (that is, an agreement between the parties reached through the intervention of the Board regional office) to 537 days for cases requiring an informal settlement agreement involving the Board staff; about 1,735 days (4.75 years) for cases decided

Table 7.5 Duration (days) between claims and decisions, by NLRA section, 2000–2009

Panel A: Sample statistics for all years from 2000–2009

	8(a)(2)	8(a)(3)	8(a)(4)	8(a)(5)	8(b)(2)	8(b)(3)
No.	69	1355	171	768	58	6
Mean	2,381	2,259	2,149	2,504	2,415	1,715
Mean in Years	6.5	6.2	5.9	6.9	6.6	4.7
Median	1,889	1,900	1,751	2,096	1,714	1,223
Median in Years	5.2	5.2	4.8	5.7	4.7	3.3
Std. Dev.	1,583	1,508	1,513	1,698	2,254	1,373

Panel B: Duration (days) between claims and decisions by year

Year Case Closed	Measure	8(a)(2)[a]	8(a)(3)[a]	8(a)(4)[a]	8(a)(5)[a]	8(b)(2)[a]	8(b)(3)[a,b]
2000	No. of citations	7	134	9	80	6	—
	Mean	2,953	2,153	2,235	2,388	2,336	—
	Median	3,102	2,018	2,333	2,237	2,377	—
	Std. Dev.	2,105	1,232	971	1,344	1,004	—
2001	No. of citations	9	174	22	99	7	1
	Mean	2,536	1,968	1,909	2,467	1,908	3,025
	Median	1,591	1,600	1,491	2,150	1,315	3,337
	Std. Dev.	2,017	1,453	1,384	1,674	1,481	***
2002	No. of citations	14	177	20	99	4	1
	Mean	2,884	2,331	2,941	2,759	1,403	3,954
	Median	2,953	2,115	2,706	2,311	1,301	3,954
	Std. Dev.	1,546	1,368	1,907	1,689	990	***
2003	No. of citations	5	147	17	92	8	2
	Mean	2,684	2,578	1,795	2,968	2,004	1,567
	Median	2,038	2,283	1,683	2,452	1,979	1,567
	Std. Dev.	979	1,729	1,071	1,774	777	1,702
2004	No. of citations	5	137	14	80	4	—
	Mean	2,219	2,215	2,589	2,596	2,999	—
	Median	1,561	2,117	2,486	2,378	3,000	—
	Std. Dev.	1,883	1,516	1,013	1,707	2,233	—
2005	No. of citations	6	143	21	78	9	—
	Mean	1,454	2,199	2,360	2,081	2,912	—
	Median	1,353	1,777	1,497	1,707	2,577	—
	Std. Dev.	877	1,566	2,409	1,309	2,231	—
2006	No. of citations	7	113	16	64	7	—
	Mean	1,176	1,933	1,523	2,202	3,911	—
	Median	1,244	1,345	1,211	1,486	1,448	—
	Std. Dev.	324	1,565	1,170	1,805	4,656	—
2007	No. of citations	5	133	19	62	9	1
	Mean	2,741	2,369	2,408	2,146	1,489	755
	Median	2,037	2,015	2,010	1,563	755	755
	Std. Dev.	1,917	1,429	1,328	1,636	1,937	***

Table 7.5   (continued)

Year Case Closed	Measure	8(a)(2)[a]	8(a)(3)[a]	8(a)(4)[a]	8(a)(5)[a]	8(b)(2)[a]	8(b)(3)[a,b]
2008	No. of citations	9	111	19	64	4	—
	Mean	2,059	2,432	2,219	2,522	3,025	—
	Median	1,614	2,218	2,069	1,917	3,337	—
	Std. Dev.	1,425	1,389	1,140	1,826	2,130	—
2009	No. of citations	2	86	14	50	—	1
	Mean	3,353	2,519	1,277	2,720	—	1,034
	Median	3,353	1,983	960	1,919	—	1,034
	Std. Dev.	1,125	1,797	910	2,169	—	***

Notes:
a. Reported mean and median values in the table reflect cases where there could have been multiple sections per citation. Excluding all cases where the employer was cited for multiple sections, the estimated durations for 8(a)(2) for the time period is 1,750 days (mean) and 1,638 days (median); for 8(a)(3) 2,159 days (mean) and 2,056 days (median); for 8(a)(4) 1,199 days (mean) and 1,255 days (median); for 8(a)(5) 2,398 days (mean) and 2,392 days (median); for 8(b)(2) 2,426 days (mean) and 2,336 (median), and for 8(b)(3) 1,991 days (mean) and 1,489 (median).
b. For these sections, the means, medians, and standard deviations are calculated only for the years which had recorded cases.

Source: National Labor Relations Board data, analyzed by the authors.

by the NLRB and 2,612 days (7.2 years) for cases securing compliance through the courts.[53] Thus, even when back pay restitution is secured through informal settlements, not involving a formal decision by the Board requires, on average, more than a year for resolution.

The long duration between initial claims and ultimate determination depicted in Table 7.5 underscores the continuing problem of delays. In the context of ULPs committed during the NLRB representation process, "justice delayed is justice denied." Analogies to the ability of the Mine Safety and Health Administration to close dangerous mining sections; the ability of the Department of Labor to embargo goods in the face of egregious violations of child labor and wage and hour standards; and the ability of the Office of Federal Contract Compliance Programs to debar contractors that flout equal employment requirements suggest the need for enhanced remedies under the NLRA.

The goal of assuring that workers have a right to choose whether they wish to have workplace issues resolved through collective bargaining should lead us as a policy matter to enable the NLRB to quickly stop potential unfair labor practices, reinstate workers, and allow the continuation of election processes pending resolution of the complaint. Once again, there are many examples of policies that could insure that election processes are not delayed, including some that are embodied in the various versions of the Employee Free Choice Act and others that could be implemented under the existing statute.

One avenue to reduce delays within the control of the NLRB is to find administrative mechanisms to triage and resolve cases more quickly so as to hasten elections through informal resolution. This has been a recurring objective of the Board (notably, the Commission on the Future of Labor Management Relations during the Clinton administration). It is not clear, however, how far such a solution can go in reducing the delays shown in Table 7.6 that in large part arise in the later stages of the administrative process (in particular, the time between an administrative law judge decision and a Board decision).[54] Fundamentally, however, since a significant incentive for the unfair labor practices is slowing the election or negotiation process, it often is not in the interests of the parties, or at least one of the parties, to informally resolve complaints.

A potentially more effective response to delays is using the NLRB's existing authority under section 10(j) of the Act to seek temporary injunctive relief in response to unfair labor practice cases. Section 10(j) empowers the Board to petition a federal District Court for an injunction to temporarily prevent unfair labor practices by employers or unions and to restore the status quo, pending the full review of the case by the Board. The section reflects Congressional concern about delays inherent in the administrative processing of unfair labor practice charges which could frustrate the Act's objectives. In determining whether the use of section 10(j) is appropriate, the Board examines whether injunctive relief is necessary to preserve its ability to remedy unfair labor practices as well as if the violator would otherwise reap the benefits of its violation.

Even absent new legislation, the NLRB could invoke 10(j) in a larger number of cases in which violations potentially undermine the conduct of fair elections.[55] Table 7.6 presents the number of 10(j) cases submitted by regional offices to Washington, DC (the first step in the process), the number of requests to pursue relief by the Board's General Counsel, and the number of authorizations for injunctive relief approved by the Board.[56] Gould (1994) notes with alarm the reduction in cases between 1982 and 1991.[57] Although the number of cases subsequently increased during the Clinton administration (during which Gould served as chair of the NLRB), it never returned to the levels in 1982–3. The number of cases submitted to the Washington NLRB and that were ultimately authorized fell precipitously during the period 2001–06, most strikingly in the number of cases submitted from the field; the number submitted in 2006 was less than one-quarter the number submitted in 1983 (which partially reflects the overall reduction in NLRB elections over this period).

Obviously the NLRB cannot rely upon the use of the courts to enjoin behavior as a day-to-day tool for resolving the problems discussed here.[58] But increasing the use of 10(j) commensurate with the growth in violations of the NLRA seems like a potential response to that growth over the last few decades. Strategic application of 10(j) could demonstrate the Board's seriousness in thwarting patterns of egregious violations or in cases with salience to other current or potential instances of violations. In so doing, use of 10(j) could potentially deter some violations by making clear the kind of behaviors that the Board would not tolerate with respect to their negative impacts on delaying elections or impeding bargaining in good faith.[59]

VI.   CONCLUSIONS

Remedies (or implied penalties) under the National Labor Relations Act (NLRA) focus on compensating for the economic injuries to employees directly affected by the violation

Table 7.6   Injunctive relief granted by the National Labor Relations Board, 1982–2006

Fiscal year of requests	Total number of 10(j) cases submitted to Washington	Number of GC 10(j) requests*	Number of Board 10(j) authorizations	Percentage of total requests receiving Board authorization
1982	255	58	53	23%
1983	309	71	51	23%
1984	195	40	30	21%
1985	168	42	38	25%
1986	163	45	43	28%
1987	155	37	37	24%
1988	166	44	43	27%
1989	163	62	62	38%
1990	157	41	39	26%
1991	142	36	38	25%
1992	116	27	26	23%
1993	137	42	42	31%
1994	207	85	83	41%
1995	259	109	104	42%
1996	131	59	53	45%
1997	124	62	53	50%
1998	104	53	45	51%
1999	115	58	45	50%
2000	154	73	68	47%
2001	99	43	43	43%
2002	87	26	16	30%
2003	90	24	17	27%
2004	70	22	14	31%
2005	61	22	15	36%
2006	69	30	25	43%

Source: For 1982–1991: Gould (1994); for 1992–2006: National Labor Relations Board data analyzed by the authors. GC refers to General Counsel (of the NLRB)

of their rights. We have shown that the benefits for individuals of winning a claim under the Act are comparatively small, meaning that the Act often fails to achieve even remediation of those whose rights have been directly violated. Further, the typical monetary costs of violating the NLRA by firing a union activist are quite small: on average, only about $11,000 of back pay per individual for section 8(a) (3), the most violated section of the Act. These expected costs represent a fraction of the benefits to employers (who are much more likely to commit violations against individuals than are labor organizations) from thwarting organizing drives. Some commentators attribute growing management resistance to unionization to increasingly competitive product markets (Wachter 2007). However, the law is supposed to operate as a constraint on management resistance. Its ability to do that seems undermined by the relatively small legal consequences of employers' illegal responses to union organizing.

While simple remediation of direct injuries may be a suitable focus for some workplace policies, it is insufficient for the NLRA given the absence of any appreciable deterrence measure to serve as a complement. It should, therefore, come as no surprise that the Act for decades has been ineffective in curbing behaviors that are antithetical to its fundamental aims. As the parties learned about the low penalties associated with the NLRA, neither labor or management seems to have been bothered by the costs relative to the benefits of violating the Act.

If the objective of the NLRA is to provide workers with a means to freely choose collective bargaining as their instrument of workplace representation, then remedial policies should seek to ensure that reinstatement is quick and that the cost to either employers or unions of thwarting that choice is significant. Our analysis in this chapter suggests that, given the large incentives for noncompliance and the limited monetary remedies available under relevant sections of the Act, it would take major changes in remedial policies to secure those ends. Given the constraints of the existing Act, an enforcement policy seeking to change behavior requires minimizing delays in the adjudicative process, maximizing retrospective monetary remedies, and expanding use of the prospective remedies available to the NLRB. Efforts to use the NLRB's existing enforcement powers to raise the implicit incentives provided by the Act should continue to be explored. In the longer run, more fundamental reform of the law that addresses the absence of sufficient deterrence incentives under the current Act will be required to assure greater compliance.

APPENDIX: STRUCTURAL ESTIMATES OF THE INCENTIVES FOR EMPLOYER COMPLIANCE WITH THE NLRA

The following exercise provides an approach to estimating the incentives for employer compliance with the National Labor Relations Act given estimated penalty costs from the tables in our study and other studies on the influence of unfair labor practices (ULPs) by employers. We present a probabilistic approach that assumes that the impact of unfair labor practices on union election losses is less than 1.[60] Our analysis starts by comparing an employer deciding between two outcomes: complying with the NLRA and not committing a ULP during the organizing campaign and not complying by committing a ULP.

If there is no illegal activity then:

$$E(\pi/legal) = U_0 \, \pi u + (1 - U_0) \, \pi_n \tag{A.1}$$

If there is illegal activity then:

$$E(\pi/illegal) = U_1 \, \pi_u + (1 - U_1) \, \pi_n - (p * F) \tag{A.2}$$

The net expected benefits from illegal activity are:

$$E(\pi/illegal) - E(\pi/legal) = (U_0 - U_1)(\pi_n - \pi_u) - (p * F) \tag{A.3}$$

The firm engages in illegal activity if the net expected benefit is positive:

$$(U_0 - U_1)(\pi_n - \pi_u) - (p * F) > 0 \tag{A.4}$$

where:

π_u=present discounted value of firm profits if union is successful;
π_n=present discounted value of firm profits if union is not successful.
Where $\pi_n > \pi_u$ (firm is more profitable if non-union):
U=probability that union is successful.
The firm can reduce U from U_0 to U_1 if it commits ULPs ($U_0 > U_1$).
p=probability that illegal activity is detected and results in a fine;
F=back pay remedies imposed by NLRB based on detected ULP.

Given the conditions in (A.4), the firm's compliance decision will be driven by:

$(\pi_n - \pi_u)$=increase in firm profits, if the union loses the election;
$(U_0 - U_1)$=decline in probability of union success arising from a ULP;
$p * F$=expected remedial payment arising from committing a ULP.

To use the above model to estimate the incentives for compliance by a typical firm under the Act, we need estimates of the three factors: the impact of committing an unfair labor practice on the probability of union organizing success; the difference in profits arising from a union versus nonunion workforce; and the expected penalty for committing a ULP. These can be obtained from existing literature and our analysis.

Change in firm profits arising from union loss of the election $(\pi_n - \pi_u)$ Lee and Mas estimate that there is a reduction in the firm value of about $40,000 per unionized worker. Since they use firms traded on the New York and American stock exchange, the size of the bargaining unit would be at least 100 (Lee and Mas 2009; Farber 1999). Therefore the total cost of having a unionized workforce would be roughly $4,000,000.

Decline in probability of winning an election from committing a ULP $(U_0 - U_1)$ There were about 17,000 elections between 2000 and 2009, and the union won about half of them (Farber 2011). Given the literature on the impact of union avoidance techniques (based on estimates from Dickens 1983; Freeman and Kleiner 1990; and Bronfenbrenner 1997), it is reasonable to assume that the influence of illegal activities is likely greater than 0.1, which is the value of $(U_0 - U_1)$. For example a recent study by Ferguson puts the parameter value as high as 0.3 (Ferguson 2008). To be conservative, we use $((U_0 - U_1) = 0.1)$.

Expected penalty from committing a ULP $(p * F)$ Based on the estimates in our data for employer violations of the Act, we use a value of F of $54,500, based on median back pay for citations for 8(a)(3) and 8(a)(5) (the most frequently violated provisions) during the 2000–09 period.

Substituting the above parameter estimates into equation (A.4) yields an estimate of the incentive to comply or not comply with the law given current penalty policies:

$$(U_0 - U_1)(\pi_n - \pi_u) - (p * F) > 0, \text{ so:}$$
$$0.1(\$4,000,000) - 1.0(\$54,500) = \$345,500 > 0 \text{ [61]}$$

That is, the relative payoff for committing ULPs that reduce the likelihood of an election victory is close to $350,000. Under these parameter assumptions, violating the Act is quite rational, especially when appeals and delays in penalties further reduce the value of the expected penalty.

NOTES

1. We thank Sheldon Friedman for his initial encouragement of the research project, and Sally M. Kleiner, Jing Cai, and Tucker DeVoe for their excellent assistance with our analysis. We also thank Diane Bridge and Jolynne Miller from the National Labor Relations Board for helping us obtain and interpret the codes for the data in the analysis. We appreciated the helpful comments from Henry Farber, Richard Freeman, William Gould and Jeffrey Hirsch on earlier versions of the chapter.
2. In our analysis of NLRB data, we focus in particular on unfair labor practices committed by employers in the process of organizing drives (that is §§ 8(a)(3) and 8(a)(4)), but also look at other unfair labor practices by employers (§§ 8(a)(2) and 8(a)(5)) and by unions (in §§ 8(b)(2) and 8(b)(3)).
3. This discussion focuses primarily on *de jure* penalties as opposed to *de facto* penalties. In fact, there are substantial differences between the two, arising from several factors: the manner in which personnel of regulatory agencies carry out enforcement; the review process provided under different statutes; judicial review of penalties; and the pressures placed on regulatory agencies by Congress, the Executive Branch, and stakeholders. The actions of stakeholders – labor unions, worker advocates, trial lawyers – may also substantially affect the manner in which laws are carried out in fact. For example, numerous studies show that labor unions increase the likelihood and intensity of enforcement activity at the workplace (e.g. Budd and McCall 1997; Weil 1991).
4. For example, the legislative effort that led to passage of the Mine Safety and Health Act in 1969 began in response to a major mining disaster in Farmington, West Virginia, which put the political coalition favoring its passage in a stronger position relative to opponents. This resulted in the original act including relatively stringent penalties and significant enforcement powers for the agency created by the legislation. In contrast, opponents of plant closing legislation held greater sway during the long political battle that ultimately led to passage of the Worker Adjustment Retraining and Notification Act (the WARN Act). This Act has a far less stringent set of penalty policies and creates no separate administrative apparatus for enforcement (Fung, Graham, and Weil 2007; Weil 2008).
5. Note that these features of incoherence can be taken advantage of in the political processes discussed earlier. That is, those arguing either in favor of or against stronger penalties can use the institutional myopia posited by Sunstein et al. (2002) to escape the potentially higher (or lower) fines suggested by legislation from another category.
6. Coglianese (2002) challenges Sunstein et al. (2002), arguing that there is greater coherence across penalty policies than meets the eye. For example, the existence of other forms of liability or availability of other remedies and differences in the state of mind of the violators or the type and size of regulatory targets may lead to sensible differences across categories of regulation that may still be rational from a category-specific perspective but lead to greater incoherence across categories. Coglianese, however, does not provide evidence of the extent of cross-category incoherence driven by these instrumental factors.
7. This view has long been established, in a series of rulings going back to Local 60, *United Brotherhood of Carpenters v. NLRB*, 365 U.S. 651, 655 (1961); *NLRB v. Seven-Up Bottling*, 344 U.S. 344, 346 (1953). See Gould (1994, pp. 119–27) for an extended discussion and Danin (2011) for a more recent analysis.
8. Posing the question in this way is not simply an exercise in academic analysis. Sunstein et al. (2002, p. 1192) point out that greater coherence could be generated: "The Office of Information and Regulatory Affairs (OIRA), within the Office of Management and Budget (OMB) should provide a full accounting of regulatory penalties, publicize it, and evaluate the existing pattern of outcomes, with recommendations both to agencies and to Congress. The longstanding mission of OMB in general and OIRA in particular has been to produce more in the way of global rationality, with respect to regulation and the budget generally. This role should be extended to better rationalization of the system of administrative penalties. Note in this regard that even without legislative change, agencies have considerable room to maneuver . . . The purpose of executive oversight would be to move agency practice in the direction of a sensible overall

pattern of penalties." In 2010, Sunstein was appointed and confirmed as the head of OIRA in the Obama administration.

9. Penalty policies may also reflect some underlying notion of justice beyond recovering the benefits of non-compliance or the harms inflicted from the violation. These would include some larger sanction for the moral wrong of committing the act itself, which underlies criminal penalties. Others argue that organizations and individuals adhere to laws more out of custom and culture than fear of financial penalties. See, for example, Earle and Peter (2009). We do not consider those aspects of penalty policy here.

10. This framework derives from Becker (1968) and Stigler (1971) and is laid out in greater detail by Polinsky and Shavell (2000). A useful summary of the deterrence literature can be found in Winter (2008). For early discussions regarding deterrence under workplace regulations, see Ashenfelter and Smith (1979) regarding the minimum wage standard of the Fair Labor Standards Act; Ehrenberg and Schumann (1983) regarding overtime provisions of that Act; Smith (1979) regarding the Occupational Safety and Health Act; and Appleton and Baker (1984) regarding the Mine Safety and Health Act.

11. There are nuances to both inspection probabilities and fines that we do not deal with here. We assume that the relevant probability is that of the inspection itself occurring. There is a separate probability function regarding whether the investigator, once on site, detects an underlying violation. We assume that this probability is 1.0. Also, the penalty initially assessed is, under most statutes, very different from the one ultimately paid. The difference arises because of the right of employers under most workplace statutes to appeal a citation or violation (Weil 2011). We assume here that penalties will be paid with complete certainty and that the penalty initially assessed on the employer is equal to the penalty it ultimately pays.

12. As we discuss below, the NLRB does not enforce provisions of the NLRA, but instead responds to complaints about violations of its provisions by employees. We can still think of p as the probability that a violation of the Act triggers a complaint to the Board and subsequent action.

13. Specifically, differentiating the expected costs of compliance with respect to the probability of complying in equation (1) gives: $d(E(C))/d\gamma = W - p(F)$. Given this, the optimal policy to minimize expected costs is where: $W - p(F) = 0$. Rearranging gives equation (2).

14. Note that the more general conclusion is that the government should consider the probability of inspections and the penalty as substitutes in achieving a desired compliance outcome given the costs of compliance W. We discuss this trade-off further below.

15. Section 10(c) of the Act states that "whenever it is charged that any person has engaged in or is engaging in any such unfair labor practice, the Board, or any agent or agency designated by the Board for such purposes, shall have power to issue and cause to be served upon such person a complaint stating the charges in that respect, and containing a notice of hearing before the Board or a member thereof, or before a designated agent or agency, at a place therein fixed, not less than five days after the serving of said complaint." 29 U.S.C. § 160(b).

16. See Weil (2005) for a discussion of the critical role played by third-party agents in the exercise of worker rights under various workplace policies. Here, the workers have an agent substantially solving the public good problems that arise in other areas of workplace rights.

17. This is not the case for all provisions of the NLRA however. Specifically, cases where workers are discriminated against by an employer for engaging in "concerted activities" for "mutual aid or protection" (§ 7 of the Act) often take place where there is no union on the scene. The probability that such instances are brought forward are therefore much lower than in the provisions we focus on in this chapter.

18. Bronfenbrenner and Warren (2011) find that almost half of serious violations are filed just prior to an election.

19. However, this rate might also reflect resource limits at the NLRB that require the Board to triage cases that are brought forward. We do not have sufficient data to rule this out.

20. In general, see Bardach and Kagan (1982) on this. See also Sparrow (2000) on inspector behavior and judgments of fairness by OSHA.

21. *Braun v. Walmart*, Case No. 19-CO-01-9790 (2008).

22. More formally, this implies that the optimal fine should be based on the marginal social cost to society of the workplace problem. As a result, from the harms-inflicted perspective, the optimal penalty policy is the result of dividing the Pigovian tax set to remedy an externality by the probability of detection.

23. The difference between the two approaches to setting policies derives from the practical problem of coming up with a penalty that most closely achieves the socially optimal goal of equating the marginal benefit of the standard (e.g., reduction in injury levels) with the marginal cost of achieving that standard. If the standard itself is set where the marginal cost and marginal benefit of the policy are equal, then the two approaches are equivalent (and the penalty level would be the same in each case). The "benefits received" approach works reasonably well where the cost structure of compliance for the standard is close to the benefits produced socially from achieving that reduction. If, however, the marginal cost of achieving that level of injury reduction is still well below the benefits produced from complying, a higher level

of compliance is desirable, thereby requiring a "harms"-based approach that would set a higher penalty to push firms to a more stringent level of compliance.

24. This is an oversimplification, however, since the decision to not comply leads to employer hiring decisions premised on a lower price for labor and, therefore, an incentive to hire more workers. Bringing the change in employment arising from noncompliance into the calculation means that both the benefits received from noncompliance include both changes in profitability to the firm arising from noncompliance and changes in harms in the net social welfare for those who are underpaid as well as for those who might not be employed if the firm complied with the law.

25. This is at best a minimum estimate: as above, the reduced labor costs arising from such discrimination changes the basis of hiring decisions by the firm. Different models of discrimination and assumptions about the operation of the surrounding labor market have implications for the economic benefits (if any) accruing to the firm from discriminatory practices. For example, under assumptions of competitive labor markets, discriminatory practices drive up (not down) the marginal cost of labor, requiring employers to pay extra for discriminatory tastes. (For example, they pay a premium in not allowing workers access to jobs because of their characteristics, even when those workers' marginal productivity would make them more attractive than other workers.) In this case, the benefits-received model implies that restitution of discrimination will lower costs through the elimination of such practices. For a summary of models, see Lang (2007).

26. 29 U.S.C. § 160(c).

27. The Mine Safety and Health Act has an explicit and detailed point system for scoring violations, made up of 12 criteria laid out in the U.S. Code of Federal Regulation. See 30 CFR 100.3(b)–(f), which is a series of tables laying out the point system, and 30 CFR 100.3(g), which converts the points into an actual penalty amount that goes up to the statutory maximum of $70,000. The above example assumes no negligence and no prior violation history on the part of the particular mine operator in both cases.

28. PL 91-173, § 104(b).

29. Section 103(a).

30. See Weil (2005, pp. 243–44). See also Weil and Mallo (2007) for evaluations of the impact of embargoes and monitoring systems on the behavior of garment contractors in New York City and Los Angeles.

31. See Weil (2010) for a more extensive discussion of the coherence of federal workplace penalty policies.

32. Note that the basis for penalties could (but does not) follow a benefits-received view of noncompliance. Such an approach would reflect, for example, the relative costs of complying with different standards (installing scaffolding; machine-guarding equipment; providing proper ventilation) and basing an assessment on the amount saved by the employer by failing to follow those standards. Such an approach is hardly antithetical to a regulatory agency: in fact, the Environmental Protection Agency (EPA) has explicitly used it since the 1980s (Lear 1998; Libber 1999; EPA 1984a, 1984b, 2004).

33. We thus focus on the costs and remedies of these violations by firms and labor organizations against individuals.

34. The period 2000–09 has the most accurate available data on dollar remedies and duration of cases in digitally readable form. Although we have access to data from the 1990s, the number of cases and the accuracy of the data for those years are questionable.

35. We also provide sensitivity estimates of the back pay for violations when only single sections of the NLRA are violated in the footnotes to the table.

36. The percentage of employees who do not receive full compensation for lost earnings because of an employer action found to be in violation of the NLRA varies according to the process of resolution, going from 20 percent of all cases for non-NLRB settlements to 15 percent for informal settlements and to 39 percent of all cases where a court ordered the settlement. Brudney's estimates are for fiscal year 2006 closed cases involving an unlawful employer discharge, where a final payment had been made to affected individuals, and are based on a comparison of the final amount actually paid to the full amount originally calculated by the regional Board office, deducting for interim earnings from other employers during the period of discharge. See Brudney (2010, Table 3, and generally, pp. 22–32).

37. In particular, the U.S. GAO (1982) found that 58 percent of workers fired for union activity and then reinstated by the NLRB were no longer working for their employers within one year and that 29 percent of those workers were fired again.

38. As noted above, the Brudney (2010) results suggest that the back pay awards probably do not always meet even this objective.

39. This estimate represents the present value of the difference in compensation costs between compensation increasing at a 2 percent rate versus a 5 percent rate over the 10-year period, with a discount rate of 5 percent over the period assumed.

40. Even more, research by Logan (2002, 2007) indicates that firms are willing to expend significant resources for union avoidance, at times far in excess of the probable wage and benefit costs of unionization. This implies an even higher upper bound on the potential costs of compliance from an employer's perspective.

41. The Appendix provides the details of this model and the parameter values we use to make these estimates.
42. In his assessment of the adequacy of remedies under the NLRA more than 25 years ago, Weiler (1983, p. 1789) notes that "at first blush, the back pay award might seem to serve both remedial and deterrent functions. Although from the employees' point of view the award is merely compensation for what has been lost, from the employer's point of view it is a financial penalty: the employer is required to pay for services it has not received. The problem is that this 'fine' – paid to the worker rather than the state – is far too small to be a significant deterrent."
43. The median number of workers receiving back pay per case for the entire 2000–09 period varies widely across NLRA sections, but is consistently smaller for union violations: management ULPs: 8(a)(2): 117, 8(a)(3): 2,458, 8(a)(4): 185, 8(a)(5): 3,820; union cases: 8(b)(2): 26, 8(b)(3): 1.
44. This is particularly illustrated by increased reporting requirements and enhanced enforcement of them under the requirements of union financial disclosure required by the Labor Management Reporting and Disclosure Act (29 U.S.C. § 401). See Fung, Graham, and Weil (2007, pp. 199–201).
45. 29 U.S.C. § 160(c).
46. *Phelps Dodge Corp. v. NLRB*, 313 U.S. 177 (1941) at 193, cited in Brudney (2010, p. 5).
47. Additionally, he advocates that "unlawfully discharged employees whose liability or backpay determination is litigated to the Board or appellate court stages should receive at least one year of back pay, again in unreduced form." The mandatory minimum penalties are modeled on cases involving the failure of employers to bargain in good faith regarding plant closures (Brudney 2010, pp. 3–5).
48. The new policy is in the decision *Jackson Hospital Corp. d/b/a Kentucky River Medical Center* (356 NLRB No. 8, at 4–5, released 10/25/10). In it, the Board determines that compound rather than simple interest better achieves the Act's intent of "making employees whole." In the decision, the Board reasons that compound interest comports with current practices of private lenders, such as credit card companies, as well as many monetary obligations imposed by federal law, such as under the Internal Revenue Code. The policy also applies retroactively to current pending cases.
49. The Employee Free Choice Act (111th Congress, H.R. 1409, S. 560) proposes two important changes to NLRA policy. First, it would increase the amount an employer would be required to pay in cases of illegal employee discharge or discrimination during an organizing campaign or first contract drive to become two times back pay in the form of liquidated damages, in addition to the back pay owed (that is, treble damages for violations in these cases). Second, it would create civil penalties of up to $20,000 per violation against employers found to have willfully or repeatedly violated employees' rights during an organizing campaign or first contract drive. Together, the proposals would move the penalty model underlying the NLRA to one closer approximating the harms-inflicted approach and potentially raise deterrent effects appreciably.
50. Weiler (1983, p. 1788) notably remarks that "if the employer's purpose had simply been to punish the worker for supporting the union, the fact that the law would effectively undo this damage at the employer's expense might discourage the use of the tactic in the future. But the real purpose of such discharge is to break the momentum of the union's organizing campaign."
51. The data in the tables are for claims that were ultimately decided by an NLRB administrative law judge, the Board, or an appellate court. We also give sensitivity estimates of the durations between the initial claim and the decision for unique citations when only single sections of the NLRA are violated in the footnotes to Table 7.5.
52. Brudney (2010) does not provide separate estimates for violations of different sections of the Act as we do in Table 7.5.
53. Brudney's estimates use Board charges as the denominator. Brudney (2010, p. 30, Table 2) also presents time estimates calculated on a per affected employee basis. The latter estimates yield even longer durations. For example, the average time between the filing of a charge and receipt of back pay through non-NLRB settlement increases to 351 days; via informal settlement, to 759 days; via compliance with a Board settlement, to 2,229 days; and via compliance with a court, to 3,869 days.
54. It is interesting to compare the estimated delays in processing unfair labor practice claims of Weiler and Gould for 1980 and 1990. In most cases, Gould's figures for 1990 show about the same or slightly reduced time elapsed between filing of claim to complaint; complaint to the close of hearings; and the close of hearings to the administrative law judge decision. However, the time required between that decision and a Board decision increased markedly (from 133 days in 1980 to 315 days in 1990). This is the primary reason that total elapsed time from filing to Board decision rose from 484 days in 1980 to 691 days in 1990.
55. The proposed Employee Free Choice Act would extend the NLRB's existing mandate to seek a temporary federal court injunction against certain forms of union misconduct (involving "secondary boycotts" and "recognitional picketing") to also include cases of employers' discrimination against employees who attempt to organize a union. While the prospects for major legislative changes to the NLRA seem limited (for reasons that have long thwarted labor law reform – see Weil 2009), increasing the *volitional* use of existing authority regarding injunctive relief, particularly when there is a pattern of violations on

the part of employers, is within the administrative purview of the Board and therefore a more tractable avenue to thwart violations of the law. See Gould (1993, pp. 158–62) for an insightful discussion of this issue. The General Counsel of the NLRB has issued a number of memoranda recently in this regard. For example, in March 2011, the NLRB announced a change to the back pay calculations to incorporate daily compounding of interest (see National Labor Relations Board, GC-11-08). The General Counsel memos regarding enforcement and other matters can be found at https://www.nlrb.gov/publications/general-counsel-memos. See Danin (2011) for a discussion of these recent initiatives in the context of past case law relating to NLRA remedies.

56. The figures from 1982–92 are from Gould (1993, Table 5.3); data for 1992–2006 are from the NLRB and are tabulated by the authors.
57. A decade earlier, Weiler (1983, p. 1801) remarked with respect to use of 10(j) that "the Board thus failed to use what was and still is, for preventive as well as for reparative purposes, the most effective weapon in its arsenal."
58. The statute also makes it difficult to move for injunctive relief in that it requires agreement by the five-member Board after the NLRB's General Counsel has sought such relief. One statutory change pursued in past attempts at labor law reform has been to give regional NLRB attorneys the same right to directly seek injunctive relief (without consent from the Board) for employer violations of the Act that they currently have under § 10(l) for certain union unfair labor practices.
59. The final column of Table 7.6 suggests that less than half of the cases from the field were ultimately moved forward by the NLRB. However, the potential deterrence effect of injunctions may arise from the volume of activity at the regional level, which might be observed as a signal of Board toleration of patterns of repeated or egregious violations of the Act. In this sense, the fall in 10(j) cases submitted to Washington over time is the most troubling in terms of its diminishing impact on prospective behavior.
60. We are grateful to Henry Farber for suggesting this approach.
61. This uses the conservative assumption that $p = 1.0$, which assumes that the ULP is both detected and results in a holding for back pay for affected workers. While it is reasonable to assume a high rate of detection for the ULP during the campaign for reasons discussed in the chapter, it is much less likely that it will always result in a ruling requiring remediation. If one uses a lower probability of detection (p), the expected value of committing ULPs increases further. The expected payoff shrinks, however, if one uses the mean values for F (Table 7.2) which are considerably higher.

REFERENCES

Apgar, Leonard. 1984. "Lane Kirkland Helps Revitalize AFL-CIO, but Difficulties Persist," *Wall Street Journal*, July 11.

Appleton, William, and Joseph Baker. 1984. "The Effect of Unionization on Safety in Bituminous Deep Mines," 5 *Journal of Labor Research* 139–47.

Ashenfelter, Orley, and Robert Smith. 1979. "Compliance with the Minimum Wage Law," 87 *Journal of Political Economy* 333–50.

Bardach, Eugene, and Robert A. Kagan. 1982. *Going by the Book: The Problem of Regulatory Unreasonableness*. Philadelphia, PA: Temple University Press.

Becker, Gary. 1968. "Crime and Punishment: An Economic Analysis," 76 *Journal of Political Economy* 169–217.

Bronfenbrenner, Kate. 1997. "The Role of Union Strategies in NLRB Certification Elections," 50 *Industrial and Labor Relations Review* 195–221.

Bronfenbrenner, Kate, and Dorian Warren. 2011. "The Empirical Case for Streamlining the NLRB Certification Process: The Role of Date of Unfair Labor Practice Occurrence." Institute for Social and Economic Research and Policy, Columbia University, Working Paper, June.

Brudney, James. 2010. "Private Injuries, Public Policies: Adjusting the NLRB's Approach to Backpay Remedies." Public Law and Legal Theory Working Paper Series No. 131, Ohio State University.

Budd, John, and Brian McCall. 1997. "The Effect of Unions on the Receipt of Unemployment Insurance Benefits," 50 *Industrial and Labor Relations Review* 478–92.

Coglianese, Cary. 2002. "Bounded Evaluation: Cognition, Incoherence, and Regulatory Policy," 54 *Stanford Law Review* 1217–38.

Danin, Ellen. 2011. "No Rights without a Remedy: The Long Struggle for Effective National Labor Relations Act Remedies." American Constitution Society for Law and Policy, Issue Brief.

Dickens, William, 1983. "The Effect of Company Campaigns on Certification Elections: Law and Reality Once Again," 36 *Industrial and Labor Relations Review* 560–75.

Earle, John, and K. S. Peter. 2009. "Complementarity and Custom in Wage Contract Violation," 91 *Review of Economics and Statistics* 832–49.

Ehrenberg, Ronald, and Paul Schumann. 1982. *Longer Hours or More Jobs? An Investigation of Amending Hours Legislation to Create Employment.* Ithaca, NY: ILR/Cornell Press.

Environmental Protection Agency. 1984a. "Policy on Civil Penalties." EPA General Enforcement Policy No. GM-21.

Environmental Protection Agency. 1984b. "A Framework for Statute-Specific Approaches to Penalty Assessments: Implementing EPA's Policy on Civil Penalties." EPA General Enforcement Policy No. GM-22.

Environmental Protection Agency. 2004. "Identifying and Calculating Economic Benefit that Goes beyond Avoided and/or Delayed Costs." Office of Enforcement and Compliance Assurance.

Farber, Henry. 2011. "Comments on 'Evaluating the Effectiveness of National Labor Relations Act Remedies: Analysis and Comparison with Other Workplace Penalty Policies.'" Labor and Employment Association Annual Meetings, Denver, January 6.

Farber, Henry, and Alan Krueger. 1993. "Union Membership in the United States: The Decline Continues," in Bruce Kaufman and Morris M. Kleiner, eds., *Employee Representation: Alternatives and Future Directions.* Madison, WI: Industrial Relations Research Association, pp. 105–34.

Ferguson, John-Paul. 2008. "The Eyes of the Needles: A Sequential Model of Union Organizing Drives, 1999–2004," 62 *Industrial and Labor Relations Review* 3–21.

Fine, Janice, and Jennifer Gordon. 2010. "Strengthening Labor Standards Enforcement through Partnerships with Worker Organizations," 38 *Politics and Society* 552–85.

Fishback, Price, and Shawn Kantor. 2000. *Prelude to the Welfare State: The Origins of Workers' Compensation.* Chicago: University of Chicago Press.

Flanagan, Robert. 2005. "Has Management Strangled U.S. Unions?," 26 *Journal of Labor Research* 33–63.

Freeman, Richard B. 1985. "Why Are Unions Faring Poorly in NLRB Representation Elections?," in Thomas A. Kochan, ed., *Challenges and Choices Facing American Labor.* Cambridge. MA: MIT Press, pp. 45–64.

Freeman, Richard B. 2005. "What Do Unions Do? The 2004 M-Brane Stringtwister Edition." NBER Working Paper Series 11410.

Freeman, Richard, and Morris M. Kleiner 1990. "Employer Behavior in the Face of Union Organizing Drives," 43 *Industrial & Labor Relations Review* 351–65.

Freeman, Richard B., and Morris M. Kleiner 1999. "Do Unions Make Enterprises Insolvent?," 52 *Industrial and Labor Relations Review* 507–24.

Freeman, Richard B., and James L. Medoff. 1984. *What Do Unions Do?* New York: Basic Books.

Freeman Richard B., and Joel Rogers. 1999. *What Workers Want.* Ithaca, NY: Cornell University Press.

Fung, Archon, Mary Graham, and David Weil. 2007. *Full Disclosure: The Perils and Promise of Transparency.* New York: Cambridge University Press.

Gould, William. 1993. *Agenda for Reform: The Future of Employment Relationships and the Law.* Cambridge, MA: MIT Press.

Gould, William. 1994. *A Primer on American Labor Law.* 3rd ed. Cambridge, MA: MIT Press.

Kleiner, Morris M. 1984. "Unionism and Employer Discrimination: Evaluation of 8(a)(3) Violations." 23 *Industrial Relations* 234–43.

Kleiner, Morris M. 2001. "Intensity of Management Resistance: Understanding the Decline of Unionization in the Private Sector." 22 *Journal of Labor Research* 519–40.

Kleiner, Morris, Robert McLean, and George Dreher. 1988. *Labor Markets and Human Resource Management.* Homewood, IL: Scott Foresman and Co.

Lang, Kevin. 2007. *Poverty and Discrimination.* Princeton, NJ: Princeton University Press.

Lear, Kelly. 1998. "An Empirical Examination of EPA Administrative Penalties." Working Paper, Kelley School of Business, Indiana University.

Lee, David, and Alexandre Mas. 2009. "Long-Run Impacts of Unions on Firms: New Evidence from Financial Markets, 1961–1999." NBER Working Paper No. 14709, February.

Leonard, James. 2000. "Hot Goods Temporary Restraining Orders under the Fair Labor Standards Act in the Agricultural Sector of the Economy: A Manual for Legal Assistance Programs." Manuscript.

Libber, Jonathan. 1999. "Impact of One Policy Change on EPA Enforcement Action." Manuscript, Environmental Protection Agency.

Logan, Jonathan. 2002. "Consultants, Lawyers and the Union-Free Movement in the United States since the 1970s." 33 *Industrial Relations Journal* 197–214.

Logan, John. 2007. "Lifting the Veil on Anti-Union Campaigns: Employer and Consultant Reporting under the LMRDA, 1959–2001," in Bruce Kaufman and David Lewin, eds., 15 *Advances in Industrial and Labor Relations* 295–332.

Polinsky, A.M., and Steven Shavell. 1998. "On Offense History and the Theory of Deterrence," 18 *International Review of Law and Economics* 305–24.

Polinsky, A.M., and Steven Shavell. 2000. "The Economic Theory of Public Enforcement of Law." 38 *Journal of Economic Literature* 45–76.

Smith, Robert. 1979. "The Impact of OSHA Inspections on Manufacturing Injury Rates." 14 *Journal of Human Resources* 145–70.

Sparrow, Malcolm. 2000. *The Regulatory Craft: Controlling Risks, Solving Problems, and Managing Compliance.* Washington, DC: Brookings Institution.

Stigler, George. 1971. "The Theory of Economic Regulation," 2 *Bell Journal of Economics and Management Science* 3–21.

Sunstein, Cass R., Daniel Kahnemann, David Schkade, and Ilana Ritov. 2002. "Predictably Incoherent Judgments." 54 *Stanford Law Review* 1153–215.

U.S. Departments of Labor and Commerce. 1994. "Commission on the Future of Worker-Management Relations," Fact-Finding Report, May.

U.S. Department of Labor, Bureau of Labor Statistics. 2012. "Union Members in 2011." March Supplements.

U.S. General Accounting Office (GAO). 1982. "Concerns Regarding the Impact of Employee Charges against Employers for Unfair Labor Practices." Washington, DC: Government Printing Office.

Wachter, Michael, 2007. "The Rise and Decline of Unions," 30 *Regulation* 23–9.

Wagner, Steven, 2002. "How Did the Taft-Hartley Act Come About?" George Mason University News Service, http://hnn.us/articles/1036.html.

Weil, David. 1991. "Enforcing OSHA: The Role of Labor Unions." 30 *Industrial Relations* 20–36.

Weil, David. 1999. "Are Mandated Health and Safety Committees Substitutes or Supplements for Labor Unions?" 52 *Industrial and Labor Relations Review* 339–60.

Weil, David. 2005. "Public Enforcement/Private Monitoring: Evaluating a New Approach to Regulating the Minimum Wage." 52 *Industrial and Labor Relations Review* 238–57.

Weil, David. 2008. "Mighty Monolith or Fractured Federation? Business Opposition and the Enactment of Workplace Legislation," in Annette Bernhardt, Heather Boushey, Laura Dresser, and Chris Tilly, eds., *The Gloves Off Economy: Problems and Possibilities at the Bottom of the Labor Market.* Champaign, IL: Labor and Employment Relations Association, pp. 287–314.

Weil, David. 2009. "Rethinking the Regulation of Vulnerable Work in the USA: A Sector-Based Approach," 51 *Journal of Industrial Relations* 411–30.

Weil, David. 2010. "Improving Workplace Conditions through Strategic Enforcement." Report to the Wage and Hour Division, U.S. Department of Labor.

Weil, David. 2011. "Exploring the Coherence of Workplace Penalties." Boston University School of Management, Working Paper.

Weil, David, and Carlos Mallo. 2007. "Regulating Labor Standards via Supply Chains: Combining Public/Private Interventions to Improve Workplace Compliance." 45 *British Journal of Industrial Relations* 805–28.

Weiler, Paul. 1983. "Promises to Keep: Securing Workers Rights to Self-Organization under the NLRA," 96 *Harvard Law Review* 1769–827.

Winter, Harold. 2008. *The Economics of Crime: An Introduction to Rational Crime Analysis.* London: Routledge.

8. The union as broker of employment rights
Stewart J. Schwab

Most employment-law rights are mandatory. Individual workers cannot decline the protections the law gives them. For example, a nonexempt worker must get at least $7.25 per hour and time-and-a-half for overtime, even if she would agree to less. A worker's pension must vest within five years. If she is injured on the job, a worker is entitled to compensation through a state system and cannot opt out in advance.

Interestingly, in these examples and others like them, the law forces its protection only on nonunionized workers. Unions in a collective bargaining contract can bargain away these rights, acting as broker in return for something more valuable to their workers.

This chapter examines the choice between waivable and mandatory employee rights and, in particular, whether some rights should be mandatory for individual workers but subject to negotiation by labor unions. Section I sets the stage with two examples. Section II explores why most employee rights are mandatory. Section III asks whether unions should be allowed to waive (or broker, to use a more palatable term) employee rights even when individuals cannot. Section IV documents the large degree to which current employment law already has this feature of mandatory individual rights that unions can broker. Section V then explores whether unions and society should welcome the role of union as broker.

I.   OPENING EXAMPLES OF UNION AS BROKER

Let me give two contrasting examples of union as broker to set the stage. The first example clearly shows the value of union waiver in some settings. The second example is the arbitral versus judicial forum, which is a more problematic use of union waiver.

Example 1: Union waiver of the eight-hour day for miners.   Consider the gold-mining industry on the California-Nevada border. Mining is brutal work, so in 1909 the California legislature passed a statute prohibiting work shifts longer than eight hours for underground miners.[1] While this statute may make sense in general, it did not optimally serve miners in San Bernardino County. Most miners there live far from the mines and commute three hours a day on narrow, winding roads to get to work. Because of the dangerous and tiring commute, they prefer a shorter workweek with 12-hour shifts compared to a longer workweek with eight-hour shifts. In 1983, the legislature amended the statute to permit 12-hour shifts if agreed to in a collective bargaining contract.[2] The unionized mines soon adopted 12-hour shifts, and the nonunion mines found themselves at a competitive disadvantage. After unsuccessfully petitioning the state labor agency for a waiver, they filed suit asking the federal court to strike down the more lenient treatment the statute gives for unionized mines. The district court held that the National Labor Relations Act (NLRA) preempts the state double standard; but the Ninth Circuit reversed and upheld the state statute allowing unionized mines to have 12-hour shifts while nonunion mines could have only eight-hour shifts.[3] In rejecting an equal protection challenge, the appellate court emphasized the greater bargaining power of unions, declaring that the legislature could rationally have believed that unionized workers have greater power to ensure safe working conditions than workers with individual employment agreements.

Four messages come from the example. First, one need not criticize the general law (here, the eight-hour shift rule) in order to see a valid role for union brokering of the law as applied to particular situations (here, to mines in a particular county with unique commuting patterns). Second, it illustrates that legislatures hesitate to allow individual workers to waive rights, for fear that their lack of bargaining power will force them to waive without any gain. Third, the example shows how unions can use legislative waivers to make unionized firms more competitive, benefiting their firms and their members. Finally, in this case the waiver was in the overall social interest as well as the workers' and the union's interest, but this point needs to be examined for particular statutes.

Example 2: Union or individual waiver of the right to court.   Title VII of the Civil Rights Act of 1964 was a landmark anti-discrimination statute, giving employees the right to go to federal court (after filing a charge with the Equal Employment Opportunity Commission) to complain of discrimination on the basis of race, color, sex, religion, or national origin. Title VII was the model for other anti-discrimination statutes protecting workers against, among other things, age and disability discrimination. The hallmark of these statutes was the right to haul the employer into federal court. Employers complained (Olson, 1997) as the number of discrimination claims skyrocketed (Clermont & Schwab, 2004). One response of employers to the burden of discrimination cases has been to create arbitration procedures for these claims, whether through the union grievance-arbitration system or, in a nonunion setting, through contracts with individual employees.

Whether unions or individual workers can waive the right to go to court over discrimination and other statutory claims (or, inversely, whether a pre-dispute arbitration agreement is enforceable) has a winding legal history and remains hotly contested. In its *Alexander v. Gardner-Denver* (1974) decision, the Supreme Court held that a unionized employee could bring a statutory discrimination claim to court, even though the employee had already lost an arbitration claim of unjust termination brought through a union grievance-arbitration procedure created by a collective bargaining agreement. *Gardner-Denver*'s effect was that a union could not waive an individual employee's right to go to court. In its later *Gilmer* (1991) and *Circuit City* (2001) decisions, the Supreme Court distinguished the union context of *Gardner-Denver* and enforced an agreement of individual employees to bring all statutory claims to arbitration, waiving their right to court. The Court emphasized a "tension between collective representation and individual statutory rights" that is not present when individuals agree to arbitration (*Gilmer*, 500 U.S. at 22).

More recently, the Court revived the union as broker of the right to a judicial forum. In *14 Penn Plaza v. Pyett* (2009), the Court upheld a collective bargaining agreement in which the union had agreed to arbitrate all employment discrimination claims arising under the ADEA. Finding nothing in the statute to preclude this choice of arbitral forum and satisfied that arbitration would protect the employees' substantive right to be free from discrimination, the Court refused to interfere in the bargained-for exchange between employer and union.

Both union and individual waivers of the right to go to court are controversial and in flux. Bills in Congress are afoot to reverse *14 Penn Plaza* and deny unions the power to waive their members' right to a judicial forum. Other bills propose to go further back in Supreme Court jurisprudence and reverse *Circuit City* and *Gilmer* by denying individual workers the power to waive a judicial forum to vindicate discrimination claims.[4] Indeed, the Franken Amendment now forbids government contractors from requiring workers to arbitrate title VII claims and other sexual harassment claims, although the language of this recent statute does not clearly cover collective agreements as well as individual agreements.[5]

All this turmoil invites two sets of questions, for individual waiver and union waiver: (1) Should individual workers want the power to waive a judicial forum for discrimination claims, and is it good public policy for individual workers to have this power; and (2) should unions want the power to waive a judicial forum for its members' discrimination claims, and should their members and public policy want unions to have this power?

On the individual-waiver questions, it is hard to distinguish whether individual workers should want the power from whether it is good public policy to allow it. In either case, as we will see, the concern is that an individual worker has little bargaining power and may have limited information and cognitive biases that prevent an appropriate decision.

On the union-waiver set of questions, the union may want this power as another chip in its bargaining arsenal. On the other hand, as we will explore, unions may feel that having the option to waive weakens their bargaining position or is not worth the exposure to costly duty of fair representation lawsuits if they do not arbitrate every case or make mistakes in the arbitral process. (It is worth pointing out that the union in *14 Penn Plaza* argued against letting the collective bargaining agreement waive a judicial forum, although it is hard to reconcile this litigation position with their actual bargaining behavior.) But even if unions want this power, it may not be in all of their members' interest, particularly minority members who may more highly value the right to go to court with discrimination claims than most members, who do not think much of this right. Unions have a long, albeit complicated, legacy of selling out the position of minority members. Finally, it is a distinctly third question whether public policy supports allowing union waiver in this context.

II.   THE MANDATORY NATURE OF EMPLOYEE RIGHTS

A.   The Rationale for Employment Laws

At its nineteenth-century, common-law, laissez-faire zenith, employment law gave most rights to employers, subject in principle to contractual waiver of the pro-employer default. For the last 100 years, workers have turned to the legislature (and more recently to the common-law courts) to change the rules. Employment laws often impose substantial costs on employers, and employers have vociferously complained. Various types of arguments justify employment laws, and often more than one for any particular law.

The usual rationale is that employment laws further some public policy. Society does not like the results of the "unregulated" labor market and so it intervenes. Within the broad category of intervention in the name of public policy are two types of intervention. First, the legislature may think that market imperfections lead to inefficient results that need correcting. Second, the legislature may think the market reaches results that are unfair, regardless of their efficiency.

An example of the first type – intervening to improve the efficiency of labor markets – may be the Employee Retirement Income Security Act (ERISA) (Freeman, 1976). A competitive labor market may provide too few pensions, in the sense that workers would prefer more of their compensation to be in the form of pensions than current wages. In a competitive market, employers look at the behavior of persons just deciding whether to work in determining the value of their pension package (i.e., firms look at whether employees are queuing up for the job or whether it is difficult to fill). But these new entrants are often younger workers, who value pensions less than most workers in the existing workforce. The older workers are trapped in their firms, however, and cannot easily signal their dissatisfaction with the level of pensions by quitting. In short, the market will be inefficient because pension rates are set according to the preferences of incoming workers who, relative to their older counterparts, prefer more in current wages and less in pensions. To remedy this, Congress enacted ERISA to encourage a higher level of pensions that workers could count on.

Probably more employment legislation is enacted because unregulated labor market outcomes are deemed too harsh rather than inefficient. Some of this legislation has distributive aims; the goal is to favor some or all workers, regardless of whether the overall pie grows or shrinks (Jolls, 2000). Some legislation is paternalistic. Even if workers are willing to trade safety for higher pay, for example, society is unwilling to allow it. The flip side of paternalism is that individuals may believe they could make themselves better off with their individual bargains than with the legislation. Where that is the case, the costs imposed by the legislation are greater than the benefits (measured by willingness and ability to pay) of the legislation. As I will show below, this means that people believe they can make themselves better off by rejecting the legislation.

Not all employment legislation is enacted with noble public policy as the goal, whether efficiency-enhancing or distributive. The public-choice theory of legislation emphasizes the coercive power of law and suggests that self-interested groups lobby for legislation that furthers their interests – rather than some larger public interest (Macey, 1986; Eskridge, Frickey & Garrett, 2000). A favorite employment-law example of public-choice theorists is the minimum wage provision of the Fair Labor Standards Act (FLSA) (29 U.S.C. § 206). Such legislation sets a floor on competition between workers for jobs. Although few union workers are directly affected by increases in the minimum wage, many empirical studies suggest that skilled or semi-skilled unionized workers are one of the prime beneficiaries of the minimum wage law, as the law prevents low-skilled workers from offering to work at a wage low enough to make them attractive compared to the higher-skilled and higher-priced workers (Burkhauser, Couch & Wittenburg, 2000; Card & Krueger, 1997; Welch, 1974).

B.   Why Make Employee Rights Mandatory?

It is not the purpose of this chapter to critique or assess the rationales described above for employment rights. I can assume (but don't have to assume for my argument) that the employment law in question has an appropriate overall social purpose. Whatever their reasons for intervening on behalf of employees, policymakers must still implicitly or explicitly decide whether to make the rights inalienable, which should turn at least in part on whether alienability is consistent with the rationale for the law in the first place.

Inalienability of individual employment rights can be defended on a few different grounds. First, some laws are enacted not to protect the affected workers but to protect others. Thus, the rights are forced on the affected workers regardless of what they individually want. The FLSA's wage and overtime provisions, for example, are sometimes explained as an attempt to prevent those workers who are willing to work long hours at low wages from undercutting.[6] If this is the purpose of the law, it is undercut by allowing workers to opt out, because the opting-out, undercutting workers harm the workers we want to protect. In a similar vein, suppose workers care about their relative income, not just how well off they are individually. In that case, worker A, by agreeing to work in a dangerous factory for an extra $10,000, hurts the relative income ranking of worker B. Occupational Safety and Health Administration (OSHA) regulations mandating safety can prevent this prisoner's dilemma by mandating safe factories. Each worker prefers a safe factory to an unsafe factory but only if the others do not sell their safety for higher wages. If OSHA regulations were waivable, the rat race would continue (Akerlof, 1976; Frank, 1985; McAdams, 1992).

The protection of a workplace public good is another rationale for making employment rights mandatory. A workplace public good is often underproduced because it is inherently non-excludable and nonrival (Samuelson, 1954). When the employer provides the benefit to one worker, it necessarily provides the benefit to other workers at little or no extra cost. For example, workplace safety is generally a public good, in that other workers at the same plant benefit at little or no cost once a single worker has, say, clean air, adequate lighting, or a safe production-line speed. An employee who initiates an OSHA inspection also benefits other workers from the abatement of the health and safety risk, but often bears the cost of initiating the inspection (the wrath of the employer) alone. An individual worker may rationally decline to bear the costs of a non-mandatory public good, hoping that another employee will bear the costs and all will benefit. For employment rights that secure public goods, making them waivable would reinstate the collective action problem the law sought to address.

A third rationale for making employment rights mandatory emphasizes the limited information workers have about the costs and benefits of many workplace goods. Individual employees often lack the necessary information to make an informed choice on whether to waive an employment right. Sometimes the information rationale for mandating rights is strongly paternalistic.[7] Policymakers believe misguided workers do not know what is in their best interest and so will foolishly waive a protection if allowed to do so. Additionally, workers may not understand the legal effect of a waiver and believe there is no harm in signing one (Kim, 1995; 1997). In other cases, particularly where employment protections involve technical data (e.g., OSHA health rights) or rights stretching out for decades (e.g., pension rights), the information rationale is weakly paternalistic. In these situations, the argument for inalienability is that workers cannot process the information or intelligently assess the risks, but if they could, they themselves would demand the protection.

Behavioral decision theory provides additional reasons for making employee rights inalienable. Workers are often risk optimists, underestimating the dangers of their work and overestimating their own ability to avoid hazards. People are particularly bad at accurately assessing low-probability events, which characterize many workplace risks such as the risk of workplace fatalities or wrongful discharge. Workers are myopic and thus have particular difficulty assessing the value of far-off events like retirement pensions (Rachlinski, 2003; Sunstein, 2002; Weiss, 1991).

Perhaps the most common reason for mandating rights is the weak bargaining power of individual workers. The fear is that workers would waive an alienable right without getting anything in return, making the legislation pointless (Schwab, 1988). For example, suppose an employee has accepted a job paying $50,000 with 10 days' vacation. Now the legislature enacts a vacation law that says a worker gets 15 days' vacation unless he or she waives the right. Will the law have any effect? The argument of no effect is that the employer will ask, and the employee will agree, to initial a vacation-law waiver and then sign the same contract for $50,000 and 10 days' vacation. People renting automobiles, for example, seem to initial waivers all the time without much hesitation or much in return for the waiver.

Counter-arguments exist to the view that giving an alienable employment right to a worker without bargaining power is giving nothing at all. Perhaps the worker will hesitate to initial a waiver, worrying that the statute reflects the approach that suits most people.[8] Cognitive biases such as anchoring effects, framing effects, and endowment effects mean that initial presumptions in statutes matter. Richard Thaler and Cass Sunstein (2009) have argued that policymakers can effectively use default rather than mandatory rules to nudge people in a wide range of situations to further "libertarian paternalism." We do not have to resolve the debates here, and can simply conclude that in many cases where workers have little bargaining power, a waivable right may not be much of a right at all.

Policymakers in such cases are left with a tradeoff in creating an employment right. If they are confident workers and the world are better off with their intervention, then rights can be made mandatory. But wise policymakers are often less sure of the appropriate outcome, or recognize that policymakers themselves are subject to cognitive biases and other limitations that sometimes make their policy prescriptions less than ideal (Rachlinski & Farina, 2002). Further, the appropriate outcome for some workers often is inappropriate for others, but legislators might have difficulty creating laws tailored to individual situations. Indeed, rules (as opposed to standards) by definition apply broadly to parties in many situations, not all of whom benefit from the rule. If the over-inclusiveness and under-inclusiveness of the rule is too great, policymakers may prefer a presumption, allowing parties to opt out if the policy is not appropriate for their circumstances. But as just discussed, allowing opt-outs may undercut the rationale for the employment right in the first place, if the right is a public good, or if limited information or cognitive biases prevent workers from accurately assessing the value of the right, or if individual workers have no bargaining power to get something in exchange for opting out.

III.   THE UNION AS BROKER

An intermediate solution exists to the dilemma of overly wooden mandates, on the one hand, and waiver by powerless individuals with limited information, on the other. That solution is to create a right that is mandatory at the individual-worker level but allows workers collectively through the union to waive the protection in favor of other benefits.

We identified above five dangers associated with allowing individual workers to waive rights: (1) undercutting or rat-race problems; (2) workplace public goods; (3) limited information; (4) cognitive biases; and (5) weak bargaining power. Let's now examine the dangers in turn to see if union brokers can overcome them.

The rat race occurs when an individual worker can get ahead of other workers by waiving a costly employment benefit such as workplace safety or maximum hours, even if each worker prefers the safety or shorter hours as long as others get them also. If the rat race occurs within the collective bargaining unit, a union can alleviate it. For example, suppose the rat race takes the form of a contest where the most productive line worker is promoted to foreman. Each worker takes on more and more hours in hopes of a promotion. An hours law limiting the workweek to 40 hours will have no effect if individual workers can waive the limitation and work an hour more than other workers, thereby setting off a rat race. But what if 40 hours is below the optimal amount for a particular worksite, all things considered, even if 40 hours is the optimal number for a national law? A union could prevent the local rat race by negotiating a collective bargaining agreement that calls for 45 hours, which workers locally might prefer to 40 hours. Without the union, the rat race might escalate to 50 or 60 hours to the detriment of workers. Union brokering cannot prevent a rat race when some of the rats in the race are beyond the collective bargaining unit. In that case, a mandatory right rather than union-broker right is needed to solve the issue.

In a similar vein, union brokering does not undermine workplace public goods in the same way that individual waivers do. An individual worker, considering whether to exercise or waive a public-good right, may waive the right even when the overall benefits to workers exceed costs, hoping to free ride on others who exercise the right. Avoiding this problem was the public-goods argument for a mandate. But the role of the union in bargaining is to consider the costs and benefits to all workers of exercising or brokering the right for something better. By internalizing the benefits to all workers in its calculus, it avoids the free-rider issue of workplace public goods.

Inadequate information is also a lesser problem for unions than individual workers, because unions have more information at their disposal and thus can make more informed decisions. Individual workers have great difficulty knowing about safety records, legal rights, and other items critical to deciding between jobs. Unions have research departments and are repeat players on many issues, learning from experience. Further, the National Labor Relations Act commands employers to bargain in good faith, with a subsidiary duty to provide the union with information to substantiate claims made during negotiations.[9]

What about the cognitive limitations that make individual waiver so problematic? Can a union avoid making the same kinds of erroneous judgments that their members might, given that unions are composed of those very same people? Unions likely have a psychological perspective on workplace risk that differs from that of the individual in two ways: First, unions lack the personal investment in avoiding injury that seems to give rise to an excess of optimism. Unions thereby can see problems from an outsider's perspective, which can reduce cognitive errors in judgment (Kahneman & Lovallo, 1995). Second, unions see workplace risk as a repeated issue that comes up in the aggregate, not one case at a time. Psychologists have found that looking at problems in an aggregate or frequentist perspective (e.g., 10 out of 100) can reduce the influence of some kinds of cognitive errors in judgment (Gigerenzer, 1991). Unions have a broader perspective on the tradeoffs than do individual workers. Workers operate from the inside while unions can step back and take an outsider's view. In doing so, unions can avoid cognitive problems that arise from taking problems one at a time (Rachlinski, 2000).

Finally, unions have bargaining power and, unlike individual workers, will not be coerced into waiving rights without getting something in return. The give and take of collective bargaining is far different from the form contracts and shopping among job offers that characterize "bargaining" in the individual context. In collective bargaining, a presumption favoring the union could strengthen its negotiating posture even if the presumption is waivable. With the presumption favoring the union, management must raise the issue if it wants change. Speaking first often weakens one's bargaining position. The idea is that unions will broker rights while individual workers waive rights. Unions will keep the rights that workers value most highly and trade less-valued rights for other benefits, while individual workers might receive nothing in return for their waiver (Schwab, 1987).

In sum, unions are often in a better position relative to individuals when it comes to brokering employment rights. Unions can prevent local rat races and promote local public goods, have more resources to gather and disseminate relevant information, are not subject to the full array of cognitive biases to which individuals are prone, and have superior bargaining power.

IV.   EXISTING EXAMPLES OF UNION BROKER OF WORKER RIGHTS

In contrast to the harsh attitude employment law takes toward individual workers waiving rights, the law often allows unions to broker rights of their members. Union waiver of rights is simply not as suspect as waiver by individual workers. This power for unions to waive rights gives unions a potential role as broker of employment-law rights.

This section outlines the various ways that current law allows unions to broker rights on behalf of members. The section's overall purpose is to show that "union as broker" is a current role of unions and not a wild-eyed dream. The section has two parts. First, I review the principles underlying union waiver of labor-law rights, to set the stage with a union brokering role that is familiar to the labor-law community. Second, I examine the current role of unions in brokering employment-law claims. This has two parts: first I review § 301 preemption of unionized workers' employment-law claims. Then I scan the broad array of employment laws in which unions currently can act as brokers – ranging from ERISA and FLSA to state wage law.

Previous commentators have extensively analyzed union waiver of labor law rights, as distinct from employment rights – that is, the waiver of rights of workers to form unions, strike, and bargain collectively or to refrain from doing so (Brosseau, 1980; Harper, 1981a; 1981b; Westman, 1974). More recently, commentators have analyzed § 301 preemption, whereby workers with rights under a collective bargaining agreement enforceable under federal law may be preempted from bringing similar claims under state law. Largely uncharted in the academic literature is the degree to which employment rights by their own terms apply differently to unionized workers (early efforts include Schwab, 1989; Estreicher, 1996).

A.   Union Waiver of Labor-Law Rights

A prime purpose behind the National Labor Relations Act (NLRA) of 1935 was to increase the bargaining power of workers through collective action. Individual workers, it was thought, had no strength to resist employer demands and would be coerced into relinquishing, in the name of freedom of contract, any putative rights the law might give them. As Senator Wagner, chief sponsor of the Wagner Act, put it:

> We are forced to recognize the futility of pretending that there is equality of freedom when a single workman, with only his job between his family and ruin, sits down to draw a contract of employment with a representative of a tremendous organization having thousands of workers at its call. Thus the right to bargain collectively . . . is a veritable charter of freedom of contract; without it there would be slavery by contract.[10]

In the early days of the NLRA, the Board and courts made clear that individual workers could not waive certain basic rights the Act gave them (Phillips, 1986). Thus the infamous "yellow dog" contracts – whereby individual workers promised never to exercise their right to join a union – were held to be unenforceable; even to propose such a contract was an unfair labor practice.[11] Individual contracts regulating how workers would select a union have likewise been held void because they differed from the Act's procedures.[12] Nor can individual workers (or the union) waive their § 8(a)(4) right to file charges before the Board without retaliation.[13]

In contrast to the prohibition against individual workers contracting away their labor-law rights, the NLRA readily countenances waiver of some Section 7 rights by unions. The preferred status of unions in waiving rights was emphasized in *NLRB v. Allis-Chalmers Mfg. Co.* (1967). The issue was whether a union-imposed fine on members who crossed the picket line during a lawful economic strike violated individual members' § 7 rights not to assist unions. The Court ruled the union did not violate its members' rights. In the Supreme Court's words, the Act "extinguishes the individual employee's power to order his own relations with his employer and creates a power vested in the chosen representative to act in the interests of all employees." Justice Black, dissenting, bemoaned that allowing union waiver means that "by joining a union an employee gives up or waives some of his § 7 rights."

Unions routinely bargain away labor-law rights of their members, both when negotiating contracts and processing individual grievances.[14] Indeed, unions regularly treat rights that are central to labor law as bargaining chips to be traded for employer concessions on other issues.[15] The clearest example is the typical no-strike clause in a collective bargaining contract. At the heart of the National Labor Relations Act is its protection of the right of workers to strike. Section 8(a)(1) of the Act makes firing workers for striking an unfair labor practice and § 13 specifically declares that "nothing in this act shall be construed as to diminish in any way the right to strike" (29 U.S.C. § 163 (1988)). Nonetheless, unions commonly waive the right of their members to strike,[16] sometimes even waiving the right to strike in protest against employer unfair labor practices.[17] We think nothing of this waiver; indeed, much of federal labor law is designed to encourage unions to waive the right to strike.[18]

Besides the right to strike, unions routinely waive other labor-law rights. Most important is the very right to bargain collectively. The mere existence of a certified union denies workers the right to bargain collectively with their employer in any other group, without any formal waiver of bargaining rights. An employer that bargains with any other group commits an unfair labor practice.[19] Further, a union often waives its own right to bargain during the term of a collective bargaining agreement through express "zipper" clauses or "management rights" clauses, through bargaining history, or through inaction.[20]

A more esoteric waiver of rights occurs when unions waive their members' *Weingarten* rights. In *NLRB v. J. Weingarten, Inc.* (1975), the Supreme Court held that the NLRA granted employees the right to have a union representative present during interrogations they reasonably believe may result in discipline. After some confusion, it is now clear that a union can waive this right in a collective bargaining agreement.[21] The Board has flip-flopped on a parallel right for nonunion workers to have a coworker present at a disciplinary interview, although the current rule gives no *Weingarten* right to nonunion workers (Higgins, 2006, pp. 225–35). All indications are that nonunion workers cannot waive whatever *Weingarten* rights they have under prevailing Board law. In the eras when all workers have the right, it is an example where unions can waive a right that nonunion employees cannot waive. An employer who feels strongly about conducting disciplinary interviews in private would be better off, all else equal, with a unionized workforce that could put such a waiver into a collective bargaining contract. If the union were a good broker who got more value in return for the waiver, employees would be better off as well.

In addition to bargaining away rights during contract negotiations, unions frequently waive rights when processing grievances or settling unfair labor practice charges. Courts sometimes acknowledge openly that they tolerate union settlements more readily than when individual workers settle cases. For example, in *Oil, Chemical and Atomic Workers v. NLRB* (1986), a union filed unfair labor practice charges on behalf of workers who were permanently replaced when they stopped work to protest unsafe working conditions. The NLRB eventually approved settlements between the employer and individual employees whereby the employees received small cash payments but waived all legal claims, including any right to reinstatement. Upon the union's petition for review, the court of appeals reversed the Board's approval of individual settlements. In an opinion by Judge Harry Edwards, a former labor law professor, the court recognized that the Board often encourages settlements between a union and the employer as furthering the collective bargaining and arbitration process. No such collective policy was furthered, however, when an individual employer settled unfair labor practice complaints with individual workers. The court remanded for further reasons why the Board should approve individual settlements.

Not all labor-law rights are waivable by unions. Unions cannot waive the rights of members freely to discuss and choose their representative. At a basic level, this means sensibly that a union cannot lock itself in as representative by waiving the right of workers to vote for another or no union. But the employees' right to choose their representative is broader than just the right to vote; for example, the union normally cannot validly waive the rights of members to distribute union literature at work (*NLRB v. Magnavox*, 1974). Nor can a union waive statutory rights that benefit third parties, such as the Act's prohibitions on hot-cargo agreements and secondary boycotts, on closed shops, and on hiring halls that favor union members.[22]

It is hard to articulate an overarching principle governing when a union can waive labor-law rights (Brousseau, 1980; Harper, 1981a; 1981b). Whatever the specific line between waivable and inalienable NLRA rights, three lessons are clear. First, labor policy encourages unions to waive rights, even "fundamental" rights like the right to strike. Second, the basic reason for accepting union waiver is that unions have the bargaining power that individual workers lack. Third, labor policy becomes skittish about union waiver when the union waives rights important for the democratic nature of the union, particularly the right of dissidents to challenge union leadership.

Unions can fairly portray their power to waive labor-law rights as a "win-win" situation for the unionized workplace. The average worker benefits from waiver because the union will not broker rights without receiving something preferable in return. Employers benefit because they can escape certain costly restraints or conditions. The mere existence of a union prevents bargaining with splinter groups of workers, and channels and filters worker demands and complaints. By contract, the union can waive other labor-law rights, the most important being the right to strike, the right to bargain continuously over mandatory subjects, and the right to route unfair labor practice complaints to the Board rather than through private arbitration. Overall, union waiver of labor rights is commonplace and beneficial to workers, assuming the union adequately represents the interests of its members.[23]

B.   Union as Broker of Employment-Law Rights

As outlined earlier, workers have a panoply of employment rights under federal and state statutes and the common law. This section surveys this panoply to illustrate where unions have a role in brokering rights, usually by negotiating language in a collective bargaining agreement that alters what would otherwise be the employment rights of covered workers.

1.   Section 301 preemption of unionized workers' employment rights
A collective bargaining agreement regulates many aspects of the employer-employee relationship, and typically creates a grievance-arbitration procedure to resolve disputes about this regulation. This regulation often overlaps with statutory or common-law employment rights of workers. For example, suppose a collective bargaining agreement creates disability insurance for injured workers, complete with a union-management panel to resolve disputes. A worker upset with erratic disability payments wants to bring a tort action complete with punitive damages alleging bad-faith handling of his insurance claim. May the worker sue in tort, or is his sole avenue the grievance-arbitration

procedure established by the collective bargaining procedure? These are the facts of *Allis-Chalmers Corp. v. Lueck* (1985), and a unanimous Supreme Court held that the tort claim was preempted.

The rationale for preemption comes from § 301(a) of the Labor-Management Relations Act (LMRA), which gives the federal courts jurisdiction to enforce collective bargaining agreements (29 U.S.C. § 1985(a) (1988)). The Supreme Court had earlier held that the LMRA requires a uniform body of federal common law to govern § 301 cases (*Textile Workers Union v. Lincoln Mills*, 1957). State-law claims that might upset the uniformity of interpreting collective bargaining agreements must be preempted. In *Lueck*, the Court required preemption of state claims where "resolution of the state-law claim is substantially dependent upon analysis of the terms of [a collective bargaining agreement]" (id. at 220).

Section 301 does not preempt all state claims with fact patterns amenable to grievance arbitration, as the Supreme Court made clear in *Lingle v. Norge Division* (1988). Lingle, working under a collective bargaining contract that protected her against being fired without just cause, was fired after she filed a workers' compensation claim. The union filed a grievance on her behalf, and ultimately the arbitrator ordered reinstatement with back pay. Meanwhile, Lingle filed a tort suit in Illinois state court for retaliatory discharge.[24] The Supreme Court held that § 301 did not preempt the tort claim even though the state court must analyze the same facts as the arbitrator. Rather, the issue is whether the state claim is "independent" of the collective bargaining agreement in that it "can be resolved without interpreting the agreement itself."

The employee in *Lingle* had argued a more expansive theory of non-preemption that, if accepted, would have eliminated differential treatment of employment claims by union workers in most cases. The employee had emphasized that, under Illinois law, the right to be free from retaliatory discharge is nonnegotiable and applies to union and nonunion workers alike. The employee argued that nonnegotiability by individuals should by itself mean that the state right could not be preempted by a collective bargaining contract. The Court rejected this analysis, however, declaring that neither nonnegotiable rights nor rights given to all state workers would ensure non-preemption. Further, the Court emphasized that union waiver of individual, non-preempted state law rights was a separate issue from § 301 preemption and left open the possibility of such union waiver if it were "clear and unmistakable."

Whether unions could waive state-law rights was touched on in a later Supreme Court case on § 301 preemption, *Livadas v. Bradshaw* (1994). When Livadas, a unionized worker, was fired, she demanded to be immediately paid the wages owed her, as guaranteed to all California workers by state law. Her store manager refused to pay immediately, however, saying company policy required that the last paycheck be mailed from the central office. Livadas complained to the California Labor Commissioner but the agency refused to process her complaint because she was covered by a collective bargaining agreement with an arbitration clause. She sued the Labor Commissioner, complaining that this policy against pursuing state-law claims of unionized workers was preempted as interfering with the federal right to bargain collectively. The Labor Commissioner defended by arguing that state processing of wage claims based on a collective bargaining agreement would itself be preempted by § 301. The Supreme Court agreed with the employee and held that the Commissioner could not refuse to vindicate unionized workers' state-law claim to prompt payment of wages simply because they worked under a collective bargaining agreement.

Most importantly for us, however, the Supreme Court made clear that state statutes creating employment rights could have opt-out provisions for unionized workers ("These 'opt-out' statutes are thus manifestly different in their operation (and their effect on federal rights) from the Commission's rule that an employee forfeits his state-law rights the moment a collective bargaining agreement with an arbitration clause is entered into." Id. at 131–2). Several amici had emphasized the broad array of state and federal laws that allow unions to waive protection for their members. The Court recognized the validity of opt-out statutes but distinguished them from the *Livadas* statute, which covered all employees without regard to union status, and noted there was no indication the union purported to bargain away the protections of the state statute merely by creating a grievance-arbitration procedure. Merely having a collective bargaining agreement with an arbitration procedure is insufficient to infer a waiver. We discuss these opt-out statutes in the next section.

The AFL-CIO argued for this distinction between state laws that allow unions to opt out and state laws that mandate a right only for nonunion workers. In the *Livadas* case, the AFL-CIO amicus brief urged a narrow holding, cautioning that "courts have just begun to consider preemption challenges raised in relation to state minimum standard laws that distinguish between unionized and nonunionized workplaces." Still, the AFL-CIO suggested support for a "nuanced" state law that allowed unionized workers to opt out if they bargained for "similar but not necessarily identical protections," because such an opt-out law "facilitates collective bargaining rather than punishes its exercise," even though it argued for preemption of the California policy that processed wage-payment claims only of nonunionized workers.

Since the Supreme Court decisions in *Lueck* and *Livadas*, lower courts have preempted dozens of state-law claims by unionized employees under § 301 while recognizing others, depending on whether the claim would require interpretation of the collective bargaining contract (see Higgins, 2006).[25] The line is not simply between tort and contract or between negotiable and nonnegotiable state-law rights, although both those lines have been articulated in the cases. Section 301 preempts most common-law claims with a contractual foundation, even if they sound in tort, including breach of the covenant of good faith and fair dealing, fraud and misrepresentation, tortious interference with contractual relations, and mishandling of health insurance or medical leave. They also include many privacy claims including improper drug testing (see Kim, 2006), which typically claim the employer created and then violated zones of privacy and thereby require interpretation of the collective bargaining contract and workplace norms it created. But the range of preempted claims is vast, ranging from wrongful discharge to misappropriation of trade secrets.[26]

Some courts have gone a long way toward preempting state-law claims based on general or boilerplate language. In *Jackson v. Liquid Carbonic Corp.* (1988), for example, a unionized employee was terminated after failing an employer drug test. He sued in state court for violation of the state constitutional right to privacy and a state privacy statute. The First Circuit held that § 301 preempted the state-law claims. The collective bargaining agreement had a general clause giving management the right "to post reasonable rules and regulations from time to time." Because this clause might give the employer the right to institute a drug test, the court would have to interpret the collective bargaining agreement in judging the state-law claim, something that § 301 forbids. Other courts require more specific language to trigger preemption.

Unions can use § 301 preemption to broker rights. By agreeing to specific language in the collective bargaining agreement that addresses state-law rights, presumably in return for worker benefits elsewhere in the agreement, the union shields the employer from a bevy of state-law claims. But § 301 preemption is an unpredictable blunderbuss, difficult to aim and uncertain in result. In particular, preemption based on the mere existence of a collective bargaining agreement is dangerous for unions and for workers, because it is unlikely the union received anything in return for the elimination of a state right. If the very existence of a collective bargaining agreement deprives workers of rights that nonunion workers enjoy, that is hardly a selling point for unions. This is why the AFL-CIO argued in *Livadas* for preemption of state laws that give rights to nonunion but not union workers, while arguing for the legitimacy of opt-out statutes whereby all workers have the state-law right unless language in the collective agreement alters the right.

C.   Employment Statutes with Collective Bargaining Opt-Outs

If § 301 preemption is a blunderbuss with unpredictable net benefits for unionized workers, opt-out statutes can be an effective tool with win-win benefits for workers and employers. Many employment laws, both federal and state, by their express terms apply differently to unionized workforces. Others allow unions to opt out or alter the general protections given workers. This section cannot catalogue all the state and federal employment laws with this feature. Rather, the goal here is to highlight important opportunities for union brokering and also to describe a few esoteric laws to give a sense of the dazzling variety of employment laws where union brokering can occur. The unifying theme in these union-waiver provisions is the legislative belief that unionized workforces do not need the full array of mandatory protections afforded weaker, nonunion workers.

State laws   A slew of state laws create employment rights that allow unions to opt out of the claims. Section I described the California law that mandates eight-hour work shifts for miners but allows a collective bargaining agreement to agree to shifts as long as 12 hours. Such opt-outs are a common feature in state statutes regulating wage payments, maximum hours, overtime, meal and rest requirements, and the like.[27] For example, in Vermont, employers must pay weekly wages within six days, but if a collective bargaining agreement calls for it, the paycheck can relate back 13 days.[28] Oregon mandates that employers immediately pay a terminated employee all earned wages unless a collective bargaining agreement provides otherwise.[29] Nevada mandates overtime pay after eight hours per day or 40 hours per week unless a collective bargaining contract says otherwise.[30] Illinois mandates a 20-minute meal break after five hours of work in a seven-and-a-half hour day unless different meal periods are established by a collective bargaining agreement.[31] Collective bargaining agreements can alter state law requirements regulating health insurance and personnel files.[32] In Montana, collective bargaining agreements can opt out of mandatory health and safety devices.[33] In

Arkansas, a collective bargaining agreement is not bound by the minimum-wage provisions of state law.[34]

ERISA   The Employee Retirement Income Security Act (ERISA) of 1974 is a complex statute regulating employer- and union-provided pension and other benefit plans (29 U.S.C. §§ 1001–461). One goal of ERISA is to encourage employers to extend benefits beyond top employees to contingent or lower-paid workers. The pension vesting requirements are a major way that ERISA attempts to protect workers who do not spend a career with a single employer.[35] ERISA requires that pension benefits completely vest (i.e., become non-forfeitable) after five years of service.[36] Compared to the lengthy requirements typical before ERISA, five-year vesting ensures that transient workers can accrue pension benefits.

Some unionized workers, however, are subject to less protective ten-year vesting requirements. In a provision added in 1986,[37] ERISA allows a multiemployer plan established by one or more collective bargaining agreements to have ten-year cliff vesting,[38] meaning that a worker can be required to wait ten years before earning any non-forfeitable pension benefits. This late-vesting exception for unionized workers is an important example of the brokering potential for unions. Apparently, both management and labor saw the provision as a potential weapon for unions when the exception was debated in Congress. Ironically, but consistent with the thesis that unions can benefit from brokering opportunities, unions pushed for lesser vesting protection for their members, while management feared giving unions this waiver opportunity.[39] Congress apparently bought the union argument that unionized employees did not need the rapid vesting schedule because they could take care of themselves through collective bargaining. Business interests opposed the relaxed vesting standards for multiemployer union plans because it would give unionized firms a competitive edge.[40] These anti-union analysts recognized that unions could benefit their firms – and thus "skew" decision-making on whether management should oppose unions – by brokering short-vesting rights that are onerous to management and not particularly useful to their members. In short, these anti-union analysts feared empowering the "union as broker" by allowing more lax regulation of unionized firms.

ERISA also gives lesser protection to unionized workers in its nondiscrimination requirements. The nondiscrimination requirements, which are perhaps the most technical sections in a technical statute, are designed to encourage employers to spread pension benefits to lower-paid workers. If the employer wants its pension and benefits plans to receive the tax breaks that ERISA gives a "qualified" plan[41] (and all employers want this), it must not discriminate in favor of highly compensated employees.[42] For example (and simplifying grossly), wage earners cannot receive lower pension benefits in percentage terms than high-paid salaried workers. ERISA excludes from the discrimination analysis "employees who are included in a unit of employees covered by an agreement which the Secretary of Labor finds to be a collective bargaining agreement between employee representatives and one or more employers, if there is evidence that retirement benefits were the subject of good faith bargaining . . ." (26 U.S.C. § 410(b)(3)(A)). Thus, unions can waive the right of its wage-earning members to receive as generous a pension as highly compensated officials of the company.[43]

Congress enacted this provision for two primary reasons: to allow employees represented by unions to pursue other (presumably more desirable) forms of compensation as an alternative to mandated pension benefits, and to make it more likely that non-union employees will benefit from membership in a qualified plan.[44] Unionized workers are sufficiently protected, under ERISA policy, by the procedural requirement that the union consciously bargain about retirement benefits.

Another ERISA provision, added in the Comprehensive Omnibus Budget Reconciliation Act of 1986 (COBRA), prohibits employers from initiating certain pension plan terminations where the action would violate the terms of an existing bargaining agreement (29 U.S.C. § 1341).[45] This might seem to discourage employers from dealing with a collective bargaining representative, but the legislative history indicates that the provision exists merely to codify prior court cases in which union contracts were construed as denying the employer the right to terminate unilaterally.[46]

FLSA   The Fair Labor Standards Act also allows unions to waive rights that are mandatory for nonunion workers. The Act prohibits employers from imposing a workweek longer than 40 hours unless hours in excess of 40 hours are compensated at "one and one-half times the regular rate" (29 U.S.C. § 207(a)(1) (1988)). However, the Act allows special workweek arrangements where collective bargaining agreements are involved. Employers need not pay time-and-a-half where union contracts provide for no more than 1,040 hours of work during a 26-week period,[47] or under certain circumstances where union workers are required to work no more than 2,240 hours during a period of 52 weeks.[48]

Congress apparently enacted the special workweek provisions for union-negotiated contracts to allow more flexible scheduling for industries such as mining and timber, which found it more efficient to employ workers for longer hours over discrete periods of time because of the remote location of their operations.[49] However, evidence of actual inclusion of such provisions in collective bargaining agreements is sparse indeed,[50] and early decisions showed that courts would give the special provision a narrow scope (see *Cabunac v. National Terminals Corp.*, 1944).

The Walsh-Healey Act provides another example of union waiver of overtime provisions (41 U.S.C. § 35 et seq.). The Walsh-Healey Act sets employment standards for federal contracts exceeding $10,000. The Act limits the workweek of employees of these contractors to 40 hours (41 U.S.C. § 35(b)). However, the section also cross-references the union-waiver provision of the Fair Labor Standards Act, thereby allowing longer workweeks as long as the employees do not exceed the maximum number of hours under FLSA for 26 weeks or 52 weeks (41 U.S.C. § 35(b)).

WARN Act   The Worker Adjustment and Retraining Notification (WARN) Act requires employers to give 60 days' advance notice before a mass layoff or plant closure. The warning procedure is technical and generally requires that the employer individually notify in writing every employee that might be affected (29 U.S.C. § 2102(a)(1)). If the employees are represented by a union, however, written notice to the union is sufficient (29 U.S.C. § 2102(a)(1)). Thus, a unionized employer can give WARN Act notice to workers for the cost of a stamp, while nonunion employers must go through the greater administrative expense of individual notification.

V.   ASSESSING THE UNION AS BROKER OF EMPLOYMENT RIGHTS

Let's get out of the weeds of individual examples and survey the swamp.

A.   Do Unions Want the Brokering Role?

Whether unions want a brokering role for employment rights is ultimately a question of bargaining power. If the union has sufficient bargaining power, it can decline to waive a valuable right but agree to negotiate over rights of less value. This power to negotiate should make its members better off. This chapter has documented instances where unions have embraced the brokering role, such as in the eight- versus 12-hour miners' day discussed in Section I. Overall, the chapter suggests that it would be in unions' interest to seriously consider the brokering role when lobbying over other employment statutes.

Still, unions often hesitate to take on this brokering role. For example, in the second example in Section I, we noted that the union in *14 Penn Plaza* argued against the brokering role that the Supreme Court ultimately endorsed – by which a collective bargaining agreement could force workers' statutory discrimination claims into arbitration and waive their right to go to court. Why would unions want to eliminate the possibility of trading rights? Under the perspective of this chapter, this is like asking when unions might willingly bind themselves to the mast like Odysseus.

One reason for unions rejecting the brokering role is that it may be complicated to justify a waiver to the membership. In the course of lengthy negotiations, it may be difficult to point to or quantify what was received in return for the waiver. For example, the union may have waived the right to an eight-hour day, but what did it get in exchange? Indeed, dissatisfied members who think the union sold them out might bring a lawsuit claiming a breach of the union's duty of fair representation, a costly and embarrassing lawsuit for a union to defend.

More generally, the value of the brokering role comes in finding win-win bargaining solutions with the employer. This requires flexibility, trust, and compromise. A union can easily be tarred as being conciliatory or even a company-controlled union if it concedes a right without a clear quid pro quo. Additionally, flexibility sometimes reduces bargaining strength. If the union burns its bridges, management knows the union cannot concede and so management may be more conciliatory. Unions attempt such postures today, with rallying cries such as "No backward steps." By the same token, unions may be in a stronger bargaining position overall if they can simply keep certain issues off the table as being inalienable. This is especially true when workers clearly value the right more than it costs employers. It may complicate bargaining with no payoff to the union to make a right formally waivable where members would never be better off from a waiver.

This suggests that unions should want a statute-by-statute approach to waivers. When a right is clearly worth more to workers than it costs employers, there is little to gain from bargaining, and the union should not want the statute to permit union brokering. But when it is less clear that workers value the right so highly, or the right clearly costs management a great deal to provide, the union may gain if the statute permits a brokering role.

B.   Does Society Want the Union as Broker?

Even when the union benefits from a brokering role, is it good public policy to allow unions to opt out of employment rights? This question has no single answer. First, if unions cannot be expected to faithfully represent their members, the legislature should balk at allowing unions to waive their members' rights. Whether and when the interests of union leaders and members are aligned is a big issue, worthy of a separate inquiry (Schwab, 1992). Second, even if the union democratically reflects the interests of its median member, some statutes are designed to protect the rights of individual or minority workers against majority control. The antidiscrimination laws immediately come to mind. It would be folly to allow a collective bargaining contract to waive the protection of Title VII for its members. Even if unions represent the majority, that majority might well agree with the employer to sell out the minority. Thus, public policy calls for some rights to be inalienable to union brokering. Some would argue that allowing unions to agree to arbitration of discrimination claims is in this category.

Laws enacted to protect third parties outside the workplace should also be immune from union brokering. Thus, a union's waiver of the right of its employees to sue for violation of public policies extending beyond the workplace would harm society at large. Common-law protections guard against discharge for the refusal to commit an unlawful act, fulfilling a public obligation, or whistleblowing. In *Nees v. Hocks* (1975), for example, the Oregon Supreme Court recognized the wrongful-discharge claim of an employee fired for being absent because of jury service, reasoning that the public policy of protecting the jury system outweighed the employer's private interest. A union waiver of the right against discharge because of jury service (which it is a little hard to imagine that a union would do) would likewise thwart the will of the community and harm the jury system, and so the waiver should not be given force. A similar rationale would prevent unions from waiving whistleblower rights of its members arising from statute or the common law. Employees are often in unique positions to know of illegal activity within their firm – for example, the illegal dumping of toxic wastes. Such illegal acts do not merely affect the one whistleblower, or even just the firm; they harm third parties or the public at large. As unions are the exclusive representatives of their bargaining unit, and not society, laws protecting third parties should not be subject to brokering.

On the other hand, many employment rights solve public-goods problems in the workplace as distinct from the larger society. The paradigmatic example here is workplace safety standards, where providing a safe speed for one worker on the assembly line provides it for all. We discussed earlier that a union can alleviate the underproduction of workplace public goods within its brokering role. Safety laws that allow unions to negotiate or opt out of otherwise mandatory standards are therefore consistent with good public policy.

Union brokering is good public policy for many other employment rights. As outlined earlier, union waiver does not suffer from problems that make individual waiver so problematic. One problem was the unequal bargaining power of the individual worker. Unions can provide that equality. Other problems were the lack of information and expertise and the cognitive biases that individual workers have in processing information on many issues. Unions, with their research staffs and institutional memory, can provide that information and expertise.

CONCLUSION

Most employment laws create rights for workers that are inalienable. This chapter has argued that, in certain contexts, it may be beneficial to unions, employees, and employers to allow unions to broker or opt out of rights that are inalienable for an individual employee. Most employment rights are mandatory for individual workers, whether to solve rat races or public goods in the workplace or to protect against information deficits, cognitive biases, or lack of bargaining power. The union as a collective body is less susceptible to the particular weaknesses of the individual – a union has the power and resources to broker a right in favor of employees into even greater value for the workers it represents, the employer it bargains with, and society as a whole. In short, unions can provide the nuance in regulation necessary for an efficient market, while still protecting the interests of workers, employers, and society at large.

Union brokering should be subject to strictures. First, legislatures should require a clear and unequivocal waiver of a specific entitlement, to prevent a far-reaching interpretation of general contract language. Second, union brokering should be proscribed when laws are meant to protect third parties (that is, parties who are not represented during collective bargaining) or meant to protect minority interests not well represented by the union.

The critical question is whether important aspects of workplace policy are best decided centrally in Washington or Sacramento, through contract between individual worker and employer, or through collective bargaining between union and employer. A long tradition suggests that this intermediate level of inquiry, collective bargaining, is optimal on many issues. The union as broker is a modern adaptation to that long-time message.

NOTES

1. CAL. LAB. CODE § 750 (West 2009).
2. CAL. LAB. CODE § 750.5 (West 2009) states: "The provisions of Section 750 shall not prohibit a period of employment up to 12 hours within a 24-hour period when the employer and a labor organization representing employees of the employer have entered into a valid collective bargaining agreement where the agreement expressly provides for the wages, hours of work, and working conditions of the employees." In 1995, the California legislature again amended the statute to allow an additional exception "when a 2/3 majority of the employees who work for a particular employer vote, in an election conducted at the expense of the employer pursuant to prescribed procedures, to adopt a policy that authorizes a regular workday of more than eight hours in a 24-hour period." CAL. LAB. CODE § 750(b) (West 2009).
3. Viceroy Gold Corp. v. Aubry, 75 F.3d 482 (9th Cir. 1995), reversing Viceroy Gold Corp. v. Aubry, 858 F. Supp. 1007 (N.D. Cal. 1994).
4. Arbitration Fairness Act of 2009, H.R. 1020, 111th Cong. (2009) (reversing *Penn Plaza*); Arbitration Fairness Act of 2007, H.R. 3010, 110th Cong. (2007) (reversing *Gilmer* and *Circuit City*).
5. Franken Amendment to the Department of Defense Appropriations Act of 2010, Pub. L. No. 111-118 § 8116, 123 Stat. 3409, 3454-55 (2010).
6. *See* Mechmet v. Four Seasons Hotels, Ltd., 825 F.2d 1173, 1176 (7th Cir. 1987) ("The first purpose was to prevent workers willing (maybe out of desperation . . .) to work abnormally long hours from taking jobs away from workers who prefer to work shorter hours. . . . The second purpose was to spread work and thereby reduce unemployment, by requiring the employer to pay a penalty for using fewer workers for the same amount of work as would be necessary if each worker worked a shorter week.").
7. For a discussion of strong and weak paternalism, see Sunstein (2006, p. 249) (describing responses to cognitive error as consisting either of "weak paternalism, through debiasing and other strategies that leave people free to choose as they wish . . . [or] strong paternalism, which forecloses choice").

8. Schwab (1988, p. 260) describes a "hesitation effect" of contract presumptions:

    Parties are often uncertain which clause will suit them best, particularly when the clause deals with remote contingencies. The parties may believe that contract presumptions reflect the standard, widely accepted solution to a contracting situation. . . . A nominal beneficiary, then, aware of his uncertainty about the value of various clauses, must be induced to take the risk that waiving the standard clause is in his interest. For this reason, beneficiaries will demand more when waiving an entitlement than they would pay to purchase the entitlement. If so, we should see that contract presumptions distribute wealth toward the beneficiary. These explanations would suggest that parties in general hesitate (that is, demand extra compensation) to waive presumptions. Let me term this the "general hesitation effect" of contract presumptions.

9. *See* NLRB v. Truitt Mfg. Co., 351 U.S. 149 (1956) (holding that employer violated its section 8(a)(5) duty to bargain in good faith when it refused to give union financial information backing its claim it could not afford a 10 cent per hour wage increase).

10. 78 CONG. REC. 3679 (1934), reprinted in 1 NLRB, Legislative History of the National Labor Relations Act, 1935, at 20.

11. Atlas Bag & Burlap Co., 1 N.L.R.B. 292 (1936) (yellow-dog contracts interfere with § 7 right to organize); Fanny Farmer Candy Shops, Inc., 10 N.L.R.B. 288, 306 (1938) (yellow-dog contracts are "invalid and of no effect").

12. R.C.A. Mfg. Co., 2 N.L.R.B. 159, 178 (1937) ("the Board's power is an exclusive one and not in any way dependent upon, or affected by . . . agreements between private parties").

13. Ingram Mfg. Co., 5 N.L.R.B. 908 (1938).

14. *See* International News Service Div., 113 N.L.R.B. 1067, 1070 (1955) ("The Board has said repeatedly that statutory rights may be waived by collective bargaining."); American Freight Sys., Inc. v. NLRB, 722 F.2d 828, 832 (D.C. Cir. 1983) ("It is well settled that a union may lawfully waive statutory rights of represented employees in a collective bargaining agreement.").

15. A student commentator aptly summarized the waiver doctrine, "[t]he Supreme Court has interpreted the [NLRA] in such a way as to make inviolable only a limited few of the rights granted therein. . . . Other rights are not, in this sense, treated as 'rights,' but rather as 'bargaining chips,' which have been granted to labor upon its being organized, and which may (and in the Court's view were *intended* to be) bargained away in exchange for employer 'concessions' during contract negotiations." Note (1986, p. 846; emphasis in original).

16. *See* NLRB v. Rockaway News Supply Co., 345 U.S. 71, 79–80 (1953) (upholding discharge of union member who engaged in sympathy strike in violation of no-strike clause); Teamsters Local 174 v. Lucas Flour, 369 U.S. 95 (1962) (right to strike implicitly waived by arbitration clause in collective bargaining agreement); Metropolitan Edison v. NLRB, 460 U.S. 693 (1983) (rejecting union's argument that right to strike may not be waived where employer had imposed sanctions on union leaders after a sympathy strike, but finding no valid waiver because the general no-strike clause in the contract did not indicate "clear and unmistakable" waiver); International Brotherhood of Electrical Workers, Local 803 v. NLRB, 826 F.2d 1283 (3d Cir. 1987) (holding that the right to engage in a sympathy strike was waived by a general no-strike clause in a collective bargaining agreement).

17. *See, e.g.,* Teamsters Local Union No. 515 v. NLRB, 906 F.2d 719, 727–8 (D.C. Cir. 1990) (holding that unfair labor practice strikes are waivable, since "merely bargaining away the right to strike does not impermissibly infringe the 'full freedom of association'").

18. *See, e.g.,* Textile Workers Union v. Lincoln Mills, 353 U.S. 448 (1957) ("Congress [in enacting the Labor Management Relations Act of 1947] was also interested in promoting collective bargaining that ended with agreements not to strike").

19. Emporium Capwell Co. v. Western Addition Community Organization, 420 U.S. 50 (1975) (affirming that once an exclusive bargaining representative is designated, attempts to compel separate bargaining are not protected by § 7 of the NLRA).

20. See Federal Labor Relations Authority v. Internal Revenue Service, 838 F.2d 567, 568 (D.C. Cir. 1988); see generally Higgins (2006, at pp. 1006–07).

21. Prudential Insurance Co., 275 N.L.R.B. 208 (1985) ("the Weingarten right, like the right to strike, is subject to being waived by the union"); *see generally* Craver (1977).

22. Plumbers & Pipefitters Local Union 520 v. NLRB, 955 F.2d 744 (D.C. Cir. 1992) (Edwards, J.).

23. Whether unions appropriately represent the interests of their members is itself a huge question, usually discussed under the topic of union democracy. I wrote an article on the subject some years back, initially conceived as a predicate to the current chapter. Schwab (1992).

24. Illinois was a leader in creating this type of tort of wrongful discharge against public policy – firing an employee for exercising a statutory right. *See* Kelsay v. Motorola, Inc., 384 N.E.2d 353 (Ill. 1978).

25. "Since *Allis-Chalmers,* lower courts applying the standard in that case have held that Section 301

preempts claims for fraud and misrepresentation, invasion of privacy, defamation, intentional infliction of emotional distress, negligence, tortious drug testing, tortious interference with contract, violation of an implied covenant of good faith and fair dealing, fraud, violation of worker compensation law, race and sex discrimination under state law, breach of a trust agreement, breach of contract, violation of state wage and hour laws, and retaliation under state workers compensation and other laws," citing some 53 preempted cases and 22 contrary, non-preempted cases. Higgins (2006, pp. 2389–93).

26.   Byrd v. VOCA Corp., 962 A.2d 927 (D.C. Ct. App. 2008) (preempting wrongful discharge claim of employee fired for reporting health and safety violations, because assessing the validity of the discharge would require interpretation of the management-rights and just-cause clauses in the collective bargaining contract); Frederick v. Federal-Mogul, Inc., 185 LRRM 3172 (E.D. Mich. 2008) (preempting employee's claim that employer misappropriated his invention for improved manufacturing process, because claim required interpretation of job duties specified in collective bargaining agreement).

27.   *See* Brief for Employers Group as Amici Curiae at B1-B6, Livadas v. Bradshaw, 512 U.S. 107 (1994) (listing 22 state laws with opt-out provisions for collective bargaining agreements).

28.   Vt. Stat. Ann. tit. 21, § 342(b).

29.   Or. Rev. Stat. § 652.140.

30.   Nev. Rev. Stat. § 608.018(2)(f).

31.   Ch. 820 Ill. Comp. Stat. § 140/3.

32.   Md. Code Ann. art. 48A, § 490L (employer-provided health insurance can not charge different copayments for mail-order pharmacies, unless insurance policy is issued pursuant to a collective bargaining agreement); Wash. Rev. Code §§ 48.44.310 & 48.44.340 (group health insurance policies shall offer coverage for chiropractic care and mental health care on same basis as any other care, unless collective bargaining agreement says otherwise); Alaska Stat. § 23.10.430(b) (employees have right to inspect personnel file, but this requirement does not supersede the terms of a collective bargaining agreement); ch. 820 Ill. Comp. Stat. § 40/2 (employees have right to inspect personnel records twice a year, unless otherwise provided in a CBA); Wis. Stat. Ann. § 103.13(2) (same).

33.   Mont. Code Ann. § 50-71-201.

34.   Ark. Code Ann. § 11-4-205.

35.   Congress intended the vesting requirements "to broaden the number of employees who are eligible to participate in their employer's pension plan," and "to reduce the loss of pension rights by employees who terminate their employment prior to retirement age." 1974 U.S.C.C.A.N. 5,177, 5,178 (statement of Sen. Williams regarding conference report on ERISA). When Congress shortened the vesting period in 1986, the Senate Report explained that "present law does not meet the needs of many workers who change jobs frequently. In particular, women and minorities are disadvantaged by the present rules because they tend to be more mobile and thus more likely to terminate employment before vesting . . . . [M]ore rapid vesting would enhance the retirement income security of low- and middle-income employees." S. Rep. No. 313, 99th Cong., 2d Sess. 589–91 (1973) (Finance Committee report regarding Tax Reform Act of 1986).

36.   ERISA § 203(a)(2)(A), 29 U.S.C. § 1053(a)(2)(A). The five-year requirement is cliff vesting, whereby the plan can completely forfeit pension benefits for an employee who leaves before five years of service. Alternatively, the plan can delay 100 percent vesting until seven years by following an ERISA schedule of partial vesting that begins with 20 percent vesting after three years. ERISA § 203(a)(2)(B), 29 U.S.C. § 1053(a)(2)(B).

37.   When enacted in 1974, ERISA mandated ten-year cliff vesting or graduated vesting schedules ranging from five to fifteen years. Employee Retirement Income Security Act of 1974, ch. 18, 88 Stat. 854–5 (1974). In 1986, Congress reduced the minimum vesting standards to allow a choice between five-year cliff vesting and three- to seven-year graduated vesting. At this time, Congress created a special provision allowing ten-year cliff vesting for multiemployer plans created by a collective bargaining agreement. Tax Reform Act of 1986, ch. 1, § 1113, 100 Stat. 2, 446–7 (1986).

38.   ERISA § 203(a)(2)(C)(ii)(I). Multiemployer plans are common in the garment industry, where there is a strong union and many small employers, and in industries such as construction where workers frequently stay within a small geographical area but frequently move from employer to employer (Conison, 1993).

39.   In Congressional hearings, the AFL-CIO promoted the relaxed vesting standards because (1) employees in industries characterized by multiemployer plans already benefit from pension portability, and shortening the vesting requirements would needlessly increase the costs of administering multiemployer plans, and (2) in these industries, the workforce size and the viability of employers tend to be very unstable, and collective bargaining is a better way to obtain better vesting: "The bill properly exempts multiemployer plans . . . . In industries characterized by multiemployer plans, the typical worker is employed by dozens, even hundreds of different employers during his or her working years. In these industries, multiemployer pooled plans have evolved which allow workers to obtain pension credits despite frequent shifts from one employer to another. This is why any vesting standard will cost a multiemployer plan more . . . . In

addition, the conditions of employment are inherently unstable in [such industries]. Contributors to these plans often include hundreds or even thousands of small companies. The incidence of business failures is relatively high and large fluctuations in the size of the work force are not uncommon. Given such conditions in these industries, collective bargaining, because of its flexibility, is the best way to achieve the goal of more liberal vesting." The Retirement Income Policy Act of 1985 and the Retirement Universal Security Arrangements Act of 1985: Hearing Before the Subcommittee on Labor-Management Relations of the Committee on Education and Labor, 99th Congress, 2d Sess., 345 (letter from Robert McGlotten, AFL-CIO).

40. For example, the Chamber of Commerce complained that, while faster vesting increases costs and reduces actual retirement security, relaxed regulations for multiemployer union plans "would skew employer decisionmaking about the type of plan with which to be involved and would disadvantage many non-unionized companies with single employer plans that compete with unionized companies [with] multiemployer plans"). *See id.* at 85 (statement of John N. Erlenborn, U.S. Chamber of Commerce; The National Manufacturers Association made essentially the same argument, *id.* at 98 (statement of James A. King, National Association of Manufacturers).

41. *See generally* Congressional Budget Office, Tax Policy [. . .] Pensions and Other Retirement Savings (1987) (explaining the tax advantages associated with qualified pension plans).

42. The relevant tax advantages for qualified plans may be found in 26 U.S.C. § 401(a). ERISA requires that a pension plan benefit "such employees as qualify under a classification set up by the employer and found by the Secretary not to be discriminatory in favor of highly compensated employees." 26 U.S.C. § 410(b)(2)(A)(i) (1988).

43. In a similar vein, ERISA's nondiscrimination requirements for "cafeteria plans" do not apply to plans maintained under a collective bargaining agreement. I.R.C. § 125(g)(1) ("For purposes of this section [on cafeteria plans], a plan shall not be treated as discriminatory if the plan is maintained under an agreement which the Secretary finds to be a collective bargaining agreement between employee representatives and one or more employers").

44. During the passage of the original ERISA bill, the House Committee on Ways and Means reported that "[f]irst, [the provision] recognizes that employees who are represented in collective bargaining agreements may prefer other forms of compensation, such as cash compensation, to coverage in a plan; and second, it makes it possible for employees who are not covered by a collective bargaining agreement to receive the advantages of coverage in a qualified plan where some employees of the same firm have elected through collective bargaining agreement not to be covered by the plan." H.R. Rep. No. 779, 93d Cong., 2d Sess. 17 (1974), reprinted in Subcommittee on Labor of the Committee on Labor and Public Welfare, 94th Cong., 2d Sess. 2606 (1976). The problem before 1974 was the requirement that a qualified plan had to cover at least 70 percent of employees, or that it be nondiscriminatory. *See* 26 U.S.C. § 410(b). Without the exemption in 26 U.S.C. § 410(b)(3)(A), when a union decided to exchange pension benefits for other compensation, nonunion employees of the same employer would not likely get to participate in a qualified plan. Specifically, in 1974 some 50 percent private-sector non-agricultural workers were not covered by pension plans. H.R. Rep. No. 779, 93d Cong., 2d Sess. 17 (1974), at 11. So the exclusion of union employees from the analysis seeks to increase pension coverage among nonunion workers and to give union employees the choice between pension benefits and other compensation.

45. 29 U.S.C. § 1341, part of Subtitle C of ERISA's Pension Benefit Guarantee Corporation authorization, allows two types of plan terminations: "standard" and "distress" terminations. 29 U.S.C. § 1341(a)(3), however, provides that "the corporation shall not proceed with the termination of a plan under this section if the termination would violate the terms and conditions of an existing collective bargaining agreement." The provision was added in 1986 as part of the Consolidated Omnibus Budget Reconciliation Act of 1985. COBRA, Pub. L. No. 99-272, § 11007, 100 Stat. 244 (1986).

46. The provision was "an endorsement of judicial decisions such as Terones [v.] Pacific States Steel Corp., 526 F. Supp. 1350 (N.D. Cal[]. 1981), holding that a company cannot unilaterally terminate a collectively bargained pension plan when such termination is in violation of the terms of any agreement between the parties." 132 CONG. REC. 3,792 (1986) (Rep. Clay, discussing conference report on the budget bill). *See generally* H.R. Rep. No. 300, 99th Cong., 1st Sess. (1985) (report by House Committee on the Budget regarding Omnibus Budget Reconciliation Act of 1985). *Terones* merely interpreted a collective bargaining agreement and concluded that it did not allow unilateral termination by the employer. Therefore, the effect may simply be to affirm a strong policy interest in preventing terminations, to which *Terones* alludes.

47. 29 U.S.C. § 207(b)(1) exempts from the workweek requirements employees employed "in pursuance of an agreement, made as a result of collective bargaining by representatives of employees certified as bona fide by the [NLRB], which provides that no employee shall be employed more than one thousand and forty hours during any period of twenty-six consecutive weeks."

48. 29 U.S.C. § 207(b)(1)–(2). 29 U.S.C. § 207(b)(2) provides, in singularly cryptic terms, that employers need

not follow the § 207(a)(1) overtime requirements for employees employed "in pursuance of an agreement, made as a result of collective bargaining by representatives of employees certified as bona fide by the [NLRB], which provides that during a specified period of fifty-two consecutive weeks the employee shall be employed not more than two thousand two hundred and forty hours and shall be guaranteed not less than one thousand eight hundred and forty hours (or not less than forty-six weeks at the normal number of hours worked per week, but not less than thirty hours per week) and not more than two thousand and eighty hours of employment for which he shall receive compensation for all hours guaranteed or worked at rates not less than those applicable under the agreement to the work performed and for all hours in excess of the guaranty which are also in excess of the maximum workweek applicable to such employee under subsection (a) of this section or two thousand and eighty in such period at rates not less than one and one-half times the regular rate . . . ."

49.   When Congress passed the original version of the FLSA in 1938, Fair Labor Standards Act of 1938, Pub. L. No. 718, 52 Stat. 1060, 1063 (1938), § 7(b)(1) exempted from the normal workweek requirements collective bargaining agreements allowing no more than 1,000 hours of work for a 26-week period, and § 7(b)(2) exempted similar agreements allowing no more than 2,000 hours for a 52-week period. However, time-and-a-half was still required for any hours above 12 per day or 56 in a week. Evidence from a conferee's explanation of the conference report suggests that the provision attempted to satisfy employers whose peculiar operations required longer workweeks. "[T]he conference agreement contains general exemptions to allow for further flexibility. . . . [The 26-week period/1,000 hour exemption] will take care of the peculiar situation which exists in isolated mining and lumber camps which are located in some cases 75 or 100 miles from civilization. . . . [The 52-week period exemption provides] an exemption from the basic maximum hours for employers who have adopted the annual wage plan." 83 CONG. REC. 9,257 (1938) (Rep. Norton, explaining conference committee report). *See also* 83 CONG. REC. 9,164 (1938) (Sen. Thomas, explaining that § 7(b) is a compromise between the alleged rigidity of the House bill and flexibility of the Senate bill; "general exceptions . . . are so drawn as to encourage under proper safeguards continuity or regularity of employment").

In 1941, Congress raised the maximum annual total for agreements covering 52-week periods to 2,080 hours. Act of Oct. 29, 1941, ch. 461, Pub. L. No. 283, 55 Stat. 756 (1941). In 1949, Congress raised the 26-week maximum to 1,040 hours; for 52-week periods, the limit was set at 2,240 hours. Act of Oct. 26, 1949, ch. 736, Pub. L. No. 392, 63 Stat. 913 (1949). That bill also added the modern language requiring a guarantee of at least 1,840 hours for annual agreements, and the modern overtime requirements for such agreements. The bill's purpose was "to provide for greater flexibility." 95 CONG. REC. 14,875 (1949) (summary of conference committee report). It also sought to conform the maximum hours under § 7(b) exemptions to an average of 40 hours per week. When employees work more than the equivalent of 40 hours per week, employers are required to pay the overtime rate. 95 CONG. REC. 14,875 (1949) (summary of conference committee report). *See also* 1949 U.S.C.C.A.N. 2,256 (conference committee report; "[new § 7(b)(1)] would permit employment under such agreements for an average workweek of 40 hours during any 26-week period"; "[new § 7(b)(2)] provide[s] for greater flexibility").

For general analysis of the legislative history of the FLSA, see generally Forsythe (1939, p. 486) (original union exemption intended to reach industries that need to send workers to remote areas, to work long hours for short periods of time); Cooper (1939, p. 346) (explaining the original language and early interpretations).

50.   The overtime pay provisions in collective bargaining agreements typically conform to the normal FLSA requirements in 29 U.S.C. § 207(a)(1). Occasionally, an agreement is negotiated which arguably falls outside the normal workweek requirements and may be valid under the § 207(b) exemptions. *See, e.g.,* Agreement, Apr. 1, 1988, State of Alaska-Inlandboatmen's Union 20–23 (providing for a workweek of seven consecutive 12-hour workdays, with seven consecutive days off following each completed workweek, and time-and-a-half for hours worked during the scheduled week off).

REFERENCES

Akerlof, George A. 1976. "The Economics of Caste and of the Rat Race and Other Woeful Tales." 90 *Quarterly Journal of Economics* 599.
Brosseau, R. 1980. "Toward A Theory of Rights for the Employment Relation." 56 *Washington Law Review* 1.
Burkhauser, Richard V., K.A. Couch, & D.C. Wittenburg. 2000. "Who Minimum Wage Increases Bite: An Analysis Using Monthly Data from the SIPP and CPS." 67 *Southern Economic Journal* 16.
Card, David, & Alan B Krueger. 1997. *Myth and Measurement: The New Economics of Minimum Wage.* Princeton, NJ: Princeton University Press.

Clermont, Kevin M., & Stewart J. Schwab. 2004. "How Employment-Discrimination Plaintiffs Fare in the Federal Courts of Appeals." 1 *Journal of Empirical Legal Studies* 429.

Conison, Jay. 1993. *Employee Benefit Plans in a Nutshell.* St. Paul, MN: West Pub. Co.

Cooper, Frank E. 1939. "The Coverage of the Fair Labor Standards Act and Other Problems in its Interpretation," 6 *Law and Contemporary Problems* 333.

Craver, Charles 1977. "The Inquisitorial Process in Private Employment." 63 *Cornell Law Review* 1.

Eskridge, William N., Jr., Philip P. Frickey & Elizabeth Garrett. 2000. *Legislation and Statutory Interpretation.* New York: Foundation Press.

Estreicher, Samuel. 1996. "Freedom of Contract and Labor Law Reform: Opening Up the Possibilities for Value-Added Unionism." 71 *NYU Law Review* 827.

Forsythe, John S. 1939. "Legislative History of the Fair Labor Standards Act," 6 *Law and Contemporary Problems* 464.

Frank, Robert. 1985. *Choosing the Right Pond: Human Behavior and the Quest for Status.* New York and Oxford: Oxford University Press.

Freeman, Richard. 1976. "Individual Mobility and Union Voice in the Labor Market." 66 *American Economics Review* 361.

Gigerenzer, G. 1991. "How to Make Cognitive Illusions Disappear: Beyond Heuristics and Biases." 2 *European Journal of Social Psychology* 83.

Harper, Michael C. 1981a. "Union Waiver of Employee Rights under the NLRA: Part I." 4 *Industrial Relations Law Journal* 335.

Harper, Michael C. 1981b. "Union Waiver of Employee Rights Under the NLRA: Part II A Fresh Approach to the Board Deferral to Arbitration." 4 *Industrial Relations Law Journal* 680.

Harper, Michael C. 1992. "Limiting Section 301 Preemption: Three Cheers for the Trilogy, Only One for Lingle and Lueck." 66 *Chicago-Kent Law Review* 685.

Higgins, John E. 2006. *The Developing Labor Law* (5th ed). Washington, DC: Bureau of National Affairs.

Jolls, Christine. 2000. "Accomodation Mandates." 53 *Stanford Law Review* 223.

Kahneman, Daniel, & Dan Lovallo. 1995. "Timid Choices and Bold Forecasts: A Cognitive Perspective on Risk Taking." 39 *Management Science* 17.

Kim, Pauline T. (1997). "Bargaining with Imperfect Information: A Study of Worker Perceptions of Legal Protection in an At-Will World." 83 *Cornell Law Review* 105.

Kim, Pauline T. 1999. "Norms, Learning and Law: Exploring the Influence on Workers' Legal Knowledge." 1999 *University of Illinois Law Review* 447.

Kim, Pauline T. 2006. "Collective and Individual Approaches to Protecting Employee Privacy: The Experience with Workplace Drug Testing." 66 *Louisiana Law Review* 1009.

Macey, Jonathan R. 1986. "Promoting Public-Regarding Legislation through Statutory Interpretation: An Interest Group Model," 86 *Columbia Law Review* 223.

McAdams, Richard. 1992. "Relative Preferences." 102 *Yale Law Journal* 1. Note. 1974. "Employees' Solicitation-Distribution Rights Supersede Contract Waiver." 26 *University of Florida Law Review* 908.

Olson, Walter. 1997. "Disabling America." *National Review* (May 5).

Phillips, P. 1986. Comment, "The Contractual Waiver of Individual Rights under the National Labor Relations Act." 31 *New York Law School Law Review* 793.

Rachlinski, Jeffrey J. 2000. "Heuristics and Biases in the Courts: Ignorance or Adaptation?" 79 *Oregon Law Review* 61.

Rachlinski, Jeffrey J. 2003. "The Uncertain Psychological Case for Paternalism." 97 *Northwestern University Law Review* 1165.

Rachlinski, Jeffrey J. & Cynthia R. Farina. 2002. "Cognitive Psychology and Optimal Government Design." 87 *Cornell Law Review* 549.

Samuelson, Paul A. 1954. "The Pure Theory of Public Expenditure," 36 *Review of Economics and Statistics* 387–89.

Schwab, Stewart J. 1987. "Collective Bargaining and the Coase Theorem." 72 *Cornell Law Review* 245.

Schwab, Stewart J. 1988. "A Coasean Experiment on Contract Presumptions." 17 *Journal of Legal Studies* 237.

Schwab, Stewart J. 1989. "The Economics Invasion of Labor Law Scholarship." in Barbara D. Dennis, ed., *Proceedings of the 41st Annual Meeting, Industrial Relations Research Association.* Madison, WI: Industrial Relations Research Association, p. 236.

Schwab, Stewart J. 1992. "Union Raids, Union Democracy, and the Market for Union Control." 1992 *University of Illinois Law Review* 367.

Stone, Katherine V. 1992. "The Legacy of Industrial Pluralism: The Tension between Individual Employment Rights and the New Deal Collective Bargaining System." 59 *University of Chicago Law Review* 575.

Sunstein, Cass R. 2002. "Switching the Default Rule." 77 *New York University Law Review* 106.

Sunstein, Cass R. 2006. "Boundedly Rational Borrowing." 73 *University of Chicago Law Review* 249.

Thaler, Richard H. & Cass R. Sunstein. 2009. *Nudge: Improving Decisions about Health, Wealth, and Happiness* (revised and expanded edition). New York: Penguin.

Weiss, D. M. 1991. "Paternalistic Pension Policy: Psychological Evidence and Economic Theory." 58 *University of Chicago Law Review* 1275.

Welch, Finis. 1974. "Minimum Wage Legislation in the United States." 12 *Economic Inquiry* 285.

Westman, T. G. 1974. Note, "Contractual Waiver by Labor Unions of Employees; Solicitation-Distribution Rights: Time For a Resolution." 49 *Notre Dame Law Review* 920.

Cases Cited

14 Penn Plaza v. Pyett, 129 S. Ct. 1456 (2009).
Alexander v. Gardner-Denver, 415 U.S. 36 (1974).
Allis-Chalmers Corp. v. Lueck, 471 U.S. 202 (1985).
American Freight Sys., Inc. v. NLRB, 722 F.2d 828 (D.C. Cir. 1983).
Atlas Bag & Burlap Co., 1 N.L.R.B. 292 (1936).
Byrd v. VOCA Corp., 962 A.2d 927 (D.C. Ct. App. 2008).
Cabunac v. National Terminals Corp., 139 F.2d 853 (7th Cir. 1944).
Circuit City Stores, Inc. v. Adams, 532 U.S. 105 (2001).
Emporium Capwell Co. v. Western Addition Community Organization, 420 U.S. 50 (1975).
Fanny Farmer Candy Shops, Inc., 10 N.L.R.B. 288 (1938).
Federal Labor Relations Authority v. Internal Revenue Service, 838 F.2d 567 (D.C. Cir. 1988).
Frederick v. Federal-Mogul, Inc., 185 LRRM 3172 (E.D. Mich. 2008).
Gilmer v. Interstate/Johnson Lane Corp., 500 U.S. 20 (1991).
Ingram Mfg. Co., 5 N.L.R.B. 908 (1938).
International Brotherhood of Electrical Workers, Local 803 v. NLRB, 826 F.2d 1283 (3d Cir. 1987).
International News Service Div., 113 N.L.R.B. 1067 (1955).
Jackson v. Liquid Carbonic Corp., 863 F.2d 111 (1st Cir. 1988).
Kelsay v. Motorola, Inc., 384 N.E.2d 353 (Ill. 1978).
Lingle v. Norge Division, 486 U.S. 399 (1988).
Livadas v. Bradshaw, 512 U.S. 107 (1994).
Mechmet v. Four Seasons Hotels, Ltd., 825 F.2d 1173 (7th Cir. 1987).
Metropolitan Edison v. NLRB, 460 U.S. 693 (1983).
Nees v. Hocks, 536 P.2d 512 (1975).
NLRB v. Allis-Chalmers Mfg. Co., 388 U.S 175 (1967).
NLRB v. Magnavox, 415 U.S. 322 (1974).
NLRB v. Truitt Mfg. Co., 351 U.S. 149 (1956).
NLRB v. J. Weingarten, Inc., 420 U.S. 251 (1975).
Oil, Chemical and Atomic Workers v. NLRB, 806 F.2d 269 (D.C. Cir. 1986).
Prudential Insurance Co., 275 N.L.R.B. 208 (1985).
R.C.A. Mfg. Co., 2 N.L.R.B. 159, 178 (1937).
NLRB v. Rockaway News Supply Co., 345 U.S. 71 (1953).
Teamsters Local 174 v. Lucas Flour, 369 U.S. 95 (1962).
Teamsters Local Union No. 515 v. NLRB, 906 F.2d 719 (D.C. Cir. 1990).
Textile Workers Union v. Lincoln Mills, 353 U.S. 448 (1957).

PART III

EMPLOYEE RIGHTS AND EMPLOYER MANDATES

9. Bias and the law of the workplace*
Christine Jolls

Shortly after noon on July 16, 2009, Henry Louis Gates, Jr., a well-known African-American professor at Harvard University, was arrested at his home after a verbal confrontation with a Cambridge police officer who was investigating a call about a possible burglary. Gates returned home from a trip to China to find the front door to his home jammed. With help from his driver, Gates forced the door open and entered the house. After neighbor Lucia Whalen called the Cambridge police to report that two men may have been breaking into the house, Sergeant James Crowley and several other Cambridge police officers arrived on the scene. The key details of what occurred next differ between Crowley and Gates. Crowley reported that Gates was aggressive, yelling very loudly, threatening Crowley repeatedly, and refusing to follow Crowley's instruction that Gates step outside.[1] Gates's account of the incident indicated that Crowley repeatedly refused to provide his name and badge number upon Gates's request (Olopade 2009). What is certain is that the incident ended with the arrest of the fifty-eight-year-old professor for disorderly conduct.

Would a hypothetical fifty-eight-year-old white man in Gates's situation have been asked to step outside upon the police's arrival at the house? Would he later have been arrested for disorderly conduct after responding in the way Gates did? Or would Magic Toyota employee Rickey Williams have been terminated if he had been white rather than (as he was) African-American?[2] We will never be certain of the answers to these questions, but plainly many observers of these and similar incidents have taken it as obvious that race played an important role – and in some cases have taken this view despite the lack of any suggestion that the protagonists were particularly ill-intended on race issues. In the Gates incident, in fact, it was frequently noted that Sergeant Crowley had been selected to instruct other police officers on awareness of issues of racial profiling (e.g., Johnson 2009).

What might account for the potential discrepancy between Sergeant Crowley's treatment of Gates and Crowley's apparent values? In some instances racial bias – defined as treating people differently from how they would have been treated had their race differed while everything else remained the same – may arise from a *cognitive error*, a mistake that the decisionmaker would prefer to avoid. Despite our best intentions, we may leap from an individual's race to particular conclusions about the individual without having any awareness of the role race played in those conclusions. Sergeant Crowley may well have earnestly believed that he was not acting because of race, yet his mental processing of the facts and circumstances of the event and his subsequent actions might well have been different had Gates been a fifty-eight-year-old white, rather than African-American, university professor. Crowley could have intended to treat individuals without any regard for race but in fact might have treated otherwise identical situations differently based solely upon that trait.

This and other exemplars of various types of "cognitive bias" are described in the next section. Cognitive bias has been a centerpiece of the burgeoning field of behavioral economics, which in turn has many points of contact with the legal regulation of the workplace. The balance of this chapter describes some of the ways that workplace law can and does respond to cognitive bias. I shall particularly emphasize legal responses that seek to reduce bias, rather than simply counteracting its effects through a traditional mandate or prohibition. Workplace law can (and I believe does) operate to decrease the level of various forms of bias, not merely to neutralize or counteract the consequences of bias. The difference is extremely significant (Jolls and Sunstein 2006a). Reducing cognitive bias, rather than trying to work around it, is generally the best place for law to begin – and many existing legal rules governing the workplace reflect an implicit recognition of this important truth.

I.   TYPOLOGY OF COGNITIVE BIAS[3]

In cognitive psychology and behavioral economics, a massive amount of attention has been devoted to *heuristics*, or mental shortcuts that function well in many settings but lead to systematic errors in others (Kahneman and Frederick 2002). This section first discusses some important heuristics and their potential role in producing various forms of bias. Second, the section describes further forms of bias that arise, not from heuristics, but from more direct misjudgments. Within the legal literature, *optimism bias* is the most commonly discussed type of these latter forms of bias and thus receives particular emphasis below.

A.   Heuristics and their Implications for Racial and Other Bias

Consider a well-known study of people's judgments about a fictional thirty-one-year-old woman, Linda, who was concerned with issues of social justice and discrimination in college. People tend to say that Linda was more likely to be a "feminist bank teller" than to be a "bank teller." This judgment is patently illogical, for a superset cannot be smaller than a set within it. The source of the mistake is the representativeness heuristic, by which events are seen to be more likely if they "look like" certain causes. In the case of Linda, the use of the representativeness heuristic leads to a mistake of elementary logic – the conclusion that characteristics X and Y together are more likely to be present than characteristic X alone.

Cognitive psychology emphasizes that heuristics of this kind frequently work through a process of "attribute substitution," in which people answer a hard question by substituting an easier one (Kahneman and Frederick 2002). People may, for example, resolve a question of probability not by investigating statistics, but by asking whether a relevant incident comes easily to mind (Tversky and Kahneman 1973). Thus, people asked how many words in a 2,000-word section of a novel end in "ing" give much larger estimates than those asked how many words have "n" as the second-to-last letter in the same material, notwithstanding the obvious fact that more words must satisfy the latter criterion than the former (Tversky and Kahneman 1983). This "availability heuristic" is a second example of the more general process of attribute substitution.

In some cases, people may deliberately choose to use a heuristic, believing that it will enable them to reach accurate results. But some of the most important heuristics have been connected to "dual process" approaches (Chaiken and Trope 1999). According to such approaches, people employ two cognitive systems. System I is rapid, intuitive, and prone to error; System II is more deliberative, slower, and often more accurate. Much heuristic-based thinking is rooted in System I, but it may be overridden, under certain conditions, by System II. Thus, for example, some people might make a rapid, intuitive judgment that a large German shepherd is likely to be vicious, but this judgment might be overcome after the dog's owner assures them that the dog is actually quite friendly. Most people would be reluctant to drink from a glass recently occupied by a cockroach; but it is possible (though far from certain) that they would be willing to do so after considering a reliable assurance that, because the cockroach had been sterilized by heat, the glass was not contaminated (Rozin 2001). Judgments about potentially harmful events are often founded in System I (LeDoux 1996), and System II sometimes supplies a corrective. (In other cases, responses within the System I domain itself may supply correctives, as discussed at some length below.)

Heuristics often produce sensible judgments and behavior for people who lack detailed statistical information, but they also can lead to significant and severe errors. Heuristics, then, can produce important biases. Thus availability bias might be said to arise when the availability heuristic leads people to make predictable errors in assessing probabilities. The prospect of errors in some cases does not suggest that the behavior in question is irrational in the sense of being arbitrary or lacking any plausible justification. The point instead is that the behavior, even if sensible in many cases, leads to systematic error in some identifiable set of them.

Assessments of members of a different race may often occur within the domain of System I – operating as largely automatic responses rather than deliberate and calculated judgments (perhaps as responses influenced by heuristics such as representativeness and availability). Consider in this connection the large body of evidence on the Implicit Association Test (IAT), which has been taken by diverse populations on the Internet and elsewhere (Greenwald, McGhee and Schwartz 1998; Nosek, Banaji and Greenwald 2002). The IAT asks individuals to perform the seemingly straightforward task of categorizing a series of words or pictures into groups. Two of the groups are racial or other categories, such as "black" and "white," and two of the groups are the categories "pleasant" and "unpleasant." In the version of the IAT designed to test for implicit racial bias, respondents are asked to press one key on the computer for either "black" or "unpleasant" words or pictures and a different key for either "white" or "pleasant" words or pictures (a stereotype-consistent pairing); in a separate round of the test, respondents are asked to press one key on the computer for either "black" or "pleasant" words or pictures and a different key for either "white" or "unpleasant" words or pictures (a stereotype-inconsistent pairing). Implicit bias against African-Americans is defined as giving faster responses when the "black" and "unpleasant" categories are paired than when the "black" and "pleasant" categories are paired. The IAT is rooted in the very simple hypothesis that people will find it easier to associate pleasant words with white faces and names than with African-American faces and names – and that the same pattern will be found for other traditionally disadvantaged groups. In fact, implicit bias as measured by the IAT has proven to be extremely widespread. Most people tend to prefer white to African-American, young to old, and heterosexual to gay

(Greenwald and Krieger 2006; Greenwald, McGhee and Schwartz 1998; Nosek, Banaji and Greenwald 2002).

Implicit racial bias of the sort found on the IAT is easily understood in System I terms. Such bias is largely automatic; the characteristic in question (skin color, age, sexual orientation) operates so quickly, in the relevant tests, that people have no time to deliberate. Indeed, it is for this reason that people are often surprised to find that they show implicit bias. In fact many people say in good faith that they are fully committed to an antidiscrimination principle with respect to the very trait against which they show a bias (Greenwald, McGhee and Schwartz 1998). From this perspective, it is entirely unsurprising that Sergeant Crowley of the Cambridge police department might have been simultaneously an esteemed instructor against racial profiling and under the sway of race in his insistent requests that Gates step outside, his later arrest of the professor, or both. According to at least one report, the entire elapsed time between the neighbor's phone call to the police and Crowley's arrest of Gates was six minutes (Herbert 2009), and in the complexly unfolding environment at the Gates home, System I may well have been more powerful than System II. None of this is to suggest that when people exhibit bias toward African-Americans, System II is never involved, but in a great many cases in America today – particularly when limited time would make it difficult to deliberate – System I may well be the culprit.

An important question about the IAT is the degree to which "IAT bias" predicts behavior or decisions (such as Sergeant Crowley's decision whether to arrest Professor Gates). Even if it is relatively uncontroversial to assume that an erroneous probability attached to the event "Linda is a bank teller" relative to the event "Linda is a feminist bank teller" – to return to an earlier example – would affect behavior in relation to Linda, it is a matter of some controversy whether faster speed in associating white faces with positive words and African-American faces with negative words on the IAT will translate into racial differentiation in real-world judgments and behavior.

It is clear, at a minimum, that implicit bias manifests itself in various forms of actual behavior coded by study observers unaware of subjects' implicit bias test results. There is evidence, for instance, that scores on the IAT and similar tests are correlated with third parties' ratings of subjects' degree of general friendliness to members of another race (Dovidio, Kawakami and Gaertner 2002; McConnell and Leibold 2001). More particularly, "larger IAT effect scores predicted greater speaking time, more smiling, [and] more extemporaneous social comments" in subjects' interactions with whites as compared to African-Americans (McConnell and Leibold 2001, p. 439). Moreover, there is evidence that the link between IAT scores and ratings of behaviors such as visual contact and use of speech illustrators is particularly pronounced when subjects' behavior is coded while the subjects must perform other cognitive tasks – that is, when subjects' response to individuals of a different race is particularly likely to be in the domain of System I rather than System II (Hofmann, Gschwendner, Castelli and Schmitt 2008). It is reasonable to speculate that the uneasy interactions observed across races could recur in the real world – and that they might be associated with biased decisionmaking.[4]

Rooth (2010) offers a first look at the connection between IAT scores and real-world decisionmaking. In Rooth's study, résumés with either Swedish-sounding or Arab-sounding names were sent in response to advertised job openings in two large Swedish cities. Rooth found that résumés with Swedish-sounding names were approximately 50 percent more likely to generate interview requests (29 percent callback rate for Swedish-sounding names versus 20 percent callback rate for Arab-sounding names). And, among recruiters from these firms who subsequently submitted to IAT testing by Rooth, differential treatment of individuals with Arab-sounding names was significantly correlated with anti-Arab implicit attitudes as measured by an Arab-white IAT.

B. Direct Misjudgments

Sometimes people's biases result not from heuristics, or mental shortcuts, but from more direct forms of misjudgment. An important bias in this category – one that has received significant attention in the legal literature on behavioral economics – is optimism bias. Optimism bias refers to the tendency of people to believe that their own probability of facing a bad outcome is lower than it actually is. Viscusi and Magat (1987, pp. 93–5), for instance, report that roughly half of consumers they surveyed considered their own household to be below average in risk, while the other half considered their household to be average in risk – yet obviously in aggregate these perceptions cannot be correct.[5]

As summarized in Jolls (1998), people typically think that their chances of a range of bad outcomes, from having an auto accident to contracting a particular disease to getting fired from a job, are significantly lower than the average person's chances of suffering these misfortunes – although, again, this cannot be true for everyone. Of course, this "above average" effect does not by itself establish that people optimistically underestimate their statistical risk (Viscusi and Magat 1987, pp. 95–6). For instance, people might believe that they are less likely than most people to contract cancer, while also having an accurate sense of the actual probability that they will contract cancer. But substantial evidence suggests that people sometimes exhibit optimism bias in the estimation of actual probabilities, not simply relative risk. For example, Armor and Taylor (2002) describe studies reporting that professional financial experts consistently overestimate likely corporate earnings, while business school students overestimate their likely starting salary and the number of offers that they will receive. People also underestimate their own likelihood of being involved in an automobile accident, and their frequent failure to buy insurance for floods and earthquakes is consistent with the view that people are excessively optimistic.[6] And it is noteworthy that these data pointing to optimism bias come from individuals making judgments that they make regularly in their everyday lives, rather than judgments far removed from those they would ordinarily make.

II. REDUCING TRADITIONAL COGNITIVE BIAS THROUGH WORKPLACE LAW

The forms of bias traditionally analyzed in behavioral economics include both biases that result from heuristics, such as the representativeness and availability heuristics, and biases related to direct misjudgments, as in optimism bias. Behavioral law and economics has emphasized the effects and desirability of a wide range of legal rules in light of such forms of cognitive bias (e.g., Jolls, Sunstein and Thaler 1998).

The most obvious path for law in response to cognitive bias is to seek to minimize the negative effects of such bias (while presuming that the bias itself will persist). Much existing work in behavioral law and economics is of this character. Consider, for instance, the large tort law literature suggesting that biased consumers believe potentially risky products to be substantially safer than they in fact are. If such beliefs exist, then the law might – and to some degree does – respond by adopting heightened standards of manufacturer liability for consumer products (e.g., Latin 1994). More generally, rules and institutions might be, and frequently are, designed to curtail individuals' decision-making freedom in the hope of immunizing legal outcomes from the effects of bias. In the existing behavioral law and economics literature, concern about cognitive bias "has been used to support the restriction of individual choice, almost without exception" (Rachlinski 2003, p. 1168).

A quite different possibility, however, is that legal policy may respond best to cognitive bias not by trying to protect outcomes from its effects, but instead by operating directly on the bias and attempting either to reduce or to eliminate it. Such approaches constitute "debiasing through law" (Jolls and Sunstein 2006a). A substantial empirical literature suggests prospects for debiasing of individuals after a demonstration of a given bias (e.g., Fischhoff 1982; Weinstein and Klein 2002), and the potential role of *law* in achieving such debiasing is a major topic of work in behavioral law and economics. Of course, not all types of bias respond to debiasing strategies (see, e.g., Fischhoff 1982). But for biases that social science evidence suggests do respond to some such strategies, debiasing through law offers the potential both to understand and to improve the legal system. The remainder of this section uses a case study of workplace law governing employee handbooks to explore this theme.

A.   The Law of Employee Handbooks

A central aspect of workplace law is the "employment at will" doctrine. Employment at will means that employees may generally be discharged at any time for any reason, unless their employment contract or (more commonly) their employee handbook provides for limits on termination. Where an employee handbook does provide for limits on termination, courts often narrowly construe employers' attempted "disclaimers" of such handbook guarantees.[7]

A leading rationale for narrowly construing employee handbook disclaimers is the belief that, under such disclaimers, employees do not adequately understand the risk of termination without good cause. Employees may not adequately understand this risk because they lack factual information, because they suffer from cognitive bias – most familiarly because of the phenomenon of optimism bias discussed above – or both. If the problem of limited employee understanding merely reflects a lack of factual information, then the traditional corrective is the provision of additional information (e.g., Stiglitz 1986, pp. 90–91). However, as the discussion above of optimism bias suggested, such bias may lead many employees to underestimate their personal risk even if they receive accurate factual information about average risk.

One potential response to employee optimism bias about the risk of termination without good cause under employee handbook disclaimers is to require that – regardless of the presence or absence of such disclaimers – employees only be terminated upon good cause (cf. Summers 1976).[8] But such an approach – seeking to protect against the effects of people's bias – would impose a uniform and inflexible regime of employment protection across the widely varying domain of American workplaces. Not all work-places may be best served by such a rule.

An alternative strategy is to use the law directly to reduce the occurrence of employee bias in the face of employee handbook disclaimers. At the broadest level, strategies for debiasing through workplace law provide a sort of middle ground between inaction or the earlier prescription (in response to a simple lack of factual information) of providing more information, on the one hand, and the aggressive strategy of uniform mandatory employment protection, on the other.[9]

B.   Empirical Evidence on Reducing Optimism Bias[10]

In the social science literature, straightforward potential strategies for debiasing in response to optimism bias include considering risk factors related to negative outcomes and suggesting reasons that negative outcomes might occur. In a set of studies, however, Weinstein and Klein (2002) find that such approaches fail to reduce optimism bias.[11] Their findings suggest that successful debiasing strategies in response to optimism bias must take an alternate form, as developed below.

1.   Reducing optimism bias through the availability heuristic

Building on Schwartz and Wilde's (1983) observation about the role of availability in risk estimation, a potentially effective response to the risk that optimistically biased indi-viduals believe "it won't happen to them" is the availability heuristic described above. Recall our earlier example of this heuristic: individuals who are asked how many words in a 2,000-word section of a novel end in "ing" give much larger estimates than individu-als who are asked how many words have "n" as the second-to-last letter. As described above, use of the availability heuristic often produces a form of judgment error; as with optimism bias, availability can lead to systematic mistakes in the assessment of prob-abilities. (Thus availability bias in the form of excessively high estimates and unavail-ability bias in the form of excessively low estimates involve complementary errors.) But because making an occurrence available to individuals will increase their estimates of the likelihood of the occurrence, availability is a promising strategy for debiasing those who suffer from excessive optimism.

One prominent method for making an occurrence available to individuals is expos-ing them to a concrete instance of the occurrence. Thus, for instance, a recent series of studies of smoking behavior finds that smokers are more likely to believe that smoking will harm their health if they are aware of specific instances of such harm (Sloan, Smith and Taylor 2003, pp. 157–79). More generally, people tend to respond to concrete, narra-tive information even when they do not respond, or respond far less, to general statistical information (Nisbett, Borgida, Crandall and Reed 1982). Concrete information appears to render the incident in question available in a way that can successfully counteract optimism bias.

As an illustration of the basic idea of debiasing through the availability heuristic in response to optimism bias, consider the finding of Weinstein (1980) that many people substantially underestimate their risk of cancer. Imagine that women asked to estimate their risk of breast cancer are told, before giving their estimates, a poignant and detailed story about a woman their age with similar family and other circumstances who was diagnosed with breast cancer. If so, then the empirical results noted above suggest that the women's estimated probabilities will typically be higher. (Of course, they may be too much higher or not enough higher; careful empirical study is needed to calibrate the legal response properly. I return to the possibility of overshooting at the end of this section.)

2.   Debiasing versus incentives

The discussion here illustrates an important general point about debiasing in response to cognitive bias. In the conception employed here, debiasing does not involve providing people with improved incentives in the hope of reducing their level of bias. In some cases, providing incentives may in fact diminish bias, and a broad definition of debiasing might embrace the use of incentives to reduce bias (Fischhoff 1982). A more conservative view, however, is that if an apparent bias is eliminated with the provision of financial incentives, then the apparent observed effect was not a bias at all, but instead a mere result of lazy or careless decisionmaking by an actor who had no reason to be other than lazy or careless.

Under the latter view, which is adopted here, debiasing occurs when bias is reduced not as a result of the provision of financial incentives, but rather as a result of intervening in and altering the situation that produces the bias. Under this conception of debiasing, individuals are not asked to repeat the very same task with the very same structure, with the sole difference that they now have greater reason to take care in making their choices; instead the environment is restructured in a way that alters not individuals' motivation but the actual process by which they perceive the world around them.

C.   Workplace Law Implications

In the context of the law governing employee handbook disclaimers, debiasing through the availability heuristic in response to optimism bias would focus on putting at employees' cognitive disposal the risk of termination from employment without good cause under such a disclaimer. Specifically, the law could specify that a handbook disclaimer, to negate the employer's legal obligation to terminate employees only upon good cause, would have to make reference to a particular, truthful account of termination of an employee whose discharge had been found in court to be without good cause; the disclaimer would have to state that such a termination would be permissible under the disclaimer. Information about termination found to be without good cause is readily available in publicly reported case judgments.

The strategy here is a cousin of the narrative strategy adopted, with great success, by Ralph Nader and Kate Blackwell (1973) in their book *You and Your Pension*. Nader and Blackwell (pp. 4, 6–7; emphasis in original) used truthful employee accounts to bring home to readers that loss of a longstanding and essential pension "could happen to them":

> Charlie Reed thought he was going to get a pension. He went to work when he was twenty-one as a coal miner for Jones & Laughlin Steel Corporation, and after twenty-three years in the mines, he was laid off . . .
>
> Thirteen years later, Reed applied for the pension he thought he had been earning during his twenty-three years in the mines. He found there wasn't one; instead, there was a rule Reed

didn't know about; he had to have twenty years of service *within the thirty years preceding his application for benefits.* The rules made no exception for miners who had been laid off . . .

If you are inclined to say, "It can't happen to me," meet some of the people who found out it could . . .

Joseph Mintz, fifty-six, of Buena Park, California, has been in aerospace work for over thirty years and has no pension coming to him. For twenty-seven years he worked for three different companies. At each job, he was laid off before he had the ten-year minimum service requirement for a pension. One company laid him off after nine years and ten months . . .

He didn't know that *you may not get a pension if you are laid off or change jobs.*

As Blackwell and Nader recognized, in effectively communicating risk, there is a world of difference between a general statement that a pension could be unavailable, even after many years of service, and several concrete accounts of people "like you and me" finding themselves without any pension after a long period of service. (Of course, an important concern is that the individual accounts could *over*compensate, rather than merely offset, the effects of optimism bias, but the concluding paragraph of this section suggests a natural limit on this concern.)

The idea of requiring actors to provide truthful accounts of harm has analogies in observed practice outside of the workplace domain as well. The American Legacy Foundation, an organization founded out of the 1998 settlement agreement between the United States tobacco industry and state attorneys general, has launched an information campaign employing what may naturally be viewed as a strategy of debiasing through the availability heuristic. The foundation has publicized, in leading national magazines and on the Internet, parting letters to children and other loved ones from parents dying of smoking-related diseases. For instance, one letter reads, "Dearest Jon, I am so sorry my smoking will cheat us out of 20 or 30 more years together. Remember the fun we had every year at the lake. I will ALWAYS love and treasure you. Linda."[12]

Of course, it is important to bear in mind that employers, not employee representatives or other employee-side actors, would be selecting the narrative to present under the legal proposal sketched above. As Glaeser (2004, p. 410) has observed, "One should expect to see a proliferation of misleading signals and other cues when incorrect beliefs are complements to buying sellers' commodities," and the same is likely to be true when incorrect beliefs are a complement to supplying labor. It is possible that employers, influenced by market pressures, would manage to subvert attempts to achieve debiasing through the availability heuristic. This influence of employers, however, reduces the overshooting concern noted above and, in addition, is itself naturally cabined by the requirement to report a narrative from an actual court decision involving a successful claim by an employee claiming termination without good cause.

III.   REDUCING IMPLICIT RACIAL BIAS THROUGH WORKPLACE LAW

Recall that implicit racial bias, like the other System I processes discussed earlier in this chapter, usually operates outside the decisionmaker's conscious awareness. Suppose, then, that Cambridge Police Sergeant Crowley both (i) would in fact have treated a hypothetical white Professor Gates, with all other circumstances the same, differently – with respect to the insistence on stepping outside, the arrest for disorderly conduct, or both – and (ii) has no awareness that he would have treated a hypothetical white Professor Gates differently (in fact would vehemently resist any such suggestion). Under these assumptions, if the law responds by directly prohibiting Sergeant Crowley's behavior as discriminatory, then the law will face a difficult challenge. If Sergeant Crowley is wholly unaware of the role race is (by hypothesis) playing in his behavior, then it is unclear how, precisely, he is supposed to alter the pattern, even if the law obligates him to do so.

An alternative legal approach – building in a general way on the discussion in the previous section – seeks to reduce people's bias directly. In fact, some features of existing employment discrimination law are likely to have just this effect, and other measures could do much more, as described below.

A.   Empirical Evidence on Reducing Implicit Racial Bias[13]

Two related lines of social science research suggest the factors that can help to reduce implicit racial bias.

1.   Evidence on the effects of diverse populations
A striking set of results in the social science literature on implicit racial bias demonstrates that diversity in the surrounding population will often shape and affect the degree of implicit bias individuals exhibit. The studies suggest that the others present in an individual's environment can significantly reduce the degree of implicit bias as measured by the Implicit Association Test (IAT) described above.

One notable study of the effects of population make-up on implicit bias showed that individuals who were administered an in-person IAT by an African-American experimenter exhibited substantially less implicit racial bias than individuals who were administered an in-person IAT by a white experimenter (Lowery, Hardin and Sinclair 2001). In other words, subjects' speed in categorizing black-unpleasant and white-pleasant (stereotype-consistent) pairs was closer to their speed in categorizing black-pleasant and white-unpleasant (stereotype-inconsistent) pairs when an African-American experimenter was standing in front of the room than when a white experimenter was standing in front of the room.

A second study paired white test participants with either white or African-American partners and then assigned the pair a task in which either the participant evaluated the partner or the participant was evaluated by the partner (Richeson and Ambady 2003). Two results from the study are notable. First, echoing the results from the study noted in the previous paragraph, participants who were paired with an African-American partner – aggregating cases in which the partner was in the superior role and the subordinate role – exhibited less implicit racial bias as measured by the IAT than participants who were paired with a white partner. Thus, the simple fact of more diversity in the immediate environment meant less overall implicit bias. Second, within pairs involving an African-American partner, participants who were told they would be evaluated by the African-American partner exhibited significantly less implicit racial bias than participants who were told to evaluate the African-American partner.

While much empirical work by psychologists (including the studies just described) involves laboratory experiments, an important study provides field evidence of the role of population make-up on the degree of implicit bias exhibited by those present (Dasgupta and Asgari 2004). The study examined levels of implicit gender stereotyping, as measured by a gender-stereotype variant of the race IAT described above, among college-age women both before and after their first year at either a coeducational or a women's college. Notably, despite the plausibility of sorting across coeducational and women's colleges based on preexisting attitudes about gender issues, the groups of women from the two particular colleges in this study exhibited indistinguishable levels of implicit gender stereotyping during the first semester of college. One year later, however, the students at the women's college exhibited no implicit gender stereotyping, while the female students at the coeducational college showed higher levels of implicit gender stereotyping than in the previous year.

What explains this substantial difference? It turns out that the central correlate of the level of implicit gender stereotyping in the second year of college is the number of female professors encountered to that point. While this was true for students at both colleges, the number of female professors encountered was far higher at the women's college, leading to overall lower levels of implicit gender stereotyping at that institution relative to the coeducational college. (Students at the women's college who had only modest numbers of female professors looked more like the students at the coeducational college.) Once again, the presence of a representative of the at-issue group in the environment significantly lowered implicit bias toward members of that group. As the authors of the study put it (p. 655), "[T]he more women see counterstereotypic ingroup members in their immediate environment[,] the more it undermines their automatic gender stereotypes."

Another sex-stereotyping study explored (again in the field rather than in a laboratory) how exposure to female chief councilors in Indian village councils affected public opinion about female leaders (Beamen, Chattopadhyay, Duflo, Pande and Topalova 2009). The study compared villages that did not have political reservation of leadership roles for women in village councils with villages that had such reservation. The study found that exposure to female chief councilors in the reserved villages led to weakened implicit stereotypes about gender roles. While both genders exhibited significant bias against women in leadership activities in villages with no reservation, exposure to a female leader significantly reduced the association among men in reserved villages. Exposure also eliminated negative bias in the perception of female leader effectiveness among male villagers.

The effects of population diversity in the environment on the level of implicit bias may stem from the availability heuristic discussed earlier; people often tend to assess probabilities based on whether a relevant event comes easily to mind. The effects of diversity may also reflect a more general role for the "affect heuristic," by which decisions are formed by reference to rapid, intuitive, affective judgments (Slovic, Finucane, Peters and MacGregor 2002). These or other System I mechanisms may lie behind the observed reductions in implicit bias across many studies.

2.   Evidence on the effects of the physical and sensory environment

The composition of a group, emphasized above, is not the only factor that appears to play a role in determining the degree of implicit racial bias. Evidence suggests that implicit bias may also be reduced by the elimination of negative stereotypes in the physical and sensory surroundings, as well as by the promotion of counter-stereotypes in those surroundings.

In one study, for instance, participants exposed to pictures of Tiger Woods (prior to the 2009 Woods scandal) and Timothy McVeigh demonstrated far less implicit bias against African-Americans as measured by the IAT than participants not exposed to such pictures (Dasgupta and Greenwald 2001). Parallel reductions in implicit bias have been observed with the display of pictures or portraits of historically important female leaders or admired gay or lesbian individuals (Dasgupta and Asgari 2004; Dasgupta and Rivera 2008).

Of course, the 2008 Presidential election provides a clear case of a prominent African-American exemplar – a phenomenon examined by Plant, Devine, Cox, Columb, Miller, Goplen and Peruche (2009). The authors found that in the midst of President Obama's successful election campaign, white college students showed significantly lower levels of implicit racial bias than in 2006. With respect to the relationship between the decline in implicit bias and exposure to Obama as a positive figure, the study found that "the tendency to have positive Black exemplars come to mind or anticipate that other people had these positive exemplars come to mind when they thought of Black people was associated with low levels of racial prejudice" (p. 963). Thus, media messages and cultural attitudes surrounding Obama's election may have decreased implicit racial bias in at least some Americans.

The academic studies just described have an intriguing potential real-world counterpart in a point familiar to (and highly evocative for) many individuals, perhaps especially university students. People frequently take note of the portraits of famous scholars or benefactors that adorn classrooms, offices, and many public spaces. Often the portraits are predominantly white. Many observers have a strong experience of these depictions as shaping and reinforcing an environment permeated in subtle ways with various forms of implicit bias, a point to which I return at the end of this section.

B.   Workplace Law Implications – Existing Employment Discrimination Prohibitions[14]

Laws regulating discrimination in the workplace are a basic component of American law. Although these laws have often been critiqued for failing to create direct legal liability for implicitly biased workplace behavior,[15] even the simplest feature of such laws – prohibiting certain hiring, firing, and promotion practices – will tend to reduce, to some degree, the level of implicit workplace bias through the simple mechanism of increasing workplace diversity.

The empirical results described above suggest that the simple fact of having a racially diverse workforce may well be an important means of reducing the level of implicit racial bias in the workplace. If someone – and perhaps especially if someone in authority – in a white employee's workplace is African-American, the evidence strongly suggests that the white employee will tend to exhibit less implicit racial bias as measured by the IAT than if everyone in the workplace is white. In a sense, the story here is the implicit-bias counterpart to the old idea that contact with members of other groups should reduce conscious bias against these individuals; while the contact hypothesis has been much discussed, the analogous concept that workplace diversity achieved through employment discrimination law can decrease *implicit* bias, without the need for various forms of "deliberate mental correction" (Krieger 1998) in response to such bias, has been overlooked in existing employment discrimination law scholarship.[16]

A natural effect of existing prohibitions on discriminatory hiring, firing, and promotion practices is of course to increase the representation of members of protected groups; and in this way these existing prohibitions should tend to reduce implicit racial bias. (Note that employment discrimination law's consistent and forceful rejection of measures such as explicit quotas counters the concern that this law might paradoxically exacerbate implicit bias through overly heavy-handed mechanisms of diversifying the workplace.[17]) The central insight is that it is possible to respond to the problem of implicit bias in ways other than creating direct legal liability for workplace conduct stemming from such bias.

To be sure, if increasing population diversity were the only means by which existing employment discrimination law tended to reduce implicit bias in the workplace, the effect of the law might not be very substantial. However, as explored below, existing law importantly affects other aspects of individuals' workplaces – beyond the diversity of the population make-up – as well. It is the *synergistic* effect of all of the provisions of existing workplace law discussed below that ultimately suggests a significant role for such law in reducing implicit racial bias.

1. Disparate treatment liability for hiring, firing, and promotion practices

Within the general category of existing prohibitions on discriminatory hiring, firing, and promotion practices, there are several causal mechanisms by which these prohibitions tend to increase workplace diversity and, thus, reduce implicit bias; a few subtleties attach to each and will be discussed in the space below.

The simplest and most obvious mechanism here is the illegalization of personnel decisions consciously made on the basis of race.[18] While this core "disparate treatment" prohibition has been at the heart of the criticism of existing employment discrimination doctrine as insufficiently responsive to the problem of implicit bias, the analysis above suggests that it is important to recognize the way in which even existing prohibitions on conscious discrimination in the workplace may have some traction against the problem of implicit bias. This analysis suggests that the degree of implicit bias is importantly affected by the level of workplace diversity. Thus, as long as existing prohibitions on conscious discrimination in hiring, firing, and promotion practices have some positive effect on workplace diversity, these prohibitions – although they do not directly illegalize personnel decisions stemming from implicit bias – will tend to decrease such bias in the workplace.

Of course, if there were no remaining consciously biased behavior in today's world to be policed by these existing employment discrimination law prohibitions, then these prohibitions would not have much, if any, effect on the level of workplace diversity. But the idea that implicitly biased behavior is the central problem in American society today certainly does not imply the absence of a significant remaining problem with consciously biased behavior. As Susan Sturm (1998, p. 641) has noted in an article primarily emphasizing the problem of implicitly biased behavior, "The classic forms of deliberate exclusion based on race and gender that were characteristic of the early stages of the civil rights regime certainly have not disappeared."

There are still two intriguing potential wrinkles in this account of the effect on implicit bias of existing disparate treatment liability for consciously biased hiring, firing, and promotion practices, however. First, as Krieger (1998, p. 1274) notes, some social science evidence suggests that "[t]he mere introduction of 'groupness' into a situation" generates various types of bias, and also that "[i]ncreasing the salience of group distinctions exacerbates these effects." Conceivably, disparate treatment liability under existing employment discrimination law, by illegalizing personnel practices based on protected traits, could "increas[e] the salience of group distinctions" – although probably not to a large degree in today's society. (Krieger does not address this issue because her focus is affirmative action rather than disparate treatment liability under existing employment discrimination law.) However, as Krieger describes, there are important countervailing effects; "racial mixing in schools, universities, neighborhoods, or interdependent cooperative workgroups results in a greater likelihood that members of different racial groups will occupy ingroups constructed along social dimensions other than race" (pp. 1275–6). That is, bias against other groups may be unavoidable, but diversity tends to affect the composition of the groups themselves. Moreover, "placing members of different social categories into situations involving cooperative interdependence and individuating social interactions also appears to reduce categorical responding" more generally (Krieger 1998, p. 1276). Thus, in the present context, the social science evidence suggests that it is at least as likely that existing disparate treatment liability for hiring, firing, and promotion practices will, on balance, reduce the salience of racial lines as that it will increase the salience of those lines; and, therefore, a countervailing increase in bias from heightening the salience of such lines is not suggested by this evidence.

A second wrinkle in the account of disparate treatment liability offered here is that some scholars have suggested that such liability makes employers reluctant to *hire* individuals from protected groups by raising such individuals' wages or making them difficult to fire – even for legitimate reasons – down the road; while the failure to hire is technically actionable, on this view practical obstacles make such hiring suits unlikely (e.g., Posner 1987). If this account is correct, then disparate treatment liability for discriminatory personnel practices under existing employment discrimination law could have the perverse effect of *reducing* workplace diversity by discouraging employers from hiring a diverse workforce in the first place.

Definitive empirical evidence supporting a reduction in workplace diversity from the imposition of disparate treatment liability has been difficult to come by, while the empirical evidence from the early history of Title VII of the Civil Rights Act of 1964 suggests that the law's protections clearly improved employment levels at least of African-Americans.[19] In the absence of contrary empirical evidence about the effects of employment discrimination law today, it seems reasonable to assume that existing employment discrimination law's core prohibition on consciously discriminatory personnel practices increases rather than decreases workplace diversity. And if this is true, then this prohibition will tend to decrease the level of implicit bias in the workplace.

2.   Disparate impact liability for hiring, firing, and promotion practices

A second way in which existing employment discrimination law tends to increase workplace diversity is the "disparate impact" branch of liability under Title VII of the Civil Rights Act of 1964. While some commentators have been dismissive of disparate impact liability on grounds of practical importance in real-world litigation,[20] there is reason to believe that the limited-importance objection has been overstated by some margin (Jolls 2001).

Commentators have emphasized that disparate impact cases require plaintiffs both to set forth identifiable employment practices that disproportionately harm their group and to present statistical evidence in support of such harm (e.g., Krieger 1995). But these same factors – while they make disparate impact cases somewhat difficult to bring and thus less frequent in practice than disparate treatment claims – also mean that each disparate impact case is likely to have far greater impact than a given disparate treatment case targeting a specific employment action taken against a particular individual. If, to take one well-known disparate impact case, a no-beard rule is struck down in a suit against a Domino's pizza franchise on grounds of its disproportionate adverse impact on African-American men, many other employers are likely to consider altering their grooming policies in response. By contrast, a finding of individual discriminatory behavior by a Domino's franchise would presumably have relatively little effect outside of that particular Domino's franchise.[21]

Different critiques of the role of disparate impact liability in increasing workplace diversity echo the groupness and hiring-disincentive points from above. While the groupness analysis carries over directly from above, a brief additional remark about the hiring-disincentive analysis is useful here. The hiring-disincentive account suggests that protection under employment discrimination law could paradoxically reduce the representation of protected groups because the legal regime may increase the costs of employing group members and thus make employers reluctant to hire them.[22] In a sense this objection is the converse of the critique of disparate impact liability discussed just above, in that the present argument assumes that disparate impact liability meaningfully affects employers' ability to fire members of the protected group, while the prior argument assumes that disparate impact liability is largely irrelevant. As noted in the above discussion of disparate treatment liability for discriminatory personnel practices, however, the empirical evidence on employment discrimination law's employment effects generally supports the conclusion that this law has had at least some positive effect on employment levels (though the studies have not been able to test specifically for the effects of disparate impact liability, as distinguished from employment discrimination law generally).

3. A further effect of existing employment discrimination law

As suggested above, the physical and sensory environment may exert significant influence over the level of implicit bias individuals exhibit on the IAT and similar measures. The evidence thus points to a further respect in which the existing employment discrimination law prohibitions discussed above – on discriminatory hiring, firing, and promotion practices – may reduce implicit racial bias. Recall the earlier discussion of the possible connection between effects of the physical and sensory environment on implicit bias and the frequent controversies in recent years over the portraiture at universities and other public places. The evidence presented above suggests the possibility of significant effects from minimizing stimuli such as the largely white portraits often observed at such institutions and, more expansively, affirmatively using portraits of important alternative figures, including a larger set of nonwhite figures, in their place. This evidence suggests that positive images of members of these groups decrease the degree of implicit bias toward group members. Thus, under the plausible assumption that the precipitating force behind greater diversity in the physical and sensory environment is often members of the underrepresented groups, employment discrimination law's effects on the population make-up of the workplace, discussed above, may – in addition to the direct effect discussed already – also have the indirect effect of altering the physical and sensory environment at the workplace and, thus, further reducing implicit bias. Put differently, adding diversity to the workplace not only will tend to reduce implicit bias directly, but also will generate a push toward a physical and sensory environment that tends to reduce further the level of implicit bias.

An example of this idea outside the workplace context is the controversy that occurred in the late 1990s at the University of Virginia School of Law over the school's decision to hang oil portraits of all of its former deans, all white men draped in black robes, in the law library.[23] "When I first did see them it was a shock," said one African-American law student. "[W]here are the representations of minorities and women? In light of that absence, it's offensive." The current dean of the law school responded by indicating that a portrait of the school's first African-American student had been commissioned.

Events at Harvard University illustrate a similar dynamic. A study revealed that only three of 302 portraits across the Harvard campus were of persons of color, and these results were reported to the university's administration. The administration responded by promising portraits of "persons of African-American, Asian-American, Latino-American and Native American backgrounds who have served Harvard with distinction" and stated that these portraits would be placed at "sites of significance" around the university campus (Gewertz 2003).

A parallel move took place at the United States Capitol, albeit in the context of omission of women rather than members of racial minorities. A few years ago a group of lawmakers and advocates for women persuaded Congress to locate a sculpture of three suffragists – Lucretia Mott, Elizabeth Cady Stanton, and Susan B. Anthony – in the Capitol's grand Rotunda. Republican Senator Olympia J. Snowe commented on the placement: "It really talks about the values of our nation and the premium that we place on the role of women in our society. Every time I see that statue, I smile, because I think that's where they belong" (Stolberg 2003).

It is important not to exaggerate the effects of the initiatives related to portraiture, and it is also important not to assume that only individuals from underrepresented groups will push for changes in portraiture. But the social science research described above suggests that Senator Snowe and others are correct to think that initiatives of this kind can have real effects on perceptions of previously underrepresented groups, and the accounts just described suggest the frequent role of underrepresented groups in undertaking these initiatives. Thus, the discussion here highlights the way in which existing provisions of employment discrimination law can work synergistically, through multiple channels, to reduce the level of implicit bias in the workplace.

C.   Workplace Law Implications – Reform of Employment Discrimination Law[24]

Until now, the discussion has focused on the effects of existing employment discrimination law. However, more could be done through this body of law to reduce implicit racial bias. I will offer one example here.

As discussed above, the evidence suggests that there are bias-reducing effects of favorable portraiture or imagery in the physical environment. Therefore, if portraiture in the workplace consistently reflects diverse exemplars, it is likely – though certainly not guaranteed[25] – that those present will show less implicit bias, with likely mechanisms once more being the availability and affect heuristics. Note that in contrast to the experimental setting, diverse exemplars in the workplace would be a recurrent rather than fleeting aspect of the individual's environment. And, parallel to the point above, the manner in which the display of exemplars were to occur would be important; if it were too heavy-handed, implicit bias might not decrease at all (and could even increase).

In light of the available evidence, it may make a good deal of sense to treat an employer's positive effort to portray diversity in the physical environment of the workplace as an express factor weighing against vicarious employer liability for hostile work environments. This approach would be parallel to the way that, under existing law governing hostile work environments, employers regularly defend against vicarious liability on the basis of actions such as manuals or training videos disseminated in the workplace.[26] The basic suggestion is that the existing legal approach to employers' vicarious liability in hostile environment cases might be extended beyond the discrete mechanisms (manuals, handbooks, videos, Internet instructional programs) contemplated by present law – at least if doing so is consistent with the First Amendment (a question that is beyond the scope of the present chapter). While many of the mechanisms contemplated by present law governing vicarious liability for hostile work environments are distinctly System II in character, the evidence suggests the important role of System I mechanisms in reducing implicit bias. The display of positive exemplars in the workplace may do far more to reduce implicit bias than yet another mandatory training session on workplace diversity.

IV.   CONCLUSION

When workplace actors exhibit the various forms of bias discussed above, law can be an important corrective. Often, as in the legal applications discussed in the two preceding sections, legal rules may reduce people's degree of bias, thereby improving decisionmaking that is erroneous *by people's own account*. If Cambridge Police Sergeant Crowley did not want to treat Professor Gates differently from how the sergeant would have treated an otherwise identical white professor, but Crowley did so treat Gates, then steps that reduce the gap between Crowley's desired course of action and his actual one should be welcomed even by Crowley himself. Of course, such steps need not derive solely from law; such measures as becoming aware of one's IAT results (Plant and Devine 2009) and participating in certain forms of training (e.g., Correll, Park, Judd, Wittenbrink, Sadler and Keesee 2007) may significantly reduce implicitly biased behavior. The discussion above, however, highlights the important role of workplace law in responding to human bias in various forms.

NOTES

*   Thanks to Vanessa Selbst for superb research assistance.
1.   Cambridge Police Incident Report No. 9005127, July 16, 2009, available at http://www.samefacts.com/archives/Police%20report%20on%20Gates%20arrest.PDF (visited Dec. 6, 2011).
2.   Equal Employment Opportunity Commission v. FLTVT, LLC (M.D. Fl. 2007).
3.   This section is an edited and expanded version of material from Section 2.1 of Jolls and Sunstein (2006a) and the Introduction and Part I of Jolls and Sunstein (2006b).
4.   For a recent overview of evidence of IAT-behavior connections in participants in a range of studies, see Greenwald, Poehlman, Uhlmann and Banaji (2009); for a study on physician subjects, see Green, Carney, Pallin, Ngo, Raymond, Iezzoni and Banaji (2007) (finding behavior-IAT correlations among physicians asked to give their responses to hypothetical patient symptom lists and then subjected to IAT testing).
5.   As described in Jolls (1998), an interesting subtlety here is that if the question is whether one's probability of experiencing a bad event is below the average probability of experiencing that event (as distinguished from the average person's probability of experiencing that event), then it is possible for most people to be below average. To illustrate, suppose that for 80% of the population the probability of being involved in an auto accident is 10%, and for 20% it is 60%. Then the average probability of being involved in an auto accident is 20% ($0.1 \times 0.8 + 0.6 \times 0.2 = 0.2$). So for 80% of the population, the probability of being involved in an auto accident (10%) is below the average probability (20%). But the average person has a 10% chance of being involved in an auto accident, and it would be impossible for more than half of the population to have a probability below this. The natural interpretation of most studies of optimism bias would seem to be that they request a comparison with the average person's probability, rather than with the average probability; the average probability would often be quite difficult to compute and not within the grasp of most subjects. Moreover, at least one study has dealt explicitly with the issue raised here and has found significant evidence of optimism bias even using the average probability benchmark (Weinstein 1980).
6.   For a discussion of the relevant studies in these domains, suggesting optimism bias in the estimation of actual probabilities rather than simply relative risk, see Jolls (1998).
7.   See, e.g., Dillon v. Champion Jogbra, Inc., 819 A.2d 703 (Vt. 2002).
8.   The requirement of termination only upon good cause could arise only if employee handbook provisions limited termination to cases of good cause or could apply to all employment relationships regardless of the existence and language of an employee handbook.
9.   In the discussion below of the law of employee handbooks, the focus is on scenarios in which employee optimism bias is thought to produce an overall underestimation by employees of the risk of termination without good cause. In general, optimism bias is context dependent and may vary across different settings (Armor and Taylor 2002). It is possible, for instance, that overoptimistic employees underestimate base-level risk of termination without good cause but then overestimate the decrease in risk from limits on such termination – conceivably creating a positive incentive for employers to undertake such measures (cf. Schwartz 1988).
10.   This subsection is an edited version of Section 3.1 of Jolls and Sunstein (2006a).
11.   Weinstein and Klein (2002) note that individualized information about risk factors was found in other studies to reduce optimism bias, but this finding is not pursued further here because it is difficult to imagine incorporating such individualized information into a general legal standard. A similar point applies to the one successful debiasing mechanism reported in Weinstein (1980) in response to optimism bias; that mechanism – in which individuals were exposed to lists made by other individuals of factors increasing the other individuals' chances of positive outcomes – again seems hard to translate into a recognizable legal standard.
12.   See http://women.americanlegacy.org/includes/pdfs/ad2.pdf.
13.   This subsection is an edited and expanded version of material from Sections 3(a) and 3(c) of Jolls (2007).
14.   This subsection is an edited version of material from Sections 3(a) and 3(d) of Jolls (2007).
15.   See Jolls (2007) for a detailed account of the critiques.
16.   For the argument that affirmative action plans voluntarily undertaken by employers will tend to reduce implicit racial bias by increasing workplace diversity, see Yelnosky (2003).
17.   Title VII of the Civil Rights Act of 1964 specifically provides that it shall not "be interpreted to require any employer . . . to grant preferential treatment to any individual or to any group because of the race, color, religion, sex, or national origin of such individual or group on account of an imbalance which may exist with respect to the total number or percentage of persons of any race, color, religion, sex, or national origin employed by any employer . . . in comparison with the total number or percentage of persons of

such race, color, religion, sex, or national origin in any community, State, section, or other area, or in the available work force in any community, State, section, or other area." 42 U.S.C. sec. 2000e–2j.

18. See, e.g., Washington v. Davis, 426 U.S. 229, 239-48 (1976) (liability for such decisions under the Equal Protection Clause of the Constitution); International Brotherhood of Teamsters v. United States, 431 U.S. 324, 335 n.15 (1977) (liability for such decisions under Title VII of the Civil Rights Act of 1964).

19. Definitive treatments of Title VII's early effects include Donohue and Heckman (1991) and Heckman and Payner (1989). The Heckman and Payner study in particular looks at employment levels (as distinguished from wages) in detail. Subsequent empirical evidence suggests that the expansion of Title VII liability in 1991 had no overall effects (either positive or negative) on employment of protected groups, although employment seems to have increased in some industries and decreased in others (Oyer and Schaefer 2002).

20. See Jolls (2007) for examples.

21. For further discussion of the Domino's disparate impact litigation, see Jolls (2001).

22. Ayres and Siegelman (1996) develop this argument in the specific context of disparate impact liability.

23. See "Univ. of Virginia Portraits of Law School Deans Focus Attention on Need for Diversity," *Jet* (1997). The quote comes from the *Jet* article.

24. This subsection is an edited version of material from Part II.B.3 of Jolls and Sunstein (2006b).

25. See Greenwald and Krieger (2006) for a cautionary note about the longer-term effects of diverse imagery.

26. See, e.g., Faragher v. City of Boca Raton, 524 U.S. 775 (1998).

REFERENCES

Armor, David A. and Shelley E. Taylor. 2002. "When Predictions Fail: The Dilemma of Unrealistic Optimism," in Thomas Gilovich, Dale Griffin and Daniel Kahneman, eds., *Heuristics and Biases: The Psychology of Intuitive Judgment.* Cambridge: Cambridge University Press.

Ayres, Ian and Peter Siegelman. 1996. "The Q-Word as Red Herring: Why Disparate Impact Liability Does Not Induce Hiring Quotas." Symposium: The Changing Workplace, 74 *Texas Law Review* 1487–526.

Beamen, Lori, Raghabendra Chattopadhyay, Esther Duflo, Rohini Pande and Petia Topalova. 2009. "Powerful Women: Does Exposure Reduce Bias?" 124 *Quarterly Journal of Economics* 1497–540.

Chaiken, Shelly and Yaacov Trope. 1999. *Dual-Process Theories in Social Psychology.* New York: Guilford Press.

Correll, Joshua, Bernadette Park, Charles M. Judd, Bernd Wittenbrink, Melody S. Sadler and Tracie Keesee. 2007. "Across the Thin Blue Line: Police Officers and Racial Bias in the Decision to Shoot," 92 *Journal of Personality and Social Psychology* 1006–23.

Dasgupta, Nilanjana and Shaki Asgari. 2004. "Seeing is Believing: Exposure to Counterstereotypic Women Leaders and its Effect on the Malleability of Automatic Gender Stereotypes," 40 *Journal of Experimental Social Psychology* 642–58.

Dasgupta, Nilanjana and Anthony G. Greenwald. 2001. "On the Malleability of Automatic Attitudes: Combating Automatic Prejudice with Images of Admired and Disliked Individuals," 81 *Journal of Personality and Social Psychology* 800–14.

Dasgupta, Nilanjana and Luis M. Rivera. 2008. "When Social Context Matters: The Influence of Long-Term Contact and Short-Term Exposure to Admired Outgroup Members on Implicit Attitudes and Behavioral Intentions," 26 *Social Cognition* 112–23.

Donohue, John J. and James Heckman. 1991. "Continuous versus Episodic Change: The Impact of Civil Rights Policy on the Economic Status of Blacks," 29 *Journal of Economic Literature* 1603–43.

Dovidio, John F., Kerry Kawakami and Samuel L. Gaertner. 2002. "Implicit and Explicit Prejudice and Interracial Interaction," 82 *Journal of Personality and Social Psychology* 62–8.

Fischhoff, Baruch. 1982. "Debiasing," in Daniel Kahneman, Paul Slovic and Amos Tversky, eds., *Judgment under Uncertainty: Heuristics and Biases.* Cambridge: Cambridge University Press.

Gewertz, Ken. 2003. "Adding Some Color to Harvard Portraits," *Harvard University Gazette.*

Glaeser, Edward. 2004. "Psychology and the Market," 94 *American Economic Review (Papers and Proceedings)* 408–13.

Green, Alexander R., Dana R. Carney, Daniel J. Pallin, Long H. Ngo, Kristal L. Raymond, Lisa I. Iezzoni and Mahzarin R. Banaji. 2007. "Implicit Bias among Physicians and its Prediction of Thrombolysis Decisions for Black and White Patients," 22 *Journal of General Internal Medicine* 1231–8.

Greenwald, Anthony G. and Linda Hamilton Krieger. 2006. "Implicit Bias: Scientific Foundations." Symposium: Behavioral Realism in Law, 94 *California Law Review* 945–67.

Greenwald, Anthony G., Debbie E. McGhee and Jordan L.K. Schwartz. 1998. "Measuring Individual

Differences in Implicit Cognition: The Implicit Association Test," 74 *Journal of Personality and Social Psychology* 1464–80.

Greenwald, Anthony G., T. Andrew Poehlman, Eric Luis Uhlmann and Mahzarin R. Banaji. 2009. "Understanding and Using the Implicit Association Test: III. Meta-Analysis of Predictive Validity," 97 *Journal of Personality and Social Psychology* 17–41.

Heckman, James J. and Brook S. Payner. 1989. "Determining the Impact of Federal Antidiscrimination Policy on the Economic Status of Blacks: A Study of South Carolina," 79 *American Economic Review* 138–77.

Herbert, Bob. 2009. "Anger Has its Place," *New York Times*.

Hofmann, Wilhelm, Tobias Gschwendner, Luigi Castelli and Manfred Schmitt. 2008. "Implicit and Explicit Attitudes and Interracial Interaction: The Moderating Role of Situationally Available Control Resources," 11 *Group Processes and Intergroup Relations* 69–87.

Johnson, O'Ryan. 2009. "Crowley Teaches Racial Profiling Class at Academy," *Boston Herald*.

Jolls, Christine. 1998. "Behavioral Economics Analysis of Redistributive Legal Rules." Symposium: The Legal Implications of Psychology, 51 *Vanderbilt Law Review* 1653–77.

Jolls, Christine. 2001. "Antidiscrimination and Accommodation," 115 *Harvard Law Review* 642–99.

Jolls, Christine. 2007. "Antidiscrimination Law's Effects on Implicit Bias," Retrieved from http://www. law.yale.edu/documents/pdf/Faculty/Antidiscrimination_Laws_Effects.pdf. Previously published in Mitu Gulati and Michael J. Yelnosky, eds., *Behavioral Analyses of Workplace Discrimination.* The Netherlands: Kluwer Academic Publishers.

Jolls, Christine and Cass R. Sunstein. 2006a. "Debiasing Through Law," 35 *Journal of Legal Studies* 199–241.

Jolls, Christine and Cass R. Sunstein. 2006b. "The Law of Implicit Bias." Symposium: Behavioral Realism in Law, 94 *California Law Review* 969–96.

Jolls, Christine, Cass R. Sunstein and Richard Thaler. 1998. "A Behavioral Approach to Law and Economics," 50 *Stanford Law Review* 1471–550.

Kahneman, Daniel and Shane Frederick. 2002. "Representativeness Revisited: Attribute Substitution in Intuitive Judgment," in Thomas Gilovich, Dale Griffin and Daniel Kahneman, eds., *Heuristics and Biases: The Psychology of Intuitive Judgment.* Cambridge: Cambridge University Press.

Krieger, Linda Hamilton. 1995. "The Content of Our Categories: A Cognitive Bias Approach to Discrimination and Equal Employment Opportunity," 47 *Stanford Law Review* 1161–248.

Krieger, Linda Hamilton. 1998. "Civil Rights Perestroika: Intergroup Relations after Affirmative Action," 86 *California Law Review* 1251–333.

Latin, Howard. 1994. "'Good' Warnings, Bad Products, and Cognitive Limitations," 41 *UCLA Law Review* 1193–295.

LeDoux, Joseph. 1996. *The Emotional Brain: The Mysterious Underpinnings of Emotional Life.* New York: Simon and Schuster.

Lowery, Brian S., Curtis D. Hardin and Stacey Sinclair. 2001. "Social Influence Effects on Automatic Racial Prejudice," 81 *Journal of Personality and Social Psychology* 842–55.

McConnell, Allen R. and Jill M. Leibold. 2001. "Relations among the Implicit Association Test, Discriminatory Behavior, and Explicit Measures of Racial Attitudes," 37 *Journal of Experimental Social Psychology* 435–42.

Nader, Ralph and Kate Blackwell. 1973. *You and Your Pension.* New York: Grossman.

Nisbett, Richard E., Eugene Borgida, Rick Crandall and Harvey Reed. 1982. "Popular Induction: Information Is Not Necessarily Informative," in Daniel Kahneman, Paul Slovic and Amos Tversky, eds., *Judgment under Uncertainty: Heuristics and Biases.* Cambridge: Cambridge University Press.

Nosek, Brian A., Mahzarin R. Banaji and Anthony G. Greenwald. 2002. "Harvesting Implicit Group Attitudes and Beliefs from a Demonstration Web Site," 6 *Group Dynamics: Theory, Research, and Practice* 101–15.

Olopade, Dayo. 2009. "Skip Gates Speaks," *The Root.*

Oyer, Paul and Scott Schaefer. 2002. "Sorting, Quotas, and the Civil Rights Act of 1991: Who Hires When it's Hard to Fire?" 45 *Journal of Law and Economics* 41–68.

Plant, E. Ashby and Patricia G. Devine. 2009. "The Active Control of Prejudice: Unpacking the Intentions Guiding Control Efforts," 96 *Journal of Personality and Social Psychology* 640–52.

Plant, E. Ashby, Patricia G. Devine, William T. L. Cox, Corey Columb, Saul L. Miller, Joanna Goplen and B. Michelle Peruche. 2009. "The Obama Effect: Decreasing Implicit Prejudice and Stereotyping," 45 *Journal of Experimental Social Psychology* 961–4.

Posner, Richard A. 1987. "The Efficiency and the Efficacy of Title VII," 136 *University of Pennsylvania Law Review* 513–21.

Rachlinski, Jeffrey J. 2003. "The Uncertain Psychological Case for Paternalism." Symposium: Empirical Legal Realism, 97 *Northwestern University Law Review* 1165–225.

Richeson, Jennifer A. and Nalini Ambady. 2003. "Effects of Situational Power on Automatic Racial Prejudice," 39 *Journal of Experimental Social Psychology* 177–83.

Rooth, Dan-Olof. 2010. "Automatic Associations and Discrimination in Hiring: Real World Evidence," 17 *Labour Economics* 523–34.

Rozin, Paul. 2001. "Technological Stigma: Some Perspectives from the Study of Contagion," in James Flynn, Paul Slovic and Howard Kunreuther, eds., *Risk, Media, and Stigma: Understanding Public Challenges to Modern Science and Technology*. Sterling, VA: Earthscan.

Schwartz, Alan. 1988. "Proposals for Products Liability Reform: A Theoretical Synthesis," 97 *Yale Law Journal* 353–419.

Schwartz, Alan and Louis L. Wilde. 1983. "Imperfect Information in Markets for Contract Terms: The Examples of Warranties and Security Interests," 69 *Virginia Law Review* 1387–485.

Sloan, Frank A., V. Kerry Smith and Donald H. Taylor, Jr. 2003. *The Smoking Puzzle: Information, Risk Perception, and Choice*. Cambridge, MA: Harvard University Press.

Slovic, Paul, Melissa Finucane, Ellen Peters and Donald G. MacGregor. 2002. "The Affect Heuristic," in Thomas Gilovich, Dale Griffin and Daniel Kahneman, eds., *Heuristics and Biases: The Psychology of Intuitive Judgment*. Cambridge: Cambridge University Press.

Stiglitz, Joseph E. 1986. *Economics of the Public Sector*. New York: Norton.

Stolberg, Sheryl G. 2003. "Face Value at the Capitol: Senator Wants to 'Promote Some Diversity' in Congressional Artwork," *New York Times*.

Sturm, Susan. 1998. "Race, Gender and the Law in the Twenty-First Century Workplace: Some Preliminary Observations," 1 *University of Pennsylvania Journal of Labor and Employment Law* 639–89.

Summers, Clyde W. 1976. "Individual Protection against Unjust Dismissal: Time for a Statute," 62 *Virginia Law Review* 481–532.

Tversky, Amos and Daniel Kahneman. 1973. "Availability: A Heuristic for Judging Frequency and Probability," 5 *Cognitive Psychology* 207–32.

Tversky, Amos and Daniel Kahneman. 1983. "Extensional versus Intuitive Reasoning: The Conjunction Fallacy in Probability Judgment," 90 *Psychological Review* 293–315.

"Univ. of Virginia Portraits of Law School Deans Focus Attention on Need for Diversity." 1997. *Jet*.

Viscusi, W. Kip and Wesley A. Magat. 1987. *Learning About Risk: Consumer and Worker Responses to Hazard Information*. Cambridge, MA: Harvard University Press.

Weinstein, Neil D. 1980. "Unrealistic Optimism about Future Life Events," 39 *Journal of Personality and Social Psychology* 806–20.

Weinstein, Neil D. and William M. Klein. 2002. "Resistance of Personal Risk Perceptions to Debiasing Interventions," in Thomas Gilovich, Dale Griffin and Daniel Kahneman, eds., *Heuristics and Biases: The Psychology of Intuitive Judgment*. Cambridge: Cambridge University Press.

Yelnosky, Michael J. 2003. "The Prevention Justification for Affirmative Action," 64 *Ohio State Law Journal* 1385–425.

10. From just cause to just notice in reforming employment termination law[1]
Rachel Arnow-Richman

INTRODUCTION

Employment at will, it is often said, means that employers can fire for any reason or no reason at any time with or without notice. For over forty years, the discourse surrounding employment termination has focused almost exclusively on a single issue: the desirability of changing the first part of this equation. Scholars of varying ideologies and methodologies have emphatically challenged or defended the idea that employers have an absolute right to terminate irrespective of their reasons for doing so.

This debate, vigorous though it has been, has come at the expense of a broader discussion of the goals of termination regulation and its inevitable costs. As currently framed, just cause advocates have the normative upper hand, having grounded their arguments in principles of fundamental fairness. However, they have given only limited attention to the costs of wrongful discharge laws and their ultimate implications for workers. Defenders of employment at will, on the other hand, have frequently invoked costs in seeking to maintain employment at will, arguing that a just cause requirement will make employment terminations more expensive. However, these scholars have not adequately grappled with the human toll exacted by unforeseen termination. Most problematic, scholars on both sides of the debate, in calling for or condemning just cause, usually compare such a system to a pure at-will regime, one in which employers enjoy almost unfettered discretion to terminate. Thus neither camp has sufficiently considered the inherent costs or the ultimate effectiveness of the prevailing employment termination system, which includes both a strong at-will presumption and numerous exceptions through which workers can question the reasons for their termination.

These failures have led to two segregated bodies of termination scholarship that are at loggerheads over the future of American termination law, but share an underlying assumption that changing the current system would necessarily involve adopting a just cause alternative. This chapter asserts that such a result is neither inevitable nor desirable. It argues that a better approach to reforming employment at will, largely ignored by existing scholarship, would be to establish a mandatory "just notice" rule that would require employers to provide advance warning of termination or, at the employer's election, pay separated workers their salary and benefits for a designated period.[2] Such a rule would overlay rather than extend existing wrongful discharge law: employers could continue to terminate for any reason not prohibited by statute or public policy, but would pay for the right to do so. Compared to a universal just cause rule, and perhaps even to the current system of "at will plus exceptions," a just notice rule is likely to engender fewer administrative costs and protect a wider swath of the workforce.

In addition to its practical value, a just notice rule, unlike a just cause rule, has a clear common law foundation in American jurisprudence. It is bedrock contract law that a party whose performance is discretionary must exercise that discretion in accordance with principles of good faith and fair dealing. Under the Uniform Commercial Code, this implied duty has been codified as a series of rules that impose obligations to act "reasonably" in specific circumstances, including contract termination. Although parties may alter these rules by agreement, their ability to do so is constrained, and they are precluded from waiving the good faith duty altogether. Thus, in a situation where a commercial contract is indefinite or severable at will, the terminating party is statutorily required to provide reasonable notice of termination to the other party. Adopting a statutory notice rule for terminating employment relationships would bring the law of employment contracts more in line with broader contract doctrine.[3]

Finally, a just notice rule would reframe the goal of employment termination law. While just cause aims to restrain employer prerogative to terminate, a just notice rule focuses on enabling employee transition. To the extent that most employers are likely to pay severance rather than actually provide notice, the system will address workers' most immediate need upon job loss – income continuity – while preserving employer discretion to determine who to terminate and why. In this way, a just notice rule operates more as an extension of unemployment compensation than as an additional constraint on employer discretion. Such an extension can be normatively justified as giving force to a fundamental component of the contemporary social contract of employment. Many employers have eschewed implicit promises of long-term employment, encouraging workers to look to the external market as the ultimate guarantor of employment security (Stone, 2001 and 2004). To the extent expectations of long-term employment have been replaced with expectations of long-term employ*ability*, it makes sense that employers be required to directly bear at least some of the costs of worker transition upon the inevitable event of job loss.

This chapter proceeds as follows. Section I presents and critiques the current debate over employment at-will reform. Section II turns to the advantages and disadvantages of a just cause rule, laying the foundation for a just notice approach that capitalizes on the best aspects of a just cause rule – the extent to which constraints on employer discretion to terminate operate as a *de facto* severance pay system for workers. Section III sketches a possible just notice system, drawing on models from foreign jurisdictions and comparing this chapter's proposal to domestic sources of law, including the federal WARN Act and the federal/state system of unemployment compensation. Section IV then turns to the doctrinal and normative bases for a just notice rule, drawing on the implied duty of good faith and social contract theory. Finally, Section V touches on some of the pragmatic implications of adopting a just notice rule, including the relative costs and benefits of such a rule and the ability of employers to insist on employee waiver of notice rights.

I.   THE TERMINATION DEBATE: ARGUMENTS AND ASSUMPTIONS

The debate over employment termination has proceeded along familiar lines. Early advocates of at-will reform appealed to principles of fairness and universal standards of decency in advocating for a just cause rule. Defenders of employment at will have mostly cited the supposed efficiency of employment at will and the increased costs of a just cause rule in opposing reform. Recently just cause advocates have attempted to engage these economic issues, but their responses have focused more on the likelihood that an existing market failure explains the prevalence of employment at will than the relative costs and benefits of a just cause system. At the same time, neither side has given sufficient attention to the practical effects of the current system, which, while grounded in employment at will, contains numerous exceptions prohibiting employers from terminating for "bad" reasons, such as those that offend public policy. The conversation has consequently reached a stalemate, with scholars debating the merits of a just cause system versus a pure – and largely hypothetical – at-will regime.

A.   The Just Cause Reform Movement

1.   A call for humane treatment

The focus on just cause as the obvious alternative to employment at will stems from the history of at-will reform efforts in the United States. That movement began with scholars voicing concerns about the welfare of workers and their vulnerability to abusive discharge. Beginning in the early 1960s, a literature emerged condemning the at-will system for its harsh effects on workers. Advocates emphasized the emotional and economic effects of job loss on workers, their families and, in the case of large-scale layoffs and company closures, whole communities (Blades, 1967; Peck, 1979; St. Antoine, 1988; C. Summers, 1976 and 2000). An emphasis on malicious and socially harmful employer behavior bolstered the emotional appeal of this argument. Literature critical of the at-will rule drew on uniquely egregious examples of employer abuse of power – terminations to punish refusals to engage in unlawful behavior, terminations in retaliation for exercising worker rights, and terminations for fulfilling public duties (Blades, 1967; C. Summers, 2000).

This picture of egregiously motivated terminations led critics to espouse a particular approach to reform – one focused on employers' reasons for terminating. If the social danger to be addressed is that employers can terminate workers for morally condemnable reasons, then the law ought to require employers to justify their termination decisions. Thus emerged a consensus view among at-will opponents that the existing system ought to be abolished in favor of a just cause rule.

In addition to addressing directly the problem of malevolent employer behavior, the just cause approach adopted by at-will opponents had an established history in the U.S. and abroad. Critics pointed to the near universal appearance of just cause clauses in American collective bargaining agreements and the prevalence of statutory protection against unjust termination in much of the Western world (C. Summers, 1976). More than 90 percent of collective bargaining agreements adopt "cause" or "just cause" as the standard for discharge (Bureau of National Affairs (BNA), 1995). Just cause provisions also figure prominently in the laws of European nations (C. Summers, 1976). Against this backdrop, employment at will appears a harsh and anomalous rule, while just cause emerges as the obvious alternative – a universal symbol of decency in employment terms.

2. The open question of costs

While just cause advocates have both moral force and foreign law to back their position, they have, until recently, mostly avoided questions of utility. Defenders of employment at will have argued, among other things, that employment at will is preferable to all parties (including workers) given the costs of administering just cause rules (Epstein, 1984; Rock & Wachter, 1996). Second generation just cause advocates have made some inroads into this position, suggesting that the prevalence of employment at will may stem from systemic market failures (Weiler, 1990; Kim, 1997 and 1999). Yet they have done little to assess whether, in a properly functioning market, rational employees would opt for such protection over other contractual terms of employment.

To some extent, just cause advocates' limited attention to questions of utility is a reflection of the underlying normative view that humane terms of employment should be mandatory regardless of their price tag. Implicit in the call for just cause is a willingness to assign additional costs to employers as a means of rectifying what is perceived as a fundamental power imbalance in the free market system. From this perspective, redistribution in the form of additional employment protection is an appropriate means of dismantling a regime that "guarant[ees the] capitalist's authority over the worker" (Feinman, 1976, pp. 132–3).

Less understandable is the disinclination of many just cause advocates to directly address the predicted consequence of increasing the cost of termination to employers – the likelihood that the cost will be passed on to workers in the form of lower wages or employment levels. A possible explanation is that just cause advocates believe that whatever costs workers ultimately bear will be worth the tradeoff. This perspective rests on two predicates: first, that market failure prevents workers from privately negotiating for this protection; and, second, that the risk and consequences of arbitrary or egregious termination to employees exceed the value of the higher wage workers supposedly enjoy under employment at will. As will be described in the next section, there is ample reason to think that obstacles to efficient bargaining do exist, a view that has been espoused not only by just cause advocates but by mainstream neo-classical economists. On the other hand, there is also reason to believe that relatively few workers would actually benefit from the implementation of a just cause rule. If so, just cause advocates are right to question employee satisfaction with employment at will, but wrong about whether just cause would offer a more valuable alternative.

Alternatively, just cause advocates' limited attention to utility may reflect a healthy skepticism about whether just cause rules will in fact prove costly to employers. Employment at will defenders argue credibly that just cause is more costly than a pure at-will system, but the American system is not purely employment at will. Given that the law is riddled with statutory and common law exceptions, many employers may already operate as if subject to a just cause regime, documenting and vetting termination decisions to ensure they can justify their actions if sued (Estlund, 2006; Hirsch, 2008). If so, formalizing that reality through a universal just cause rule may add little additional expense to employers, who in turn would have little to pass on to workers (Hirsch, 2008). However, such thinking still assumes that just cause is the best type of employment protection regime for workers. There may well be a more valuable form of protection that employees can secure for the same cost, however modest, that they would bear in a just cause system.

Either way, just cause advocates' failure to fully develop their arguments on these issues has ceded ground to law and economics-based defenses of employment at will. Absent serious consideration of the benefits of a just cause rule to employees relative to the costs and how those costs will be shared, the at-will reform movement remains vulnerable to the critique that its proposal would ultimately do workers more harm than good.

B.   In Defense of the Status Quo

For their part, traditional defenders of employment at will have staked their claim on the belief that employment at will is efficient, or at least more efficient than a just cause alternative. From this perspective, the prevalence of at-will contracts is testament to the desirability of that rule on the theory that an unfettered market necessarily reflects the preferences of its participants. That assumption is then bolstered by a critical assessment of a proposed just cause regime.

As a defense of the current system, however, both aspects of the argument are vulnerable. The first, grounded in the supposed preferences of workers, fails to account for the now widely accepted possibility that the terms of individual employment contracts reflect systemic market failures. By contrast, the second aspect of the argument, which invokes the administrative costs of a just cause system, offers a legitimate critique of that proposal, but applies equally to the current system of employment at will plus exceptions. Thus, while the arguments of at-will defenders succeed in questioning the value of a just cause rule, they also affirm the need for significant reform of the current system.

1.   Faith in the market
The starting point for traditional defenses of employment at will is a basic expression of faith in the market. As employment at will's principal defender Richard Epstein puts it, "It is hardly plausible that contracts at will could be so pervasive in all businesses and at every level if they did not serve the interest of employees as well as employers" (Epstein, 1984, p. 955). If employees truly preferred job security, they would be willing to pay for it through a reduction in wages. The fact that the vast majority of parties retain employment at will rather than contracting around the default suggests that employees as well as employers prefer this arrangement, at least in the sense that employees do not value job security more than the cost to the employer of providing it (Verkerke, 1995).

As a descriptive matter, however, it is not at all clear that at-will arrangements appear with "the same tenacity in relations between economic equals and subordinates" (Epstein, 1984, pp. 965–6). Empirical evidence shows that executive employment contracts almost invariably contain termination clauses that limit or penalize termination without cause (Schwab & Thomas, 2006). In addition, as previously noted, just cause provisions are standard fare in unionized workplaces, where workers enjoy enhanced bargaining power through collective representation (BNA, 1995). At-will defenders have largely ignored this central point in the scholarship of at-will critics.

The stratification of job security protections depending on the worker's degree of economic power strongly suggests the possibility of recurring flaws in the bargaining process. The work of "second generation" neoclassical economics recognizes such realities, including the possibility of asymmetric information that impedes efficient bargaining (Deakin, Chapter 11 in this volume). More recent just cause scholarship has leveraged such arguments and bolstered them with empirical research that questions the premises of traditional law and economics defenses of employment at will. For instance, Professor Pauline Kim's research documents that employees seriously miscomprehend the background rules that govern employment termination (1997 and 1999). Employees not only suppose that employers are constrained from terminating without reason, they overestimate the degree to which a "just cause" rule would actually protect them. Importantly, such beliefs persist even when workers are presented with explicit employer policies that reinforce their at-will status (Kim, 1997 and 1999). Such an observation directly challenges the conclusions of at-will defenders who ground their claims on the prevalence of at-will clauses in employer-drafted documents (Verkerke, 1995). If employees do not understand either the existence or meaning of employment at will, their failure to bargain for just cause protection cannot be viewed as a rational decision to maintain the default rule.

In the same vein, other insights from behavioral law and economics suggest that employment at will may be an especially "sticky" default, casting doubt on the degree to which its prevalence reflects workers' preference. Workers may be reluctant to seek a deviation from the default for fear of signaling to potential employers that they are marginal workers (Weiler, 1990; Kamiat, 1996) or they may perceive the default rule as having special legitimacy (Sunstein, 2002). On the flip side, the default rule may create endowment effects that lead employers to overvalue their right to freely terminate and make it difficult for employees to "buy" just cause protection (Sunstein, 2002). Such arguments, based on widely accepted principles of contemporary economics, seriously undermine the premise of early at-will defenders that the prevailing rule is necessarily efficient.

2. Estimating the utility of a just cause rule

At-will defenders are on surer footing in questioning the value of a just cause rule from a cost/benefit perspective. Scholars have argued that a just cause rule is unnecessary in light of existing workplace norms and that juridification would serve only to create transaction costs (Rock & Wachter, 1996). Employers would be forced to engage in close monitoring of work performance and might be unable to verify their reasons for termination if challenged in court (id.).

Since those extra labor costs would presumably be visited on employees, cost concerns have significant bearing on the degree to which employees are likely to benefit from a just cause rule. Consequently, if one accepts the claim of just cause advocates that enhanced legal protection for workers is a normative imperative, the arguments of at-will defenders raise important questions about whether adopting a just cause rule is the best way to proceed. At the same time, arguments about the difficulties of monitoring and verifying cause call into question the efficiency of the current system of employment at will plus exceptions in which employers (and consequently employees) already bear many of the same costs associated with universal just cause protection. Thus, at-will defenders have succeeded in seriously questioning both the benefits of just cause and the desirability of maintaining the status quo.

The scarcity of arbitrary termination   Defenders of employment at will have argued against just cause based in part on the notion that employers will act in accordance with just cause principles even in the absence of legal regulation (Rock & Wachter, 1996). Employers have every reason to retain productive, and even marginal, workers in order to reap the benefits of their labor and avoid hefty replacement costs; thus, implicit commitments to terminate only for cause are largely self-enforcing (Rock & Wachter, 1996). This does not mean that employers will never terminate arbitrarily, but rather that such events are too infrequent to justify the costs inherent in legal intervention.

Advocates of just cause implicitly concede this point in describing the harm of arbitrary termination. Scholars frequently cite the statistic that employers perpetrate between 150,000 and 200,000 arbitrary terminations per year, an estimate drawn from labor arbitration data examined in the early 1980s (Craver, 1998; Hirsh, 2008; St. Antoine, 1988; Stieber, 1985). Contemporary defenders of employment at will have churned this statistic, concluding that the risk of arbitrary termination for any one employee is less than 0.02 percent per year (Freed & Polsby, 1989; Morriss, 1996). Even if this estimate understates the incidence of arbitrary termination, the risk to any employee of such an event is still negligible.

This point not only undermines advocates' claims about the need for a just cause rule, it also calls into question the focus of their advocacy. In contrast to the number of arbitrary terminations, millions of workers are terminated each year for economic reasons, particularly in times of significant economic hardship, like the Great Recession of 2008. These separations are not immune from legal action. Like arbitrary terminations, economic terminations are vulnerable to the claim that the employer's "business" reason is pretextual, and a just cause rule would make it easier to ferret out instances where termination is unlawfully motivated (Estlund, 1996). However, legitimate economic terminations are permissible under just cause, and their consequences have been far removed from the central concerns of just cause scholars. Most appear content to allow laid-off workers to obtain redress exclusively through the unemployment insurance system (UI), which provides partial income replacement to involuntarily terminated workers unable to find replacement employment. That system is funded by an "experience-rated" employer payroll tax under which the rate of contribution is loosely calibrated to the degree of unemployment caused by the particular employer (Lester, 2001). However, UI does not regulate the conduct of employers who terminate for economic reasons; it does not provide any direct obligations on employers to provide either advance notice of termination or full-scale severance pay.

No doubt there are good reasons why at-will reform advocates have targeted the more culpable act of arbitrary termination over economic layoffs. While the latter is a justified, often a necessary, exercise of business discretion, the former is a morally condemnable exercise of power. However, the contemporary incidence of economic dislocation raises broader questions about the goals and scope of termination reform. Employees terminated for economic reasons likely experience many of the same personal and financial losses that arbitrarily terminated workers face. Indeed, advocates of at-will reform have drawn on psychological studies of the effects of plant closings in making the case for a just cause rule (C. Summers, 1976 and 2000). Assuming that workers will pay at least some portion of any costs associated with enhanced job protection, employee advocates should take seriously at-will defenders' argument that most terminated workers will gain little from adoption of a just cause rule. While at-will defenders conclude from this point that efforts to impose a just cause rule are pointless and should be abandoned, employee advocates ought to consider whether to change gear, advocating a more inclusive type of reform, one that reaches a wider pool of workers.

The difficulty of establishing arbitrary termination Along the same lines are at-will defenders' purported concerns about verification under a just cause system. Scholars have argued that even where cause for termination exists, it is easy to dispute but difficult to detect and prove (Freed & Polsby, 1989; Morriss, 1996). This means that courts will not necessarily do a better job than managers in assessing whether firing a particular worker was justified and, consequently, a just cause rule will result in little to no reduction in agency costs for employers (Freed & Polsby, 1989). At the same time, employers will have to expend efforts in monitoring, documenting and ultimately demonstrating cause in court, sometimes in the context of frivolous claims. This means that employers will occasionally be held liable for terminations justified in fact, but unverifiable in court.

To the extent defenders of employment at will present these administrative costs of a just cause system as a burden to employers, it is perhaps not surprising that their argument has been unpersuasive to advocates of reform. Just cause proponents begin from the presumption that employers should be strictly accountable for their decisions. Given the human toll termination exacts on workers, the fact that an employer may in some instances be held liable in error or incur the cost of defending a justified decision garners little sympathy.

Yet what makes just cause objectionable to *employers* should be of equal if not greater concern to those seeking greater protection for *employees*. Under the union model, which inspired much of the early scholarship supporting just cause, employers have the burden of justifying their termination decisions; however, as a matter of common law, the burden of proof generally falls on the employee, who must prove an improper basis for the termination (*Pugh v. See's Candies, Inc.*, 1981). He or she must do this relying almost entirely on evidence that is created and within the control of the defendant, such as performance evaluations, job descriptions, and accounts of supervisors. At the same time, the employee is far less likely than the employer to have the resources to pursue this type of fact-intensive lawsuit (Estlund, 1996; McGinley, 1996).

Added to these procedural obstacles to employee success is the history of judicial deference to management decisions concerning termination. Arbitrators who decide employee grievances in the union context employ a highly contextualized standard of cause. They are charged with applying the "law of the shop," that is, determining not only whether actual cause to terminate existed, but whether the decision to do so was appropriate in the particular situation (*United Steelworkers of America v. Warrior & Gulf*, 1960). In contrast, the standard for cause adopted by courts in the context of individual employment rights requires merely that the employer have a "fair and honest cause or reason regulated by good faith" (*Pugh v. See's Candies, Inc.*, 1981). This means that employers need not even be right about the facts giving rise to the termination, provided they acted in good faith based on reasonable assumptions.

In sum, what makes a just cause rule costly from the perspective of employers also makes it a relatively weak form of protection for employees. At least that is true under the version of just cause – with its management-friendly substantive standard and burden of proof rules – that is likely to take hold in court based on common law precedent. Given the difficulty of proving arbitrary termination under such a rule, and the relatively small number of employees who are terminated for such reasons to begin with, very few workers are likely to succeed in obtaining redress under a just cause system.

At the same time, arguments about the administrative costs of identifying and verifying the reasons for termination resonate beyond the debate over just cause to implicate the current system of employment at will. The cost-based defense of at will is at its strongest when evaluating the difficulties of administering a just cause rule against a system that grants employers complete discretion to terminate – a purely hypothetical comparison. Current law carves out numerous statutory and common law exceptions to employment at will that proscribe certain wrongful reasons for termination (Estlund, 1996). It also recognizes the possibility that an employee may have implied contractual rights to termination only for cause (*Pugh v. See's Candies, Inc.*, 1981). This means employers *already* spend time and resources preparing for the possibility that they will be called on to verify cause for termination in an adjudicative forum, and that employees *already* bear at least part of the associated costs (Weiler, 1990; Hirsch, 2008). Some have suggested that, in light of this, there is little lost by going to a full-fledged just cause system (Hirsch, 2008). On the other hand, it may mean that both camps are wrong. If a just cause rule is costly and inefficient, so too is the current system of employment at will plus exceptions.

C.   Stalemate

As it stands, scholars on both sides of the employment termination debate have valid arguments. Critics of the current system have the moral high ground. At-will defenders simply do not ask whether as a normative matter it makes sense to reshuffle the deck in favor of worker protection. Workers may want just cause protection and be unable to afford it, a fair expression of market principles, but one that many scholars and policymakers might be loathe to live with.

On the other hand, at-will defenders deserve credit for deeply questioning the effectiveness of a just cause system. While such thinkers tend to frame their arguments in terms of the cost to employers, their observations regarding the limited utility of a just cause rule should give pause to advocates of greater protection for workers.

At the same time, arguments about the administrative costs of a just cause rule implicitly raise concerns about the efficiency of the prevailing system of employment at will plus exceptions. Thus, the logical question to emerge from the scholarly stalemate is whether the law might fashion a more effective, more inclusive, and less costly system of worker protection than either just cause or the prevailing version of employment at will. The next section tackles this problem.

II.   RETHINKING JUST CAUSE

A.   Fixing What's Broken?

One way to respond to the legitimate arguments of at-will defenders is to troubleshoot the problems associated with a just cause rule, such as its enforcement costs. Contemporary proposals for a universal just cause rule, for instance, generally seek to emulate the streamlined, worker-friendly procedures of the collective bargaining regime, albeit without its worker-friendly burden of proof. Thus, the Montana Wrongful Discharge in Employment Act (MWDEA), the only state statute establishing a just cause system, creates incentives for parties to choose private arbitration rather than judicial resolution of just cause claims (Mont. Code Ann. § 39-2-914 (1987)). The much-discussed but unadopted Model Employment Termination Act (META) makes arbitration the default forum, and creates a mechanism for prevailing workers to obtain attorneys' fees (META §§ 6, 7 (1991)). Various scholarly proposals for employment termination reform adopt these features as well (Hirsch, 2008; Porter, 2008).

Such initiatives go a long way toward enhancing worker access to third-party review of suspect termination decisions. They may be relatively palatable to employers who tend to favor arbitration as a means of reducing the expense of litigation. However, they do not address the verification problem, that is, workers' ability not only to initiate and pursue claims, but to obtain vindication. Leveling the playing field to enable deserving workers to prevail requires more than the installation of a just cause default coupled with an alternative dispute resolution system. It may require the adoption of a stricter definition of cause and a reversal of the burden of proof, akin to the version of just cause that governs collective bargaining relationships. Few just cause advocates call for so drastic a move, perhaps because it would make their proposals even more controversial. A shift in the burden of proof or a narrower definition of cause would draw intense opposition from employers who would argue, not without legitimacy, that adoption would increase the risk of frivolous claims and unfounded awards.

Even if such political opposition could be overcome, there remains a more basic limitation of a just cause system – the scope of protection. No matter how strictly the law examines employers' proffered explanations for termination, companies remain free in a just cause system to terminate for any non-arbitrary reason irrespective of whether the employee is at fault or the degree to which he or she will be harmed. In contemplating this issue it is useful to consider the universe of possible lawful reasons for termination – those terminations sanctioned by the current system of employment at will – on a continuum between unjustified terminations and highly justified terminations based on the culpability of the employee (see Figure 10.1).

In this depiction, "arbitrary" termination anchors the left-hand side of the line graph, representing terminations perpetrated for no legitimate reason and not based on the behavior of the employee.[4] Next are "economic" terminations, those actions necessitated by legitimate business reasons but likewise involving no employee fault. Following from left to right are terminations based on the performance or conduct of the employee, with increasing employee culpability as one moves toward "misconduct" on the far right. A just cause system protects only a subset of workers not already protected by existing law – those who are arbitrarily terminated and able to establish this before a third-party decisionmaker. As a practical matter, it might also enhance the rights of unlawfully terminated employees – those fired for wrongful reasons but who face an uphill battle proving their cases in court (Estlund, 2006). But most employees who are not already protected under the current system would continue to be without recourse.

Enhancing worker access to outside review and intensifying judicial or arbitral scrutiny of termination decisions would increase the number of workers in the arbitrarily terminated category who are capable of obtaining redress. It would also, as some at-will defenders fear, make it more likely that decisionmakers will assign liability for a subset of

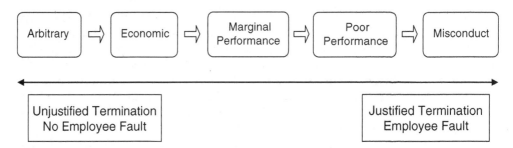

Figure 10.1   Continuum of reasons for termination

decisions in the "marginal performance" category, or even the "poor performance and-misconduct" categories, insofar as a less deferential standard for cause may lead judges or arbitrators to second guess the decision of the employer. However, even under the most exacting definition of cause, employers would remain free to lay off workers as a result of full or partial cessations of operations, strategic changes in direction, takeovers or mergers, or any number of business reasons without incurring any direct liability. As described previously, such terminations dwarf those perpetrated for arbitrary reasons and, however justified, pose significant and far more widespread hardship to employees.

B.   Capitalizing on What Works

In rethinking the call for just cause reform, it is also useful to keep sight of the merits of such proposals. This requires an examination of how the law operates in practice, not just in theory. One way to respond to the argument that relatively few employees would prevail under a just cause system is to point out that employers' reaction to reform would likely benefit a far larger swath of workers than those technically "covered" by a just cause rule.

In this respect, management's response to judicial innovations in employment termination law during the 1980s is instructive. The recognition of various common law "exceptions" to employment at will during this time period stoked fears among employers of a flood of wrongful discharge litigation and, for a time, fueled an employer-supported movement in favor of statutory just cause reform (Gould, 1987; Krueger, 1991). The work of Lauren Edelman, Steven Abraham and Howard Erlanger, studying the incidence of and response to this "threat," suggests that employers vastly overstated the risk of liability (Edelman, 1992). This insight likely explains the prevalence of common human resource practices, such as employer reluctance to terminate absent documentation of cause, the prompt settlement of lawsuits brought by terminated workers claiming wrongful discharge, and the use of "severance and release" agreements offering terminated workers temporary salary continuation in exchange for a waiver of claims. Indeed, survey research on the use of voluntary severance by employers reveals that "avoidance of litigation" is the number one cited reason for the adoption of such policies by employers (Lee Hecht Harrison, 2008).

If the likely response of employers to the implementation of a just cause rule is to redouble their risk avoidance practices, the success of the system from a worker protection perspective may depend little on whether employees are capable of proving the absence of cause in court. Employers' internal screening processes will limit the number of arbitrary terminations, and severance or settlement payments can be expected for those workers whose terminations are at all suspect. In the likely event that management implements its risk avoidance techniques in the form of general practices, such as a universal severance program, workers terminated for economic reasons and, in some instances, for marginal performance, poor performance or misconduct are also likely to benefit.

Such insights not only suggest that just cause is more beneficial to workers than previously argued, they also offer renewed justification for such a rule from the perspective of employers. To the extent that companies rely on costly risk avoidance practices in managing existing wrongful discharge law, a just cause rule may result in little additional cost, while reducing some of the expenses associated with the current state of legal uncertainty (Hirsh, 2008; Dannin, 2007).

On the other hand, the prevalence of risk avoidance measures, particularly the use of severance and release agreements, suggests that a just cause rule is valuable not so much as a means of protecting workers' jobs but rather as a proxy for compensation upon termination. For a variety of reasons, even in instances where an arbitrary or wrongful termination is actionable under the current system, it is relatively rare for successful employees to be reinstated outside the labor arbitration context (West, 1988). More often than not, employees receive frontpay in lieu of reinstatement, backpay, and, if available for the particular cause of action, compensatory and punitive damages. Rather than rehabilitating just cause, it might be wise to consider approaches that accomplish more directly what just cause, in the best of circumstances, does circuitously – require a set payment to terminated workers. The next section imagines more fully this possibility.

III.   THE "JUST NOTICE" ALTERNATIVE

One way to rethink termination reform is to focus on how employers execute their decisions as opposed to why they choose to terminate. Whereas just cause proposals attack the principle that employers can fire with or without reason, an alternative approach to reform might tackle the second component of the at-will rule – the employer's right to terminate at any time with our without notice.

As previously described, the existing "at will" system already proscribes terminations perpetrated for particularly "bad" or socially harmful reasons. Thus, the critical question facing at-will reform advocates is how to regulate the remaining terminations, consisting loosely of arbitrary terminations and economically or otherwise "justified" terminations. A just cause approach to at-will reform would essentially extend the inquiry that applies under current wrongful termination doctrines to discretionary terminations, asking whether the employer's motivation for any particular termination was a proper or improper exercise of business discretion under the circumstances. Decisions whose justifications fall short would be prohibited and would subject the employer to liability.

In contrast, a "just notice" approach to at-will reform would abandon this inquiry into the motivation and justification for discretionary terminations in favor of a universal notice requirement. This would not change the rules that currently prohibit wrongful terminations. However, it would impose an additional obligation in such instances, and a new obligation in the case of most "lawful" terminations, under which employers would be required to provide a designated amount of advance notice, or, at the employer's election, severance pay, to the terminated worker. Much like unemployment compensation, this obligation would apply to all terminations – wrongful, arbitrary or justified – absent serious misconduct by the worker. This section considers the purpose of, and possible models for, this type of reform.

A.   Enabling Job Transition

A just notice rule offers different advantages and advances different goals than a just cause rule. Unlike just cause, just notice would grant workers upfront compensation (either in the form of severance pay or continued salary during the "working notice" period) rather than a delayed award of damages in the event of a successful claim. Because it would create an entitlement for all employees absent serious misconduct, it would address the problem of the limited scope of just cause protection, reaching the large ranks of workers who suffer economic dislocation. At the same time, it would avoid the problem of increased litigation associated with just cause reform by eschewing fact-intensive inquiries into the quality of the employer's reason for termination.

More importantly, a just notice rule would further the goal of employment transition. A just cause rule discourages unjustified termination and offers compensation to victims who unfairly suffer job loss. In contrast, a just notice rule assumes no entitlement to continued employment; in fact, to the extent it covers economic dislocations, just notice implicitly accepts the employer's prerogative to terminate absent a legally prohibited reason. Rather, a just notice rule focuses on the employer's obligations to its workers in their quest to find new work. It represents a policy choice to affirm employers' business discretion in determining who to terminate and why, while holding employers directly responsible for funding at least part of the worker's inevitable transition costs.

In this way, a just notice rule serves more to supplement social security benefits and existing plant closing laws than to fill gaps in wrongful termination doctrine. Assuming that employers are most likely to comply by offering severance, the rule would partially supplant current government-sponsored unemployment insurance (UI). Under UI, qualifying workers terminated involuntarily and without fault are entitled to temporary partial income replacement, provided they are willing and able to seek alternate work (Lester, 2001). In this way, UI acts as a public safety net, insulating terminated workers against the risk that new work might not be available. The system also spreads that risk across employers roughly in proportion to the amount of dislocation they cause by "experience rating" employers' contribution rates to state/federal unemployment funds.

The focus of UI, however, is on systemic obstacles to re-employment. The system is silent on the normative question of employers' responsibility to the worker in exercising the right to terminate. As will be described in greater detail, contemporary employers often promise workers, explicitly or implicitly, that they will obtain valuable skills and experience that will allow them to leverage the external labor market for future employment (Cappelli, 1999; Stone, 2001 and 2004). To the extent these employers have encouraged workers to look to the larger market for long-term security and have benefited from a more entrepreneurial and self-reliant workforce, it makes sense that they assume some responsibility in the inevitable event of job loss. Unlike UI, "just notice" would impose a direct obligation on the employer to pay terminated workers their full salary for a designated period of time. This would create an interim step between termination and UI eligibility, making UI a true stop gap program available only after the conclusion of the mandatory notice or severance period.

In situations where the employer chooses to provide notice, the rule would function more like an expansion of the federal Worker Adjustment Retraining & Notification Act (WARN) than a UI alternative. The federal WARN Act requires large employers to provide sixty days' advance notice of a plant closing or statutorily defined mass layoff event (29 U.S.C. §§ 2101(a)(3), 2102). The purpose of the Act is to reduce the duration of unemployment and help prepare workers and communities for the consequences of widespread job loss. However, because of high thresholds for coverage under the Act, the duty to warn applies only to a fraction of termination decisions.[5] The Act also contains a broad exception for terminations resulting from "unforeseeable business circumstances" (29 U.S.C. § 2102(b)(2)(A)). Such an exclusion makes sense insofar as the Act requires actual advance notice of termination. Employers face genuine difficulties predicting whether immediate business challenges will ultimately require drastic action, and an inflexible notice rule might lead companies to announce layoffs prematurely, exacerbating their financial situation. However, if the goal of providing notice is to give workers a temporary income stream while seeking reemployment, that can be accomplished by providing severance at the time of termination for the same duration as the notice period. Such is the effect of a just notice rule. In addition to extending the right to receive notice of termination to individual workers, it would replace the unforeseeable circumstance defense with a severance alternative for those employers who are unable (or unwilling) to give advance notice.

B. Models for a Just Notice System

Like calls for just cause, the idea of a just notice rule is well grounded in the collective bargaining model of labor relations. Most union contracts not only require terminations to be justified by cause, they also recognize the need to cushion necessary economic terminations. Most collective bargaining agreements create a process for selecting workers for layoff ("last in, first out") and provide affected workers with recall and transfer rights (BNA, 1995). They thus offer a modest degree of predictability about job loss. More importantly, many collective bargaining agreements require that workers receive notice of an impending layoff and some amount of severance pay and benefits continuation upon termination (BNA, 1995; Pita, 1996). These amounts are generally modest – one week per year of service is common – but they offer some cushion for workers as they search for new employment (BNA, 1995; Pita, 1996).

In addition, statutory notice rules are a standard feature of the regulatory law of most Western countries. These include many of the European nations frequently cited by at-will reform advocates in support of universal just cause protection. In such countries, employees have statutory protection against unjust dismissal and an entitlement to advance notice (or severance pay) for both unjust and most justified terminations. Thus, in the United Kingdom, workers receive one week's notice per year of service, or pay in lieu thereof ("PILN"), for up to twelve weeks upon termination for any reason other than serious misconduct (Employ. Rts. Act, ch.18, § 86). Germany is slightly more gener-ous, requiring a minimum of four weeks' notice up to a maximum of seven months for workers employed for twenty years or more (Bürgerliches Gesetzbuch [BGB] § 622(1), (2), 2002). Exceptions exist for terminations justified by a "compelling reason," gener-ally understood to mean serious misconduct by the employee, and parties may agree to reduced notice in the case of a probationary employee (BGB § 626, 2002). But under both the British and German laws, the obligation to provide notice (or pay) pertains even where the termination is economically motivated.

While the call to emulate European-style just cause laws has been all but defeated in the United States, calls to adopt just notice legislation would not necessarily meet a similar fate. Indeed, European notice law would appear to be a far more viable candidate for transplant insofar as it provides a set of relatively modest, scheduled fees rather than the open-ended liability associated with just cause rules. In contrast to the numerous calls for the latter, there has been only one sustained scholarly treatment of the possibility of a notice-based system (Libenson, 2006) and no state-initiated or model legislation advanc-ing a no-fault right to notice or severance pay. Arguably the closest employee advocates have come to seriously entertaining such an idea has been the "opt out" provision of the Model Employment Termination Act (META). META Section 4 provides that an employee may, by written agreement, waive the just cause default set out in the model law and reinstate employment at will, provided the employer agrees to pay at least one month's severance per year of service up to thirty months (META § 4, 1991). However, as this high rate of compensation suggests, the notice provision of META is more akin to a statutory penalty for violating the just cause norm than a no-fault obligation imposed even in the case of a justified termination.

There is no reason, however, why the concept of scheduled payments to workers must be conjoined with a system that regulates the allowable reasons for termination. Canadian law offers an isolated, but valuable, example. The law in most Canadian provinces permits companies to terminate employees "at will" – that is, for any lawful reason or for no reason – provided they give workers reasonable notice of termination or its equivalent in pay.[6] This obligation is partially statutory and partially common law and applies to all terminations, including those proscribed by other law, absent serious misconduct by the worker. Every Canadian jurisdiction has enacted notice of dismissal statutes that can be satisfied either by providing "working notice," in which case the employee continues to work until the notice period ends, or pay in lieu of notice ("PILN") (Gilbert et al., 2006). These statutes mostly require modest periods of notice tied to the length of the employee's service, much like U.K. law. However, Canada also recognizes a common law duty of reasonable notice which requires the employer to provide notice based on individual circumstances (*Bardal v. The Globe & Mail Ltd.*, 1960). This duty has generally been construed to require amounts well beyond the statutory minimums (England, 2008). Of paramount consideration in determining the appropriate amount of notice or pay is the likelihood of the employee finding replace-ment work (*Bardal v. The Globe & Mail Ltd.*, 1960). Thus, Canadian law in the majority of provinces implicitly recognizes that workers are freely terminable and respects the employer's prerogative to make decisions about its need for labor. At the same time, it places an obligation on the employer to facilitate the reemployment of those workers it chooses to terminate.

C.   Toward an American Notice Rule

Canadian law offers perhaps the best model for a U.S. notice system. Like the approach proposed here, Canadian law is designed not to compensate the worker for job loss, but rather to facilitate reemployment. The viability of that goal is supported by empirical research that, while mixed, tends to show that advance notice reduces the likelihood of unemployment and its duration (Addison & Blackburn, 1997; Ehrenberg & Jakubson, 1989; Friesen, 1997; Zippay, 1993). Thus a just notice rule provides a significant benefit to employees. As for employers, they remain free under such a rule to terminate for any lawful reason, but they must pay part of a worker's transition cost in exchange for that privilege.

On the other hand, the Canadian approach poses difficult administrative challenges. The common law portion of the rule, which requires whatever amount of notice is "reasonable" under the circumstances, would seem to introduce significant legal uncertainty. Interestingly, this has not been the case in Canada, where a developed body of case law has yielded adequate guidance to employers and their attorneys about the appropriate duration of notice in particular cases (Gilbert et al., 2006). Litigation over such issues appears to be the exception rather than the rule (Nielsen, 1999). However, it would be highly optimistic to assume that these practices and legal culture could be transplanted along with the Canadian notice rule. Indeed, research on the treatment of employment disputes in Canada versus the United States reveals that American workers are more likely to dispute termination and to pursue legal claims than their Canadian counterparts (Nielsen, 1999).[7]

Nor is it necessary to take that risk. It is possible to emulate the Canadian model while adopting a statutory form of the law that establishes fixed obligations. By applying a flexible standard, the Canadian common law rule ensures that the period of notice or amount of pay is appropriate to the particular employee's needs without over- or under-compensating. In contrast, statutory notice laws, in both Canada and Europe, set the duration of the notice period based on length of service. Using length of service may be a means of approximating the loss to the employee under the theory that long-standing employees have a stronger property interest in their jobs or suffer a greater wrong than their more junior counterparts. Length of service may also serve as a proxy for employ-ability, consistent with the notion that as employees gain firm-specific skills they are likely to be more valuable to their current employer and less valuable in the general market (Schwab, 1993). To the extent years of service correlates with age, it also implicitly addresses the possibility that bias will impact the ability of older workers to find new work. Although it is surely a cruder tool, a fixed obligation tied to years of service can accomplish much of what the Canadian common law rule achieves, while ensuring predictability in application.

The more challenging question is how to select a base amount (or number of weeks' salary) for each year of tenure. The reality is that if a notice system were to be considered for U.S. adoption, the number of weeks required would be the product of political compromise rather than a studied effort to tie the amount of notice or pay to the needs of employees. It is beyond the scope of this chapter to determine or predict that amount. As previously noted, there is an existing body of research on the degree to which advance notice facilitates reemployment, and more study could be commissioned (Addison &

Blackburn, 1997; Ehrenberg & Jakubson, 1989; Friesen, 1997; Zippay, 1993). Ideally, legislators would take account of available data on the positive effects of notice, as well as the risk that long-term income replacement might disincentivize work search efforts, in crafting politically viable legislation.

IV.   LEGAL AND THEORETICAL FOUNDATIONS FOR JUST NOTICE

So just notice is a well-established feature of foreign legal systems that would fill certain gaps in American social security and plant closing law. But that does not dictate that it should be adopted. Nor should pragmatic considerations alone drive the development of employment termination law. Rather, the case for adopting a just notice approach must be legally and theoretically sound. This section returns to the call for just cause reform, comparing the doctrinal and policy considerations at stake in the choice between a just cause and a just notice rule. It argues that just notice for termination, unlike just cause, is an established feature of the contractual duty of good faith as applied to indefinite commercial relationships. It therefore has firm doctrinal roots in American common law that support its statutory adoption in the employment context. In addition, just notice, with its emphasis on reemployment over job preservation, accords with contemporary expectations about long-term employment. This reality provides a theoretical basis for adoption that is consistent with previously developed inroads into employment at will.

A.   Just Notice and the Implied Duty of Good Faith

The notion that "reasonable notice" is required for contract termination is an established feature of the law of commercial relationships grounded in the implied duty of good faith. In contrast to mainstream contract law, the implied duty of good faith in employment relationships has been interpreted to reach only a narrow category of cases dealing with the deprivation of vested benefits and has never been equated with a procedural obligation to provide notice of termination. A reexamination of the implied duty in employment relationships yields a doctrinally sound basis for adopting just notice reform, while bringing the law of employment contracts more in line with general contract law.

1.   The implied duty in contract law
The duty of good faith is implied in every contractual relationship (Uniform Commercial Code (UCC) § 1-304, 2001; Restatement 2d of Contracts (RST) § 205, 1981). Its force is felt principally in areas in which the contract itself grants discretion to one party that could be exercised adversely with regard to the other. Its effect is to preclude behavior that otherwise would be permitted under a strict reading of the parties' written document.

Two well-developed theoretical approaches to good faith have framed the contemporary understanding of the scope of the duty: Robert Summers' "excluder" approach and Steven Burton's "forgone benefit approach." The excluder approach embraces a broad notion of good faith, incapable of specific definition, that prohibits a variety of behaviors that may occur during performance – evasion, willful underperformance, obstructing performance and similar conduct (R. Summers, 1968). In contrast, the forgone benefit approach finds a breach of the duty only where a party abuses contractually conferred discretion to recapture opportunities sacrificed at contract formation (Burton, 1981). Under such an approach the implied duty applies principally to situations in which a party attempts to withhold or obstruct the flow of benefits rightfully allocated by the contract to his or her opponent.

As a matter of general contract doctrine, the broad excluder approach has won the day. The Restatement of Contracts explicitly adopts an expansive view of good faith, one that "emphasizes . . . consistency with the justified expectations of the other party" and excludes conduct that "violate[s] community standards of decency, fairness or reasonableness" (RST § 205, cmt. a & d). Article 2 of the UCC, applicable to contracts for the sale of goods, draws on this approach in setting forth a number of substantive default rules that amount to an elaboration of the doctrine. These all impose an obligation to act "reasonably" or "in good faith" with respect to matters on which the contract is either vague or silent (UCC §§ 2-305, 2-306, 2-309, 2002).

Contract termination is an example. Commercial relationships of indefinite duration, like employment relationships, are construed as terminable at the will of either party (UCC § 2-309, 2002). Unlike the law of employment relationships, however, the UCC "requires that reasonable notification be given" to the losing party (UCC § 2-309(3), 2002). The comment explains that this requirement "recognizes that the application of principles of good faith and sound commercial practice normally call for such notification of termination . . . as will give the other party reasonable time to seek a substitute arrangement" (UCC § 2-309 cmt. 8, 2002). In other words, the law allows parties to terminate indefinite relationships for any or no reason, but requires that the terminating party mitigate the harm to the loser by giving due warning of the inevitable loss.

Case law in this area further explicates how the notice requirement and the concept of at-will termination comfortably co-exist. *Pharo Distributing v. Stahl* (1989) involved an oral contract between a franchisee of Schlitz Beverage and a sub-distributor. On June 9, 1987, after many years working together, the franchisee advised the sub-distributor that it had purchased its own distributorship and that the contract would end on June 15. The agreement did not contemplate a fixed duration, and the court presumed that the franchisee had the right to terminate the relationship. Notwithstanding, it awarded damages to the sub-distributor. The court explained:

> It is not the termination of an at-will contract that constitutes the breach; the right to terminate is inherent in the nature of the contract. Nor is it relevant that a party losing an at-will contract suffers losses . . . Rather, it is the failure to give reasonable notice before termination that constitutes breach (*Pharo Distrib. v. Stahl*, 1989 at 638).

That requirement, the court explained, is intended to afford the party losing the contract "an opportunity to make appropriate arrangements" (*Pharo Distrib. v. Stahl*, 1989 at 638). This might include finding a replacement supplier, unloading inventory and making workforce adjustments. It is an obligation, said the court, grounded in "fairness and equity"; its purpose is to grant the losing party time to "'get[] his house in order' to proceed in absence of the former relationship" (*Pharo Distrib. v. Stahl*, 1989 at 638).

This duty to provide advance notice of termination, and the implied duty of good faith more generally, are effectively mandatory obligations. Although parties may limit the scope of the duty of good faith, allocating particular benefits or preserving areas of discretion in drafting, the Code makes clear that "[t]he obligations of good faith, diligence and reasonableness and care . . . may not be disclaimed by agreement" (UCC § 1-302(b), 2001). Parties' ability to limit or dispense with the "default" notice rule under UCC 2-309 is similarly constrained. Section 1-302(b) specifies that when the Code provides for an action "to be taken within a reasonable time," parties may fix a particular time frame that is not "manifestly unreasonable" (UCC § 1-302(b), 2001). Similarly, the commentary to Section 2-309 states that an agreement limiting or dispensing with notice is unenforceable if it would "create an unconscionable state of affairs" (UCC § 2-309, cmt. 8, 2001). This provision could be interpreted to disallow immediate termination based on hardship to the losing party, notwithstanding a contract provision purporting to grant that right (*Intergraph v. Intel*, 1998). Thus, the general contract duty of good faith simultaneously recognizes parties' unfettered discretion to determine whether to terminate a commercial relationship, while at the same time establishing a baseline rule requiring sufficient advance notice to allow the losing party to recoup sunk costs and find a replacement.

2.   The implied duty in employment law

Employment law has veered from this basic understanding of the operation of good faith. Although both the UCC and the common law treat the duty of good faith as an inherent feature of every contract, some courts have refused to recognize the implied duty in the employment context (*Murphy v. Amer. Home Products*, 1983). Those that do have adopted Burton's definition to the exclusion of Summers'. The only factual context in which good faith claims by employees have enjoyed a modicum of success has been where the plaintiff's termination results in the deprivation of a promised benefit. Thus courts have recognized a limited cause of action for deferred payments, such as commissions or bonuses, or the value of a vested benefit where the termination was motivated by a desire to avoid payment (*Fortune v. Nat'l Cash Register*, 1977).

Even in those cases that fit this factual paradigm, courts have not permitted recovery absent a demonstration of actual bad faith in the form of an intent to deprive the worker of the lost benefit, a standard not applicable in commercial law relationships (*Fortune v. Nat'l Cash Register*, 1977). In addition, courts have refused even in successful cases to award damages for lost employment generally, as in lost wages (*Gram v. Liberty Mut. Ins. Co.*, 1984). For this reason, some scholars have eschewed the doctrine altogether in favor of relying on other common law theories in seeking to expand workers' termination rights (Lillard, 1992; Parker, 1995). The claim's principal value appears to be in settlement negotiations where a plaintiff might trade on the risk that an idiosyncratic court will appeal to the doctrine in a case involving egregious facts.

This rigid treatment of the duty of good faith is doctrinally problematic. The conclusion that the employment at will default somehow trumps other implied duties relies on the misapplication of a rule of interpretation that pertains to express contract language. The reasoning of *Murphy v. American Home Products* (1983), the key New York Court of Appeals case rejecting the availability of a good faith claim in an indefinite employment relationship, illustrates the error. *Murphy* involved a good faith claim by an accountant who had been fired allegedly for reporting internal mismanagement, or, as the plaintiff described it, for doing his job. Although the court acknowledged the existence of the duty of good faith as a general matter of contract law, it rejected the plaintiff's claim, holding that the application of the duty must be limited by "other terms of the agreement" (*Murphy v. Amer. Home Products*, 1983 at 91). Noting that the law accorded the employer "an unfettered right to terminate the employment at any time," the court asserted that "it would be incongruous to say that an inference may be drawn that the employer impliedly agreed to a provision which would be destructive of his right of termination" (*Murphy v. Amer. Home Products*, 1983 at 91).

However, the court's conclusion does not follow from general contract interpretation principles. It is true that contract law permits parties to avoid some of the consequences of the good faith duty by providing in their agreement that a party has the right to do that which the duty would otherwise preclude. But employment at will was not an express term of Murphy's contract; Murphy had no written agreement. In that context, employment at will, like good faith, was a provision supplied by law. The court erred in elevating that default principle to the status of an explicit reservation of discretion in a written instrument.

Even if Murphy had signed a generic at-will recital, it does not follow that the court's conclusion would have been compelled. The tradition of contract law interpretation is to reconcile competing sources of contract terms wherever possible to achieve a consistent whole (UCC § 1-303(e), 2001). Such a reconciliation is easily achieved in the context of employment relationships that are "terminable at will," just as it is in the case of terminable at-will commercial relationships. The inherent inconsistency between the implied duty of good faith and such a written reservation of discretion arises only when good faith is equated with a substantive limitation on the power to terminate. But as commercial law demonstrates, it is possible to understand the duty of good faith as a procedural obligation, one that requires parties to act fairly in carrying out decisions that are otherwise immune from substantive review. Consistent with commercial contract law, it would make sense for the duty of good faith in employment law to be understood to require employers to provide advance notice of termination irrespective of their reasons for terminating.

Such an approach accords with the more prevalent "excluder" interpretation of the duty of good faith which views the implied duty as a "'safety valve' to which judges may turn to fill gaps and qualify or limit rights and duties *otherwise arising under rules of law and specific contract language*" (R. Summers, 1982 at 812; emphasis added). Indeed, good faith notice does not contradict employers' right to terminate for any or no reason so much as limit when that right can be exercised. In this way, it offers a more coherent explanation of the existing jurisprudence recognizing a limited good faith claim for deprivation of vested benefits. The wrong in such cases is not the termination, but the timing – the employer's action severs the relationship between the earning of an entitlement and payment under the employer's deferred compensation policy. A UCC-like notice rule would in theory ensure that the employee receive sufficient advance notice of termination such that he or she could fully realize any deferred, previously earned benefits before final separation or else receive the amount of the entitlement in the form of pay and benefits provided in lieu of notice.[8]

Even in the case of a direct conflict between the parties' written agreement and this interpretation of the duty of good faith, it is unlikely that contract law would defer to the writing. For instance, a provision in a written employment agreement might reserve power to terminate for any reason, as well as the right "to terminate at any time" or, in an even stronger formulation, to terminate "with or without notice." Clearly the intent of such a provision would be to dispense with any implied obligation to provide reasonable advance notice of termination. However, as previously noted, the implied duty of good faith may be limited, but not be waived. There is a strong argument that courts should not sanction a complete waiver of the duty to provide notice of termination, at least in those situations where the losing party is constrained in finding a replacement party that will satisfy its commercial needs. Thus, in *Intergraph v. Intel*, a district court found chip-maker Intel in breach of contract for terminating its relationship with Intergraph, a manufacturer of computer workstations, despite language in the parties' agreement allowing termination "at any time without cause."[9] The court based its decision on Intel's "greatly disproportionate bargaining power" in the industry, the fact that Intel had unilaterally drafted the agreements in question, and the investment Intergraph had made in configuring its machines to accept Intel chips.[10]

The concerns expressed in *Intergraph* present with even greater force in cases involving immediate termination of employment. Almost invariably the employee will have made a significant financial and personal investment in the relationship and will need lead time to find an alternative "buyer" to match his or her services. Indeed, given the background contract law, the current state of the duty of good faith in employment relationships is puzzling. As a policy matter, one would expect the law of good faith to resonate most strongly in those contexts, like employment, that involve relationships of dependence and the risks associated with non-diversifiable investments. Instead, commercial parties in arm's length transactions appear to have greater good faith obligations to one another than companies do in dealing with individual workers.

It is not the purpose of this chapter to advocate for judicial reinterpretation of the duty of good faith in employment, although that would be both logical and welcome. Such a sea change in the law would probably require legislative intervention. Certainly the enactment of a statutory notice schedule of the type proposed here would require legislation. The point is that the implied duty of good faith supplies an existing common law foundation for such an exercise, and precedent for codification can be found in the strong default rules of the Uniform Commercial Code. A statutory notice rule would enhance worker rights, preserve the key feature of employment at will, and realign employment law with mainstream contract law.

B.   Just Notice and Implicit Contract Theory

The previous section suggests a legal foundation for reinterpreting employment at will. The fact that a just notice rule can be doctrinally supported, however, does not make it good policy. This section seeks to justify as a normative matter the adoption of a just notice rule based on social contract theory. It argues that the policy underlying the UCC reasonable notice rule – the idea that good faith requires a terminating party to grant the loser an opportunity to replace the lost relationship – resonates strongly with the contemporary social contract of employment. In today's global economy, employers implicitly promise to help workers achieve long-term security by equipping them with skills and experience that they can leverage in the external labor market. A just notice rule gives legal force to that understanding.

1.   Just cause and life-cycle employment

Discerning a theoretical foundation for just notice requires some examination of the theory undergirding just cause. Both scholarly support for and judicial adoption of just cause exceptions to employment at will grew out of the social contract of the mid-twentieth century, which reflected the dominance of internal labor markets. Beginning in the early part of the century, many companies adopted systems of workplace management founded on Frederick Taylor's scientific management theories, which emphasized sharply differentiated job classifications requiring minimal skill and repetitive work (Stone, 2001 and 2004). This structure gave management a strong degree of control over its workforce and its output, but it also engendered morale problems. The solution was a system of rewards and benefits tied to job tenure (Stone, 2001 and 2004). Companies implemented fixed promotion ladders heavily dependent on firm-specific training. In exchange for their loyalty and commitment, workers could look forward to increasing pay, consistent advancement and long-term employment security (Stone, 2001 and 2004).

This social contract, however, was not a contract at all; rather it was a shared expectation drawn against the backdrop of employment at will. Workers who joined unions were able to formalize their understanding with management through the collective bargaining apparatus. Indeed, many unions adopted management's symbiotic vision of the dominant social contract in negotiating on behalf of workers. The typical features of collective bargaining agreements – set job classifications and promotion ladders, structured pay scales and seniority systems, work preservation clauses and elaborate grievance and arbitration procedures – dovetail with what, at the time, was the prevailing social contract relied upon by management as well as workers (Stone, 2001 and 2004).

Non-unionized workers, however, had to rely on the good will of management and the questionable effect of reputational consequences to employers willing to "breach" the dominant social contract. By the 1970s, some companies found themselves either unable or unwilling to sustain their implicit promises, and by the early 1980s appellate courts were facing termination claims by workers on the losing side of such understandings. A series of cases, primarily from employee-friendly jurisdictions in which union density was strong, sought to remedy these "breaches" by recognizing the viability of an implied contract to job security based on such things as employer practices and policies, assurances about continued employment, and applicable industry standards – all indications of the company's efforts to inculcate the expectation of long-term employment (*Pugh v. See's Candies*, 1981; *Woolley v. Hoffman-La Roche*, 1985).

Consistent with the social contract account of this jurisprudence, Stewart Schwab (1993) has explained judicial inroads into employment at will in terms of internal labor market theory. Under the career employment model of wages, employers structure pay to rise over time both as a means of motivating workers and as a method of sharing the costs of initial worker training (Schwab, 1993). The employee is paid less than his or her marginal value to the employer from the outset of the relationship through mid-career, then recoups that amount at the conclusion of the relationship when wages continue to rise despite a decline in marginal product. Schwab's work suggests that courts leveraged contract theory as a way of monitoring points in the career relationship when an employer might have an incentive to opportunistically breach the agreement, most notably at the end of the relationship, but also in early relationships where a worker has made an initial investment in accepting employment but has not had time to recoup those sunk costs (Schwab, 1993). In such cases an employer might have an incentive, particularly with long-term employees, to terminate arbitrarily to avoid paying deferred compensation.

Thus, from a law and economics perspective, the judicial retreat from employment at will can be explained as an effort to capture situations in which the parties' mutual expectations are not self-enforcing. Similar to good faith cases that redressed the denial of a promised bonus or commission, decisions like *Pugh* implicitly recognized that workers who invested in a long-term employment relationship were entitled in late career to recoup part of the surplus they had generated for their employers. Thus, adoption of an implied contract cause of action elevated the social contract to a legally binding agreement. Dismissal absent just cause violated the terms of the deal, and an employer's reasons for terminating consequently became a legitimate source of judicial (or arbitral) scrutiny.

2.   Just notice and the spot market for labor

Of course, the life-cycle model of employment is neither universal nor inviolate. At the time Schwab set forth his theory in the early 1990s, some had begun to wonder, as Schwab himself acknowledged, whether internal labor markets might be on the wane (Schwab, 1993). Hindsight suggests that the cases that enforced implicit contracts were in fact signs of the system's imminent collapse. Since that time, the technological and communication innovations of the late twentieth century have resulted in a global marketplace, one which requires companies to quickly develop new products and services to meet fluctuating demands and compete against a broader pool of international competitors (Cappelli, 1999; Stone, 2001 and 2004). In this environment, employers require innovative, self-motivated workers with access to the newest and most marketable skills, skills that are likely to change frequently over time.

Achieving this flexibility requires greater reliance on short-term and need-specific employment. Indeed, the last quarter of the twentieth century witnessed an increase in explicitly contingent employment relationships. Temporary, leased, part-time and other "non-core" workers accounted for 40–50 percent of domestic jobs created during the period 1980 to 1993, a growth rate that was 40–75 percent faster than the growth rate in the overall workforce (Belous, 1995).[11] Overall job tenure rates also declined during this period. Median tenure for male workers (though not for women) fell for all age groups between 1983 and 2000.[12] By 2000, 36–39 percent of workers had less than two years' tenure, while just over 10 percent had twenty years or more (Rajnes, 2001).

Anecdotal evidence also suggests a shift in employer practices. Through statements of managerial strategy, human resources policy, and company hiring and firing practices, employers have conveyed to their workers that employment relationships are always contingent on financial success and the needs of the business (Cappelli, 1999; Stone 2001). Workers' financial security thus depends not on their current employer, but rather on their external marketability. As Ken Dau-Schmidt describes it:

> The American workplace is undergoing a transformation from a place that was dominated by internal labor markets with corporate administrative rules and expectations of long-term employment to one which is governed by an international spot market for labor with no rules or expectations except payment for product and the prospect of constant change (Dau-Schmidt, 2001 at p. 2).

In other words, companies have come to expect a "just in time workforce" (Hipple, 2001).

This movement away from internal labor markets has required a shift away from the old social contract of employment. The implicit understanding between employee and employer is no longer premised on long-term employment, but on the prospect of long-term marketability. In exchange for strong performance, innovative thinking and good occupational citizenship, companies offer valuable experience and the opportunity to cultivate marketable skills (Cappelli, 1999; Stone, 2001 and 2004). While continued employment with any particular company in any particular capacity is not assured, workers can reasonably expect that they will be well positioned to take advantage of new opportunities in the event that their current relationship ends.

To be sure, the contemporary model of short-term relationships has not wholly replaced past practices. Long-term employment remains the norm in some industries, and exceptions can be found even among those employers that have widely embraced external labor market practices (Jacoby, 2000). What has changed, however, is the expectation that any particular job, indeed any particular firm, will survive long-term. Thus, the rise of external labor market practices calls into question the theoretical underpinnings of twentieth century implied contract jurisprudence. Arguably a right to continued employment is no longer an accurate legal translation of contemporary workplace understandings.

To the extent employers have replaced implicit promises of job security with implicit promises of marketability, the guiding theory of worker protection ought to focus on enabling continued labor market participation rather than preserving particular employment relationships. In this way, just notice offers a more appropriate legal rule than just cause insofar as it gives the terminated party an opportunity to prepare for loss of the relationship and seek an appropriate replacement consistent with the parties' understanding. Even if an employer has not made such an implicit promise in a particular case, both the worker and society have a stake in continued employability that may justify the modest burdens of just notice. Such a rule provides a window of income security in which terminated employees can conduct a job search, invest in training, or do whatever else might be necessary to promote themselves in the external labor market. It thus translates the expectation of employability into a concrete obligation enabling employees to realize and enforce the benefits of the new social contract of employment.

V.   THE CONSEQUENCES OF A JUST NOTICE RULE

Thus far this chapter has aimed to expose the limits of a just cause rule and lay the doctrinal and normative foundation for a just notice alternative. This section turns to the practical effect of adopting a just notice system. To the extent that employers choose to pay workers severance as the primary method of complying with their just notice obligations, a just notice rule will essentially operate as an extension of unemployment compensation. This in turn raises questions about the cost of such an extension and the degree to which employees will ultimately benefit. This section offers preliminary thoughts on the extent to which a just notice rule will increase the price of termination, how that additional cost will be paid, and whether the parties should be permitted to override just notice obligations through contract. In so doing, it raises questions that policymakers will have to weigh in enacting just notice legislation. It also identifies several areas in which empirical study or economic modeling may be useful in fully assessing the cost of changing the law.

A.   Costs and Savings under a Just Notice Rule

Estimating the cost of a just notice system might begin with an assessment of the amount of additional wages employers would be obligated to provide to workers who would have been terminated immediately under a pure at-will rule. The per-termination cost of a just notice system might thus be stated as the average amount of additional pay provided to terminated workers as a result of the just notice rule. From this perspective, just notice would appear a more costly proposition than just cause reform, which, as previously described, benefits only a handful of workers whose terminations cannot be justified by a business reason. A just notice rule would impose an upfront obligation upon termination for any reason (other than for serious misconduct), while a just cause rule would require an employer to pay only arbitrarily terminated employees and only upon proof before the requisite tribunal. Payments exacted in the latter situation might be higher than payments owed to just notice beneficiaries (depending on factual circumstances and the predilections of particular decisionmakers), but they would be less frequent.

   This conceptualization of cost oversimplifies in several respects. Under the system envisioned here, amounts owed to employees do not represent a total loss to the employer. The employer has the option of providing actual notice as opposed to severance, thereby capturing the benefit of the worker's continued labor. In such cases, the cost to the employer will consist of any reduction in the worker's marginal product resulting from the notice, rather than the full cost of the worker's additional weeks' salary.

   More importantly, a just notice rule in the form of a fixed statutory obligation offers employers the advantage of a predictable obligation in managing terminations. This may reduce the cost of legal uncertainty inherent in the current system of employment at will plus exceptions. Proponents of statutory just cause reform have at times traded on this argument, asserting that employers will benefit from a universal, codified law of termination that avoids the duplication of claims and disparities in coverage, remedies and standards of proof that currently pertain (Dannin, 2007; Hirsch, 2008; Porter, 2008).

   Depending on how the system is structured, just notice could offer some comparable advantages. Just notice could not supersede the whole of contemporary wrongful discharge law like the more aggressive just cause proposals (Hirsch, 2008). This is because the "no fault" nature of the system, combined with the relatively modest amounts of notice or severance that it would impose, would not deter or adequately capture the social costs of affirmatively wrongful conduct. However, it would make sense in codifying a just notice rule to preempt at least a subset of common law claims. At a minimum, the law should explicitly preempt those claims alleging breach of an oral or implied promise of job security insofar as the system is designed to replace those theories in particular. While implied contract claims have not been an especially significant source of liability for employers, they have been a key focus of risk management efforts (Edelman,

1992). Preemption will thus allow employers to avoid at least some of the costs they currently incur through liability avoidance strategies.

Even if the scope of direct preemption is relatively small, under a just notice system employers are likely to experience a decline in other forms of employment litigation. Some scholars have speculated that a subset of discrimination claims are brought by employees who are terminated unfairly, but not unlawfully (Hirsch, 2008). The same may well be true of other claims alleging wrongful reasons for termination, like those based on whistleblower laws or common law public policy torts. With the benefit of advance notice or income continuity, employees will likely have less need to resort to such theories to address the legitimate hardship and perceived unfairness of at-will termination. Nor is it likely that a just notice regime will itself inspire costly litigation insofar as it avoids the observation and verification problems associated with current wrongful discharge litigation and universal just cause proposals.

Finally, employers might reap direct savings from a just notice rule in the form of lower unemployment premiums. To the extent the rule succeeds in enforcing the contemporary social contract of employment, it will smooth transitions for terminated workers, reducing demand for unemployment benefits. Where employers provide the requisite advance notice, some terminated workers should be able to find new jobs during the working notice period, avoiding unemployment altogether. Where employers chose to provide pay rather than notice, these payments (like voluntary severance) should delay employee eligibility for unemployment benefits. If the terminated employee finds new work before losing this stream of income, he or she will have no need to resort to the unemployment system. Even if employees do not avoid unemployment completely, they will likely draw benefits for a shorter time assuming they begin their search for re-employment during the mandatory notice or pay period. Thus, a just notice system should reduce the overall demand on the unemployment system, resulting in reduced premium payments from employers under the current experience rating system.

In short, there is reason to think that a just notice system will be less costly than adopting a just cause rule, and may be cost neutral relative to the current system of employment at will plus exceptions. Currently the cost of termination to employers is higher than the actual cost of liability to terminated employees due to the costs of litigation and liability avoidance techniques. In addition, many employers already pay voluntary severance payments to separated workers, whether as an offensive strategy or as a matter of corporate benevolence. A key question in determining the net cost of a just notice obligation, if any, is the extent to which such costs might be displaced, a matter that will ultimately require empirical study. The possibility that adopting a just notice rule might actually be cost *saving* is suggested by Laura Beth Nielsen's (1999) case study of the human resources practices of a transnational firm operating in the U.S. and in Canada. Notwithstanding Canada's reasonable notice requirement, Nielsen found that the company's U.S. office spent more on terminations than the Canadian office, albeit in payment to lawyers rather than to workers.

In sum, it is likely that the total cost to employers of a just notice rule will be less than the aggregate amount of wages owed, pursuant to statute, for each terminated worker. A more accurate statement of costs would be that amount *minus* the value of any work provided by terminated employees during the applicable statutory period, the amount of any voluntary severance the employer would have made absent a just notice obligation, the cost of any claims preempted or avoided as a result of the law (including the costs associated with defending such claims), and any reduction in unemployment insurance premiums resulting from employees' reduced need for benefits. In light of these considerations, economic modeling may be useful to more fully understand the relationship between the statutory obligation proposed here and the actual cost to employers.

B.   The Potential Employment and Wage Effects of a Just Notice Rule

The previous section suggested reasons why a just notice rule might prove less costly than initially anticipated. If, however, the costs associated with such a change in the law prove significant, then a key question in determining whether employees will ultimately benefit from a just notice rule is how those additional costs will be distributed. Because employers control wages, mandating notice or severance could lead employers to reduce pay or employment levels. In the event they reduce pay, the value of any notice or severance pay would be offset by a front-end loss of income that workers might otherwise have used to insure against the risk of job loss. In the event employers reduce hiring, the benefits to incumbent workers will be offset by losses to those in the job market.

Such risks have frequently been invoked in objection to other types of employment protection measures, including just cause reform (Autor et al., 2006; Bird, 2008; Friesen, 1996; Lazear, 1990). There is some empirical data showing small employment declines in the wake of judicial adoption of tort and contracts-based exceptions to employment at will in the United States (Autor et al., 2006; Dertouzos & Karoly, 1992). However, researchers studying the impact of employment protection laws reach different conclusions about the size and cause of such effects (Deakin, Chapter 11 in this volume). In addition, there are conflicting accounts of the effects of wrongful discharge law on firm performance. At least one study suggests that judicial innovations have adversely affected firm profitability (Bird & Knopf, 2009), while another suggests that such laws improve firm innovation (Acharya et al., 2010).

By contrast, there is only limited data isolating the economic impact of mandatory notice or severance laws; but that which exists confirms the risk of negative effects to employees. A study of European laws found an adverse effect on employment levels based on European data (Lazear, 1990), while a Canadian study of notice requirements found a downward effect on wage levels, at least for non-unionized employees (Friesen, 1996). One study of the adoption of the WARN Act in the United States found adverse effects on growth, but positive effects on productivity (Deakin and Sarkar, 2008).

However, it is difficult to know what lessons to take from these studies. As previously described, the WARN Act applies only to a subset of U.S. termination events, and other variables may explain its supposed impact (Deakin & Sarkar, 2008; Addison & Blackburn, 1997). As for the Canadian and European studies that deal with universally applicable notice laws, it is unclear to what extent similar effects would be felt in the United States which has different background laws, weaker labor unions and a different legal culture. Thus, additional research would be required to determine the economic consequences of adopting an American just notice rule. If the risk of adverse effects on wages or employment levels is significant, policymakers will have to consider whether to cushion those effects, for instance through a tax credit to employers or via direct government funding.[13]

C.   The Viability of Contractual Waiver

A final policy consideration that bears on the cost and effectiveness of a just notice rule is the degree to which employers will be permitted to contract out of the notice obligation and its attendant costs. In light of the risk that employers will seek waivers of rights as a matter of course, the best approach to this question might be to allow waivers only under delineated circumstances, in effect instituting just notice as an especially "strong" default rule.

For instance, it would be appropriate to allow an exception to the just notice requirement for probationary employees. Many statutory just cause proposals incorporate such a period, during which employers may terminate freely without the additional costs imposed by protective legislation (Montana Code Ann. § 39-2-904(2), META § 3(b); Hirsch, 2008). Just notice legislation could similarly require that workers be employed for a threshold period of time before becoming eligible for notice or severance. This would soften the risk employers face in making new hires.

It would also make sense to allow employers to escape just notice obligations for temporary workers, at least where such workers are explicitly hired for a discrete task or employment term. In such cases, the parties' written contract specifying the duration of the relationship serves much the same purpose as just notice, enabling the temporary worker to predict the need to find alternate work at a specified time and search for his or her next position while still employed.

Allowing such an exception will, of course, have the effect of creating an employer preference for temporary versus "permanent" hires. This has posed a problem in European countries that have created alternative forms of employment that enjoy less protection from prevailing laws. The risk is arguably less significant here, where all that is at stake is a single, and not especially costly, right to notice or severance rather than access to the panoply of protections afforded to full-status employees in unjust dismissal jurisdictions. To be sure, the problem of "second-class" employees exists in the United States: the proliferation of "independent contractor" relationships has removed many workers from the protections of antidiscrimination and labor laws (Befort, 2003). However, adoption of a just notice rule is unlikely to exacerbate it. In fact, employers' ability to leverage the exception will likely be relatively constrained, assuming that a written commitment to a fixed term is a necessary prerequisite. Employers could not simply designate a class of workers as "temporary" for an indefinite period. Rather they could avail themselves of the exception only if willing to substitute a form of (short-term) job security for the worker's lost notice and severance rights.

The more difficult question is whether to permit employers the flexibility to contractually waive just notice obligations absent a commitment to a fixed term of employment. Employer solicitation of waivers of rights through contractual documents, such as pre-dispute arbitration agreements, is an increasingly common practice (Bodie, 2004; Malin & Ladenson, 1993; Schwartz, 1997; Stone, 1996). Such waivers are facilitated by the use of form documents produced by professional human resources departments and in-house counsel's offices (Arnow-Richman, 2007). Many of these documents likely are viewed by employees as routine paperwork and are signed as a matter of course without serious consideration of their content or the worker's background rights. In some instances they are also provided to employees after employment begins, at which point employees have extremely limited power of exit (Arnow-Richman, 2006 and 2007). Given these realities, allowing contractual waivers as a matter of course could effectively sanction the reinstitution of employment at will by unilateral employer action.

This conflict between protecting rights and ensuring individual autonomy has led some scholars, in the context of other employment terms, to take an intermediate stance on issues of waiver. Under a "conditional waiver" approach to employment protections, the contractual relinquishment of background rights may only be enforced under designated circumstances (Estlund, 2006; Sunstein, 2001). For a conditional waiver approach to be effective in policing such agreements, it must impose both procedural and substantive prerequisites to enforcement. In the just notice context, conditional waiver ought, at a minimum, to be predicated on compliance with meaningful disclosure requirements. Employers should be obligated to provide a detailed statement of the rights being waived, including the statutory notice schedule, to the employee prior to his or her acceptance of the job offer. Procedural fairness might also require that the employer provide the employee with a choice between waiver and employment at a lower salary or benefit level.

Given the various reasons why employees might be unwilling or unable to bargain, however, policymakers should devise additional substantive requirements to ensure not only that waiver represents an actual choice by employees, but that waivers are executed on fair terms. Policymakers could devise a menu of alternative terms or benefits – including, perhaps, just cause protection – which, if promised by the employer, could be treated as prima facie evidence of a fair and enforceable waiver. The result would, in effect, create an inverse of the Model Employment Termination Act – a law that establishes a default notice rule, requiring employers to provide notice or severance upon termination unless they "opt in" to a just cause regime (META § 4, 1991).

This notion of a conditionally waivable notice right is also in keeping with the previously described constraints on commercial parties' ability to contract out of the implied duty good faith and the UCC notice obligation. Although contract law doctrines such as unconscionability are generally understood to impose a high threshold on voiding contract terms, the limited case law on waivers of notice in the commercial context reflect judicial willingness to set aside such provisions where enforcement would result in a significant loss to the weaker party (*Intergraph v. Intel*, 1998). Such courts are in effect evaluating the terms of the parties' relationship as a whole in determining whether a contractual provision dispensing with notice is enforceable. The same concerns that justify that approach in the commercial context – the need to protect a weaker party's investment in the relationship – support a fixed requirement that the employer provide a meaningful quid pro quo in exchange for any employee waiver of just notice rights.

CONCLUSION

This chapter has suggested a fundamental shift in the long-standing debate over employment at will. Existing scholarship has focused on just cause reform as the natural alternative to the current system. However, a just cause rule requires the worker to prove that termination was arbitrary, a relatively rare occurrence that is difficult to prove, while leaving workers vulnerable to the more prevalent problem of economic-based termination. In addition, profound changes in the contemporary labor market, including the need for increased employer flexibility and the rise in short-term and contingent labor, challenge the premise of many just cause proposals that preserving workers' existing relationships with a particular employer is itself an important goal.

Rather than constrain employer discretion to terminate, a better approach to at-will reform would assist workers in the inevitable situation of job loss. Under the just notice approach proposed here, employers would remain free to terminate at will, but would be obligated to pay for that right by providing either advance notice or severance pay.

Such a system has several advantages. It would bring employment law in line with contract law, which has long required contracting parties to provide reasonable notice of termination in severing an at-will relationship. Just notice would also bring the law in line with the dominant social contract of employment. To the extent that contemporary employees anticipate obtaining marketable skills and experience in lieu of long-term employment, it makes sense that employers should be required to underwrite some portion of their workers' costs in the event of termination.

A just notice rule would grant workers an immediate and universal benefit that recognizes both the challenges and the inevitability of job transition. Rather than compensating a subset of individuals for the arbitrary loss of particular jobs, just notice would provide all workers with a window of income security during which to search for their next opportunity.

NOTES

1. Portions of this chapter are based on a prior article, Arnow-Richman, 2010.
2. At various points in this chapter I refer to my proposal as a "mandatory" just notice rule. As will be described, *infra*, I allow both for exceptions to this general rule and for the limited possibility of contractual deviation from its provisions. However, these circumstances would be significantly constrained, making just notice far closer to a mandate than a true default. Some scholars have referred to this mid-way point in the spectrum between mandates and defaults as "conditionally waivable" rules (Estlund, 2006), a topic I take up in Section V.C.
3. To be clear, this chapter focuses solely on the contract obligations of employers. In the commercial context, the duty of good faith is reciprocal: whoever invokes the right to terminate at will must provide the other party with reasonable notice. The proposal advanced here, on the other hand, imposes an explicit notice obligation only on the employer. In this way the analogy to contract common law and the UCC is only partially apt. In practice, however, under the current system of employment at will, workers are generally expected to provide notice of voluntary departure, either through an explicit employer policy or as a matter of workplace culture. Thus, the behavior of departing workers already conforms to some extent with the principles of good faith I seek to impose on employers. Whether it makes sense to formalize this obligation of employees as well as employers is beyond the scope of this chapter.
4. This figure focuses only on the universe of permissible reasons for termination under the current system of employment at will plus exceptions; it thus omits unlawfully motivated terminations, which are proscribed by law and would remain so under the proposed just notice rule. There may be a sixth category of terminations that violate social norms but not any legal prohibition. For the purposes of this figure, such terminations may be deemed "arbitrary" – that is, permissible under the at-will rule, but not motivated by any legitimate business reason.
5. Although the Bureau of Labor Statistics (BLS) reports data on "mass layoffs," its definition differs from the definition of a covered termination event under WARN. It is therefore impossible to determine with precision the percentage of terminations that trigger WARN Act obligations. However, an examination of reported data suggests that WARN applies to far less than a third of all terminations. For instance, in

the first quarter of 2009, at the height of the Great Recession, mass layoffs (as defined by BLS) resulted in over 500,000 job losses (Dept. of Labor, BLS, May 2009). In contrast, new unemployment claims during the same period neared or exceeded 600,000 for each month of the quarter (Dept. of Labor, BLS, Feb. 2009, Mar. 2009, Apr. 2009).

6. The exceptions are the provinces of Quebec and Nova Scotia, which have general unlawful dismissal statutes that apply to workers with a specified amount of job tenure. (Employees of the federal government also have greater protections, as they do in the U.S.) Thus the law in these two provinces is similar to that of many European countries in requiring both just cause and mandatory notice (or severance pay).

7. It is unclear, however, the extent to which these realities are endogenous to the law. The patchwork nature of American employment law, coupled with employees' documented misconception about the degree of employment protection, may breed confusion and discontent, leading to more frequent disputes. Thus, it is difficult to predict the effect of importing a distinct legal doctrine, like Canada's reasonable notice rule, which would establish a clear universal entitlement but with a benefit to be determined case by case. On the other hand, it is also possible that the greater litigiousness of American employees owes not to the state of the law but to structural aspects of the American system, including greater accessibility to lawyers and courts, stronger rights to jury trials, and higher aggregate damage awards (Nielsen, 1999). Regardless, the adoption of an open-ended standard of reasonableness would likely be met with significant skepticism by both employers and lawmakers.

8. On the other hand, a statutory version of the "just notice" rule that imposed a graduated amount of notice (or severance) based on years of service might be somewhat less effective in serving this goal. A true reasonable notice rule, like the default imposed by the UCC, would consider all aspects of the parties' relationship, including sunk investments in the relationship and the expectation for future benefits, whereas a fixed notice period calculated based on years of service may or may not cover the deferred compensation period established by the employer in a particular case.

9. Notably the contract language in *Intergraph* purported to allow termination "at any time," but did not explicitly allow termination "without notice." Yet the court subjected it to the unconscionability test applicable to "agreement[s] dispensing with notification" under Section 2-309 (UCC § 2-309(3), 2002; *Intergraph v. Intel*, 1998). This suggests that a more strictly drafted termination clause would not have changed the result. The degree to which commercial parties may alter the reasonable notice default under current contract doctrine is beyond the scope of this chapter. However, in Section V.C. I take up more directly the question whether as a policy matter a statutorily adopted just notice rule ought to be non-waivable.

10. This conclusion was subsequently rejected by the Federal Circuit Court, which heard the appeal in the case pursuant to its jurisdiction over patent disputes. (*Intergraph v. Intel*, 1999). The court failed to address UCC § 2-309 and principally took issue with the district court's remedial power to extend the disputed contract by twenty months. It is not surprising that courts would disagree as to the unconscionability of a commercial party's chosen contract terms. In contrast, the employment context, in which a "no notice" provision would allow an individual worker to immediately lose his or her only stream of income without any advance warning, presents a much starker example of what the UCC would likely conceive of as "an unconscionable state of affairs."

11. The given range reflects different results in measuring the growth rate of the contingent workforce depending on how contingency is defined (Belous, 1995). The most accurate rate is likely between the two reported benchmarks.

12. Overall tenure among female workers rose between 1951 to 2000, with a large rise throughout the 1960s and more modest growth between 1983 and 2000. These figures reflect the continuing migration of women into the labor force, presumably owing to changing work/family dynamics and increased economic pressure requiring two-income households (Rajnes, 2001). Thus, isolating the effects on male workers gives a more accurate depiction of the trend toward external labor market practices. Notably, while all male workers experienced declines in tenure, older workers were hardest hit, with job tenure declining more than five years for males aged 55–64 and 3.3 years for males aged 45–54 (Rajnes, 2001).

13. For instance, assuming just notice were to be adopted at the federal level, Congress could choose to make any severance payments or wages paid during an employee's notice period tax deductible in the same way that employer contributions to group health plans and other employee benefits are currently treated. It could also choose to contribute directly some portion of the overall cost to employers through general tax funds, much as it chose to do under the American Recovery and Reinvestment Act of 2009 in helping unemployed workers pay the cost of continued health insurance coverage under COBRA (the Consolidated Omnibus Budget Reconciliation Act).

REFERENCES

Acharya, Viral V., Subbu Subramanian, & Ramin Baghai. 2010. "Wrongful Discharge Laws and Innovation." Available at SSRN: http://ssrn.com/abstract=1570663.

Addison, John T., & McKinley L. Blackburn. 1997. "A Puzzling Aspect of the Effect of Advance Notice on Unemployment." 50 *Industry and Labor Relations Review* 268–88.

American Law Institute. 1981. Restatement (Second) of Contracts. Sec. 205.

American Law Institute & National Conference on Commissioners on Uniform State Laws. 2001. Uniform Commercial Code. Art. 1. Sec. 304.

American Law Institute & National Conference on Commissioners on Uniform State Laws. 2002. Uniform Commercial Code. Art. 2. Sec. 305 *et seq.*

Arnow-Richman, Rachel. 2006. "Cubewrap Contracts and Worker Mobility: The Dilusion of Employee Bargaining Power via Standard Form Noncompetes." 2006 *Michigan State Law Review* 963–92.

Arnow-Richman, Rachel. 2007. "Cubewrap Contracts: The Rise of Delayed Term, Standard Form Employment Agreements." 49 *Arizona Law Review* 637–64.

Arnow-Richman, Rachel. 2010. "Just Notice: Re-reforming Employment at Will." 58 *University of California, Los Angeles, Law Review* 1.

Autor, David H., et al. 2006. "The Costs of Wrongful-Discharge Laws." 88 *Review of Economics and Statistics* 211–31.

Befort, Stephen. 2003. "Revisiting the Blackhole of Workplace Regulation: A Historical and Comparative Perspective of Contingent Work." 24 *Berkeley Journal of Employment and Labor Law* 153–78.

Belous, Richard S. 1995. "The Rise of the Contingent Work Force: The Key Challenges and Opportunities." 52 *Washington and Lee Law Review* 863–78.

Bird, Robert C. 2008. "An Employment Contract 'Instinct with an Obligation': Good Faith Costs and Contexts." 28 *Pace Law Review* 409–28.

Bird, Robert C., & John D. Knopf. 2009. "Do Wrongful-Discharge Laws Impair Firm Performance?" 52 *Journal of Law and Economics* 197.

Blades, Lawrence E. 1967. "Employment At Will vs. Individual Freedom: On Limiting the Abusive Exercise of Employer Power." 67 *Columbia Law Review* 1404–35.

Bodie, Matthew T. 2004. "Questions about the Efficiency of Employment Arbitration Agreements." 39 *Georgia Law Review* 1–79.

Bureau of National Affairs. 1995. *Basic Patterns in Union Contracts*, 14th ed. Washington, DC: Bureau of National Affairs.

Burton, Steven J. 1981. "Good Faith Performance of a Contract within Article 2 of the Uniform Commercial Code." 67 *Iowa Law Review* 1–30.

Cappelli, Peter. 1999. *The New Deal at Work: Managing the Market Driven Workforce*. Cambridge, MA: Harvard Business School Press.

Craver, Charles B. 1998. "Why Labor Unions Must (and Can) Survive." 1 *University of Pennsylvania Journal of Labor and Employment Labor* 15–48.

Dannin, Ellen. 2007. "Why At-Will Employment is Bad for Employers and Just Cause is Good for Them." 58 *Labor Law Journal* 5–16.

Dau-Schmidt, Kenneth G. 2001. "Employment in the New Age of Trade and Technology: Implications for Labor and Employment Law." 76 *Indiana Law Journal* 1–28.

Deakin, Simon & Prabirjit Sarkar. 2008. "Assessing the Long-run Economic Impact of Labour Law Systems: A Theoretical Reappraisal and Analysis of New Time Series Data." 39 *Industrial Relations Journal* 453–87.

Dertouzos, James N., & Lynn A. Karoly. 1992. *Labor-Market Responses to Employer Liability*, RAND Institute for Civil Justice. Available at http://www.rand.org/pubs/reports/2007/R3989.pdf.

Edelman, Lauren B. 1992. "Professional Construction of Law: The Inflated Threat of Wrongful Discharge." 26 *Law and Society Review* 47–83.

Ehrenberg, Ronald G., & George H. Jakubson. 1989. "Advance Notification of Plant Closing: Does it Matter?" 28 *Industry Relations* 60–71.

England, Geoffrey. 2008. *Essentials on Canadian Law: Individual Employment Law*, 2nd ed. Toronto: Irwin Law, Inc.

Epstein, Richard A. 1984. "In Defense of the Contract at Will." 51 *University of Chicago Law Review* 947–82.

Estlund, Cynthia L. 1996. "Wrongful Discharge Protections in an At-Will World." 74 *Texas Law Review* 1655–92.

Estlund, Cynthia L. 2002. "How Wrong are Employees about their Rights, and Why does it Matter?" 77 *New York University Law Review* 6–35.

Estlund, Cynthia L. 2006. "Between Rights and Contract: Arbitration Agreements and Non-Compete Covenants as a Hybrid Form of Employment Law." 155 *University of Pennsylvania Law Review* 379–445.

Feinman, Jay M. 1976. "The Development of the Employment at Will Rule." 20 *American Journal of Legal History* 118–35.

Freed, Mayer G., & Daniel D. Polsby. 1989. "Just Cause for Termination Rules and Economic Efficiency." 38 *Emory Law Journal* 1097–144.

Friesen, Jane. 1996. "The Response of Wages to Protective Labor Legislation: Evidence from Canada." 49 *Industrial and Labor Relations Review* 243–55.

Friesen, Jane. 1997. "Mandatory Notice and the Jobless Durations of Displaced Workers." 50 *Industrial and Labor Relations Review* 652–66.

Gilbert, Douglas G., et al. 2006. *Canadian Labour and Employment Law for the U.S. Practitioner*, 2nd ed. Washington, DC: Bureau of National Affairs.

Gould IV, William B. 1987. "Stemming the Wrongful Discharge Tide: A Case for Arbitration." 13 *Employment Relations Law Journal* 404–25.

Hipple, Steven. 2001. "Contingent Work in the Late-1990s." 124 *Monthly Labor Review* 3–27.

Hirsch, Jeffrey M. 2008. "The Law of Termination: Doing More with Less." 68 *Maryland Law Review* 89–159.

Jacoby, Sanford M. 2000. "Melting into Air? Downsizing, Job Stability, and the Future of Work." 76 *Chicago-Kent Law Review* 1195–244.

Kamiat, Walter. 1996. "Labor and Lemons: Efficient Norms in the Internal Labor Market and the Possible Failures of Individual Contracting." 144 *University of Pennsylvania Law Review* 1953–70.

Kim, Pauline T. 1997. "Bargaining with Imperfect Information: A Study for Worker Perceptions of Legal Protection in an At-Will World." 83 *Cornell Law Review* 105–60.

Kim, Pauline T. 1999. "Norms, Leaning, and Law: Exploring the Influences on Workers' Legal Knowledge." 1999 *University of Illinois Law Review* 447–515.

Krueger, Alan B. 1991. "The Evolution of Unjust-Dismissal Legislation in the United States." 44 *Industrial and Labor Relations Review* 644–59.

Lazear, Edward P. 1990. "Job Security Provisions and Employment." 1990 *Quarterly Journal of Economics* 699–726.

Lee Hecht Harrison. 2008. "Severance and Separation Practices: Benchmark Study 2008–2009." Available at http://www.lhhitalia.com/it/Documents/LHH_SevStudy08.pdf.

Lester, Gillian. 2001. "Unemployment Insurance and Wealth Redistribution." 49 *UCLA Law Review* 335–93.

Libenson, Daniel J. 2006. "Leasing Human Capital: Toward a New Foundation for Employment Termination Law." 27 *Berkeley Journal of Employment and Labor Law* 111–77.

Lillard, Monique C. 1992. "Fifty Jurisdictions in Search of a Standard: The Covenant of Good Faith and Fair Dealing in the Employment Context." 57 *Missouri Law Review* 1233–300.

Malin, Martin H., & Robert F. Ladenson. 1993. "Privatizing Justice: A Jurisprudential Perspective on Labor and Employment Arbitration from the Steelworkers Trilogy to Gilmer." 44 *Hastings Law Journal* 1187–240.

McGinley, Ann C. 1996. "Rethinking Civil Rights and Employment at Will: Toward a Coherent National Discharge Policy." 57 *Ohio State Law Journal* 1443–524.

Miles, Thomas J. 2000. "Common Law Exceptions to Employment at Will and U.S. Labor Markets." 16 *Journal of Law, Economics, and Organization* 74–101.

Morriss, Andrew P. 1996. "Bad Data, Bad Economics, and Bad Policy: Time to Fire Wrongful Discharge Law." 74 *Texas Law Review* 1901–41.

Nielsen, Laura Beth. 1999. "Paying Workers or Paying Lawyers: Employee Termination Practices in the United States and Canada." 21 *Law and Policy* 247–82.

Parker, J. Wilson. 1995. "At-Will Employment and the Common Law: A Modest Proposal to De-Marginalize Employment Law." 81 *Iowa Law Review* 347–405.

Peck, Cornelius J. 1979. "Unjust Discharges from Employment." 40 *Ohio State Law Journal* 1–50.

Pita, Cristina. 1996. "Advance Notice and Severance Pay Provisions in Contracts." 119 *Monthly Labor Review* 43–50.

Porter, Nicole B. 2008. "The Perfect Compromise: Bridging the Gap between At-Will Employment and Just Cause." 87 *Nebraska Law Review* 62–124.

Rajnes, David. 2001. "A 21st Century Update on Employee Tenure." 22 *EBRI Notes* Number 3.

Rock, Edward B., & Michael L. Wachter. 1996. "The Enforceability of Norms and the Employment Relationship." 144 *University of Pennsylvania Law Review* 1913–52.

Ruhm, Christopher. 1992. "Advance Notice and Postdisplacement Joblessness." 10 *Journal of Labor Economics* 1–32.

Schwab, Stewart J. 1993. "Life-Cycle Justice: Accommodating Just Cause and Employment at Will." 92 *Michigan Law Review* 8–62.

Schwab, Stewart J., & Randall S. Thomas. 2006. "An Empirical Analysis of CEO Employment Contracts: What Do Top Executives Bargain For?" 63 *Washington and Lee Law Review* 231–69.

Schwartz, David S. 1997. "Enforcing Small Print to Protect Big Business: Employee and Consumer Rights Claim in an Age of Compelled Arbitration." 1997 *Wisconsin Law Review* 33–132.

Schwartz, Kenneth D. 2005. "A Lawyer's Perspective on Planning a Reduction in Force." 29 *Economic Perspectives* 94–107.

St. Antoine, Theodore J. 1988. "A Seed Germinates: Unjust Discharge Reform Heads toward Full Flower." 67 *Nebraska Law Review* 56–81.

Stieber, Jack. 1985. "Recent Developments in Employment-at-Will." 36 *Labor Law Journal* 557–63.

Stone, Katherine V.W. 2001. "The New Psychological Contract: Implications of the Changing Workplace for Labor and Employment Law." 48 *UCLA Law Review* 519–659.

Stone, Katherine V.W. 2004. *From Widgets to Digits: Employment Regulation for the Changing Workplace.* Cambridge: Cambridge University Press.

Stone, Katherine Van Wezel. 1996. "Mandatory Arbitration of Individual Employment Rights: The Yellow Dog Contract of the 1990s." 73 *Denver University Law Review* 1017–50.

Summers, Clyde W. 1976. "Individual Protection against Unjust Dismissal: Time for a Statute." 62 *Virginia Law Review* 481–532.

Summers, Clyde W. 2000. "Employment at Will in the United States: The Divine Rights of Employers." 3 *University of Pennsylvania Journal of Labor and Employment Law* 65–86.

Summers, Robert S. 1968. "'Good Faith' in General Contract Law and the Sales Provisions of the Uniform Commercial Code." 54 *Virginia Law Review* 195–267.

Summers, Robert S. 1982. "The General Duty of Good Faith – Its Recognition and Conceptualization." 67 *Cornell Law Review* 810–40.

Sunstein, Cass. 2001. "Human Behavior and the Law of Work." 87 *Virginia Law Review* 205–73.

Sunstein, Cass R. 2002. "Switching the Default Rule." 77 *New York University Law Review* 106–34.

U.S. Department of Labor, Bureau of Labor Statistics. 2009, February. *The Employment Situation: January 2009.* (Report No. USDL 09-0117). Retrieved from http://www.bls.gov/news.release/archives/empsit_02062009.pdf.

U.S. Department of Labor, Bureau of Labor Statistics. 2009, March. *The Employment Situation: February 2009.* (Report No. USDL 09-0224). Retrieved from http://www.bls.gov/news.release/archives/empsit_03062009.pdf.

U.S. Department of Labor, Bureau of Labor Statistics. 2009, April. *The Employment Situation: March 2009.* (Report No. USDL 09-0328). Retrieved from http://www.bls.gov/news.release/archives/empsit_04032009.pdf.

U.S. Department of Labor, Bureau of Labor Statistics. 2009, May. *Extended Mass Layoffs in the First Quarter of 2009.* (Report No. USDL 09-0506). Retrieved from http://www.bls.gov/news.release/archives/mslo_05122009.pdf.

Verkerke, J. Hoult. 1995. "An Empirical Perspective on Indefinite Term Employment Contracts: Resolving the Just Cause Debate." 1995 *Wisconsin Law Review* 837–917.

Weiler, Paul C. 1990. *Governing the Workplace: The Future of Labor and Employment Law.* Cambridge, MA: Harvard University Press.

West, Martha S. 1988. "The Case against Reinstatement in Wrongful Discharge." 1988 *University of Illinois Law Review* 1–65.

Zippay, Allison. 1993. "The Effects of Advance Notice on Displaced Manufacturing Workers: A Case Study." 1993 *Labor Studies Journal* 43–57.

Cases and Legislation

Bardal v. The Globe and Mail Ltd., 24 D.L.R. (2d) 140 (1960).

Bundesgesetzblatt. 2002. Sec. 622(1)–(2). Bürgerliches Gesetzbuch.

Employment Rights Act. 1996. Chap. 18. Sec. 86. United Kingdom Statutes.

Fortune v. National Cash Register Co., 364 N.E.2d 1251 (Mass. 1977).

Gram v. Liberty Mutual Insurance Co., 461 N.E.2d 796 (Mass. 1984).

Intergraph Corp. v. Intel Corp., 3 F. Supp. 2d 1253 (N.D. Ala. 1998).

Intergraph Corp. v. Intel Corp., 195 F.3d 1346 (Fed. Cir. 1999).

Model Employment Termination Act. 1991. Sec. 3 *et seq.* The National Conference of Commissioners on Uniform State Laws.

Montana Wrongful Discharge from Employment Act. 2009. Chap. 39. Sec. 2-904(1)(b) *et seq.* Montana Code Annotated.

Murphy v. American Home Products Corporation, 558 N.Y.S.2d 920 (App. Div. 1990).

Pharo Distributing Co. v. Stahl, 782 S.W.2d 635 (Ky. Ct. App. 1989).

Pugh v. See's Candies, Inc., 116 Cal. App. 3d 311 (1981).

Title 29. Sec. 185a. 2007. Laws of Puerto Rico Annotated.

United Steelworkers of America v. Warrior & Gulf Navigation Co., 363 U.S. 574 (1960).

The WARN Act. 1988. Chap. 29. Sec. 2101 *et seq.* United States Code.

Woolley v. Hoffman-La Roche, Inc., 491 A.2d 1257 (N.J. 1985).

11. The law and economics of employment protection legislation
Simon Deakin*

I. INTRODUCTION

Employment protection legislation (EPL) has a long history in some jurisdictions, having been introduced in Weimar Germany and the French Third Republic in the inter-war period in forms which are recognizable to modern labour lawyers (Vogel-Polskey, 1986). 'Unjust' or 'unfair' dismissal legislation is the principal example of this type of statutory intervention, but the term 'employment protection' is capable of embracing other legal mechanisms aimed at promoting job security, including legislation setting minimum notice periods for dismissal and requiring the payment of redundancy compensation. The rights created generally vest in individual employees, but also potentially relevant in the present context are laws which grant collective information or consultation rights over dismissal, sometimes extending to codetermination or joint decision-making, to worker representatives. EPL is not, generally, taken to include social insurance or other social security legislation, through which unemployment compensation or social assistance is paid to the individual by the state, not the employer, nor does it extend to legislation which mandates basic labour standards on hours and wages. EPL is nevertheless complementary to these forms of regulation and to some extent overlaps with them. In this chapter, for reasons of space, the focus will be on the core of EPL as it is conventionally defined, that is to say, unjust or unfair dismissal laws and laws relating to layoff and redundancy.

This chapter will show that the law and economics analysis of EPL has proceeded through a series of stages which reflect theoretical developments in the wider field of labour economics, the emergence over time of new data sources, and a growing policy interest in this area. What might be thought of 'first-generation' studies were highly critical of EPL, regarding it as one among a number of legislative impositions on the autonomy of the parties to the employment contract which could not be justified in efficiency terms (Epstein, 1984). These contributions reflected the traditional neoclassical origins of the law and economics field and the focus of the early literature on the US case, in the context of which the possible erosion of at-will employment was a lively issue.

In time, a 'second generation' of analyses influenced by so-called 'modern neoclassical' approaches (Wachter and Wright, 1990), sometimes referred to as the 'new institutional economics' (Kaufman, 2009), came to the fore. These used models based on transaction costs, asymmetric information and adverse selection that created some scope for an efficiency-based argument in favour of EPL, although potential inefficiencies were also recognized (Bertola, 2009). The emergence of new data, on a cross-state basis in the USA and at cross-country level in the case of indicators constructed by the Organisation for Economic Co-operation and Development (OECD) (1994, 2004) and World Bank (various years), gave rise to new opportunities for empirical research, which tended to confirm the indeterminate position adopted by new institutional theory.

Most recently, these studies have been challenged by a 'third generation' of evolutionary models (Amable, Demmou and Gatti, 2007; Deakin and Sarkar, 2008; Gatti, 2010). These view the various different types of EPL not as an exogenous interference with contractual relations, but as endogenously generated solutions to coordination problems arising in labour markets. Alongside these theoretical developments, time-series datasets are starting to fill in the gaps in knowledge left by the limited cross-sectional indices of the OECD and World Bank (Deakin, Lele and Siems, 2007). The resulting studies are providing a more fully rounded explanation for cross-national diversity in the forms of EPL and a more complete account of its potential economic effects.

As a result of these various developments, the skepticism towards EPL initially shown by economists and law and economics scholars has given rise to a more cautious and qualified assessment, which accepts, to some degree, the efficiency case for legislative interventions of this kind, at least in certain national contexts and under particular market conditions. In providing an account of this developing literature, Section II of this chapter introduces the concept of employment protection legislation, defines basic terms, and outlines the various functions and goals attributed to this kind of legislation. Section III outlines different theoretical approaches to the economic analysis of EPL. Section IV describes the main data sources used in the study of EPL, while Section V discusses some methodological issues which arise in relation to their use in econometric analysis. Section VI provides an account of the main lines of the empirical literature. Section VII concludes.

II.   FORMS AND FUNCTIONS OF EMPLOYMENT PROTECTION LEGISLATION

The basic structure of the forms of EPL which exist within national systems can be seen from a consideration of the most influential international law standard on termination of employment, namely International Labour Organization (ILO) Recommendation 119 of 1963. The Recommendation sets out as a first principle the proposition that 'termination of employment should not take place unless there is a valid reason for such termination connected with the capacity or conduct of the worker or based on the operational requirements of the undertaking, establishment or service' (Art. 2(1)). This is the starting point for more or less all systems of unfair dismissal legislation: the employer must have a good reason for dismissal based either on the capabilities or behaviour of the employee who is being dismissed, or on the organizational or economic needs of the enterprise. The Recommendation goes on to identify reasons for dismissal which should never be regarded as valid: these are reasons based on trade union membership or participation in trade union activities; seeking to be or acting as a worker representative; making a good faith complaint of employer violation of relevant laws or regulations; and dismissal on prohibited, discriminatory grounds (the race, colour, sex, marital status, religion, political opinion, national extraction or social origin of the employee) (Art. 2(3)). With respect to reasons that are potentially valid or fair, the Recommendation essentially prescribes a set of procedural standards. Dismissal without notice should only take place for serious misconduct, and a worker accused of such misconduct should be given an opportunity to put forth his or her side of the case, where appropriate with the assistance of a representative (Art. 10(5)). In cases of economic dismissal, the employer, in conjunction with other parties including worker representatives, should take steps to avert job loss as far possible 'without prejudice to the efficient operation' of the enterprise. Selection for dismissal on economic grounds should avoid discrimination and balance the efficiency needs of the employer with consideration of the ability, skills and qualifications of the employees affected, their seniority, and their family circumstances (Art. 15).

As Büchtemann (1993) argues, there are many different meanings in practice to the term 'job security', and it is not clear how far these are reflected in the type of legislative structure reproduced in Recommendation No. 119. Job security, in the specific sense of the right of a worker to retain a particular employment, can be contrasted with employment security in a wider sense of the availability of employment opportunities within a given market or economy. The concept of 'security' implicit in EPL lies somewhere between these two cases. Virtually no EPL systems confer complete job security on employees in the sense of giving them a veto over the removal of the job or, what may amount to the same thing, a unilateral change of job definition. This makes the notion of job property or 'ownership of jobs' (Meyers, 1964) somewhat problematic (Collins, 1993, ch. 1), although the protection given to some workers against arbitrary termination of employment has been conceptualized as akin to a property right, or 'new property', in some jurisdictions, such as the USA (Reich, 1964). The idea of property in work has also been invoked to explain workers' collective consultation or codetermination rights (Njoya, 2007). Some countries grant civil servants the right not to be dismissed except for good cause defined as gross misconduct or incapability, in effect giving them protection against dismissals for economic reasons, but these categories of workers often have to accept, as a quid pro quo, obligations of redeployment that give the employer considerable leeway to redefine the core terms of the employment relationship. Mostly, EPL systems give employees a right, within limits, not to be subjected to arbitrary managerial decision-making; hence a core feature of such laws is the presence of 'explicit or implicit rules and provisions putting a restraint on the ability of firms to dismiss workers "at will"' (Büchtemann, 1993, p. 8). Another idea which reflects the form and function of EPL in jurisdictions which emphasize the human rights dimension of labour and employment law is that 'the employee's interest in job security is . . . a right to dignity combined with the establishment of conditions for autonomy and freedom' (Collins, 1993, p. 28).

Other interests may be served by EPL. Many laws owe their origins to attempts by legislatures to use this type of law to improve organizational efficiency, and from time to time this kind of intervention has been actively supported by employer groups. One of the justifications for the original unjust dismissal legislation of 1920s Germany was the corporatist aim of binding workers to the firm, a view which was compatible with a 'communitarian' view of the enterprise in which workers and the employer had reciprocal duties of loyalty and trust. The German law idea of the worker's *Tatbestand* or 'factual adhesion to the enterprise', a process conferring 'a status equivalent to membership of a community' (Supiot, 1994, p. 18), was on the one hand deeply rooted in pre-contractual notions of service, but also a useful legal adaptation to the emergence of large, vertically integrated firms in the last decades of the nineteenth century and first decades of the twentieth (Ahlering and Deakin, 2007).

In the UK, dismissal laws arrived as part of a later corporatist experiment, in the 1970s. The Donovan Commission of 1968 proposed unfair dismissal legislation as part of an attempt to regularize and proceduralize workplace industrial relations. The legislation which arrived in 1971 as part of the then Conservative government's Industrial Relations Act had 'a dual purpose' in which employment protection was to be combined with 'managerial efficiency' (Anderman, 1986, p. 416). The British Redundancy Payments Act of 1965, which provided a right to compensation based on seniority for loss of employment on economic grounds, was adopted by a legislature keen to encourage firm-level restructuring and the movement of labour away from declining industries; for a critic of the Act, 'to claim that the provisions of the statute amount to an improvement in employment security is akin to suggesting that legislating for insurance cover for a proportion of road users would be about road safety' (Fryer, 1973, p. 3).

In the course of the 1970s, unfair dismissal laws were widely adopted in many market-based economies, both developed and developing. The US case, in which employment at will remained the prevailing rule in the absence of a federal job security statute and only minimal legislative initiatives at state level, was an outlier by international standards. US workers are not entirely without dismissal protection; public sector workers are generally entitled to the protection of due process in matters relating to termination of employment, and unionized workers, in both the public and private sectors, normally benefit from protections set out in collective agreements. It is possible to exaggerate the difference, in this respect, between the US and other industrialized countries. Partial judicial erosion of the employment at will rule took place from the 1970s onwards, with exceptions introduced for discriminatory or retaliatory discharges and, in some states, terminations which did not comply with contractual commitments made by employers. The threat of litigation arising out of these developments appears to have had an impact on employer behaviour (see Autor et al., 2004).

Beginning in the 1980s, those countries which had adopted unfair dismissal legislation in the preceding decades began to limit the protection they conferred. This initially took the form of a tightening of qualifying conditions. Public policy switched from the goal of protection to the aim of enhancing labour market 'flexibility', which in practice meant partial deregulation. However, no system has repealed its unfair dismissal laws completely. Most of them retain significant levels of legal job security for 'core' workers, that is, those employed on indefinite-duration or 'permanent' contracts, while narrowing the scope of coverage. Thus growing 'legislative dualism' has seen the exclusion from protection of a significant proportion of casual, fixed-term and part-time employees, and the legitimation of temporary agency work in systems which had previously prohibited or tightly regulated it (Veneziani, 2009). These developments – the controversy over employment at will in the USA and the partial retreat of dismissal laws elsewhere – have made EPL contested terrain politically, while stimulating a considerable body of economic and empirical research into its effects.

III.   ECONOMIC-THEORETICAL ACCOUNTS OF EPL

The economic analysis of EPL begins with accounts that see labour law regulation in general as an exogenous intervention in, and hence interference with, the operation of the market. In the neoclassical model, wages and other terms and conditions of employment, including those relating to termination of employment, are set by the interaction of supply and demand for labour. The market operates as an implicit regulator of the decisions of private parties. If workers value job security, firms that make inadequate provision for employment protection risk losing their workers to competitors, just as workers who overbid for this type of protection risk exclusion from employment as firms substitute capital for labour or cease to trade. The spontaneous movement of the market to equilibrium should ensure that the optimal level of job security, in any particular case, is arrived at through the autonomous action of the parties.

In this 'first-generation' model, legislative intervention is not just unnecessary, but positively harmful. Labour laws are seen as originating in decisions made in the political sphere and reflect rent-seeking, or distributional demands, by collective groups. Rent-seeking, as it is aimed at redistribution rather than value creation, imposes a deadweight loss on the economy and so constitutes a source of inefficiency. Further inefficiencies arise from distortions in the operation of the market that are induced by legal interferences with bargaining. EPL artificially raises firing costs by imposing procedural and, in some cases, substantive constraints on the employer's power to end the employment relationship at will. These costs impact back on the hiring decision, making employers more reluctant to hire labour which they will find difficult to shed at a later point. This in turn depresses the demand for labour and results in the exclusion from the market of those it is designed to help, that is, those regarded as most vulnerable to dismissal in the first place (Minford, 1985). From this point of view, EPL, like other forms of labour legislation, is not just inefficient, but discriminatory and unjust in its effects (Epstein, 1984).

By contrast, 'second-generation' modern neoclassical or new-institutionalist perspectives view unregulated labour markets as affected by imperfections or rigidities of various kinds. The presence of structural imperfections arising from transactions costs, information asymmetries and externalities can be used to justify labour law intervention on efficiency grounds (Manning, 2003, p. 24). A clear illustration of this is the monopsony-based case for wage regulation. Where employers have significant market power, they are able to act as monopsonists (that is, as 'monopoly buyers'). This means that they can set wages and terms and conditions below the 'equilibrium' rate at which markets would clear if they were fully competitive. As wages are then 'artificially' low, workers have less incentive to offer their labour to employers and so labour supply is reduced. Minimum wage legislation, by restoring wages to a level closer to the market-clearing rate, can bring about an increase in wages without a compensating decline in employment. In some situations, employment will also rise as the labour supply increases. The surplus that employers were previously able to capture by virtue of their monopsony power meets the costs of employing additional workers. Society is better off because resources are being more efficiently allocated than they were before (Manning, 2003, pp. 15–16). This argument can be extended to other aspects of the wage-work bargain, including those falling within the remit of EPL.

Neoclassical economics has long accepted that there are rigidities in labour markets which could justify regulation. A widely held view among neoclassical economists, however, is that monopsony is not a good explanation for observed rigidities, since few employers have sufficient market power to distort the workings of the price mechanism (see Kaufman, 2009, pp. 17–20). A possible response to this critique is that monopsony is just one of a number of cases illustrating the role of asymmetric information in labour markets (Manning, 2003). For markets to self-correct in response to rigidities and shocks of various kinds, and hence arrive at a welfare-maximizing equilibrium, workers and employers must be well informed not just about prevailing prices but also about alternative trading possibilities. Employer power is the result not simply of limited competition between firms, but also of limits on the information available to both workers and employers concerning alternative employment opportunities, and the resulting costs of matching employment offers to the skills and capacities of workers (see Manning, 2003, p. 132).

Levine (1991) develops a model of information asymmetries to explain the specific potential efficiency-enhancing effects of unfair dismissal legislation. In the same way that they may pay an 'efficiency wage' above the market-clearing rate in order to induce workers to invest in firm-specific skills, employers may offer guarantees of job security in order to enhance workers' commitment to the firm. Prior to the hiring, however, workers cannot perfectly observe the likely quality of the job that they are being invited to undertake, and, in particular, may find it difficult to judge whether employers' commitments to stable employment are serious or sustainable. Knowing this, employers may be reluctant to make such commitments. Thus an equilibrium can arise in which employers may not offer, and/or workers may not be prepared to accept, contractual arrangements which would otherwise be in their mutual interests. Unfair dismissal legislation enhances the credibility of employers' offers of job security, thereby promoting efficiency in contracting. In effect, legal intervention shifts outcomes from a low-level equilibrium 'trap' to one in which all parties are better off.

From a modern neoclassical or new-institutional perspective, the weakness in the traditional neoclassical approach is to assume that labour law regulations act upon a market which is already at an optimal equilibrium point (Manning, 2003, p. 58). Demonstrating the contingency of this assumption makes it possible to refute certain neoclassical arguments for deregulation. However, it does not follow that labour law regulation is always justifiable on efficiency grounds. It may be far from clear what, in practice, the hypothetical optimal equilibrium is. It is unlikely that minimum wage laws can mimic the market-clearing wage in a completely accurate way; so, in the same way, heroic assumptions have to be made to believe that unfair dismissal laws precisely reproduce the terms of hypothetically perfect employment contracts under conditions of efficiency wage bargaining. More realistically, EPL, in common with other forms of labour law regulation, can only be regarded as offering an approximate solution for the effects of market failure. It is also possible to view EPL, from a new-institutionalist perspective, as inducing market failures of its own. Thus, in an adaptation of the efficiency-wage approach, 'insider-outsider' models see employment protection in terms of the ability of unionized workers to capture firm-specific rents, to the detriment of less well organized workers who are displaced into a 'secondary' market of casualized employment (Lindbeck and Snower, 1989).

It is also possible, within the modern neoclassical or new-institutional approach, that 'spontaneous' solutions to market failures will arise, based on private ordering, thereby removing the need for legal intervention. This is suggested by 'signaling' models (Akerlof, 1982). Firms wishing to offer secure, high quality employment to employees may find ways to signal their capacity to do so by absorbing the high costs of employment-related benefits which are beyond the means of their less productive competitors. More productive employees, conversely, can signal their capabilities by voluntarily undergoing firm-specific training which carries a short-term cost in the form of reduced wages, in return for seniority-based increments later (Spence, 1973). More generally, standards based on firm or industry-level practices, which incorporate some of these signalling effects, may work better than legislatively imposed mandates (see Kaufman, 2009, pp. 43–4). The potential role of private ordering outside or beyond the law formed part of the basis for Epstein's influential defence of the US employment at will rule at a time when judicial attacks on the doctrine were at their height (Epstein, 1984).

Modern neoclassical and new institutional approaches to law and economics, notwithstanding their differences from traditional neoclassical models, share a conception of legal rules as exogenous to market relations, and hence as an external imposition upon them. There is also a related tendency to see legislative solutions as complete in the sense of being certain in the scope of their application and self-executing in their implementation. By contrast, third-generation 'systemic' or 'evolutionary' models see legal rules as endogenous in various ways to the market settings in which they operate as well as incomplete in their application (Deakin and Sarkar, 2008). This approach has a number of implications for the law and economics of labour law.

In the systemic-evolutionary approach, legal rules are understood as devices for coordinating the expectations of actors under conditions of uncertainty (Aoki, 2010). Laws that mandate certain outcomes, and hence appear to operate in a top-down, hierarchical way, often do no more than crystallize social norms or conventions that first emerge at the level of the market, in the form of behavioural patterns or routines, and that then go on to acquire greater formality in contractual agreements and legislative texts. Most labour law rules have openly redistributive aims and give expression to widely held beliefs on what constitutes fair treatment. These beliefs operate as 'focal points' that assist bargaining and the mutual adjustment of disputes (Hyde, 2006). The employment contract is a complex legal 'institution' that embodies a number of these focal points. The core of the employment model is a trade-off between norms granting powers of coordination to the employer (Coase, 1988), and those providing the employee with access to income-smoothing and insurance mechanisms which offset risks arising from wage-dependence (Simon, 1951). Labour law institutions, of which EPL is one alongside collective bargaining and social insurance, express this fundamental trade-off in various ways, reflecting the compromises struck in particular national and regional settings (Supiot, 1994).

It follows that labour laws are not exogenously 'imposed' upon an otherwise 'unregulated' market, but are endogenous to the markets in which they operate and to the political structures that give rise to them. 'Endogenous laws' are solutions to coordination problems which emerge over time in response to certain market and political contexts. In part because they are generated by the rough and tumble of politics in which distributive outcomes are fought over between rival interests groups, these legal solutions are necessarily incomplete. They are also imperfect in their mode of operation. They are neither self-executing, nor capable of being made operational by enforcement alone. They cannot be successfully implemented in the absence of shared understandings and beliefs on the part of market actors beyond the limits of the legal system (Aoki, 2010). Thus the operation of legal rules, and hence their potential costs and benefits for firms and workers, are dependent on contextual factors that vary across time and space.

This implies that we cannot say much, a priori, about the economic effects of labour laws, including EPL. Because the origins of these laws are context-specific, their impact will not be constant across given sets of firms, industries or national systems. The nature of their implementation turns on factors beyond the legal system, at the level of social norms and self-regulation by industry actors. It also varies across the economic cycle. Labour laws may have offsetting positive and negative effects on efficiency. Thus models predicting the effects of legislative interventions need to take into account these diverse contextual conditions if they are to have any traction in real-life situations.

In an extreme form, this 'indeterminacy hypothesis' (Deakin and Sarkar, 2008) could tip over into a claim about the law's triviality. This is the view that, precisely because of its endogeneity in the sense just described, the legal system is no more than a conduit for the operation of wider economic forces. The legal origins hypothesis offers a corrective to this view (La Porta et al., 2008). This maintains that the substantive content of legal rules, and, in turn, their economic impact, are shaped by the nature of a given country's 'legal infrastructure' or 'regulatory style'. Apart from a few parent systems, most countries have inherited their 'legal origin' in the sense just described through an exogenous event such as conquest or colonization. Even cases of conscious adoption of an external model are relatively rare. Legal origin can thereby be understood as a variable with long-run causal effects of its own, which can help to account for the economic trajectories of different countries, and hence the persistence of cross-national diversity (La Porta et al., 2008).

In this vein, it is argued that common-law origin systems tend to favour market-creating rules and take a laissez-faire approach to economic regulation. Civil-law systems, by contrast, are said to contain a bias towards government ownership and regulation of the economy, and to favour redistributive solutions. Two potential 'channels' have been identified as mechanisms linking legal infrastructure with the substantive content of legal rules. Through the 'adaptability channel', common-law systems, since they give more discretion to judges to shape the law, are likely to produce more flexible rules in their response to economic conditions as they change over time (Beck et al., 2003). The alternative 'political channel' posits a process according to which the regulatory bias of civil-law systems gives rise to greater opportunities for rent-seeking, and hence to deadweight losses for the relevant national economies (Rajan and Zingales, 2003).

It has been argued that the legal origins hypothesis is based on a greatly over-simplified account of the divide between common-law and civil-law systems (Armour et al., 2009a). Nevertheless, in identifying the legal system as a source of path-dependence and institutional lock-in in the development of national economies, it has made a significant theoretical contribution and this in turn has generated a large and growing empirical literature. The 'strong form' of legal origins theory predicts that differences in regulatory style will be reflected in economic performance outcomes, with common-law systems experiencing more dynamic growth. This claim is not supported empirically, however (see La Porta et al., 2008, pp. 301–2). A weak form of the legal origins hypothesis may be more easily defended: this sees legal infrastructure as having a long-run influence on economic growth, but with legal institutions co-evolving alongside economic and political structures rather than as exogenously determining them (Ahlering and Deakin, 2007; Armour et al., 2009a, 2009b).

A coevolutionary perspective of this kind is also compatible with the comparative political science approach of varieties of capitalism theory. This views national systems dividing between 'liberal market' and 'coordinated market' economies (Hall and Soskice, 2001). This distinction maps on to that between the common-law and civil-law legal families, but does not see legal origin as the main explanatory variable. Rather, the emphasis is on the role of political structures and the make-up of interest-group coalitions in shaping the content of labour legislation and related rules in the areas of finance, corporate governance and antitrust or competition law (Roe, 2003; Pagano and Volpin, 2005). This emphasis on the political economy of legislative change implies an empirical research agenda which looks at possible links or 'complementarities' between legal, economic and political institutions. For example, labour law rules that are typical of coordinated market systems, such as stringent EPL and codetermination, may be complementary to certain features of the financial and corporate governance environment, such as concentrated share ownership and bank-led monitoring. Conversely, flexible labour markets and liquid capital markets, underpinned respectively by minimal levels of EPL and strong shareholder rights regimes, may operate in a complementary way within liberal market systems (Ahlering and Deakin, 2007). This again implies a need for data on the key legal and institutional variables. With this point in mind, we will now turn to an examination of data sources on EPL.

IV.   DATA SOURCES ON EPL

New datasets have emerged to quantify the content of legal rules in the labour law field as well as in related areas of economic regulation including company and insolvency law. This has happened in part as a result of the growing interest in the legal system as a causal variable capable of influencing economic outcomes in its own right, as well as by virtue of the growth in comparative analysis of economic institutions and performance outcomes. The first such index in the labour law field was the one developed by the OECD for the purpose of analyzing the 'strictness' of EPL. This currently tracks the law in almost 30 OECD member states. It is based in large part on an index first developed by Grubb and Wells (1993). Four main data-gathering exercises have taken place, in the late 1980s, the late 1990s, 2003 and 2008. The index is made up of three components: rules affecting dismissal of workers with regular (that is, indefinite or indeterminate) employment contracts; rules governing fixed-term and temporary agency work; and collective dismissal procedures. The country scores are expressed on a scale from zero to 6; 6 represents maximum 'strictness'. The three sub-indices are combined to arrive at an overall strictness indicator for each country. The collective dismissals indicator is weighted at 40 percent of the other two on the grounds that it operates in a way that is largely supplementary to the workings of laws regulating the individual employment relationship (OECD, 2004; Venn, 2009).

An alternative index, which offers wider coverage in terms of the countries and subject-matter covered but does not provide a time series, is the labour regulation index of Botero et al. (2004). This index was informed by the methodology of legal origins theory (see La Porta et al., 2008). It contains codings for the labour laws of over 80 developed and developing countries. The index makes use of more than 60 indicators covering employment law, collective labour relations law and social security law. For each indicator, a score is supplied which is intended to indicate the strength of worker protection for a given country. The higher the score on a zero to 1 scale, the greater the protection. Botero et al. provide coding protocols or algorithms which explain how the scores were worked out. A number of approaches are used; mostly, assumptions are made about the operation of the law on the basis of its formal content alone, although in some cases cardinal variables, based for example on mandated legal minima for dismissal compensation, are used. The sources for the coding are mostly described as 'the laws of each country', with the reader being directed to secondary sources such as textbooks or legal encyclopaedias. More specific legal sources, such as statutes or judicial decisions, are not provided. The index is not time-variant, and refers to the state of laws in the late 1990s.

The methods pioneered by the early legal origins papers were used to inform the *Doing Business* reports of the World Bank (various years). As part of its *Doing Business* project, the World Bank developed an 'employing workers index'. This incorporated a 'rigidity of employment index' covering, among other things, firing costs. This index is based in part on surveys of businesses, local and official, and takes the form of a time series going back to 2004. Following criticism from a sub-committee of the US Senate, the World Bank's approach to the coding of labour laws is currently under review (see World Bank, 2011, p. 94).

Notwithstanding their different approaches to coding, the OECD and World Bank datasets reach similar conclusions on the nature and extent of cross-national variation in labour laws in general and EPL in particular. Labour regulation seems to be highly correlated with legal origin, with French-origin countries, as a group, scoring higher (indicating greater worker protection) than German-origin or common-law origin countries (Botero et al., 2004). The OECD gives lower scores (indicating less EPL 'strictness') to the USA and UK. Northern European, east Asian and Nordic countries are in the middle range, while southern European ones score more highly. Much of the variation in scores in the OECD index stems from the role played by laws governing temporary and fixed-term employment. The major change over time has been a gradual deregulatory trend, which has also led to convergence across systems.

The use of synthetic indices to code labour laws and regulations has been the subject of intensive debate. The World Bank's approach makes the strong assumption that the firm in question completely abides by the law in question, ignoring the possibility of non-enforcement. It also takes no account of the possibility that firms would provide contractual job security in the absence of legal mandates. The authors of the OECD index have accepted that their EPL measure suffers from problems 'inherent to most synthetic indices', namely 'problems of subjectivity, the difficulty of attributing scores on the basis of legal provisions that may be applied differently in practice, and the choice of the weighting scheme used to calculate the summary indicator form from the various sub-components' (OECD, 2004, p. 99). They have sought to deal with these by incorporating data on court practice and collective bargaining, an approach which creates further problems since not all countries provide such data (OECD, 2004, p. 66).

The labour regulation index developed by the Cambridge Centre for Business Research (CBR) seeks to address the methodological shortcoming of these other approaches (Deakin, Lele and Siems, 2007). This index includes information from collective agreements and other self-regulatory mechanisms that operate as the functional equivalents

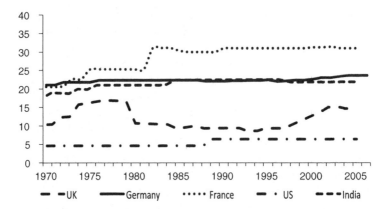

Source: Deakin, Lele and Siems 2007.

Figure 11.1   Labour regulation in five countries, 1970–2006 (aggregate index: maximum score is 40)

to formal laws in some countries. It also makes use of coding protocols that reflect how far labour law rules take the form of defaults that only apply unless the parties agree otherwise, as opposed to mandates. The CBR index uses graduated variables, as opposed to binary ones employed in the legal origins literature, so that the differences between legal mandates, default rules and self-regulation can be captured in the relevant scores. In the case of federal systems, the federal law is used where it is realistic to assume that it applies, and where state laws generally improve on or alter federal minima, the laws of a more heavily industrialized or populated state are used. Full explanations for the codings, including primary legal sources, are provided. The most important difference between the CBR index and its rivals is that it takes the form of a complete time series, going back, for some countries, to the early 1970s.

The CBR index contains 40 indicators, and has five sub-indices covering the form of the employment contract, working time, dismissal, employee representation and industrial action. Indices based on the same methods have been constructed for shareholder protection and creditor protection, so that it is possible to test for complementarities across labour, company and insolvency law.

A comparison of the CBR indices for the three 'parent' systems (the UK, France and Germany) and those of the USA and India confirms the suggestion of Botero et al. (2004) that civil-law systems are more protective of worker interests than common-law ones (see Figure 11.1). Nevertheless, India does not conform to expectations; its labour laws are closer to those of Germany rather than to the 'parent' British system. The long time series provided by the CBR index reveals substantial change over time in the content of labour laws. The marked divergence of French and British labour law in the early 1980s is associated with the election of the socialist president François Mitterand in France and the election of the Conservative government of Margaret Thatcher in the UK. The first socialist government of the Mitterand presidency adopted an ambitious programme of labour law reforms, the Auroux Laws, at the same time as the Thatcher

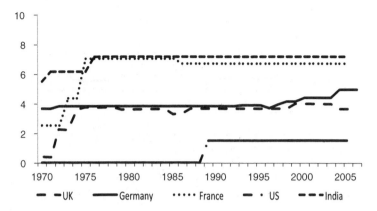

Source: Deakin, Lele and Siems 2007.

Figure 11.2 Labour regulation in five countries, 1970–2006 (dismissal law sub-index: maximum score is 9)

governments were implementing a programme of labour law deregulation. Thus shifts in the political environment brought about significant changes in the substance of labour law, casting doubt on the idea of stable cross-country differences derived from legal origin, and emphasizing the endogeneity of the law to local political contexts (Deakin, Lele and Siems, 2007; Deakin and Sarkar, 2008).

Figures 11.2 and 11.3 show trends in two of the sub-indices from the CBR dataset, those on dismissal protection and the regulation of flexible forms of employment, that are most relevant for present purposes. The dismissal law sub-index contains nine variables. These indicate whether the law provides for minimum periods of notice by the employer prior to dismissal; whether the employer has to pay redundancy compensation or severance pay in the event of economic dismissal; the minimum period of qualifying service required for general unfair dismissal protection; the extent of procedural constraints on individual dismissal, that is, those relating to hearings and appeals; the extent of substantive constraints, that is, restriction of the reasons for dismissal; how far reinstatement is the normal remedy for dismissal; whether notification of dismissal to the government or a third party is a precondition for the effectiveness in law of that dismissal; whether the law imposes restrictions on selection for redundancy or economic dismissal; and whether the law contains rules on priority in re-employment for those dismissed on economic grounds.

It can be seen from Figure 11.2 that there was a significant strengthening of dismissal protection in the 1970s. India's dismissal law sets a high level of protection against dismissals or 'retrenchments' by international standards. Dismissal law is by no means a phenomenon confined to developed countries. French dismissal law was strengthened in the 1970s and has remained at a consistently high level since. Dismissal law in the UK was not the main focus of deregulation in that system; the more far-reaching changes in the 1980s were those which occurred in respect of working time, the law relating to worker representation, and strike law. In Germany, dismissal law, which was already

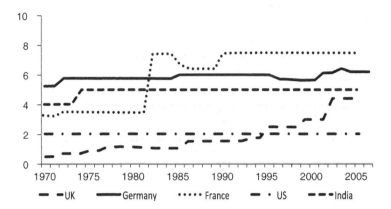

Source: Deakin, Lele and Siems 2007.

Figure 11.3   *Labour regulation in five countries, 1970–2006 (alternative employment contracts sub-index: maximum score is 8)*

strong at the start of the period covered by the index, has not changed much since. The so-called Hartz reforms of the mid-2000s, which were intended to introduce a degree of flexibility into the labour market, were mostly concerned with changes to unemployment compensation and related aspects of social security law, not employment protection law.

The United States data present a very different picture. The absence of unfair dismissal legislation either at federal level or in virtually all of the states is reflected by the very low score on the US indicator for dismissal law. The index does not attempt to code for the modifications to the employment at will rule which occurred in some states from the 1980s onwards. Although significant by US standards, and generating considerable debate there, these changes were very minor by international standards, and so do not justify a change in the score in the context of an index which is intended to compare the degree of legal regulation across different countries, as this one is. In this respect, the CBR index follows the same approach to coding US law as the OECD and World Bank indices. The one change in the score for the US relates to the adoption of the federal Worker Adjustment and Retraining Notification Act ('WARN') in the late 1980s. This introduced provision for minimum notice periods and severance pay and notification requirements in economic dismissals.

It is possible that the CBR index underscores the actual costs to employers of dismissal in the US system. This is for various reasons. A minority of US workers are protected by job security clauses in collective agreements and by laws or regulations governing public-sector employment. Workers whose employment contracts are, in principle, at will may benefit from de facto protections conferred by employer handbooks and by the possibility (however distant) of litigation under one of the exceptions to the at-will presumption (Autor et al., 2004). Discrimination law, not coded in the CBR index, is also a significant factor shaping termination decisions in the US context. These caveats aside, there is little doubt that the US is an outlier, by international standards, in not providing for a general right to protection against arbitrary dismissal. The relatively unchanging position of the

US over time, by comparison to other industrialized and large economies, is captured in the time series provided by the CBR dataset.

Figure 11.3 charts developments in the law relating to the definition of the employment relationship and the regulation of labour flexibility. The variables covered here are concerned with how strictly the law regulates the definition of the employment contract (and how much leeway, conversely, the parties have to avoid labour law regulation by adopting self-employment or another contract form which is either wholly or partly outside labour law protection); whether the law contains a principle of equal treatment for part-time workers, relative to those employed full-time; whether the cost of dismissing a part-time worker is the same, in proportionate terms, as dismissing a full-time one; whether the law allows the use of fixed-term employment contracts only under specified circumstances; whether fixed-term workers have the right to equal treatment with those employed on a permanent or indefinite basis; after what period of time (if any) or number of renewals a fixed-term contract of employment is deemed to become permanent; whether the law imposes restraints on the use of temporary agency work; and how far the law requires agency workers to be treated equally with directly employed workers of the user undertaking.

Figure 11.3 clarifies the extent to which the civil-law systems of France and Germany make this area of law a priority for protection. The increase in the rights of 'flexible' workers in France during the 1980s is particularly marked. In the UK case, this area of regulation was the focus of considerable legislative intervention from the mid-1990s onwards. The law on part-time workers' rights was strengthened in 1995 following a ruling of the European Court of Justice on the implications of sex discrimination law for part-time workers' right to equal treatment. After the election of a Labour government in 1997 and the reversal of the UK's 'opt-out' from the Social Chapter of the Maastricht Treaty, the UK acceded to European Union labour law directives concerning the equal treatment of part-time and fixed-term contract workers. Thus the steady rise in the UK score after 1997 reflects in part a change of government, and in part the growing alignment of UK labour law with that of other EU member states, a consequence of the EU's labour law harmonization programmes at that time.

In common with the OECD and World Bank indices, the CBR index measures formal or de jure law, as opposed to the de facto operation of the law in particular industrial sectors or enterprises. It does not take into account the extent of the enforcement of the law, as measured by state support for enforcement mechanisms or by the extent of use of labour courts or similar institutions, nor the degree to which, in a given system, the rules created by the legal system enjoy general legitimacy. These considerations would seem greatly to limit the value of indices of this type, but there are reasons for not including enforcement or legitimacy measures directly in the relevant indicators (see Deakin, Lele and Siems, 2007, for discussion). One is the value that can be obtained from having a measure of formal legal change in its own right; the influence of politics and of the macroeconomic context on the state of the formal law is one of the issues of interest that can be explored using such data. Secondly, data on the extent of enforcement and of legal legitimacy are available from other indicators, such as the World Bank's Rule of Law index, and these other data sources can be combined with legal indices, either as control variables or as part of a structural regression, in such a way as to take the variability of legal enforcement or observance in practice into account. Thirdly, in developing country contexts, the extent of observance of the law may not be independent of the content of formal legal rules, in the sense that excessive regulation may create incentives for avoidance or evasion. For this reason, too, it may be helpful to have a measure of the content of the formal law.

V.   METHODOLOGICAL ISSUES IN THE ECONOMETRIC ANALYSIS OF EPL

With data on legal trends available, it becomes possible to undertake statistical analysis aimed at isolating the economic impacts of labour laws. At this point, a number of new methodological issues arise. Botero et al.'s (2004) finding that higher labour regulation is associated with lower male employment, higher youth unemployment and a larger informal economy has been much cited. However, this study uses cross-sectional analysis, which takes no account of changes in labour law rules over time, and is based on bivariate correlations, with few controls for other possible explanations for the observed effects. Even allowing for these limitations, the reported coefficients imply a small impact of the law on economic outcomes, and the statistical significance of the results is low (Pozen, 2006).

As the OECD (2004) has recognized, bivariate, cross-sectional analyses tell us little about the direction of causation from the assumed independent or explanatory variable (legal rules) to the dependent or outcome one (economic effects). Even a statistically significant correlation between the two variables may not establish causation. Where the explanatory variable is correlated with the error term in the regression equation, a false result can be obtained. Where stricter EPL is correlated with higher unemployment it could be that the latter causes the former, as would be the case if a rise in joblessness creates new demand for laws regulating termination of employment.

The problems of 'reverse' or 'simultaneous' causation (where causal influences flow both ways) can be addressed in a number of ways. One way is to make use of an 'instrumental' variable that can be safely assumed to be correlated with the explanatory variable, but not with the error term. In the legal origins literature, the common-law or civil-law origins of a given country's laws were initially used as instrumental variables in this sense. It was assumed that legal origin was correlated with the content of legal rules in such areas as shareholder, creditor and workers' rights, but that it could not be correlated with outcome variables such as financial development or labour productivity. This was because legal origin was thought to have been fixed for each country (with the exception of the parent systems) by an external event such as conquest or colonization that, because it preceded industrialization, could not be said to have been endogenous economic or political factors in that country. Once a correlation between legal origin and various economic outcomes was established, it could be more confidently postulated that laws caused economic growth rather than vice versa (La Porta et al., 1998).

However, the instrumental variable approach is not free of difficulty. First, some subjective judgment is unavoidable in the choice of an appropriate instrument. Secondly, a variable will not be a good instrument if it could have had a causal impact on the outcome variable through channels other than that of the supposed independent variable. In later papers in the legal origin series, La Porta et al. came to the conclusion that legal origin might have an influence on the path of economic development through various routes, including approaches to interpretation and enforcement of laws. They therefore came round to the view that legal origin should be seen as a causal or exogenous variable in its own right (La Porta et al., 2008, p. 298). This approach creates new problems since it rests on the disputable assumption that regulatory styles, once fixed, cannot be altered at all by economic or political influences (see Deakin, 2009; Armour et al., 2009a, 2009b).

Another technique used for getting round the problem of endogeneity is the 'difference-in-differences' approach. This is suitable for dealing with time-series data covering more than one case, such as a state or country, with different legal rules. The experience of the two countries or states can be compared using a 'before and after' analysis, in a kind of 'natural experiment'. The statistical method in question involves comparing the differences in the means of the before-and-after differences of the two cases. This method was famously used by Card and Krueger (1995) in their analysis of minimum wages increases in US states in the early 1990s. They used Pennsylvania, a state in which no increase had taken place, as a control for New Jersey, a state where there had been a rise. They found that, after controlling for the impact of the national recession on both states, employment had risen in New Jersey by comparison with Pennsylvania, a result they explained by the presence of monopsony effects which had enabled employers to depress wages below the equilibrium rate prior to the enactment of the minimum wage increase.

Card and Krueger's minimum wage studies have been the subject of a long-running controversy, with critics claiming, among other things, that negative effects of minimum wage increases can be identified if longer time series are used (Neumark and Wascher, 2008). While these critiques appear to have convinced many US commentators of the negative effects of minimum wage laws (for discussion see Kaufman, 2009), the recent experience of the introduction of national minimum wage in the UK, a process accompanied by stable or rising employment in virtually all sectors affected by the legislation (Metcalf, 2007), offers some support for Card and Krueger's analysis. More generally, the difference-in-differences methodology which they helped to popularize has proved extremely influential as a way of studying the impact of legal change in a wide range of contexts including those relating to the operation of labour laws.

Some limitations of the difference-in-differences approach should nevertheless be borne in mind. To be used, it requires a control case or group which is not subject to the legal change being examined. Thus it should not be used to study legal changes which affect a number of jurisdictions in the same way, or for a single country study. It is also inappropriate for the analysis of longer time series, where the problem of 'autocorrelation', implying false or spurious results, may arise (Bertrand et al., 2004).

In long time series, covering a number of years, data may display the statistical property known as 'non-stationarity'. Such time series do not follow a regular path, but are prone to unpredictable deviations without returning to the previous trend. The error terms of two time series, one or both of which are non-stationary, are liable to autocorrelate, giving rise to a false result. This problem was identified by statisticians in the formative stages of the emergence of time-series analysis (Yule, 1926), but has only recently been addressed by mainstream econometrics. The pioneering work of Engle and Granger (1987) showed how techniques of 'cointegration' could be used to identify ways in which non-stationary time series could be shown to be linked by a common, stationary trend. Granger had earlier shown how problems of reverse causality could be addressed in the analysis of long time series (Granger, 1969). So-called Granger causality techniques involve regressing current values of the outcome variable against past values of itself and of the explanatory variable. If the addition of the past values of the explanatory value makes a difference to the outcome, it is conventional to attribute a causal effect to the explanatory variable, although strictly speaking it is safer to talk of precedence rather than causation in this context. Cointegration can be used to study the impact of legal change in a single country or for a panel of countries, but generally only where very long time series, containing at least 25 yearly observations, are available (see Deakin and Sarkar, 2008).

In principle, time-series analyses give more reliable results than cross-sectional ones. Long-run and short-run effects can be distinguished from each other, and the direction of causation can be more safely (if perhaps not completely reliably) identified. Now that very long time series are available for the study of EPL, along with national-level data on employment, unemployment, productivity and GDP, we are in a better position to assess the impact of legal change in this area.

VI. EMPIRICAL ANALYSIS OF THE ECONOMIC EFFECTS OF EMPLOYMENT PROTECTION LEGISLATION

A. Cross-National Studies on the Impact of EPL on Productivity, Employment and Unemployment

Because EPL is generally stricter in western Europe than in the US or other industrial economies, the divergence between the European and American experiences of job growth since the 1970s has been the focus of a number of studies. In the 1960s, the USA had higher unemployment than western Europe, but in the 1980s this relationship was reversed, with the USA enjoying faster employment growth in comparison to the sluggish European record on job creation. In France and Germany there was a significant increase in the intensity of job security legislation in the 1970s, while in the US context there was, relatively speaking, very little change (Deakin, Lele and Siems, 2007).

In the late 1980s and early 1990s this divergence in the legal environment was used in a number of influential analyses (Emerson, 1988; Lazear, 1990), culminating in the OECD's Jobs Study (1994), to argue for the negative effects of EPL. However, these early studies used data on the strength of EPL which can now be seen to be somewhat rudimentary. In 2004 the OECD, using its more developed EPL indicator, which incorporated a time-series element, reported only weak evidence of a link between EPL strictness and flows into and out of unemployment (OECD, 2004). There was no overall link between EPL and cross-national variations in unemployment levels. This study found some evidence of a reduction in unemployment associated with greater flexibility in the use of temporary and fixed-term employment, but more recent studies suggest that relaxation of dismissal rules in the case of these forms of employment is more often associated with a rise in dismissals which is not compensated for by increased hirings (see Guell and Rodríguez Mora, 2010).

The impact of EPL also needs to be studied alongside other potential explanatory variables. When this is done, EPL emerges as a less significant factor in shaping macroeconomic outcomes than unionization rates, interest rate policy and the degree of central bank independence (Baker et al., 2005; Baccaro and Rei, 2007).

The lack of a clear finding in these broadly framed, national- and transnational-level studies has encouraged a more finely grained approach to the analysis of EPL that recognizes its multiple and potentially offsetting effects. On the one hand, stricter EPL should cause unemployment as the costs of hiring are increased in an upturn. In addition, EPL may slow down the movement of workers from less productive firms and sectors of the economy to more productive and growing ones (Saint-Paul, 1997). On the other, stricter EPL may reduce unemployment by making firms more reluctant to dismiss in a downturn. EPL can also induce productivity gains by ensuring the more efficient matching of firms and workers (Levine, 1991). Firms subject to stricter EPL come under incentives to train workers for more productive employment, thereby compensating for restrictions on their ability to hire and fire at will (Koeniger, 2005).

Another step in a more precisely calibrated analysis of EPL is to focus on the extent to which this type of legal regulation is endogenous to economic or political contexts and, relatedly, complementary to the working of other institutions. This approach to empirical work is consistent with the 'evolutionary-systemic' theoretical perspective set out above (Section III). As we have seen, it is plausible to see dismissal legislation as endogenous to (in the sense of having evolved from) the type of employment practices that are found in sectors with stable, bureaucratically organized employment. If this is correct, legal mandates in the EPL field should have more of an impact on employment and productivity in sectors with casualized employment practices and high levels of labour turnover. Bassanini and Venn (2007) take this approach in their analysis of the role of the law in 'EPL-binding' industries, which they characterize as those where firms are more likely to dismiss workers in a downturn. They report a negative impact of EPL on productivity in those sectors. However, using the same approach, they find a positive impact of minimum wage legislation on productivity in such low-paying sectors, and a positive impact of parental leave laws in industries with a higher level of female employment.

Complementarities between EPL and institutional variables such as product market regulation and corporate governance structures are being examined by a growing number of studies. In this vein, Amable, Demmou and Gatti (2007) find that, in OECD countries, product market deregulation produces higher GDP growth only if a high level of EPL is preserved. They suggest that product market regulation, rather than high EPL, was a cause of Europe's sluggish employment growth after 1980. Gatti (2009) reports that high levels of EPL are complementary to concentrated corporate ownership in coordinated market systems, with this conjunction leading to high rates of GDP growth. Low levels of EPL strictness are combined with dispersed ownership and liquid capital markets in liberal market systems.

Similar complementarities can be found in Deakin and Sarkar's (2008) analysis of the CBR indices. They undertake a time-series analysis of changes in labour law over time and trends in employment and productivity growth in France, Germany, the USA and UK. In the light of the claims made for the beneficial economic impacts of deregulatory labour market reforms in the UK in the period the late 1970s onwards (see, e.g., Minford, 1985), their analysis should have found positive long-run effects of these legal reforms on employment and labour productivity. No such impacts were found. In Germany, on the contrary, a positive impact of stricter dismissal law on productivity growth was identified. In France there was a positive relationship between working time reductions and employment growth. These findings suggest that EPL (and related forms of labour law legislation such as working time controls) may have had beneficial economic impacts in coordinated market (and civil-law origin) systems. In such systems, the potentially negative effects of EPL, in terms of disincentives for hiring and a reduction in the intensity of flows into and out of employment, are countered by the positive institutional influences of active labour market policy and state support for training (Hall and Soskice, 2001). In the same way, a stable corporate governance environment may operate alongside strict dismissal laws and legally mandated codetermination, to produce circumstances conducive to a high level of mutual investments by employers and workers in firm-specific human capital. This in turn tends to foster the long-run growth of capital-intensive, high-productivity orientated firms (Jackson et al., 2005).

The analysis for the US suggest that the strengthening of dismissal laws there in the late 1980s (in the form of the WARN laws that required employers to give notice of dismissal and make severance payments when downsizing their workforces) was associated with productivity gains, but at the expense of employment growth. This result implies that for a liberal market regime, such as the US, dismissal legislation can bring about efficiency gains through better utilization and motivation of labour in parts of the economy, but at the expense of slowing down overall employment adjustments, which are then reflected in higher unemployment. The finding should also be put in the context of wider trends in the US economy at this time. There was a sharp fall in the employment growth rate between 1989 and 1991, at a point when GDP was also falling in the context of a recession. The relationship between the WARN law and productivity growth identified by Deakin and Sarkar (2008) is arrived at after controlling for the rate of growth of GDP. After 1992 US employment growth resumed again, but for most of the period since then the rate of growth has been lower than it was in the 1970s and 1980s. It is unlikely, in principle, that this long-run trend can be ascribed solely or even mainly to the WARN law, which was limited in scope and to a large extent may simply have codified pre-existing practices concerning notice and severance pay (see Addison and Blackburn, 1994). It is also possible that the adoption of the law itself was endogenous to wider change in the US economy at this time. The WARN law was a response to concern, in the mid-1980s, about the erosion of internal labour markets and the rise in unemployment which accompanied deregulation and growing international competition in product markets.

In a separate study, Deakin and Sarkar (2011) look at the relationship between the changing state of labour law and the macroeconomic and political context in India. They use a cointegration-based approach to test for the presence of correlations between the Indian labour law index and changes in unemployment and industrial output, and also to identify the direction of causation. They find that the strengthening of labour law was linked to rises in industrial output and in the size of the organized employment sector, and that its weakening was linked to rises in unemployment. In each case, the direction of causation ran from the economic to the legal variable: in other words, it was economic development and growing formality of employment which stimulated growing labour law protection, and it was rising unemployment and informality which triggered labour law deregulation. The Indian experience suggests, firstly, that a high level of labour law regulation is not incompatible with rapid economic growth in a developing country context. Secondly, the protective role of labour law emerges in response to the growth of the organized employment sector and in line with a rise in industrial output; labour law, in the Indian context, is more a result of economic development than its cause. Thirdly, there is no evidence in the case of India that enhancing labour law regulation leads to unemployment, but there is evidence that rising unemployment and, in so far as it is related to it, informality of employment lead to political pressure for labour law deregulation.

B.   The Effects of the Erosion of Employment at Will in the USA

As noted above, there is no federal-level unfair dismissal legislation in the US, and the common-law regimes of nearly all the states observe a version of the 'employment at will' rule, by virtue of which the employer can terminate the employment relationship without just cause or, in some jurisdictions, the giving of notice. This does not mean that American workers altogether lack job security. Many employers recognize limits to the right to dismiss as a matter of practice, to the extent that it is possible to speak of a wide degree of acceptance of tacit or social norms setting standards of workplace fairness (Rock and Wachter, 1996). In addition, a significant proportion of the workforce, probably around a third (Verkerke, 2008), are covered either by public sector civil service laws or by collectively or individually negotiated job security clauses. Moreover, personnel practices designed to avoid litigation under a raft of antidiscrimination and antiretaliation laws import a measure of procedural protection against arbitrary dismissal. The main difference between the US and other systems is the absence of formal legal regulation on these issues; many US employers are likely to have regard, in practice, to the non-legal costs of dismissals, including reputational effects, as supporters of the at-will rule have argued (Epstein, 1984).

From the 1970s onwards the employment at will rule has been partially eroded in a majority of states, although, as we have seen, the changes introduced by case law were negligible by international standards, to the extent of being almost invisible in cross-national comparisons. The most comprehensive studies of the effects of these legal changes are those by Autor and his colleagues. These report some evidence that the most far-reaching of the modifications to employment at will, the 'implied contract' exception, led to an increase in unemployment in the states affected, without any countervailing improvements in productivity (Autor et al., 2004). To reach this result, Autor et al. constructed a sophisticated index that timed changes in the law to the point at which pro-worker decisions were first reported in the press and would thereby have come to the attention of employers. An alternative approach to coding, based on rulings that marked a shift in doctrine at the level of the appellate courts as opposed to all decisions marking a shift to a pro-worker approach, found no evidence of a disemployment effect (Walsh and Schwarz, 1996). In further analysis, Autor et al. (2007) found evidence that pro-worker rulings were associated with a rise in both employment and productivity in manufacturing sectors, but with a decline in total factor productivity in these industries. The general picture to emerge from this line of work is that changes in the legal framework which are derived from developments in case law are particularly difficult to code, and that even if it is possible to come up with a reliable measure of legal change, the balance of the econometric evidence is not clearly against this type of protection, as a number of conflicting and potentially offsetting effects appear to be present.

C.   EPL and Innovation

A body of work is beginning to investigate the relationship between EPL and innovation. There are two possible routes by which they might be related in a positive way. One possibility is that EPL, by raising dismissal costs, provides incentives for firms to move to, or remain on, a 'high road' to competitive success, based on continuous product and process innovation, as the condition for being able to maintain a credible commitment to job security. This also implies a greater commitment by firms to training and upgrading of the labour force. A second possible route depends on the effect of EPL in reducing the downside costs to employees of risk-taking of the kind associated with high-innovation practices.

There is some evidence to support both these sets of claims. With respect to the first, Koeniger (2005) finds that a high level of EPL at country level is associated with more innovation and with firm-level training. With respect to the second, Acharya et al. (2010a) use the CBR labour regulation index to examine the effects of changes in EPL over time on patenting activity. Using a difference-in-differences approach, they find a positive correlation which can be interpreted as a causal relationship, with the law stimulating higher innovation. In a separate study (Acharya et al., 2010b), they have applied the same methodology to the study of the effects of the erosion of the employment at will rule in US states from the 1970s onwards. Again, stricter controls over dismissal are found to be correlated with higher innovation rates, with the direction of causation running from the former to the latter.

This is an area that would repay further study. There has been a tendency to associate innovative activity with the 'high velocity' labour markets, and minimal EPL, of the Silicon Valley model of venture capital funding (Hyde, 2006), but this may not be the only type of interface between employment law and innovation (see Hyde, this volume).

D.   EPL, Enforcement, and Labour Courts

Studies of the formal law, as already suggested, can only give a partial account of the operation of EPL. In practice the economic effects of EPL will depend to a great degree on the way that legal institutions, in particular labour courts and arbitration mechanisms, work. There is considerable evidence that these institutions and mechanisms differ greatly across jurisdictions, and this cross-national variation needs to be taken into account in empirical research on and policy assessments of EPL.

The importance of in-depth comparative analysis in elucidating these issues can be gauged from the important study of the UK and Germany carried out by Blankenburg and Rogowski (1986). Both countries relied on specialized employment tribunals or labour courts to resolve individual employment disputes on EPL and related matters, but the differences between them were striking. At the point in the mid-1980s when the original research was conducted, there were almost 400,000 filings each year before labour courts in West Germany, but just under 50,000 in Britain. The West German and British labour courts had jurisdiction over roughly the same sets of issues. After controlling for population size and employment levels, litigation rates in West Germany were six times higher than in the UK. Moreover, the West German case load had increased by 40 percent in the preceding decade, whereas in Britain there had been a small decline. Ninety percent of German disputes were settled or withdrawn prior to the hearing, whereas only 66 percent of British cases were dealt with this way. Of those disputes which reached a hearing, employees had a 50 percent success rate in West Germany compared to one of just under 30 percent in Britain.

Blankenburg and Rogowski showed that the differences in litigation levels, settlement rates and success rates between the two systems were rooted in their very different institutional trajectories. The German labour court system dated back to the period, in the 1920s, when employment protection laws had first been introduced. Throughout most of their history, and in particular after 1945, the German labour courts had been strongly supported not just by the trade unions but also by the employer side. In the UK, labour courts (industrial tribunals) were introduced in the 1960s, again coterminously with the first (and much later) EPL laws. British trade unions regarded the industrial tribunals, at this point, as a second-best to voluntary collective bargaining, an attitude that has only slowly changed since then as collective bargaining in Britain has declined. British employers tended to regard tribunals as a source of extra costs, and this attitude is still prevalent. In general, the legitimacy of labour courts within the wider industrial relations system is a major influence on the way the system works and the use made of it by the parties.

Different attitudes to the legal system in general and to the use of law to resolve disputes also affect the way that EPL is administered in practice. The German labour courts studied by Blankenburg and Rogowski were, and are, staffed by career judges with a specialized training in labour law. Many of these officials are left-leaning and active in public-sector trade unions. In the British case, industrial tribunals in their early years were chaired by generalist lawyers, most of whom had no labour law training, and, thanks to the more usual commercial law background, were often unsympathetic to the aims of the legislation they were applying. The population of employment judges has changed over time and they now make up a specialized cadre more akin to their German counterparts, but this development has only been slowly achieved.

There remain significant differences in the way in which the two systems process employment disputes. German labour court judges, consistently with the continental European 'inquisitorial' approach to civil procedure, have the power to intervene in arguments and to shape the outcome of a hearing to a much greater extent than British employment judges do. In addition, a German labour court judge has the power to arrange conciliation, a function granted to a separate government agency in the British case. As a result, 'the inquisitorial discretion that [the German judge] enjoys allows him to shift back and forth between mediation, arbitration and adjudication, using the letter of the law to encourage parties to settle' (Blankenburg and Rogowski, 1986, p. 83). The procedures of British employment tribunals were intended to be relatively flexible by the standards of the regular courts system. However, in a comparison with the way German labour courts operate, they appear as highly formal and adversarial. Thus while German legislation is, on the face of it, significantly more protective than the British equivalent, the more flexible German model of dispute resolution tempers the apparent rigidity of the law.

Further consideration of the British case highlights the complexity and ambiguity of EPL in practice even in a context where labour law rules are well developed and there is a fully operational employment tribunal system. Applications to employment tribunals in Britain increased rapidly in the early 1990s to reach around 70,000 a year and they then carried on rising to reach over 200,000 by 2008. This is still below the equivalent German (post-unification) figure of 600,000 annual filings, but nevertheless represents a significant rise. In response to employer complaints about the 'burden' of employment tribunal claims, legislative policy in Britain has been aimed at reducing the number of tribunal hearings since the early 2000s, but without success. Reforms aimed at sifting out unmeritorious claims, introduced in 2004, only had the effect of displacing the costs of dispute resolution on to employers, who were required to process a greater number of claims internally. Yet, access to tribunals was still highly costly for the non-unionized workforce, representing around 70 percent of the total, and a much lower success rate could be observed in claims brought by applicants not represented by a union or by a legal adviser (Pollert, 2005). The ineffectiveness of the tribunal system in providing substantive protection to the unrepresented must be taken into account in any assessment of the 'rigidity' of EPL in the British case.

VII.   CONCLUSION

This chapter has shown that an economic case can be made for employment protection legislation, but that the operation of this kind of labour law cannot be viewed in isolation from the operation of complementary institutions in labour, product and capital markets. In the law and economics of EPL, a growing interest in cross-national, comparative analysis has prompted the emergence of new data sources, in the form of indices of labour regulation, and the utilization of statistical methods which can throw light on the nature of causal influences running from the law to the economy and vice versa. Through work of this kind, a more complete account of the economic effects of EPL and other forms of labour law regulation is slowly emerging.

The traditional neoclassical view that informed the development of the law and economics field took the view that unregulated markets were, on the whole, competitive, and so maintained that EPL, like other forms of labour regulation, was an exogenous source of inefficiencies, leading to unemployment and slower economic growth. Modern neoclassical or new institutional accounts, by contrast, see EPL as having a number of complex and potentially offsetting effects. In particular, dismissal laws may have positive impacts on productivity through their encouragement of training and innovation at firm level. The emerging evolutionary approach goes further in stressing that the effects of EPL, like those of other labour laws, cannot be predicted in an a priori way. Models of apparently universal application have little value when the economic effects of legislation depend on the interaction of legal rules with a number of national, regional and industry-specific conditions and with complementary institutions in capital markets and product markets. This implies a need for better and more reliable data on the content of the law, on modes of operation, and on the context in which legal rules are applied.

Is the upshot of this likely to be the greater use of evidence from empirical studies in the policy-making process? The prospects for evidence-based policy are, in practice, uncertain. One reason for this is that the status of the knowledge produced by empirical research remains, to some degree, contingent. Many of the questions to which policy-makers would like to have answers are not susceptible to empirical research given the current state of data resources. As we have seen, it is only recently that data have become available on legal systems in a form which can be used in cross-national comparisons. In addition, statistical analyses involve limitations and trade-offs which may (or should) qualify any policy recommendations.

There are, moreover, wider constraints on evidence-based policy. Theory plays a more significant role in shaping the policy-making process. Although the traditional neoclassical model of competitive markets has been undermined by recent empirical research, there is only a limited degree of feedback from the empirical literature to the theoretical core which forms the basis for the approach of mainstream economics (and law and economics) to understanding how labour markets work. A theory such as this remains functional, in the eyes of its adherents, as long as it can generate meaningful research questions which can then be analysed using appropriate empirical techniques. According to this point of view, the theory does not need to be realistic, and so cannot be invalidated by new empirical findings alone. New methods which cast doubt on previous findings, such as those associated with development in time-series and panel-data analysis, are a different matter, as are new data sources, in particular the new longitudinal datasets of legal change which are currently emerging, in so far as they give rise to different types of findings. But progress is slow.

At the level of the political process, the theory of competitive markets informs an ideological commitment to labour market flexibility and deregulation that, while weakening, continues to influence policy-makers. As we have seen, the empirical basis for the deregulatory approach is not very strong. It is perhaps surprising then to find the international financial and economic institutions continuing to advise national governments that, as the World Bank *Doing Business* report for 2008 puts it, 'laws created to protect workers often hurt them' (World Bank, 2008, p. 19). But this is perhaps a reflection of the marginal role accorded to empirical social science, as opposed to dogma and vested interests, in the formation of public policy.

NOTE

*   I am grateful to the editors for comments on an earlier draft of this chapter.

REFERENCES

Acharya, V., R. Baghai-Wadji, and K. Subramanian. 2010a. 'Labor Laws and Innovation', NBER Working Paper No. 16484.
Acharya, V., R. Baghai-Wadji, and K. Subramanian. 2010b. 'Wrongful Discharge Laws and Innovation', Working Paper, NYU-Stern Business School.
Addison, J. and M. Blackburn. 1994. 'Policy Watch: the Worker Adjustment and Retraining Notification Act', 8 *Journal of Economic Perspectives* 18–90.
Ahlering, B. and S. Deakin. 2007. 'Labour Regulation, Corporate Governance and Legal Origin: A Case of Institutional Complementarity?' 41 *Law and Society Review* 865–98.
Akerlof, George. 1982. 'Labor Contracts as Partial Gift Exchange', 97 *Quarterly Journal of Economics* 543–69.

Amable, B., L. Demmou, and D. Gatti. 2007. 'Employment Performance and Institutions: New Answers to an Old Question', IZA Discussion Paper No. 2731.

Anderman, S. 1986. 'Unfair Dismissal and Redundancy', in R. Lewis, ed., *Labour Law in Britain*. Oxford: Basil Blackwell.

Aoki, M. 2010. *Corporations in Evolving Diversity*. Oxford: Oxford University Press.

Armour, J., S. Deakin, P. Lele, and M. Siems. 2009a. 'How Do Legal Rules Evolve? Evidence from a Cross-Country Comparison of Shareholder, Creditor and Worker Protection', 57 *American Journal of Comparative Law* 579–630.

Armour, J., S. Deakin, V. Mollica, and M. Siems. 2009b. 'Law and Financial Development: What We are Learning from Time Series Evidence', 2009 *Brigham Young University Law Review* 1435–500.

Autor, D., J. Donohue, and S. Schwab. 2004. 'The Employment Consequences of Wrongful Discharge Law: Large, Small or None at All?' 93 *American Economic Review Papers and Proceedings* 440–46.

Autor, D., W. Kerr, and A. Kugler. 2007. 'Do Employment Protections Reduce Productivity? Evidence from US States', IZA Discussion Paper No. 2571.

Baccaro, L. and D. Rei. 2007. 'Institutional Determinants of Unemployment in OECD Countries: Does the Deregulatory View Hold Water?' 61 *International Organization* 527–69.

Baker, D., A. Glyn, D. Howell, and J. Schmitt. 2005. 'Labour Market Institutions and Unemployment: A Critical Assessment of Cross-Country Evidence', in D. Howell, ed., *Fighting Unemployment: The Limits of Free Market Orthodoxy*. Oxford: Oxford University Press.

Bassanini, A. and R. Duval. 2006. 'Employment Patterns in OECD Countries: Reassessing the Role of Policies and Institutions', OECD Social, Employment and Migration Working Paper No. 35.

Bassanini, A. and D. Venn. 2007. 'Assessing the Impact of Labour Market Policies on Productivity: A Difference-in-Differences Approach', OECD Social, Employment and Migration Paper No. 54.

Beck, T., A. Demirgüç-Kunt, and R. Levine. 2003. 'Law and Finance: Why Does Legal Origin Matter?' 31 *Journal of Comparative Economics* 653–75.

Bertola, G. 2009. 'Labour Market Regulation: Motives, Measures, Effects', ILO Conditions of Employment and Work Research Series.

Bertrand, M., E. Duflo, and S. Mullainathan. 2004. 'How Much Should We Trust Difference-in-Differences Estimates?' 119 *Quarterly Journal of Economics* 249–75.

Blankenburg, E. and R. Rogowski. 1986. 'German Labour Courts and the British Industrial Tribunal System: A Socio-Legal Comparison of Degrees of Judicialisation', 13 *Journal of Law and Society* 67–92.

Botero, J., S. Djankov, R. La Porta, F. Lopez-de-Silanes, and A. Shleifer. 2004. 'The Regulation of Labor', 119 *Quarterly Journal of Economics* 1340–82.

Büchtemann, C. 1993. 'Introduction: Employment Security and Labor Markets', in C. Büchtemann, ed., *Employment Security and Labor Market Behavior: Inter-Disciplinary Approaches and International Evidence*. Ithaca, NY: Cornell University Press.

Card, D. and B. Krueger. 1995. *Myth and Measurement: The New Economics of the Minimum Wage*. Princeton: Princeton University Press.

Coase, R.H. 1988. 'The Nature of the Firm', reprinted in R.H. Coase, *The Firm, the Market and the Law*. Chicago: University of Chicago Press.

Collins, H. 1993. *Justice in Dismissal*. Oxford: Clarendon Press.

Deakin, S. 2009. 'Legal Origin, Juridical Form and Industrialisation in Historical Perspective: The Case of the Employment Contract and the Joint-Stock Company', 7 *Socio-Economic Review* 35–65.

Deakin, S. and P. Sarkar. 2008. 'Assessing the Long-Run Economic Impact of Labour Law Systems: A Theoretical Reappraisal and Analysis of New Time Series Data', 39 *Industrial Relations Journal* 453–87.

Deakin, S. and P. Sarkar. 2011. 'Indian Labour Law and its Impact on Unemployment, 1970–2006: A Leximetric Study', 54 *Indian Journal of Labour Economics*, 607–29.

Deakin, S., P. Lele, and M. Siems. 2007. 'The Evolution of Labour Law: Calibrating and Comparing Regulatory Regimes', 146 *International Labour Review* 133–62.

Emerson, M. 1988. 'Regulation or Deregulation of the Labour Market', 32 *European Economic Review* 775–817.

Engle, R. and C. Granger. 1987. 'Cointegration and Error Correction: Representation, Estimation, and Testing', 55 *Econometrica* 251–76.

Epstein, R. 1984. 'In Defense of the Contract at Will', 51 *University of Chicago Law Review* 947–82.

Fryer, R. 1973. 'The Myths of the Redundancy Payments Act', 2 *Industrial Law Journal* 1–16.

Gatti, D. 2009. 'Macroeconomic Effects of Ownership Structure in OECD Countries,' 18 *Industrial and Corporate Change* 901–28.

Granger, C. 1969. 'Investigating Causal Relations by Econometric Models and Cross-Spectral Methods', 37 *Econometrica* 424–38.

Grubb, D. and W. Wells. 1993. 'Employment Regulation and Patterns of Work in EC Countries', 21 *OECD Economic Studies* 7–58.

Guell, M. and J. Rodríguez Mora. 2010. 'Temporary Contracts, Incentives and Unemployment', CEPR Discussion Paper No. DP 8116.

Hall, P. and D. Soskice. 2001. 'Introduction to Varieties of Capitalism', in P. Hall and D. Soskice, eds., *Varieties of Capitalism: The Institutional Foundations of Comparative Advantage*. Oxford: Oxford University Press.

Hyde, A. 2006. 'What is Labour Law?' in G. Davidov and B. Langille, eds., *Boundaries and Frontiers of Labour Law*. Oxford: Hart.

Jackson, G., M. Höpner and A. Kurdelbusch. 2005. 'Corporate Governance and Employees in Germany: Changing Linkages, Complementarities, and Tensions', in H. Gospel and A. Pendleton, eds., *Corporate Governance and Labour Management: An International Comparison*. Oxford: Oxford University Press.

Kaufman, B. 2009. 'Labor Law and Employment Regulation: Institutional and Neoclassical Perspectives', in K. Dau Schmidt, S. Harris, and O. Lobel, eds., *Labor and Employment Law and Economics*. Cheltenham, UK and Northampton, MA, USA: Edward Elgar.

Koeniger, W. 2005. 'Dismissal Costs and Innovation', 88 *Economics Letters* 79–85.

Koeniger, W. and A. Vindigni. 2003. 'Employment Protection and Product Market Regulation', IZA Discussion Paper No. 880.

La Porta, R., F. Lopez-de-Silanes and A. Shleifer. 1998. 'Law and Finance', 106 *Journal of Political Economy* 1113–55.

La Porta, R., F. Lopez-de-Silanes and A. Shleifer. 2008. 'The Economic Consequences of Legal Origins', 46 *Journal of Economic Literature* 285–332.

Lazear, E. 1990. 'Job Security Provisions and Employment', 105 *Quarterly Journal of Economics* 699–726.

Lee, S., D. McCann and N. Torm. 2008. 'The World Bank's "Employing Workers" Index: Findings and Critiques – A Review of Recent Evidence', 148 *International Labour Review* 416–32.

Levine, D. 1991. 'Just-Cause Employment Policies in the Presence of Worker Adverse Selection', 9 *Journal of Labor Economics* 294–305.

Lindbeck, A. and D. Snower. 1989. *The Insider-Outsider Theory of Employment and Unemployment*. Cambridge, MA: MIT Press.

Manning, A. 2003. *Monopsony in Motion: Imperfect Competition in Labor Markets*. Princeton: Princeton University Press.

Metcalf, D. 2007. 'Why has the British National Minimum Wage had Little or No Impact on Unemployment?' CEP Discussion Paper No. 781, The London School of Economics and Political Science.

Meyers, F. 1964. *Ownership of Jobs: A Comparative Study*. Los Angeles: University of California Press.

Minford, P. 1985. *Unemployment: Cause and Cure*, 2nd ed. Oxford: Basil Blackwell.

Neumark, D. and W. Wascher. 2008. *Minimum Wages*. Cambridge, MA: MIT Press.

Njoya, W. 2007. *Property in Work: The Employment Relationship in the Anglo-American Firm*. Aldershot: Ashgate.

Organisation for Economic Co-operation and Development (OECD). 1994. *OECD Jobs Study, Evidence and Explanations, Part I: Labour Market Trends and Underlying Forces of Change*. Paris: Organisation for Economic Co-operation and Development.

Organisation for Economic Co-operation and Development (OECD). 2004. *Employment Outlook*. Paris: Organization for Economic Cooperation and Development.

Pagano, M. and P. Volpin. 2005. 'The Political Economy of Corporate Governance', 95 *American Economic Review* 1005–30.

Pollert, A. 2005. 'The Unorganized Worker: The Decline in Collectivism and the New Hurdles to Individual Employment Rights', 34 *Industrial Law Journal* 217–38.

Pozen, D. 2006. 'The Regulation of Labor and the Relevance of Legal Origin', 28 *Comparative Labor Law and Policy Journal* 43–56.

Rajan, R. and L. Zingales. 2003. 'The Great Reversals: The Politics of Financial Development in the Twentieth Century', 69 *Journal of Financial Economics* 5–50.

Reich, C. 1964. 'The New Property', 73 *Yale Law Journal* 33–87.

Rock, E. and M. Wachter. 1996. 'The Enforceability of Norms and the Employment Relationship', 144 *University of Pennsylvania Law Review* 1913–52.

Roe, M. 2003. *Political Determinants of Corporate Governance*. Oxford: Oxford University Press.

Saint-Paul, G. 1997. 'Is Labour Rigidity Harming Europe's Competitiveness? The Effect of Job Protection on the Pattern of Trade and Welfare', 41 *European Economic Review* 499–506.

Simon, H. 1951. 'A Formal Theory of the Employment Relationship', 19 *Econometrica* 293–305.

Spence, M. 1973. 'Job Market Signaling', 87 *Quarterly Journal of Economics* 355–74.

Supiot, A. 1994. *Critique du Droit du Travail*. Paris: Presses Universitaires de France (PUF).

Veneziani, B. 2009. 'The Employment Relationship', in B. Hepple and B. Veneziani, eds., *The Transformation of Labour Law in Europe*. Oxford: Hart Publishing.

Venn, D. 2009. 'Legislation, Collective Bargaining and Enforcement: Updating the OECD Employment Protection Indicators', OECD Social, Employment and Migration Working Paper No. 89. Paris: OECD.

Verkerke, J. 2008. 'The Law and Economics of Discharge', John M. Olin Program in Law and Economics Working Paper No. 50, University of Virginia Law School.

Vogel-Polsky, E. 1986. 'The Problem of Unemployment', in B. Hepple, ed., *The Making of Labour Law in Europe*. London: Mansell.

Wachter, M. and R. Wright. 1990. 'The Economics of Internal Labor Markets', 29 *Industrial Relations* 240–62.

Walsh, D. and J. Schwarz. 1996. 'State Common Law Wrongful-Discharge Doctrines: Up-Date, Refinement and Rationales', 33 *American Business Law Journal* 645–89.

Williamson, O., M. Wachter, and J. Harris. 1975. 'Understanding the Employment Relation: The Economics of Idiosyncratic Exchange', 6 *Bell Journal of Economics and Management Science* 250–78.

World Bank. Various years. *Doing Business Reports*. Washington, DC: International Bank for Reconstruction and Development.

Yule, G. 1926. 'Why Do We Sometimes Get Nonsense-Correlations between Time-Series? A Study in Sampling and the Nature of Time Series (with Discussion)', 89 *Journal of the Royal Statistical Society* 1–64.

12. Intellectual property justifications for restricting employee mobility: a critical appraisal in light of the economic evidence

*Alan Hyde**

An employee of Employer 1 proposes to quit his or her job and either go to work for a competing employer in the same industry (Employer 2) or to found his or her rival company. Employer 1 wishes to prevent this. May it do so or plausibly threaten litigation that might slow or discourage the employee's moving to a rival? In many cases, the answer is yes. Lawyers for Employer 1 will study at least the following five legal theories, which, as applied to this scenario, comprise the subject of this chapter:

1. Duty of loyalty. Every state implies a duty of loyalty running from incumbent employees to their current employer. While an employee may make "preparations" to join or start a rival, the employee may not, while on Employer 1's payroll, "solicit" customers or fellow employees for the new venture or divert opportunities from Employer 1.
2. Patent or copyright infringement. Employee might be sued for infringement if his or her duties at Employer 2 threaten to make use of Employer 1's patents or copyrights.
3. Trade secrets. Every state imposes a duty on employees and former employees not to disclose trade secrets, a very broad category, of their former employer.
4. Noncompete (or covenant not to compete). Most states enforce "reasonable" covenants by employees not to compete with their former employer.
5. Invention assignment agreements. Like noncompetes, these are creatures of contract, not imposed by obligation of law. However, Employer 1 may enforce a promise by an employee to turn over to it any inventions developed for some period of time after leaving employment. This may have the practical consequence of dissuading hiring by Employer 2 (or venture capital in support of Employee's start-up).

Legal scholarship normally disaggregates these five areas of law. This is a perfectly valid approach. Each has distinct origins, applications, and, in some cases, professional bar. Patent infringement suits all apply federal law and are often highly technical. Patent lawyers often have engineering degrees and must in any case be able to understand highly technical expert testimony. The other doctrines are creatures of state law that vary, sometimes significantly, from state to state. The duties of loyalty, and to preserve trade secrets, are imposed by law in every state, though the first is common (judge-made) law and equity, while the duty to keep trade secrets is statutory in forty-five states and common law and equity in the rest. By contrast, noncompetes and invention assignments must be signed by the individual employee, though normally this is done when the employee initials a general employment contract or handbook. Distinctions of this kind, which could be multiplied, are properly the raw material of much legal analysis. A drawback of this legal perspective is that a book chapter would not suffice to explain the law. Five multi-volume treatises would be required just to explore the differences among states, and subtle distinctions, within state law, among grossly similar fact patterns. It follows that this chapter will inevitably paint with a broad brush and ignore many distinctions important to legal readers.

This chapter instead develops two premises that stand as alternatives to the disaggregative legal approach. First, despite their legal diversity, all of these doctrines may be approached as aspects of a single economic problem: restrictions on employee mobility. From an economic perspective, any restriction on employee mobility is suspect, likely to impede efficient adjustment of labor markets and, like any restriction on competition, harms the public. Second, in most, though not all, applications, the case for restricting employee mobility comes down entirely to an evaluation of the intellectual property, broadly defined, claimed by Employer 1. This is obviously the case if Employer 1 sues for appropriation of trade secrets (Lemley, 2009) or infringement of patents. However, litigation on noncompetes and the duty of loyalty also often turn on the intellectual property interest of Employer 1. Only "reasonable" noncompetes may be enforced, and whether a given noncompete is reasonable often reflects whether it is necessary to protect Employer 1's interest in training or trade secrets.[1] Similarly, in deciding whether an employee was disloyal, courts often analyze his or her approaches to Employer 1's customers, and this often turns into an inquiry into whether that customer list is a trade secret.[2] Cases of this type suggest that much of this unruly field can be disciplined by intense scrutiny of the intellectual property interests of employers as against their departing employees – that is, the rights of employers to the information residing in their departing employees' heads.

This chapter will analyze the economic literature addressing this question. Most of it falls into one of two categories. Most analysis produced by economists in economics departments and business schools is situated within the economics of growth. It assumes that nonrivalrous information is a, perhaps the, crucial factor in economic growth, and that any restriction on the production or distribution of nonrivalrous information calls for careful analysis. This branch of economics is heavily empirical. A typical study will compare rates of growth, or business start-ups, or venture capital investment, in jurisdictions with different regimes of employee intellectual property. Since these studies are open to empirical demonstration or refutation, their picture cannot be final. But so far it is extraordinarily consistent. In *every* such study, the jurisdiction with weaker employer intellectual property experiences greater growth. This literature finds there are *no* provable social advantages in intellectual property-based restrictions on employee mobility.

This chapter will also consider a second school of economic analysis, one that is more popular in law schools. This school analyzes intellectual property restrictions on employee mobility as a problem in the economics of contracting. The problem is assumed to be transaction costs that impede the formation of efficient contracts between employers and employees. The authors model likely contract formation under different ex ante allocations of intellectual property. While there are many insights here, the models tend to prove precisely what they assume. The consensus though not universal position is that, for any allocation of intellectual property rights, or even in the absence of any intellectual property rights, efficient contracts may be reached between Employer 1 and Employee. Employer 1 can normally prevent loss of intellectual property simply by outbidding Employer 2, and this arrangement is more efficient than ex ante specification of intellectual property rights. Allocation of formal property rights has little or no impact on this negotiation. Labor markets can reach efficient allocations even where none of the relevant ideas is protected by intellectual property, for example the market for French chefs (Fauchart and von Hippel, 2008). In such cases informal norms arise that efficiently substitute for property rights.

The chapter will follow the following plan. Section I will summarize the trends by which most workplace know-how became conceptualized as the property of the employer, which by the 1990s gained the corresponding ability to impede employee mobility to start-ups or rivals. Section II will summarize four social and intellectual trends that have led very recently to reconsideration of this allocation of intellectual property: (a) advances in the economic analysis of nonrivalrous information; (b) greater attention to the process of entrepreneurship and start-ups; (c) particular attention to Silicon Valley, the region around Stanford University in California, which combines rapid innovation and start-ups with a highly restricted regime of employer intellectual property, raising the question whether this represented an alternative model to the normal US regime, or merely a coincidence; and (d) the apparent weakening in the US of implicit contracts for lifetime employment, in which employers both demanded and extended loyalty, and their replacement by much greater use of planned employee mobility, market-mediated hiring and temporary employment. Section III will look in depth at economic analysis of intellectual property restrictions on employee mobility that is either empirical, or within a framework of the economics of growth, or both. It will demonstrate the remarkable unanimity of studies suggesting that restricting employer claims of intellectual property is positive for business start-ups, venture capital and economic growth. As we shall see, at the firm level, for firms with research and development (R&D) expenditure (Andersson et al., 2008) or that use advanced technology (Abowd et al., 2007), employee mobility is positive for growth. Comparing either jurisdictions with different intellectual property law, or the same jurisdiction before and after a change, every study shows the positive influence of employee mobility on start-ups, venture capital and growth. In other words, Silicon Valley is no aberration but a legal model worth emulating. Section IV will examine the contrasting studies that approach employee intellectual property as a problem in the economics of contract, and that suggest that the formal allocation of intellectual property rights is largely irrelevant to efficient contracting. These studies suggest that contractual restrictions on employee mobility serve mainly as a way of permitting Employer 1 to restrict competition, which the literature reviewed in Section III suggests is counterproductive for firms and for society. Section V concludes with suggestions for future research.

I. OVERVIEW OF THE LAW: CONCEPTUALIZING WORKPLACE KNOWLEDGE AS EMPLOYER INTELLECTUAL PROPERTY

Fisk (2009) describes the slow process, extending from the late 19th to late 20th century, through which knowledge of most ordinary manufacturing processes became conceptualized as the intellectual property of the employer. By the early 20th century, often in contradiction to earlier decisions or industrial practice, the employer could patent inventions by employees "hired to invent" even without any formal assignment from the employee; enforce a "shop right," a nonexclusive, nontransferable right to use inventions by employees not hired to invent; demand invention assignments by independent contractors that effectively left them unable to work or consult elsewhere in their area of expertise; protect "trade secrets" that earlier generations had not recognized, such as ideas, general knowledge unreduced to written formula, and negative knowledge (that is, what does not work); and enforce all these rights through negative injunctions forbidding former employees from taking specific jobs.

Fisk shows that the legal device that accomplished all these ends was the implied contract. The concept of "intellectual property" came late to the law. Earlier cases had approached all these as problems of property, normally concluding that inventive individuals owned the fruits of their labor. By contrast, "implied contracts" permitted courts to reallocate economically valuable information in ways that seemed to them fair and efficient, despite the absence of formal agreement by employer and employee, and often in the teeth of contrary trade custom. As we shall see, contemporary academic literature on implied contracts often serves this century-old purpose of permitting judicial specification of property in pursuit of larger goals.

Developments from the Second World War into the 1990s greatly expanded the scope of employers' intellectual property justifications for restricting employee mobility or claiming employee invention (see also Coriat and Weinstein, 2009). The following developments are among the highlights, though the literature could use a comprehensive account. First, while courts retained the traditional formula under which "reasonable" covenants by employees not to compete would be enforced, the category of "reasonable" covenants expanded; in particular, negotiated covenants for "unreasonable" duration or geographic scope were increasingly rewritten by courts into reasonable form, and then enforced against the employee. Second, a Uniform Trade Secrets Act, adopted in nearly all US jurisdictions, tried to put trade secrets claims on a uniform statutory footing, away from the uncertainties of common law. Systematic differences between Uniform Act jurisdictions and the other five are not easy to observe. Both now term "trade secrets" practices that were centuries old and widely practiced, such as using a reserve to sweeten chardonnay, or sweeping nut dust into the batter for chocolate chip cookies.[3] Third, the federal Bayh-Dole statute encouraged universities to claim as their own intellectual property the intellectual creations of university faculty. Fourth, a 1996 federal criminal statute, the Economic Espionage Act, 18 U.S.C. § 1832, made most ordinary misappropriation of trade secrets, defined by the Uniform Trade Secrets Act, into a federal criminal offense (though prosecutions have been rare (Ghosh, 2009)). The result of these and other trends is to make litigation a threat almost any time an employee valued by Employer 1 attempts to leave for a competitor (cf. Agarwal et al., 2009).

There was little economic analysis of these developments before the 1990s. A small critical literature argued for a kind of moral property right for inventors in their inventions (Neumeyer, 1971; Cherensky, 1993; Stedman, 1970). But as information and ideas became an increasingly large share of the value held by both businesses and employees, litigation and scholarly interest grew accordingly.

Evan Brown's case is an example of application of these legal principles that many people would now find extreme. Brown was a computer programmer for a communications company. In his job he often had to work with code in older programming languages and developed some algorithms for his own use in working with the older code. His employer did not sell software. Nevertheless it was able to persuade the Texas courts that Brown's algorithms were its property, and obtained a court order requiring him to disclose them (*Brown v. Alcatel USA, Inc.*, 2004 Tex. App. LEXIS 5687). The case is legally unremarkable but became a cause célèbre on the Internet – an example of social and economic trends, to which we now turn, that have been occasioning questions about the law's expansive concept of employer intellectual property.

II.   QUESTIONING THE BREADTH OF EMPLOYER INTELLECTUAL PROPERTY CLAIMS

Economic inquiry into the breadth of employer intellectual property claims has, since the early 1990s, been propelled by four loosely related intellectual and socio-economic developments: (a) Advances in the economic analysis of nonrivalrous information; (b) greater attention to the process of entrepreneurship and start-ups; (c) particular attention to Silicon Valley, the region around Stanford University in California, which combined rapid innovation and start-ups with a highly restricted regime of employer intellectual property; and (d) the apparent weakening in the US of implicit contracts for lifetime employment, in which employers both demanded and extended loyalty, and their replacement by much greater use of planned employee mobility and temporary employment.

A.   Advances in the Economic Analysis of Nonrivalrous Information

Economic analysis of markets for information is still in its infancy, and most potential applications of this analysis to labor markets lie in the future. Until the 1990s or so, economists typically assumed that information had economic value only insofar as it was held as property, typically intellectual property. This simplifying assumption is still encountered. For example, a leading and quite brilliant textbook on the economics of innovation, Aghion and Howitt (1998), contains, as nearly as I can see, not a single reference to information that is shared by multiple users and therefore nobody's property.

Economic reference to such shared information typically took place, if at all, within the framework of "spillover" (e.g. Arrow, 1962). In this framework, normal production of goods and services has, as a kind of unintended consequence, the production of information, for example, about what kinds of production are and are not possible. This information then "spills over" to rival firms without compensation. "Spillover" models before the 1990s saw this as a problem, not a blessing. Since the social value of production exceeded the private return to the producer, there would be a tendency for firms to invest in R&D at levels below the socially optimum (e.g. Arrow, 1962). Economic models of this type were obviously compatible with the legal regime described above in which knowledge of workplace processes is indeed the property of the employer.

In the New Economics of Growth (Romer, 1990; Lucas, 1988, 1993), by contrast, nonrivalrous and nonexcludable information, the property of no one, becomes the most important factor in economic growth or economic "miracles."[4] Most of this nonrivalrous information is produced by private firms, as opposed to general scientific or technological facts. Firms produce information, whether or not they can exclude others from using it, because it provides the best return on investment, and they do not, a priori, need special legal monopolies in technical information in order to produce it. As we shall see, this single insight lies behind most recent critical examination of employment intellectual property law. Space does not permit treatment of other aspects of Romer's or Lucas's New Economics of Growth, or the economic work it has inspired, or any other applications of the new economics of markets in information to labor markets. Markets for information are now well-understood to have many features that distinguish them from conventional markets for goods and services: difficulty in measuring units, multiple equilibria, information asymmetries and signaling, increasing returns and network effects. The application of these findings to labor markets is mostly yet to be explored by future scholars.[5]

B.   Economic Literature on Start-Ups and Entrepreneurship

Scholarship on management was heavily focused on large corporations during the years when employers' intellectual property rights were consolidated (e.g. Chandler, 1990; Coase, 1937). The large corporation that achieved economies of scale and scope (e.g. Chandler) by purchasing inputs in internal, not external, markets (Coase) was assumed to be the only superior form of economic organization.

Scholarly attention to entrepreneurship and processes of creation of new firms thus arose late as a subject of analysis. Such new firms are typically founded by employees of existing firms in the industry who depart to start their own (Franco and Filson, 2006). Franco and Filson apply their model to the disk drive industry where, the better the original firm's technology, the more likely it was to generate spin-outs *and* the more likely those spin-outs were to survive. The result was a competitive industry with lower prices to consumers. Medical device manufacturers similarly perform better, and are financed more quickly, when founders leave established firms. But this is not (judging from patent citations) because those founders are taking patented information; they simply have better knowledge, ability and contacts (Chatterji, 2009). Analysis of massive Census data reveals that, while highly paid employees are less likely to leave firms, when they do, they are more likely to go to a start-up than to an existing firm (Campbell et al., 2009). Legal rules vesting intellectual property in employers, which may seem fair and efficient in the context of stable careers in stable firms, suddenly look problematic when seen as potential impediments to start-ups.

C.   Economic Literature on Economics of Agglomeration and Industrial Districts

Employer intellectual property rights also began to seem problematic within a third strain of economic literature that had been dormant for decades but was revived in the 1980s and 1990s. Alfred Marshall, in the 1920 edition of his *Principles of Economics*, noted the tendency of competing firms in the same business to locate in geographic proximity, and attributed this to the efficiency advantage of what we (following Romer) have been calling nonrivalrous and nonexcludable information. In such districts, Marshall wrote, the "mysteries of the trade become no mysteries; but are as it were in the air, and children learn many of them unconsciously." (I.271 [iv.x.527]). There was little further development of this point in the economics literature until the revival of interest in economic geography sparked by Piore and Sabel's (1984) rediscovery of the "industrial district." It became obvious that, if there was anything to Marshall's observation, the "mysteries of the trade" necessary to the success of industrial districts could not be the trade secret of any individual employer.

These two strands of economic literature, on start-ups and industrial districts, combined with particular force in the 1990s as the United States came to identify its global economic role with the high technology sectors of information, communication, pharmaceutical and other technology. These growth industries saw many start-ups and spinouts from existing firms, and are often geographically concentrated in Silicon Valley CA, Route 128 MA, the Research Triangle NC, and similar communities. Silicon Valley, the area around Stanford University, came to be seen as a prototype. None of its leading firms succeeded because of the kind of vertical integration associated with Chandler's work on economics of size and scope (Langlois, 1992). Instead, firms succeeded by rapidly meeting changing technology and markets, and this success necessitated the flexible structure of small start-up and spin-out firms.

These smaller firms succeed as parts of networks. They are typically located in an industrial district (like Silicon Valley), where they leverage the human capital in other firms through outsourcing, cooperative vendor-purchaser relations, informal social ties, and recruitment of personnel from rivals (Langlois, 1992; Saxenian, 1994). "The functional boundaries between firms are porous in a network system, as are the boundaries between firms themselves and between firms and local institutions such as trade associations and universities" (Saxenian, 1994: 3). Firms' participation in networks enables them to thrive in emerging global networks, in which technology products are brought to market by inventors, engineers, managers, capitalists, and manufacturers, perhaps each on a different continent (e.g. McKendrick et al., 2000). Nonrivalrous and nonexcludable information turned out not to be just an academic construct. It is the precise explanation of how small firms that spend little on R&D acquire the knowledge that enables them to produce disproportionate numbers of new products and innovations (Audretsch, 1998). Excessively broad employer intellectual property no longer seemed harmless. It has the potential to impede economic growth in precisely the sectors that appeared to be leading the US economy. It seemed no accident that Silicon Valley is in California, which never enforces employee covenants not to compete (Gilson, 1999).

D.   Economic Literature on Implicit Employment Contracts

Large US employers, during the decades in which they consolidated legal control of workplace know-how, independently developed a characteristic implicit contract of employment. This contract was first described by Edward Lazear (1979) but thereafter elaborated in hundreds of economic articles, then legal articles after its introduction to the legal community in Wachter and Cohen (1988). Large firms effectively offered lifetime employment to their managerial and technical personnel, and often to ordinary workers as well. Top jobs were reserved to employees who had risen through the ranks of an internal labor market. External recruiting for top jobs was rare. Pension plans and health insurance, attractive to older employees, were also used to induce employees to spend entire careers with a single employer. Compensation was not reduced even after employees' most productive years were passed. These contracts were implicit, in the sense that none of these practices was (in the 1950s and 1960s) legally enforceable (except for some unionized employees). But they were common practice in large employers. While implicit contracts were in no way legally linked to employer intellectual property, they helped give a kind of moral sense to that concept. The employer that voluntarily offered lifetime employment might more readily be seen to have a claim on employee inventions and a right to impede employee mobility. Implicit contracts and strong internal labor markets also ensured that employers would rarely have to seek legal enforcement of their intellectual property rights, since there was little market for mid-career knowledge workers.

For a variety of complex reasons explored elsewhere in this volume, many employers began repudiating such implicit employment contracts in the late 1970s and 1980s, making clear to newly hired employees that they should not expect such stability (Stone, 2004). There were sharp increases in voluntary and involuntary terminations, decreases in average job tenure for men, and increased employment through temporary help agencies and other less stable arrangements. Silicon Valley was a leader in all these dimensions, too (Hyde, 2003; Fallick et al., 2006). This decline in career employment certainly led to more litigation – not only wrongful discharge claims by employees complaining of employers' ex post renunciation of commitments that had been efficient ex ante, but also employers suing to prevent employees from departing to new opportunities. It also led many to question the concepts of intellectual property that underlay those employer claims. It is not easy to say why a high-tech start-up that hires its workforce through a temporary help agency or professional employer organization that serves as its nominal employer, offers no pensions or health insurance, and makes it clear that services are hired for a specific project and will end with that project, should have the same rights to impede employee mobility, through legal doctrines like covenants not to compete and trade secrets, that were developed for old-style employers with implicit employment contracts.

III.   ECONOMIC ANALYSIS OF INTELLECTUAL PROPERTY RESTRICTIONS ON EMPLOYEE MOBILITY: EMPIRICAL STUDIES IN THE ECONOMICS OF GROWTH

"The non-rival nature of knowledge was explored and identified as a key ingredient in modern endogenous growth theory." (Acs et al., 2009, citing Romer, 1986). Much recent work by economists on growth, including economics of international trade and market structure, starts from this central importance of nonrivalrous, nonexcludable knowledge. When information is held by a corporation as a monopoly, it does not grow as rapidly as nonexcludable information (Romer, 1990), does not spill over across networks that promote regional growth (Saxenian, 1994), does not provide the best incentives to employees (Motta and Rønde, 2002), and dissipates rents in duplicative and delayed research (Cheung, 1982).

Economic analysis of nonrivalrous information is often a challenge to legal analysis, in which information is often assumed to have value only as someone's property, and concepts of public domain, or information commons, are often poorly specified (but see

Benkler, 2006; Boyle, 2008; Lessig, 2001; Gordon, 1993). Future scholars will doubt-less apply, to our problem of intellectual property justifications for impeding employee mobility, insights from this wider economic literature on nonrivalrous information. For reasons of space, this chapter will restrict itself to work within this framework that focuses specifically on the economic analysis of employee mobility. This literature asserts, with a clarity that is unusual in economic (or at least empirical) analysis, that there is a vital public interest in unimpeded employee mobility and no public interest in its restriction. The very concerns about intellectual property, often supposed to justify restrictions on employee mobility, actually support removing those restrictions.

This section will develop five propositions that are firmly established in the economic literature:[6]

(a)   High employee mobility (and low returns to experience) is positive for productivity in particular firms, especially those that spend heavily on R&D or hold valuable patents.
(b)   While the reasons for this are complex, they at least include: (1) the valuable nonri-valrous information spread by mobile employees; (2) incentives to creative employ-ees; and (3) noninterference with work opportunity as a clause in the new implicit employment contract for mobile employees.
(c)   Legal restrictions on employee mobility can actually be shown to be detrimental to regional growth.
(d)   Employers can protect themselves quite adequately against loss of key intellectual property without formal intellectual property rights, usually by matching outside bids for employees, or through norms and customs that are as efficacious as legal rules in protecting intellectual property. We can thus be confident that many employer suits, assertedly to protect intellectual property, are instead intended to raise rivals' costs and diminish competition.
(e)   In labor markets where no information is protected by intellectual property, infor-mal norms arise that facilitate both employee mobility and protection of innova-tion. Consequently, it is likely that similar norms would arise in the wake of any shrinking of formal intellectual property.

A.   High Employee Mobility is Positive for Productivity at Certain Firms

Census and other data now permit a more nuanced picture than was possible a decade ago of the rise and incidence of what this author has termed "high-velocity labor markets" in America. We can reject some assertions common in the 1990s. Traditional labor markets have not disappeared. Twenty years or more with one employer is as common among men retiring today as it was thirty years ago (Stevens, 2005). On the other hand, employers and industries with very rapid turnover are also encountered; this was not a 1990s fad that companies have re-evaluated. A man working in the computer industry in California has a 56 percent greater likelihood of changing jobs this month than an average Californian (Fallick et al., 2006).

This rapid turnover occurs because it is productive for certain employers. Andersson et al. (2008) used Census data to match productivity among electronics firms with various human resource practices. For firms with high R&D expenditure, high rates of hiring, hiring at multiple points of entry, and performance incentives were positive for firm productivity. Firms that did not spend much on R&D did not realize productivity gains from frequent hiring. Abowd et al. (2007) used Census data to distinguish firms using advanced technologies from firms that do not. The firms that don't use advanced technology reward experience, just as normal economic models of employment contracts predict. But the firms using advanced technology do not. Firms with the highest levels of expenditure on computer technology are more likely to hire high-ability workers and less likely to hire the most experienced workers. If all else were equal, one would normally expect experienced workers to be more productive than less experienced workers. But all else is not equal.

Firms that understand that rapid turnover is positive for their productivity do not disrupt this system by suing departing employees. Although trade secret law permits many, if not most, employers to assert plausible claims against departing employees, many Silicon Valley employers cultivate a reputation for not asserting such claims against departing employees, while others that have brought such suits have discovered that asserting intellectual property rights hurts their reputation in the recruiting process (Hyde, 2003) and in the stock market (Carr and Gorman, 2001).

Germany has given us a natural experiment of a self-conscious attempt to build a culture of high-tech start-ups without changing the employment contract. It failed. The German government thought, not implausibly, that the paucity of start-ups reflected the difficulties of investing venture capital in an excessively rigid securities market, and developed an alternative market to encourage venture capital. It turned out that the problem was not, or not just, a rigid investment market, but also a rigid labor market. Germany has the second-lowest rate of mobility of scientific and technical personnel in Europe (only Italy's is lower). There is no labor market for mid-career German scientists and it would be folly for any to leave Siemens or SAP for a start-up (Vitols and Engelhardt, 2005).

B.   Why is Short Job Tenure Positive for Productivity at High R&D, High-Technology Firms?

There is no single answer to this question, but the data strongly suggest a combination of at least three factors: (1) mobile employees spread the nonrivalrous knowledge that is the most crucial factor in endogenous growth; (2) employees have greater incentives to create knowledge if they can trade on it in an external labor market than they have as career employees in a large firm with an internal labor market; and, (3) in order to induce employees to accept uncertain work relations, a term of their new implicit employment contract requires employers not to interfere with employee mobility. The first point is more firmly supported by data than the last two, but there is no significant data telling against any of the three.

1.   Mobile employees spread the nonrivalrous knowledge that is the crucial factor in endogenous growth

Remarkably, the very factor that supposedly supports legal restrictions on employee mobility – the value of the knowledge in employees' heads – instead shows why unimpeded mobility is in the public interest.

In order for firms to make lawful use of technical and scientific information, hiring an employee familiar with the technology is vastly superior to acquiring that information through professional journals or conferences. The basic insight is not new (see Almeida and Kogut, 1999; Cooper, 2000; Audretsch, 1998). A famous study a generation ago showed that a particular type of laser, every element of which was in the public domain, was never in fact successfully constructed except by laboratories that employed someone who had done it before (Collins, 1974). Earlier studies documented the common practice, however uncomfortable its fit with legal models of intellectual property, of engineers asking counterparts at other firms whether they had seen particular problems, for copies of recent programs or hardware, and similar questions (Sitkin, 1986; von Hippel, 1988). Surveys revealed the willingness of technology employees to share information across firm boundaries, even in violation of legal rules (Feldman, 2003).

Only in the last few years, however, has it been possible to document, largely through patent citations, the sheer scope of employee mobility as a source of transmission of information. An early contribution was Almeida and Kogut's 1999 study of patent citations in semiconductor technology, showing the importance of physical location. In regions dominated by one semiconductor manufacturer, such as IBM in upstate New York or Texas Instruments in Texas, that firm's patents cited mainly its other patents. At the time of their study, Silicon Valley stood alone as the only region in which patent applications significantly cited patents of other companies – mostly, other Valley firms. This was significant support for Saxenian's account of Silicon Valley: collaboration across firm lines leading to flexibility and growth. While Saxenian emphasized production networks that spanned firm boundaries, and informal social ties (while also mentioning employee mobility), Almeida and Kogut singled out employee mobility as the explanation for the Valley's unusual pattern of nonexcludable information.

A decade on, that pattern is no longer unique to Silicon Valley. Fleming et al. (2007) analyzed collaboration in over two million patents, drawing maps showing networks of collaborators branching out from particular firms or universities. Having worked together before, or being connected through a very short network, is crucial in producing any patentable knowledge. "Inventors are less likely to read documentation, textbooks, or scientific literature and more likely to approach a friend or colleague who has appropriate experience or does read the scientific and technical literature" (at 940). Most of this knowledge sharing raises no legal concern. The collaboration necessary to bring any patentable invention to completion will concern academic knowledge, scientific facts, information created by corporations or universities but now in the public domain: nonrivalrous and nonexcludable. However, given the legal breadth of the concept of trade secret, it is simply not possible for such collaboration to take place without some sharing of corporate intellectual property. If sharing simply concerned scientific facts established in the academic literature, there would be little reason for it to depend so heavily on previous work relations and geographic proximity. However, the sad and difficult truth is that the production of knowledge – the key element in economic growth – necessarily involves taking information that is nonrivalrous by its nature, and making it legally nonexcludable. As Fleming et al. put it: "The conflict between regional welfare and firms' protection of their intellectual property strikes us as an important topic for future research" (at 951).

Agrawal et al. (2006) show that social ties formed by proximity outlive geographic proximity. They studied inventors who moved, patenting from different locations and affiliated with different organizations. Knowledge flows are 50 percent more likely to flow to the inventor's former region than would have been expected had the inventor never lived there. "[T]he identified effect is not the result of institutional knowledge management systems designed explicitly to direct flows across different locations within the same organization, but rather it is the result of personal relationships, formed within an institutional context, that endure over time, space, and institutional boundaries" (at 583). The effect was strikingly strong when the inventor and the citer worked in different fields. Even more amazing, perhaps, is the finding of Corredoira and Rosenkopf (2010) that firms are more likely to cite patents from the firms to which their former employees have departed. In other words, losing an employee does not necessarily mean a loss of knowledge. It is more likely to mean an expansion of a knowledge network. Why? It is very hard for relevant knowledge to pass from one field to another without such personal relationships (though the instant volume is an attempt). The enduring importance of social ties among mobile inventors fits well with the rise of globalization since Saxenian's book. Knowledge flows through employee mobility are no longer just a matter of flowing from Shockley to Fairchild to Intel. Knowledge now flows to the firm's former employees now returned home to China, India, or Israel, and from them back to the US region where they once worked (Kerr, 2008). We will return to this point.

The importance, for information flow, of enduring personal ties and geographic proximity may just seem like common sense, like something your mother used to tell you. But it is not obvious, and it is not what everybody used to believe. We all remember predictions, still encountered, that in the future everyone would work at computers linked to all the other computers in the world and that physical location would thus become irrelevant. There is some truth here but it is wildly overstated. Certainly some kinds of knowledge do not require physical proximity. Irwin and Klenow (1994) found that, when new chips come onto the market, chip manufacturers around the world seemed equally able to use them to improve their own. It did not matter whether the two manufacturers had ever been in a joint venture, were across the road, or in different continents. However, the lesson of the studies by Almeida and Kogut (1999), Fleming et al. (2007), Agrawal et al. (2006), and Corredoira and Rosenkopf (2010) is that, for other kinds of knowledge, location and personal ties matter a lot.

The importance of proximity is the only conceivable economic reason for the immigration of many technical employees. Firms lobby for visas to bring, for example, computer programmers from Bangalore to San Jose even though much programming work is outsourced to Bangalore and the "human capital" of the programmers is identical in each location. They are however more productive, now and in the future, if they have worked, at least for a time, in San Jose.

2.   Mobile employees have greater incentives to invent than do career employees

Little systematic is known about employee incentives in high-velocity labor markets. Undoubtedly there are many individuals who will do their best work in secure, sheltered, quiet environments, and it is good when they can gravitate toward universities, research institutes, and older corporations with internal labor markets and long time horizons (Azoulay et al., 2009). However, and to the surprise of many observers, there are other individuals who appear to thrive in labor markets in which they change employers frequently, or try out stints of self-employment. Barley and Kunda (2004) interviewed these workers. They typically chose contingent work because they loved engineering and technical challenges and hated organizations, which they experience as obstacles to technical rationality. They experience their networks of contacts at all the firms where they have worked as a source of greater job stability than career employees who can be laid off at any time. Motta and Rønde (2002) model incentives for mobile employees. They point out that if compensation cannot be adjusted – a feature of Lazear-type implicit contracts for lifetime employment – and employees are bound not to compete with employers, they have no incentive to innovate at all. Lester and Talley (2000), and Kräkel and Sliwka (2009), also model incentives for employees under different regimes of intellectual property, suggesting greater incentives for creativity if employees can retain the ability to trade on their inventions.

While more research is needed, we can provisionally assume that firms institute or at worst tolerate high-velocity labor markets in part to create greater incentives in some fraction of their creative workforce. It is not necessary that employees hold formal intellectual property. It is essential that they be able to carry information to new firms without fear of being enjoined. An employee free to acquire such market recognition has high incentives to create even if he or she does not hold any formal intellectual property. An analogy might be to software developers who participate, without direct compensation, in development of open source software. They can attain community recognition for their achievements that can be very valuable when next they change jobs, even though they hold no intellectual property in their contributions (Roberts et al., 2006). We will return to the irrelevance of formal intellectual property.

3. Employers promise not to interfere with mobility as part of a new implicit employment contract for high-velocity labor markets

Similarly, little systematic is known about what, if any, implicit promises are made in employment contracts that are understood to be short term, unaccompanied by promises of benefits or tenure, and flexible as to compensation. The present author in 1996 interviewed a number of Silicon Valley employees about their understandings of their employment contracts. An IT professional whom I interviewed, when asked to describe his implicit contract, stated: "I normally get a year to show what I can do; I get a month's notice before I'm let go; and I will be more marketable when I leave this job than I was when I got here" (at 68). Lewis and Yao (2006) model the implicit contract when engineers with high bargaining power demand an "open" firm environment in which they will be able to exchange information with colleagues at rival firms and universities, and eventually depart without litigation. Møen (2005), Franco and Filson (2006), and Balsvik (2011), show that employees earn more at Employer 2 by virtue of having been previously employed at firms with valuable patents and other intellectual property. If this is true, employees may need no special implicit promises to induce them to accept quite contingent employment – except for the crucial implicit promise not to interfere with their future employability.

The literature cited earlier in Section III.A suggests that a high-velocity labor market, of the type observed in technology clusters, arises when it is in the mutual interest of employers and employees. This kind of high-velocity labor market is not something that vicious monopsonistic employers impose on helpless workers, and, despite Lewis and Yao, is not something that employees with high bargaining power extract from unwilling employers. However, little systematic is known about the implicit employment contracts in a high-velocity labor market. Their future elaboration is a major intellectual challenge.

C.   Legal Restrictions on Employee Mobility are Negative for Growth

Despite these uncertainties, the literature on endogenous growth, the role of nonrivalrous information and its transmission through employee mobility, and the broader culture associated with these phenomena, have suggested to some legal scholars that it is time to re-evaluate legal impediments to that mobility (Gilson, 1999; Hyde, 2003; Stone, 2004; Arnow-Richman, 2001; Lobel, 2009). Very recently, several economists and other scholars have constructed more rigorous tests of the impact of legal restrictions on employee mobility. All of the empirical analyses to date concern the enforceability of covenants not to compete, the legal issue for which differences among jurisdictions are starkest. Some compare jurisdictions horizontally; others are event studies. While this work is in its infancy, so far it *all* suggests that the public would be better served by reducing employer ability to impede employee mobility.

The earliest empirical study is Valletta (2002), who simply compared rates of growth by state in the computer services sector and noted the disproportionate growth rates in California and Colorado, which do not enforce noncompetes. Similarly, Stuart and Sorenson (2003) found more biotech firms founded in states that do not enforce noncompetes.

Samila and Sorenson (2011) compared metropolitan areas based on a more sophisticated index with varying levels of enforcement of noncompetes, depending on which of a list of relevant legal doctrines had been adopted in a given state. They found that full enforcement of noncompetes reduces venture capital, business start-ups, and patenting. The finding on patenting is crucial. The sole legitimate reason for enforcing noncompetes, as we have seen, is their supposed tendency to encourage employer investment in training and information, investment that, supposedly, will never take place if employees are free to depart. If there is anything to this scenario, it is outweighed by its opposite. "[N]ot only does the enforcement of non-compete agreements limit entrepreneurship . . . but also it appears to *impede* innovation" (at 23; emphasis in original). Another interesting feature of the Samila-Sorenson study is that its results remain robust even if the San Francisco Bay area is entirely omitted from the comparisons. In other words, the association between employee mobility and economic growth is not limited to the specific conditions of information technology, or Silicon Valley in the 1990s. Similarly, Garmaise (2011), who studied executive compensation, shows that managers in jurisdictions that enforce noncompetes are less mobile, are paid less, and take more poorly paid jobs if they change jobs. They invest less in their own human capital. As a result, employers in jurisdictions that do not enforce noncompetes are more productive and better able to attract financing.

Michigan in 1985 repealed, apparently inadvertently, its previous California-like statutory restrictions on the enforcement of noncompetes and began to enforce noncompetes. This created a natural experiment analyzed by Marx, Strumsky, and Fleming (2009) by studying patents. Mobility among inventors dropped 8.1 percent, with higher drops among inventors with more human capital. There was no social benefit from this decline in mobility. In particular, there was no increase in patents. Michigan employers may have gained the power to impede their employees' mobility, but they did not do anything useful with this power. The results did not change significantly if the automobile industry was completely excluded. The authors believe this provides confirmation for the prediction of Motta and Rønde (2002): "If individuals cannot extract the full value of their contributions to the company because they are prevented from exploring their market value through external opportunities, will they in turn be less productive or creative?" (Marx, Strumsky, and Fleming, 2009: 887). Marx, Singh and Fleming (unpublished) then tracked inventor mobility nationally, through the patent database, and found a significant brain drain from states that enforce noncompetes to states that do not, controlling for general economic conditions. The most productive, and most networked, patenting inventors are the most likely to move from enforcing to nonenforcing states. The result does not change if California is left out of the analysis entirely.

What happens to employees who are subjected to a covenant not to compete? The first such study is by Marx (2011), who interviewed around sixty inventors in the automatic speech recognition industry. He found that the waste of human capital is enormous. A significant number were unable to use their skills again. They switched industries, or absorbed the cost of being out of work for the duration of the noncompete. Those that decided to change jobs anyway were much likelier to go to a large firm that could afford litigation with Employer 1 than to a smaller firm.

So far the empirical literature deals only with covenants not to compete. Application to other impediments to employee mobility awaits further research. The application of these methods to trade secret law will be difficult. As mentioned, most American jurisdictions have enacted a Uniform Trade Secrets Act. While there remain subtle distinctions among jurisdictions, it will require some care to form an index of how vigorously they enforce trade secrets. It seems likely that distinctions will need to be made among traditional trade secrets developed by the firm, perhaps in the past (for example recipes, pharmaceutical formulas); "trade secret" claims to employee inventions; and newer, mostly unsuccessful claims that departing employees will "inevitably disclose" some unspecified trade secret, to name only three types of trade secret litigation.

Still, even limited to noncompetes, the unanimity of the early studies is striking. Using different data sets and methodologies, none has found *any* social advantage in enforcing noncompetes. Enforcing covenants not to compete reduces employee mobility, start-ups, venture capital, patenting, employee compensation, and growth. Enforcement harms employees (considerably), regions, and, in most cases, the enforcing firm itself. It has no economic function except to raise rivals' costs and decrease competition for consumers. There is, therefore, no more reason to enforce an employee's promise not to compete than any analogous agreement in which producers agree to limit competition.

D. Labor Markets in which No Idea is Protected by Intellectual Property Develop Efficient Informal Norms

Possibly the most important recent economic contribution to understanding employee intellectual property is Fauchart and von Hippel (2008), who studied French chefs.

Recipes of leading French chefs are unprotected by any formal system of intellectual property. Moreover, the relevant community includes chefs in many different countries in several continents. Nevertheless norms have arisen, without legal sanction, that are adhered to strictly. Recipes are not to be copied exactly; a recipe shared with another chef must not be given to a third; credit must be given when recipes are used. Chefs who violate these norms are not given further information. We have already mentioned research into similar norms among California information technology employees (Feldman, 2003) and programmers on open-source projects (Roberts et al., 2006). Future research will reveal other informal norms of intellectual property. The basic point, however, is that decreasing legal enforcement of intellectual property rights that impede employee mobility will not result in a state of nature; informal norms will arise, and those may be more efficient than legal rules.

IV.   ECONOMIC ANALYSIS OF INTELLECTUAL PROPERTY RESTRICTIONS ON EMPLOYEE MOBILITY: ECONOMICS OF CONTRACT MODELS

A second and more theoretical body of economic literature approaches negotiated restraints on employee mobility as a problem in the economics of contracting, specifically incomplete contracting. As with any incomplete contract, the background property rights will continue to be salient even when contracts are actually negotiated (e.g. Hart and Moore, 1990). There is a large literature, well-known in law schools, modeling efficient contracting under the assumptions that contracts are incomplete and ex ante property rights thus salient. I will discuss only the small literature devoted specifically to predicting the impact of various allocations of intellectual property rights between employers and employees on the efficiency of, and allocation of gains from, employment contracts. Doubtless there are insights from the wider literature on incomplete contracting that future scholars might apply to employment contracts and the allocation of rights to exploit intellectual property.

There is no necessary conflict between this literature and the literature, discussed in the last section, looking to empirical data on economic growth. For example Garmaise (2011) also presents several complex models of employer-employee contracts under different assumptions respecting employee human capital. But this second body of literature relies much more heavily on models and assumptions than on data. The models vary considerably in their assumptions, and the conclusions they reach are highly responsive to these assumptions. Space does not permit detailed presentation of all this literature, but I will present representative examples.

The modeling literature tends to fall into two categories: (a) the models that show the irrelevance, to efficient contracting, of formal allocation of intellectual property rights contrast with (b) those that assume that formal intellectual property rights can facilitate or impede contracts between employers and employees, for example by reallocating incentives or creating relation-specific assets. Models in this second genre generally claim to identify reasons of efficiency for law to grant intellectual property rights to employers instead of employees.

A.   Efficient Contract without Clear Ex Ante Allocation of Intellectual Property Rights

Under many plausible assumptions, employers and employees may reach efficient agreements over the right to exploit valuable information even when that information is in
the public domain or solely inside the employee's head, or when its property status is
unclear. Indeed, formal ownership of intellectual property is usually irrelevant in new
economy ventures (Hayton, 2005).

Pakes and Nitzan (1983) model an optimum labor contract to hire scientists for a
project "when one takes explicit account of the fact that the scientist may be able to use
the information acquired during the project in a rival enterprise." (at 345). They focus
on negotiations as the employee departs, which they assume will reach a Pareto-optimal
outcome, in which the employer will or will not make an offer to the employee that will
induce him or her to stay. Under this assumption, the optimal hiring policy is thus one
that permits the scientist to depart at any time, free to trade on information acquired
on the previous job. This is optimal because, as Pakes and Nitzan assume, Employer
1 should always be able to outbid either a second employer or a start-up. Employer
1 knows more about the employee than does either the rival enterprise or the venture
capitalists financing the employee's own start-up. The rival will have start-up costs. If,
prior to the scientist's departure, Employer 1 is a legal monopolist over the information,
its bargaining position is even stronger. Competition will divert to consumers some of
the gains that would otherwise accrue to Employer 1, the monopolist. Thus, as to any
employee threatening to defect, Employer 1 should be able, should it choose, to offer a
bonus that would offset the amounts that would be made by moving to a rival or start-
up. Pakes and Nitzan specifically mention stock options, common in Silicon Valley when
they wrote in 1983 and even more common now.

In other words, formal ownership of property rights, or impediments to mobility like
a noncompete, are really irrelevant. If Employer 1 wants to keep an employee, it can do
so. If it doesn't outbid the competition, the departing employee's information might be
worthless, or commonly known. In such a case the employee will leave, and the region
will experience increasing returns to nonrivalrous and, now, nonexcludable information.

Pakes and Nitzan's appears to be the oldest economics article that addresses the question of employer-employee disputes over the ownership of intellectual property. It long
predates the Grossman-Hart-Moore approach to property rights and firm boundaries
(Grossman and Hart, 1986: Hart and Moore, 1990), and Oliver Williamson's work (e.g.
1985) sensitizing (over-sensitizing) us to bargaining issues such as firm-specific human
capital, fixed investments, hold-up, and end-game bargaining. For many employment
contexts, such as Silicon Valley's, Pakes and Nitzan are more realistic than Williamson,
for none of these bargaining problems may exist. There will be little firm-specific human
capital not widely known to contractors and allies. Rival firms and venture capitalists
will provide accurate information about the employee's alternative earnings. There is
little information asymmetry.

Recent models basically confirm Pakes and Nitzan on these issues. Kräkel and Sliwka
(2009) review various employment contracts and conclude that the most efficient is the
contract under which Employer 1 simply decides whether or not to match an outside
offer, rather than extracting an enforceable covenant not to compete. Bernhardt and
Dvoracek (2009) find that employers already pay such wage premia to prevent employee

departure. Consistent with this finding, Carnahan et al. (2010), with a large census data-base, show that highly paid employees are much less likely to depart from firms where their earnings are high relative to others in that firm, confirming that the most efficient way an employer can prevent key employees from leaving is to pay them properly, rather than sue them.

Anton and Yao show that the presence of unclear intellectual property rights does not alter this conclusion. They model (1994) the contract of an inventor whose invention is not protected by any property right, perhaps because it is too closely related to prior art to receive a patent, or too conceptual to protect. He cannot develop the idea himself, yet any buyer or employer to whom he reveals the idea might steal it. Is a contract possible? Anton and Yao show that it is, even if the inventor has no wealth. The inventor reveals the idea to one investor, who now shares with the inventor a monopoly position and an incentive to contract to preserve this monopoly position. Their 1995 article applies the model to the situation in which the inventor is an employee deciding whether to disclose her idea – also unprotected by intellectual property – to the employer. Like Pakes and Nitzan, Anton and Yao assume that Employer 1 should be able to outbid other bidders if it chooses. It will not, however, pay more than the added value of monopoly over duopoly, so there will be a set of cases when the employee will form a spin-out independent of Employer 1 even if the joint profit potential of a duopoly is greater. A recent application of Anton and Yao's model of bargaining in the absence of enforceable property rights is Bar-Gill and Parchomovsky's (2009) analysis suggesting that the boundaries of technology firms demonstrate Anton and Yao's model. Baccara and Razin (2007) present what is in effect a more complex version of this model with multiple bidders. In both models, property rights are not exogenously given but emerge endogenously through bargaining.

These are interesting efforts to model efficient contracting in the absence of intellectual property rights. One wonders, however, why any employer or investor would price the invention as a monopoly (or duopoly) if it is unprotected by any intellectual property and already known to one inventor in a high-velocity labor market. Any monopoly in such a labor market lasts only until shared with an employee who leaves. The price of an idea that gives the owner only first-mover advantages should be less than a real monopoly.

Franco and Mitchell (2008) do not assume monopolies or duopolies in information. In their model, Employer 1 evaluates at the time of hiring the likelihood of Employee's learning and departure. If such a departure would lower firm profits, Employer 1 will, if unable to enforce a noncompete, pay the employee not to leave. Again, efficient contracts can be reached even if intellectual property rights are not specified ex ante and are assumed to be weak. As in Møen (2005), and Balsvik (2011), employees who work for firms with valuable technology are paid less, in effect paying for their acquisition of the knowledge of that technology, on which they will trade when they move to Employer 2. Franco and Mitchell then model employment contracts under the opposite assumption, in which noncompetes are enforceable. Employers pay less, and initially gain an efficiency advantage. However, over time, Franco and Mitchell show jurisdictions that do not enforce noncompetes overtaking jurisdictions that restrict employee mobility. The enforcing jurisdiction will have fewer spin-outs and will lose out on the growth that competition from spin-outs creates in the nonenforcing jurisdiction.

B.   Bargaining Problems Allegedly Necessitating Ex Ante Property Rights

More popular among law professors are articles that, by contrast, maintain that ex post contracting between employers and employees cannot reach efficient results absent firm ex ante property rules lodging intellectual property in employers. Articles by law professors tend to blend several strands of economic analysis that are too familiar in law schools to require summary here: (1) concern about the boundaries of the firm ("make or buy") (Coase, 1937); (2) skepticism about ex post contracting in conditions of bilateral monopoly, lock-in, hold-ups, etc. (Williamson, 1985); (3) specification of ex ante property rights as a solution both to the boundaries of the firm and the avoidance of ex post bargaining (Grossman-Hart-Moore); and (4) theories of human capital deriving from Becker (1993). In combination, these analyses normally support strong ex ante property rights in employee inventions, held by the employer, with concomitant power to frustrate employee mobility. Writers in this tradition have not yet responded to the two bodies of economic literature, summarized above, that support weak property rights and high employee mobility: applications, mostly empirical, of the economics of growth (Almeida and Kogut, 1999; Samila and Sorenson, 2011, Marx et al., 2009); and models predicting that efficient contracts can be made where intellectual property rights are either unclear or held by the employee (Pakes and Nitzan, 1983; Anton and Yao, 1994; Franco and Mitchell, 2008; Kräkel and Sliwka, 2009; Baccara and Razin, 2007). It is idle to speculate how they would respond.

Much the most sophisticated treatment in this vein is Merges (1999). Merges analyzes invention assignment agreements in which employees agree to transfer to the employer present and future inventions. Merges' chief concern is with the employee-owner of a patent on an invention that is complementary to his employer's assets, that is, each asset has value only when combined with the other. The employee-owner of such a complementary asset, Merges argues, would be able to extract such a high price from the employer as to frustrate agreement, and R&D itself. Merges is also concerned that permitting employees to patent in their own names gives them incentives to pursue private projects rather than the employer's, applying familiar models of multi-task principal-agent contracts (e.g. Holmström and Milgrom, 1991). He would thus enforce invention assignment agreements by employees, though not by independent contractors.

It is worth noting at the outset that invention assignment agreements probably have less impact on nonexcludable information than do noncompete agreements, which have attracted more attention from economists. Blocking the departure of an employee necessarily prevents the diffusion of some nonexcludable information, while a patentable invention is destined to be somebody's property, and the question is simply whether it should be the property of employee or employer.

That being said, Merges' analysis is subtle, and considers many examples. Since, as we have seen, there is no empirical data available on invention assignments, Merges' is a good starting-point for analysis, if limited to that particular context. However, recent scholarship on the economic importance of employee mobility casts a different light on some of Merges' assumptions, for in practice enforcement of an invention assignment often deprives the employee of the ability to depart for a rival or start-up and make the best economic use of his or her ideas. The literature also does not clearly support Merges' assumption that there is a problem in ex post negotiations at the time of employee departure. These negotiations take place every day in Silicon Valley and other technology sectors; in what Pakes and Nitzan (1983), Anton and Yao (1995), and Kräkel and Sliwka (2009), among others, have shown to be efficient practice, firms routinely decide whether or not to outbid rivals. Employer 1 is at no systematic disadvantage in these discussions (unless we presuppose some entitlement on its part to keep the information to itself). On the contrary, Employer 1 knows more about the employee and his or her past projects than Employer 2, or venture capitalists, are likely to know. Much economic literature overstates the difficulty in contracting for technological information (as argued in Arora et al., 2001; Lamoreaux and Sokoloff, 1999). Merges deals with a tiny subset of these exit negotiations: those in which the employee invention is complementary to firm assets in the sense that neither has value without the other. It seems unlikely that there are many such examples, certainly not in information technology where there are few secrets and many firms that can capitalize on good ideas. However, if the employee's invention has value only in an Intel product, the employee will have little ability to leave Intel. Colorful talk of hold-ups just begs the question of who is holding up whom.

Another important touchstone for the law-and-economics crowd is Becker's 1993 analysis of human capital, which has been applied in a pair of articles to support enforcement of covenants not to compete. Becker hypothesized that firms would only train employees in "firm-specific" human capital that employees could not exploit elsewhere. They would not, Becker hypothesized, pay for general training to at-will employees. (Pigou, 1932: IV.12.4 conjectured the same thing, but for some reason law professors always cite Becker.) Employees therefore paid for such training themselves through lower wages, which they would recoup either internally or externally in the form of higher marginal productivity. If this were both true and complete, covenants not to compete would serve no legitimate purpose, since the employees would already have paid for their general training, while their firm-specific human capital would be of no value to a competitor.

Rubin and Shedd (1981) suggested, however, that covenants not to compete should be enforceable to protect the employer's investment in a third, intermediate kind of knowledge: general knowledge that is very useful to other employers but too expensive for employees to pay for. They also pointed out that such covenants create incentives for each side to behave opportunistically: the employer by not providing the general training, and the employee by breaching. E. Posner, Triantis, and Triantis (2004/09) similarly defend the efficiency of noncompete agreements as incentives for employers to provide training, based on an analogy with stipulated remedies for breach of contract.

There are a couple of problems with these analyses on their own terms, apart from the critique provided earlier in this chapter. First, contrary to their assumption, employers do pay for general training (Acemoglu and Pischke, 1999; Chang and Wang, 1996; Katz and Ziderman, 1990). Second, self-enforcing contracts are available if the employer fears loss of this training. One common example is a Lazear-delayed payment contract, without any special legal subsidy, paying the worker less than his or her opportunity wage during the training period, then back-loading benefits to induce the worker not to leave. Neither of the papers cited above explains why this assertedly self-enforcing arrangement does not protect most employer knowledge without adding the heavy hand of an injunction against the employee's departure. The charm of the Lazear contract was supposed to be its implicit, self-enforcing quality. To the extent that legal remedies need to be added to that contract to prevent opportunism, they would have to be extended to each side. Third, and more importantly, employers pay for training even in a high-velocity labor market in which the employer hires the worker only on a short-term basis. Even temporary help agencies train temps in computer skills (Autor, 2001). Employers need no special legal grants of property, or other subsidies, to make this decision. In other words, the entire supposed problem of employers not training employees because they can't enforce noncompetes lacks empirical support. (Recall the literature discussed in Section III.C showing greater patenting, venture capital, and growth in jurisdictions that do not enforce noncompetes at all.) Finally, the concept of opportunism is stretched beyond meaning when applied to the voluntary departure of an employee at will. E. Posner et al. recognize that such a departure is not a breach of contract, but then argue that Employer 1 should be entitled to injunctive relief as if it were a plaintiff seeking remedies for breach of contract. I understand why believers in long-term employment relations sometimes need to be convinced of this, but for law-and-economics scholars to model employment as a lifelong contract at the sole option of the employer is, well, opportunistic.

However, the more important problems with the analysis lie in its ignoring the literatures discussed earlier, on (1) the social costs of impeding employee mobility, and (2) models of ex post bargains at the time of departure. As we have seen, enforcing noncompetes does not, in fact, provide any observable incentive for employers to train; it clearly lowers incentives for employees and venture capitalists to invest in information, and is always negative for growth. Moreover, negotiations between employers and employees who are free to depart are perfectly adequate, in theory and in practice, to resolve intellectual property concerns. Finally, informal norms arise in labor markets without formal intellectual property, and seem efficient. It would be idle to speculate how the authors might respond to these facts.

V.   CONCLUSION AND SUGGESTIONS FOR FURTHER RESEARCH

There is thus a significant tension between dominant legal conceptions of intellectual property at work and recent economic scholarship. Law gives employers many plausible threats against employee mobility, usually in the name of intellectual property: the departing employee threatens to disclose employer trade secrets or analogous information, which makes a signed noncompete "reasonable." Recent economics scholarship, by contrast, establishes the social importance of employee mobility, not in tension with innovation and intellectual property, but in pursuit of it. Economists have modeled efficient contracts, and efficient informal norms, in the absence of legally enforceable property rights that impede employee mobility.

Further research will clarify many of these issues. Here are some questions that cannot yet be answered and will occupy researchers over the next decade or two, if not longer.

1.   Has excessive focus on information technology in California distorted our picture of employee intellectual property? In information technology there really are few secrets: employees share information across firm boundaries (Feldman, 2003; Sitkin,

1986; Saxenian, 1994; von Hippel, 1988); the half-life to obsolescence of information is rapid; nearly all products can be reverse-engineered (Irwin and Klenow, 1994). Much research is needed into other sectors. Are there particular industries or sectors that require more protection of intellectual property than software in California? There has been little attention to pharmaceutical manufacturers or biotechnology firms that do realize competitive advantage in being the first to patent and market drugs. How do they protect secrets: contracts, informal norms, lawsuits? Are their employees as mobile as software engineers? There is plenty of inter-organizational cooperation in biotechnology (Powell, 1996), but little systematic knowledge about its personnel practices.

2. How do managers actually manage intellectual property, given short-tenured mobile employees and dubious legal enforceability of restrictive covenants? Do they consciously seek more patents in jurisdictions in which enforcement of noncompetes and trade secrets is weak? It is sometimes alleged that employers that fear loss of proprietary information limit its dissemination among employees or divide tasks so that no departing employee is in a position to harm the firm. This author found no evidence of such personnel practices in Silicon Valley – people usually laughed out loud when I asked about them – but, again, they might be found in less innovative industries.

3. What are the micromechanisms by which employee mobility contributes to firm productivity (Abowd et al., 2007; Andersson et al., 2008)? We now know that rapid employee turnover can indeed be positive for productivity in certain firms, but we do not know why. Research reviewed above suggests some combination of knowledge transmission, incentives in employees to create, and inducements to employees to accept precarious employment. This cannot be a complete picture. Many mobile employees carry little information of value to employers: software testers or programmers hired on short-term nonimmigrant visas. Moreover, since employees often share information with employees at rival firms even without necessarily moving there themselves (von Hippel, 1988; Sitkin, 1986; Feldman, 2003), the precise role of employee mobility as a device to lower information costs is not well understood, particularly as compared with other modalities of information spillover. Similarly the suggestion of increased incentives for employees' creativity is a black box. Interviews with managers would illuminate these questions.

4. Informal norms in different industries. With greater understanding of the informal norms of intellectual property, in industries other than French haute cuisine, will come more refined understanding of the interaction between legal and informal rules.

5. Behavioral economics undoubtedly has much to contribute to this problem but little use has been made of it. Machlup (1952), long before the advent of behavioral economics, mordantly noted the social benefit from granting illusory monopolies, such as in intellectual property, that monopolists wrongly believe are secure; the supposed monopoly may encourage investments in innovation, but the failure to enforce the monopoly allows imitators to arise quickly and create competition. This author asserted that this well describes trade secret law in Silicon Valley, which encourages companies to believe that they own information that in fact diffuses rapidly to competitors. Chu (2007) attempts to apply recent behavioral economics to the

relationship between overconfidence and R&D activity. There are many possibilities for the application of behavioral economics to issues in intellectual property.

6. Comparison among countries. Many countries have high economic growth, technology sectors, innovation, or little Silicon Valleys. To my knowledge, only Israel and India among technology leaders follow California in forbidding restrictive covenants. Other countries (e.g. Germany) do not rely on the supposed benefits of employee mobility. Are they all suffering? If we understood precisely what employee mobility does (3 above), we might understand what might substitute for it. Government-brokered joint ventures in which firms exchange technical information (Japan; see Irwin and Klenow, 1994)?

7. Globalization. The most important intellectual challenge is to integrate our understanding of knowledge and employee mobility into the globalization of the economy, specifically the economics of international trade and migration. Amazingly little is known about the employer's choice between: (a) manufacturing at home, importing workers; (b) manufacturing abroad, importing finished products; (c) investing in a foreign manufacturer; (d) buying finished products from a foreign manufacturer. Only in economics departments is factor mobility a complete substitute for trade. Does the economics of information spillover play a role in this decision? Is there a difference between local and global knowledge spillover (other than the greater efficacy of the former)? Might an American look benignly on information flowing from one Californian firm to another, yet hold reservations about the same information accompanying mobile engineers home to China or India (Kerr, 2008)? Samuelson (2004), in one of his last papers, argued that accepted models of gains from free trade break down here. Suppose it is true that both Britain and Portugal will experience gains from trade if each pursues its comparative advantage in making cloth and wine respectively. It does not follow that this model can be applied to the US pursuing comparative advantage in information and China pursuing comparative advantage in manufacturing in a world in which the information, nonrivalrous or embodied in mobile workers, can pass costlessly from one country to another. To what extent is global migration of professionals driven by information, and what are the implications for makers of trade, immigration, or industrial policy?

NOTES

* April M. Franco and Mark Lemley made very helpful comments. Brian N. Biglin provided research assistance.

1. For example, the New York Court of Appeals, the state's highest court, once seemed to hold that noncompetes would be enforced against employees only if the employee either threatened use of employer trade secrets, or possessed unique or extraordinary skills. Employee knowledge of Employer 1's operation did not make a noncompete reasonable unless that knowledge involved trade secrets. Reed, Roberts Associates Inc. v. Strauman, 353 N.E.2d 590 (N.Y. 1976). It is doubtful, however, that all subsequent New York cases that enforce noncompetes really fall into one of these two categories. In any state, an employer seeking to enforce a noncompete must demonstrate a "legitimate interest," and simply disliking competition is not such a legitimate interest.

2. See, e.g., Retirement Group v. Galante, 176 Cal.App.4th 1226, 98 Cal.Rptr.3d 585 (2009) (departing employee may solicit customers of Employer 1 so long as trade secrets not used).

3. See Kendall-Jackson Winery v. Steele (Cal.Super.unreported) (the chardonnay case); Peggy Lawton Kitchens, Inc. v. Hogan, 466 N.E.2d 138 (Mass.App. 1984) (the cookies case).

4. Romer distinguishes between rivalrous and excludable information. His theory is limited to information that is both nonrivalrous and nonexcludable. "Rivalry is a purely technological attribute. A purely rival good has the property that its use by one firm or person precludes its use by another; a purely nonrival good has the property that its use by one firm or person in no way limits its use by another. Excludability is a function of both the technology and the legal system. A good is excludable if the owner can prevent others from using it." Romer, 1990: 573–4. This chapter will follow Romer's terminology. When a given court refuses an injunction to plaintiff Employer 1, and permits Employee to found or join a rival, it is allocating both rivalrous and nonrivalrous (and now, by definition, nonexcludable) information. The rivalrous information is the "tacit information" or "know-how" of employee, not reducible to code. Information lodged in a human body that can be in only one place at one time is technologically rivalrous, in Romer's terminology. The departing employee will also carry formulas, algorithms, ideas, and negative information that are nonrivalrous – many firms may use them – and, should the court deny an injunction, nonexcludable. So far as I know, Romer's is the first economic analysis of legally nonexcludable information as a factor in economic growth rather than what earlier analysts called "spillover." The term "spillover" is however now often used, somewhat confusingly, to denote this nonrivalrous, nonexcludable information.
5. One should mention, however, the line of recent scholarship criticizing the system of patent law for discouraging innovation and raising costs of producing and diffusing information. Bessen and Meurer, 2008; Boldrin and Levine, 2008; Jaffe and Lerner, 2004; Williams, 2010. This scrutiny of the patent system helps reinforce this similar scrutiny of trade secrets and restrictive covenants.
6. Literature before 2002 is discussed in Hyde (2003). This chapter will be devoted almost exclusively to literature published since that date.

REFERENCES

Abowd, John M., John Haltiwanger, Julia Lane, Kevin L. McKinney, and Kristin Sandusky. 2007. "Technology and the Demand for Skill: An Analysis of Within and Between Firm Differences." National Bureau of Economic Research Working Paper 13043.

Acemoglu, Daron, and Jörn-Steffen Pischke. 1999. "The Structure of Wages and Investment in General Training." 107 *Journal of Political Economy* 539–72.

Acs, Zoltan J., Claire Economidou, and Mark Sanders. 2009. "Knowledge Spillovers from Creation to Exploitation: A Theoretical Model with Implications for Firms and Public Policy." Utrecht School of Economics, Tjalling C. Koopmans Research Institute, Discussion Paper Series 09-32.

Agarwal, Rajshree, Martin Ganco, and Rosemarie H. Ziedonis. 2009. "Reputations for Toughness in Patent Enforcement: Implications for Knowledge Spillover via Inventor Mobility." 30 *Strategic Management Journal* 1349–74.

Aghion, Philippe, and Peter Howitt. 1998. *Endogenous Growth Theory*. Cambridge MA: MIT Press.

Aghion, Philippe, and Jean Tirole. 1994. "The Management of Innovation." 109 *Quarterly Journal of Economics* 1185–209.

Agrawal, Ajay, Iain Cockburn, and John McHale. 2006. "Gone but not Forgotten: Knowledge Flows, Labor Mobility, and Enduring Social Relationships." 6 *Journal of Economic Geography* 571–91.

Almeida, Paul, and Bruce Kogut. 1999. "Localization of Knowledge and the Mobility of Engineers in Regional Networks." 45 *Management Science* 905–17.

Anand, Bharat N., and Alexander Galetovic. 2000. "Weak Property Rights and Holdup in R&D." 9 *Journal of Economics and Management Strategy* 615–42.

Andersson, Fredrik, Clair Brown, Benjamin Campbell, Hyowook Chiang, and Yooki Park. 2008. "The Effect of HRM Practices and R&D Investment on Worker Productivity," in Stefan Bender et al., eds., *The Analysis of Firms and Employees: Quantitative and Qualitative Approaches*. Chicago: University of Chicago Press, pp. 19–43.

Anton, James J., and Dennis A. Yao. 1994. "Expropriation and Inventions: Appropriable Rents in the Absence of Property Rights." 84 *American Economic Review* 190–209.

Anton, James J., and Dennis A. Yao. 1995. "Start-ups, Spin-offs, and Internal Projects." 11 *Journal of Law, Economics, and Organization* 362–78.

Arnow-Richman, Rachel S. 2001. "Bargaining for Loyalty in the Information Age: A Reconsideration of the Role of Substantive Fairness in Enforcing Employee Noncompetes." 80 *Oregon Law Review* 1163–244.

Arora, Ashish, Andrea Fosfuri, and Alfonso Gambardella. 2001. *Markets for Technology: The Economics of Innovation and Corporate Strategy*. Cambridge MA: MIT Press.

Arrow, Kenneth. 1962. "Economic Welfare and the Allocation of Resources for Invention," in *The Rate and Direction of Inventive Activity: Economic and Social Factors*. Princeton: Princeton University Press.

Audretsch, David B. 1998. "Agglomeration and the Location of Inventive Activity." 14 *Oxford Review of Economic Policy* 18–29.

Audretsch, David B., and Maryann P. Feldman. 1996. "R&D Spillovers and the Geography of Innovation and Production." 86 *American Economic Review* 630–40.

Audretsch, David B., and Maryann P. Feldman, and Paula E. Stephan. 1996. "Company-Scientist Locational Links: The Case of Biotechnology." 86 *American Economic Review* 641–52.

Autor, David H. 2001. "Why Do Temporary Help Firms Provide Free General Skills Training?" 116 *Quarterly Journal of Economics* 1409–48.

Azoulay, Pierre, Joshua S. Graff Zivin, and Gustavo Manso. 2009. "Incentives and Creativity: Evidence from the Academic Life Sciences." National Bureau of Economic Research Working Paper 15466.

Baccara, Mariagiovanna, and Ronny Razin. 2007. "Bargaining Over New Ideas: The Distribution of Rents and the Stability of Innovative Firms." 5 *Journal of the European Economic Association* 1095–129.

Balsvik, Ragnhild. 2011. "Is Labor Mobility a Channel for Spillovers from Multinationals? Evidence from Norwegian Manufacturing." 93 *Review of Economics and Statistics* 285–97.

Bar-Gill, Oren, and Gideon Parchomovsky. 2009. "Law and the Boundaries of Technology-Intensive Firms." 157 *University of Pennsylvania Law Review* 1649–89.

Barley, Stephen R., and Gideon Kunda. 2004. *Gurus, Hired Guns, and Warm Bodies: Itinerant Experts in a Knowledge Economy*. Princeton: Princeton University Press.

Becker, Gary S. 1993. *Human Capital*, 3rd edition. Chicago: University of Chicago Press.

Benkler, Yochai. 2006. *The Wealth of Networks*. New Haven: Yale University Press.

Bernhardt, Dan, and Vladimir Dvoracek. 2009. "Preservation of Trade Secrets and Multinational Wage Premia." 47 *Economic Inquiry* 726–38.

Bessen, James, and Michael Meurer. 2008. *Patent Failure: How Judges, Bureaucrats and Lawyers Put Innovators at Risk*. Princeton: Princeton University Press.

Boldrin, Michele, and David K. Levine. 2008. *Against Intellectual Monopoly*. New York: Cambridge University Press.

Boyle, James. 2008. *The Public Domain: Enclosing the Commons of the Mind*. New Haven: Yale University Press.

Campbell, Benjamin, Martin Ganco, April M. Franco, and Rajshree Agarwal. 2009. "Who Leaves, Where To, and Why Worry?: Employee Mobility, Employee Entrepreneurship, and Effects on Source Firm Performance." U.S. Census Bureau, Center for Economic Studies, CES 09-32.

Carnahan, Seth, Rajshree Agarwal, Benjamin Campbell, and April Franco. 2010. The Effect of Firm Compensation Structures on Employee Mobility and Employee Entrepreneurship of Extreme Employers. U.S. Census Bureau, Center for Economic Studies, CES 10-06.

Carr, Chris A., and Larry Gorman. 2001. "The Revictimization of Companies by the Stock Market Who Report Trade Secret Theft under the Economic Espionage Act." 57 *Business Lawyer* 25–53.

Chandler, Alfred Dupont, Jr. 1990. *Scale and Scope: The Dynamics of Industrial Capitalism*. Cambridge, MA: Belknap Press of Harvard University Press.

Chang, Chun, and Yijiang Wang. 1996. "Human Capital Investment under Asymmetric Information: The Pigovian Conjecture Revisited." 14 *Journal of Labor Economics* 505–19.

Chatterji, Aaron K. 2009. "Spawned with a Silver Spoon?: Entrepreneurial Performance and Innovation in the Medical Device Industry." 30 *Strategic Management Journal* 185–206.

Cherensky, Steven. 1993. "A Penny for their Thoughts: Employee-Inventors, Preinvention Assignment Agreements, Property, and Personhood." 81 *California Law Review* 597–669.

Cheung, Steven N.S. 1982. "Property Rights in Trade Secrets." 20 *Economic Inquiry* 40–53.

Chu, Angus C. 2007. "Confidence-Enhanced Economic Growth." 7 *Berkeley Electronic Journal of Macroeconomics* no. 13.

Coase, R.H. 1937. "The Nature of the Firm." 4 *Economica* 386–403.

Collins, H.M. 1974. "The TEA Set: Tacit Knowledge in Scientific Networks." 4 *Science Studies* 165–86.

Cooper, David P. 2000. "Innovation and Reciprocal Externalities: Information Transmission via Job Mobility." 45 *Journal of Economic Behavior and Organization* 403–25.

Coriat, Benjamin, and Olivier Weinstein. 2009. "Intellectual Property Right Regimes, Firms, and the Commodification of Knowledge." 5(3) Comparative Research in Law and Political Economy, Research Paper 17/2009, Osgoode Hall Law School, York University, Toronto.

Corredoira, Rafael A., and Lori Rosenkopf. 2010. "Should Auld Acquaintance be Forgot?: The Reverse Transfer of Knowledge through Mobility Ties." 31 *Strategic Management Journal* 159–81.

Delerue, Hélène, and Albert Lejeune. 2010. "Job Mobility Restriction Mechanisms and Appropriability in Organizations: The Mediating Role of Secrecy and Lead Time." 30 *Technovation* 359–66.

Fallick, Bruce, Charles A. Fleischman, and James B. Rebitzer. 2006. "Job Hopping in Silicon Valley: Some Evidence Concerning the Micro-foundations of a High Technology Cluster." 88 *Review of Economics and Statistics* 472–81.

Fauchart, Emmanuelle, and Eric von Hippel. 2008. "Norms-Based Intellectual Property Systems: The Case of French Chefs." 19 *Organization Science* 187–201.

Feldman, Yuval. 2003. "Experimental Approach to the Study of Normative Failures: Divulging of Trade Secrets by Silicon Valley Employees." 2003 *University of Illinois Journal of Law, Technology and Policy* 105–80.

Fisk, Catherine L. 2009. *Working Knowledge: Employee Innovation and the Rise of Corporate Intellectual Property, 1800–1930*. Chapel Hill: University of North Carolina Press.

Fleming, Lee, Charles King III, and Adam I. Juda. 2007. "Small Worlds and Regional Innovation." 18 *Organization Science* 938–54.

Fosfuri, Andrea, Massimo Motta, and Thomas Rønde. 2001. "Foreign Direct Investment and Spillovers through Workers' Mobility." 53 *Journal of International Economics* 205–22.

Franco, April Mitchell, and Darren Filson. 2006. "Spin-outs: Knowledge Diffusion through Employee Mobility." 37 *RAND Journal of Economics* 841–60.

Franco, April M., and Matthew F. Mitchell. 2008. "Covenants Not to Compete, Labor Mobility, and Industry Dynamics." 17 *Journal of Economics and Management Strategy* 581–606.

Garmaise, Mark J. 2011. "Ties that Truly Bind: Noncompetition Agreements, Executive Competition, and Firm Investment." 27 *Journal of Law, Economics, and Organization* 376–425.

Ghosh, Shubha. 2009. "Open Borders, Intellectual Property Policy, and Federal Criminal Trade Secret Law." University of Wisconsin Law School, Legal Studies Research Paper Series 1091.

Gilson, Ronald J. 1999. "The Legal Infrastructure of High Technology Industrial Districts: Silicon Valley, Route 128, and Covenants Not To Compete." 74 *New York University Law Revew* 575–629.

Gordon, Wendy J. 1993. "A Property Right in Self-Expression: Equality and Individualism in the Natural Law of Intellectual Property." 102 *Yale Law Journal* 1533–609.

Grossman, Sanford, and Oliver Hart. 1986. "The Costs and Benefits of Ownership: A Theory of Vertical and Lateral Integration." 94(4) *Journal of Political Economy* 691–719.

Hart, Oliver, and John Moore. 1990. "Property Rights and the Nature of the Firm." 98(6) *Journal of Political Economy* 1119–58.

Hayton, James C. 2005. "Competing in the New Economy: The Effect of Intellectual Capital on Corporate Entrepreneurship in High-Technology New Ventures." 35 *R&D Management* 137–55.

Holmström, Bengt, and Paul Milgrom. 1991. "Multitask Principal-Agent Analysis: Incentive Contracts, Asset Ownership, and Job Design." 7 *Journal of Law, Economics, and Organization* (special issue) 24–52.

Hyde, Alan. 2003. *Working in Silicon Valley: Economic and Legal Analysis of a High-Velocity Labor Market*. Armonk, NY: M.E. Sharpe.

Irwin, Douglas A., and Peter J. Klenow. 1994. "Learning-by-Doing Spillovers in the Semiconductor Industry." 102 *Journal of Political Economy* 1200–27.

Jaffe, Adam B., and Josh Lerner. 2004. *Innovation and its Discontents: How our Broken Patent System is Endangering Innovation and Progress, and What to Do About It*. Princeton: Princeton University Press.

Katz, Eliakim, and Adrian Ziderman. 1990. "Investment in General Training: The Role of Information and Labour Mobility." 100 *Economic Journal* 1147–58.

Kerr, William R. 2008. "Ethnic Scientific Communities and International Technology Diffusion." 90 *Review of Economics and Statistics* 518–37.

Kräkel, Matthias, and Dirk Sliwka. 2009. "Should You Allow Your Employee to Become Your Competitor? On Noncompete Agreements in Employment Contracts." 50 *International Economic Review* 117–41.

Lamoreaux, Naomi R., and Kenneth L. Sokoloff. 1999. "Investors, Firms, and the Market for Technology in the Late Nineteenth and Early Twentieth Centuries," in Naomi R. Lamoreaux, Daniel M.G. Raff, and Peter Temin, eds., *Learning by Doing in Markets, Firms, and Countries*. Chicago: University of Chicago Press, pp. 19–57.

Langlois, Richard N. 1992. "External Economies and Economic Progress: The Case of the Microcomputer Industry." 66 *Business History Review* 1–50.

Lazear, Edward. 1979. "Why Is There Mandatory Retirement?" 87 *Journal of Political Economy* 1261–84.

Lemley, Mark. 2009. "The Surprising Virtues of Treating Trade Secrets as Intellectual Property Rights." 61 *Stanford Law Review* 311–53.

Lessig, Lawrence. 2001. *The Future of Ideas: the Fate of the Commons in a Connected World*. New York: Random House.

Lester, Gillian, and Eric L. Talley. 2000. "Trade Secrets and Mutual Investments." University of Southern California 00-15.

Lewis, Tracy R., and Dennis Yao. 2006. "Innovation, Knowledge Flow, and Worker Mobility." http://www.people.hbs.edu/dyao/LewisYaoMobility.pdf.

Lobel, Orly. 2009. "Intellectual Property and Restrictive Covenants," in Kenneth Dau-Schmidt, Seth Harris and Orly Lobel, eds., *Encyclopedia of Labor and Employment Law and Economics*. Cheltenham, UK and Northampton, MA, USA: Edward Elgar.

Lucas, Robert E. 1988. "On the Mechanics of Economic Development." 22 *Journal of Monetary Economics* 3–42.

Lucas, Robert E. 1993. "Making a Miracle." 61 *Econometrica* 251–72.

Machlup, Fritz. 1952. *The Economics of Sellers' Competition: Model Analysis of Sellers' Conduct.* Baltimore: Johns Hopkins University Press.

Marshall, Alfred. 1961 [1920]. *Principles of Economics*, 9th (Variorum) edition. London: Macmillan.

Marx, Matt. 2011. "The Firm Strikes Back: Non-compete Agreements and the Mobility of Technical Professionals." 76 *American Sociological Review* 695–712.

Marx, Matt, Deborah Strumsky, and Lee Fleming. 2009. "Mobility, Skills, and the Michigan Non-Compete Experiment." 55 *Management Science* 879–89.

Marx, Matt, Jasjit Singh, and Lee Fleming. Unpublished. "Regional Disadvantage: Non-compete Agreements and Brain Drain."

McKendrick, David G., Richard F. Doner, and Stephen Haggard. 2000. *From Silicon Valley to Singapore: Location and Competitive Advantage in the Hard Disk Drive Industry.* Stanford: Stanford University Press.

Merges, Robert P. 1999. "The Law and Economics of Employee Inventions." 13 *Harvard Journal of Law and Technology* 1–63.

Møen, Jarle. 2005. "Is Mobility of Technical Personnel a Source of R&D Spillovers?" 23 *Journal of Labor Economics* 81–114.

Motta, Massimo, and Thomas Rønde. 2002. "Trade Secret Laws, Labor Mobility, and Innovations." Discussion Paper 3615. London: Centre for Economic Policy Research. www.cepr.org/pubs/dps?DP3615. asp.

Neumeyer, Fredrik. 1971. *The Employed Inventor in the United States: R&D Policies, Law, and Practice.* Cambridge MA: MIT Press.

Pakes, Ariél, and Shmuel Nitzan. 1983. "Optimum Contracts for Research Personnel, Research Employment, and the Establishment of 'Rival' Enterprises." 1 *Journal of Labor Economics* 345–65.

Pigou, Arthur C. 1932. *The Economics of Welfare.* London: Macmillan.

Piore, Michael J., and Charles F. Sabel. 1984. *The Second Industrial Divide: Possibilities for Prosperity.* New York: Basic.

Posner, Eric, Alexander Triantis, and George Triantis. 2004/09. "Investing in Human Capital: The Efficiency of Covenants Not to Compete." unpublished.

Powell, Walter W. 1996. "Inter-Organizational Collaboration in the Biotechnology Industry." 152 *Journal of Institutional and Theoretical Economics* 197–215.

Roberts, Jeffrey A., Il-Horn Hann, and Sandra A. Slaughter. 2006. "Understanding the Motivations, Participation, and Performance of Open Source Software Developers: A Longitudinal Study of the Apache Projects." 52 *Management Science* 984–99.

Romer, Paul M. 1986. "Increasing Returns and Long Run Growth." 94 *Journal of Political Economy* 1002–37.

Romer, Paul M. 1990. "Endogenous Technological Change." 98 *Journal of Political Economy* S71–102.

Rønde, Thomas. 2001. "Trade Secrets and Information Sharing." 10 *Journal of Economics and Management Strategy* 391–417.

Rubin, Paul H., and Peter Shedd. 1981. "Human Capital and Covenants not to Compete." 10 *Journal of Legal Studies* 93–110.

Samila, Sampsa, and Olav Sorenson. 2011. "Non-compete Covenants: Incentives to Innovate or Impediments to Growth." 57 *Management Science* 425–38.

Samuelson, Paul A. 2004. "Where Ricardo and Mill Rebut and Confirm Arguments of Mainstream Economists Supporting Globalization." 18 *Journal of Economic Perspectives* 135–46.

Saxenian, AnnaLee. 1994. *Regional Advantage: Culture and Competition in Silicon Valley and Route 128.* Cambridge, MA: Harvard University Press.

Sitkin, Sim B. 1986. "Secrecy in Organizations: Determinants of Secrecy Behavior among Engineers in Three Silicon Valley Semiconductor Firms." Ph.D. dissertation, Graduate School of Business, Stanford University.

Stedman, John C. 1970. "The Employed Inventor, the Public Interest, and Horse and Buggy Law in the Space Age." 45 *New York University Law Review* 1–32.

Stevens, Ann Huff. 2005. "The More Things Change, the More they Stay the Same: Trends in Long-Term Employment in the United States 1969–2002." National Bureau of Economic Research Working Paper 11878.

Stone, Katherine Van Wezel. 2004. *From Widgets to Digits: Employment Regulation for the Changing Workplace.* Cambridge, UK: Cambridge University Press.

Stuart, Toby E., and Olav Sorenson. 2003. "Liquidity Events and the Geographic Distribution of Entrepreneurial Activity." 48 *Administrative Science Quarterly* 175–201.

Valletta, Rob. 2002. "On the Move: California Employment Law and High-Tech Development." Federal Reserve Bank of San Francisco Economic Letter, No. 2002-24 (August 16). http://www.frbsf.org/public ations/economics/letter/2002/el2002-24.html.

Vitols, Sigurt, and Lutz Engelhardt. 2005. "National Institutions and High Tech Industries: A Varieties of Capitalism Perspective on the Failure of Germany's 'Neuer Markt.'" Discussion Paper SP II 2005-03, Wissenschaftszentrum Berlin für Sozialforschung.

von Hippel, Eric. 1988. *The Sources of Innovation*. New York: Oxford University Press.

Wachter, Michael L., and George M. Cohen. 1988. "The Law and Economics of Collective Barganing: An Introduction and Application to the Problems of Subcontracting, Partial Closure, and Relocation." 136 *University of Pennsylvania Law Review* 1349–417.

Williams, Heidi. 2010. "Intellectual Property Rights and Innovation: Evidence from the Human Genome." National Bureau of Economic Research Working Paper 16213.

Williamson, Oliver E. 1985. *The Economic Institutions of Capitalism: Firms, Markets, Relational Contracting*. New York: Free Press.

13. Antidiscrimination in employment: the simple, the complex, and the paradoxical
Samuel Issacharoff and Erin Scharff

A paradox lies at the heart of employment discrimination law. Why would an employer choose to discriminate against any qualified potential employee? After all, any unilateral employer decision to limit the range of potential qualified applicants necessarily constricts the supply of labor. Any employer indulging such a "taste for discrimination" (Becker, 1971) on the basis of antipathy for a particular group (as with black applicants) or a mistaken indulgence in stereotyped thinking about the abilities of a group to perform certain work (as with women) would find the applicant pool limited and the cost of labor correspondingly increased. To the extent that such discriminatory behavior was widespread, the wage premium to the preferred group would also then rise.

Under such circumstances, the market should serve as a strong corrective force. Any employer freed from the stereotyped rejection of qualified employees would find a broader pool of potential workers and would presumably save on labor costs. Without having to pay the premium for this undesirable indulgence in discrimination, the tolerant employer would have an advantage in the market for goods and services. Generalized across the economy, a competitive market should squeeze the margins necessary for any employer's willingness to indulge inefficient discrimination.

Despite the logic of the market, discrimination abounds in employment markets around the world. Employers may be cushioned from market accountability by customer prejudices, co-worker prejudices or even legalized mechanisms of discrimination, as in the Jim Crow South, that prevented potential black employees from acquiring the skills necessary to participate in the workforce. Hence the need for employment discrimination laws. By prohibiting employers from using certain protected characteristics as a basis for employment decisions, these laws condemn the subjugation of protected groups for a variety of reasons – prejudice, fear, unconscious motivations, cognitive distortions and assumed characteristics. They even prohibit capitulation to these biases among co-workers, customers or the public at large.[1] This anti-subjugation principle is rooted in the promise of the Equal Protection Clause[2] and has been applied, through the Commerce Clause,[3] to correct discriminatory distortions in the private markets.[4]

But employment discrimination laws are not merely exhortations against the wrongs occasioned by retrograde views. All employment discrimination laws are, at least implicitly, redistributive. There is a tacit understanding that there are classes of persons who have benefitted from the privileged social status of their group and corresponding classes who are on aggregate worse off. Without mandating redistribution, the cumulative effect of employment discrimination laws must be to redress some of the historic advantages and disadvantages resulting from ingrained past injustices. After all, there would be no compelling reason for antidiscrimination laws' sweeping intrusion into market-based employment decisions about hiring, promotion and pay, unless there were a corresponding belief that the revealed market preferences are somehow wrong. Even Title VII of the Civil Rights Act of 1964,[5] the most axiomatic of non-discrimination laws, was more than a statement that hostility to blacks in the workplace is opprobrious.[6] Rather, advocates hoped that Title VII would also address the lack of employment opportunity for blacks. First and foremost among these consequences was the denial of jobs, promotions and income as a result of invidious discrimination.

While even Title VII claims occasionally floundered when they forced the courts to confront directly the question of who should bear the costs of remedying past racial discrimination,[7] the tension between the anti-subordination and redistributive goals of employment discrimination law reveal themselves most clearly in the jurisprudence of other protected classes: pregnant women, older workers and people with disabilities. In place of the original civil rights syllogism, which argued that *but-for* invidious discrimination, employers would treat members of protected classes just like any other job candidate or employee, these new protected classes require not equal treatment, but rather special treatment to ensure equal opportunities for workforce participation. In these cases, discrimination might be economically rational. Thus, for example, even benevolent employers might worry about the productivity losses inherent in maternity leave (whether paid or unpaid) or the fixed costs of making an office or store accessible to an employee with a disability.

With the passage of the Pregnancy Discrimination Act (PDA),[8] the Age Discrimination Employment Act (ADEA)[9] and the Americans with Disabilities Act (ADA),[10] antidiscrimination law was forced to confront its redistributive norm and to struggle with the difficult question of who should bear the costs of providing equal opportunity. In this chapter, we explore at some length the problems of pregnancy discrimination, age discrimination and disability discrimination to highlight claims that are not easily resolved within the traditional civil rights paradigm of antidiscrimination law. These claims strain the boundaries of antidiscrimination law because they push to the foreground questions of cost allocation and the accompanying policy judgments that tax the institutional capabilities of courts. Instead of relying on a conventional equality of treatment model of antidiscrimination, which focuses on combating discrimination that was at its core economically irrational, newer legislation sought to provide workforce opportunities to specific groups deemed vulnerable in the labor market, raising difficult policy issues not easily handled by employment discrimination law.

Section I of this chapter will offer a broad overview of the development of employment discrimination law as it moves from problems of subordination and irrational discrimination to issues of redistribution and economically rational discrimination. Section II addresses the strains placed on employment discrimination law as it confronted demands of accommodation increasingly removed from a simple *but-for* model, looking specifically at the PDA, the ADEA, and the ADA. Section III offers suggestions for future development of this area of law. Section IV concludes.

I.   THE *BUT-FOR* MODEL AND ITS DEMISE

In its first and most successful iteration, employment discrimination law targeted the most blatant, and most vulnerable, form of categorical discrimination against blacks.

Such discrimination also proved to be economically irrational discrimination. These cases followed the simple syllogism that *but-for* irrational discrimination, two employees (or potential hires) would be judged as equals and would move toward equivalent positions in the labor market.

In this phase, Title VII addressed forcible occupational segregation by race such that black employees were hired only for the lowest-paying and most unattractive jobs. The presumption of these cases was that irrational discrimination explained differences in the labor market distribution of black and white workers. Only discrimination, not personal preference, could explain why white workers took jobs as over-the-road truck drivers while black workers were over-represented among the lower-paid local delivery drivers. Absent discrimination, the syllogism would presume that black workers, just like white workers, would prefer the better paid job; black workers would prefer to move into the skilled trades in the steel industry rather than serve in the dirty and dangerous position of coal shovelers.[11] These early cases were relatively easy to prove since the discrimination was oftentimes notoriously overt and the resulting workforce segregation was oftentimes absolute.

Further, employer resistance was undermined by the fact that ending discrimination increased market efficiency. When employers constrict the full range of employees as a result of either their own discrimination or that of co-workers or customers, the market exacts costs – higher wages due to their demand from a smaller supply of labor. Absent a legal requirement of equal treatment, even employers who were not themselves prone to be discriminatory had reasons to be concerned over a unilateral decision to integrate their labor forces. They feared revolt from their employees that might decrease productivity and sanctions from consumers that could lead to decreased demand. Title VII offered employers an excuse to do what had long been in their ultimate economic self-interest.[12]

Title VII's removal of the discriminatory barriers proved the underlying premise of equal aspirations among black and white workers to be strikingly robust; racial prejudice blocked black workers' access to more desirable positions, and Title VII was remarkably successful in weeding out these inefficient market preferences (Heckman and Verkerke, 1990; Heckman and Payner, 1989). The perfectly predictable consequence was a corresponding redistribution of income and opportunity (Donohue, 2007; Donohue and Heckman, 1991).

That comfortable alliance between equal opportunity and labor market efficiencies did not readily carry forward past the early cases. The key to the effectiveness of these early Title VII cases was the ease with which the *but-for* syllogism fit the problem of racial discrimination in hiring: *but-for* the invidious discrimination, blacks and whites would be similarly situated and would obtain an equitable distribution of social opportunities. Second generation discrimination law struggled to address personnel decisions and employment policies that did not fit as well into this *but-for* model. Complications arose in reaction to several changes in both doctrine and litigation trends.

In many of these second generation cases, employers could point to legitimate economic rationales for treating employees or job applicants differently. While the effectiveness of first generation discrimination claims rested on discrimination law's general alignment with employer self-interest, second generation claims often conflicted with employers' bottom lines. Further, the law's anti-subordination norms served to camouflage these differences and the potential redistributive effects of requiring employers to treat unequal employees as equals.

Four changes in particular proved especially difficult to wrestle within the context of the simple syllogism: (1) the shift to disparate impact rather than disparate treatment claims; (2) the increasing emphasis on the need for diversity in the workforce and the resulting increase in workplace affirmative action programs; (3) the shift in the Title VII docket toward oftentimes nuanced firing and promotion claims and away from categorical hiring discrimination; and (4) the expansion of antidiscrimination law to cover workers whose unequal workforce participation could not be explained solely by invidious discrimination, such as pregnant women or older workers.

The first major challenge to the *but-for* syllogism was the shift toward disparate impact claims. Early cases recognized expansive statistical proof under disparate impact theory and held employers to a high burden of justification for any claimed hiring requirements above the bare minimum needed to perform the tasks at hand. In the blue-collar jobs commonly at issue in these cases, this standard of proof easily fit patterns of discrimination and protected black applicants from the compounding effects of broader societal discrimination.

The key legal ruling came in 1971 when the Supreme Court, in *Griggs v. Duke Power Company* (1971), first recognized disparate impact claims under Title VII. In *Griggs*, black workers challenged Duke Power's hiring requirement of a high school diploma or minimum score on a standardized intelligence test for certain skilled positions. The Court accepted the plaintiffs' argument that high school graduation was not necessary to perform the relevant jobs and that the diploma requirement disproportionately disqualified otherwise capable black workers from these more skilled positions.

Unlike disparate treatment claims, which can be defeated by the establishment of a non-discriminatory justification for a personnel decision, disparate impact claims can be sustained even in the presence of such justification if a hiring qualification was not deemed a truly necessary precondition for a particular job. Thus, disparate impact claims could reach personnel policies enacted in the absence of discrimination. For example, the doctrine of disparate impact denies employers the option of taking advantage of a surplus of overqualified workers and demanding higher-level credentials in their workforce, or even of paying a wage premium for overqualified employees in the hopes that their productivity gains outweigh the concomitant increase in wages. By reducing hiring criteria to the minimum level of competence rather than the most credentialed employees the employer could attract or might be willing to pay for, the early disparate impact cases anticipated some of the potential economic losses associated with later reasonable accommodation demands under the disability discrimination laws (Jolls, 2001).

Affirmative action programs further complicated the *but-for* paradigm. As disparate impact law took hold, the absence of women or minorities in the workforce began to create an informal presumption that the hiring criteria might be suspect. In turn, the composition of the workforce provided a safe haven for claims of discrimination since it forced any claim of discrimination from the statistically driven disparate impact line of cases into the more difficult proof of invidiously motivated disparate treatment. Employers turned increasingly to affirmative action to buttress the representation of historically excluded groups, thereby altering the composition of their workforce.

This created pressure for the preferential hiring and retention of qualified applicants from historically excluded groups, even if they were not the most qualified by existing employment standards (some of which, but certainly not all of which, were subject to challenge for their true job relatedness). The effect was to level the qualifications standards that employers could seek, presumably having some adverse effects on efficiency. At the very least, the employers were forced by the pressures for diversification of their workforces to depart from the criteria that they believed best served their hiring needs, even if the requirements of test performance, educational attainment or job-related experience may have had in themselves no relation to any overt or even covert discriminatory objective.

The third major challenge confronted in the second generation was the shift from point-of-hire to promotion and retention claims. Because early Title VII cases focused primarily on point-of-hire employment decisions, courts could for the most part avoid the hard question of how to distribute the costs of their findings of discrimination. Employers, paying damages to individual plaintiffs, bore the costs of their discriminatory decisions and the altered hiring practices had a diffuse effect on unspecified other applicants in the labor pool. By 1971, however, the number of Title VII claims based on retention decisions exceeded the number of claims based on discrimination in hiring, and this divergence continued to widen over time (Donohue and Siegelman, 1991). This trend has continued (Nielson et al., 2008; Neumark, 2008). With this shift, discrimination law became a form of incumbency protection for covered workers, and this raised the distributive stakes of employment discrimination law, particularly since non-covered employees were subject to the general legal presumption of at-will employment.

This change was probably inevitable once the early cases of outright refusal to hire women or minorities began to fade away. When dealing with individual claims, a refusal-to-hire case is much more difficult to prove, especially when the number of applicants outnumbers positions available and when many factors unknown to the potential litigant could have been taken into consideration. In contrast, a terminated employee has nothing to fear from and plenty of animosity toward her former employer and can more easily build a case of discrimination. It is unusual for "[a]n individual who is not hired [to] build up the bitterness and hostility toward the prospective employer that is necessary to carry a suit through trial" (O'Meara, 1989, p. 28). Compounding these difficulties of proof, the monetary stakes in failure-to-hire claims (especially when plaintiffs can find other, comparable work) are lower than those in wrongful termination cases (Posner, 1995). Thus, potential plaintiffs in discharge cases are more likely to seek out representation and to find lawyers willing to take such cases under the contingency success fee of the employment discrimination laws.

While the shift to termination claims has happened across the board, it has been most noticeable in the ADEA context, where plaintiffs are end-stage employees at the peak of their earnings history – the economics of which we address below. An opportunistic firing feels like a betrayal of trust, leaving employees bitter and essentially unemployable because no other employer would assume the burden of a high-wage, late-stage employee. While this pattern is perhaps most obvious in the ADEA context, other workers can advance claims of wrongful termination under other anti-discrimination statutes.[13] Older white male workers turn to the ADEA because it is the one piece of federal legislation that protects them.

Finally, newly protected classes brought an even more significant challenge to the *but-for* syllogism's success in the second generation of employment discrimination laws. The ADEA and the PDA are both examples of second generation employment discrimination's attempt to fight a two-front battle. There is no question that some personnel decisions involving the hiring, promotion and retention of pregnant and older workers were premised on unfounded stereotypes reflecting ageism and sexism, and these decisions fit the *but-for* model. As Paul Samuelson once remarked, women are just men with less money. Nevertheless, many (perhaps most) personnel decisions targeted by the ADEA and PDA's bans on age and pregnancy discrimination were not economically irrational.

As we will discuss more extensively below, employers had real reasons to be concerned about retaining an older worker at wage levels that reflected years of experience and not necessarily increases in productivity. They also worried about the productivity costs in hiring women who, because of family obligations, were significantly more likely to leave the workforce than their male counterparts. Invidious discrimination does not fully explain employer preferences for younger workers and workers not likely to bear children. Instead, employers are relying on what has come to be called "statistical discrimination," in which a job candidate is judged not solely on her own merits but also on common characteristics of her class. Such statistical discrimination may be perfectly rational; it is simply cheaper and more reliable for employers to rely on the statistically defensible heuristic that women are more likely to leave the workforce rather than try to get a truthful response from a female potential-hire as to her true intentions about remaining with a particular firm.

As it confronted these challenges, the *but-for* model began to hang on second generation discrimination claims like an ill-fitted suit, still wearable, but not particularly dashing. By the third generation, however, the claims no longer fit at all. The ADA jettisoned the *but-for* model completely. Recognizing that differences between workers with recognized disabilities and those without such disabilities cannot be explained simply by invidious discrimination and that equal treatment will not suffice to open the labor market to this protected class, the ADA affirmatively requires accommodation for workers with disabilities. The tacit cost burden of accommodation that was implicit in the *Griggs* command that the baseline for employment decisions be the minimum level of competence suddenly came to the fore. The difficult question in all ADA suits was the reasonableness of the cost of accommodation, a question which had been studiously avoided in the early disparate impact cases.

The *but-for* model worked well initially, especially in the context of invidious racial discrimination. In this first generation, employment discrimination law was unusually successful for market regulation; it freed employers to make economically rational choices. As second generation employment discrimination law shifted to tackling issues of equity that could only partially be explained through the *but-for* model and its emphasis on invidious discrimination, regulatory solutions became more complicated. By the third generation, employment discrimination law abandoned its mandate of equal treatment. The next section of this chapter focuses on the ways new protected classes challenge the *but-for* model.

II.   CRACKS IN THE MODEL

We now turn to three examples of the broader reaches of employment discrimination law to explore civil rights legislation that protects pregnant women (the PDA), older workers (the ADEA) and people with disabilities (the ADA). All three of these efforts invoked the inclusive equality concerns of the Civil Rights Movement, yet each tests the core premise of equality of opportunity that characterized, at least rhetorically, the initial model.

A.   The Pregnancy Discrimination Act

Under the terms of the Pregnancy Discrimination Act of 1978 (PDA), any employment-based classification based on pregnancy is presumptively unlawful.[14] The fundamental assumption of the PDA is that obstacles to equal workforce participation by women of child-bearing age are primarily based on invidious employer discrimination against such women. Accordingly, the literal terms of the Act prevent the contemplation of pregnancy status in the allocation of any job-related benefits or responsibilities.

If, however, pregnancy is a likely source of workforce disruption for women of child-bearing age, there are two possible employer reactions. An employer who provides maternity leave could face legal repercussions if such leaves were expressly triggered by pregnancy – meaning that under the statute there could be liability if such a benefit were allowed only for women. Such an employer could potentially avoid liability by allowing family leave, thereby making those men who are willing to stay at home for child care the beneficiaries of the law. But more centrally, what of an employer who provided no leave for pregnancy or childbirth? That would clearly have an adverse impact on the ability of women to work continuously and acquire firm and professional seniority. Yet, under the strict equal treatment mandate of the PDA, such a policy would face no legal prohibition.

The affirmative need for some form of pregnancy accommodation shows the strained match between the equal treatment premise of Title VII and problems occasioned by actual biological differences between the sexes that require affirmative steps to accommodate the career goals of working women. Pregnant workers and their employers incur real, economic costs as a result of the childbirth, and the antidiscrimination model is at best a clumsy vehicle for addressing the difficult question of resource allocation that is necessarily implicated in accommodating employees who face specific and predictable obstacles to achieving security in the workplace.

Women (and their families) pay a price, in reduced wages and reduced career opportunities, because of the combined demands of childbearing and modern workforce participation. While the pay equity gap has narrowed since the 1970s, the average man still makes more than the average woman.[15] This persistent pay gap cannot be attributed solely to invidious discrimination, but also results from women's discontinuous participation in the workforce (Blau and Kahn, 2000). This is not, however, a new problem; as economist Solomon Polachek explained in 1975:

> The result of this discontinuous labor force participation is that females both enter occupations requiring lesser amounts of training and train less even when in professions typified by much on

the job training. As a result, we observe females being overrepresented in lower-paying occupations while also receiving lower pay in the higher-paying professions.

Continuous workforce participation continues to play an important role in perpetuating the wage gap (O'Neill, 2003), and this is especially true for higher-skilled workers (Blank and Shierholz, 2006). This discontinuous workforce participation by women corresponds to the demands of childbirth and childcare. In light of the strong effects that childbearing has on women's participation in the workforce, it is unsurprising that businesses would be concerned about young female hires' likely permanence in the workforce. In those positions in which employers must invest in training or job-specific skills, shorter anticipated workforce participation translates into a shorter time period in which to recoup training costs.

The expectation of shorter female job tenure is reflected in the behavior of women who are in the workforce and those who are entering it. Women may logically respond to the expectation of leaving the workforce by reducing their investment in training or pre-workforce education, i.e., human capital formation in economic terms. It is also reflected in the actions taken by firms in anticipation of sex-differentiated participation patterns in the workforce. Firms may similarly face incentives to track women away from certain career ladders.

Thus pregnancy discrimination law must fight a battle on two fronts. First, the law must protect women against statistical discrimination, i.e., an employer's assumption that because a woman is of childbearing age, she is likely to become pregnant. Second, the law must counteract an employer's rational concerns about the costs associated with employing a pregnant woman (including health care costs, temporary labor costs and retraining costs if the woman decides not to return to the workforce). The *but-for* model, however, responds in cases of invidious stereotype, not real differences in cost.

Not surprisingly, the theoretical difficulties in the application of the simple antidiscrimination model to pregnancy accommodation are reflected in the case law from the PDA. Because the PDA focuses on combating employers' invidious discrimination, the model applied was an equal treatment approach in which the objective was equality of opportunity. Consequently, the law failed to explicitly address the question of whether classifications that benefit working women were permissible, particularly in cases in which additional benefits were provided in order to facilitate continuous female employment. This silence led to inevitably conflicting judicial constructions of the Act, as the courts struggled to apply this anti-subordination framework to what is essentially a redistributive problem that tries to address the accommodation of women's distinct issues in the workforce.

In *California Federal Savings & Loan Ass'n v. Guerra* (1987), the Supreme Court confronted Californian legislation aimed at assisting working women that mandated up to four months of unpaid pregnancy and maternity leave for childbirth, with a right of reinstatement at the conclusion of that period. Since the pregnancy of an employee was the triggering event for the benefit, the Californian statute was presumptively in direct violation of the PDA's strictures against all pregnancy-based classifications. Only by disregarding the plain language of the PDA and transforming it into an awkwardly framed pregnancy benefits bill did the Supreme Court save the Californian legislation from the PDA's rigid antidiscrimination model.

Following *Guerra*, one might have expected that the Supreme Court would continue to interpret the PDA in a way that would permit special treatment of pregnancy. That expectation was not realized when the Court next fronted a special treatment policy. In *UAW v. Johnson Controls* (1991), the Court struck down a company-imposed 'fetal protection' program that excluded all fertile women from certain job categories on the grounds that the Pregnancy Discrimination Act forbids all pregnancy classifications, regardless of source or motive. In contrast to the majority reasoning in *Guerra*, the Court relied heavily on the language and legislative history of the PDA to mandate unequivocal equal treatment of pregnancy. This approach, while consistent with the language of the PDA, simply restated the problem of applying a simple antidiscrimination norm outside of its natural boundaries.

Further, even when the question is equal treatment, courts have also been reluctant to draw an easy inference of invidious motive in claims of disparate treatment based on pregnancy. A striking example is found in *Troupe v. May Department Stores* (1994), where the Seventh Circuit held that termination of an employee based on a belief that she would not return to work following maternity leave did not, in itself, violate the PDA. In *Troupe*, a pregnant woman who had been late to her job on several occasions because of severe morning sickness was fired the day before she was scheduled for extended maternity leave. Writing for the court, Judge Posner explained that in order to prevail under the PDA, the plaintiff would have to demonstrate not merely that her discharge was related to her pregnancy, but that she had been treated differently from a hypothetical Mr. Troupe, who was about to take an extended medical leave, or some other employee who had actually taken such a leave. The plaintiff would prevail if, and only if, she could show that the defendant would not have fired Mr. Troupe, or some other similarly situated male who was thought unlikely to return to work after an extended leave. Since no such showing had been made, the plaintiff could not prevail. Judge Posner expressly rejected what he termed feminists' "urgings" – an interpretation of the PDA which would require an employer to "make it as easy [for female employees], say, as it is for their spouses to continue working during pregnancy" (id. at 738). Thus, the court emphasized that the PDA does not require employers to accommodate pregnancy in any way – an approach that would require subsequent amendment through legislative initiatives like family leave and which will be discussed below.

B.   The Age Discrimination in Employment Act

Federal age discrimination legislation is characterized by a similar disjuncture between the legislative model and the underlying problem of discrimination the legislature addresses.[16] In 1967, Congress passed the Age Discrimination in Employment Act (ADEA). Modeled on Title VII of the Civil Rights Act, the ADEA made it illegal for an employer "to fail or refuse to hire or to discharge any individual or otherwise discriminate against any individual with respect to his compensation, terms, conditions, or privileges of employment, because of such individual's age."[17] The group the ADEA sought to protect, however, lacked the discrete and insular quality of other protected groups, such as racial minorities or even women. The elderly represent the normal unfolding of life's processes for all persons, and all employees may at some point be expected to move within that category.

Though the language of the ADEA tracked the original language of Title VII, Congress recognized that the Act addressed something other than traditional discrimination. The legislative history reflects Congress's understanding that age discrimination in employment is complex and necessarily "based on many interrelated factors."[18] Unlike the victims of traditional forms of discrimination, the labor market does not pay aging employees, as a class, lower wages. Since wages tend to rise with time in the firm or in continuous workforce employment, "it costs more money to employ [older workers]."[19]

The economics of age discrimination account for the marked disparity between the stated congressional aim of redressing barriers to job acquisition by older employees and the actual effect of the statute. Congress initially set its sights on workforce exclusion of older employees triggered presumptively by some irrational bias. Any employment offering that stated "No applicants over 50" would seemingly be offensive to an equality of treatment norm and would be redressable through the same prohibitions as were used in Title VII. Though the Act had an immediate impact on formal barriers to employment, such as maximum age listings for job openings, the removal of the barriers failed to solve, or even reduce, the problem of long-term unemployment among older workers. During periods of economic contraction, including in the current recession, older workers have enjoyed the advantages of seniority and have been better able to avoid layoffs than their younger co-workers, but once unemployed, older workers face a much more difficult time in the job market (Kazzi and Madland, 2009). As a result, older workers are over-represented among the long-term unemployed, those without a job for six months or more (Kazzi and Madland, 2009; PBS NewsHour, 2009).

The career-term model of employment that was the norm in American labor markets until the 1980s explains some of the protective effects of job tenure and also some of the particular vulnerability of older employees in the labor market. Standard neoclassical models would view employment as a spot market in which a quantum of work was exchanged for a corresponding quantum of pay, presumably renegotiated each day (at least tacitly) between the employee's willingness to arrive for work and the employer's willingness to pay. As in all such markets in which price is set at the margin, the greater the marginal product, the greater the marginal pay. The at-will rule of freely terminable employment relationships corresponded to the notion that, in the absence of an express contract for a fixed term, both employees and employers freely renegotiated their employment relationship on a daily basis and there was no more reason to restrict the free sale and purchase of labor than there was to restrict the exchanges held daily at the corner greengrocer.

Observed reality in the U.S. in the period after World War II was largely to the contrary. Long-term employment relationships were better analogized to "relational contracts" that adjust for the long-term expectations of the parties. The career-wage market rewarded longevity in the workplace by providing what was in effect an annuity for contributions to the firm during an employee's years of peak productivity (Schwab, 1993). Employee wages went up over time, terminating at the point of mandatory retirement. In the early stages of a career, an employee was paid below his marginal productivity, but recouped that in later years as productivity leveled off, while wages continued to rise. Under this theory, any disruption to a career-wage profile has adverse effects on an employee's long-term employment prospects, regardless of whether an employee is discharged late in the career cycle (Jacobson et al., 1993) or simply does not build up labor force continuity.

An employee under this arrangement faces distinct risks. The primary risk is that an employer under financial stress may come to see an expensive senior employee as an unaffordable luxury, regardless of implicit contractual obligations. Traditionally, employers refrained from this opportunistic behavior because of the adverse impact on employee morale and firm reputation; encouraging highly productive mid-stage employees to stay with the firm would be difficult if they observed widespread termination of employees at the next stage of employment (Rock and Wachter, 1996). Nonetheless, competitive pressures for downsizing in the 1980s and an increase in global competition provided sufficient incentive for employers to engage in such opportunistic breaches of obligations to long-term employees. The temptation to discharge long-term employees was compounded by the mergers and acquisitions boon of the 1980s, as the management that inherited these obligations viewed itself as divorced from, and consequently not subject to, them. This trend was accentuated in 1986 with an amendment to the ADEA that forbade mandatory retirement for all but a small number of employees.[20] Without a natural termination point for long-term employment relations, employers faced increasing competitive pressures to remove older employees from their payrolls, which in turn prompted not only more ADEA litigation but common law wrongful termination claims, as the career-wage model would predict.

A second risk directly tied to the first is that if an employee were to lose her job, there would be a strong disincentive to any subsequent employer hiring her. Any new employer hiring an older worker at her then-current wage scale would be assuming a wage premium for services delivered in the past to another employer. An older employee already at (or near) the end stage of the employment cycle would present an unduly expensive investment for a new employer. The employer would have to invest in firm-specific training of the older worker, the worker would expect a higher wage, and the new employer would not be able to realize the pay-in represented by the earlier stages of the employee's career. For an employer to hire an older employee at the wage such an employee would normally command within the firm's employment scale would be economically irrational. Further, because a reduction in pay to a level approximating productivity would appear to be a dignitary affront to the employee and would be potentially disruptive within the firm, the life-cycle wage pattern had the predictable effect of freezing unemployed older workers out of the job market altogether.

The 1967 Act, which set its sights on express age discrimination in hiring, was insufficient to solve the problem of long-term unemployment. The "No Elders Need Apply" signs came down, but the reluctance to hire older workers remained. As might be expected, the tension between the simple antidiscrimination form of the ADEA and the complicated economic underpinnings played out doctrinally as well. The problem is highlighted by a comparison of age cases to early race discrimination cases. In *Furnco Construction Corp. v. Waters* (1978), then-Justice Rehnquist articulated the justification for the relaxed use of presumptions of discrimination in favor of black plaintiffs:

> A prima facie case . . . raises an inference of discrimination only because we presume these acts, if otherwise unexplained, are more likely than not based on the consideration of impermissible factors. And we are willing to presume this largely because we know from our experience that

more often than not people do not act in a totally arbitrary manner, without any underlying reasons, especially in a business setting. Thus . . . it is more likely than not the employer, whom we generally assume acts only with some reason, based his decision on an impermissible consideration such as race.[21]

Justice Rehnquist's attention in *Furnco* focused on the shifting of the burden of production upon a relatively minimal plaintiff's showing, which is known as the *McDonnell Douglas* approach in Title VII law.[22] While the *Furnco* rationale may hold in the context of race or even sex, it fails to justify a presumption of age discrimination.[23] Unlike race or sex,[24] age is not a constitutionally protected class[25] nor has there been a credible claim made that older Americans are subject to arbitrary state laws inspired purely by animus.[26] In age cases, as opposed to racial discrimination claims, the alternative explanation is ever present. In simple doctrinal terms, courts have been forced to recognize that cost-based discrimination may serve as a defense to an age-based classification in circumstances in which comparable defenses would be unavailing were the challenged classifications to be triggered by race or sex. For example, several courts have held that a legitimate business reason or economic purpose could justify a differentiation in benefits based on age.[27]

In its most recent ADEA decision, *Gross v. FBL Financial Services* (2009), the Supreme Court made clear that doctrinally the ADEA is its own boat, separate from the Title VII jurisprudence. At issue in *Gross* was the relationship between the ADEA and a 1991 amendment to Title VII that ensured plaintiffs could still establish discrimination claims under Title VII even when an employer was acting with mixed motivations. As amended, Title VII allowed the plaintiff to establish his or her claim with evidence "that race, color, religion, sex, or national origin was *a motivating factor* for any employment practice, even though other factors also motivated the practice."[28] In *Gross*, the court rejected this mixed-motive analysis in the context of the ADEA, insisting that "a plaintiff must prove that age was the 'but-for' cause of the employer's adverse decision" (*Gross*, at 2350).

The Court thus confirmed what first became apparent after *Furnco*. Differences between age considerations and the categories that typically give rise to societal animus would lead to doctrinal distinctions between the ADEA and other strains of employment discrimination law. *Gross* strengthened the *but-for* rule the Court had established in *Hazen Paper Co. v. Biggins* (1993), which rejected a "finding of disparate treatment under the ADEA when the factor motivating the employer was some feature other than the employee's age" (id. at 609) – even if that feature happened to correlate with age. *Hazen* doomed attempts to prove a prima facie case of age discrimination by showing that employer reliance upon a proxy for age – such as seniority, income level or pension status – was sufficient to establish the discriminatory intent necessary for liability under the Act.

This result in turn exposes the paradox of the ADEA. Concern about employer opportunism against older employees may prove to be well founded. For long-term employees, the source of vulnerability is that financially strapped employers, having enjoyed the period of superprofits during the middle stages of employee careers, might seek to evade the obligations that underlie the career-wage relationship. This contractual opportunism may be wrong, but it is not at the core of the anti-subjugation principles of Title VII. Moreover, because the employer can assert that it is acting for apparently rational economic considerations, the relaxed evidentiary burdens of Title VII do not apply. Like the PDA, the ADEA attempts to end discrimination against a protected class but fails to tailor its redress to the kind of discrimination faced by this class.

C.   The Americans with Disabilities Act

Like the PDA and the ADEA, the Americans with Disabilities Act (ADA) patterned itself after Title VII.[29] The Act proclaims as its primary purpose providing "a clear and comprehensive national mandate for the elimination of discrimination against individuals with disabilities."[30] The statute begins simply enough by invoking the standard antidiscrimination formula by making it illegal for an employer to "discriminate against a qualified individual with a disability because of the disability of such individual in regard to job application procedures, the hiring, advancement, or discharge of employees, employee compensation, job training, and other terms, conditions, and privileges of employment."[31] This language is accompanied by florid claims in the legislative history drawing an unbroken line from the Civil Rights Act of 1964 to the ADA.[32]

This analogy works in so far as people with disabilities, though not a constitutionally recognized class,[33] can lay claim to the "discreteness and insularity" that characterizes heightened scrutiny classes. Certainly, there is a long history of irrational animus impeding the integration of people with disabilities into the workforce. Particularly when the disabilities are manifest, a host of unjustified reactions, ranging from presumptions about overall capacity to perform, termed a "spread effect" by Samuel Bagenstos (2000), to visceral rejection, may serve as a barrier to the integration of prospective employees fully capable of performing the job in question.

Nevertheless, the ADA is a departure from the prevailing non-discrimination norm of equal treatment. The Act defines its objectives not simply in terms of combating the irrational barriers created by animus, but as the failure to reasonably accommodate differences. Though the issue of accommodation is essential to the PDA and redistributive questions are at the core of the ADEA, neither law explicitly requires employers to accommodate members of its protective class, and, in both cases, subsequent judicial interpretation has limited the laws' protections. Thus, the ADA should be seen as the high water mark of redistribution in non-discrimination law. It is the first employment discrimination law that does not attempt, even as a formal matter, to derive redistributive objective from a simpler equality of treatment command.

From the outset, the ADA defines disability discrimination as a failure of redistribution, not invidious discrimination.[34] While the core of the anti-subjugation command is that similarly situated persons should be treated similarly, the ADA is concerned with equal opportunity for people not similarly situated.[35] The basic accommodation claim under the ADA accepts the employer's ability to measure productivity while simultaneously arguing that there is an intervening duty to alter the work environment,[36] even if a disabled employee may never be as productive as a non-disabled potential employee. Thus, the claim, at least in part, is not that employers are enslaved to irrational preconceptions, but that even if the preconceptions reflect actual differences in productivity, there is an independent duty to accommodate a job candidate with a disability at some unspecified cost to the employer.

There are two critical levers in the application of the ADA: the definition of disability and the question of what constitutes a reasonable accommodation. The questions of how much accommodation is due and at what cost put courts in an uncomfortable regulatory role, with little to guide them from other branches of discrimination law. Accordingly, the initial attempts to grapple with the scope of the ADA turned primarily on the question of what constituted a covered disability, a matter left open by the original statutory language of the ADA (Harris, 1998) and by the interpretative guidelines issued by the Equal Employment Opportunity Commission (EEOC).[37]

In a series of cases, the Supreme Court and lower courts limited the reach of the Act by narrowing the triggering conditions for a disability. For example, in *Sutton v. United Air Lines* (1999), two sisters applied for pilot positions with United and were rejected because of their poor eyesight. The sisters argued that their eyesight was correctable and that United denied them reasonable accommodation due to their disability or perceived disability. The Supreme Court rejected their claim, holding that poor vision was not a disability under the ADA. In *Toyota Motor Manufacturing, Kentucky, Inc. v. Williams* (2002), a worker with carpel tunnel syndrome sued under the ADA after being fired from her quality inspection job. The Court held that an inability to perform certain work activities did not, of itself, constitute a disability under the ADA if the plaintiff could still perform household chores (id. at 199–202). Other cases similarly restricted the ADA's reach.[38] Congress responded to these judicial limitations when it enacted the ADA Amendments Act of 2008, significantly expanding and clarifying the definition of disability.[39] In addition to explicitly overruling the Court's decisions in *Sutton* and *Williams*,[40] the new law defines a disability as "a physical or mental impairment that substantially limits one or more major life activities of such individual"[41] and, unlike previous law, also defines major life activities.[42] As a result, ADA litigation is expected to shift away from its prior focus on the threshold disability determination and toward developing a more robust jurisprudence around reasonable accommodation (Hensel, 2009).

As noted, the reasonable accommodation requirement represents the ADA's unique contribution to antidiscrimination law, explicitly requiring the court to weigh the costs of accommodation with the benefits of inclusion.[43] The statute rejects equal treatment as a defense to liability and indeed defines liability by a refusal to treat disabled employees with sufficient levels of specific accommodation. The ADA directs that the finding of a disability that substantially limits a major life activity triggers a duty of reasonable accommodation, and now that Congress has expanded the definition of disability, the statutory pressure will move to determining the level of accommodation required.

Congress intended that courts use a case-by-case approach in analyzing reasonable accommodations, as evidenced by the plain language and the legislative history of the ADA. For example, the statute expressly defines reasonable accommodations to include:

> [J]ob restructuring, part-time or modified work schedules, reassignments to a vacant position, acquisition or modification of equipment or devices, appropriate adjustment or modifications of examinations, training materials or policies, the provision of qualified readers or interpreters, and other similar accommodation for individuals with disabilities.[44]

The legislative history further confirms that Congress intended this formulation to be illustrative as the "other similar accommodation" formulation would indicate.[45] This case-specific approach is also reflected in the ADA's safe harbor provision, which allows employers to claim that an unreasonable accommodation "would impose an undue hardship on the operation of [its] business."[46]

The professed antidiscrimination norm of the statute does nothing to clarify the extent of the burden demanded by its redistributive obligations. Like other antidiscrimination legislation, the burden to comply with the ADA's employment provisions is triggered by the existence of a job applicant or an employee who is a member of a protected class, but only the ADA defines discrimination to include a firm's failure to accommodate productivity costs due to a member of the protected class's employment. As a result, the ADA distributes the burden of paying for necessary accommodation based on the happenstance of which applicant happens to apply where, a cost burden that may fall arbitrarily.[47] Any individual employer may be subject to costs of unknown dimensions while her competitors are not. Further, the extent of the accommodation standard is defined not by a uniform obligation across all employers, but by the ability of any employer to pay, regardless of fault or ensuing competitive disadvantage (Kelman, 1999).

III. THE LIMITS OF THE ANTIDISCRIMINATION NORM

Congress has, on some occasions, responded to the limits of the antidiscrimination model by directly mandating accommodation and facing up to at least some of the cost consequences of such statutory regimes. In contrast to the limited non-discrimination norm of the PDA, for example, we have the Family Medical Leave Act of 1993 (FMLA), which seeks to provide actual benefits to pregnant women and working parents. This much-heralded legislation was designed in large part to provide some accommodation to working women for the time of childbirth and recovery.[48] The FMLA allows permanent employees to take unpaid leave for serious domestic emergencies, including not only pregnancy but also family crises, such as the illness of a close family member.[49] Although working women were the intended primary beneficiaries, the FMLA was designed to be "non-discriminatory" in its provision of benefits. Part of this is an artifact of Congress seeking to legislate under the powers constitutionally conferred over interstate commerce, rather than the more limited confines of the Equal Protection Clause. But the FMLA also represented Congress's broader commitment to creating safety valves for working people faced with domestic dislocations. Accordingly, the FMLA does not specifically focus on women. Instead, pregnancy is addressed as part of a broad pattern of leave provisions for family-related emergencies.[50]

That said, in acknowledging the costs associated with a direct accommodation benefit, the FMLA then places the costs on the employees themselves. Any leave under the FMLA is unpaid. Few women can afford to take three months off work without pay, especially at the same time that their households (and household expenses) are growing. Second, the FMLA covers only those firms with more than 50 employees.[51] This limitation means that almost 40 percent of the workforce is unaffected by the legislation,[52] and these smaller firms are the ones that are least likely to offer such benefits absent this regulation.

Even this limited benefit, however, is costly to the smaller employers it does cover. The FMLA provides that the employer must continue payment of benefits during the period of leave.[53] In addition, there are likely to be search and training costs associated with finding temporary replacements for permanent employees. Moreover, to the extent that the work of a firm is not routine but depends on personal client connections or specific employee skills, temporary labor is likely to be far less efficient.

By assigning these secondary costs of leave to firms, particularly the smaller of covered firms, the FMLA reintroduces an incentive to discriminate against women at the hiring stage. For example, during testimony in 1989, the House Subcommittee on Labor-Management Relations was told in no uncertain terms:

> Faced with mandated parental leave, a business owner choosing between two qualified candidates – one male and one female – would be tempted to select the male. Direct and hidden costs to employers will compel them to think twice before hiring additional employees.[54]

Thus, the FMLA, like the ADA, requires employers to provide certain reasonable accommodations to their employees with family responsibilities and distributes the cost of those accommodations arbitrarily across employers.[55]

A different approach to the anticipated costs of family leave could accomplish the objective of permitting women not to interrupt their careers at points of childbirth, while also not disincentivizing employers from hiring women of childbearing age. For example, it would be possible to construct a social insurance model of pregnancy leave which would tax all employers for the cost of potential leave and then reimburse the firms that confront the actual costs. One approach would be to finance pregnancy leave insurance through the existing unemployment infrastructure, with a uniform employer contribution based on payroll.[56] Such an approach would provide benefits for both pregnant women and the employers who cover them, with the latter benefits helping to ease the dislocation costs of an employee's maternity leave.

While no state has adopted a pregnancy leave model that includes such an employer benefit, several states have adopted some version of social insurance for parental leave. California was the first to adopt a comprehensive system.[57] California's system is based on employee contributions to its State Disability Insurance (SDI) program, with employees able to take up to six weeks of partially paid leave during each 12-month period.[58] Since then, Washington State[59] and New Jersey[60] have both adopted paid family leave programs. Several other states provide some paid leave through their temporary disability programs.[61]

By contrast, no effective cost allocation mechanisms have emerged in the United States for addressing the accommodation of people with disabilities. Academic commentators have long recognized the issue and tried to address the cost consequences. Professors Karlan and Rutherglen (1996), for example, early on argued that the ADA operates as implicit insurance against the common risk that anyone *could have been* the individual with a disability. Others have suggested that the accommodation requirement imposed by the ADA is significantly more limited than the ADA's language suggest. For example, Professor Bagenstos argues that the ADA, as interpreted by the courts, "simply demands that defendants provide redress for their own wrongful conduct that uniquely disadvantages a protected class," and that some of the statutory burden be assumed by restructuring other employment-related benefits, such as health insurance coverage (Bagenstos, 2004b, p. 24). This does not appear to have taken hold in the case law under the statute.

There are, however, other approaches within employment law that could encourage either an efficient match between job seekers with disabilities and employers or an insurance model that spreads costs evenly through the job market. Germany has adopted one such model. German disability employment law is a "pay or play" regime, placing a hiring quota on all public and private employers with more than 20 workers. Currently, the quota requires these employers to ensure that 5 percent of their workers are people with severe disabilities, and companies that fail to meet this quota must pay fines (IDRM, 2007; Kock, 2004). Such a system allows employers, workers with disabilities and the electorate to assess openly the costs, as well as the benefits, associated with employing the severely disabled. Further, because employers have the option of opting out of employing workers with disabilities in exchange for paying a fee to the government, *all* employers contribute toward the admirable societal goal of full employment of those with disabilities, and this ensures these costs are predictable. The penalty that employers must pay goes into a fund which pays for employment benefits for workers with disabilities and their employers (Kock, 2004).

The German system is one example of a legal regime that addresses the unique needs of workers with disabilities without relying on an ill-fitting non-discrimination model. It does not offer a perfect solution; studies suggest the system has become less successful at improving employment prospects of those with disabilities over time (Bagenstos, 2003). Further, such a system fails one objective of disability rights advocates in that it does not create an across-the-board mandate for integrative mainstreaming. Rather, it would allow an intermediate level of accommodation consistent with some level of cost limitations.

At issue in these further examples is whether the laudable aims of promoting the integration of subordinated social groups and achieving more equitable redistribution can be achieved within the framework originally conceived to redress the complete legal subordination of black Americans. Perhaps it is not surprising that antidiscrimination law has been poorly positioned to tackle these problems. Social insurance programs, like California's paid family leave insurance, offer one possibility of reform. Germany's mandates for integrating people with disability offer a different kind of regulatory solution.

Even accepting that traditional civil rights concepts are unlikely to ever be transformative in the way they once were, there remains a secondary role for established legal doctrines to help redress newer forms of subordination. Recall that Title VII's doctrinal force was not simply a matter of its affirmative commands, but also its ability to ferret out more subtle forms of discrimination or exclusion through the development of procedural doctrines of burden shifting, in effect imposing a burden on defendants to produce evidence of benign intent in order to justify even facially neutral criteria that perpetuated prior exclusions. In the wake of Title VII and federal enforcement programs, the business world created affirmative action programs that achieved levels of diversification of the workforce well beyond any of the liability standards of Title VII. Similar burden shifting might incentivize further institutional investment in the kind of benefits and accommodations that would help working mothers and people with disabilities succeed in the workforce. For example, the absence of a family or childcare leave programs (other than those mandated by the FMLA or state law) could establish a rebuttable presumption under the PDA. The absence of human resources devoted to disability accommodation (like adaptive technology) could perhaps serve a similar purpose under the ADA.

The advantage of all of these suggestions (social insurance programs, inclusionary mandates and burden shifting) is that they remove the goal of integration from the narrow confines of antidiscrimination law.

IV.   CONCLUSION

There is a world beyond the scope of this chapter. The antidiscrimination norm draws its force not from its relation to market efficiencies but from the deep moral offense occasioned by historic discrimination. The claim here is not that discriminatory behavior in employment should be either held to or defended by its relation to efficiency or market rationality. Far from it. Rather, it is that the legal intervention to remedy employment discrimination should comprehend the market forces that may help or hinder its objectives. As a general rule, antidiscrimination commands that most correspond to employer economic self-interest are likeliest to sail with the wind at their backs, while those that are indifferent to the cost consequences of claims for accommodation are most likely to falter.

Matching the various stages of employment discrimination law against the economic implications on the labor market helps clarify some of the difficulties with the doctrinal applications across the various statutory frameworks, as with the application of disparate impact to ADEA claims, for instance. As we set out, the key development is the breakdown of the *but-for* model of discrimination as changes in litigation patterns and employment discrimination law have required the courts to confront labor market inequalities that could not be attributed solely to invidious discrimination either by employers or others. In 1964, few probably could have predicted how quickly the hiring norms of Jim Crow would prove vulnerable to legal challenge. In retrospect, it is perhaps not surprising that employers' disparate treatment in hiring would be easy to root out; aligning regulatory policy with economic self-interest creates a powerful force.

Subsequent generations of employment discrimination law are tackling more difficult, and perhaps more intractable, problems of inequality in the labor market. The remarkable success of the early antidiscrimination cases was attributable to the overt practices challenged (recall the prevalence of signs announcing that no blacks or women need apply) and the close fit between the *but-for* model of discrimination and the actual labor market equity problem faced by workers. As both the cases brought under Title VII and the reach of subsequent antidiscrimination laws began to depart from that fit, discrimination law became less responsive to the problem. Court-enforced regulatory mandates allowed Congress to avoid answering the hard distributive justice questions raised by offers of equal opportunity employment to working mothers and older workers. Third generation discrimination law could not avoid these questions. Since the equal treatment norm would accomplish too little in the disability rights realm, the ADA jettisoned the *but-for* model of discrimination while retaining the rhetorical force of antidiscrimination law.

Perhaps paradoxically, legislation currently pending before Congress reintroduces some of the earliest impulses of employment discrimination law. The Employment Non-Discrimination Act (ENDA) would prohibit employers from discriminating on the basis of sexual orientation and gender identity.[62] Since there would seem to be no economic reason for employers to prefer heterosexual workers or to assume that homosexual employees would self-segregate away from desirable employment, the *but-for* model would suggest that differences in employment patterns may be, at least in part, attributed to discrimination by employers, co-workers or even customers. Although the current version of ENDA explicitly eschews overbroad comparisons to Title VII, there is a strong parallel in providing a statutory club to reinforce the market rationale for hiring from the pool of all potentially qualified employees.

As ENDA wends its way through the legislative process, employment law looks back to its most striking successes: enacting bans on economically irrational, invidious discrimination. Nevertheless, the challenges presented by second and third generation discrimination claims will remain and the uncertain relation between accommodation and discrimination will continue to challenge this area of law.

NOTES

1. *See* Palmore v. Sidoti, 466 U.S. 429, 433 (1984) ("The Constitution cannot control such prejudices but neither can it tolerate them. Private biases may be outside the reach of the law, but the law cannot, directly or indirectly, give them effect.").
2. U.S. Const. amend. XIV, § 1.
3. U.S. Const. art. I, § 8, cl. 3.
4. *See* Fitzpatrick v. Bitzer, 427 U.S. 445, 548 (1976) (Stevens, J., concurring) ("[T]he commerce power is broad enough to support . . . the 1972 Amendments to Title VII."); *id.* at 458 (Brennan, J., concurring) ("Congressional authority to enact the provisions of Title VII at issue in this case is found in the Commerce Clause."); Heart of Atlanta Motel, Inc. v. United States, 379 U.S. 241, 249–62 (1964) (holding that the Civil Rights Act of 1964 was a valid exercise of Commerce Clause powers).
5. Civil Rights Act of 1964, Pub. L. No. 88-352, 78 Stat. 241 (codified as amended in scattered sections of 28 U.S.C. & 42 U.S.C.).
6. *See* Civil Rights Act of 1964, tit. VII, 42 U.S.C. §2000e-2 (2006); see also 110 CONG REC. 6548 (1964) (noting that Title VII's focus was on opening employment opportunities for blacks in occupations traditionally closed to them, in part to combat "the plight of the Negro in our economy"). This pattern is repeated with other major employment discrimination statutes. *See, e.g.,* Age Discrimination in Employment Act, 29 U.S.C. § 621(b) (2006) (noting that the congressional purpose is to "promote employment of older persons").
7. *See, e.g.* Wygant v. Jackson Bd. of Educ., 476 U.S. 267, 270–73, 283 (1986) (rejecting an affirmative action policy in which teachers of color were given protection from layoffs over non-minority teachers with greater seniority because it "impose[d] the entire burden of achieving racial equality on particular individuals, often resulting in serious disruption of their lives.").
8. Pregnancy Discrimination Act of 1978, Pub. L. No. 95-555, 95 Stat. 2075 (codified at 42 U.S.C. §2000e(k) (2006)).
9. Age Discrimination in Employment Act of 1967, Pub. L. No. 90-202, 81 Stat. 602 (codified as amended at 29 U.S.C. §§ 621–34 (2006)).
10. Americans with Disabilities Act of 1990, Pub. L. No. 101-336, 104 Stat. 327 (codified at 42 U.SC. §§ 12101–213 (2006) (amended 2008)).
11. *See, e.g.,* Int'l Brotherhood of Teamsters v. United States, 431 U.S. 324, 348–9 (1977) (holding that a promotion system effectively "freezing" minority workers into undesirable positions by maintaining the status quo violated Title VII); McDonnell Douglas Corp. v. Green, 411 U.S. 792, 800 (1973) (stating the purpose of Title VII was to "eliminate those discriminatory practices and devices which have fostered racially stratified job environments to the disadvantage of minority citizens.").
12. Professor Epstein (1992) has extended this argument to claim that all employment discrimination laws should be repealed on the grounds that market pressures will eliminate irrational tastes for discrimination. Per Epstein, such economically irrational discrimination is often the by-product of restrictive laws or other coercive entry barriers.
13. However, succeeding on an ADEA claim does offer a significant benefit. Unlike Title VII, the ADEA's right to back pay is not discretionary; it is a matter of right. Further liquidated damages provide double recoveries where the employer committed a willful violation of the statute and awards of back pay include damages for lost wages, pension benefits and insurance benefits.

14. This subsection draws on material from Issacharoff and Rosenblum (1993).
15. According to the Bureau of Labor Statistics (2009), in 2008, the most recent year available, women working full-time earned 79 percent of their male co-workers. In 1979, the first for which such data is available, women made 62 percent as much as men. The narrowing has not been continuous. In the more economically prosperous years of 2005 and 2006, women earned 81 percent of men's wages.
16. This subsection draws on material from Issacharoff and Harris (1997).
17. 29 U.S.C. § 623(a)(1).
18. *See Age Discrimination in Employment: Hearing on H.R. 3651, H.R. 3768, and H.R. 4221 Before the Gen. Subcomm. on Labor of the House Comm. on Educ. and Labor*, 90th Cong. 6 (1967) (statement of Rep. John H. Dent).
19. *Id.* at 69 (statement of Peter J. Pestillo, U.S. Chamber of Commerce).
20. Age Discrimination in Employment Amendments of 1986, Pub. L. No. 99-592, § 2, 100 Stat. 3342, 3342 (1986) (codified as amended at 29 U.S.C. § 623 (2006)).
21. *Furnco* at 577.
22. *See* McDonnell Douglas Corp. v. Green, 411 U.S. 792, 802–03 (1973) (setting forth burden shifting under Title VII disparate treatment claims). *But see* St. Mary's Ctr. v. Hicks, 509 U.S. 502, 506–12 (1993) (restricting *McDonnell Douglas* burden shifting by forcing plaintiff to prove ultimate issue of discriminatory treatment even when defendant has failed to discharge intermediate burden of production).
23. Almost immediately after the decision in *Furnco*, courts began to question the applicability of the strict *McDonnell Douglas* test to age discrimination cases. As expressed by the Sixth Circuit, "[t]his factor of progression and replacement is not necessarily involved in cases involving the immutable characteristics of race, sex, and national origin. . . . Thus we do not believe that Congress intended automatic presumptions to apply whenever a worker is replaced by another of a different age." Laugesen v. Anaconda Co., 510 F.2d 307, 313 n.4 (6th Cir. 1975).
24. *See, e.g.*, Parents Involved in Cmty. Sch. v. Seattle Sch. Dist. No. 1, 551 U.S. 701, 746 (2007) (citing precedent to reaffirm that race is a suspect class); United States v. Virginia, 518 U.S. 515, 532–33 (1996) (describing heightened scrutiny accorded to facial sex discrimination).
25. *See* Mass. Bd. of Ret. v. Murgia, 427 U.S. 307, 313–14 (1976) (per curium) (rejecting age as heightened scrutiny classification).
26. This concept of state action that is comprehensible only on the grounds of class-based animus was the rationale by which the Supreme Court struck down a Colorado constitutional amendment limiting conferral of legal benefits on homosexuals. *See* Romer v. Evans, 517 U.S. 620, 631–2 (1996). The Court did so despite the fact that gays and lesbians as such do not enjoy constitutional protection as a discrete and insular group.
27. *See, e.g.*, Potenze v. N.Y. Shipping Ass'n, 804 F.2d 234, 238 (2d Cir. 1986) (ruling that plan that offset Social Security benefits for those workers over 60 choosing to participate in the employee retirement incentive program (ERIP) was not subterfuge because plan was justified by legitimate business reasons); Cipriano v. Bd. of Educ., 78 F.2d 51, 57–8 (2d Cir. 1986) (reasoning that ERIP with age ceiling would not constitute subterfuge to avoid ADEA if employer could provide legitimate reason for excluding workers over 60 from participating); Crosland v. Charlotte Eye, Ear and Throat Hosp., 686 F.2d 208, 215 (4th Cir. 1982) (holding that provision excluding workers over 55 from pensions plan was not illegal if "the provision was motivated by a legitimate business or economic purpose which, objectively assessed, reasonably justified it"); *see also* 29 U.S.C. § 623(f)(2)(B) (2006) (allowing age-based discrimination when observing terms of bona fide employee benefit plan).
28. 42 U.S.C. § 2000e-2(m) (2006) (emphasis added).
29. This subsection draws on material from Issacharoff and Nelson (2001).
30. 42 U.S.C. § 12101(b)(1) (2006 and Supp. 2008).
31. § 12112(a).
32. Senator Edward Kennedy directly invoked Dr. Martin Luther King as the symbol for greater inclusiveness, 136 Cong. Rec. 17,360–61 (1990), while Senator Robert Dole drew a direct analogy to the 1964 Civil Rights Act. 136 Cong. Rec. 18,879 (1990).
33. *See* City of Cleburne v. Cleburne Living Ctr., Inc., 473 U.S. 432, 44243 (1985) (refusing heightened scrutiny for the developmentally disabled).
34. Michelle T. Friedland (1999) argues that the ADA requires affirmative accommodation rather than simply the prevention of discrimination. Thus, an employer failing to conform to this affirmative command is not discriminating, per se, but rather failing to properly redistribute according to the ADA's mandate (Travis, 2000).
35. *See also* Erickson v. Bd. of Governors, 207 F.3d 945, 949, 951 (7th Cir. 2000) ("The ADA's main target is an employer's rational considerations of disabilities . . . . The ADA goes beyond the antidiscrimination principle . . . ."). But Professor Bagenstos (2004a) has questioned this distinction between accommodation and antidiscrimination.

36. *See Erickson*, 207 F.3d at 949 ("Title I of the ADA, by contrast, requires employers to consider and to accommodate disabilities, and in the process extends beyond the antidiscrimination principle.").
37. *See* 29 C.F.R. § 1630.2(h)(1)–(2) (2000).
38. *See* Murphy v. United Parcel Serv., 527 U.S. 516, 521–5 (1999) (denying coverage for high blood pressure); McKenzie v. EAP Mgmt. Corp., 40 F. Supp. 1369, 1375-76 (S.D. Fla. 1999) (steel rod in limb); and Kidwell v. Shawnee County, 928 F. Supp. 2d 1201, 1219–20 (D. Kan. 1998) (breathing difficulties around smoking).
39. The ADA Amendments Act of 2008, Pub. L. No. 110-325, 122 Stat. 3553.
40. *Id.* § 2.
41. *Id.* (to be codified at 42 U.S.C. 12102(1)(A)).
42. *Id.* (to be codified at 42 U.S.C. 12102(1)(B)).
43. There is a significant empirical debate about the success of the ADA in increasing the workforce participation of people with disabilities. Studies suggest that since the implementation of the ADA, their workforce participation has decreased, but there is much dispute about the causal relationship in the drop (Jolls and Prescott, 2004; Acemoglu and Angrist, 2001).
44. 42 U.S.C. § 12111(9)(b) (2006).
45. The Senate noted that its list of illustrations was "not meant to be exhaustive; rather it is intended to provide general guidance about the nature of the obligation . . . .[T]he decision as to what reasonable accommodation is appropriate is one which must be determined based on the particular facts of the individual case." S. REP. No. 101-116, at 31 (1990) (Sup. Docs. No. Y1.1/8:101-4.85/pt.3). In fact, this passage expressly adopts the history of the prior disability acts as its model: "This fact-specific case-by-case approach to providing reasonable accommodation is generally consistent with interpretation of this phase under sections 501, 502, and 504 of the Rehabilitation Act of 1973." *Id.*
46. 42 U.S.C. § 12112(b)(5)(A) (2006); *see also id.* § 12111(10) (defining undue hardship). This defense is no less fact-specific than any other provision of the ADA. The statute identifies numerous factors to be weighed, including "the nature and cost of the accommodation needed," "the overall financial resources of the facility," and "the type of operation or operations of the covered entity." *Id.* § 12111(10)(B)(i)–(iii).
47. Congress does subsidize some costs of compliance for small businesses. *See* I.R.C. § 44 (2006) (providing a tax credit equivalent to 50 percent of ADA compliance costs in excess of $250 but less than $10,250 for businesses with gross receipts of less than $1 million or who employ less than 31 full-time workers).
48. The Act was prompted by Congressional concern that women of childbearing age were increasingly likely to be in the workforce. A Congressional report found, for example, that 57.5 percent of married women with children under the age of three were in the workforce in 1992, as opposed to 32.6 percent in 1975. See H.R. Rep. No. 103-8, pt. 2, at 11–12 (1993).
49. *See* 29 U.S.C. § 2612(a) (2006). The FMLA provides that an eligible employee is entitled to 12 workweeks of unpaid leave during any 12-month period if the employee gives birth or fathers a child, adopts or accepts a child into foster care; or cares for a seriously ill employee unable to perform the functions of the position of such employee. *See id.* To qualify for leave, an employee must have been working with that employer for 12 months and for at least 1,250 hours of service. Employees are eligible if at least 50 people work at their worksites or if their employers employ more than 50 people with 75 miles of their worksites. *See id.* § 2611(2). The FMLA was recently amended to provide additional benefits for family members of injured military service members and for families of service members called on duty. *See* National Defense Act of 2010, Pub. L. No. 111-84, 123 Stat. 2309 (to be codified as amended at 29 U.S.C. §§ 2611–13).
50 For an argument that providing parental leave equitably to both mothers and fathers is essential to ensuring gender equality in the workplace and ending gender stereotypes, see Nev. Dep't of Res. v. Hibbs, 538 U.S. 721, 968, 969 (2003).
51. § 2611(2)(B)(ii).
52. *The Fifteenth Anniversary of the Family Medical Leave Act: Achievements and Next Steps: Hearing Before the Subcomm. on Workforce Protections of the H. Comm. on Education and Labor*, 110th Cong. 53 (2008) (statement of Debra Ness, President, National Partnership for Women & Families).
53. 29 U.S.C. § 2614(c).
54. *Family and Medical Leave Act of 1989: Hearing Before the Subcomm. on Labor-Management Relations of the House Comm. on Education and Labor*, 101st Cong., 102 (1989) (statement of Dr. Earl Hess, U.S. Chamber of Commerce).
55. However the duty imposed by the FMLA is less rigorous than that imposed by the ADA, which is triggered every time a job applicant with a disability seeks a job at a particular firm. The FMLA is only triggered after 12 months of employment.
56. For a fuller description of this proposal, see Issacharoff and Rosenblum (1993).
57. Paid Family Leave Act, 2002 Cal. Stat. 901 (codified as amended at CAL. UNEMP. INS. CODE §§ 3300–06 (Deering 2009)).

58. The law applies to businesses with at least one employer, though public employees and self-employed individuals are not required to participate (Milkman and Appelbaum, 2004).
59. *See* WASH. REV. CODE § 49.86 (2008). Washington's paid leave was supposed to go into effect in 2009, but the State has decided to delay implementation until 2012 because of the recession. *See* 2009 Wash. Sess. Laws 544.
60. *See* N.J. REV. STAT. § 43:21–5 et seq. (2009).
61. For a complete list of state family leave legislation, see National Conference of State Legislatures (2008).
62. H.R. 2981, 11th Cong. (2009); S. 1584, 11th Cong. (2009).

REFERENCES

Acemoglu, Daron and Joshua Angrist. 2001. "Consequences of Employment Protection? The Case of the Americans with Disabilities Act," 109 *Journal of Political Economy* 915–57.
Bagenstos, Samuel R. 2000. "Subordination, Stigma, and 'Disability,'" 86 *Virginia Law Review* 397–534.
Bagenstos, Samuel R. 2003. "Comparative Disability Employment Law from an American Perspective," 24 *Comparative Labor Law and Policy Journal* 649.
Bagenstos, Samuel R. 2004a. "The Supreme Court, the Americans with Disabilities Act, and Rational Discrimination," 55 *Alabama Law Review* 923–49.
Bagenstos, Samuel R. 2004b. "The Future of Disability Law," 114 *Yale Law Journal* 1–83.
Bagenstos, Samuel R. 2006. "Comparative Disability Employment Law from an American Perspective," 24 *Comparative Labor Law and Policy Journal* 649–68.
Becker, Gary. 1971. *The Economics of Discrimination.* 2nd ed. Chicago: University of Chicago Press.
Blank, Rebecca M. and Heidi Shierholz. 2006. "Exploring Gender Differences in Employment and Wage Trends among Less-Skilled Workers," NBER Working Paper No. 124949.
Blau, Francine D. and Lawrence M. Kahn. 2000. "Gender Differences in Pay," NBER Working Paper No. 7732.
Bureau of Labor Statistics (BLS). 2009. "Highlights of Women's Earnings in 2008," Report 1017.
Donohue, John J. 2007. "The Law and Economics of Antidiscrimination Law", in A.M. Polinsky and Steven Shavell, eds., *The Handbook of Law and Economics.* Oxford: Elsevier B.V.
Donohue, John J. and James L. Heckman. 1991. "Continuous versus Episodic Change: The Impact of Civil Rights Policy on the Economic Status of Blacks," 29 *Journal of Economic Literature* 1603–43.
Donohue, John J. and Peter Siegelman. 1991. "The Changing Nature of Employment Discrimination Litigation," 43 *Stanford Law Review* 983–1033.
Epstein, Richard. 1992. *Forbidden Grounds: The Case against Employment Discrimination Laws.* Cambridge, MA: Harvard University Press.
Friedland, Michelle T. 1999. "Note: Not Disabled Enough: The ADA's 'Major Life Activity' Definition of Disability," 52 *Stanford Law Review* 171–203.
Harris, Erica Worth. 1998. "Controlled Impairments under the Americans with Disabilities Act: A Search for the Meaning of 'Disability,'" 73 *Washington Law Review* 575–608.
Heckman, James J. and Brook S. Payner. 1989. "Determining the Impact of Federal Antidiscrimination Policy on the Economic Status of Blacks: A Study of South Carolina," 79 *American Economic Review* 138–77.
Heckman, James J. and J. Hoult Verkerke. 1990. "Racial Disparity and Employment Discriminations Law: An Economic Perspective," 8 *Yale Law and Policy Review* 276–98.
Hensel, Wendy F. 2009. "Rights Resurgence: The Impact of the ADA Amendments Act on Schools and Universities," 25 *Georgia State University Law Review* 641–97.
International Disability Rights Monitor (IDRM). 2007. *Regional Report on Europe.* Chicago: International Disability Network.
Issacharoff, Samuel and Erica Worth Harris. 1997. "Is Age Discrimination Really Age Discrimination?: The ADEA's Unnatural Solution," 72 *New York University Law Review* 780–840.
Issacharoff, Samuel and Justin Nelson. 2001. "Discrimination with a Difference: Can Employment Discrimination Law Accommodate the Americans with Disabilities Act?" 79 *North Carolina Law Review* 307–58.
Issacharoff, Samuel and Elyse Rosenblum. 1993. "Women and the Workplace, Accommodating the Demands of Pregnancy," 94 *Columbia Law Review* 2154–221.
Jacobson, Louis S., R.J. Lalonde and D.G. Sullivan. 1993. "Earnings Losses of Displaced Workers," 83 *American Economic Review* 685–709.
Jolls, Christine M. 2001. "Antidiscrimination and Accommodation," 115 *Harvard Law Review* 642–99.

Jolls, Christine and J.J. Prescott. 2004. "Disaggregating Employment Protection: The Case of Disability Discrimination," NBER Working Paper No. 10740.

Karlan, Pamela S. and George Rutherglen. 1996. "Disabilities, Discrimination, and Reasonable Accommodation," 46 *Duke Law Journal* 1–41.

Kazzi, Nayla and David Madland. 2009. *Mixed News for Older Workers.* Washington, DC: Center for American Progress.

Kelman, Mark. 1999. *Strategy or Principle? The Choice Between Regulation and Taxation.* Ann Arbor, MI: University of Michigan Press.

Kock, Martin. 2004. "Disability Law in Germany: An Overview of Employment, Education and Access Rights," 5 *German Law Journal* 1373–92.

Milkman, Ruth and Eileen Appelbaum. 2004. "Paid Family Leave in California: New Research Findings," in Ruth Milkman, ed., *The State of California Labor 2004.* Berkeley, CA: University of California, Berkeley, Institute of Industrial Relations.

National Conference of State Legislatures. 2008. "State Family and Medical Leave Laws that Differ from the Federal FMLA." Available at: http://www.ncsl.org/print/employ/fam-medleave.pdf.

Neumark, David. 2008. "The Age Discrimination in Employment Act and the Challenge of Population Aging," NBER Working Paper No 14317.

Nielson, Laura Beth, et al. 2008. *Contesting Workplace Discrimination in Court: Characteristics and Outcomes of Federal Employment Discrimination Litigation 1987–2003.* Chicago: American Bar Foundation.

O'Meara, Daniel P. 1989. *Protecting the Growing Number of Older Workers: The Age Discrimination in Employment Act.* Philadelphia: Industrial Research Unit, Wharton School, Vance Hall, University of Pennsylvania.

O'Neill, June. 2003. "The Gender Gap in Wages, circa 2000," 93 *American Economic Review* 309–14.

PBS NewsHour. 2009. "Older Workers Face New Challenges in a Tough Job Market." PBS Television Broadcast (Dec. 10).

Polachek, Solomon W. 1975. "Discontinuous Labor Force Participation and its Effects on Women's Market Earnings," in Cynthia B. Loyd, ed., *Sex, Discrimination, and the Division of Labor.* New York: Columbia University Press.

Posner, Richard. 1995. *Aging and Old Age.* Chicago: University of Chicago Press.

Rock, Edward B. and Michael L. Wachter. 1996. "The Enforceability of Norms and the Employment Relationship," 144 *University of Pennsylvania Law Review* 1913–52.

Schwab, Stewart J. 1993. "Life-Cycle Justice: Accommodating Just Cause and Employment at Will," 92 *Michigan Law Rev*iew 8–62.

Travis, Michelle A. 2000. "Leveling the Playing Field or Stacking the Deck? The 'Unfair Advantage' Critique of Perceived Disability Claims," 78 *North Carolina Law Review* 901–1011.

Cases and Statutes Cited

California Federal Savings & Loan Ass'n v. Guerra, 479 U.S. 272 (1987).

Cipriano v. Board of Education, 78 F.2d 51 (2d Cir. 1986).

City of Cleburne v. Cleburne Living Center., Inc., 473 U.S. 432 (1985).

Crosland v. Charlotte Eye, Ear & Throat Hospital, 686 F.2d 208 (4th Cir. 1982).

Erickson v. Board of Governors, 207 F.3d 945 (7th Cir. 2000).

Fitzpatrick v. Bitzer, 427 U.S. 445 (1976).

Furnco Construction Corp. v. Waters 438 U.S. 567 (1978).

Gross v. FBL Financial Services, 129 S.Ct. 2343 (2009).

Hazen Paper Co. v. Biggins, 507 U.S. 604 (1993).

Heart of Atlanta Motel, Inc. v. United States, 379 U.S. 241 (1964).

International Brotherhood of Teamsters v. United States, 431 U.S. 324 (1977).

Kidwell v. Shawnee County, 928 F. Supp. 2d 1201 (D. Kan. 1998).

Laugesen v. Anaconda Co., 510 F.2d 307 (6th Cir. 1975).

Massachusetts Board of Retirement v. Murgia, 427 U.S. 307 (1976) (per curium).

McDonnell Douglas Corp. v. Green, 411 U.S. 792 (1973).

McKenzie v. EAP Management Corp., 40 F. Supp. 1369 (S.D. Fla. 1999).

Murphy v. United Parcel Services, 527 U.S. 516 (1999).

Nevada Department of Human Resources v. Hibbs, 538 U.S. 721 (2003).

Palmore v. Sidoti, 466 U.S. 429 (1984).

Parents Involved v. Seattle School District No. 1, 551 U.S. 701 (2007).

Potenze v. New York Shipping Ass'n, 804 F.2d 234 (2d Cir. 1986).

Romer v. Evans, 517 U.S. 620 (1996).

St. Mary's Center v. Hicks, 509 U.S. 502 (1993).

Sutton v. United Air Lines, 527 U.S. 471 (1999).
Toyota Motor Manufacturing, Kentucky, Inc. v. Williams, 534 U.S. 184 (2002).
Troupe v. May Department Stores, 20 F.3d 734 (7th Cir. 1994).
UAW v. Johnson Controls, 499 U.S. 187 (1991).
United States v. Virginia, 518 U.S. 515, 532–33 (1996).
Wygant v. Jackson Board of Education, 476 U.S. 267 (1986).

Legislation

Age Discrimination in Employment Act of 1967, Pub. L. No. 90-202, 81 Stat. 602 (codified as amended at 29 U.S.C. §§ 621–34 (2006)).
Age Discrimination in Employment Amendments of 1986, Pub. L. No. 99-592, § 2, 100 Stat. 3342, 3342 (1986) (codified as amended at 29 U.S.C. § 623 (2006)).
Americans with Disabilities Act of 1990, Pub. L. No. 101-336, 104 Stat. 327 (codified at 42 U.SC. §§ 12101–213 (2006) (amended 2008)).
Civil Rights Act of 1964, Pub. L. No. 88-352, 78 Stat. 241 (codified as amended in scattered sections of 28 U.S.C. & 42 U.S.C.).
Employment Non-Discrimination Act, H.R. 2981, 11th Cong. (2009); S. 1584, 11th Cong. (2009).
Family Medical Leave Act of 1993 29 USC §§ 2601 et seq. (2006).
National Defense Act of 2010, Pub. L. No. 111-84, 123 Stat. 2309.
N.J. Rev. Stat. § 43:21–25 et seq. (2009).
Paid Family Leave Act, 2002 Cal. Stat. 901 (codified as amended at Cal. Unemp. Ins. Code §§ 3300–06 (Deering 2009)).
Pregnancy Discrimination Act of 1978, Pub. L. No. 95-555, 95 Stat. 2075 (codified at 42 U.S.C. §2000e(k) (2006)).
Wash. Rev. Code § 49.86 (2008).

14. The forum for adjudication of employment disputes

Samuel Estreicher and Zev J. Eigen*

INTRODUCTION

This chapter focuses on the appropriate design of the forum for adjudication of employment disputes. By the term "adjudication," we refer to the resolution of "rights" disputes – disputes over the application of a contract or the application of a statutory or regulatory rule or policy to a particular situation. We are not referring to "interests" disputes – disputes over the substantive content of an initial labor-management contract or renewal agreement, or the analog in a non-unionized setting, such as the construction of rules to govern the workplace. In considering the design question, we assume that all involved actors (employees, employers, unions, etc.) retain whatever endowments they currently possess in terms of intelligence, energy, income, occupational status, access to resources, union representation, and statutory and contractual rights. Holding these endowments constant, we ask what institutional arrangements for adjudicating rights disputes would do the best job of resolving those disputes in a fair, efficient manner for workers, managers and the public generally.

The fundamental problem of the current system is that the overwhelming majority of U.S. workers lack access to a fair, efficient forum for adjudicating their disputes with their employers. They have, in a theoretical sense, a right of access to a court system that is, properly viewed as, the envy of the world, but the costs of access to the system – not so much filing fees, but access to competent counsel – are prohibitive (Estreicher, 2005). Workers with viable claims are often left with the unpalatable choice of either filing a complaint with an administrative agency poorly resourced to handle a large volume of claims, representing themselves in court, or simply giving up. Class actions, an ingenious, lawyer-driven device of the equity courts that has done much good, are also poorly designed for fact-intensive, day-to-day disputes of employees who complain of an improper termination of employment or other adverse personnel decision. No other country in the developed world relies on ordinary civil courts for employment disputes; rather, they use some form of employment tribunal with limited rights of appeal to the courts (Estreicher, 2008).

I. THE CURRENT SYSTEM IN THE UNITED STATES

A. Reliance on Courts for Employment Disputes

The U.S. litigation system has been characterized as a system of "cadillacs for the few, rickshaws for the many" (Estreicher, 2001). The features of the U.S. system that cause it to stand out among developed countries as a plaintiff-friendly system – allowance of a 30 percent (or greater) contingent attorney's fee, non-responsibility of losers for winner's attorney's fees, civil jury trials, recovery of "pain and suffering," and the possibility of a punitive damages award – spell an attractive source of leverage for well-paid litigants who can afford competent counsel; they receive the "cadillacs for the few". For the overwhelming number of U.S. workers, however, the U.S. court system is, for all practical purposes, *terra incognito*; they receive, at best, the "rickshaws for the many." This is because, at least in employment cases where jury awards tend not be astronomical, competent lawyers are not available for individuals who cannot afford to pay a non-trivial hourly fee (at least $200–300 per hour in major American cities) even if they are willing to be partially compensated by a contingent fee (payable only if they win) (Estreicher, 2005; Hadfield, 2000; Sherwyn, Tracy, and Eigen, 1999). Lawyers who are paid exclusively on a contingent-fee basis do not handle many employment disputes, and tend either not to be proficient in employment matters or are not likely to invest very much of their time and effort in cases they do handle, often hoping to be compensated out of a "nuisance" payment from the employer (Rosenberg and Shavell, 2006; Sherwyn, Tracy, and Eigen, 1999). Statutes providing for one-way fee shifting (for prevailing plaintiffs only) have improved access for particular claims but without fundamentally altering the picture.

The United States arrived at this state of affairs, in part, because our legal culture is very much enamored of the courts. Over a century ago, de Tocqueville wrote about the Americans' penchant for turning all interesting political and policy issues into legal questions. American attitudes in this regard have not changed. Americans like the ideal of an assumedly impartial judicial system adjudicating disputes that they are unable to resolve on their own (Merry, 1990; Merry and Silbey, 1984). The jury trial, both for criminal and civic cases, is an important component of the American ideal of justice and procedural fairness. Courts also play an extremely important role in providing a bastion against the power of the state and, for this reason, have found favor on both the left and the right.

B.   Declining Union Representation

A second important factor is that American regulation of the employment relationship started first with "labor law," i.e., workers' collective rights to representation and collective bargaining, before it turned to "employment law," i.e., workers' individual rights under contract, various statutes or regulations. This occurred in part because early efforts at legislated improvements were overturned by courts, and organized labor developed a philosophy of "voluntarism," of looking for lasting improvements in the welfare of their members through collective action and contract (Estreicher, 2010b; Tucker and Mucalov, 2010).

At a time when U.S. labor unions represented one-third of all workers in private companies, and many non-union companies seeking to avoid union campaigns felt compelled to replicate the compensation, benefits and working conditions (including grievance procedures) obtained in the unionized sector (Ewing, 1989), it made sense to think of the U.S. employment adjudication system as grounded principally in the grievance and arbitration process provided jointly by the employer and union in the union sector.

This model of union-based workplace representation was (and is), in many ways, advantageous to the parties concerned. The costs of the system were shared by the employers and unions. The familiarity of the union with collective bargaining agreements it negotiated – not only the text but the bargaining history and the practices of the parties under the agreement – made it an efficient, low-cost provider of representational services. Unions often used their business agents, rather than lawyers, to represent them before arbitrators when workplace disputes arose. Arbitrators also understood that the labor union, even more than the employer, was an institutional repeat player likely to represent employees and be involved in choosing arbitrators for future disputes as well. A high premium was placed on informal resolution; often grievances were resolved in the less formal early steps of grievance procedures and never escalated to arbitration. Particularly difficult cases might be subject to a non-legal resolution via continuation of the bargaining process between the parties.

Not all was perfect, however, with the union-based model. The union's integrative role in representing employees in rights disputes was invariably accompanied by a redistributive role in seeking wages and benefits not required of competitors (Estreicher, 2009). Historically, unions affiliated with the railroad crafts and building trades barred African-Americans from membership and the better jobs – leading to a judicially created duty of fair representation (Malamud, 2005). Even when unions actively support non-discriminatory policies, they have difficulty mediating claims of groups of workers where those claims cannot be easily resolved by a rule favoring length of service in the particular department or the particular employer (Kleiman and Frankel, 1975). This may be part of the reason unions generally are reluctant to overtly assert claims of racial or other discrimination even where the labor agreement authorizes such claims. Indeed, even if there are no issues of discrimination or other concerns over dividing workers into factions, the fact that a given grievance or arbitration could have significance for other workers and other possible disputes might in some cases work to the benefit of all represented workers but in other cases could lead to "horsetrading" resulting in the sacrifice of valid claims ostensibly for the greater good (Summers, 1977).

C. The Rise of Employment Law

Through much of the first six decades of the twentieth century, many laws enacted to regulate the workplace assumed an ongoing role for union representation and collective bargaining (Kochan, Katz, and McKersie, 1986). But unions and collective bargaining have faded instead of flourishing. While unions have declined as a force within the private sector (a slide that began in earnest in the mid-1970s), the civil rights movement of the 1960s prompted the enactment of important state and federal legislation giving the individual worker the right to sue employers (and unions) for discriminatory employment decisions. State courts followed suit with new causes of action challenging certain employer actions. In short, Employment Law has come to displace Labor Law as the dominant feature of legal regulation of the workplace.

Unions remain important forces in government offices and continue as collective bargaining agents in several important private industries, such as hospitals, big-city construction, film and television, and trucking. But the system of collective bargaining agreements with progressive discipline, "just cause" provisions, and grievance systems culminating in final, binding arbitration is not the common experience of most American workers. And even where unions are present, they remain reluctant to assert discrimination and other statutory claims, preferring to rely on purely contractual grounds that pose less of a danger of dividing workers. (This may change with the Supreme Court's 2009 *Pyett* decision, which authorizes the parties to a collective bargaining agreement to negotiate a binding arbitration process in lieu of lawsuits even for statutory discrimination claims (Green, 2012; Cummins and Seiler, 2010).) With the emergence of individual rights as the primary building block of workplace regulation, not surprisingly employment rights enforcement has almost entirely shifted away from the tripartite model of collective representation to reliance on legal advocacy on an individual or class action basis.

One question about this shift is whether an effective rights-based adjudicatory system requires (at least from the employees' perspective) some measure of institutional power – the employees' ability to impose significant costs of disagreement on the employer to secure their objective without expending resources on case-by-case adjudication. When union representation was the dominant model of dispute resolution, employees derived institutional power from the unions. The union presence enhanced the leverage of workers with low-dollar value claims, and introduced, or brought to the surface, the risk of extra-legal disputes that might create serious industrial unrest if left unaddressed. Even where the courts sought to channel rights disputes into the contractual grievance and arbitration process, the threat of a work stoppage or of recurring difficulties on the shop floor created a powerful disincentive for employers to continue on a course of conduct opposed by the union.

By contrast, in a workplace without union representation, employees have much less institutional power. Where the employee does not have significant individual bargaining power, his or her sole means of imposing costs of disagreement on the employer is by quitting or threatening to sue the employer. Quitting is obviously costly and not likely to be pursued where jobs are scare. So, too, lawsuits by current employees are costly and not likely to be pursued, in part for fear of employer retaliation (Eigen, 2008). Rather, claims are asserted, if at all, only by former employees (Donohue and Siegelman, 1991). Even if we assume that the actions of former employees are likely to have important feedback effects that influence the relationship between current employees and the employer (Estreicher, 2010a), the individual-rights model has some obvious deficiencies. First, employees are not likely to obtain competent counsel for their retail claims. Second, the damages the employee might be able to levy against the employer are, for all practical purposes, tied directly to how much money the employee earns, suggesting that the prospect of a damages recovery, standing alone, may not always influence employer behavior. Finally, for all employees, regardless of earnings, there is no institutionalized means of bringing lawful non-legal pressure to bear on the employer.[1]

There are long-standing debates in the industrial relations literature implicated by these results and this chapter more broadly. For instance, is workplace conflict inevitable or is it something that may be reduced so that it becomes functionally non-existent? John R. Commons and Karl Marx disagreed on this point. Commons and his fellow "Institutionalists" believed that conflict is naturally occurring in the workplace, as it is a function of the division of labor. It therefore requires accommodation, but no ultimate solution that resolves to some utopian result; conflict is an ongoing part of work

(Commons, Saposs, Sumner, Mittelman, Hoagland, Andrews, and Perlman, 1946). Marx believed that there is no way of regulating conflict in an equitable or effective way via the law. He posited that conflict is a precursor of revolution stemming from the discord between labor and those who control the means of production and distribution. This chapter takes the view held by Commons that conflict is naturally occurring in the structure of work, and the law has a role to play in helping manage it effectively.

A related debate provoked by the rise and current dominance of the individual-rights model for adjudicating workplace disputes is the question of whether employee "voice" is important. Voice is the decision to complain about a perceived deteriorated condition or engage in individual or group activity to bring actual and desired conditions closer together, rather than to exit from the firm (Hirschman, 1970). Both voice and exit are alternative mechanisms for mediating conflicts between workers and their employer. Unions are conduits for employee voice for employees with a diminished exit option; the focus of their efforts are on "inframarginal" workers, i.e., those with little ability to exit the firm because their compensation, job security or other benefits are tied to length of service or because they have put down roots in the local community (Freeman and Medoff, 1984). Other theorists define voice as the ability to have meaningful input into decisions, and argue that voice is an "intrinsic standard of participation," meaning that it is an important end in itself for "rational human beings in a democratic society" (Budd, 2004: 13). For Budd, Clegg (1975), and Institutionalists like Commons, voice is an essential part of a vibrant, pluralist democracy. By contrast, for writers from the human resource management (HRM) perspective, voice is seen more in instrumental, functional terms, perhaps closer to Hirschman's. For these scholars, voice is nice, but not a necessary and important component of a viable workplace relations system, and therefore should not factor heavily in a normative discussion of how workplace rights disputes ought to be adjudicated. This view would suggest less of a focus on procedural fairness and perceived fairness. In any event, employee unwillingness to reveal true preferences, in part because of fear of employer retaliation and legal strictures against non-union representation, makes it very difficult to design a significant employee voice mechanism in a non-union environment (Dunlop, 1958; Estreicher, 1994; Leibowitz, 1998).

The current rights-based litigation system evolved out of the prior collective, labor-management system for adjudicating workplace disputes. The two parallel systems remain intact, although individual rights are now the dominant mode of dispute resolution. The rights-based litigation system is not an efficient means of resolving non-legal disputes or establishing new rules for regulation, because the system is almost entirely predicated on *legal* rights. It is slower and costlier than the collective method, allocating many of the costs of its administration to taxpayers and incurring the avoidable costs of an outside bureaucracy. It also lacks the intimate knowledge of industries' peculiarities, and flexible specialization of the "law of the shop" (Wheeler, Klaas, and Mahony, 2004). Some argue that the current system's lack of pluralistic, democratic employee voice carries significant negative implications and costs in terms of loyalty, productivity, and other important metrics (Kochan, Katz, and McKersie, 1986). But even if individual-right litigation is viewed exclusively as a system for resolving rights disputes, access costs reduce the likelihood of an adjudication on the merits in most cases. It is extremely difficult to obtain competent lawyers to represent even indisputably wronged employees who are not paid enough to warrant the attention of competent counsel (Sherwyn,

Tracy, and Eigen, 1999). The current system arguably sets different de facto standards of legal compliance for employers of low-wage earners versus high-wage earners. Lastly, the current system is better suited to terminated relationships, but relatively ill equipped to resolve disputes occurring in ongoing relationships (Eigen, 2008). Essentially, the individual-rights system is analogous to divorce proceedings, but does very little in the way of counseling couples interested in staying together.

But the current system is not all bad. There are some clear advantages to the individualized rights-based model. Most of these claimed benefits are based on the comparable advantage of judges and juries deciding employment matters. For instance, interpretation of the laws is relatively consistent because judges bound by precedent tend to interpret the law consistently across industries, employers and fact patterns. Significantly, the adjudicators (judges) are not chosen by the parties. This lends transparency to the process and reduces (if not eliminates) the oft-cited – in our view, overstated – disadvantage of arbitration as a means of resolving employment disputes – the so-called, "repeat-player effect" (Bingham, 1997; Bingham and Sarraf, 2004). On the other hand, a number of studies raise the question whether judges are unfairly biased against discrimination claimants (Clermont and Schwab, 2009).

The current rights-based system's means of resolving disputes affecting a group of employees is the class-action lawsuit. Proponents of this method of adjudicating workplace rights disputes make two empirical arguments for it as a superior means of resolving disputes, particularly as compared to arbitration. First, some assert that only class actions will afford relief to plaintiffs with claims that are too small to justify being brought individually. Second, it is argued that class actions provide an important means of enhancing employer compliance by reducing employers' abilities to benefit by delaying and forcing numerous plaintiffs to reprove the same facts or relitigate the same issues. However, it is unclear to what extent these claims are always true. In fact, there is evidence suggesting that, with the exception of certain wage and hour class actions brought under the Fair Labor Standards Act, or equivalent state statutes, the estimated individual recoveries would warrant the assertion of individual claims in an appropriately designed low-cost forum (Estreicher and Yost, 2009). Others question whether the class action is really the optimum means of eradicating discrimination or even addressing most of the rights-based problems in the contemporary workplace (Nielsen, Nelson, and Lancaster, 2010).

D.   The Diminished Significance of the Administrative Agency

The original conception of U.S. lawmakers (evidenced, for example, in the Fair Labor Standards Act of 1938) was that while there might be a modest role for the private lawsuit, the primary enforcement drive would come from a specialized administrative agency knowledgeable about technical and industry-specific issues and able, without regard to the earning power of the affected employees, to obtain not only recovery for the employees but also systemic relief capable of deterring future violations. Administrative agencies could also provide a special adjudicatory forum (evidenced, for example, in the National Labor Relations Act of 1935) that did not rely on the courts and would be less formal and forbidding to ordinary workers and their representatives.

Although administrative agencies continue to play an important role, the legislation of the 1960s and on has largely displaced the agency as the principal enforcers and adjudicators in favor of the private lawsuit and the courts. This has occurred in part because administrative agencies operate under significant budgetary restraints, which become even more limiting when government is controlled by opponents of the underlying legislation. Courts, on the other hand, operate under budgets that are not tied to particular legislation, and hence are less likely to come under the budgetary scrutiny of opponents of the legislation. There are also questions of public administration that suggest that agencies are not likely to be able to recruit and retain quality personnel to handle efficiently and fairly retail disputes. Like the class action plaintiff bar, the administrator is likely to focus on high-profile "impact" cases rather than address the needs of most workers.

E.   The Challenge of Employer-Initiated ADR

Paradoxically, the costs of the litigation system, coupled with fear of jury trials and class actions, have prompted many employers to unilaterally adopt systems of alternative dispute resolution (ADR) and other means of resolving rights-based workplace conflict such as human resource management (HRM).

Generally speaking, ADR includes two components: mediation and arbitration; some programs combine both, some use one to the exclusion of the other. Several surveys of participant experience with private mediation and arbitration show high levels of participant satisfaction (Lipsky and Seeber, 2006; Lipsky, Seeber, and Fincher, 2003). Introduction of an informal internal process or mediation before arbitration tends to increase participant satisfaction (Bendersky, 2003). A strength of employment mediation in particular is that it can help bridge power differentials, offering employees a useful mechanism to get their employer to listen to them, and enabling the parties to explore innovative solutions (Carnevale, 1986; Moore, 2003). Third-party assisted mediation can reduce barriers to conflict resolution by avoiding some of the perils of dyadic negotiations such as escalation of commitment and conflict spirals (Brett, Shapiro, and Lytle, 1998; Lewicki, Weiss, and Lewin, 1992).

Employment arbitration is the more controversial of the ADR components. Studies to date have reported on outcomes in arbitrations conducted under the auspices of the American Arbitration Association (AAA). The positive side is that arbitral proceedings are a good deal quicker than litigation, employees are more likely to be able to proceed pro se to hearing than they would in trials, and claimants earning lower salaries than plaintiff in employment law trials obtain hearings on the merits. On the other hand, claimant win rates and median awards in arbitration tend to be lower than plaintiff win rates and awards in court actions (Colvin, 2011; Sherwyn, Estreicher, and Heise, 2005). Sound comparisons between arbitration and litigation are difficult to make, however, because different types of cases and claimants may end up in arbitration than in litigation. Moreover, the intensive screening process that goes on during litigation suggests a more substantial winnowing-down process than occurs in arbitration. In addition, cases are more likely to go to hearing in arbitration irrespective of merit than would be true of the more expensive, more formal litigation process (Sherwyn, Estreicher, and Heise, 2005; Sherwyn, Tracy, and Eigen, 1999). Because the overall story is positive from the employee standpoint, some prominent early critics have reassessed their views of employment arbitration (St. Antoine, 2008).

A persistent criticism of employment arbitration is the so-called "repeat player effect"

– that is, because employers are like to face several claimants in the process, they will fare better than a single claimant who is a one-time player (Bingham, 1997). As a later study suggests (Bingham and Sarraf, 2004), the effect disappears when certain minimum rules of fairness, such as the widely adopted "Due Process Protocol," are observed. The repeat-player effect is, in any event, irrelevant to the present discussion because it simply reflects the advantages that large employers would have under any system, arbitration or litigation (Colvin, 2011). Whatever reputational and informational benefits the employer has are largely mirrored on the claimant side by the organized plaintiff employment bar (Estreicher, 1997; Estreicher, 2001). A claim that does point to a possible systematic advantage for employers is the "repeat arbitrator effect" – that is because the same arbitrator will be appearing in more than one dispute with the employer, that arbitrator might be inclined to give close calls to the employer (Colvin, 2011). This, too, can be minimized by appropriate disclosure rules.

Other research challenges head-on that employers are unfairly and systematically favored by neutral third parties in employment ADR over employees (Sherwyn, Tracy, and Eigen, 1999; Wheeler, Klaas, and Mahony, 2004). These researchers maintain that arbitrators tend to be retired judges and other long-time practitioners with interests in maintaining their established reputations for integrity and neutrality. Also, arbitrators are jointly selected by both sides. They are often not selected by employers or employees, as such, but by the legal counsel representing each party; lawyers are the real repeat players. As with the selection of labor arbitrators in a unionized context, each side's counsel is able to vet arbitrators based on available information. This system of bipartite selection reduces or eliminates the repeat-player effect when both employer and employee are represented by counsel. However, it does not eliminate the risk of bias when employees represent themselves or where arbitral rosters are skewed to favor employers.

Another criticism of employment arbitration is that it is being used by employers to immunize themselves from the deterrent effect of class actions (Gilles, 2005). Until the Supreme Court got involved, first reading silence in arbitration agreement as authorizing classwide arbitration and more recently reversing the presumption, arbitration was not commonly associated with class claims. Under the Court's recent *Stolt-Nielsen* (2010) ruling, silence in the agreement does not support arbitrator authority to proceed on a classwide basis. The Court will still, however, need to resolve whether employees covered by an otherwise binding arbitration agreement cannot be named representatives of, or otherwise participate in, a class action where the federal statute in question indicates a legislative policy favoring the class action mechanism for claims under that statute.

The overarching principle is that employer-provided employment arbitration of statutory claims involves only a change of forum – certainly, the loss of a civil jury trial – but no change in the substantive rights of employees (*Gilmer*, 1991). Although some employers may still try, most employers today understand that the arbitrator has to apply applicable law and award legally available remedies if violations are found.

The related concern is that employers have too much control, under current law, to customize an ADR system, and that ADR in its current incarnation reflects management fiat imposed as a condition of employment on job applicants and employees. For some, management control of program design may reduce the degree of employee trust in the process, the potential for expression of meaningful employee voice, and may reduce its perceived procedural fairness (Bingham, 1997; Eigen, 2008; Lipsky, Seeber, and Fincher,

2003; Stone, 1996). Existing employees are not likely to invoke the ADR system when they fear reprisal and conflict of interest, especially when the appeal procedure goes through the same decision makers who control employees' advancement in the firm (Rowe, 1997). A related weakness is the fact that employees in the non-union setting are often not represented by anyone, while the employer has the benefit of its human resources and legal departments.

In addition to ADR, HRM is often included in the array of models for reducing and resolving workplace disputes (McCabe and Lewin, 1992). HRM is construed broadly here to encompass work practices that emanate from the philosophy of conflict-avoidance in the workplace. As Kochan, Katz and McKersie put it, the aim of HRM is to "increase the participation and involvement of individuals and informal work groups so as to overcome adversarial relations and increase employee motivation, commitment, and problem-solving potential" (1986: 147). Examples of HRM practices aimed at reducing and resolving workplace conflict include quality of working life (QWL), quality circles (QC), employee involvement (EI), labor-management participation teams, and high-performance work systems (HPWS). As demonstrated by several empirical studies, these measures tend to have either a neutral or slightly positive effect on firm productivity, and a positive effect on employee attitudes, grievance and absenteeism rates (Freeman and Kleiner, 2000; Godard and Delaney, 2000; Kochan, Katz, and McKersie, 1986). Similarly, Spencer (1986) found a positive relationship between hospitals' adoption of HRM strategies like employee-management meetings, counseling services, ombudsman services, question and answer programs and survey feedback and employee satisfaction and high retention rates. Relying on British data, Bryson, Willman, Gomez and Kretschmer (2007) have demonstrated a similar, positive correlation between HRM and several key measures of reduced workplace conflict.

HRM does not itself supply a forum for adjudicating rights disputes but, like a well-functioning mediation, "open door," or ombudsman process (Rowe, 1997), it helps create a supportive environment to promote employee acceptance and utilization of the ADR system. It may also help identify and rectify causes of disputes before they blossom into more serious affairs (Ichniowski, Kochan, Levine, Olson, and Strauss, 1996). The strength of such systems ultimately rests on the degree to which employees are aware of their surroundings, identify themselves as individuals committed to their jobs and their employers, and employers make reciprocal commitments to their employees. Because HRM is likely to take root where the employment relationship is one of mutual trust and dependence, it is not surprising that positive employee attitudes toward HRM practices correspond with greater employee satisfaction and pluralistic democratic participation in work (Rusbult, Farrell, Rogers, and Mainus, 1988).

II. PROPOSED REFORM

A. Improvements Not Requiring Legislation

1. An updated due process protocol
In thinking of how to improve the current system, the initial focus should be on making improvements that do not require new legislation, which is politically difficult to achieve.

One such important first step is to build on the 1995 task force representing employer and employee representatives and arbitration service providers that promulgated "A Due Process Protocol for Mediation and Arbitration of Statutory Disputes Arising Out of the Employment Relationship" (Bales, 2005; Dunlop and Zack, 1997). The Due Process Protocol has been widely adopted by companies and, importantly, is used by the AAA and JAMS (Judicial Arbitration and Mediation Services) to screen the kinds of employer-promulgated ADR programs they are willing to administer.

As it has been fifteen years since its promulgation, the time is ripe for an updating of the Protocol, to capture the issues that have become salient in the interim. Everyone is going to have his or her own favorite list, but provisions rejecting employer-promulgated changes in the otherwise legally applicable limitations period and available statutory or contractual remedies should be featured. Also, employees should not be required to pay forum or arbitrators' fees if the arbitration is pursuant to an employer-promulgated agreement or program; the most an employee should have to pay would be the equivalent of court costs. In addition, the Protocol should develop tightened disclosure standards to require potential arbitrators to disclose any prior decisions or other ties involving the same employer or its representative or employee or his or her representative. The AAA has begun to publish its awards in redacted form. The revised protocol might state that such publication should be required as a condition of judicial enforcement. Such an admonition would not be binding on the courts, but would help promote best practices and may influence judicial standards (*Cole*, 1997).

The Equal Employment Opportunity Commission (EEOC), which enforces federal antidiscrimination in employment laws, and other federal and state agencies, should consider adopting a policy of abstaining from investigating any charge in which the charging party is subject to an arbitration agreement that complies with the revised Due Process Protocol. The agency would not be forswearing jurisdiction but, rather, deferring its action until completion of the ADR process. After an award has been rendered (and possibly after it has been confirmed), the agency might dismiss the charge (or, under certain statutes, issue a right-to-sue letter) if it approved the process and the result or bring an enforcement action if it found serious fault with either (*Waffle House*, 2001; Estreicher, 1990).

Work should be done, perhaps as part of the Protocol revision process, to facilitate research on employment ADR. For example, a tracking system should be implemented by the AAA, JAMS, and other participating arbitration service organizations to obtain data on the income of the claimant, whether the claimant is represented, whether the claimant had to go through some earlier process, such as mediation, before invoking arbitration, if the case settles (and for which relief), length and nature of any discovery. All of this can be done in a manner that preserves the anonymity of the parties.

2. Pro se representation

The major challenge for any ADR system is to reduce costs and complexity so that pro se claimants are able to participate meaningfully on their own in the adjudication. Perhaps as part of the revised protocol, any forum fee (to be paid by the employer) could pay for provision of a staff facilitator to help pro se claimants with pleadings, discovery notices and the like. An effort also should be made by the adherents to the Due Process Protocol to encourage pro bono offices of major law firms and clinics of major law schools to undertake the representation of relatively low-salaried claimants in the ADR process. Unions also may have a role to play in supplying representation.

B.   Legislated Improvements

On the legislative front, we oppose current efforts in Congress to amend the Federal Arbitration Act to prohibit predispute arbitration agreements (Rutledge, 2009). At least if applied in the employment context, this is a case of throwing out the baby with the bath water, as first argued more than a decade ago (Sherwyn, Tracy, and Eigen, 1999). Employment arbitration, if it is properly structured and regulated, improves the likelihood that employees, and most especially those who are relatively low-paid, will be able to obtain an adjudication on the merits of their rights disputes with the employer. Abolition of employment arbitration simply relegates those employees to the courts to fare as best they can on their own in a complex, formal litigation environment (Landsman, 2008).

Legislation abolishing predispute employment arbitration would not, of course, pre-clude employer-promulgated mediation programs. Even if mediation is required as a condition of employment, most claimant representatives will agree to mediation if the relevant statute of limitation is tolled. Although some employers rely on mediation alone (Malin, 2004), the question is whether most employers will be willing to pay for the costs of mediation if they cannot preclude a lawsuit in most cases. We believe most will not.

Based on what is practically and politically feasible as of this writing, employer-promulgated ADR should be the basis of an employment adjudication system that supplements the work of courts, administrative agencies and, in the union sector, the grievance and arbitration process. We say this because unless adequate resources are provided to administrative agency adjudicators or courts to handle responsibly the vast increase in self-represented employee claims – which we think unlikely – the appropri-ate legislative response even for critics of employer-promulgated ADR is to develop safeguards that help minimize their concerns without driving employers to abandon the process entirely.

If we were starting from scratch, we would be inclined to consider a system similar to Great Britain's. In the United Kingdom, complaints are initially referred to the Advisory, Conciliation and Arbitration Service (ACAS) for attempted conciliation. If unresolved, complaints are heard by tripartite industrial tribunals. Employees with less than fifty-two consecutive weeks of work are exempted from general statutory protection against unjust dismissal. The burden is on the employer to show a legitimate reason for the discharge, such as misconduct. The law has been interpreted to require only good faith and reasonable belief, not that the employee in fact committed the infraction (Estreicher, 2008). Unsatisfied employees may appeal tribunal decisions to an Employment Appeals Tribunal (EAT) and to courts of law for questions of law. While reinstatement is a pos-sible result, employees tend to prefer a monetary award (doubled where an order of reinstatement is rejected by the employer). Wrongful dismissal awards are subject to a statutory cap; discrimination awards are not. These awards tend to be modest – certainly by U.S. standards (Estreicher, 2008; Hirsch, 2013).

The UK approach started as a wrongful dismissal statute and over time also assumed adjudicatory authority over discrimination claims. The UK system mixes government-supplied mediation services with a tripartite government-funded, public adjudication. The system supersedes any common law cause of action for breach of the employment agreement and employment statutes; employment disputes that go to the regular civil courts are limited to libel and slander, certain torts and claims for injunctive relief for breach of restrictive covenants. Class actions are not authorized.

There may be some institutional features of the UK approach that are difficult to replicate here. One such feature is the tripartite adjudicatory structure used in England. With our low union density in private companies and the fact that employers tend not to form representative associations in the employment law field, it will take some ingenuity to develop a regularized procedure for selecting employer- and employee-side adjudicators.

The more difficult question is whether there is any political will to adopt something like the UK system. Lawyers representing employees would not necessarily oppose such legislation if they could remove all caps on recovery and retain their ability to bring lawsuits (including class actions) in the courts. Employers might support such legislation, if it did not include abolition of employment at will and there was some institutional guarantee of modest awards of the UK variety. Most employees, we believe, would be better off under the UK approach but we cannot get there politically. Therein lies the dilemma for law reform.

We do believe, however, that, working with what is in place at many companies, much can be done to improve employer-promulgated ADR to pick up many of the desirable features of the UK approach, but with an American flavor responsive to U.S. legal and popular culture.

NOTES

1.   Although certainly not an institutional means, one could argue that the increasingly available and low-cost option of publicizing information about employers via electronic outlets in real time presents a growing lawful, non-legal way of bringing pressure to bear on an employer. However, there are significant limitations to this mechanism. For instance, many employers are not in the public eye and are not worried about their public reputation (Estreicher, 2010a).

REFERENCES

Articles, Chapters and Books

Bales, Richard A. 2005. "The Employment Due Process Protocol at Ten: Twenty Unresolved Issues, and a Focus on Conflicts and Interests." 21 *Ohio State Journal on Dispute Resolution* 165–97.
Bendersky, Corrine. 2003. "Organizational Dispute Resolution Systems: A Complementarities Model." 28 *Academy of Management Review* 643–56.
Bingham, Lisa B. 1997. "Employment Arbitration: The Repeat Player Effect." 1 *Employee Rights and Employment Policy Journal* 189–220.
Bingham, Lisa B. and Shimon Sarraf. 2004. "Employment Arbitration before and after the Due Process Protocol for Mediation and Arbitration of Employment: Preliminary Evidence that Self-Regulation Makes a Difference," in Samuel Estreicher and David Sherwyn, eds., *Alternative Dispute Resolution in the Employment Arena: Proceedings of the New York University 53rd Annual Conference on Labor*, vol. 53, The Hague: Kluwer Law International.

Brett, Jeanne M., Debra L. Shapiro, and Anne L. Lytle. 1998. "Breaking the Bonds of Reciprocity in Negotiations." 41 *Academy of Management Journal* 410–24.

Bryson, Alex, Paul Willman, Rafael Gomez, and Tobias Kretschmer. 2007. "Employee Voice and Human Resource Management: An Empirical Analysis using British Data." *Research Discussion Papers, Policy Studies Institute.*

Budd, John W. 2004. *Employment with a Human Face: Balancing Efficiency, Equity, and Voice.* Ithaca, NY: ILR Press.

Carnevale, Peter. 1986. "Strategic Choice in Mediation." 2 *Negotiation* 41–56.

Clegg, H. A. 1975. "Pluralism in Industrial Relations." 13 *British Journal of Industrial Relations* 309–16.

Clermont, Kevin M. and Stewart J. Schwab. 2009. "Employment Discrimination Plaintiffs in Federal Court: From Bad to Worse?" 3 *Harvard Law and Policy Review* 3–35.

Colvin, Alexander J.S. 2011. "An Empirical Study of Employment Arbitration: Case Outcomes and Processes." 8 *Journal of Empirical Legal Studies* 1–23.

Commons, John R., David J. Saposs, Helen L. Sumner, E. B. Mittelman, H. E. Hoagland, John B. Andrews, and Selig Perlman. 1946. *History of Labour in the United States.* New York: Macmillan.

Cummins, Brendan D. and Bryan M. Seiler. 2010. "The Law of the Land in Labor Arbitration: The Impact of *14 Penn Plaza LLC v. Pyett.*" 25 *ABA Journal of Labor and Employment Law* 159–72.

Donohue, John J. and Peter Siegelman. 1991. "The Changing Nature of Employment Discrimination Litigation." 43 *Stanford Law Review* 983–1033.

Dunlop, John T. 1958. *Industrial Relations Systems.* New York: Holt.

Dunlop, John Thomas and Arnold M. Zack. 1997. *Mediation and Arbitration of Employment Disputes.* San Francisco: Jossey-Bass Publishers.

Eigen, Zev J. 2008. "The Devil in the Details: The Interrelationship among Citizenship, Rule of Law and Form-Adhesive Contracts." 41 *Connecticut Law Review* 1–50.

Estreicher, Samuel. 1990. "Arbitration of Employment Disputes without Unions." 66 *Chicago Kent Law Review* 753–97.

Estreicher, Samuel. 1994. "Employee Involvement and the 'Company Union' Prohibition: The Case for Partial Repeal of Section 8(a)(2) of the NLRA." 69 *New York University Law Review* 125–61.

Estreicher, Samuel. 1997. "Predispute Agreements to Arbitrate Statutory Employment Claims." 72 *New York University Law Review* 1344–75.

Estreicher, Samuel. 2001. "Saturns for Rickshaws: The Stakes in the Debate over Predispute Employment Arbitration Agreements." 16 *Ohio State Journal on Dispute Resolution* 559–70.

Estreicher, Samuel. 2005. "Beyond Cadillacs and Rickshaws: Towards a Culture of Citizen Service." 1 *New York University Journal of Law and Business* 323–34.

Estreicher, Samuel. 2008. "Unjust Dismissal Laws: Some Cautionary Notes," in S. Estreicher and M. Cherry, eds., *Global Issues in Employment Law.* St. Paul, MN: Thomson, West, pp. 74–85.

Estreicher, Samuel. 2009. "Think Global, Act Local: Employee Reputation in a World of Global Labor and Product Market Competition." 4 *Virginia Law & Business Review* 81–95.

Estreicher, Samuel. 2010a. "Employer Reputation at Work." 27 *Hofstra Labor & Employment Law Journal* 1–11.

Estreicher, Samuel. 2010b. "Trade Unionism under Globalization: The Demise of Voluntarism?" 54 *Saint Louis University Law Journal* 415–26.

Estreicher, Samuel and Kristina Yost. 2009. "Measuring the Value of Class and Collective Action Employment Settlements: A Preliminary Assessment." 6 *Journal of Empirical Legal Studies* 768–92.

Ewing, David. 1989. *Justice on the Job: Resolving Grievances in the Nonunion Workplace.* Cambridge, MA: Harvard Business School Press.

Freeman, Richard B. and Morris M. Kleiner. 2000. "Who Benefits Most from Employee Involvement: Firms or Workers?" 90 *American Economic Review* 219–23.

Freeman, Richard and James Medoff. 1984. *What do Unions Do?* New York: Basic Books.

Gilles, Myriam. 2005. "Opting Out of Liability: The Forthcoming, Near-Total Demise of the Modern Class Action." 104 *Michigan Law Review* 374–430.

Godard, John and John T. Delaney. 2000. "Reflections on the 'High-Performance' Paradigm's Implications for Industrial Relations as a Field." 53 *Industrial and Labor Relations Review* 482–502.

Green, Michael. 2012. "Reading *Ricci* and *Pyett* to Deliver Racial Justice Through Union Arbitration." 87 *Indiana Law Journal* 367–419.

Hadfield, Gillian. 2000. "The Price of Law: How the Market for Lawyers Distorts the Justice System." 98 *Michigan Law Review* 953–1006.

Hirsch, Jeffery N. 2013. "A Comparative Perspective on Unjust Dismissal Laws" in *Global Labor and Employment Law: Reports from Law Offices Worldwide (Samuel Estreicher & Michael J. Gray eds., 2014).*

Hirschman, Albert O. 1970. *Exit, Voice and Loyalty.* Cambridge, MA: Harvard University Press.

Ichniowski, Casey, Thomas A. Kochan, David Levine, Craig Olson, and George Strauss. 1996. "What Works at Work: Overview and Assessment." 35 *Industrial Relations* 299–333.

Kleiman, Bernard and Carl B. Frankel. 1975. "Seniority Remedies under Title VII: The Steele Consent Decree – Union Perspective," in Bruno Stein, ed., *Proceedings of New York University Twenty-Eighth Annual Conference of Law*. New York: Little, Brown.

Kochan, Thomas, Harry Katz, and Robert McKersie. 1986. *The Transformation of American Industrial Relations*. Ithaca, NY: ILR Press.

Landsman, Stephan. 2008. "The Growing Challenge of Pro Se Litigation." 13 *Lewis & Clark Law Review* 439–60.

Leibowitz, Ann G. 1998. "The 'Non-Union Union'?" in Samuel Estreicher, ed., *Employee Representation in the Emerging Workplace: Alternatives/Supplements to Collective Bargaining*, vol. 50. Cambridge, MA: Kluwer Law International, pp. 235–48.

Lewicki, Roy J., Stephen E. Weiss, and David Lewin. 1992. "Models of Conflict, Negotiation and Third Party Intervention: A Review and Synthesis." 13 *Journal of Organizational Behavior* 209–52.

Lipsky, David B. and Ronald L. Seeber. 2006. "Managing Organizational Conflicts," in John G. Oetzel and Stella Ting-Toomey, eds., *The Sage Handbook of Conflict Communication: Integrating Theory, Research, and Practice*. Thousand Oaks, CA: Sage Publications.

Lipsky, David B., Ronald L. Seeber, and Richard D. Fincher. 2003. *Emerging Systems for Managing Workplace Conflict: Lessons from American Corporations for Managers and Dispute Resolution Professionals*. San Francisco: Jossey-Bass.

Malamud, Deborah. 2005. "The Story of *Steele v. Louisville & Nashville Railroad*: White Unions, Black Unions, and the Struggle for Racial Justice on the Rails," in Laura J. Copper and Catherine L. Fisk, eds., *Labor Law Stories*. New York: Foundation Press.

Malin, Donna M. 2004. "Johnson & Johnson's Dispute Resolution Program: A New Formula for Achieving Common Ground," in Samuel Estreicher and David S. Sherwyn, eds., *Alternative Dispute Resolution in the Employment Arena: Proceedings of New York University 53rd Annual Conference on Labor*, vol. 53. The Hague: Kluwer Law International, pp. 235 –42.

McCabe, Douglas M. and David Lewin. 1992. "Employee Voice: A Human Resource Management Perspective." 34 *California Management Review* 112–23.

Merry, Sally Engle. 1990. *Getting Justice and Getting Even: Legal Consciousness among Working-Class Americans*. Chicago: The University of Chicago Press.

Merry, Sally Engle and Susan S. Silbey. 1984. "What Do Plaintiffs Want: Reexamining the Concept of Dispute." 9 *The Justice System Journal* 151–78.

Moore, Christopher W. 2003. *The Mediation Process*. San Francisco: Jossey-Bass.

Nielsen, Laura Beth, Robert L. Nelson, and Ryon Lancaster. 2010. "Individual Justice or Collective Mobilization? Employment Discrimination Litigation in the Post Civil Rights United States." 7 *Journal of Empirical Legal Studies* 175–201.

Rosenberg, David and Steven Shavell. 2006. "A Solution to the Problem of Nuisance Suits: The Option to Have the Court Bar Settlement." 26 *International Review of Law and Economics* 42–51.

Rowe, Mary. 1997. "Dispute Resolution in the Non-Union Environment," in S. E. Gleason, ed., *Workplace Dispute Resolution: Directions for the Twenty-First Century*. East Lansing, MI: Michigan State University Press.

Rusbult, C. E., D. Farrell, G. Rogers, and A. G. Mainus. 1988. "The Impact of Exchange Variables on Exit, Voice, Loyalty, and Neglect: An Integrative Model of Responses to Declining Job Satisfaction." 31 *Academy of Management Journal* 599–627.

Rutledge, Peter B. 2009. "Arbitration Reform: What we Know and What we Need to Know." 10 *Cardozo Journal of Conflict Resolution* 579–86.

Sherwyn, David S., Samuel Estreicher, and Michael Heise. 2005. "Assessing the Case for Employment Arbitration: A New Path for Empirical Research." 57 *Stanford Law Review* 1557–91.

Sherwyn, David S., J. B. Tracy, and Zev J. Eigen. 1999. "In Defense of Mandatory Arbitration of Employment Disputes: Saving the Baby, Tossing Out the Bathwater and Constructing a New Sink in the Process." 2 *University of Pennsylvania Journal of Labor and Employment Law* 73–150.

Spencer, Daniel G. 1986. "Employee Voice and Employee Retention." 29 *Academy of Management Journal* 488–502.

St. Antoine, Theodore J. 2008. "Mandatory Arbitration: Why it's Better than it Looks." 41 *University of Michigan Journal of Law Reform* 783–812.

Stone, Katherine V. W. 1996. "Mandatory Arbitration of Individual Employment Rights: The Yellow Dog Contract of the 1990s." 73 *University of Denver Law Review* 1017–50.

Summers, Clyde W. 1977. "The Individual Employee's Rights under Collective Agreement: What Constitutes Fair Representation?" 126 *University of Pennsylvania Law Review* 251–80.

Tucker, Sean and Alex Mucalov. 2010. "Industrial Voluntarism in Canada." 65 *Industrial Relations Quarterly Review* 215–35.
Wheeler, Hoyt N., Brian S. Klaas, and Douglas M. Mahony. 2004. *Workplace Justice Without Unions.* Kalamazoo, MI: W.E. Upjohn Institute for Employment Research.

Court Decisions

Cole v. Burns Int'l Sec. Servs., 105 F.3d 1465 (D.C. Cir. 1997).
EEOC v. Waffle House, Inc., 534 U.S. 279 (2002).
14 Penn Plaza, LLC v. Pyett, 129 S. Ct. 1456 (2009).
Gilmer v. Interstate/Johnson Lane Co., 500 U.S. 20 (1991).
Goodman v. Lukens Steel Co., 482 U.S. 656 (1987).
Stolt-Nielsen S.A. v. AnimalFeeds Int'l Corp., 130 S. Ct. 1758 (2010).

PART IV

CONCLUDING PERSPECTIVES

15. The striking success of the National Labor Relations Act
Michael L. Wachter[1]

INTRODUCTION

In the United States today, less than 10 percent of private sector employment is union-ized.[2] After peaking at 35 percent of employment in the early 1950s, union membership has been in decline for the last 59 years. This decline represents one of the most impor-tant institutional shifts in the United States economy. Reflecting this decline, a common theme among academic legal commentators is that the law governing unionization and collective bargaining, the National Labor Relations Act (NLRA), has been a terrible failure. In this chapter I will make the counter-claim – that the NLRA has been largely successful and in one key area exceedingly successful. Its presumed failure, if the word failure needs to be maintained, is largely due to its successes.

Before judging the NLRA to be a success or failure, measures of success have to be identified. I will judge the success of the NLRA by whether the two explicit goals of the Wagner Act of 1935 have been achieved. The goals are industrial peace and a greater balance in bargaining power between employers and employees.

The first of the goals is industrial peace. The preamble of the Wagner Act starts by identifying that the "denial by some employers of the right of employees to orga-nize" and bargain collectively had led "to strikes and other forms of industrial strife or unrest."[3] Industrial strife and unrest at the time of the passage of the Wagner Act meant more than the inconvenient strikes that we sometimes experience today. Instead, it meant violent strikes that paralyzed the national economy and frequently required the deployment of the National Guard or federal troops to restore order. Indeed, in the midst of the Great Depression the question was whether the then-prevailing political economy would survive. Critical to the stability of the political economy was adopting a legal regime for labor that would replace industrial strife with industrial peace.

A second goal is to redress "inequality of bargaining power." In the words of the Act, "[t]he inequality of bargaining power ... substantially burdens and affects the flow of commerce, and tends to aggravate recurrent business depressions, by depress-ing wage rates and the purchasing power of wage earners in industry and by preventing the stabilization of competitive wage rates and working conditions within and between industries."[4] The goal was not true equality but rather giving employees meaningful bargaining power.

To evaluate the success of the NLRA, I will treat it as one of four alternative legal regimes, all of which have actually existed in the United States since the beginning of the New Deal, and will ask which of the four is most likely to achieve the two goals. In terms of terminology, I note that the NLRA has been amended several times since the original

Act – the Wagner Act – was first passed in 1935. When I use the term NLRA, I refer to the labor law as it exists today.

The first of the alternative legal regimes is the National Industrial Recovery Act (NIRA) of 1933, which was the first attempt in the United States to give workers the right to act in concert without employer interference and to encourage collective bargaining. The second is the original NLRA – the Wagner Act – as passed in 1935. The third is today's NLRA, which includes the major Taft-Hartley Amendments of 1947. The fourth legal regime is the patchwork of employment laws that regulate today's non-union sector.

It is also useful to think of these legal regimes as constituting alternative political economies. Here the four legal regimes constitute three alternative political economies since the NLRA of today and the non-union sector of today constitute a single political economy. Since both the NIRA and the Wagner Act envisioned widespread unionization, I do not discuss the non-union sectors that co-existed when those laws were in effect.

In addition, each of the four legal regimes corresponds with a distinct economic model. The economic model of the NIRA was cartelization, where both wages and prices were set collectively with government oversight. The economic model of the Wagner Act was also a cartelization model, but only of the labor market. It was envisioned that collective bargaining would become the primary vehicle for wage setting and would, in time, embrace most eligible workers. Hence, wages would be set by the dictates of the collective bargaining process and not the dictates of the marketplace. Unions would have monopoly power in the labor market, but firms would not have monopoly power in their product markets.

The third legal regime is the modern NLRA, which includes the Taft-Hartley Amendments. That legal regime envisioned that unionization would not spread throughout the economy and that non-union employers would emerge within each industry to compete with unionized employers. The resulting model has a union sector where wages are set by collective bargaining and a non-union sector where wages are set competitively.

The fourth legal regime is today's non-union sector. The economic model that fits the non-union sector is the competitive model, but with an important twist. Competition operates in the external labor market (ELM) where firms seek workers and workers seek jobs. Wages overall are set competitively in the ELM. However, after being hired, an employee works inside a firm, and the firm can be viewed as having its own internal labor market (ILM). The ILM inside non-union firms is a complex organizational structure where norms rather than legal rules prevail.[5] Importantly, the ILM is not a textbook competitive model. In addition to the norms of the ILM, the employment relationship is regulated by statutory rules that govern the entire labor force, such as the Fair Labor Standards Act (FLSA), the Occupational Safety and Health Act (OSHA) and the Employee Retirement Income Security Act (ERISA). These statutory regulations govern both the union and the non-union labor market, but I discuss them as part of the non-union market.

The analysis below proceeds as follows: In section I, I analyze in depth the two goals of the NLRA: first, industrial peace and, second, equalization of bargaining power. Since the former emerges as the key of the two goals, section II presents a history of the major events whereby industrial strife was slowly replaced by industrial peace. The industrial strife of this period was marked by strikes of uncertain legal standing which often turned violent. In section III, I present the four legal regimes, introduced above, describing their main features and matching each with an economic model that captures the spirit of the legal regime. In section IV, I evaluate the success of the four legal regimes in achieving the goals of industrial peace and equalization of bargaining power. Section V concludes with the claim that today's NLRA can be judged to be successful because of the sharp decline in strike activity and related violence. In addition, perhaps unexpectedly, the non-union sector has become a vibrant part of the American economy. I argue that the success of the non-union sector is partly a result of the incentives created by the NLRA, which gives an escape valve for poorly treated non-union workers and a costly penalty to non-union opportunistic employers.

I. THE BROAD GOALS OF THE NLRA

A. Industrial Peace

The preamble of the Wagner Act first lists the goal of reducing industrial strife. On one level, this goal means reducing the number of strikes or the economic effects of strikes. But that barely scratches the surface of this goal. Industrial strife in the late 19th and early 20th centuries went far deeper, raising the question of whether the employees would accept the basic rules of the game. For instance, would workers cooperate in a political economy that did not provide for a legally protected right to organize and to strike? Would workers act to change the political system itself, whether lawfully or not, if their key demands were not respected? Would the United States electorate tolerate a political economy that regularly needed to call on the National Guard or federal troops to be deployed in American cities to break strikes, often using lethal force in the process?

Not only was industrial peace given top billing by the Act itself, it was also specifically cited as the basis for declaring the Act constitutional. In *Jones & Laughlin Steel* the Supreme Court spoke of the deleterious impact of industrial strife on interstate commerce, noting especially the immediate and potentially catastrophic effects of a steel strike on the economy.[6]

Prior to 1932, there was no federal legal right to strike, even peacefully; and indeed many strikes were illegal under state law or the federal common law followed in federal courts.[7] Employers often required that workers agree not to join a union or be involved in union activities during the term of their employment, and the federal courts held such agreements binding. Concerted activity by employees was not protected. If workers went out on strike and did not return to work when served with a state court ordered injunction, the striking workers were in contempt of court.[8] When confronted by police or Pinkerton guards, strikes would often turn violent. The next move in many strikes was for the state governor to call out the National Guard to restore order.

In the Great Railroad Strike of 1877 federal troops were deployed in six states in major cities, including Baltimore, Pittsburgh, Chicago and St. Louis. Striking workers often resisted, resulting in considerable violence and many deaths. Certainly one could understand President Rutherford Hayes' concern that a revolution might be in the making (Brecher, 1997; Zinn, 2003).[9] Imagine that scene today playing out on television and the

Internet. Industrial turmoil persisted well into the 20th century, as demonstrated below, further underscoring the desire to achieve industrial peace.

Hence, when I use the term "industrial peace" to describe what Congress was seeking, I am not only referring to a reduction in the number of work days lost from peaceful and lawful work stoppages. My focus is – and Congress' focus was – on the unrest that led to riots and to the eventual use of police or military force to restore order.

A legal regime was needed to legitimize both unionization and strikes, but also to steer those activities into peaceful channels. In this chapter I will focus on this first goal of industrial peace because it was arguably the most important in terms of the workings of the economic system.

B.   Equality of Bargaining Power

A second goal of unions is to redress "inequality of bargaining power."[10] Whereas the goal of industrial peace is straightforward, the same is not true of the equality of bargaining power. Indeed, the goal is not only complex, but also based on a flawed theory of economics, and, as a consequence, is internally inconsistent.

First, the goal is complex because it has both procedural and substantive elements. On the procedural element, Senator Wagner himself said that the goal was satisfied if workers were represented by unions. I will adopt Senator Wagner's interpretation by equating the procedural element with workers' achievement of collective bargaining status.[11] This provides a clear and measurable goal. The greater the percentage of workers belonging to unions and engaging in collective bargaining, the more successful is the Act. Hereafter, I use the term "union density" to denote the percentage of workers who belong to unions.

The substantive element is raising wages, which it was hoped would reduce the likelihood or severity of depressions. The traditional indicator of whether unions raise wages is the union wage premium, or the percentage difference between the union wage and the non-union wage.[12] Collective bargaining and higher wages were linked. It was always understood that the collectively bargained wage would be higher than the wage achieved in the non-union sector.

At this point in the analysis the goal, albeit complex, can be cabined in what appears to be a consistent manner. Simply stated, the procedural goal is achieved when workers join unions and engage in collective bargaining and the substantive goal is achieved when the collectively bargained wage is set above otherwise-prevailing wages in an unorganized labor market. But that understanding of the second goal of the Act brings us to a problem that is not easily resolved. The Wagner Act was passed in 1937, before the development of the neoclassical model of economics and the modern theory of business cycles. Fundamentally the second goal of the Wagner Act was based on flawed and now outdated theories of wage determination and of business cycles.

The labor market analysis at the time of the Great Depression was still rooted in the theories of Thomas Malthus and John R. Commons. Malthus claimed that population growth would always leave a pool of unemployed workers that would keep wages at the subsistence level (Malthus, 1803). John R. Commons, one of the original giants of industrial relations, extended the claim, saying that "cutthroat competition" among workers set the market wage at the wage that the "cheapest laborer" would be willing to accept

(Commons and Andrews, 1927). To remedy the problem, unions were needed to address the inequality of bargaining power.[13]

The modern concept of competitive labor markets was undeveloped at this time. It was not until 1932 that John Hicks published *The Theory of Wages* and laid the framework for the neoclassical theory of wage determination; and it was several decades later before it became widely known or accepted (Hicks, 1963). In the modern theory of wage determination, the competitive wage is the wage that equates supply and demand. Both employers and employees are "price takers;" neither exercises bargaining power. The competitive wage may be a depressed wage in terms of some norm of acceptable living conditions, but it is the market outcome. But the conventional wisdom among policymakers when labor law was being developed in the 1930s was that of Commons and not Hicks.[14]

The business cycle language of the Act creates problems as well in light of modern neoclassical economic theory. The statutory language looks to unions to raise wages to counter an ongoing deflationary cycle where declining wages result in under-consumption and thus increased unemployment. The under-consumption story was a neat one but there was never any solid economic support for it,[15] and it was in the course of being replaced by Keynesian economics even as the Act was passed. Keynesian economics posited that a combination of fiscal and monetary policy could reduce the severity of business cycles and maintain wages. That theory has been applied with considerable success ever since.

Today's economics textbooks do not refer to "under-consumption" and there is no business cycle theory that utilizes it. Mark Barenberg (1993) investigated the under-consumption story and confirmed these conclusions; he referred to under-consumption as part "of the popular 'new economics,' but it was the new economics of the 1920s."

C. What Do We Make of the Two Goals?

Two alternative stories can be told in putting these two goals together. The first story is the one told by the framers of the Wagner Act. Industrial peace is an important, clear, and coherent goal of the Wagner Act. Moving from a regime of violent strikes and industrial strife to one of industrial peace is an extraordinarily important goal, if it can be achieved. Replacing industrial strife and unrest with industrial peace makes both employers and employees better off, and has enormous benefits for social welfare. On the other hand, a violent regime of illegal strikes, riots and the recurring exercise of police power bears the hallmarks of a failed industrial relations system.

In this story, the goal of equalization of bargaining power seems to fit neatly with the goal of industrial peace. Workers needed the protection of a collective bargaining apparatus that could resolve labor disputes peacefully. With this interpretation of the equalization of bargaining power, the two goals are complementary and both are needed for either to be realized.

The second story reaches a very different conclusion, at least in a competitive economy. First, by the lights of neoclassical economic theory, the procedural and substantive aspects of the goal of equalizing bargaining power are inconsistent. The higher the union wage, the lower is the level of employment in the union sector. The substantive goal of a high wage thus pulls in one direction, while the procedural goal of more workers·covered by collective bargaining pulls in the other direction. Second, there is a potential inconsistency between the substantive goal of higher union wages and the goal of industrial peace. The higher the union wage level rises above the non-union wage, the greater will be the opposition of management to paying union demands (and indeed to union organizing efforts generally), thus resulting in a greater likelihood of strikes.

The inconsistency in the goals, however, depends very much on the political economy: the more competitive the economy, the greater the inconsistency. In a competitive economy there would be a strong tradeoff between higher union wages and high rates of unionization, because both cannot be maintained.[16] If the political economy is less competitive, the tradeoff is less dramatic: the greater the degree of cartelization of markets, the greater the ability to achieve both goals at the same time. And that indeed was the nature of the political economy envisioned by President Roosevelt's first New Deal legislative agenda. But the U.S. economy has become increasingly competitive since the New Deal, with the shift away from a coordinated economy and toward a commitment to antitrust principles and with the rise of deregulation and liberal trade policies. In this new environment, the tradeoff between higher union wage rates and union density has become sharper. The substantive and procedural dimensions of the goal of increasing workers' bargaining power have become irreconcilable.

The complexities and potential inconsistencies inherent in this second goal of the NLRA is one reason for emphasizing the more straightforward goal of industrial peace. But another reason lies in the dramatic statutory revisions of 1947. When Congress enacted the Taft-Hartley Amendments to the NLRA, there was little question that it was seeking to promote industrial peace, and to confine the scope and conduct of labor disputes, even at the obvious cost of curbing unions' bargaining power. So it is fair to say that industrial peace was the one goal shared by the congressional majorities that passed the Wagner Act and the Taft-Hartley Amendments.

II.   INDUSTRIAL STRIFE

This section focuses on the meaning of industrial peace and its opposite, industrial strife. The section develops the meaning of industrial peace through a brief historical narrative. Unlike the decades that are chronicled in this section, the United States today has little or no industrial strife. Consequently, it may be difficult for us to picture the state of industrial relations in the decades beginning with the railroad strikes of 1877 running through the passage of the Taft-Hartley Amendments of 1947.

The genius of the labor law reforms of the 1930s and 1940s lay in the fact that through trial and error they replaced a system marked by violent confrontational labor-management strife with a system where disagreements were channeled into a peaceful mechanism that avoided major disruptions to interstate commerce. Although a full survey of U.S. labor history is beyond the scope of this chapter, well-recognized and readily available scholarly references develop a good picture of the state of industrial and labor relations during this period. However, in order to assess the labor laws' objective of industrial peace, it is helpful to review what "industrial conflict" actually meant in the decades leading up to the period of major national labor legislation.

The violent strikes of the late 19th and early 20th centuries had a choreography of their own. Companies frequently employed their own security forces to defeat strikes, whether the strikes were legal or not. In that setting, the strikes often led to violence and confrontations with local police. If the local police were unable to contain the violence and the riot conditions that sometimes developed, the governors of the affected states or the president would call out the National Guard or federal troops. The result would be a violent one, often with some deaths, before the military was able to restore order. To the authors of the Wagner Act, industrial strife did not mean orderly strikes. Instead it meant violence and, in the extreme, riots that had the potential to paralyze an entire city or region.

The meaning of industrial strife in the 1930s was informed by a 70-year period of disruptive labor-management strife. The Great Railroad Strike began in 1877 in the midst of a severe national depression that led to deflation in prices and wages (Dubofsky, 1994). After the Baltimore and Ohio Railroad cut wages and intensified workloads, workers went on strike in West Virginia and disrupted the movement of train traffic. Fighting began in West Virginia where state officers determined that they lacked sufficient police power to resume train traffic; they asked for the aid of the federal militia to end the strike (Dubofsky, 1994). Although federal troops successfully restored order in West Virginia, violence intensified as the railroad strike spread to three other states. The arrival of state militia initiated street battles between the troops and strikers. On several of these occasions, employers called in the Pinkerton Detective Agency, which supplied spies, agents, and private armed forces ready and willing to combat unruly workers. Many blame their aggressive tactics for intensifying the fighting.

The conflict soon spread beyond West Virginia. For nearly two days Pittsburgh was known as the "smoky city" as nearly 80 buildings were burned, over 2,000 railroad cars were destroyed, and 24 people were left dead (Brecher, 1997). Before the strike ended, it had spread to other cities, including Baltimore, Cincinnati, Chicago and St. Louis. The state militia failed in its efforts to retain order in almost every instance, leading state officials to request federal military intervention. President Hayes granted all of these requests and dispatched federal troops to six states.

Labor unrest was hardly limited to the railroads. As organized labor quickly grew in size, reaching nearly 3 million members shortly after the turn of the century, the incidence of strikes and violence also increased. A few other examples of the strike scene in the United States prior to the New Deal illustrate this point. From 1903–05 the Colorado mining industry was immersed in a war between management and workers over wages. Unable to control the strike, the governor declared martial law and federal troops were used to break the strike at the request of management. The period between 1910 and 1915 was commonly referred to as an "age of industrial violence" as unions struck back at anti-union employers, culminating in the 1910 bombing of the *Los Angeles Times* building. After America declared war in 1917, more than 4,000 strikes broke out involving over 1 million workers. Citywide strikes broke out in cities such as Springfield, Illinois; Kansas City, Missouri; Waco, Texas; and Billings, Montana (Brecher, 1997).

The primary legal tactic adopted by employers prior to the New Deal was the labor injunction. It was a highly effective tool to cripple or end strikes.[17] If an employer whose facilities were affected by a strike could allege a danger of irreparable injury that was too imminent to risk delay, a judge could issue a temporary restraining order pending a preliminary hearing. The preliminary hearings often resulted in the issuance of a temporary injunction on the basis of employers' allegations alone (Summers, Wellington and Hyde,

1982). Judges had wide discretion in granting injunctions and employers often succeeded in their attempt to choose a pro-business judge. Once an injunction was issued, workers who continued to pursue the strike might find themselves in contempt of court, and thrown in jail without a jury trial; or they might respond with violence when the authorities sought to enforce the judicial action. But if the workers abided by the preliminary injunction and suspended their strike, the cause was often lost before the case could be heard on the merits.

Industrial strife worsened during and in the aftermath of World War I. First, the shortage of workers during World War I helped galvanize unions to push for higher wages, and, in addition, the number of workers who belonged to unions increased sharply. In this regard, the year 1919 was pivotal. There were 3,000 strikes involving 4 million workers, many involving mass riots and bombings. Even the police walked out in the dramatic Boston police strike. A major strike involving steel workers was broken up by federal troops and U.S. marshals. Widespread strike activity broke out again during the summer of 1922 among the coal miners and the railroad shop craft workers (Dubofsky, 1994). More specifically, the coal miners' strike of 1922 was considered one of the largest strikes in American history, comprising workers in both bituminous and anthracite mines. The early 1920s also saw the first national railroad strike since 1894, comprising 400,000 railroad shopmen and non-operating railroad workers.

Adding to the tension and the political stakes, two American communist parties appeared, both with some presence in the growing labor movement. Many business and political leaders feared that labor demands might become more broadly political and less narrowly tied to improving wages and working conditions (Dubofsky, 1994). Violent strikes where federal troops or National Guard units were deployed might enflame the more radical elements in the labor movement that aimed to change the political regime. To the political establishment, the need for a peaceful resolution of labor strife became more vital than ever.

The transformational decade for organized labor came with the Great Depression. As the Depression set in, public demands for federal intervention and reform brought Franklin Roosevelt to the presidency. The new Democratic administration sought substantive labor law reform that might avoid the strife that would likely accompany the severe downturn in business. The result was the National Industrial Recovery Act (NIRA) of 1933. The Act guaranteed workers minimum wages, maximum hours, and the right to form unions (Dubofsky, 1994).

Rather than bringing industrial peace, the legislative gains for unions resulted in more organizing activity, which itself became a major source of industrial strife. Worker militancy increased as unions demanded the right to bargain collectively and employers remained equally adamant in resisting labor's efforts (Dubofsky, 1994). Labor historian Irving Bernstein (1970) describes the industrial struggle during this period as including "strikes and social upheavals of extraordinary importance, drama, and violence which ripped the cloak of civilized decorum from society, leaving exposed naked class conflict."

Roosevelt attempted to calm the industrial strife with the creation of the National Labor Board (NLB). Although the NLB did have some success, it ultimately lacked the power needed to successfully resolve disputes (Dubofsky, 1994). Hopes for industrial peace ended when mass violence broke out in Toledo during the auto-parts worker strike of 1934 (Bernstein, 1970). Demanding a wage increase and union recognition, workers took to the streets to picket in mass numbers and to block the plant. Facing a crowd of 10,000, police attempted to enforce an injunction that limited the number of picketers. Fighting erupted when police attempted to arrest five picketers (Bernstein, 1970). The struggle continued over the next few days as tear gas, gunfire, and flying bricks left numerous people seriously injured. The arrival of the National Guard initially intensified the fighting, wounding 15 and killing two, but their presence eventually calmed the situation (Bernstein, 1970).

Similar struggles broke out across the country the following year. Coal miners and truckers in Minneapolis and longshoremen in San Francisco waged bloody battles for recognition, while a cotton and textile strike spread from Maine to Alabama. With over 400,000 strikers, and crowds nearly impossible to control, battles commenced on the streets of many of the nation's cities. Strikers struggled with police, using clubs, baseball bats and pipes, while newspapers denounced strikers, running publications with the headline "Communists capturing our streets." As casualty numbers mounted, the National Guard was summoned to restore order on all three occasions (Bernstein, 1970). On May 27, 1935, the Supreme Court found the NIRA unconstitutional in *Schechter*.

The passage of the National Labor Relations Act (NLRA) in 1935 was thus President Roosevelt's second attempt. Conditions did improve in some ways – in terms of enabling employees to form unions and seek bargaining. But industrial strife continued. Unions were emboldened by the new legislative endorsement of collective bargaining, while hostile employers refused to abide by the new legislative restrictions, assuming that the NLRA, like the NIRA, would also be declared unconstitutional by the Supreme Court (Gross, 1974). Finally, in 1937, the Court upheld the constitutionality of the NLRA, based on a massive factual record detailing past industrial strife and its disastrous effect on interstate commerce (Gross, 1974).

The Supreme Court's ruling in favor of the NLRA curbed the concerted employer defiance of the Act, but it did not succeed in achieving industrial peace. In late 1937, steelworkers waged battle against the steel companies across four states. Violence broke out as police attempted to disperse a massive crowd of strikers. In Chicago, fighting turned deadly. On a day known in labor history as the "Memorial Day Massacre," police killed ten strikers and wounded dozens (Dubofsky, 1994). Also in 1937, a wave of sit-down strikes involved close to 400,000 workers (Brecher, 1997). The union victory in the General Motors sit-down of 1937 turned the sit-down into a popular strike device. The Ford Motor Company experienced mass picketing at its River Rouge plant in the spring of 1941 after it failed to enter into negotiations with the United Auto Workers (UAW) (Bernstein, 1970). As workers attempted to organize, management did everything in its power to prevent unionization. Armed with baseball bats and clubs, union picketers took on Ford's special police, who attacked their picket lines with bars and knives (Bernstein, 1970).

While workers were fighting for recognition, newly forming industrial unions were battling the traditional craft unions for members at both the workplace and federation levels. Although the leaders of the Congress of Industrial Organizations (CIO) once proclaimed themselves allies to the American Federation of Labor (AFL), their affiliation with the AFL quickly crumbled, and the AFL and the CIO began to compete over membership (Bernstein, 1970; Dubofsky, 1994). The CIO supported industrial unionism

(Bernstein, 1970); it represented the more diverse and porous ranks of industrial workers, and became known for its more militant and socially conscious labor strategies. In contrast, the AFL largely kept to its practice of craft unionism and the representation of skilled workers (Dubofsky, 1994). The internecine conflict between the AFL and the CIO only added to the level of industrial turbulence at the time.

When the United States became involved in World War II, President Roosevelt met with the nation's top labor and corporate leaders to develop a wartime labor relations system. The AFL and the CIO put their differences aside for the moment, and all parties agreed to condemn lockouts and strikes for the duration of the war (Dubofsky, 1994). Although initially a success, the wartime system quickly crumbled. By 1943 workers were engaged in a wave of unauthorized wildcat strikes that threatened production (Dubofsky, 1994). The strikes were unauthorized, but the unions often used the resulting instability to increase their contract demands (Dubofsky, 1994). After several wartime strikes that outlasted his mediation efforts, an angry Roosevelt condemned the "selfish preoccupations of civilians" and in 1944 supported a National Service Act that would require Americans to either work or fight (Blum, 1976).

The War Labor Board attempted to resolve industrial disputes without strikes or lockouts. But when dispute resolution failed, the government had a new policy option to help the parties resolve their disputes: executive orders allowing the government to seize companies.[18] During the war, there were no fewer than 18 executive orders centering on labor regulation (Sparrow, 1996). President Roosevelt and President Truman conducted 71 industrial seizures (Sparrow, 1996). In fact, the number of seizures increased during each year of the war, and peaked in fiscal year 1944 and fiscal year 1945 (Sparrow, 1996).[19] Of the top 100 American corporations, more than one-third were seized either in whole or in part (Sparrow, 1996). Among those seized were railroads, coalmines, and even the Montgomery Ward department store (Perrett, 1973).

Roosevelt was not the only one frustrated by union demands. By the end of the war many members of Congress and voters no longer viewed organized labor as the underdog it had once been in the 1930s. Rather, it was seen by many, including some of its erstwhile allies, as abusing its new powers (Dubofsky, 1994). Political and public frustration with labor's tactics after World War II, along with Republicans' sweep of Congress in 1946, led to the passage of the Taft-Hartley Amendments in 1947, which had the votes to overcome President Truman's veto of the legislation.

The passage of the Taft-Hartley Amendments marked a major change in the legal regime and political economy established by the Wagner Act. The Taft-Hartley Act reframed the basic policy of the NLRA from one of encouraging unionization and collective bargaining to one of neutrality, and of protecting employees' choice to unionize or not. It also matched the original set of employer unfair labor practices with a set of union unfair labor practices that arguably targeted labor's most effective and disruptive economic tactics – the very tactics that had proven most effective in enhancing unions' bargaining power.

Industrial peace would continue to be elusive for several years, but the passage of Taft-Hartley was the historical marker that represented the peak in industrial strife. Strikes thereafter were largely peaceful and more narrowly confined to the immediate parties involved in the labor disputes. Moreover, in the emerging postwar prosperity, the public attitude toward unions and the ongoing frequent strike activity turned from being supportive to being opposed. Overall there was a political shift toward conservatism that undercut public support for unions.

Although the decline in strike activity was to take place gradually over several decades, one critical and immediate result of the Taft-Hartley Amendments was the disappearance of violent strikes. The near century of serious industrial strife ended with Taft-Hartley. The National Guard and federal troops were no longer called upon to restore order and encourage peaceful negotiations,[20] the employers' private police were less frequently deployed, and the president did not see the need to seize companies in order to protect the public interest. A new system of industrial relations began to take shape as employers and union leaders learned to successfully negotiate either an initial collective bargaining contract or a follow-up contract in a relationship that both sides assumed to be ongoing (Dubofsky, 1994).

In the new relationship, most disputes either centered on contract interpretation, which was often resolved in arbitration by a new cadre of labor relations arbitrators, or the development of a new contract, which was worked on by specialized labor lawyers. The result was that the parties developed a kind of day-to-day cooperation, which enabled them to resolve disputes in a more peaceful manner off the streets and usually outside of the public courts (Dubofsky, 1994).

Although the level of strikes was lower in the 1950s than before the passage of Taft-Hartley, it remained high by current standards. By the 1960s, most strikes and confrontations between employers and employees took on a ritualistic character in which neither the future of the union nor the achievement of a collective agreement was in doubt. Industrial conflict lost its association with political militancy, unruliness and violence. Yes, strikes were often still part of the ritual, but a new and more peaceful choreography had taken hold (Dubofsky, 1994).

The outright collapse in strike activity occurred in the 1980s with the election of President Reagan. The election of President Reagan and the repudiation of President Carter's attempt for a second term speak to the underlying change in the electorate. The single dramatic seismic event in the labor landscape was President Reagan's decision to replace the striking air traffic controllers in 1981. That critical decision emboldened employers to use economic weapons available to them under the NLRA, such as the replacement of striking workers when impasse was reached.

For the last 20 years, strike activity has been a fraction – and a declining fraction – of its former self. What I describe as a maturation of an employment relationship into a peaceful mode was to union activists the beginning of the end for their particular vision of labor unionism. The idea that unionization would become the spearhead of a more radical reform of the workplace or of society dropped off the mainstream political agenda. In the widespread political consensus that emerged after World War II, industrial peace and continued economic prosperity were favored over radical labor law reform or radical social change of any kind.[21]

III.   THE FOUR LEGAL REGIMES

In this section, I discuss the capacity of each of the four legal regimes to achieve the goals of industrial peace and equality of bargaining power. I focus on only a few of the most salient features of each legal regime as they affect the achievement of the statutory goals, since a comprehensive treatment of even one of the four is beyond the scope and page limits of this chapter. I also match the legal regime with the economic model that best captures the rules of the regime.

A.   The National Industrial Recovery Act (NIRA): Taking Wages out of Competition

The NIRA was the centerpiece of President Roosevelt's first New Deal. Of the alternative legal regimes it had a critical feature that might have supported wide-scale unionization in the United States: a coordinated policy of reform that would affect not only labor law, but also antitrust and corporate law. The theme was to replace "free competition" with managed "fair competition."[22]

The legal structure of the NIRA is known as corporatism. Corporatism emphasizes cooperation among interest groups or constituencies – especially labor and capital – and between those constituencies and the government. The role of the government is to define an objectively cognizable "public interest" that is developed through active collaboration with the relevant constituent groups. Once the public interest is expressed, firms and other associations are challenged to adapt their policies so as to support the public interest.

Within the consultative process, individual companies would be represented at the policy table by a trade association. Labor unions would also have a seat at the policy table representing employees' interests. At the national level, these constituencies are assembled hierarchically, with "peak associations" at the top holding the most influence with government policymakers. These peak associations are groups like organized industry-wide business associations or national labor federations, the broad membership of which is thought to discourage narrow conceptions of political interest. These peak groups are also expected to exert discipline among their constituent local groups so as to maintain cohesive support for national policies.

In the incipient corporatism of the early New Deal, the constituency groups had to come together at the policy table to develop industry codes of practice. To bring this about, the administration sought to convene corporate leaders and union leaders from most of the major industries to deal with economic problems. One problem with this scheme was that unions represented only a small percentage of the private labor force at that time. Without labor unions that broadly represent employees' interests, industry codes would likely be unbalanced, reflecting only the interests of business.

To provide a countervailing power to corporations, the NIRA actively encouraged unionization. The result was that union membership grew exponentially in the period following the adoption of the NIRA. In August 1932 there were 307 federal and local unions affiliated with the AFL. In July and August 1933, immediately after the passage of the NIRA, 340 new charters were issued to federal and local unions. In the following year, an additional 1,196 charters were issued.[23]

Codes of practice were adopted for most industries. Businesses were not forced into associations against their will. Instead there were enormous incentives to join the process since the codes enabled firms to legally fix prices. At the level of the individual firm, participation in the process was critical since the codes were legally binding on the entire industry. For the individual firm to protect its own interests it had to join the process.

Similar incentives existed at the industry level. If the trade association in a particular industry was a reluctant player, that reluctance usually gave way because the NIRA could adopt a code for an industry that failed to adopt one (Brand, 1988).[24]

The economic model of the NIRA legal regime, stripped to its essentials, was to cartelize industry in order to prevent price and wage competition from feeding deflation. With higher prices and no price competition, companies could pay the higher wages demanded by newly unionized workers. The term "cartel" was not used to describe the codes' agreements, but that is what they represented; and it was this feature of the NIRA that encouraged corporations to participate. The opportunity to cartelize the product market to dampen price competition under state policy is a plum that should not be underestimated.

In return for allowing businesses to fix prices, codes had to grant employees the right to participate in union activities (Hosen, 1992). At the heart of the NIRA's labor policy was section 7(a), which required that each code recognize the rights of employees "to organize and bargain collectively through representatives of their own choosing free from employer interference." Section 7(a) was breakthrough legislation for the union movement, providing labor the right to organize and to do so without interference from employers.[25] The exact scope of the right to be free from interference was never clarified, but it did provide the basis for limiting the employer's right to hire and fire based on an employee's interest in unionization (Brand, 1988).

Most importantly, the NIRA held out the promise of a truly cooperative relationship between labor and capital. The two constituencies needed each other. The cartelization of labor markets by unions helped employers to avoid price-cutting by competitors. The cartelization of product markets also provided the extra revenue to fund the higher wage. From a political perspective, management associations and labor unions worked together to form the codes of behavior that would guide individual actors. The national unions and even more so the federations were to be consulted on all industrial policy issues affecting their membership.

The corporatist moment was too short-lived in the United States to provide a picture of how the fully formed policies might have functioned. However, the NIRA was the most radical attempt of the Roosevelt administration to reset the political economy of the country. If the NIRA had survived, the history of the labor union movement would look very different.

With its emphasis on fair rather than free competition, the economic model of the NIRA does not fare well under the scrutiny of neoclassical economics. From a welfare perspective, an economy built around cartelized industries leads to various inefficiencies. Wages are high, but because they are high relative to equilibrium market-clearing wages, the result is unemployment. Cartelized economies can also be inefficient because they stifle change. The conflict between neoclassical economics and the NIRA is hardly surprising, however, since the goal of the NIRA was largely to replace the market mechanisms that are the cornerstone of neoclassical economics.

The policies of the NIRA would have proved much more appealing if the view of economics held by the Roosevelt administration had been correct. If the dynamics of capitalism did indeed have a tendency to regularly produce a deflationary cycle, then unions would have played a critical function. By engaging in collective bargaining they would prevent downward pressure on wages, thus sustaining purchasing power and averting the development of a deflationary cycle that was the plague of the Great Depression.

B.   The Wagner Act: Promoting the Spread of Unionization

Congress was at work on a successor statute to the NIRA well before the latter was struck down by the Supreme Court. The heart of the Wagner Act, Section 7, was largely a carryover from Section 7(a) of the NIRA.[26] Workers were given a right to join labor organizations, to bargain collectively and to engage in concerted activity such as strikes, without "interference, restraint or coercion" by management.[27] Unlike the NIRA, which was broad in scope but lacked detail, the NLRA provided a detailed set of rules for both union recognition and collective bargaining. It forbade many employer tactics that discouraged unionization, including the creation of management-dominated employee representation plans; set up machinery for determining the union designated as their representative by a majority of the employees; and directed employers "to bargain collectively" with the chosen representatives in good faith.

The intent of the Wagner Act was to foster collective bargaining, and its proponents appeared to assume that the result of the Act would be that most workers, at least in the major industries, would eventually become unionized. Unlike the predecessor NIRA, however, the Wagner Act offered no financial benefits or inducements for employers to join in this endeavor. Moreover, while Section 8 contained a list of employer practices that would constitute an unfair labor practice, there was no comparable list for unfair union practices. This represented a remarkable empowerment of unions to organize new sectors and win extensive contracts. While the employer faced many constraints in resisting union gains, the unions had few constraints in using their economic weapons.

The Wagner Act also sought to solve an endemic problem of the NIRA, namely the lack of effective enforcement powers. The National Labor Board under the NIRA was created through an executive order and only had the power to mediate disputes. The Wagner Act created a new body, the National Labor Relations Board (NLRB), to conduct secret-ballot representation elections and to remedy unfair labor practices. The NLRB was established as a quasi-judicial body, with the general counsel investigating and prosecuting unfair labor practice complaints. Cases were to be heard by an administrative law judge, whose decisions could be appealed to the NLRB and then to the U.S. Court of Appeals.

To achieve its goal of promoting industrial peace, the Wagner Act provided for a legal strike mechanism which channeled concerted activity into a peaceful form: employees were given the right to strike, but that right was required to be exercised in a peaceful fashion. It was assumed that violence would render strike activity unprotected and subject to existing state criminal and civil laws. What was not entirely clear was whether Section 7 trumped existing state laws and protected all peaceful union activity.[28]

It was also hoped that, by granting employees the right to bargain collectively, the Act would make employers understand the fundamental changes to rules of the employment relationship. Compelled to live with unions, perhaps employers would learn to cooperate with them. The result would be a more cooperative spirit where the parties would resolve differences through negotiations.[29]

The cooperative spirit envisioned by Senator Wagner was an impossible dream from the beginning. If unions and employers found it difficult to cooperate under the NIRA, how could they be expected to cooperate under the NLRA? Under the NIRA, higher union wages would be paid for by consumers in the form of higher profits protected by the codes of conduct. Under the NLRA, however, higher union wages were to be paid for out of corporate profits since the employers could be forestalled from increasing prices by product market competition from non-union producers or those with weaker unions.

Whereas the economic model of the NIRA was to cartelize both product and labor markets, the economic model of the NLRA was to cartelize the labor market only. The difference is critical. In the economic model of the Wagner Act, product market competition continues unabated. There is no win-win here, only win-lose. That did not provide the foundation for industrial peace. Whereas the NIRA, if successful, could take wages out of competition, the Wagner Act could only take wages out of competition if the entire industry, including all new entrants, were unionized and wages were bargained at the industry level. Under the best of circumstances that would take time to develop. But from the outset, staying non-union under the Wagner Act gave firms much lower labor costs, which provided a great inducement to stay non-union.[30]

Under the original Wagner Act, unions had considerable bargaining power over employers. For example, since there were no union unfair labor practices, the strike weapon could be used freely under the Wagner Act in support of union recognition (subject to the uncertain force of state law). For example, when a union met resistance from an employer it hoped to unionize, it could boycott the employer, set up a "recognitional" picket line, and then pressure that employer's business customers or suppliers, through strikes or boycotts, to refuse to deal with the target employer. Through the secondary boycott, unionized workers in one firm could pressure their employer to put pressure in turn on a resisting company, either to recognize a union or to sacrifice its business relationship with the initial company.[31]

The Wagner Act also allowed for "closed shop" rules which provided another powerful source of union strength. Under this system, employers committed themselves contractually to hire only union members; thus employees had to be members of the union before being hired, and had to remain members or else they would be fired. This was a very powerful organizing device. The closed shop concept fits the assumption of the Wagner Act that most workers would organize. If most workplaces were closed shops, then workers would end up being a member of a bargaining unit whose terms and conditions of employment were set in collective bargaining.[32]

Importantly, the closed shop also gave the union the power to discipline its own members. Members who engaged in a wildcat strike could be expelled from the union and would thus lose their jobs. The closed shop rule made the worker a loyal union member first and a loyal employee second, as the union might control employees' access to most or all of the jobs in the trade, while the employer only controlled those jobs in its own enterprise.

In addition, the Act favored collective bargaining as the preferred form of the employment relationship and, implicitly, favored spreading collective bargaining throughout the economy. With collective bargaining, the wage that would emerge would be higher than the competitive wage. The Act imposed upon employers a duty to bargain in good faith with "respect to wages, hours, and other terms and conditions of employment." As a result, the union could impose costs on the employer by using its strike weapon. The competitive wage would be the floor, and the effectiveness of the strike weapon would determine the pay premium that the union could achieve.

In effect, unions were given the right to exercise monopoly power in the labor market by setting wages collectively. From an efficiency perspective, the higher union wages and benefits would be expected to cause a lower level of employment than would occur in a competitive market. The union's bargaining effect on economic variables is similar to that of a monopolist in the product market where the firm garners higher profits by restricting supply.

C.   The NLRA after Taft-Hartley: Competition between Union and Non-Union Firms

The Taft-Hartley Amendments left the preamble statement of the Act largely intact and, in that respect, did not explicitly alter the goals of the legislation.[33] There were, however, some highly significant modifications that implicitly changed the Act's goals. Archibald Cox in his famous article from 1947 argued that Taft-Hartley changed the NLRA from actively encouraging unionization to being neutral toward it.

Nowhere is this clearer than in the revised Section 7, entitled "the rights of employees." In the original Wagner Act, Section 7 contained the sweeping language that employees had the right to join a union, to bargain collectively, and to engage in concerted activity such as strikes. The Taft-Hartley Amendments left those rights in place, but added that workers "have the right to refrain from any or all of such activities." Taft-Hartley thus approved the legitimacy of the non-union employment relationship and removed one of the effective tools that union organizers had used since the NIRA; namely, the claim that, by unionizing, workers were following the policy adopted by two very popular presidents, FDR and Harry Truman.

Taft-Hartley shared with the Wagner Act the goal of industrial peace. It sought to reduce the industrial strife that continued after the passage of the Wagner Act and accelerated during World War II, and it did so not by strengthening unions but by weakening them. Most of the changes brought by Taft-Hartley reduced the scope and effectiveness of the economic weapons available to the union in organizing new workers. The secondary boycott, a very powerful but disruptive and often violent tool in unionizing new establishments, was outlawed. In addition, the Taft-Hartley Amendments sharply restricted the use of strikes or picketing for recognition when another union was certified as the exclusive bargaining representative, or in the absence of majority support. As noted in the section on strike history, battles between unions to organize workplaces that were already organized were a major cause of industrial strife after World War II.

Critically, the Taft-Hartley Act also outlawed the closed shop. Under the "union shop" rules that replaced the closed shop, employees did not need to be members of a union as a condition of employment. Instead, the collective bargaining agreement could require that an employee join the union and was given at least 30 days from the date of hire to join. Under the so-called "union shop," unions lost control of the employer's available labor supply. The employer could hire a worker directly rather than through the union.

The union shop framework was a middle ground that loosened the control of the union while still retaining a strong union identification for employees. Although the loss of closed shop status was important to unions, it was minor compared to the effect of the "open shop," which severed the link between employment and union membership and gutted labor union control of the labor supply.[34] And that was precisely what the Taft-Hartley Act allowed the states to do, in what remains the Act's one explicit concession to state law.

Under § 14(b) states were permitted to pass "right to work" laws mandating the "open shop." In a right-to-work state, employees hired into a bargaining unit job did not have to join the union or pay dues. The effect of the right-to-work laws, which were especially popular in the South, was to make it much more difficult for a union to organize and sustain a bargaining unit. The open shop creates a powerful free-rider effect so that even workers who are in favor of a union have an incentive not to join the union because they can enjoy the benefits without paying dues.

Taft-Hartley also added a new Section 8(c) to clarify that employers have the right to express their views about unionization in response to a union organizing drive. Prior to Taft-Hartley, some NLRB rulings had put in doubt whether the employer could wage its own campaign against a union seeking to organize its labor force; Taft-Hartley made it clear that employers could do so. The enhanced ability and willingness of employers to fight unionization of their companies was an important factor in stopping the spread of unionization.

The main effect of Taft-Hartley was to limit the spread of unionization throughout the economy. Consequently, the economic model of the Taft-Hartley legal regime is one with both a union sector and a non-union sector. The relative difficulty of organizing, as well as the ban on the "closed shop," guarantees that there will be a vibrant non-union sector, especially in the "right-to-work" states that require an "open shop." In the right-to-work states, a non-union sector would likely develop even in industries that were heavily unionized in other states.

The economic model of the Taft-Hartley Act has a non-union sector competing actively with a union sector. The automotive industry presents an important example of the competition between union and non-union firms in the same industry. The traditional unionized automobile assembly manufacturers and parts suppliers are located in the industrial belt around Detroit and Ohio, while non-union (and foreign-owned) assembly plants and domestic automotive parts suppliers set up shop mostly in the right-to-work states. As a consequence of the lower labor costs, the non-union manufacturers can deliver a less expensive product. The result is steady erosion in the profits of the unionized plants and a concomitant reduction in union employment. The key point is that, for both parts and final products, prices are being determined at the margin, and the non-union companies are the ones at the margin and thus determining price. Union companies have little to no ability to pass through cost differences to buyers (Hirsch, 2008).[35]

Commentators stress the importance of international trade, and competition from domestic or foreign companies' plants overseas, in promoting a non-union sector that can undercut union businesses in the United States. Globalization of markets makes the story easier to tell, and is important, but the same outcomes are likely without that story because of the persistence and cost advantages of the non-union sector in the U.S.[36]

D.   The Non-Union Sector: The Norm-Based Employment Relationship (and its Competitive Advantage)

The non-union sector has its own legal regime, one that has come to dominate the U.S. labor market in all but a few industries and regions. Obviously, the employees in this sector have not exercised their right to union representation (or have not managed to garner majority support in the face of strong management opposition) and hence are not regulated by most of the provisions of the NLRA. The employees have little to no bargaining power and must act individually. Very few of them enjoy the protections of an enforceable contract, or of "just cause"-type job security, and they do not have a bargaining agent to represent their interests before the employer. In a sense, the legal regime is marked more by the absence of rights than by the presence of rights.

This legal regime has two components. The first is the employment-at-will doctrine, which governs the norms of the workplace. The second is a set of government mandates such as the FLSA, OSHA and ERISA, as well as Title VII and other antidiscrimination laws.

The employment-at-will doctrine is often stated in the following stark form: that an employer can fire an employee for good reason, bad reason, or no reason at all (Ehrenberg, 1989). As I have argued elsewhere, the doctrine of employment-at-will is more of a jurisdictional boundary than a legal rule that is applied in its literal meaning (Rock and Wachter, 1996). By stating the employer's prerogatives as broadly as possible, the employee who believes that she was wrongfully discharged simply cannot sustain a claim. (There are exceptions, such as race or gender discrimination or whistleblowing, that complicate the picture; but let us ignore them for now.)

Take the case of a non-union employee who works in a production or non-supervisory position and is discharged for what she believes to be false or frivolous reasons.[37] She may be able to bolster her complaint with evidence showing that she was never told of poor performance, that her regular job reviews were good, or even that the supervisor was lying about her performance. If the employee were to sue, under the strict employment-at-will doctrine, the case would be dismissed for failure to state a claim. The reason for discharge, or the quality of the employer's evidence, would be simply irrelevant. The purpose of stating employment-at-will so broadly is thus to cut off judicial scrutiny of such claims, and to avoid enforcement through the legal system. The courts accept this jurisdictional boundary by dismissing the suit, leaving the dispute to be settled without judicial interference. The employer thus retains almost complete discretion as to when it can discharge a worker. Moreover, under employment-at-will, employers can change terms and conditions of employment at will, too.

If taken literally, this rule seems to promote rampant opportunism and unfairness. Some particular kinds of unfairness have been addressed, to be sure, by legislation and a variety of tort doctrines arising under the aegis of "public policy." Yet employment-at-will survives insofar as employers have no general duty to justify discharge decisions; they may terminate employment for any reason or for no reason at all (as long as they do not do so for a reason that violates some statute or public policy).

What then explains the almost universal fact that the non-union employment relationship works without use of an enforceable contract for most of its terms? One possible answer is that employers are able to exploit their superior bargaining power over employees and impose this unfair arrangement. But that begs the question of why some employers have not found it worthwhile to offer job security, perhaps in exchange for lower wages, to attract employees who value job security. A more complete answer to this question takes us to the economic model of the non-union sector. Having discussed above the workings of the non-union ELM, the focus here turns to the workings of the labor market inside the firm; that is, the ILM. As a consequence, the appropriate model is the neoclassical theory of the non-union ILM, which is a component of the neoclassical theory of the firm.

We first need to consider why a firm decides to bring an activity inside the firm (the "make" decision) versus leaving the activity outside the firm and buying the services from another firm or entity (the "buy" decision). When the decision is made to bring the activity inside the firm, decision making with respect to the activity is done through the firm's own hierarchy. The individuals involved in the activity do not contract with the employer regarding most terms and conditions; rather most decisions are made unilaterally by the employer. The theory of the firm reaches a stark conclusion on this issue: when contracting is inexpensive and the firm has no core competency in the area, the firm will "buy;" it will contract for the service or good to be provided by an outside entity. However, when contracting is expensive or when the firm has a core competency in the area, the firm will "make," or bring the activity inside the firm.

At the heart of the contracting decision is the level of transaction costs associated with the activity. High transaction costs make contracting costly and thus favor bringing the activity inside the firm. Low transaction costs make contracting straightforward and less costly, and favor leaving the activity to the market. Transaction costs are the costs associated with negotiating, writing and enforcing contracts. High transaction costs occur when the parties interact frequently, when the interactions are connected rather than independent events, and when the environment in which the parties interact evolves over time. These conditions are all present in an ongoing relationship such as the employment relationship inside the firm. The greater the number of contingencies that affect the relationship over time, the greater is the cost of contracting. Finally, the contracting costs are higher relative to the gains when the value at stake in each individual contingency is low. When the transaction is a low-value event, the benefit of contracting to protect the transaction is low, and hence even moderate contracting costs may cut deeply into the profits generated by the transaction.

Transaction costs are typically high in the employment relationship due to a full range of factors such as whether the employee's training is firm-specific and has little use at other firms, and if the employer has access to information, such as job risks, not available to the employee (Williamson, Wachter and Harris, 1975). When transaction costs are high and contract governance is too expensive, the relationships are brought inside the firm, where they are governed by the intra-firm hierarchical governance structure. From the perspective of transaction cost theories, the decision to bring relationships within the firm is the decision to opt for the intra-firm governance structure over contractual governance within markets.

With one important exception, the decision to bring the activity inside the firm means that the activity will not be governed in most of its particulars by contract terms; there is a contract, but it is radically incomplete, in that its terms are largely open and subject to employer discretion. The one exception is, of course, the unionized firm in which the employees' rights and obligations are delineated in an enforceable collective contract. In the union sector, an employer's violation of the contract is prohibited by contract law – albeit a distinctive federal common law of the collective bargaining contract that is invariably enforceable through an internal grievance and arbitration system and only in rare cases through litigation in court. Moreover, the union's bargaining rights are protected by the NLRB against employer interference.

This account of the non-union employment relationship, however, raises a serious legitimacy question: is this discretion used wisely and fairly enough so as to protect the reasonable expectations of the employees? Employment-at-will seems facially to encourage opportunism by employers. At least in past decades many employers may indeed have acted in this manner; hence the outbreak of strikes and violence. Today, employment-at-will is an accepted part of the non-union employment relationship, at least to the extent that it is not a serious topic of labor law reform at either the national or state level. In addition, although many labor and employment law scholars are adamantly opposed to employment-at-will, I know of no empirical studies that claim that it facilitates employer opportunism.

What explains the relative lack of employer opportunism in today's non-union sector? The answer is to be found in the unique nature of the employment relationship. The employment relationship is distinctive because it is an intensively repeat-play game. The employer and the employees are in frequent interactions with each other over an extended period. The tasks evolve over time to meet new contingencies. Monitoring is costly and thus incomplete. It is now well known that informal norm governance works best in such situations because self-help methods are much more effective. In this situation, an employer that engages in bad play by not following prevailing norms can be sanctioned by the employees through techniques running from work slowdowns to outright sabotage at the individual or collective level. In this situation it is the firm that arguably lacks bargaining power, since the remedy – increased monitoring – can be prohibitively expensive for the same reasons that contract writing is prohibitively expensive (Rock and Wachter, 1996).

This is not the place to recount the various self-enforcing norms that operate within the workplace, although one example will be helpful. The employment relationship is typically marked by the parties investing in their match. Starting a new job typically requires the employee to acquire firm-specific skills that are useful in the current job, but not with a different employer (Wachter and Wright, 1990). Firm-specific investments create a wedge between the employee's value to her current employer versus her value to a new employer. If the employer pays all the costs associated with the firm-specific investments, then the employee's problem is obviated, but now the firm is vulnerable if the employee holds up the firm by threatening to quit. If the employee has paid all the costs, then the employee can be held up by the firm through a threat of discharge. The solution to the problem is for the costs to be split. The employee is paid a lower wage during the training period, but not a wage that reflects all of the training costs. After the training is completed and the employee now has valuable firm-specific skills, the surplus from those skills should be divided between the parties in the form of a higher wage for the employee and a more productive worker for the employer. The contract is self-enforcing because both sides then lose their investment if the relationship is terminated early.

In addition to the self-enforcing structure of norms, other factors are also at work. Reputational effects can be a strong deterrent to employer opportunism. Historically industrial strife often followed as a consequence of employers cutting pay during severe downturns in the economy. These downturns, and the resulting pay cuts, occurred at a time when the industrial economy was a fairly new development and employers were still learning how it worked. Nowadays, employers understand that opportunistic treatment of employees during the downturn will make it difficult for employers to hire during the inevitable upturn in the economy. Even during normal conditions, quit rates, or the percentage of workers who voluntarily quit a job each year, are remarkably high, with most of the turnover occurring in the early years of employment. As a consequence, the employer is constantly forced to hire in the competitive job market even to retain a given size.

The ultimate deterrent to employer opportunism is the threat effect of unionization. A non-union firm will become much less profitable if unionized (Williamson, Wachter and Harris, 1975). Wage and benefits will likely be raised above competitive levels and the firm will have the transaction costs of negotiating a collective bargaining agreement that will also impose restrictions on its ability to unilaterally manage its workforce.

The second component of the non-union legal regime is the extensive set of government mandates such as the FLSA, OSHA, and ERISA, as well as Title VII and other antidiscrimination laws. Describing these mandates is beyond the scope of this chapter. They do however serve an important function in the workings of the non-union employment relationship, particularly regulating areas of the relationship that are prone to employer opportunism. Mandates such as ERISA and OSHA serve to remedy potential problems of information asymmetries. In the context of both employee benefit programs and workplace safety, the complexity of the issues and the employer's superior knowledge of them create a potential market failure. The employer could tell its employees that the jobs are safe and that the pension plan is well invested when, in fact, the jobs are very risky and the pension plan is entirely invested in the company's own common stock. The problem is resolved by forcing the employer to disclose relevant information and imposing standards on pension plans and workplace safety.

The solution in this case is government regulations that require the companies to meet certain safety standards for both the jobs and the pensions. In addition, the regulations force the employer to disclose relevant facts to its employees. Violations of the law leave the company facing civil or criminal sanctions imposed by the relevant agency or class-action suits brought by aggrieved employees.

Mandates such as minimum wages, child labor prohibitions and discrimination-free employment serve a different function. Rather than correcting a market imperfection, these impose a public moral standard. Such regulations impose minimum standards on the theory that market-determined outcomes are unacceptable as a matter of national policy (Bennett and Taylor, 2002). In such cases, the outcomes of a $1 wage or the employment of a child under 10 may be efficient in that they do not hamper the operation of the price mechanism. But maximizing social welfare is not coincidental with economic efficiency. Society can declare as a national policy that certain outcomes, whether economically efficient or not, are simply unacceptable outcomes. Such policies, by reflecting the social welfare function, increase overall welfare and are thus the correct actions to take.

If government regulation proves to be an acceptable policy response to major norm failures when they emerge, the non-union sector can benefit from a bifurcated enforcement mechanism. In cases where norm governance rules, such as employment-at-will, the enforcement mechanism is left to the private ordering of the parties. Where the employment relationship works poorly and employer opportunism is most likely to occur, as was the case with occupational health and safety and job discrimination, government intervention is used to resolve those specific problems with targeted regulatory solutions. This allows employers to use very inexpensive, informal contracting mechanisms in all but those identifiable areas where management opportunism is most likely to occur.

IV.   WHICH LEGAL REGIME CAN BEST ACCOMPLISH THE GOALS OF THE WAGNER ACT?

In this section I will evaluate which of the four legal regimes is or was most successful in accomplishing the goals of the Wagner Act: industrial peace and equalization of bargaining power.

A.   The NIRA

Analyzing the NIRA in terms of its ability to achieve the goals of the Wagner Act is arguably unfair to the NIRA because the Act's reform – the implementation of a corporatist political economy – was abandoned when the NIRA was declared unconstitutional. The time period for evaluating the success of the policy is therefore too short to get a reliable reading. In addition, the NIRA, as workable legislation, was only a start.

Even with these caveats, the NIRA receives some credit for being the first federal labor law legislation to provide for the right to engage in lawful concerted activity: both to unionize and to strike without interference from employers. The Norris-LaGuardia Act, passed in the final year of the Hoover Administration and only a year before the NIRA, had already provided for the right to concerted activity against federal court injunctions prohibiting such activities; but the NIRA recognized that employer interference was also a serious impediment to workers' right to unionize.

The NIRA was an improvement over Norris-LaGuardia from labor's perspective, but it was very much a work in progress. Its language was aspirational and hortatory, and badly lacking in specific guidance. In contract law, mandatory rules that cannot be varied by contract are rare because the relationship is entirely voluntary. But the union-employer relationship is not the product of mutual voluntary choice. To ensure the viability of the union sector, core mandatory terms such as the requirement to bargain in good faith are necessary. In addition, mounting an organizing drive and bargaining collectively are not simple matters in an adversarial relationship, especially one that is new. Consequently a more detailed legislative mandate was needed.

The goal of the NIRA was to change the political economy of the United States in a fundamental manner: free competition was to be replaced by fair competition. The new political economy would achieve industrial peace by creating a system of reciprocal benefits in the form of higher prices for employers and higher wages for employees.

The benefits would not only lead to industrial peace, but would also reduce the tendency toward deflationary cycles in wages and profits. In this system, employers might plausibly accept unionization. Although the employer might lose discretion in having to deal with the union, the cartelization of the product market would generate the higher prices necessary to pay for the higher costs of being unionized.

As a practical matter, the NIRA failed on the ground, and the problems showed up almost immediately. Price-fixing proved difficult to accomplish. No sooner had the fair price been set than cartel members started cheating on the price to gain market share (Brand, 1988).[38] Non-compliance begot further non-compliance, as code-abiding business executives began to feel the pinch of competition from cheating firms. The hoped-for stable higher prices were not achieved.

The NIRA was no more successful in labor relations than it was at fixing prices. In the NIRA framework, unions and business were expected to exercise self-restraint in their bargaining demands in order to support national priorities. Self-interest was to give way to the national interest. That did not happen (Brand, 1988; Wachter, 2007).[39] Organizational strikes became more frequent and bargaining demands grew in response to labor's perception that they had the Roosevelt administration and the law on their side, that disruptive disputes would lead to mediation, and that mediators would back up their demands (Dulles, 1960).[40] President Roosevelt's call for moderation in bargaining was ignored. Instead strikes continued to be frequent and violent, requiring the National Guard to be called out regularly to enforce the peace.

The historical record of strike activity, as brief as it is for the NIRA, illustrates the failure of the NIRA to reduce industrial strife. Instead of providing for greater labor stability, the number of workdays lost to strikes tripled over the first three years of the NIRA (Brand, 1988). Also, as shown in Table 15.1, the average annual number of strikes increased dramatically from 766 in 1930–32 to 1,831 in 1933–35.

The NIRA does much better with the goal of equalization of bargaining power. First, on the procedural element, the NIRA scores high since the percentage of workers from the private sector belonging to unions increased from 15.5 percent in 1933 to 16.3 percent in 1934, as shown in Table 15.2 below. More importantly, the NIRA was the catalyst behind the surge in union membership that occurred in the 1930s as the new unions formed during these two years provided the impetus behind organized labor in general. Early organizing efforts were just beginning to show results. As discussed above, the advocates of the Act, including Senator Wagner, viewed collective bargaining as the antidote to unequal bargaining power. Hence, I can use union density as a measure of the procedural element of the goal.

On the substantive element, the NIRA was also successful. Although it is difficult to find a time series of union premiums – that is, the union wage percentage differential with respect to the non-union sector – the data suggest a union wage premium of roughly 20 percent over the entire period covered by this chapter. Although the exact premium differs by industry and over time, the evidence uniformly supports the existence of a high union wage premium over the entire period studied here.[41]

Overall, the NIRA scores high as the first major legislation to grapple with the problems of industrial strife and unequal bargaining power. Much more statutory work needed to be done, but the NIRA was a good first attempt. In addition, it is worth noting that the NIRA was the most pro-union political economy of those studied in

Table 15.1   Number of strikes or lockouts, average annual, over relevant periods

Relevant Period	Years Covered	Number of Strikes, Average Annual
Pre-NIRA Period	1930–32	766
NIRA Period	1933–35	1831
Wagner Act Period	1935–48	3539
Taft-Hartley Period	1948–81	4398

Notes: The averages were calculated using data on work stoppages from 1929–81 from the U.S. Bureau of Labor Statistics (BLS): *Handbook of Labor Statistics*, 1975, Bulletin number 1865, Table 159; *Handbook of Labor Statistics*, 1983, Bulletin number 2175, Table 128; *Handbook of Labor Statistics*, 1989, Bulletin number 2340; and the BLS internet site, available at http://hsus.cambridge.org/HSUSWeb/search/searchTable. do?id=Ba4954-4964. This data set included all strikes and lockouts except those that involved fewer than six workers. After 1981, the data were no longer calculated in this manner and are unavailable.

this chapter. The success of unions depends heavily on their place within the overall legal and economic structure of the country. The NIRA experiment provided unions with a seat at the NIRA policy table, a high-level policy position that they would not have thereafter. The NIRA also reflected an understanding that reforming labor law meant reforming other laws that guided the manner in which employers dealt with labor unions. If unions were to bargain for higher wages, the firms needed to have a way of paying for the higher wages without facing competition from non-union firms that had a lower cost structure.

The question is whether the NIRA was a workable policy in a large and diverse economy such as the United States where competitive pressures are strong. The government would have to wield a big stick to keep companies from undercutting each other's prices and to keep unions from making immoderate demands for better wages and working conditions. In any event, corporatism ran up against constitutional objections, and apparently lacked the political support it would have needed to surmount those objections. President Roosevelt abandoned corporatism, and thus the NIRA, after it was declared unconstitutional, rather than attempting to revise the policy to meet the Court's objections.

B.   The Original Wagner Act's Ability to Achieve its Goals

One would expect that the Wagner Act would be successful in achieving its own goals. The law of unintended consequences might get in the way, but otherwise the Act should have gotten off to a good start. The record is more mixed.

With respect to industrial peace, the Wagner Act created a legal strike mechanism that turned many strikes from violent ones to non-violent ones. President Roosevelt, at least prior to World War II, was reluctant to call in federal troops, although governors might still do so. The battles were still serious and disruptive, but now they were more likely to be union picketers fighting management's private police. With President Roosevelt favoring the unionization of the labor force, labor posed far less of a threat to the legitimacy of the established order. This was an important change.

Although less threatening to the established order, industrial strife, which had already increased during the years of the NIRA, increased further under the Wagner Act. As shown in Table 15.1, in the years prior to the adoption of the NLRA, 1933–35, the average number of strikes and lockouts per year was 1,831. In the period between the passage of the Wagner Act and the adoption of the Taft-Hartley Amendments, the annual number of strikes was 3,539. Rather than bringing industrial peace, the number of strikes and lockouts nearly doubled under the Wagner Act.[42]

There are several explanations for the worsening in industrial strife under the NLRA. First, particularly in the late 1930s, many new unions were forming, undertaking their organizing drives and bargaining for their first contract. A high level of strike activity is not unexpected during this period. Second, the legal regime was particularly favorable to unions. For example, as noted above, the fact that there were no unfair labor practice standards restricting union action meant that the strike weapon could be used freely except as constrained by state law. Third, the aspirations of union leaders and workers increased along with the more favorable legal regime, and rising aspirations translated into more costly bargaining demands which were difficult to resolve without strikes.

The jump in industrial strife went along with a sharp increase in union density. As shown in Table 15.2, union density in the private sector or the percentage of workers represented by unions was 14.2 percent when the Wagner Act was passed in 1935. By 1939 it was 22.8 percent, and by 1945 it was 33.9 percent. So while the Wagner Act was unable to reduce industrial strife, it was able to increase union representation. That is, while the first goal was proving unattainable, the second goal was being achieved. This underscores one of the themes of this chapter; namely that the goals of the Wagner Act were potentially inconsistent. While a surge of initial organizing drives may worsen industrial strife, it does advance the second goal of equalization of bargaining power.

A potential inconsistency in the Act turns into an actual inconsistency once the substantive goal of equalizing bargaining power is taken into account. Concomitant with the increase in union density, the newly organized union members were able to achieve higher wages and thus gained the union wage premium. Herein lies the problem. Who would pay for the higher wages?

The NIRA had one answer: the consumers would pay. Higher prices would compensate the firms for the higher wages, reducing the likelihood that firms would take a strong stance against the wage gains. The NLRA had a different answer and that was the source of the inconsistency: firms would pay for the higher wages through reduced profits. Although firms might be able to pass on some of the wage increases to consumers, there is no reason to suppose that they could pass on the bulk of the increase.

The key question was whether all the firms in the product market could be unionized or cartelized. An aspiration of the Wagner Act was for the entire labor force to be unionized, thus eliminating competition between lower cost non-union firms and higher cost union firms. But achieving that goal would always prove elusive. As long as non-union firms could earn higher profits than union firms, firms would always have an incentive to oppose unionization and, more specifically, the higher labor cost bargaining demands of unions.

Consequently, at the heart of the inconsistency in the Wagner Act goals was the idea that the collective wage would be higher than the market wage. In other words, it is the

Table 15.2   Private sector union density (1929–2010)

Year	Union Density	Year	Union Density	Year	Union Density
1929	12.4	1957	34.7	1985	14.3
1930	13.3	1958	33.9	1986	13.8
1931	14.0	1959	32.3	1987	13.2
1932	15.2	1960	31.9	1988	12.7
1933	15.5	1961	31.9	1989	12.3
1934	16.3	1962	31.6	1990	11.9
1935	14.2	1963	31.2	1991	11.7
1936	15.0	1964	31.0	1992	11.4
1937	19.5	1965	30.8	1993	11.1
1938	21.9	1966	30.3	1994	10.8
1939	22.8	1967	30.5	1995	10.3
1940	24.3	1968	29.9	1996	10.0
1941	25.9	1969	29.0	1997	9.7
1942	28.1	1970	29.1	1998	9.5
1943	30.8	1971	28.2	1999	9.4
1944	32.4	1972	27.3	2000	9.0
1945	33.9	1973	*24.5	2001	9.0
1946	34.1	1974	*23.6	2002	8.6
1947	34.9	1975	*21.7	2003	8.2
1948	34.7	1976	*21.5	2004	7.9
1949	34.9	1977	21.7	2005	7.8
1950	34.6	1978	20.7	2006	7.4
1951	34.7	1979	21.2	2007	**7.5
1952	35.2	1980	20.1	2008	**7.6
1953	35.7	1981	18.7	2009	**7.2
1954	35.6	1982	17.6	2010	**6.9
1955	35.1	1983	16.5		
1956	34.7	1984	15.3		

Notes:

*   Adjusted by Hirsch (2008).
**   Added using data from www.unionstats.com.
The figures for 1929–72 were compiled by Troy and Sheflin (1985) from union financial reports. Figures from 1973 onward are compiled from CPS household data (Hirsch and Macpherson, 2011, updated at http://www.unionstats.com). The union density figure is calculated by determining the percentage of employed workers who are union members.

Source: Hirsch (2008), Figure 1.

substantive aspect of the second goal that would prove to be the problem. Would industrial strife have declined after the collective bargaining relationship matured? Again, there is no obvious reason to suppose that a mature relationship would have become less cantankerous.

In fact, the higher level of industrial strife continued throughout World War II, even in industries where unions were well established. This helped generate public support for what became Taft-Hartley, a retreat from the expansive power granted to unions by the NLRA. However radical the goals of the original Wagner Act might have been, at least in the eyes of its most progressive supporters, much of the public was not buying the result.

In summary, the Wagner Act scores high on the goal of equalizing bargaining power. With respect to the key goal of industrial peace, however, the Wagner Act was not a success. Strikes did become less violent compared to the strikes of the late 19th century, but violence was still a frequent feature of strike activity. In addition the level of strike activity increased dramatically, and this, combined with the continuing incidence of violence, was eventually deemed to be unacceptable. Whatever its success in promoting the bargaining power of workers, it was doomed to be replaced because it failed to achieve industrial peace.

C.   Did the Taft-Hartley Amendments Achieve the Goals of the NLRA?

The Taft-Hartley Amendments transformed the original Wagner Act into a very different regime. It certainly changed the Wagner Act's balance between employers and unions in favor of employers. It also supported the development of a vibrant non-union sector in almost every industry, thus raising the likelihood of direct product market competition between union and non-union companies vying to sell to the same customers.

With respect to the goal of industrial strife, the post-Taft-Hartley NLRA has been much more successful than the Wagner Act. While the Wagner Act had some success in reducing the level of violence and the political threat associated with strike activity, highly disruptive strikes continued in large numbers and the state of labor-management relations during World War II was an especially sorry story. The labor relations problems of World War II, however, were not repeated during the Korean War, which followed the passage of Taft-Hartley. Indeed, after Taft-Harley, violent strikes and the need for federal troop intervention finally disappeared.

Table 15.3 includes two strike activity calculations. In column 2, the average annual number of strikes is presented. Although informative, focusing on the number of strikes over an extended period of time can be misleading. The United States economy boomed after World War II and the growth in the economy, both in terms of output and in the size of the labor force, continued with only brief interruptions, at least until the last few years. In terms of its economic effect, even an unchanging number of strikes meant a lessening of industrial strife and that is what the data show.

As shown in Table 15.3, which provides decade averages in the number of strikes, the absolute number of strikes declined very slowly after the passage of the Taft-Hartley Act. (Note that the data are for strikes involving over 1,000 workers. This series is presented because the Bureau of Labor Statistics stopped collecting the number of all strikes with less than 1,000 workers in 1981.) The decline in the number of strikes, adjusted for the size of the economy, is more gradual and continuous.

A factor that stands out in the unadjusted strike activity data is the apparent effect of the election of Ronald Reagan in 1981 and the subsequent firing of the air traffic controllers for engaging in an illegal strike on August 3, 1981.[43] Specifically, while the average number of strikes during the 1970s was roughly 289 per year, this same figure was roughly 83 during the 1980s. Since 2000, the average number of strikes per year has been around 20. But attributing the success of the Taft-Hartley Act in reducing

Table 15.3   Average number of strikes (involving 1,000 or more workers) by decade

Decade	Average Number of Strikes (Unadjusted)	Average Number of Strikes (Adjusted to 1947 Employment)
1947–59	330.3	310.2
1960–69	282.9	225.1
1970–79	288.8	191.0
1980–89	83.1	45.7
1990–99	34.7	16.0
2000–09	20.1	8.2

Notes: This table was calculated from BLS statistics (1947–2009). The data were reported as strikes involving 1,000 or more workers. The number of strikes was averaged over relevant periods in column 2. Column 3 shows average number of strikes adjusted to 1947 employment. This column was created by using 1947 employment as a base and then dividing the number of strikes by employment for the given year adjusted to the base of 1947.

industrial strife to Ronald Reagan's action some 33 years after the passage of the Act is far too simplistic. After all, there was never a question as to the authority to replace workers who were striking unlawfully. What changed were the social norms of labor relations.

The election of Ronald Reagan, like the passage of Taft-Hartley, speaks to the changing mood of the electorate toward strikes. The effect of that election and especially of the Professional Air Traffic Controllers Organization (PATCO) firings was immediate and jarring for existing unions and their strategies. The decision emboldened employers to make more use of the economic weapons available to them under the NLRA, particularly the right to permanently replace striking workers after impasse is reached in the midst of a strike.[44]

What accounts for the success of Taft-Hartley in reducing industrial strife, following the failure of the Wagner Act to achieve the goal? One of the theses of this chapter is that a key underlying factor – and this is indeed attributable to Taft-Hartley – is the growth of the non-union sector. One of the distinguishing differences between the Wagner Act and the Taft-Hartley Act is that the former took an activist pro-union stance, while the latter switched to a neutral position. While the former envisioned a country where most workers would belong to unions, the latter did not. It was the Taft-Hartley vision that won out. While the United States economy was booming, with a few recessions but no depressions, virtually all of the growth occurred in the non-union sector. Even without the Reagan effect, industrial peace would have been achieved.

Non-union companies became a factor in nearly every industry. Mounting a costly strike in a unionized plant or firm carried a much higher probability that the effect of any resolution of the strike would be a loss of union employment. Higher labor costs and disruptions in the supply of any particular good or activity made it all the more likely that the buyer would switch to a non-union competitor who had lower costs and where disruptions due to strikes were extremely unlikely. The higher probability of losing a strike decreased the incidence of its use by unions.

The growth of the non-union labor force takes us back to the second goal of the

Wagner Act and my thesis that the goals are in conflict with each other. While industrial peace was finally being achieved, the gains in the equalization of bargaining power were being undone. The data on union density are shown in Table 15.2. In 1947, the year which marked the passage of the Taft-Hartley Act, union density almost reaches a peak. Union density plateaus around this level through the Korean War (1950–53). After the Korean War period, a steady decline sets in. As of 2010, union employment as a proportion of total private sector employment is 6.9 percent.

In summary, the Taft-Hartley legal regime achieved the goal of industrial peace, but not the goal of union representation. With the Wagner Act, industrial strife increased rather than declined, but union representation grew strongly as well. This is reversed under the Taft-Hartley legal regime. Industrial peace is achieved, but not the equalization of bargaining power. Instead, a vibrant union sector is replaced by a vibrant non-union sector.

D. Does the Non-Union Sector Achieve the Goals of the NLRA?

In analyzing the success of the NLRA as amended by Taft-Hartley, one needs to address the non-union sector as well as the union sector. As noted above, a key development in the passage of the Taft-Hartley Act was that the regulators moved from a one-sided goal of encouraging unionization and collective bargaining to one of neutrality, allowing the non-union sector to blossom. Consequently, we are interested not only in the effects of the legislation on the union sector; we also want to evaluate its effects on the vitality of the non-union sector.

The short answer to the question of whether the non-union sector achieves the goals of the NLRA would seem to be "no," at least with respect to inequality of bargaining power. Certainly the non-union sector is one where employers unilaterally set pay and working conditions. There is no explicit collective action involving employers and employees. If equalization of bargaining power is equated with collective bargaining, then the answer is definitional: the non-union sector has failed in the goal of equalization of bargaining power.

Is there a longer answer that affords the non-union sector more credit for fulfilling the public policy of the Wagner Act? There is, and, perhaps ironically, it makes the non-union sector one of the great success stories of the NLRA. The longer answer starts by recognizing the importance of peace; it ends by questioning whether non-union employees truly lack bargaining power.

With respect to industrial peace, the non-union sector in the decades prior to the passage of the NLRA was frequently a dysfunctional labor market, particularly during recessions and depressions. Remember that the industrial strife and unrest that is documented above occurred in the non-union sector, largely among employers that refused to cross over into the union sector and bargain with their employees' representatives. From a historical perspective, the episodes of violent strikes in non-union plants made that sector an incubator of industrial strife and unrest. Clearly, in those instances the so-called self-enforcing norms of the non-union sector, elaborated above, were not actually self-enforcing.

The non-union employment relationship is no longer a source of industrial strife. Employees are apparently not so frustrated by their inability to organize a union and get employer recognition that they take to the streets, which they did in large numbers before the Wagner Act.

What has changed? One obvious answer is that the non-union worker can now trigger the union option if the employer proves untrustworthy. Employees have a legal right to organize whenever they choose to do so.[45] The threat of unionization is a powerful one. By replacing the non-judicially enforceable norms of the individual employment relationship with a collective bargaining agreement, unionization significantly increases the transaction costs of the firm. Replacing market wages with the significantly higher union wages and benefits reduces the competitiveness of the non-union firm. Consequently, the threat to unionize is a powerful deterrent that has likely caused the non-union employer to act in a more trustworthy manner, living up to the accepted norms of the workplace. However, the threat effect of unionization cannot be the entire story, especially as union density in many sectors of the labor market approaches zero.

The employment relations practices of non-union firms have also likely improved over time. Self-governing norms take time to develop and to be tested for effectiveness. In the wake of the decline in union density, a consulting industry has been established which can give employers either an off-the-shelf set of norms or norms targeted to their specific employment relationship. Those norms are embodied in employee handbooks as well as much of modern human resources (HR) practice. Since labor costs are such a large component of total costs, the efficiency of the non-union employment relationship is big business.

With respect to the equality of bargaining power, the non-union sector lacks the collective bargaining apparatus, but it can make other claims to satisfy some aspects of the second goal of the NLRA. As noted above, the language of the Wagner Act points to the "stabilization of competitive wage rates." There is little doubt among economists that the United States labor market is highly competitive, with the exception that wages are downwardly rigid during recessions. Although this rigidity appears to be in conflict with the idea of the market being highly competitive, downward wage rigidity serves a separate competitive purpose; namely it is a component of self-enforcing norms in the non-union sector (Wachter, Chapter 2 in this volume). The United States economy has gone through a number of recessions since the Great Depression, yet no one has made the 1930s' claim that the downturn in the economy was due to depressed wages resulting from an absence of collective bargaining. Non-union workers may not act in concert or articulate their preferences through a participatory process; but the need to act in concert – at least to achieve the goal of wage stabilization – is not needed in today's competitive labor markets. The non-union sector does have a governance structure in the form of the self-enforcing norms that constrain management. Self-enforcing norms work silently, through the invisible hand, as it were, in terms of their adoption and retention. Although there is no formal "offer/acceptance" process, employees show constructive acceptance when they consent to employment and then do not quit with knowledge of workplace norms. Quit rates, in the form of workers voluntarily leaving an employer, are highly concentrated in the first few years of employment. This suggests that workers do search and reject jobs that they do not like. Similarly, employers show adherence to workplace norms when they respect them, even though it is costly to them in the short run. Moreover, there is evidence that the norms of the non-union workplace do change over time in a way that reflects changes in social norms.

V. CONCLUSION: THE SUCCESSES OF THE NLRA

I return to the original question raised in this chapter: has the NLRA as it now stands been successful in achieving the goals of the original Wagner Act? According to my analysis, the NLRA has been strikingly successful in achieving its explicit legislative goals. It has not been completely successful because the Wagner Act's second goal of higher union wages and higher union employment is internally inconsistent in the competitive labor market of the United States: it is not possible both to increase union employment and to increase wages in the union sector above competitive levels.

My positive assessment of the NLRA rests in part on the notion that the overriding goal of the Wagner Act was really to achieve industrial peace. It is illegitimate as a matter of national policy and deeply destabilizing to the social order to shoot striking workers as regularly occurred during the decades of industrial strife. The NLRA, as amended by Taft-Hartley, solved the problem of industrial warfare by creating a legalized regime of union representation elections and a legalized strike weapon that has been choreographed into a peaceful series of steps between the union and the employer.

Once the Taft-Hartley Act shifted the NLRA from being proactively pro-union to being neutral, however, the embedded conflict in the goals of the NLRA emerged as an insurmountable hurdle. While the Act favored higher pay, it also supported competition between the union and non-union employment alternatives. By favoring the substantive goal of above-market wages, the union sector has largely priced itself out of the competitive labor marketplace.

Critical to the success of the NLRA is the transformation of the non-union sector from a dysfunctional labor relations system that was an incubator for riots and violence into one in which employees can trust the employer most of the time to enforce the norms of the workplace. The NLRA gets a lot of the credit for the transformation of the non-union sector, however unfortunate and certainly ironic this may be. As long as employees can exercise their inalienable NLRA rights to organize and bargain collectively, the non-union employer has to play fair. The cost of employer opportunism is too high; namely that the profitable company will have to engage in inefficient bargaining, write an enforceable employment contract that introduces rigidities and, in addition, pay higher wages and benefits than the non-union competitor.

In a very real sense, the union sector is a victim of the success of the NLRA in achieving industrial peace and incentivizing the emergence of a viable non-union employment relationship. Although a goal of the NLRA was to create a vibrant union sector, it seems to have created a vibrant non-union sector instead. Whether from the threat of unionization or simply the realization that acting opportunistically toward one's workforce is unproductive, the non-union sector has emerged as a central component of the NLRA's striking success.

Could a different system have worked better in generating high union employment and industrial peace? The United States tried one of the legal regimes that would have made it all work, corporatism as developed in the NIRA. In the corporatist regime, all workers could be unionized – or at least covered by the major economic terms of union agreements. That would secure both the procedural and substantive elements of the equalization of bargaining power. The workers could bargain collectively at the firm level and their national or federation union would have a seat at the highest level of policymaking, thus securing industrial peace. But that was not the choice that Roosevelt and the American voters made.

NOTES

1. The author gratefully acknowledges the contribution of the criticisms and suggestions made by Cynthia Estlund, Sarah Gordon, Barry Hirsch, Sophia Lee and Howard Lesnick. The author also thanks Natalie DiTomasso, Sarah Edelson, Marisa Kirio and Conor McNally for research assistance.
2. Hirsch and Macpherson (2011) report that less than 8 percent of private sector workers belong to unions.
3. This is from the preamble to the NLRA, 29 U.S.C. § 151 (2006): "The denial by some employers of the right of employees to organize and the refusal by some employers to accept the procedure of collective bargaining lead to strikes and other forms of industrial strife or unrest, which have the intent or the necessary effect of burdening or obstructing commerce . . . ."
4. This is from the preamble to the NLRA, "The inequality of bargaining power between employees who do not possess full freedom of association or actual liberty of contract, and employers who are organized in the corporate or other forms of ownership association substantially burdens and affects the flow of commerce, and tends to aggravate recurrent business depressions, by depressing wage rates and the purchasing power of wage earners in industry and by preventing the stabilization of competitive wage rates and working conditions within and between industries."
5. See Wachter (Chapter 2 in this volume) for a discussion of the ILM and the features that distinguish it from the ELM.
6. NLRB v. Jones & Laughlin Steel Corp., 301 U.S. 1 (1937) ("[T]he fact remains that the stoppage of those operations by industrial strife would have a most serious effect upon interstate commerce. In view of respondent's far-flung activities, it is idle to say that the effect would be indirect or remote. It is obvious that it would be immediate and might be catastrophic.").
7. Many states, maybe even most, recognized some right to strike. But even in those that did, the federal courts could enjoin strike activity under the "general common law" and their own version of "equity," both informed by a broad "liberty of contract."
8. See Forbath (1991) for a more detailed discussion on labor injunctions.
9. Zinn (2003, p. 251): ("When the great railroad strikes of 1877 were over, a hundred people were dead, a thousand people had gone to jail, 100,000 workers had gone on strike, and the strikes had roused into action countless unemployed in the cities. More than half the freight on the nation's 75,000 miles of track had stopped running at the height of the strikes.").
10. This is from the preamble to the National Labor Relations Act, 29 U.S.C. § 151 (2006).
11. 78 CONG. REC. 3678, 3679 (1934) (statement of Senator Wagner) ("The primary requirement for cooperation is that employers and employees should possess equality of bargaining power. The only way to accomplish this is by securing for employees the full right to act collectively through representatives of their own choosing. . . . The fathers of our Nation did not regard freedom of contract as an abstract end. They valued it as a means of insuring equal opportunities, which cannot be attained where contracts are dictated by the stronger party.").
12. The union wage premium over the last 90 years has been calculated to be around 20 percent. The work of Lewis (1963) is regarded as authoritative for the first half of the 20th century up until the 1970s. Pencavel and Hartsog (1984) agreed with Lewis's findings and placed the premium somewhere between 18 and 26 percent for the period from 1920–80. More recently, Hirsch and Macpherson (2011) show the premium to hover right around 20 percent since 1973. There has, however, been a decline in the premium in recent years.
13. Commons and Andrews' support for this claim was meager, citing to Tawney's (1915) study of the tailoring industry that concluded, "as a rule, the girls work better if they are paid more." See also Ernst (1993) for an intellectual history of the Commons school and the economic theories it relied on.
14. Hicks was 28 years old when he published *The Theory of Wages*. Since he was not well established until his influential *Value and Capital*, published in 1939, his ideas spread slowly.
15. But see Estlund (1993, p. 973) (The theory of "underconsumption" or "mass purchasing power," which underlay much of the New Deal program, was featured prominently in the Act's preamble, and was repeatedly invoked by the Act's key supporters.
16. To Senator Wagner, workers' participation in collective bargaining was more important than achieving the substantive goal of higher wages. See Barenberg (1993).
17. See Summers, Wellington and Hyde (1982) (Enacted in 1932, the Norris-La Guardia Act put serious

restrictions on the federal courts' ability to grant labor injunctions, made yellow-dog contracts illegal, and acknowledged the right of workers to engage in concerted activities. Section 4 of the Act prohibits injunctions against peaceful union activities such as striking or picketing. Section 7 of the Act goes on to further limit the issuance of such injunctions to instances where for example "substantial and irreparable injury" will occur to plaintiff's property and the "complaint has no adequate remedy at law."). See also Frankfurter and Greene (1930).

18. Of 85 seizures from the Civil War period to the steel seizure of 1952, inclusive, only 18 or 19 appear to have been undertaken for reasons having nothing to do with labor disputes. See Kleiler (1953) (referencing Appendix II attached to Justice Frankfurter's opinion in Youngstown Sheet and Tube Co. v. Sawyer, 343 U.S. 579 (1952)).

19. Court settlements, however, peaked in 1941. Perhaps this indicates a shift in tactics by the Roosevelt administration as labor-management disputes affected defense production.

20. However, the National Guard was summoned for assistance twice during the year of 1970. They were first called in during the 1970 postal strike when the president declared a national emergency and summoned both the National Guard and the U.S. Army to deliver vital pieces of mail that, if not delivered, threatened to cripple large businesses. Troops were called in again during the 1970 Teamsters wildcat strike. The unauthorized strike quickly spread across the country. Violence broke out in Ohio, forcing the governor to call in 4,100 members of the National Guard to control the rioting crowds and rock-hurling strikers. The strike continued for 12 weeks and concluded with a union victory. See Brecher (1997, pp. 273–6).

21. Economic prosperity allowed labor to tend to its already organized industrial and craft base and gain higher wages and benefits. The reduction in new organizing in the private sector meant that unions were limiting their influence to the sectors that had already been unionized. Consequently, unionization would not become a national movement.

22. The goal of "fair competition" was featured in the preamble of the National Industrial Recovery Act of 1933, ch. 90, 48 Stat. 195 ("To encourage national industrial recovery, to foster fair competition, and to provide for the construction of certain useful public works, and for other purposes."). Section 3 of the Act provides for "Codes of Fair Competition."

23. William Green, president of the AFL, credited Section 7(a) with adding 1.5 million new union members, a more than one-third increase, by the time of the October 1933 convention. See Eisner (2000).

24. Note Section 7(b) permitted the establishment of standards regarding maximum hours of labor, minimum rates of pay and working conditions in the industries covered by the codes, while Section 7(c) authorized the president to impose such standards on codes when voluntary agreement could not be reached.

25. Section 7(a) states, "[E]mployees shall have the right to organize and bargain collectively through representatives of their own choosing, and shall be free from the interference, restraint, or coercion of employers of labor, or their agents, in the designation of such representatives or in self-organization or in other concerted activities for the purpose of collective bargaining or other mutual aid or protection; [and] (2) that no employee and no one seeking employment shall be required as a condition of employment to join any company union or to refrain from joining, organizing, or assisting a labor organization of his own choosing . . .".

26. The change from the NIRA to the NLRA and the early days of the National Labor Relations Board are described in great detail in Gross (1974). Gross's work on the NLRB remains the premier discussion of these issues.

27. National Labor Relations Act, 29 U.S.C. § 157 (2006).

28. But did Section 7 trump existing state laws and protect all peaceful union activity, including secondary activity? Almost certainly not. When challenged on the "one-sidedness" of the Wagner Act, proponents said several times that there was no need to create unfair labor practices since state law already regulated union activity. So the Board and the courts would have had to figure out just how far Section 7 protected activity that was restricted by state law. We can be quite sure that Section 7 would not have protected all non-violent concerted activity. But that interpretive process was cut short by the relatively quick enactment of Taft-Hartley, which itself regulated union activity. Subsequently, the Supreme Court concluded that Congress had occupied the field of labor relations and preempted state regulation, except for violent events. For a compelling discussion of this issue, see Estlund (2002).

29. Barenberg (1993) makes this point most strongly.

30. An alternative argument that used to be popular and is still included in textbook treatments of the labor market is the monopsony model. The claim is that firms have monopsony power in labor markets. If firms can exercise market power in setting wages, they can set the wage below competitive levels. The result is higher profits but at the cost of below competitive wages and employment levels. In this setting, the union arrives as a rescuer of both the employee and society. The union can raise the wage to competitive levels, thereby offsetting the firm's monopsony power. Moreover, in doing so, the union leads the parties to the competitive result where employment increases as well as wages. Unfortunately, I am not aware of any

literature that makes a serious claim that the labor market, outside of a few isolated pockets, is marked by monopsony power that can be exercised by firms.

31. For a discussion of a secondary boycott, see Frankfurter and Greene (1930).
32. Closed shop is different from what became known as the "union shop." Under the "union shop," which was permitted by Taft-Hartley as long as state law allowed it, an employee once hired by the employer was required to join the union.
33. But see Gross (1995) ("Taft and his supporters in the Senate argued that the conference committee bill left undisturbed the act's essential theory that [in Taft's words] 'The solution of the labor problem in the United States is free, collective bargaining.' Whatever the merits of Taft's claim . . . [t]he majority of the House did not intend to promote collective bargaining as the solution to labor problems. Their statement of policy, not only in its omission of any reference to collective bargaining but also in its historical context, was intended at least to weaken, and possibly eliminate, collective bargaining.").
34. "Open shop" is a system that Taft-Hartley did not mandate but does permit states to mandate. Outside the 22 right-to-work states, unions can negotiate for a "union shop" by which employees have to join (or now pay an agency fee) within 30 days of starting work.
35. See also Hirsch's contribution to this volume.
36. A virtue of focusing on the globalization point is that it takes away any onus that may have been placed in the above analysis. If the competition is only within the United States, then the unionized firms that lose market share are less likely to find political support. If union workers in Michigan receive higher wages than non-union workers in North Carolina, where they are doing comparable levels of work, then it is easy to make a normative argument to support the competitive markets that lead to work leaving Michigan to go to North Carolina. If the work is migrating to lower wage firms in China, or now Vietnam, then the normative story is different. Almost no one would favor United States wage levels to fall to the level in the Chinese market. Hence, if the competitive advantage arises from the low wage level in China, then a policy argument to protect American workers from such competition is easier to make (at least to American voters). On the other hand, almost no one would favor building in constraints that would prevent jobs from migrating from Michigan to North Carolina. Yes, the migration benefits one group of American workers over another group of American workers. But if both groups of workers are doing the same work, then it is unclear why government policy should favor one group over another. For a detailed discussion of this issue, see Cowie (2001).
37. There is a contract, of course, even if it's terminable at will, and even if its terms can be altered at will by the employer prospectively. The contract provides for a specific wage or salary, certain job duties, etc., all subject to change by the employer. It may have almost no prospective impact, but as to work that has been done, the contract governs. Most non-union, non-managerial employees probably work under a contract that is expressly terminable at will, by the terms of an employee handbook or other document that many courts are willing to give legal effect.
38. Referring to a "crisis in compliance" by fall of 1933.
39. See Brand (1988, p. 94) (noting that the Depression did not elicit the "level of virtuous self-restraint" necessary for NIRA compliance).
40. See Dulles (1960, pp. 271–2) (describing the precipitous increase in strikes under NIRA as workers fought for higher wages and union recognition).
41. As mentioned above, Pencavel and Hartsog (1984) confirmed Lewis's (1963) findings and placed the premium between 18 and 26 percent for the period of 1920–80. Hirsch and Macpherson's (2011) data show that the wage premium has typically been between 15 and 20 percent since 1973.
42. Although the number of strikes increased between the Wagner Act period and the Taft-Hartley period, the percentage increase in strikes decreased dramatically. Additionally, the number of strikes adjusted for the size of the labor force had declined.
43. The Professional Air Traffic Controllers Organization (PATCO) went on strike on August 3, 1981, seeking better working conditions and a shorter workweek. As a government union, PATCO violated 5 U.S.C. § 7311, which prohibits government unions from striking. Historically, the government had been lax in punishing violations of this law, so it was surprising when President Reagan used it to order the strikers back to work within 48 hours of the announcement of the strike. The public was supportive of Reagan's tactics because the strike seemed to lack moral content; "the salaries and working conditions of the strikers scarcely generated sympathy among a public conscious of high levels of inflation and unemployment" and "the strikers had not only defied the law but also, as constantly emphasized by the Administration, had broken their oath." See Meltzer and Sunstein (1983, p. 760) (referencing Gallup polls as well as editorials from the major newspapers).
44. The battle between the UAW and Caterpillar is a primary example. See Corbett (1994, p. 822) and Bearak (1995).
45. There is considerable debate on the question as to whether the legal right to organize is fully effective. See, for just two examples, Weiler (1990) and Gould (1996).

REFERENCES

Barenberg, Mark. 1993. "The Political Economy of the Wagner Act: Power, Symbol, and Workplace Cooperation," 106 *Harvard Law Review* 1381–496.

Bearak, Barry. 1995. "UAW Gives Up, Orders Caterpillar Strikers Back: Labor Directive Ends 17-Month Walkout, Letting Firm Impose its Own Terms on 9,000 Union Workers. Their Rejection of Latest Company Offer is Moot," *Los Angeles Times* (December 4).

Bennett, James T., and Jason E. Taylor. 2002. "Labor Unions: Victims of their Own Political Success?" in J. T. Bennett and B. E. Kaufman, eds., *The Future of Private Sector Unionism in the United States*. Armonk, NY: M.E. Sharpe.

Bernstein, Irving. 1970. *Turbulent Years: A History of the American Worker, 1933–1941*. Boston, MA: Houghton Mifflin.

Blum, John Morton. 1976. *V was for Victory: Politics and American Culture during World War II*. San Diego, CA: Harcourt Brace & Company.

Brand, Donald R. 1988. *Corporatism and the Rule of Law: A Study of the National Recovery Administration*. Ithaca, NY: Cornell University Press.

Brecher, Jeremy. 1997. *Strike!* 3rd ed. Cambridge, MA: South End Press.

Commons, John R., and John B. Andrews. 1927. *Principles of Labor Legislation*. Revised ed. New York: Harper and Brothers.

Corbett, William L. 1994. "A Proposal for Procedural Limitations on Hiring Permanent Striker Replacements: 'A Far, Far Better Thing' Than the Workplace Fairness Act," 72 *North Carolina Law Review* 813–903.

Cowie, Jefferson. 2001. *Capital Moves: RCA's 70-Year Quest for Cheap Labor*. New York: The New Press.

Cox, Archibald. 1947. "Some Aspects of the Labor Management Relations Act, 1947," 61 *Harvard Law Review* 1–49.

Dubofsky, Melvyn. 1994. *The State and Labor in Modern America*. Chapel Hill, NC: The University of North Carolina Press.

Dulles, Foster Rhea. 1960. *Labor in America: A History* (2nd rev. ed.). New York: Crowell.

Ehrenberg, Ronald G. 1989. "Workers' Rights: Rethinking Protective Labor Legislation," in D. Lee Bawden and Felicity Skidmore, eds., *Rethinking Employment Policy*, Washington, DC: Urban Institute Press.

Eisner, Marc Allen. 2000. *Regulatory Politics in Transition*. Baltimore, MD: The Johns Hopkins University Press.

Ernst, Daniel. 1993. "Common Laborers? Industrial Pluralists, Legal Realists, and the Law of Industrial Disputes, 1915–1943," 11 *Law & History Review* 59–100.

Estlund, Cynthia. 1993. "Economic Rationality and Union Avoidance: Misunderstanding the National Labor Relations Act," 71 *Texas Law Review* 921–92.

Estlund, Cynthia. 2002. "The Ossification of American Labor Law," 102 *Columbia Law Review* 1527–612.

Forbath, William A. 1991. *Law and the Shaping of the American Labor Movement*. 2nd ed. Cambridge, MA: Harvard University Press.

Frankfurter, Felix, and Nathan Greene. 1930. *The Labor Injunction*. New York: Macmillan.

Gould, William. 1996. *Agenda for Reform: The Future of Employment Relationships and the Law*. Cambridge, MA: MIT Press.

Gross, James A. 1974. *The Making of the National Labor Relations Board*. Albany, NY: State University of New York Press.

Gross, James A. 1995. *Broken Promises: The Subversion of American Labor Relations Policy, 1947–1994*. Philadelphia, PA: Temple University Press.

Hicks, John R. 1963. *The Theory of Wages*. 2nd ed. London: Macmillan and Company.

Hirsch, Barry T. 2008. "Sluggish Institutions in a Dynamic World: Can Unions and Industrial Competition Coexist?" 22 *The Journal of Economic Perspectives* 153–76.

Hirsch, Barry T., and David A. Macpherson. 2011. *Union Membership and Earnings Data Book 2011: Compilations from the Current Population Survey*. Washington, DC: Bureau of National Affairs.

Hosen, Frederick E. 1992. *The Great Depression and the New Deal: Legislative Acts in their Entirety (1932–1933) and Statistical Economic Data (1926–1946)*. Jefferson, NC: McFarland.

Kleiler, Frank M. 1953. "Presidential Seizures in Labor Disputes," 6 *Industrial and Labor Relations Review* 547–56.

Lewis, H. Gregg. 1963. *Unionism and Relative Wages in the United States*. Chicago, IL: The University of Chicago Press.

Malthus, Thomas R. 1803 (1958). *An Essay on the Principle of Population; or, a View of its Past and Present Effects on Human Happiness; with an Enquiry into our Prospects respecting the Future Removal or Mitigation of the Evils which it occasions*. London: J.M. Dent & Sons Ltd.

Meltzer, Bernard D. and Cass Sunstein. 1983. "Public Employee Strikes, Executive Discretion, and the Air Traffic Controllers," 50 *University of Chicago Law Review* 731–99.

Pencavel, John, and Catherine E. Hartsog. 1984. "A Reconsideration of the Effects of Unionism on Relative Wages and Employment in the United States, 1920–1980," 2 *Journal of Labor Economics* 193–232.

Perrett, Geoffrey. 1973. *Days of Sadness, Years of Triumph: The American People 1939–1945*. Madison, WI: The University of Wisconsin Press.

Rock, Edward B., and Michael Wachter. 1996. "The Enforceability of Norms and the Employment Relationship," 144 *University of Pennsylvania Law Review* 1913–52.

Sparrow, Bartholomew H. 1996. *From the Outside In: World War II and the American State*. Princeton, NJ: Princeton University Press.

Summers, Clyde, Harry Wellington, and Alan Hyde. 1982. *Cases and Materials on Labor Law*. 2nd ed. Mineola, NY: Foundation Press.

Tawney, R. H. 1915. *The Establishment of Minimum Rates in the Tailoring Industry: Under the Trade Boards Act of 1909*. London, UK: G. Bell and Sons Ltd.

Troy, Leo and Neil Sheflin. 1985. *U.S. Union Sourcebook: Membership, Structure, Finance, Directory*. West Orange, NJ: Industrial Relations Data and Information Services.

Wachter, Michael. 2007. "Labor Unions: A Corporatist Institution in a Competitive World," 155 *University of Pennsylvania Law Review* 581–634.

Wachter, Michael and Randall D. Wright. 1990. "The Economics of Internal Labor Markets," 29 *Industrial Relation* 240–62. Reprinted in D. J. B. Mitchell and M. A. Zaidi, eds., *The Economics of Human Resource Management*. Oxford, UK: Basil Blackwell.

Weiler, Paul C. 1990. *Governing the Workplace: The Future of Labor and Employment Law*. Cambridge, MA: Harvard University Press.

Williamson, Oliver E., Michael L. Wachter, and Jeffrey E. Harris. 1975. "Understanding the Employment Relation: The Analysis of Idiosyncratic Exchange, 6 *The Bell Journal of Economics* 250–78. Reprinted in L. L. Putterman and R. S. Kroszner, eds., 1996, *The Economic Nature of the Firm*. Cambridge, UK: University of Cambridge Press.

Zinn, Howard. 2003. *A People's History of the United States*. New York: HarperCollins.

Cases and Statutes Cited

A. L. A. Schechter Poultry Corp. v. United States, 295 U.S. 495 (1935).

Anti-Injunction (Norris-La Guardia) Act, ch. 90, 47 Stat. 70 (1932) (codified at 29 U.S.C. §§ 101–15 (2006)).

Labor Management Relations (Taft-Hartley) Act, Pub. L. No. 81-101, 61 Stat. 136 (1947) (codified as amended at 29 U.S.C. §§ 141–87 (2006)).

National Industrial Recovery Act, ch. 90, 48 Stat. 195 (1933) (repealed 1966).

National Labor Relations (Wagner) Act, Pub. L. No. 74-198, 49 Stat. 449 (1935) (codified as amended at 29 U.S.C. §§ 151–69 (2006)).

NLRB v. Jones & Laughlin Steel Corp., 301 U.S. 1 (1937).

Youngstown Sheet & Tube Co. v. Sawyer, 343 U.S. 579 (1952).

16. Why workers still need a collective voice in the era of norms and mandates

*Cynthia L. Estlund**

The drastic decline of union representation in the United States has opened up a large and by now familiar "representation gap" in the workplace – a gap between "what workers want," to cite Freeman and Rogers' (1999) important book on the question, and what they have by way of voice at work. But what workers want does not necessarily command the attention of policymakers. Is workers' desire for greater voice at work any more compelling than their desire for higher wages, paid vacations, or any number of terms and conditions of employment that are left almost entirely to the tender mercies of labor markets and individual bargaining?

On some accounts, workers no longer need collective representation (whether or not they want it) because their interests are adequately protected by a combination of legally enforceable mandates and self-enforcing norms. I will argue in this chapter that these accounts are wrong and workers are right: most workers not only want but need some form of collective representation in order to enforce the mix of legal mandates and informal norms by which they are currently governed at work.

The existing patchwork of employment mandates has indeed supplied what some commentators view as a kind of union substitute. But minimum standards are often quite minimal, and are underenforced in many workplaces. The default regime of individual contract thus continues to exert a powerful gravitational pull on actual wages and working conditions both above and below the mandatory floor. The nature of the individual employment contract in the non-union sector has also changed since the 1930s, and on some views has created a different kind of union substitute: a regime of non-legally enforceable yet mostly self-enforcing norms that have displaced the arbitrary and harsh labor management practices that drove many workers in the past to demand union representation. But the informal enforcement of workplace norms depends on "reputational sanctions" that are certain to vary across employers and across different classes of workers, leaving many workers vulnerable to unfair and opportunistic employer practices.

So workers not only still want collective representation at work; they need collective representation to enforce the regime of mandates and norms by which most workers are actually governed at work. But both the nature of the collective representation that workers need and the path by which they might achieve it differ for workers at the top and the bottom of the labor market.

Section I reviews the story of declining union density, and the nature of the "representation gap" that has grown in its wake. Section II maps the current regime of employment mandates by which the public now governs private employment relations, and the stubborn problems of enforcement that undermine the efficacy of mandates. Section III turns to the default regime of individual contract and informal norms by which the overwhelming majority of private sector employees are governed nowadays, and the widely divergent implications of that regime for workers at the top and the bottom of the labor market. Section IV widens the lens to include non-labor market forces that may magnify or refract the role of both mandates and informal norms in constraining employer behavior, and that help to explain the wide divergence between "high road" and "low road" employers. Finally, Section V briefly sketches a two-track approach to workplace governance reform, and to labor law reform, that responds to both the shared need and desire for collective representation and the distinct barriers and opportunities that workers face at the top and the bottom of the labor market.

I.   THE FALL OF COLLECTIVE BARGAINING AND THE "REPRESENTATION GAP": WHAT WORKERS WANT AND WHAT THEY HAVE BY WAY OF COLLECTIVE VOICE

The fall of collective bargaining is a familiar tale, but it is worth a brief reprise here. That will set the stage for a review of the evidence of what workers say they want in terms of collective voice at work, and what they say they have.

A.   The Fall of Collective Bargaining

Declining union density obviously reflects both the demise and shrinkage of unionized firms and the slow pace of new organizing. Scholars continue to disagree over the extent to which those phenomena are a product of employer resistance – and the limited legal restrictions and remedies associated with employer resistance – or of sheer economic forces. In the present volume alone, Epstein, Hirsch, and Wachter all weigh in on the side of economic forces, while Kaufman, Sachs, Kleiner and Weil emphasize the role of employer opposition, legal and illegal. But all would probably agree that employer resistance to unions is not independent of economic forces.

Consider four sources of declining union density. First, through the normal workings of "creative destruction" in a capitalist economy, some existing business operations die every year, freeing up capital for new operations. Some of the former are unionized; all of the latter start out non-union and remain so unless a majority of employees chooses to form a union. So union jobs are constantly being replaced by non-union jobs even if unionization as such plays no role whatsoever in firms' fortunes or decisions; that compels unions to engage in constant new organizing just to keep union density from falling.

Second, among the operations that shrink or die each year, the casualty rate is likely to be higher for union operations that compete in same product market with non-union operations. Unions tend to raise wages and benefits – that is their main selling point, after all – and thus labor costs; but they tend not to bring significant gains (or losses) in productivity (Hirsch, Chapter 4 in this volume). Freeman and Medoff's important book, *What Do Unions Do?* (1984), popularized a more positive account of the impact of unions on productivity based on some encouraging early studies. But by 2007, reflecting on more than 20 years of subsequent empirical research, Freeman acknowledged that the data had shown the positive productivity story to be "overly optimistic," while confirming unions' negative impact on profits (Freeman, 2007). The result for unionized operations is higher prices, lower profits, or some of each, and a competitive disadvantage in product markets and capital markets.

We have said nothing yet about conscious union avoidance by firms, but that is the unsurprising third contributor to declining union density. The costs normally associated with unionization will tend to lead firms to deliberately direct investment and production away from union facilities and toward new or non-union facilities. Undoubtedly ideological, cultural, and psychological factors contribute to managers' union avoidance decisions. But it is hard to separate those factors from the fact that unions tend to reduce profits. Whatever its underlying motives, union avoidance as such appears to be a significant, routine consideration in employer decisions about where to locate production, and about whether to invest in modernization or expansion of existing facilities (Craver, 1993; Estlund, 1993).

Fourth and finally, there is the familiar fact of vehement employer resistance to new organizing. In a system like ours, in which union firms are nearly all in competition with non-union firms (including new entrants), and union operations are in competition with non-union operations even within the same firm, employers will predictably resist and avoid unionization. Indeed, they may be punished by product and capital markets if they fail to do so.

This dynamic of union decline is not independent of our policy choices. It reflects in part the basic structure of labor relations under U.S. labor law, by which organizing and wage bargaining is conducted, with rare exceptions, at the level of the bargaining unit rather than at the sectoral level; in that system, wages and other labor costs remain subject to market competition within the same national market. By contrast, in corporatist labor law systems such as those in Europe and elsewhere, wages are generally negotiated between large employer federations and the largest trade unions, and then extended to the sector as a whole; moreover, many employee benefits are statutory. The result – and the aim of this system – is to take wages and benefits out of competition (within national boundaries).[1] But the corporatist path was rather decisively rejected in the U.S. after a brief early-New Deal experiment, and is unlikely to be reopened (Wachter, 2007). In our system, employers in any competitive product market sector with a significant non-union presence are under pressure to resist unionization and to resist union bargaining gains.

None of this either justifies employers' illegal anti-union conduct or refutes the rationale for making that conduct illegal. Both employers' union avoidance in the location of production (as in the "runaway shop") and their resistance to union organizing efforts may take forms that are illegal under the National Labor Relations Act (NLRA) even if they are economically rational (Estlund, 1993). Law in a civilized society frequently constrains economic actors from doing things that may be economically advantageous for themselves but harmful in the aggregate for the society or simply contrary to public values. Pouring toxic waste into public waterways may reduce production costs, and some forms of employment discrimination may attract customers; but both are illegal, and justifiably so.

Still, the economic logic behind much anti-union behavior makes it unusually challenging to enforce employee rights under the NLRA. That is because those employee rights take the form of an option, not a mandate; their costs fall not on all firms in the jurisdiction (as in the case of minimum labor standards), but on the firms whose employees choose to exercise their option to form a union. Firms that deal with a union and pay a union premium thus compete with firms that do not. So employers have a stronger incentive to resist their employees' exercise of these rights than to resist, say, uniform safety standards. As a result, those charged with enforcing the NLRA are rowing against a powerful economic current (and, according to many observers, are up a creek without a paddle, given their limited remedial powers (Kleiner and Weil, Chapter 7 in this volume)). But it hardly means it is wrong for society to undertake that challenge.

The affirmative case for promoting unionization and collective bargaining rests on several pillars, which I will only touch on here: a commitment to employees' basic freedom of association rights (long enshrined in international law instruments to which the U.S. subscribes), a belief in the civic virtues of democracy within the workplace, an egalitarian effort to boost wages by enhancing workers' bargaining power, and the promotion of "labor peace" through the legitimation and regulation of labor–management conflict. Unfortunately, these goals may not all be compatible with each other. For example, the goal of labor peace may be advanced by Taft-Hartley-like restrictions on the scope of concerted labor activity that dramatically reduce workers' bargaining power (Wachter, Chapter 15 in this volume). And the goal of increasing workers' bargaining power and wages – to the extent that drives employers to resist and avoid unionization – may be in tension with the goal of promoting workplace democracy through wider unionization (id.). The latter tension could be dissolved if higher union wages are offset by productivity gains. As noted above, the voluminous studies on this question suggest that, as a general matter, they are not.

Many contemporary proponents of collective bargaining contest that bleak empirical conclusion, and tout the possibility of mutual gains and greater productivity through creative and cooperative labor–management partnerships. Although the empirical studies find no general link between unionization and higher productivity, they do not exclude the possibility of raising productivity through labor–management cooperation (Hirsch, Chapter 4 in this volume). Unfortunately, such partnerships may simply be too rare to show up in the aggregate data. It takes two to tango, after all. Unions cannot create a cooperative labor relations climate unless employers agree to cooperate with them. And without many successful models of labor–management cooperation, the idea is a hard sell to skeptical managers (and investors), to whom it may appear less familiar, more difficult to execute, and riskier than the increasingly conventional labor relations strategy of maximizing managerial discretion and resisting and avoiding unions. The economics may drive much of the anti-union ideology of U.S. employers, but anti-union ideology in turn stacks the economic deck against unions by impeding the development of a climate of trust and cooperation in which unions might be able to contribute to economic successes.

That is a short and stylized version of the story behind the decline of private sector union density to single digits, and of the reasons for pessimism about any dramatic turnaround. We will return to elements of this story, but for present purposes there are a few important points. First, unionization is currently viewed by the vast majority of U.S. employers as a dire fate but a mostly avoidable one. Second, partly as a consequence, the overwhelming majority of U.S. workers are in fact covered not by collective contracts but only by individual contracts (subject to the web of rights and mandates to which we will shortly turn). Third, the very low unionization rate is unlikely to rise much in the foreseeable future, with or without labor law reform.

B.   What Workers Want and What They Have by Way of Collective Representation

The decline of union representation has led to a growing "representation gap" – an unmet desire for collective representation. In their massive, in-depth survey of worker attitudes, Freeman and Rogers found support for the labor movement's view that what many non-union workers want (30 to 40 percent) is independent union-like representation (Freeman and Rogers, 1999, pp. 81–92). But they also found that even more workers want a less adversarial form of representation: fully 85 percent of non-managerial employees say they prefer an organization that is "run jointly" by employees and management (and that is almost certainly illegal under the National Labor Relations Act (NLRA)) (ibid., pp. 84–8). Indeed, when asked to choose between an organization with which management cooperated but that had no power, and an organization that had more power but that management opposed, employees said they preferred the former by a margin of 63 percent to 22 percent (id.).

What most workers say they want is subject to divergent interpretations: union backers can fairly argue that the preference for cooperative, jointly run forms of employee representation is an "adaptive preference" – adaptive to the stubborn fact of management opposition to unions – rather than a genuine, uncoerced choice. Others may argue that workers' preference for a form of participation that is cooperative by design, and that elicits management's cooperation, is both realistic and sensible. But it is important to keep in mind that not all workers express that preference. While there is a widely shared desire for some kind of collective or institutionalized representation, different workers prefer different forms of representation and participation, depending partly on how much trust and confidence they have in their managers and partly on how much individual influence they feel they have (ibid., pp. 79–81).

Unfortunately, the NLRA both fails to enable most workers to form a union when that is what they want, and prohibits the alternative forms of representation that most workers say they prefer. Section 8(a)(2) prohibits employer domination of or assistance to "labor organizations"; that term is defined to include any organization "in which employees participate," and that "deals with" the employer on terms and conditions of employment. That makes it unlawful for employers to maintain, or even for workers to choose, an organization "run jointly" by employees and management. To be sure, there are no serious sanctions for violating Section 8(a)(2); at worst an employer may be ordered to disestablish an unlawful organization. The fact remains, though, that federal law prohibits employers from maintaining representative structures through which employees can meaningfully discuss workplace concerns unless they are entirely independent of the employer.

Section 8(a)(2) was probably the single most controversial provision of the NLRA, partly because it prohibited not only representative structures that were designed to fend off majority-backed demands for union recognition, but also some that were not, and that enjoyed strong support from employees. For a New Deal Congress that sought to promote collective bargaining throughout the economy, all company-backed representation schemes tended to discourage the growth of independent unions. The "union or nothing" approach of the NLRA remained in place even after Congress in 1947 recast the goal of the labor laws as the protection of employee "free choice," and even today when union density has fallen to single digits. Under U.S. labor law, it is legitimate for employees to choose not to be represented by a union, and for employers to pay good wages and treat employees fairly in hopes of avoiding unionization. But it is not lawful for employees to choose, or for employers to supply, a less adversarial, less independent, and less powerful form of employee representation than a union.

In the meantime, the rest of the world has moved in a very different direction. Most developed countries now *mandate* some form of employee representation (Deakin and Koukiadaki, 2012). No country broadly prohibits voluntary forms of non-union representation or worker–management cooperation as does the U.S. (Freeman and Rogers, 2006, pp. 205–08). Even Canada, whose labor laws are largely modeled on our own, maintains a narrower "company union" ban, and permits forms of worker representation that are illegal here (id.; Taras, 1997).

So what most workers say they want in the U.S. is not legally available. And yet consider what U.S. workers say they have. In one recent study, 34 percent of non-union respondents reported having some form of management-established representation structure at work (Godard and Frege, 2011; see also Taras and Kaufman, 2006; Freeman and Rogers, 1999: 92–3). These are not identity-based affinity groups (which were tracked separately); nor are they mere "quality circles." Many (42 percent) involved discussions of wages and benefits (Godard and Frege, 2011). Workers mostly seem to like these representation schemes (as one would expect given their expressed preferences). Most participants rated them highly in terms of consulting with workers (54 percent) and standing up for them (51 percent) (id., p. 16).[2] These structures are almost certainly illegal under the NLRA.

We know little about how these management-established schemes function. Many employers appear willing to violate Section 8(a)(2) by creating these structures, but few are willing to discuss them publicly. Moreover, it seems certain that some employers – especially large, high profile firms with strong "compliance" structures and norms – are discouraged by the law from setting up such organizations, and that more employees would have access to these forms of representation if they were not illegal.

So we find that the overwhelming majority of workers say they want a form of collective representation that the law says they cannot have; and that a significant minority of employers are in violation of the law by giving employees what they say they want. These are facts worth reckoning with. But perhaps workers' own stated preferences are not a sufficient basis for reform. Some observers argue that workers no longer need collective representation because their interests are adequately protected by a combination of legally enforceable mandates and self-enforcing norms. I will argue in the next two sections that, contrary to these accounts, most workers not only want but need some form of collective representation in order to enforce the mix of legal mandates and informal norms by which they are currently governed at work.

II.   WORKPLACE MANDATES AND THE ENDURING ROLE OF THE INDIVIDUAL EMPLOYMENT CONTRACT

The default mode of regulating employment relations in the U.S. is by individual contract, the peculiarly incomplete nature of which will occupy us below. Yet the default regime of individual contract, and the unregulated labor market that is constituted by such contracts, has not had free rein in the U.S. for over a century. The New Deal constructed not only a framework for collective self-help and collective bargaining through unionization, but also a mandatory minimum floor on wages and working conditions. That floor has since been furnished with a growing number of built-in fixtures in the form of non-waivable labor standards and employee rights.

On some accounts, legislative mandates have conferred upon workers many of the protections they might have sought through unionization, and have functioned as a kind of union substitute. Yet the floor that is set by these mandates is quite low, and is full of holes that are especially evident at the bottom of the labor market. For the enforcement of mandates is largely in the hands of employees themselves, and is beset by both collective action problems and the fear of reprisals. That is partly because U.S. law does not mandate protection against unjustified dismissal. Employees' lack of legally enforceable job security, whatever its economic virtues (Wachter, Chapter 15 in this volume), undermines employees' ability to enforce other workplace rights (Estlund, 1996). So the regime of mandates on which the society has come to rely for the protection of employees is itself plagued by a "representation gap." I have elaborated on this problem at length elsewhere (Estlund, 2010), and will be brief here. In short, employment mandates have not displaced the individual contract from its central role in employment relations, and have not supplanted the need for collective voice, without which mandates are bound in many settings to be underenforced.

A.   Labor Standards and their Underenforcement

Since the mid-19th century, many employer advocates and economists have argued that regulation of wages above what the market would bear – that is, above the wage that some worker would be willing to accept given the labor market alternatives – hurts workers and the economy by pushing employers out of business and workers out of work. Similarly, costly non-wage mandates are bound to reduce wages or employment levels, given employers' residual freedom to decide whether and at what wage level to employ labor (Epstein, 1984; Posner, 1998). It was better, they argued, to leave employees free to bargain or shop around for their preferred terms and conditions in competitive labor markets. Even safety could be left to the market, for workers would demand a wage premium for work that exposes them to uncompensated injury or illness, and such wage premiums induce "efficient" levels of safety precautions.[3]

This story contains a number of "ifs": if labor markets are competitive, frictionless, and efficient; if workers are fully informed and rational about risks and working conditions, and if they internalize all the costs of poor conditions. Scholars have questioned those "ifs," and argued on efficiency grounds for some regulations (Jolls, 2007; Kaufman, Chapter 3 in this volume; Rose-Ackerman, 1992; Revesz and Livermore, 2008). Debates about the efficiency and consequences of mandates and minimum labor standards continue. But, in the meantime, so does the proliferation of employment mandates – albeit to a lesser degree in the U.S. than in most of the developed world.

The first major round of labor standards mandates centered on wage levels and hours of work. In the midst of the Great Depression, labor market forces were seen to have pressed wages too low and hours too high to satisfy the legitimate economic and social needs of workers and their families. The New Dealers believed that market mechanisms for the allocation of goods, services and labor, though worth preserving, were intrinsically flawed (Kaufman, Chapter 3 in this volume; Sunstein, 1987). Competition needed to be "fair" rather than "free," lest it generate a destructive "race to the bottom" in which responsible firms were undercut and the public injured by exploitative cost-cutting (Wachter, 2007). After a short-lived experiment with corporatist-style management of the economy, New Dealers turned to regulation as the primary mechanism for protecting the public interest against market failures and destructive competition (Wachter, 2007; Stever, 1994). Corporatism left a bigger imprint in the labor arena, where collective bargaining, rather than direct regulation, was to serve as the main mechanism for engendering "fair competition" and improving labor standards (Wachter, 2007). But direct regulation also gained a foothold with the Fair Labor Standards Act of 1938 (FLSA), which set a nationwide minimum wage and mandatory overtime premium and banned most child labor in leading sectors of the private labor market. Above that fairly low nationwide floor, the parties to the employment relationship were free to bargain, either collectively or individually.

A few decades passed before the next major federal labor standards law was enacted. The Occupational Safety and Health Act of 1970 (OSHA) sought to take workplace safety out of competition by establishing publicly enforced minimum standards. The Employee Retirement Income Security Act of 1974 (ERISA) regulated the administration, funding and insurance of employee pension and benefit plans.[4] Later came the Worker Adjustment and Retraining Notification Act of 1988 (WARN), which required employers to give advance notice of plant closings and mass layoffs, and the Family and Medical Leave Act of 1993 (FMLA), which regulated and expanded parental and medical leave policies. Notwithstanding persistent complaints from employers about the burdens they impose, none of these mandates has ever been significantly cut back.

Whether or not these employment laws have contributed to the decline of collective bargaining, they have effectively taken its place as the primary source of protection against the vicissitudes of the market for most employees. Yet those regulatory regimes have themselves proven inadequate to the task of regulating labor standards in millions of workplaces across the country. In part that is because of the challenge of setting uniform standards that meet the needs of workers and the capabilities of employers across the breadth of the labor market (Freeman and Medoff, 1984; Weiler, 1990); that has tended to produce labor standards well below the level that many employees demand and many employers are capable of supplying. But even those rather minimal labor standards are underenforced, and non-compliance is widespread, especially in the lower reaches of the labor market.

The problem under the wage and hour laws is illustrative: Whenever there are workers willing to work for less than the law requires – as poor and undocumented immigrants often are – employers are sorely tempted to pay less. Traditional enforcement mechanisms fail to raise the cost of non-compliance high enough to outweigh the immediate savings from non-compliance, and employers risk little by underpaying employees and hoping to avoid enforcement (Weil, 2002; 2003). One study in the apparel industry found that the cost of compliance (that is, the added cost of paying employees a lawful wage and overtime) was nearly nine times the basic cost of non-compliance (that is, the average civil penalty discounted by the probability of detection) (Weil, 2003).

Not surprisingly, many employers evade or ignore the law (Bobo, 2009; Greenhouse,

2008; Weil, 2003; Bernhardt et al., 2007). Some employers at the very bottom of the market simply ignore minimum wage and overtime laws, or refuse to pay workers the promised wage after the work is done. Some exact "off-the-clock" work or alter employees' time cards after the fact. Some illegal pay practices are veiled by misclassification of employees as "independent contractors" who are exempt from labor standards laws (Goldstein et al., 1999; GAO, 2009). These practices are found even in some major firms; Wal-Mart, for example, lost or settled scores of lawsuits over its "off-the-clock" work policies. But wage and hour violations are especially common among marginal producers that have little fixed capital or stake in their reputation, and that rely heavily on undocumented immigrant workers who are too fearful or desperate to complain (Wial, 1999; Wishnie, 2004; Bernhardt et al., 2007).[5]

Occupational health and safety laws confront a more complex economic calculus than do the wage and hour laws. Clearly the law is not all that drives firms to invest in safety. Some precautions have indirect benefits (for example, reducing lost-time accidents and turnover) as well as direct and indirect costs (for example, slowing down production). Depending partly on the difficulty of replacing workers, one side of the equation or the other may loom larger. But to the extent that the law is needed to promote safe and healthy working conditions, it is not up to the job. Tort law and its deterrent function have been replaced by worker compensation regimes that are far from fully compensatory (though more predictable). OSHA enforcement is plagued by rare inspections, low penalties and long delays (McGarity and Shapiro, 1993; Lierman, 2010). Firms seeking to compete by squeezing labor costs may be sorely tempted to do so in part by failing to take safety precautions, or by driving workers at a pace that forces them to ignore safety.

The problem of underenforcement under the FLSA and OSHA reflects in part a chronic shortfall in public enforcement capacity. There is simply no way for public agencies and their inspectors to monitor and enforce compliance with labor standards in millions of covered workplaces. Rather, employees themselves must take the lead role in monitoring and enforcing their own labor standards. But that points to another problem: decent labor standards are "public goods" within the workforce. The public goods dimension of workplace safety is particularly clear, and figures in some neoclassical economic arguments in favor of health and safety laws (Burton and Chelius, 1997). But collective action problems plague many terms of employment, for employers govern their employment relations largely through policies and practices, not through individualized agreements. For example, a single employee's effort to challenge an employer's exaction of "off-the-clock" work faces a "free rider" problem if the practice affects multiple employees; both the cost to the employer and the benefit to employees of correcting the practice far exceed the benefit to the individual complainant.

The public goods nature of workplace terms and conditions suggests, and empirical studies confirm, the value of a collective voice for workers in achieving compliance with those minimum standards (Freeman and Medoff, 1984; Morantz, 2009; Weiler, 1990). Unfortunately, employees in the U.S. without union representation have no lawful, legally sanctioned avenue for collective participation in enforcement, either under the labor standards statutes or otherwise; they have only the individual right to file a complaint or to contact regulators (Bennett and Kaufman, 2002; Brudney, 1996).

As we have seen, non-union forms of employee representation, far from being nearly mandatory as they are in much of the developed world, are basically illegal under the

NLRA's broad ban on "company unions." Section 8(a)(2) stands as a legal obstacle to efforts (by states or regulatory agencies, as well as employers), to institute non-union representation schemes; and political obstacles have defeated efforts to amend the statute. Both employers and organized labor are suspicious, albeit for opposite reasons, of any form of non-union employee representation. Employers fear that workplace committees would become a point of entry for union organizing, while unions fear that they would become management-dominated tools for deflecting or quashing union sentiment.[6] The decline of union representation and the lack of any other legally sanctioned vehicle of collective employee voice produce a workplace "representation gap" that contributes in turn to the underenforcement of labor standards.

Minimum labor standards are meant to set a floor on terms and conditions at the low end of the labor market; they are not meant to and do not bind employers above the floor. But widespread non-compliance with minimum labor standards means that labor market forces and individual employment contracts are still setting most workers' terms and conditions both above and often below the official floor. We will return to the representation gap below. But first let us fold in the other subset of employment mandates: employee rights, particularly against discriminatory treatment.

B.   Employee Rights and Underenforcement

Employee rights, like labor standards, were central to the original New Deal labor regime. But rights under the NLRA – to form a union, to discuss workplace concerns, and to engage in peaceful concerted activity – were meant to support collective bargaining, and were enforceable only through the NLRB. The idea of the workplace as a domain of civil rights and liberties was extended and transformed with Title VII of the Civil Rights Act of 1964, which proscribed discrimination in terms and conditions of employment based on race, sex, religion, color and national origin.[7] The banner of equal opportunity has proven to be politically formidable and adaptable. Congress has extended it to new categories (age, pregnancy, disability and genetic endowment), added new remedies, and overruled judicial decisions that restricted liability.[8] State and local laws protect additional groups and add remedies and judicial fora. Most of these statutory equality rights, state and federal, are enforceable both by public agencies and by individuals; a jury trial is generally available, and remedies include compensatory and exemplary damages, as well as attorney fees.[9]

Employment discrimination law gave momentum to the idea of the workplace as a domain of legally cognizable rights and liberties. It also gave birth to a plaintiffs' employment bar, which pressed for additional employee rights of privacy and dignity on and off the job, and of freedoms of belief, association and expression at work. Those claims challenged the employers' presumptive power under employment at will to terminate employment at any time for good reason, bad reason or no reason at all (Summers, 2000). But the civil rights laws had already dealt a mortal blow to the legitimacy of firing employees for "bad reasons," and opened the door to legislative and judicial recognition of other unacceptably bad reasons for discharge. Beginning in the 1960s, employment at will became riddled with "wrongful discharge" exceptions, and common law courts invoked public policy to afford redress to employees fired for refusing to violate the law, for claiming a legal right, or for "blowing the whistle" on violations of the law.[10]

Legislatures also entered the fray. By the 1970s, it became common, in legislation regulating private firms' conduct, to prohibit retaliation against employees who report violations of the law. OSHA and Title VII both contain such provisions, as do environmental, consumer protection, tax, and securities statutes. Some of these statutory "whistleblower" protections, like OSHA's, lack robust enforcement procedures and remedies; others, like Title VII's, allow private enforcement and broad remedies. These provisions recognize that firms' compliance with their legal obligations to workers, consumers, shareholders and the public at large depends upon the willingness of individuals inside those firms to abide by the law and to report violations. That in turn required the recognition of employee rights against discrimination or retaliation for doing their part.

These rights and liabilities have had some of the deterrent impact that tort liability is supposed to have: They have induced employers to take precautions against liability. Some employer precautions aim to minimize "accidents" – that is, decisions that might be found wrongful – by creating internal procedures for the review and appeal of disciplinary and discharge decisions. There is little doubt that the threat of litigation and liability has helped to transform personnel practices and workplace demographics, at least among "leading firms," as we will see.

The expansion of employee rights should not be overstated, of course. The scope and strength of those rights vary from state to state and often from case to case; and they are circumscribed by deference to managerial prerogatives and undermined by the background regime of employment at will (Estlund, 1996). Moreover, enforcement is left largely to affected employees themselves. Given the cost of litigation and the difficulty of proving an unlawful motive, many employees are unable or unwilling to challenge a discharge or other adverse action they believe to be illegal (Maltby, 2003). Some employees, especially low-wage immigrants, may be so unlikely to sue to enforce their rights that employers can safely ignore those rights. In short, some employee rights, like labor standards laws, are underenforced, at least at the bottom of the labor market.

Part of the problem is that even individual employee rights against discrimination and retaliation often face collective action problems. First, the very nature of discrimination lies in treating individuals differently based on their group identity; absent "smoking gun" evidence, discrimination may not be recognized, much less provable, unless employees are able to share and collect information about how other members of the group are treated. That information is a public good. Second, as Title VII doctrine itself recognizes, much discrimination occurs not through one-off personnel decisions, but through policies and practices that affect many employees at once. Those policies and practices may be challenged through both "pattern-and-practice" lawsuits and "disparate impact" claims, and the law allows for aggregate litigation to mitigate the collective action problems that face such lawsuits. Yet workforce-wide theories of liability and aggregate lawsuits face many hurdles, legal and practical, especially in the wake of the Supreme Court's 2011 decisions overturning class certification in the Wal-Mart case,[11] and striking down the major doctrinal barrier to employer efforts to bar aggregate claims through mandatory arbitration schemes.[12] Aggregate forms of discrimination, and the collective action problems that follow, are not matched by effective aggregate forms of redress.

Nor are aggregate forms of discrimination matched by effective collective mechanisms for addressing discrimination internally. Unions might be able to do that – though unions, as majoritarian institutions, have not always represented minority group concerns effectively (Frymer, 2007). At least in the non-union workplace, there is no internal mechanism for pooling employees' information and interests in relation to discriminatory policies and practices. Once again, the "representation gap" – and the lack of any meaningful collective employee voice in the vast majority of workplaces – undermines effective enforcement of rights that are mandated by law.

So for a variety of reasons across a wide range of employment mandates, both above and below official minimum standards, the individual employment contract and the market forces that operate on parties to the contract effectively govern most terms and conditions of employment most of the time for most employees. That is especially true at the top and the bottom of the labor market. So let us turn to the nature of that employment contract.

III. INCOMPLETE CONTRACTS AND UNDERENFORCED NORMS

The employment contract is highly incomplete. Most of its terms are relegated to employer discretion, informal norms, and reputational sanctions, and are not legally enforceable. On one account, that is as it should be. In any event, that is how it is. The question is whether employees in the non-union workplace are adequately protected against the risk of employer opportunism in this norm-based regime.

A.   The Incomplete Employment Contract in Theory, and the Limits of Non-Legally Enforceable Norms

According to the economic theory of the firm, firms "make" rather than "buy" – they employ labor internally rather than contracting with other market actors for the relevant products or services – when the nature of the work requires close monitoring, firm-specific knowledge or both (Wachter, Chapter 15 in this volume; Williamson et al., 1975). In such cases, both the transaction costs associated with the negotiation and enforcement of detailed contracts with outsiders and the productivity gains from workers' accumulation of firm-specific skills are likely to be high; when that is the case, it is more cost-effective to hire employees to perform the work within the firm, subject to managerial control, than it is to contract with outside actors. As a result, the nature of individual employment contracts inside the firm is fundamentally different from the nature of ordinary contracts for goods or services: Their raison d'être is the avoidance of explicit contracting costs, and their terms are largely open-ended, leaving much to employer direction and discretion and informal interaction. Thus arise "internal labor markets," in which match-specific investments and asymmetric information create the possibility of both joint gains and opportunism of the sort that are generally thought to be absent in competitive external labor markets.

Some have argued that the problem of opportunism in internal labor markets offers a neoclassical economic justification for the role of collective bargaining, which avoids many of the costs of contracting with external actors, as well as the costs of judicial enforcement, while addressing the problem of employer opportunism (Wachter and

Wright, 1990; Dau-Schmidt, 1992; Weiler, 1990). Others have argued that the still-substantial contracting costs associated with collective bargaining, even with non-judicial enforcement of the collective contract, puts it in tension with the economic logic of the firm's decision to "make" through employees rather than "buying" through outside contractors (Wachter, 2007). Whatever the virtues of collective bargaining as a response to employer opportunism, employers have overwhelmingly resisted it; and, given the law's weak constraints on employers' anti-unionism, they have largely succeeded in avoiding it. So the problem of opportunism that arises in internal labor markets in the *non-union* workplace remains to be reckoned with.

One solution lies in discerning and enforcing the terms of the individual contract. But the economic theory of the firm suggests that legal enforcement of the terms of individual employment contracts is presumptively inefficient because it imports into the employment relationship many of the costs that the relationship was formed to avoid (Wachter, Chapter 2 in this volume; Rock and Wachter, 1996; Wachter and Wright, 1990). Crucially, legal enforcement is also said to be unnecessary to protect employees, for workplaces are governed by norms of fairness, and employers face the threat of informal sanctions against the violation of norms of fair treatment (Rock and Wachter, 1996).

To say that workplaces are governed by norms of fairness reveals little about what those norms are and what counts as "fair" in any given workplace. As a general matter, it means fulfillment of employer promises and reasonable employee expectations – but what do employers promise and what do employees reasonably expect? For most workers, fairness may require reasonable business-related reasons for both advancement and adverse employment decisions, and maintenance or improvement of basic economic terms of employment absent serious economic necessity. But in some industries – for example, in high-tech sectors – job security may be of less concern to employees than job mobility, and the ability to quit and compete without legal restraints (Hyde, Chapter 12 in this volume; Hyde, 2003). Those sectors may see the rise of norms against the use of non-compete covenants. Whatever the content of norms of fairness, and whether they arise from employer promises or from employees' own sense of what is fair, those norms are said to be "self-enforcing" – backed by informal reputational sanctions – and not properly enforceable by courts.

Professors Rock and Wachter (1996) thus contend that legal enforcement of employer promises of job security is unnecessary, costly, and ultimately counterproductive for workers. Legal enforcement is unnecessary, they argue, because employers are already bound by informal norms of fair treatment backed by reputational sanctions: current employees can punish the employer for breaching promises or acting unfairly through voluntary quits, reduced effort, or even covert sabotage.[13] And prospective employees can either avoid or demand higher wages from an employer that gains a reputation for opportunism or unfairness. In sum, employers who act opportunistically or arbitrarily will have to pay higher wages, will depress workers' morale and productivity, or will lose good workers to employers who do abide by social norms of fairness. Legal enforcement is also costly: both the sheer expense of litigation and the less calculable cost of erroneous decisions by outside decisionmakers are high due to the open-endedness of many terms of employment and the cost and difficulty of monitoring employee performance. All that being the case, legal enforcement is ultimately counterproductive for workers because those costs are greater than the incremental gain in job security, and will be borne by employees in the form of lower wages. In short, workers are *and rationally should be* unwilling to pay for the benefit of legal enforceability; it is simply not worth the price.

Or so the story goes. Prospective employees may have difficulty gaining reliable information about employment practices; even something as basic as an employee manual may not be available to outsiders, while non-compete covenants or arbitration agreements may not be presented until after hiring, when the employee's options have narrowed (Estlund, 2007). Even as to current employees, employers may be able to conceal opportunistic behavior (for example, by portraying unfair discharges as fair or as voluntary resignations); and they may be able to detect and deter employees' own countermeasures (reduced effort, for example) by closer monitoring and the threat of termination. Moreover, current employees' decision to quit – their primary recourse in response to unfairness – may be quite costly, especially for employees who have accumulated firm-specific skills and knowledge, and especially in slack labor market conditions. The point is not that informal sanctions do not work at all, but that they work imperfectly and to varying degrees.

Scholars are likely to divide along rather familiar lines over the question of whether informal norms and sanctions protect workers from employers' opportunistic or abusive behavior. But there should be agreement on the following: first, informal norms and reputational sanctions will better protect the expectations of workers with scarce and higher-level skills than of workers who lack those skills; the latter are easier to replace and easier to monitor, thus reducing the cost to the employer of its own opportunism. Second, informal norms and sanctions will be more effective in disciplining the behavior of larger and more established firms with robust reputations, and less effective in disciplining smaller and more marginal firms with less history, less of a public profile, and less of a stake in cultivating a good reputation. In other words, even if informal norms and sanctions were perfectly adequate to protect the most skilled and valued workers in Fortune-500-type firms, they might leave a sizable gap between workers' reasonable expectations and employer behavior among less skilled workers, especially in smaller and more marginal firms.

There is another problem among those workers at the bottom of the labor market: Employers may simply make no promises or raise no expectations of fair treatment. The problem in that case is not one of protecting employees from employer "opportunism," nor is the solution likely to be found within the employment contract, with or without legal enforcement. The problem at the bottom of the labor market is one of enforcing minimum standards of fair and decent treatment at work, a task that has proven challenging, as we have seen.

B.   The Incomplete Employment Contract in Fact

So there should be agreement that norms and non-legal sanctions, even if they can be effective in protecting workers in theory, will work less well among the most fungible workers and among smaller and less-capitalized firms. There should also be agreement on this: whatever its efficiency or desirability in theory, informal norm-based workplace governance has largely prevailed in practice. That is, non-union workplaces in the U.S. are in fact largely governed by non-legally enforceable norms (and legal mandates), not by formal contract. Although courts are hardly guided by the "theory of the firm" when faced with employee claims of unfair treatment and broken promises, they reach much the same result through doctrines that ensure a high degree of managerial discretion over how employment relations are to be governed. Managerial discretion and the predominance of norm-based governance was supported by one set of legal doctrines for much of the 20th century, and then, after a decade or two of transitional uncertainty, by another set of doctrines.

Until the 1960s or 1970s, individual employee claims of unfair treatment were mostly kept out of the courts by a very robust presumption of employment at will, fortified by a cluster of doctrines requiring that employer promises be unusually specific, often in writing, and supported by extraordinary consideration and "mutuality" of obligation. As long as employees were free to quit at will, courts were loath to find employers bound even to express promises of job security; and as long as employers were free to fire employees at will, they were free to condition continued employment on virtually any terms of employment they chose. The result was that, except in rare circumstances (and still putting aside the then-minor role of legal mandates), employers were constrained only by non-legally enforceable norms and informal sanctions, not by legally enforceable contracts.

Starting in the 1970s, the legal fortifications around employment at will began to crumble, and courts began to see many employment disputes that were readily constructed as breaches of contract. Relatively few employees had secured individual written promises regarding job security or the conditions of future employment; but many could attest to oral representations of fair treatment or implied promises of job security, or could point to employee handbook provisions that promised fairness in discipline and discharge decisions. Courts struggled, and disagreed, over whether employee expectations arising from oral and implied representations and employee handbooks were sufficiently definite and supported by consideration (or detrimental reliance) to be legally enforceable. But courts in most states opened one or more avenues of legal recourse to employees claiming that employers had broken promises, particularly promises of job security, in discharge decisions.

Employers responded with some alarm to the news that past assurances and existing policy documents might open them up to lawsuits by employees who were fired or laid off without adequate proof of good cause (Autor et al., 2006).[14] But even as courts opened the door for employees' contract claims, they instructed employers on how to close that door. As the New Jersey Supreme Court put it in the *Woolley* decision, a landmark employee handbook case, for an employer that wishes to avoid these lawsuits, "there are simple ways to attain that goal":

> All that need be done is the inclusion in a very prominent position of an appropriate statement that there is no promise of any kind by the employer contained in the manual; that regardless of what the manual says or provides, the employer promises nothing and remains free to change wages and all other working conditions without having to consult anyone and without anyone's agreement; and that the employer continues to have the absolute power to fire anyone with or without good cause.[15]

Woolley set a rather stringent standard for the clarity and prominence of disclaimers. Some courts, along similar lines, find ambiguity in the combination of a disclaimer and promissory language, and allow such cases to go to a jury.[16] But for the most part, a reasonably prominent boilerplate disclaimer in an employee handbook or job application forecloses nearly all employee contract claims, whether based on an oral contract, implied contract, or an employee handbook (Estlund, 2010).[17]

Once employers rewrote their manuals and job applications to incorporate the requisite disclaimers, as most did, they largely defused the threat of contract litigation for newly hired employees. For incumbent employees with potentially enforceable expectations of job security, the process took a bit longer. Some courts required formal acceptance or consideration for modifications disclaiming prior promises of job security. But whether by virtue of doctrine or of workplace realities, well-advised employers have generally been able to condition continued employment on employees' acceptance of new (at-will and non-legally enforceable) terms for the future. And once employers had effectively regained the power to fire employees at will, they also regained the power to impose other new terms prospectively as a condition of continued employment – including harsher working conditions, stingier benefits, suspicionless drug tests, or other restrictions on private life or freedom of speech and association. Some of those terms may be subject to public policy constraints and statutory employee rights and mandates; but they are largely immune from challenge based on employees' reasonable expectations about their terms and conditions of employment.

It took a decade or two of litigation in most states for the new legal rules to be worked out and for employers to modify their employment practices accordingly. The process was drawn out, messy and somewhat costly for employers. But, in hindsight, this was a transitional problem that left employer prerogatives largely intact. The new law of the employment contract, much like the old, allows employers to adopt a regime of norms without legal enforceability. For, at the end of the day, contract law is about enforcing promises, and employers largely decide for themselves whether and how much to promise employees.

The difference between the old regime and the new (again, apart from the growing role of employment mandates) is that, at least in theory, the new regime is more above-board. The doctrinal shift had much the same information-forcing effect as a hypothetical "penalty default" rule rendering norms (especially those regarding job security) enforceable: employers had to make explicit their commitment to employment at will and their avoidance of contractual constraints (Issacharoff, 1996). If employees read and understand the disclaimer language by which they are bound, they now realize that any promises or expectations of fair treatment are only as reliable as their employer is trustworthy, and are not backed up by the courts. (In fact, many appear to believe otherwise (Kim, 1997); employees' faulty information about the law's content points to another "public goods" problem.) In theory, if they are unsettled by their lack of legal protection, or by employer actions that demonstrate untrustworthiness, they can go elsewhere or simply put forth less effort; indeed, in theory, they could form a union, and reject the regime of non-legally-enforceable norms in favor of collective contract and arbitral enforcement. In reality, each of those courses of action may be quite costly or simply unavailable. The upshot is that, most private sector employees are back in the domain of non-legally enforceable norms and informal sanctions.

Under the modern law of the employment contract, employers can and generally do choose to govern the workplace largely on a discretionary basis, within boundaries set by market forces, informal norms, and external law, but without the constraints of legally enforceable contractual obligations. The limited reach of formal contract should not be overstated: employer promises regarding compensation for work that has already been done are generally enforceable, for example.[18] Moreover, some workers with special skills, talents, and experience that are valued in the external labor market can deploy their bargaining power to secure enforceable contractual promises on issues that matter to them – whether that is job security, job mobility, compensation, or something else. But for most employees, employment is subject to termination at will, and its terms and conditions are subject to prospective change at will, without contractual constraints or third party review. The nature of most employment contracts – as employers have constructed them – is to leave such issues to employer discretion and to the domain of norms.

Outside the small and shrinking union sector, and beyond the domain of mandates, workers thus depend heavily on non-legally enforceable norms and non-legal (especially reputational) sanctions to protect their interests. Yet the incompleteness and modifiability of employment contracts, by leaving wide room for employer discretion, create the potential for employer abuse and opportunism. Employers may make tacit or explicit promises to induce employees to accept employment, to stay on the job, and to invest in firm-specific skills and know-how; and employees may rely on those unenforceable promises in deciding to take a job or stay on. Reputational sanctions for broken promises and opportunistic behavior will be relatively weak where employers can readily find the skills they need on the external labor market, where they can easily monitor employee performance and punish those who slack off, or where they can conceal their opportunism – for example, by portraying unfair dismissals as justified, as voluntary quits, or as economically necessary layoffs. Especially in slack labor markets these conditions may prevail even for relatively skilled workers.

The vagaries of non-legal enforcement are exacerbated by the fact that, on many or even most matters of concern to employees, employers' compliance with informal norms and fulfillment of promises of fair treatment, and information about that compliance, is a public good among the workforce. Compliance is usually a wholesale and not a retail matter – a matter of policy, not individual case-by-case decisionmaking. The cost of compliance to the employer is often much greater than the benefits to each employee, so that, even apart from employees' fears of employer reprisals, each employee is tempted to free-ride on others' efforts to enforce norms or promises made to a group of workers.

We have seen that employer practices – both their individual contracting practices and their successful resistance to unions and collective bargaining – have effectively avoided legally enforceable contractual obligations of any kind; they have created the norm-based individual employment relationships that neoclassical economic theory favors and that employers obviously prefer. But the serious potential for employer opportunism in such a regime, and the "public goods" nature of employer compliance with informal norms of fair treatment, give rise to a "representation gap" – an unmet need and desire for some form of organized collective employee representation in workplace governance.

IV.   THE RACE TO THE BOTTOM AND THE RACE FOR TALENT: DIVERGENT CHALLENGES AND OPPORTUNITIES FOR IMPROVING WORKPLACE GOVERNANCE

The picture painted thus far highlights the problems of underenforced labor standards, underenforced employee rights, and underenforced norms. These problems are obviously greatest among workers at the bottom of the labor market. But we have already intimated that the outlook for some employees is considerably brighter. For the "talent" in the "race for talent" – that is, the sought-after workers with scarce and valued skills – and for many of those who work for large, branded firms with a significant stake in their reputations, the law's meager inducements to improve labor standards and vindicate employee rights are supplemented by labor market forces, and may be magnified by reputational rewards and sanctions in consumer and financial markets. So what we see is not a uniformly depressing landscape for workers but one that features lofty peaks and lush valleys for some, and arid and unforgiving terrain for others. That highly variegated landscape poses a challenge to efforts to improve compliance with both norms and mandates in the workplace. Yet it also reveals potential footholds and leverage for reform.

Recall the pivotal role of reputational sanctions in the defense of non-legally enforceable norms in lieu of formally enforceable contract terms: reputational sanctions are supposed to do enough work to render unnecessary formal enforcement of employer representations about matters such as job security. Yet reputational sanctions are undermined in both external and internal labor markets by information deficits, and at least in internal labor markets by firm-specific investments and other frictions that raise employees' cost of exit.

For some employees, however, reputational sanctions may be exacted not only in labor markets but in product and financial markets. One might – indeed, should – be skeptical that an employer's reputation for how it treats its employees could meaningfully affect its reputation among consumers and investors, and its product or share price. But that very proposition underlies much of the corporate social responsibility (CSR) enterprise. Firms themselves seek to cultivate a reputation for maintaining a diverse and inclusive workplace environment, or a "culture of safety," among their own ranks. In both cases, firms proclaim their commitment to going "beyond compliance" to some higher standard of "best practices" and "corporate social responsibility."

Importantly, firms claim to act responsibly not just because it is the right thing to do, but because it makes good business sense. These arguments harken back to old debates about whether corporate managers should pursue the public good, or simply the interests of shareholders (Bratton and Wachter, 2008; Elhauge, 2005). The shareholder-primacy position has basically prevailed; but the CSR movement, along with the growth of the regulatory state, has managed to ensure that the corporation's impact on workers, communities and the public at large – or at least the perceived impact – must itself be of concern to both shareholders and managers.

The "business case for diversity," and for CSR generally, rests on a rarely interrogated mix of motives. Some of the business arguments are genuinely operational (for example, pollution may go hand in hand with inefficient production methods; workplace diversity may be essential to recruit and retain talent in a diverse labor force; safe and decent working conditions can reduce lost work days and costly turnover and can improve morale). But much of the business case for CSR depends on legal and reputational sanctions dealt out by external actors, and especially the damage that scandals can do to (or the good that positive publicity can do for) a brand. It seems clear that reputational sanctions can drive significant corporate investments in at least the appearance of, or reputation for, compliance with socially salient norms of workplace conduct.

There are important limitations on the extent to which consumers and investors can be expected to deliver reputational rewards or sanctions based on workplace practices. First, reputation in product and financial markets is likely to be a significant motivator only for relatively large branded companies. Second, information deficits undoubtedly impair the accuracy of corporate reputations for social responsibility, including decent employment practices, among consumers, investors and other outsiders, and even among current and prospective employees. The problem of information deficits suggests the value of requiring companies to publicly disclose accurate information about their workplace practices (Estlund, 2011). It also reinforces the case for some mechanism of collective employee voice, which can help to gather, verify and disseminate information about workplace practices to interested outsiders. To the extent that the public relies on reputational sanctions to promote compliance with public law – and that is increasingly so, by choice or default – the public should also seek to elicit the information that can allow stakeholders and market participants to keep reputations in line with reality.

With those caveats, let us consider the potential reputational impact of poor workplace practices – that is, practices that violate either legal mandates or the workplace norms that largely supplant formal contracts. Those are two areas in which we have found serious gaps in enforcement; the question is whether outside reputational sanctions can help to close either of those gaps.

The reputational impact of legal non-compliance may be significant. A few studies have sought to measure empirically the adverse impact of lawsuits or judgments on a firm's share price (which presumably reflects in large part the perceived impact on the brand, and ultimately the price of its products). The findings have been mixed or modest (Selmi, 2003; Blose and Calvasina, 2002; Ursel and Amstrong-Stassen, 2006). Still, large branded firms act as though their reputations are damaged by credible claims that they have violated the employment laws; some firms undertake costly remedial efforts in the wake of such claims, and many others invest significant resources to avoid such claims. Witness, for example, Coca-Cola's response in 2000 to claims of race discrimination (Winter, 2000), and Wal-Mart's attempt at a corporate identity makeover, beginning in 2005, after a barrage of lawsuits pointing to widespread off-the-clock work demands and to a record-setting sex discrimination lawsuit (Briones, 2009). These are not isolated cases. In a recent book, sociologist Frank Dobbin traces the fascinating process by which a hazy but potent threat of discrimination litigation or loss of federal contracts helped to spur the development and dissemination of corporate policies promoting fairness, diversity and inclusiveness, and family-friendliness; those policies went well beyond what the law could plausibly be read to require (Dobbin, 2009).

It may be fair to assume that these corporate investments are founded on something real, even if it is hard to document empirically. Lawsuits, especially successful ones, have a way of crystallizing the otherwise-diffuse information on which reputations are based; they enable stakeholders to coalesce around credible and concrete claims, and to call upon whatever societal consensus underlies the relevant laws as well as the general opprobrium attached to lawbreaking (Sachs, 2008). At the very least they are an irritant worth avoiding. That helps drive many large branded firms to try to avoid litigation, to stay ahead of the legal curve, and to portray themselves as reaching beyond compliance with socially salient legal standards. For those firms, the apparently weak deterrent force of many employment laws, given the probability and formal legal consequences of their enforcement, is magnified by a range of reputational consequences.

It is less clear whether and how workplace norms might be backed by these sorts of reputational sanctions. Some such norms may come within the "penumbra" of legal mandates – the margin by which leading firms may go "beyond compliance" in order to insulate themselves from the threat of litigation and scandal. For example, the non-discrimination mandate may promote greater fairness and "due process" in connection with discipline and discharge. To that degree, and in those leading firms, legal mandates may do some work on behalf of non-legally enforceable norms that shape employee expectations. Otherwise, much of what allows legal enforcement and lawsuits to serve as effective spurs to corporate compliance is missing in the case of non-legally enforceable workplace norms. Such norms are often diffuse, as is evidence of their violation, and are not necessarily backed by a broad societal consensus. There is no counterpart to the crystallizing, coalescing and credibility-enhancing impact of lawsuits. We have already surmised that labor market forces may do a good deal to enforce workplace norms that affect "the talent" – the sought-after skilled workers at the top of the labor market. But even in large branded companies, consumer and investor pressures are unlikely to come to the aid of less skilled workers claiming breach of non-legally enforceable workplace norms.

So it is that the law of the workplace must grapple with an extreme heterogeneity of workplace settings, and particularly a sharp divergence between the firms and workers at the top of the heap and those at the bottom. For those at the top, incomplete contracts are supplemented and inadequate legal sanctions are magnified by highly imperfect yet significant reputational sanctions in labor, product and financial markets that induce significant investments in compliance and "beyond compliance." For those at the bottom, however, the force of both law and norms is weakened by collective action problems and fear of reprisals that virtually disable many low-wage employees from playing their indispensable role in enforcement. Of course, many workers fall in between the top and the bottom, and have neither the considerable advantages of high-skill workers in big firms nor the severe disadvantages of low-skill workers in marginal firms.

It would be helpful to be able to gauge the relative size of the top and bottom layers of the labor market and of the layers in between. But those questions are only partly empirical in nature, and are sure to be hotly contested. Some neoclassical labor economists regard what is described here as the "bottom" of the labor market as a small and marginal phenomenon limited largely to firms and jobs populated by undocumented immigrants; above that lowest layer of the labor market, they count mainly on labor market competition to discipline employers and protect employees (Wachter, 2007). Others, including economists of the institutional and industrial relations persuasions, see more impediments to labor market competition, more room for employer exploitation – of information asymmetries, of labor market frictions, of bargaining power, and accordingly of employees – and a greater role for collective representation and regulation in protecting a larger swath of the labor market (Kaufman, Chapter 3 in this volume). I do not pretend to resolve these disputes, but adopt the latter view here, based partly on concerns about the extent of information deficits and asymmetries in employment (Estlund, 2011). A rash of recent accounts suggest that large chunks of the workforce in the manufacturing, retail, service, and transportation sectors experience substandard conditions and growing insecurity (Greenhouse, 2008; Bobo, 2009; Appelbaum, Bernhardt, and Murnane, 2003).

V.   A TWO-TRACK STRATEGY FOR NARROWING THE WORKPLACE REPRESENTATION GAP

We have identified an enforcement gap with regard to both workplace fairness norms and employment law mandates, especially among workers who lack individual market power and in firms that lack a significant stake in their reputations. The enforcement gap is traceable in large part to collective action problems and fear of reprisals by individual (at-will) employees. To that degree it is traceable as well to the lack of collective employee representation or voice in most workplaces, for collective employee representation is well-suited to addressing both collective action problems and fear of reprisals.

It is no surprise that the "representation gap," or the demand and the need for a collective employee voice, is greatest among those workers with the least labor market power and in those firms that are least subject to reputational sanctions. The supply of collective representation of the traditional union variety for those workers has been constrained by aggressive employer resistance, driven in part, to be sure, by competitive pressures in product and capital markets, as well as by unions' own limited ability and will to invest in organizing low wage workers. We will turn to these problems below. For now, it is enough to observe that collective worker voice is most needed at the bottom, though likely to be valuable well above the bottom in enforcing workplace norms and mandates.

Any effort to address the workplace representation gap will lead us straight into the thicket of labor law reform from which no significant legislation has emerged for over 50 years. I will explore a two-track labor law reform proposal that seeks to address the rather different problems that employees face, and that holds out some (admittedly slim) hope of breaking the logjam that has stymied past labor law reform proposals.

Narrowing the workplace representation gap will aid in the enforcement of both internal workplace norms and external mandates. But obviously the public has greater leverage and greater legitimacy in seeking to improve the enforcement of publicly imposed mandates. So that is where we will look in the first instance for solutions to the workplace representation gap. We must bear in mind as we do so that the sharply divergent conditions faced by employees at the top and the bottom of the labor market will affect not only the incidence of illegality – minimum wage violations, for example, are obviously concentrated at the bottom – but also the efficacy of regulatory strategies. Firms vary in both the will and the capacity to comply with norms and mandates. As a shorthand, we may refer to "high-road" and "low-road" employers. But undoubtedly many employers are somewhere in between – complying unless it is too costly or unless competitors are getting away with cheating, or sitting on the fence and observing how different strategies fare. A one-size-fits-all regulatory strategy – for example, one that either assumes or ignores the disposition to comply with the law or the potential for reputational sanctions to magnify legal deterrence – may misfire, fall short, or waste scarce enforcement resources (Ayres and Braithwaite, 1992; Estlund, 2010).

Let us begin at the top.

A.   Redefining Responsibility for High-Road Employers

Employment law, for all its deficiencies as an instrument of workplace governance, has become a prolific fount of duties and liabilities. Employers have pushed back, pleading for deregulation and relief from the "litigation crisis."[19] But, at the same time, they have had to manage their liabilities. Title VII and the resulting wave of discrimination litigation generated an upsurge of internal grievance procedures and equal employment offices to redress potential discrimination complaints (and avoid lawsuits). OSHA spurred the growth of corporate health and safety departments. Parallel compliance structures were put in place to manage liabilities under environmental, securities, consumer safety and other regulatory regimes.

The rise of corporate self-regulation has coincided with a growing scholarly critique of the postwar regime of "command-and-control regulation" or "adversarial legalism" (Kagan and Bardach, 1982), which is said to be losing its grip in the face of complex and rapidly changing markets, technology and firm structures (see Breyer, 1982; Dorf and Sabel, 1998). In the workplace context, critics argue that uniform minimum standards are unable to address the range of concerns and contexts that workers face (Weiler, 1990); civil litigation is a costly, slow and often inaccessible mechanism for securing workplace rights and adjudicating disputes (U.S. Commission, 1994; Estreicher, 2001; Outten, 1999; Sternlight, 2004).

In view of both growing corporate compliance capabilities and doubts about the efficacy of traditional regulatory strategies, scholars have argued that law should be reconceived and retooled as an instrument to encourage and steer employers' self-regulatory efforts rather than primarily as a direct instrument of control (Estlund, 2010; Lobel, 2004). In some respects the ideas underlying regulated self-regulation are compatible with a sophisticated deterrence theory, and with a view of law and liability rules as shaping the incentives of rational economic actors, including firms, their managers, and employees within the firm (Arlen and Kraakman, 1997). But most theories of regulated self-regulation rely on a more complex account of organizational dynamics and individual motivations, one that recognizes the potential for firms and individuals to internalize public values and regulatory aims (Estlund, 2010).

The idea of fostering self-regulation has begun to shape the external law of the workplace. The federal Organizational Sentencing Guidelines, and reigning standards for prosecutorial charging decisions, reward companies that maintain an "effective compliance program" (Estlund, 2010). Agencies have experimented with cooperative programs designed to encourage self-regulation and to reduce the role and cost of "adversarial legalism" (Lobel, 2004). Courts have begun to formalize the role of internal compliance regimes, and to shape and reward them, by according employers a partial shield against litigation and liability based on those regimes. Firms now institute and craft internal compliance regimes not simply to comply with the law but to secure the legal advantages of self-regulation and a partial shield against regulatory and judicial intervention. These developments bring the main locus of enforcement of both rights and regulations inside the firm or under the firm's control.

In short, the law has begun to create multiple enforcement tracks, and to treat responsible self-regulating organizations differently from those organizations that lack either the capacity or the will to self-regulate. The former correspond roughly to the organizations that aspire to norms of corporate social responsibility, while the latter include many small and marginal entities as well as some opportunistic firms that may be both capable and ostensibly compliant.

The move toward more and less regulated versions of self-regulation, and toward multiple regulatory tracks, is widespread. Across regulatory arenas, and across much of the world, there has been a shift away from direct regulation and toward mechanisms for encouraging organizations to self-regulate (Braithwaite and Drahos, 2000). Skeptics see a disguised form of deregulation, with a high risk of "cosmetic compliance" and window-dressing (see Arthurs, 2005; Blackett, 2001; Krawiec, 2003). Proponents acknowledge the risks but see the evolution of more efficient and effective systems for enforcing legal norms (Ayres and Braithwaite, 1992; Kagan and Bardach, 1982; Estlund, 2010). Much turns on whether courts and regulators can distinguish effective from ineffective systems of self-regulation, or high-road from low-road actors. The difficulty of that task poses perhaps the greatest challenge to the emerging model of regulated self-regulation.

For that very reason, a crucial dimension of effective self-regulation is meaningful participation of stakeholders – the beneficiaries of the relevant laws, whether they are consumers, environmentalists, patients or workers – in the self-regulatory enterprise (Ayres and Braithwaite, 1992). Stakeholder involvement, particularly in monitoring compliance, is a crucial safeguard against "cosmetic compliance" and cheating by firms and against capture or inattention on the part of regulators (id.). What that obviously entails in the workplace is meaningful participation of the workers who are the law's beneficiaries and best monitors (Estlund, 2010). That requires not only avenues for individual reporting and complaints, but some organized form of collective representation to overcome the collective action problems associated with the "public good" of legal compliance, as well as the fear of reprisals that inhibits individual employees from monitoring compliance. Workers collectively can blow the whistle on employers who are masquerading as responsible self-regulators, and can help to keep a system of regulated self-regulation honest.

Unions would seem to fit the bill, both in theory and experience; employee rights and labor standards tend to be better enforced in unionized workplaces (Morantz, 2009; Craver, 1998; Rabin, 1991). But for reasons explored briefly above, few private sector workers in the U.S. have union representation or are likely to get it in the foreseeable future. Nor do those workers generally have access to any other form of organized, legally sanctioned employee representation within the firm. That is a troubling state of affairs for U.S. workers, particularly as regulation moves inside of organizations. But it is a state of affairs that calls for different solutions and different strategies at the top and the bottom of the labor market.

The partial migration of employment law and its enforcement inside firms – especially among "responsible" organizations – creates not only the need but also the opportunity to revive employees' voice inside firms. That is because the law can and does impose conditions on firms' ability to secure the legal advantages of self-regulation. Those conditions should be designed to ensure the efficacy of self-regulation, and should include meaningful collective participation of the employees whose rights and working conditions are at stake. In short, any self-regulatory privileges that the law and legal actors deal out in the employment arena – partial defenses to liability, more congenial and cooperative enforcement tracks – should be reserved for firms that maintain an effective system of self-regulation in which employees have meaningful collective representation (or what I have called "co-regulation"). Unlike much of what now passes for corporate self-regulation, a system of co-regulation would provide safeguards against the cosmetic compliance and against "self-deregulation" that critics legitimately fear.

Given the current statutory constraints on non-union forms of employee representation, congressional action in support of co-regulation is necessary. One simple and straightforward reform would be a revised definition of "effective compliance and ethics programs" under the federal Organizational Sentencing Guidelines to include meaningful representation of stakeholders, and of employees in the case of workplace laws. Those guidelines have been extremely influential in shaping at least the superficial attributes of corporate compliance programs. Express congressional action to require stakeholder (employee) representation as an element of "effective compliance" could simultaneously take down the hurdle that Section 8(a)(2) of the NLRA now poses to internal employee representation schemes and strongly encourage corporations to institute or permit such schemes. That would open the door to external examination and comparison of various schemes, assessment of their efficacy, and development of "best practices" regarding stakeholder (employee) representation.

Alternatively, co-regulatory reform could be pursued piecemeal – one statutory regime or even one state at a time – provided that the 8(a)(2) roadblock were removed. Indeed, with that same proviso, it would be possible to make progress without further legislation, and to pave the way for future legislation, by injecting the idea of co-regulation and stakeholder representation into the evolving concept of corporate social responsibility.

Corporate social responsibility is often an ill-defined concept, but it is also protean and evolving. Nowadays, for a firm that has embraced the CSR project (as the entire Fortune 500 has done to varying degrees), corporate responsibility entails, among other things, a commitment to a diverse and inclusive workforce and to a safe and healthy workplace; and each of those commitments entails further organizational reforms designed to put those commitments into practice. The transformation of equal opportunity and affirmative action programs into commitments and programs for workforce diversity and inclusion is perhaps the most striking case in point (Dobbin, 2009). Increasingly, and perhaps more surprisingly, a responsible corporation is one that ensures that its *suppliers* comply with labor, environmental and human rights standards, even when there is no colorable claim of legal responsibility for those suppliers' actions. The gap between corporate professions of responsibility and actual performance is notorious, sometimes scandalously so. But scandals often beget further precautions and reforms, not only on the part of the firm that has been exposed but on the part of others seeking to avoid their own scandal. The CSR juggernaut is not all that it purports to be, but its impact is real, and it seems to be here to stay.

Each of the dimensions of responsible corporate citizenship emerged out of a conscious reform effort emanating from both outsiders – stakeholders and advocates – and insiders within large firms. "Social regulation," backed by a mix of legal and reputational pressures, seeks to induce leading firms to adopt "best practices," and not merely to comply with legal requirements (Dobbin, 2009). Those past successes offer a model for promoting co-regulation, and the entirely reasonable proposition that a socially responsible employer must maintain collective mechanisms for employee representation, union or non-union, especially on matters of shared employee concern and compliance with employment laws.

Of course that would still require a significant loosening of the NLRA's legal constraints on non-union forms of employee representation. The case for doing so has been rehearsed too often to bear repetition here (Barenberg, 1993; Estreicher, 1993; 1994; Kaufman, 1999) except for what I have tried to add to that case here and elsewhere: Some form of meaningful collective employee representation is essential to carrying out the combined regime of norms and mandates by which U.S. society has chosen to govern workplaces and regulate terms and conditions of employment. In that light, and in light of the very small fraction of workers who now enjoy union representation, it no longer makes sense to prohibit employers from establishing or supporting non-union employee representation structures (Estlund, 2010).[20]

As for how employee representation could be structured, models are available across the world. Some are found within the foreign operations of U.S.-based multinational corporations, such as those that are subject to the European Works Councils Directive and the more recent Information and Consultation Directive (Deakin and Koukiadaki, 2012). Others may be found in Canada, whose labor laws largely follow the U.S. "Wagner model" but diverge from the Wagner Act, among other ways, in allowing much more space for both employer-initiated and legally mandated forms of non-union employee representation (Taras, 1997). Indeed, as we have seen, the germ of non-union employee representation schemes appears to exist even within the U.S., according to the many U.S. employees who claim to already have some form of non-union collective representation (supra p. 468). Apart from the fact that most employees rate these schemes quite favorably, we know very little about how they are structured, or how well they work. The shadow of illegality that the NLRA casts over non-union employee representation takes an enormous toll on our ability to understand or improve whatever schemes exist. Some combination of legislative intervention and coordinated private ordering through CSR channels would help to promote the emergence of "best practices," or at least better practices, in employee representation.

B.   Recalibrating the "Union Threat" to Target Low-Road Employers

Unfortunately, neither a revision of the Organizational Sentencing Guidelines nor a redefinition of corporate social responsibility in the employment context will deliver meaningful representation to workers at the bottom of the labor market, especially at the hands of low-road employers. Those workers still need strong state-directed enforcement of labor standards laws and, given the inevitable shortfall in direct state oversight, independent and adversarial representation. In principle, and in some pockets of the labor market, that might be through something other than a union, such as a worker center. But for most low-wage workers, union representation is still their best recourse for seeking compliance with decent labor standards.

That brings us back to the quixotic quest for labor law reform of the more traditional sort. Over the past forty-five years, unions have lobbied for a variety of reforms that would make it easier to organize employees, including access to the workplace for union organizers, mandatory card check recognition, and bans on "captive audience meetings" and on permanent replacement of strikers. They have failed to break through the unyielding and unified opposition of businesses and their congressional allies.

But the political landscape of labor law reform might look different if we understood union organizing not only as an employee right but also as a de facto sanction against low-road employers. Employers seem to regard unionization as a fearsome fate that is well worth avoiding; perhaps that fear can be made to work *for* workers instead of only against them. Professor David Doorey has recently argued in the Canadian context for a labor law reform strategy founded on that view (Doorey, forthcoming). He proposes a more-or-less standard package of labor law reforms (access, card check, etc.) that would make it easier to organize a union, but that would apply only to employers that have been found in violation of wage and hour laws, health and safety laws, or the like.

A union-friendly labor law track for demonstrably low-road employers would allow unionization to serve simultaneously as punishment, remedy, and deterrent against violation of employment law mandates. It would enable employees to "punish" employers for violating labor standards by forming a union; that fitting and fearsome sanction would beef up the rather meager arsenal of sanctions that labor regulators can now bring to bear on violators. Union representation would also function as a prospective remedy for violations by enhancing employees' ability to enforce their own labor rights and standards going forward. At the same time, the increased threat of unionization entailed by the union-friendly labor law track would deter labor standards violations and encourage employers to maintain at least minimally decent conditions in order to avoid unionization.

The idea that a "union threat effect" can induce managers to improve wages and working conditions is not new, of course. What is new in Doorey's elaboration is the idea of sharpening and calibrating the union threat effect to address the problem of non-compliance with labor standards. It is an elegant partial solution to the stubborn intertwined problems that workers face at the bottom of the labor market: chronic underenforcement of labor standards and a lack of collective power and voice. It is still a partial solution because it depends on enforcement of employment laws to ensure the identification of "low-road" employers. But here, too, the Doorey proposal offers leverage: unions would have an incentive to identify "low-road" employers and to help bring about enforcement actions, for findings of non-compliance would trigger union-friendly labor law rules and thus facilitate organizing.

C.   A Two-Track Labor Law Reform Proposal

In the U.S. context, the creation of a union-friendly labor law track for demonstrably bad employers could be coupled with one revision to the "regular" labor law track for other employers: a narrowing of Section 8(a)(2)'s ban on "company unions," or non-union forms of employee representation. The resulting opening for non-union representation schemes would have to be crafted so as to ensure the continued availability of independent union representation for all employees. Moreover, this opening would be available only to employers that have *not* been found guilty of serious employment law violations.

Confining Section 8(a)(2) reform to "good" (or not demonstrably "bad") employers would help guard against the most cynical deployment of non-union representation schemes as a weapon of union avoidance. But it would allow responsible employers – those that are respecting their employees' basic legal rights and labor standards – to offer employees a less adversarial form of collective voice; and that would help to avoid the accumulation of grievances that might lead employees to seek union representation. Just as employers are now free to offer employees better wages, benefits and a humane work environment in order to preempt interest in unionization, they would be free under this proposal to offer a non-adversarial form of employee voice as well.

A two-track labor law reform proposal – one that coupled pro-union reforms for certifiably "low-road" employers with a narrower "company union" ban for the rest – might shake up the political stalemate over labor law reform. First, it might fracture the united front that the business community has heretofore maintained with regard to across-the-board labor law reform. "High-road" employers might feel relatively unthreatened by such a labor law reform package, and might even recognize a benefit in putting greater enforcement pressure on "low road" competitors. That might allow the emergence of a political constituency – or, more realistically, a handful of moderate votes in the Senate in some foreseeable political future – for the proposition that, even if most employers can be trusted to treat their workers right, some employers are bad enough to deserve the supposedly dire fate of unionization.

VI.   CONCLUSION

There is a workplace representation gap both among "high-road" and "low-road" employers. But the solutions to that representation gap are different at the top and the bottom of the labor market – among the leaders and the laggards – because of the divergent pressures that product markets and capital markets as well as labor markets exert on the leaders and the laggards. I have sketched a two-track regulatory strategy that links together labor law and employment law, and that harnesses both a range of reputational mechanisms and the robust and persistent fear of unionization that operate on employers at different layers of the market. The animating idea is to appeal to both the higher reputational aspirations of responsible employers and the fears of irresponsible employers, and to thereby nudge both high-road and low-road employers toward better compliance (or better than compliance) with the labor standards, rights and norms that protect workers, and toward some mechanism of employee representation that can help workers to enforce their own labor standards, rights and reasonable expectations.

Most employers probably travel on what we might call the "middle road": They do not have the means or the motivation to invest in extensive internal compliance structures, but they mostly try to live within the constraints of employment mandates as long as they understand them and can afford to abide by them, and as long as they are not being undercut by non-compliant low-road competitors. They want more flexibility and lower transaction costs than formal employment contracts or collective bargaining would afford, but they try to meet employee expectations of fair treatment as long as they can afford to do so, and as long as there is not too much to be gained from defying them. The middle-roaders are watching both the high road and the low road – how the leaders and the laggards are behaving and how they fare in both the market and the legal system. The two-track regulatory strategy advanced here aims to ensure that the middle-roaders will see both a viable high-road model of responsible workplace governance to which they can aspire, and a low road that is risky, unrewarding, and well worth avoiding.

NOTES

*   The author would like to thank Michael Wachter for thoughtful comments on earlier drafts and Dennis Chanay and Kari Wohlschlegel for excellent research assistance.
1.   See, e.g., the description of French wage bargaining in Vigneau (2003).
2.   By way of comparison, unions got high marks from 41 percent of members (for consulting with members) and 54 percent (sticking up for members) (Godard and Frege, 2011, p. 16).
3.   The idea of compensating wage differentials was invoked in support of the old tort rules that foreclosed most personal injury tort actions by employees against their employers in the 19th century. *See, e.g.*, Farwell v. Boston & Worcester R.R. Corp., 45 Mass. (4 Met.) 49 (Mass 1842). For modern analogues of the argument, *see* Lambert (2004) and Viscusi (1983).
4.   ERISA does not require employers to provide pensions or other employee benefits, but it requires them to properly fund and administer whatever benefits are offered. Many ERISA provisions target the "defined benefit" pension plans that were prevalent in 1974; indeed, ERISA may in fact have contributed to the dramatic shift toward "defined contribution" plans, and toward placing greater risk on employees (Blair, 2004; Drummonds, 2007).
5.   This layer of the labor market has grown with the trend among larger firms to outsource work that is peripheral to their "core competencies" (Stone, 2004). Outsourcing allows firms to reduce costs for services such as maintenance, security, food and laundry, while potentially insulating them from liability for the labor standards violations that may follow from cost-cutting competition among contractors (Bernhardt et al., 2007).
6.   These dynamics helped to doom a Clinton-era effort to reform OSHA, in part by mandating workplace health and safety committees (Kovach et al., 1997; Rabinowitz and Hager, 2000; Seidenfeld, 2000).
7.   *See* Civil Rights Act of 1964, Pub. L. No. 88-352, § 703, 78 Stat. 241, 255 (codified as amended at 42 U.S.C. § 2000e-2 (2000)).
8.   *See* Age Discrimination in Employment Act of 1967, Pub. L. No. 90-202, 81 Stat. 602 (codified as amended at 29 U.S.C. §§ 621–34 (2000)); Pregnancy Discrimination Act, Pub. L. No. 95-555, 92 Stat. 2076 (1978) (codified at 42 U.S.C. § 2000e (2006)); Americans with Disabilities Act of 1990, Pub. L. No. 101-336, 104 Stat. 327 (codified as amended at 42 U.S.C. §§ 12101–213 (2000)); Genetic Information Nondiscrimination Act of 2007, S. 358, H.R. 493, 110th Cong. (2007); Civil Rights Act of 1991, Pub. L. No. 102-166, 105 Stat. 1071 (1991).
9.   Before 1991, race discrimination plaintiffs could seek damages and a jury trial under 42 U.S.C. § 1981(a). After the 1991 amendments, a jury trial and damages (subject to caps) were available under Title VII itself.
10.   *See, e.g.*, Luedtke v. Nabors Alaska Drilling, Inc., 768 P.2d 1123, 1136–7 (Ala. 1989) (discharge for refusing random drug tests); Petermann v. Int'l Bhd. of Teamsters, Local 396, 344 P.2d 25, 27 (Cal. Ct. App. 1959) (discharge for refusing to give perjured testimony); Nees v. Hocks, 536 P.2d 512, 516 (Or. 1975) (discharge for serving jury duty).
11.   *See* Wal-Mart Stores, Inc. v. Dukes, 131 S.Ct. 2541 (2011).
12.   *See* AT&T Mobility LLC v. Concepcion, 131 S.Ct. 1740 (2011).
13.   Some features of the workplace setting help to support "self-enforcing" norms in this story. In particular, both employers and employees are "repeat players" with the ability to anticipate, observe, and respond to the others' actions. *See* Rock and Wachter (1996) (citing Ellickson); Ellickson (1991).
14.   Empirical studies have sought to discern just how much alarm these doctrines caused. One major study found that judicial innovations in the law of the employment contract had a significant (though still small) impact on employment levels (whereas, e.g., the public policy exception to employment at will had no significant impact). See Autor, Donohue and Schwab (2006).
15.   Woolley v. Hoffman-La Roche, Inc., 491 A.2d 1257 (N.J. 1985).
16.   Dillon v. Champion Jogbra, Inc., 819 A.2d 703 (Vt. 2002).

17. The implied covenant of good faith and fair dealing also sounds in contract in most jurisdictions. See, e.g., Foley v. Interactive Data Corp., 765 P.2d 373 (Cal. 1988). Its scope is not entirely settled, and varies by jurisdiction, but it has generally been narrowly construed, and offers no independent protection against discharge, in the case of at-will employees. See, e.g., Guz v. Bechtel National, Inc., 8 P.3d 1089 (Cal. 2000); Murphy v. American Home Products Corp., 448 N.E.2d 86 (NY 1983).

18. Some of these claims to "vested" benefits or deferred compensation (like commissions and bonuses) for work already performed are governed by ERISA, but some are still governed by state law. The latter tends to distinguish between "vested" benefits and other terms that may be modified prospectively without breach of contract. *See* Simko (1996). In Rock and Wachter's strong version of "non-legally enforceable norms," even this exception would threaten to breach the "jurisdictional boundary" between the norm-based employment contract and formally enforceable contracts outside the employment context; even so, they appear to concede the legal enforceability of "vested benefits." Rock and Wachter (1996, p. 1936, n. 47).

19. For critical accounts of employer responses to litigation and regulation, see Edelman et al. (1992); McGarity and Shapiro (1996).

20. Provided they do not use those non-union structures to discriminate against union supporters or to deflect demands for recognition of a majority-supported union (Estlund, 2010).

REFERENCES

Appelbaum, Eileen, Anette Bernhardt, and Richard J. Murnane, eds. 2003. *Low-Wage America: How Employers are Reshaping Opportunity in the Workplace*. New York: Russell Sage Foundation.

Arlen, Jennifer and Reinier Kraakman. 1997. "Controlling Corporate Misconduct: An Analysis of Corporate Liability Regimes," 72 *NYU Law Review* 687–779.

Arthurs, Harry W. 2005. "Private Ordering and Workers' Rights in the Global Economy: Corporate Codes of Conduct as a Regime of Labour Market Regulation," in Wesley Cragg, ed., *Ethics Codes, Corporations, and the Challenge of Globalization*. Cheltenham, UK and Northampton, MA, USA: Edward Elgar.

Autor, David H., John J. Donohue III and Stewart J. Schwab. 2006. "The Costs of Wrongful-Discharge Laws," 88 *The Review of Economics & Statistics* 211–31.

Ayres, Ian and John Braithwaite. 1992. *Responsive Regulation: Transcending the Deregulation Debate*. New York: Oxford University Press.

Bardach, Eugene and Robert A. Kagan. 1982. *Going by the Book: The Problem of Regulatory Unreasonableness*. Philadelphia, PA: Temple University Press.

Barenberg, Mark. 1993. "The Political Economy of the Wagner Act: Power, Symbol, and Workplace Cooperation," 106 *Harvard Law Review* 1379–496.

Bennett, James T. and Bruce E. Kaufman. 2002. *The Future of Private Sector Unionism in the U.S. – Assessment and Forecast*. Armonk, NY: M.E. Sharpe.

Bernhardt, Annette, Siobhán McGrath, and James DeFilippis. 2007. "Unregulated Work in the Global City: Employment and Labor Law Violations in New York," Technical Report, Brennan Center for Justice at New York University School of Law. Available at: http://nelp.3cdn.net/cc4d61e5942f9cfdc5_d6m6bgaq4.pdf.

Blackett, Adelle. 2001. "Global Governance, Legal Pluralism and the Decentered State: A Labor Law Critique of Codes of Corporate Conduct," 8 *Indiana Journal of Global Legal Studies* 401–47.

Blair, Margaret M. 2004. "The Great Pension Grab: Comments on Richard Ippolito, Bankruptcy and Workers: Risks, Compensation and Pension Contracts," 82 *Washington University Law Quarterly* 1305–12.

Blose, Laurence E. and Gerald E. Calvasina. 2002. "Employment Discrimination Litigation and the Value of the Firm," 5 *Journal of Legal, Ethical and Regulatory Issues* No. 2.

Bobo, Kim. 2009. *Wage Theft in America: Why Millions of Working Americans Are Not Getting Paid – and What We Can Do About It*. New York: The New Press.

Braithwaite, John and Peter Drahos. 2000. *Global Business Regulation*. Cambridge, UK: Cambridge University Press.

Bratton, William W. and Michael L. Wachter. 2008. "Shareholder Primacy's Corporatist Origins: Adolf Berle and 'The Modern Corporation,'" 34 *Journal of Corporation Law* 99–152.

Breyer, Stephen G. 1982. *Regulation and its Reform*. Cambridge, MA: Harvard University Press.

Briones, Rowena. 2009. "Did Wal-Mart Wake Up? How Strategic Management Handled Wal-Mart's Reputation," Case Study, Arthur W. Page Society. Available at: http://www.awpagesociety.com/images/uploads/Wal-Mart_CaseStudy.pdf.

Brudney, James J. 1996. "Reflections on Group Action and the Law of the Workplace," 74 *Texas Law Review* 1563–600.

Burton, John F. and James R. Chelius. 1997. "Workplace Safety and Health Regulations: Rationale and Results," in Bruce E. Kaufman, ed., *Government Regulation of the Employment Relationship*. Madison, WI: Industrial Relations Research Association.

Craver, Charles B. 1993. *Can Unions Survive? The Rejuvenation of the American Labor Movement*. New York: New York University Press.

Craver, Charles B. 1998. "Why Labor Unions Must (and Can) Survive," 1 *University of Pennsylvania Journal of Labor and Employment Law* 15–48.

Dau-Schmidt, Kenneth Glenn. 1992. "A Bargaining Analysis of American Labor Law and the Search for Industrial Peace," 91 *Michigan Law Review* 419–514.

Deakin, Simon and Aristea Koukiadaki. 2012. "Capability Theory, Employee Voice and Corporate Restructuring: Evidence from UK Case Studies," 33 *Comparative Labor Law and Policy Journal* 427–58.

Dobbin, Frank. 2009. *Inventing Equal Opportunity*. Princeton, NJ: Princeton University Press.

Doorey, David J. Forthcoming. "A Model of Responsive Workplace Law," *Osgoode Hall Law Journal*. Available at: http://ssrn.com/abstract=1625044.

Dorf, Michael C. and Charles F. Sabel. 1998. "A Constitution of Democratic Experimentalism," 98 *Columbia Law Review* 267–473.

Drummonds, Henry H. 2007. "The Aging of the Boomers and the Coming Crisis in America's Changing Retirement and Elder Care Systems," 11 *Lewis and Clark Law Review* 267–304.

Edelman, Lauren B., Steven E. Abraham and Howard S. Erlanger. 1992. "Professional Construction of Law: The Inflated Threat of Wrongful Discharge," 26 *Law and Society Review* 47–84.

Elhauge, Einer. 2005. "Sacrificing Corporate Profits in the Public Interest," 80 *New York University Law Review* 733–869.

Ellickson, Robert C. 1991. *Order Without Law: How Neighbors Settle Disputes*. Cambridge, MA: Harvard University Press.

Epstein, Richard A. 1984. "In Defense of the Contract at Will," 51 *University of Chicago Law Review* 947–82.

Estlund, Cynthia. 1993. "Economic Rationality and Union Avoidance: Misunderstanding the National Labor Relations Act," 71 *Texas Law Review* 921–92.

Estlund, Cynthia. 1996. "Wrongful Discharge Protections in an At-Will World," 74 *Texas Law Review* 1655–92.

Estlund, Cynthia. 2007. "Between Rights and Contract: Arbitration Agreements and Non-Compete Covenants as a Hybrid Form of Employment Law," 155 *University of Pennsylvania Law Review* 379–445.

Estlund, Cynthia. 2010. *Regoverning the Workplace: From Self-Regulation to Co-Regulation*. New Haven, CT: Yale University Press.

Estlund, Cynthia. 2011. "Just the Facts: The Case for Workplace Transparency," 63 *Stanford Law Review* 351–408.

Estreicher, Samuel. 1993. "Labor Law Reform in a World of Competitive Product Markets," 69 *Chicago-Kent Law Review* 3–46.

Estreicher, Samuel. 1994. "Employee Involvement and the 'Company Union' Prohibition: The Case for Partial Repeal of Section 8(a)(2) of the NLRA," 69 *New York University Law Review* 125–61.

Estreicher, Samuel. 2001. "Saturns for Rickshaws: The Stakes in the Debate over Predispute Employment Arbitration Agreements," 16 *Ohio State Journal on Dispute Resolution* 559–70.

Freeman, Richard B. 2007. "What Do Unions Do? The 2004 M-Brane Stringtwister Edition," in James T. Bennett and Bruce E. Kaufman, *What Do Unions Do? A Twenty-Year Perspective*. New Brunswick, NJ: Transaction Publishers.

Freeman, Richard B. and James L. Medoff. 1984. *What Do Unions Do?* New York: Basic Books.

Freeman, Richard B. and Joel Rogers. 1999. *What Workers Want*. Ithaca, NY: Cornell University Press.

Frymer, Paul. 2007. *Black and Blue: African Americans, the Labor Movement, and the Decline of the Democratic Party*. Princeton, NJ: Princeton University Press.

Godard, John and Carola Frege. 2011. "Union Decline, Alternative Forms of Representation, and Workplace Authority Relations in the United States," unpublished paper presented at 2011 Labor and Employment Relations Association meeting.

Goldstein, Bruce, Marc Linder, Laurence E. Norton II, and Catherine K. Ruckelshaus. 1999. "Enforcing Fair Labor Standards in the Modern American Sweatshop: Rediscovering the Statutory Definition of Employment," 46 *UCLA Law Review* 983–1163.

Greenhouse, Steven. 2008. *The Big Squeeze: Tough Times for the American Worker*. New York: Alfred A. Knopf.

Hyde, Alan. 2003. *Working in Silicon Valley: Economic and Legal Analysis of a High-Velocity Labor Market*. Armonk, NY: M.E. Sharpe, Inc.

Issacharoff, Samuel. 1996. "Contracting for Employment," 74 *Texas Law Review* 1783–812.

Jolls, Christine. 2007. "Employment Law," in A. Mitchell Polinsky and Steven Shavell, eds., *The Handbook of Law and Economics*. Amsterdam: Elsevier Academic Press.

Kagan, Robert A. and Eugene Bardach. 1982. *Going by the Book: The Problem of Regulatory Unreasonableness*. Philadelphia, PA: Temple University Press.

Kaufman, Bruce E. 1989. "Labor's Inequality of Bargaining Power: Changes over Time and Implications for Public Policy," 10 *Journal of Labor Research* 285–98.

Kaufman, Bruce E. 1999. "Does the NLRA Constrain Employee Involvement and Participation Programs in Nonunion Companies? A Reassessment," 17 *Yale Law & Policy Review* 729–812.

Kim, Pauline T. 1997. "Bargaining with Imperfect Information: A Study of Worker Perceptions of Legal Protection in an At-Will World," 83 *Cornell Law Review* 105–60.

Kovach, Kenneth A., Nancy Greer Hamilton, Thomas M. Alston, and Judith A. Sullivan. 1997. "OSHA and the Politics of Reform: An Analysis of OSHA Reform Initiatives before the 104th Congress," 34 *Harvard Journal on Legislation* 169–90.

Krawiec, Kimberly D. 2003. "Cosmetic Compliance and the Failure of Negotiated Governance," 81 *Washington University Law Quarterly* 487–544.

Lambert, Thomas A. 2004. "Avoiding Regulatory Mismatch in the Workplace: An Informational Approach to Workplace Safety Regulation," 82 *Nebraska Law Review* 1006–87.

Lierman, Brooke E. 2010. "'To Assure Safe and Healthful Working Conditions': Taking Lessons from Labor Unions to Fulfill OSHA's Promises," 12 *Loyola Journal of Public Interest Law* 1–37.

Lobel, Orly. 2004. "The Renew Deal: The Fall of Regulation and the Rise of Governance in Contemporary Legal Thought," 89 *Minnesota Law Review* 342–470.

Maltby, Lewis L. 2003. "Employment Arbitration and Workplace Justice," 38 *University of San Francisco Law Review* 105–18.

McGarity, Thomas O. 1994. "Reforming OSHA: Some Thoughts for the Current Legislative Agenda," 31 *Houston Law Review* 99–118.

McGarity, Thomas O. and Sidney A. Shapiro. 1993. *Workers at Risk: The Failed Promise of the Occupational Safety and Health Administration*. Westport, CT: Praeger Publishers.

McGarity, Thomas O. and Sidney A. Shapiro. 1996. "OSHA's Critics and Regulatory Reform," 31 *Wake Forest Law Review* 587–646.

Morantz, Alison D. 2009. "The Elusive Union Safety Effect: Towards a New Empirical Research Agenda," Proceedings of the 61st Annual Meeting 130, Labor and Employment Relations Association.

Outten, Wayne N. 1999. "Negotiations, ADR, and Severance/Settlement Agreements: An Employee's Lawyer's Perspective," 604 Practising Law Institute: Litigation and Administrative Practice Course Handbook Series 235.

Posner, Richard A. 1998. *Economic Analysis of Law*. 4th ed. New York: Aspen Publishers.

Rabin, Robert J. 1991. "The Role of Unions in the Rights-Based Workplace," 25 *University of San Francisco Law Review* 169–264.

Rabinowitz, Randy S. and Mark M. Hager. 2000. "Designing Health and Safety: Workplace Hazard Regulation in the United States and Canada," 33 *Cornell International Law Journal* 373–434.

Revesz, Richard and Michael Livermore. 2008. *Retaking Rationality: How Cost-Benefit Analysis Can Better Protect the Environment and Our Health*. New York: Oxford University Press.

Rock, Edward B. and Michael L. Wachter. 1996. "The Enforceability of Norms and the Employment Relationship," 144 *University of Pennsylvania Law Review* 1913–52.

Rose-Ackerman, Susan. 1992. *Rethinking the Progressive Agenda: The Reform of the American Regulatory State*. New York: The Free Press.

Sachs, Benjamin I. 2008. "Employment Law as Labor Law," 29 *Cardozo Law Review* 2685–748.

Sachs, Benjamin I. 2010. "Enabling Employee Choice: A Structural Approach to the Rules of Union Organizing," 123 *Harvard Law Review* 655–728.

Seidenfeld, Mark. 2000. "Empowering Stakeholders: Limits on Collaboration as the Basis for Flexible Regulation," 41 *William and Mary Law Review* 411–502.

Selmi, Michael. 2003. "The Price of Discrimination: The Nature of Class Action Employment Discrimination Litigation and its Effects," 81 *Texas Law Review* 1249–335.

Simko, Darryl B. 1996. "Of Public Pensions, State Constitutional Contract Protection, and Fiscal Constraint," 69 *Temple Law Review* 1059–79.

Sternlight, Jean R. 2004. "In Search of the Best Procedure for Enforcing Employment Discrimination Laws: A Comparative Analysis," 78 *Tulane Law Review* 1401–500.

Stever, Donald W. 1994. "Experience and Lessons of Twenty-Five Years of Environmental Law: Where We Have Been and Where We Are Headed," 27 *Loyola of Los Angeles Law Review* 1105–120.

Stone, Katherine V.W. 2004. *Widgets to Digits: Employment Regulation for the Changing Workplace*. Cambridge, UK: Cambridge University Press.

Summers, Clyde W. 2000. "Employment at Will in the United States: The Divine Right of Employers," 3 *University of Pennsylvania Journal of Labor and Employment Law* 65–86.

Sunstein, Cass R. 1987. "Constitutionalism After the New Deal," 101 *Harvard Law Review* 421–510.

Taras, Daphne G. 1997. "Why Non-Union Representation is Legal in Canada," 52 *Industrial Relations* 761–86.

Taras, Daphne G. and Bruce E. Kaufman. 2006. "Nonunion Employee Representation in North America: Diversity, Controversy, and Uncertain Future," 37 *Industrial Relations Journal* 513–42.

Ursel, Nancy D. and Marjorie Armstrong-Stassen. 2006. "How Age Discrimination in Employment Affects Stockholders," 27 *Journal of Labor Research* 89–99.

U.S. Commission on the Future of Worker-Management Relations. 1994. *The Dunlop Commission on the Future of Worker-Management Relations: Final Report.* Washington, DC: U.S. Departments of Labor and Commerce.

U.S. Government Accountability Office (GAO). 2009. "Employee Misclassification: Improved Coordination, Outreach, and Targeting Could Better Ensure Detection and Prevention," Report to Congressional Requesters. Available at: http://www.gao.gov/products/GAO-09-717.

Vigneau, Christophe. 2003. "Labor Law between Changes and Continuity," 25 *Comparative Labor Law and Policy Journal* 129–41.

Viscusi, W. Kip. 1983. *Risk by Choice: Regulating Health and Safety in the Workplace.* Cambridge, MA: Harvard University Press.

Wachter, Michael L. 2007. "Labor Unions: A Corporatist Institution in a Competitive World," 155 *University of Pennsylvania Law Review* 581–634.

Wachter, Michael L. and Randall D. Wright. 1990. "The Economics of Internal Labor Markets," 29 *Industrial Relations* 240–62.

Weil, David. 2002. "Regulating Noncompliance to Labor Standards: New Tools for an Old Problem," 45 *Challenge* 47–74.

Weil, David. 2003. "Compliance with the Minimum Wage: Can Government Make a Difference?" Working Paper. Available at: http://papers.ssrn.com/sol3/papers.cfm?abstract_id=368340.

Weiler, Paul. 1990. *Governing the Workplace: the Future of Labor and Employment Law.* Cambridge, MA: Harvard Univ. Press.

Wial, Howard. 1999. "Minimum-Wage Enforcement and the Low-Wage Labor Market," Working Paper, Keystone Research Center. Available at: http://mitsloan.mit.edu/iwer/pdf/tfwial.pdf.

Wilborn, Steven L., Stewart J. Schwab, John F. Burton Jr., and Gillian L. Lester. 2007. *Employment Law: Cases and Materials.* 4th ed. Albany, NY: LexisNexis.

Williamson, Oliver E., Michael L. Wachter, and Jeffrey E. Harris. 1975. "Understanding the Employment Relation: The Analysis of Idiosyncratic Exchange," 6 *The Bell Journal of Economics* 250–78.

Winter, Greg. 2000. "Coca-Cola Settles Racial Bias Case," *New York Times* (Nov. 17). Available at: http://www.nytimes.com/2000/11/17/business/coca-cola-settles-racial-bias-case.html.

Wishnie, Michael J. 2004. "Emerging Issues for Undocumented Workers," 6 *University of Pennsylvania Journal of Labor and Employment Law* 497–524.

Index